Introduction to Sociology

Introduction to Sociology

Situations and Structures

By JACK D. DOUGLAS

and

Donald W. Ball

Lindsey Churchill

Robert E. Cole

Randall Collins

Norman K. Denzin

John Scott Fuller

James M. Henslin

Jerry Jacobs

John M. Johnson

Ivan Light

Stanford M. Lyman

Peter K. Manning

Harvey Molotch

Clarice Stasz Stoll

Carol A. B. Warren

Paul Weaver

Norbert Wiley

The Free Press, New York
Collier Macmillan Publishers, London

Copyright © 1973 by The Free Press
A Division of Macmillan Publishing Co., Inc.
Printed in the United States of America
All rights reserved. No part of this book may be
reproduced or transmitted in any form or by any means,
electronic or mechanical, including photocopying, recording,
or by any information storage and retrieval system,
without permission in writing from the Publisher.

The Free Press
A Division of Macmillan Publishing Co., Inc.

Collier–Macmillan Canada Ltd., Toronto, Ontario

Library of Congress Catalog Card Number: 75–163608

printing number
1 2 3 4 5 6 7 8 9 10

Biographical Notes

Donald W. Ball
received his Ph.D. from U.C.L.A. He is Associate Professor in the Department of Sociology at the University of Victoria and Associate Editor of *Pacific Sociological Review*. He wrote Chapter 5, "The Biological Bases of Human Society."

Lindsey Churchill
received his Ph.D. from Harvard University. He taught at U.C.L.A. and Cornell University and was at the Russell Sage Foundation. Dr. Churchill wrote Chapter 10, "Purposes and Problems of Social Research." He is Associate Professor in the Department of Sociology at the Graduate Center, City University of New York.

Robert E. Cole
received his Ph.D. from the University of Illinois. He wrote *Japanese Blue-Collar* and is Associate Professor in the Department of Sociology at the University of Michigan. He wrote Chapter 15, "Comparative Sociology and Economic Development."

Randall Collins
received his Ph.D. from the University of California, Berkeley. He is the author of *The Discovery of Society* and is now Associate Professor, Department of Sociology, University of California, San Diego. Dr. Collins wrote Chapter 13, "Politics in Society."

Norman K. Denzin

received his Ph.D. from the University of Iowa. He has written, edited, and co-edited several books including *The Mental Patient* (with Stephen P. Spitzer), *The Research Act, Sociological Methods, The Values of Social Science,* and *Social Relationships.* Currently Associate Professor in the Department of Sociology at the University of Illinois, Dr. Denzin wrote Chapter 8, "Self and Society."

Jack D. Douglas

received his Ph.D. from Princeton University. The author and editor of many articles and books including *American Social Order* (The Free Press), *Relevance of Sociology, Social Meanings of Suicide, Crime and Justice in American Society, Research on Deviance,* and *Understanding Everyday Life,* he is currently Professor, Department of Sociology, University of California, San Diego. Dr. Douglas is the editor of this book, *Introduction to Sociology: Situations and Structures,* and the author of the Part introductions as well as six chapters: Chapter 1, "The Importance of Sociology Today"; Chapter 2, "The Emergence of Modern Sociology"; Chapter 3, "The Progress of Modern Sociology: Social Psychology, Small Groups, and Functionalism"; Chapter 4, "The Progress of Modern Sociology: Field Research, Interactionism, and Phenomenology"; Chapter 20, "Deviance and Social Control"; and Chapter 21, "The Future of Sociology in America."

John Scott Fuller

is at the University of California, San Diego. His major research interests are in theoretical sociology, socio-linguistics, and he is now doing a study of medical ethics in hospitals. He is the co-author (with Jerry Jacobs) of Chapter 7, "Socialization."

James M. Henslin

received his Ph.D. from Washington University. He is the editor of *Studies in the Sociology of Sex* and *Down to Earth Sociology* (The Free Press) and the co-editor (with Larry T. Reynolds) of *American Society* and *Social Problems in American Society.* Currently Associate Professor, Department of Sociology, at Southern Illinois University, Dr. Henslin is the author of Chapter 6, "Sex and Love," and Chapter 9, "The Sociology of Everyday Life."

Biographical Notes

Jerry Jacobs
received his Ph.D. from U.C.L.A. He is the author of several books including *The Search for Help, A Study of the Retarded Child in the Community,* and *Adolescent Suicide.* Currently Associate Professor in the Department of Sociology at Syracuse University, Dr. Jacobs is the co-author (with John Scott Fuller) of Chapter 7, "Socialization."

John M. Johnson
received his Ph.D. from the University of California, San Diego. He is an Assistant Professor in the Department of Sociology at Arizona State University. Dr. Johnson is the co-author (with Stanford M. Lyman and Carol A. B. Warren) of Chapter 18, "American Social Problems."

Ivan H. Light
received his Ph.D. from the University of California, Berkeley. The author of *Ethnic Enterprise in America,* he is currently an Assistant Professor in the Department of Sociology at U.C.L.A. Dr. Light is the author of Chapter 16, "Formal Organizations: Freedom and Control."

Stanford M. Lyman
received his Ph.D. from the University of Berkeley. The author of *A Sociology of the Absurd* and *Revolt of the Students* (both with Marvin Scott) and *The Asian in the West* and *The Black American in Sociological Thought,* Dr. Lyman is Professor in the Department of Sociology at The New School for Social Research. He is the co-author (with John M. Johnson and Carol A. B. Warren) of Chapter 18, "American Social Problems."

Peter K. Manning
received his Ph.D. from Duke University. He is the co-editor (with Marcello Truzzi) of *Youth and Sociology* and the author of *Youth, Divergent Perspectives.* Currently Associate Professor, Department of Sociology and Psychiatry, Michigan State University, Dr. Manning is the author of Chapter 11, "Language, Meaning, and Action."

Harvey L. Molotch
received his Ph.D. from the University of Chicago. The author of *Managed Integration: Dilemmas of Doing Good in the City,* he is Associate Professor

in the Department of Sociology, University of California, Santa Barbara. Dr. Molotch is the author of Chapter 19, "Urban Society."

Clarice Stasz Stoll

received her Ph.D. from Rutgers University. She is the co-editor of *Simulation and Gaming in Social Science* (with Michael Inbar) and the co-author of *Simulation Games for the Social Studies Teacher* (with Samuel Livingston), both published by The Free Press. Dr. Stoll is book review editor of *Stimulation and Games* and Assistant Professor in the Department of Sociology, Sonoma State College. She is the author of Chapter 17, "Computers, Sociology, and Society."

Carol A. B. Warren

received her Ph.D. from the University of California, San Diego. She is Assistant Professor, Department of Sociology and Anthropology, University of Southern California. She is the co-author (with John M. Johnson and Stanford M. Lyman) of Chapter 18, "American Social Problems."

Paul H. Weaver

received his Ph.D. in Political Science from Harvard University. His current research is on the mass media and their political influence. He is now an Assistant Professor of the Department of Government at Harvard. Dr. Weaver is the author of Chapter 12, "Society and Mass Communication."

Norbert Wiley

is Associate Professor of Sociology at the University of Illinois. His current research includes papers on "America's Unique Class Politics" and "The Ethnic Mobility Trap." Dr. Wiley is the author of Chapter 14, "Social Stratification."

Contents

List of Inserts — xiii

List of Tables and Figures — xvi

Acknowledgments — xvii

A Note to the Reader — xviii

Preface — xix

PART I   **Modern Sociology** — 1

CHAPTER 1
The Importance of Sociology Today
by Jack D. Douglas — 2

CHAPTER 2
The Emergence of Modern Sociology
by Jack D. Douglas — 26

CHAPTER 3
The Progress of Modern Sociology: Social Psychology, Small Groups, and Functionalism
by Jack D. Douglas — 59

CHAPTER 4
The Progress of Modern Sociology: Field Research, Interactionism, and Phenomenology
by Jack D. Douglas — 86

PART II The Development of Man and Society — 117

CHAPTER 5
The Biological Bases of Human Society
by Donald W. Ball — 118

CHAPTER 6
Sex and Love
by James M. Henslin — 139

PART III The Analysis of Social Situations: The Sociology of Everyday Life — 167

CHAPTER 7
Socialization
by John Scott Fuller and Jerry Jacobs — 168

CHAPTER 8
Self and Society
by Norman K. Denzin — 209

CHAPTER 9
The Sociology of Everyday Life
by James M. Henslin — 227

CHAPTER 10
Purposes and Problems of Social Research
by Lindsey Churchill — 250

PART IV Language and Communication in Society — 277

CHAPTER 11
Language, Meaning, and Action
by Peter K. Manning — 278

CHAPTER 12
Society and Mass Communications   303
by Paul H. Weaver

PART V Politics and Stratification: Authority, Power, and Prestige   327

CHAPTER 13
Politics in Society   328
by Randall Collins

CHAPTER 14
Social Stratification   356
by Norbert Wiley

CHAPTER 15
Comparative Sociology and Economic Development   387
by Robert E. Cole

PART VI The Technological Society, Computers, and Social Research   409

CHAPTER 16
Formal Organizations: Freedom and Control   410
by Ivan H. Light

CHAPTER 17
Computers, Sociology, and Society   439
by Clarice Stasz Stoll

PART VII Social Problems and Social Order   471

CHAPTER 18
American Social Problems   472
by Stanford M. Lyman, John M. Johnson, and Carol A. B. Warren

CHAPTER 19
Urban Society   498
by Harvey L. Molotch

CHAPTER 20
Deviance and Social Control
by Jack D. Douglas   537

PART VIII Conclusion   561

CHAPTER 21
The Future of Sociology in America   563
by Jack D. Douglas

Glossary of Key Concepts   570

Bibliography   588

Index   637

List of Inserts

INSERT NO. 1	On Robert W. Friedrichs' *A Sociology of Sociology*	10
INSERT NO. 2	On Alvin W. Gouldner's *The Coming Crisis of Western Sociology*	12
INSERT NO. 3	On Herbert J. Gans' *The Urban Villagers*	14
INSERT NO. 4	On Gerald D. Suttles' *The Social Order of the Slum*	16
INSERT NO. 5	On Emile Durkheim's *Suicide*	34
INSERT NO. 6	Emile Durkheim	38
INSERT NO. 7	Auguste Comte	40
INSERT NO. 8	Herbert Spencer	43
INSERT NO. 9	Karl Marx	47
INSERT NO. 10	C. Wright Mills	50
INSERT NO. 11	Max Weber	52
INSERT NO. 12	Vilfredo Pareto	55
INSERT NO. 13	Georg Simmel	56
INSERT NO. 14	William Graham Sumner	60
INSERT NO. 15	Lester F. Ward	63
INSERT NO. 16	Albion Small	64
INSERT NO. 17	"The Invasion from Mars"	68
INSERT NO. 18	Ferdinand Tönnies	70
INSERT NO. 19	Sociometry	72

xiv   Lists of Inserts

INSERT NO. 20	On Peter M. Blau's *Exchange and Power in Social Life*	75
INSERT NO. 21	On W. I. Thomas and Florian Znaniecki's *The Polish Peasant in England and America*	78
INSERT NO. 22	On Robin M. Williams' *American Society: A Sociological Interpretation*	82
INSERT NO. 23	Robert E. Park	88
INSERT NO. 24	On William Foote Whyte's *Street Corner Society*	92
INSERT NO. 25	On Herbert J. Gans' *The Levittowners*	95
INSERT NO. 26	Charles H. Cooley	98
INSERT NO. 27	George Herbert Mead	100
INSERT NO. 28	Edmund Husserl	104
INSERT NO. 29	Alfred Schutz	106
INSERT NO. 30	On Peter L. Berger and Thomas Luckmann's *The Social Construction of Reality*	110
INSERT NO. 31	Pop Ethology	120
INSERT NO. 32	Monkey Mothers and Monkey Others: The Experiments of the Harlows	134
INSERT NO. 33	Bronislaw Malinowski	144
INSERT NO. 34	The Kinsey Report	158
INSERT NO. 35	Noam Chomsky	174
INSERT NO. 36	Jean Piaget	178
INSERT NO. 37	The Beauty Parlor as Backstage by Carol A. B. Warren	232
INSERT NO. 38	Self-Presentations of Homosexuals by Carol A. B. Warren	240
INSERT NO. 39	John Stuart Mill's Methods for Establishing Causation	254
INSERT NO. 40	On Robert Freed Bales's *Interaction Process Analysis*	258
INSERT NO. 41	Claude Levi-Strauss	284
INSERT NO. 42	Ludwig Wittgenstein	286

List of Inserts

INSERT NO. 43	The Craft of Reporting	320
INSERT NO. 44	On Kingsley Davis' *Human Society*	377
INSERT NO. 45	Modernization and Communist Party Strength	402
INSERT NO. 46	On Jacques Ellul's *The Technological Society*	412
INSERT NO. 47	On Melville Dalton's *Men Who Manage*	422
INSERT NO. 48	On William Kornhauser and Warren O. Hagstrom's *Scientists in Industry: Conflict and Accommodation*	424
INSERT NO. 49	"On the Meaning of Alienation" by Melvin Seeman	430
INSERT NO. 50	Computers	441
INSERT NO. 51	Artificial Intelligence	448
INSERT NO. 52	On Norbert Wiener's *Cybernetics*	455
INSERT NO. 53	"Chalk One Up for Humans vs. Computers"	459
INSERT NO. 54	How Much Does the Federal Government Know About You?	465
INSERT NO. 55	Trailer Parks as a Social Problem	478
INSERT NO. 56	On Norton Long's "The Community as an Ecology of Games"	522
INSERT NO. 57	On Robert K. Merton's "Social Structure and Anomie"	544
INSERT NO. 58	On Kai T. Erikson's *Wayward Puritans*	546
INSERT NO. 59	On Howard S. Becker's *Outsiders*	550
INSERT NO. 60	On David Matza's *Becoming Deviant*	552
INSERT NO. 61	"Practical Reasons for Gundecking" by John M. Johnson	554
INSERT NO. 62	"The Situated Morality of a Nudist Camp" by Martin S. Weinberg	556

List of Tables and Figures

Figure 3–1.	Simplified Picture of the Functional Model of Society	84
Figure 4–1.	Symbolic Interactionist Model of Social Action	102
Figure 6–1.	U.S. Marriages, Divorces, 1940–1968	159
Table 10–1.	Father-Son Occupational Identity Diagram	262
Table 10–2.	Client Activity Related to Case Result	268
Table 10–3.	Hypnosis Data	272
Table 10–4.	Orne and Evans' Design and Results	273
Figure 14–1.	Degree of Inequality	358
Table 14–1.	Distribution of Family Units According to Income (in percentages)	360
Table 14–2.	Percentage Distribution of World Income Earned by Each Fourth of World's Population for Selected Years	361
Table 14–3.	Percent of National Personal Income Before Taxes Received by Each Income Tenth	364
Table 14–4.	Percentage of 1958 Total Income Paid in Federal, State, and Local Taxes, by Income Class	365
Figure 15–1.	Predicted Relationship between Level of Economic Development and Communist Party Strength	402
Figure 16–1.	The Organization Chart of a Large American School System	415
Figure 16–2.	Flow-Chart Model of Typical Control-Alienation Spiral in Bureaucracies	420
Table 16–1.	Manufacturing Establishments in the United States by Employment, Size of Establishment, Percent of Total Manufacturing Employment, and Percent of Total Manufacturing Value Added: 1963	426
Figure 17–1.	Computer Programming	445
Figure 20–1.	Durkheim's Theory of Suicide	542
Figure 20–2.	Outline of the Social Disorganization Theory of Deviance	548

Acknowledgments

The greatest contribution has been made by the authors who put so much creative work into fulfilling our purpose. But we also owe much to others. Irving Naiburg of The Free Press not only made important contributions by his strong support for the idea of this new kind of text from its inception, but also helped by criticizing the work at many stages. David McDermott of The Free Press has been of crucial importance in seeing the book through the difficulties of production. Clarice Stoll has been of vital importance as a critical reviewer, as well as an author. Carol Warren has aided us greatly by her research for the whole volume and by writing many of the inserts that help to enliven the book. Coleen Carpenter and her co-workers have done beautiful work in typing and retyping the whole work. Others too numerous to name have contributed by their critical readings of chapters.

Jack D. Douglas
La Jolla, California

A Note to the Reader

We have tried to provide the reader of this text with a maximum of help in comprehending its topics, and we suggest that his studies will be more enjoyable and rewarding if he uses these devices. Each part and chapter includes an introduction describing its contents and its relationship to the rest of the book. Every chapter includes cross-references and editorial notes that will help the reader to locate additional information on the subject under discussion.

Technical terms and phrases have been defined, with important alternative meanings indicated, in the Glossary. Each chapter has an annotated list of Suggested Readings related to that chapter. The general bibliography at the end of the book, to which references are made in the body of the volume, may serve as an additional guide.

Finally, the boxed inserts in each chapter provide a wealth of important and interesting material on the topics, works, and individuals in sociology.

Preface

There are two vital perspectives in sociology today: the sociology of everyday life situations and the sociology of social structures. Usually, these perspectives are treated as totally independent. One is presented and then the other, with little indication of how they are related to each other. Yet sociology is dependent on the analysis of social situations and of social structures and on the synthesis of these forms of analysis. The only social reality we can directly observe is the face-to-face, everyday interaction of members of society in concrete situations. The sociology of everyday life constitutes this foundation of sociology. But we must go beyond concrete situations to the analysis of their structural relations if we are to gain knowledge about society crucial to understanding social problems.

An integrated presentation of sociology is the primary goal of this text. Only in this way can we show what sociology is about and how it is important to solving social problems. Only in this way can we show the sense of discovery and excitement that now animates much of sociology.

Because this synthesis is still in progress, we cannot present it as a completely finished product. Our attempts to synthesize the analysis of everyday life situations and social structures have necessarily given this text an unusually creative approach. But I believe this creative approach will give a greater sense of what is going on today in sociology and a feeling for the excitement of this effort.

An Age of Sociology

The last decades of the twentieth century promise to be a great age of sociology. Until recently, common sense social thought has been dominated by an individualistic or psychologistic perspective. Social events—the creation of new nations, the destruction of the old, the outbreak of wars, or the making of peace—were explained primarily in terms of individual values, desires, thoughts, and actions. But by the middle of the twentieth century what C. Wright Mills called the *sociological imagination* had become public property: people began to explain social events at least partially in terms that seemed to transcend the individuals involved, speaking of "sociological forces" with no fear of being misunderstood.

Sociology has come of age after only four decades as a major academic discipline in the United States. Many Americans turned to sociology to understand a technological and urban society. As college students have become more concerned with these problems, the numbers of those studying sociology have grown rapidly.

At the same time, sociology has become far more complex, making it difficult for students to understand its basic ideas. This difficulty has been accentuated in the past decade by the rapid development of the *sociology of everyday life*. The development of this perspective on society transformed our basic understandings of man and society.

The two basic perspectives in sociology are the *structural perspective* and the *everyday life* (or *interactionist*) *perspective*. The older of these is the structural, which may be called the classical perspective of sociology. This is the perspective of Durkheim and most other early sociologists. Its basic idea, as stated by Durkheim, is that society transcends the individuals comprising it. The structural, or macrosocial, perspective sees society as a whole and focuses on the interdependence of a society's parts.

The everyday life, or microsocial, perspective developed primarily in the United States, though important contributions to it are found in the earlier works of the European sociologists Georg Simmel and Max Weber. It was based on the idea that the individual members of society and their observable communications and actions are the primary reality of society from which structural generalizations must be derived. The early students of everyday life had the journalist's fascination with what went on in the teeming cities of America. Robert Park, one of the most important of the Chicago sociologists, had been a newspaper reporter before he became a sociologist, and he never lost his interest in the daily affairs of the city. In contrast to abstract ideas of the European structuralists, who sometimes took their intellectual abstractions to be the primary realities and saw everyday life merely as examples of those abstractions, these early American sociologists were convinced that the activities they could directly observe and describe constituted the substance of society. They would look at, describe, and analyze everyday events first, and only then derive their abstract, theoretical ideas about society from those observations and descriptions of everyday life. They studied life in Chicago's "gold coast," slums, rooming houses, skid rows, gangs, and taxicab dance halls.

The symbolic interactionists, especially George Herbert Mead and Charles Cooley, first began to construct the theoretical ideas that underlie the sociology of everyday life. Their work was further developed by that of Erving Goffman, Howard S. Becker, and other recent students of everyday life who have followed in their tradition. More recently, their work has been complemented and advanced by the introduction of linguistic analysis and phenomenological sociology into American sociology.

To say that sociology must be based on the study of everyday life does not mean that we should be content with only the analysis of the microlevel of social action. Sociology has two basic goals: to gain scientific knowledge of society and to provide knowledge that may help the members of society to solve the complex problems of our increasingly technological and urban society. The first goal can best be served by studies of everyday life, as only such studies allow us to feel confidence in the reliability and validity of our work. But the second goal can be achieved only by analyzing the broader, macrolevel patterns and forces in society. Social problems are related to broad patterns of developments in society, rather than only to some small part that can be studied by the very intensive methods of the sociology of everyday life. Thus, we must further develop both our understanding of everyday life and our structural analyses of society.

We need a progressive synthesis of the sociology of everyday life with structural analyses of social problems. A number of earlier works have begun this synthesis. This is also the purpose of this introduction to sociology. Many chapters in this volume contain creative contributions to this goal, as well as a synthesis of earlier works.

Chapter 1 is concerned primarily with the commitment of sociology to providing scientific knowledge about society that can be used to implement practical attempts to solve social problems. This knowledge can be provided only by intensive studies of everyday life situations, including studies of such activities as government planning and operations. But sociology can provide useful knowledge only if it is able to understand the complex structural relations among many everyday situations. We must, then, go from studies of concrete situations to theories enabling us to see relations among the many situations.

In Chapters 2, 3, and 4 we deal with the emergence and progress of sociology over the last several centuries. We find a steady growth among sociologists of the recognition that sociological research and theory must be fundamentally concerned with the *social meanings of social actions*. We also find progress in the analysis of those social meanings and their relations to social actions. Much of this progress came from sociologists' recognition that we cannot know the structure of society without knowing what situations make up the structure, or what the situations are from which structures are inferred. Sociologists have come to see the need to determine the realities of the concrete situations of everyday life and then to determine the structural relations among these situations.

In Part II, "The Development of Man and Society," we shall be concerned with the early development of the human individual and of human society. Chapter 5 deals with the rudimentary forms of communication among animals, showing some of the important properties of meaning, communication, and society. Indirectly, it contributes to our concern with the relations between situations and structures by showing that organized social life can be built upon a minimal culture but that animal social organization is very restricted in its complexity by the lack of man's abstract, symbolic capacities. Chapter 6, "Sex and Love," deals with the most basic human situations, those which, as in the case of animal social organization, are closely related to our biological capacities. Sex and love, and the many complex family relations built upon them, are found in all human societies and thus constitute the most universal human social situation.

Part III, "The Analysis of Social Situations: The Sociology of Everyday Life," develops further the account of theory and research on social situations and social structures. Chapter 7, "Socialization," shows the early stages of socialization that lead an individual to develop basic self-concepts, values, and ideas that enable him to move beyond his concrete situation into the broader social world. After dealing with the informal socialization of the family, this chapter deals with formal education and the problems it faces in our society today. Chapter 8, "Self and Society," is largely concerned with the theoretical relationship between the analysis of social situations and the analysis of social structures, showing how the members of society construct social order out of their everyday situations. Chapter 9, "The Sociology of Everyday Life," is concerned with the ways in which individuals construct meanings for each other in concrete situations and present themselves to each other in everyday life situations. Chapter 10, "Purposes and Problems of Social Research," deals with both traditional research methods and the methods of participant observation.

Part IV, "Language and Communication in Society," concerns the way social actors construct meanings and actions in concrete situations, especially through the use of language. Chapter 11, "Language, Meaning, and Action," begins with considerations of the uses of language in constructing meanings in concrete situations and proceeds to considerations of how language and communications are related to the development of social structures. Chapter 12, "Society and Mass Communications," considers the ways in which the media construct messages and factors that determine what kinds of messages are constructed, and discusses the ways in which the oligopolistic ownership of the media today may affect the messages being communicated.

In Part V, "Politics and Stratification: Authority, Power, and Prestige," we become predominantly concerned with social structures. Still, Chapter 13, "Politics in Society," begins with strategies used by would-be political leaders to gain political power and then proceeds to show how political structures such as political parties are affected by these strategies. Finally, the author discusses the importance of pluralistic social structure. We also become more directly concerned with the social problems related to these basic social patterns. Chapter 14, "Social Stratification," takes up the history and nature of social inequality. We find no simple, monolithic structure of social strata in American society but, instead, a number of factors such as wealth, education, and political influence that are important in determining one's class position. It is, then, necessary for individuals to deal with and make use of these factors in various ways for the situations they face in their everyday lives. But there are some important patterns to these situations and the ways in which inequality is related to them, especially financial inequalities. The author goes on to show how these structures or patterns of inequality are related to social problems. Chapter 15, "Comparative Sociology and Economic Development," considers the comparative analysis of economic development, especially in relation to social problems such as pollution.

Part VI, "The Technological Society, Computers, and Social Research" is concerned with the nature and problems of bureaucratic organizations and technological production in modern America. Chapter 16, "Formal Organizations: Freedom and Control," begins with an analysis of the nature of bureaucratic, or formal, organizations in our society, arguing that we must begin our studies and analyses of organizations with detailed considerations of the concrete, everyday situations of the organizations. Chapter 17, "Computers, Sociology and Society," discusses the development and nature of computers and their effects on sociology. Then, after considering the importance of computers in our technological society, the author examines the effects of the properties of computer operations upon the kinds of decisions that can be made with them, especially the built-in bias toward precision and quantification which may distort decisions in an imprecise and qualitative world. In this chapter, we warn of the potential danger offered by computers to personal freedom. Chapter 18, "American Social Problems," analyzes the social definitions of social problems, or what members of society, from their own practical experiences, consider our social problems. The sociologist must understand this perspective, as well as the objective patterns of social events seen to constitute the problem, if he is to propose any solutions. In Chapter 19, "Urban Society," we consider the nature of urban society, including everyday experience in an urbanized world. We go on to consider the present nature of our urban crisis, its causes, and the prospects for dealing effectively with it. In Chapter 20, "Deviance and Social Control," we consider ways in which individuals construct the meanings of social rules in their everyday lives and make use of rules, in conjunction with such factors as social power, to try to construct social order or to build the structure of society they desire.

In the Conclusion, we consider the problems of social forecasting and try to anticipate some fundamental social trends.

Because sociologists' attempts to synthesize the analysis of social situations with the analysis of social structures still suffer from important factual and theoretical gaps, it is inevitable that some of these gaps will appear in this work. But our focus has been on integrating the analyses of situations and structures as much as possible, while presenting the vital aspects of both the sociology of everyday life situations and the sociology of social structures.

In courses on introductory sociology, teachers and students are concerned with achieving four kinds of knowledge: (1) a knowledge of the basic concepts and ideas shared by all sociologists, (2) a knowledge of basic facts about society, (3) a knowledge of the major lines of historical development of sociology, including its major personages and works, and (4) an integrated view of what sociology is about—what sociologists are doing, how, and why. Almost all texts concentrate on communicating the first three kinds of knowledge. First, they cut the sociology pie into its many specialized parts and proceed to give the student a quick view of "social roles," "stratification," "deviance," "marriage and the family," "the Founders," "social theory," and other interesting but seemingly disconnected sights. The result is that often sociology appears to be made up of disconnected concepts to be memorized, with no vital center. Often, this approach leaves the student wondering if there is any reason why all these topics are under the one roof of sociology.

But basic theoretical concerns and ideas form the vital center of sociology. There are important disagreements, as in every discipline, but even the most meticulous study of a particular everyday life situation and the most grandiose theory of universal social structures are tied together by common sociological questions, methods, and ideas.

There has been a progressive development in sociology, from the nineteenth-century attempt to exclude common-sense meanings from social theory to the attempt to substitute the ideas of sociologists for those of members of society to the more recent concern of sociologists with scientifically studying the meanings of social actions for those performing the actions. Though there has been no unilinear development in these fundamental ideas of sociology, the progress of sociological ideas has been clear. It is sensible to integrate the presentation of sociology around the historical development of fundamental ideas about society up to the present. It seems sensible to present the basic concepts of sociology in the historical context in which they were created. This path is followed in the first four chapters. These chapters present an integrated overview of the fundamental concepts and ideas of sociology. Chapter 1 deals with the basic questions of why we study sociology and what sociology as a whole is. Systematically, Chapters 2, 3, and 4 present the historical progress of sociology and of the basic concepts that tie sociology—and this book—together. There is some overlap among the first four chapters and the succeeding ones, but it has been limited to an amount that seemed optimal for integrating the book.

Some of the ideas we present may at first seem difficult to grasp. This is true of any serious intellectual discipline. We have not tried to present a closed universe with all questions answered. We have tried to inform your thinking about society to aid you in making your own critical evaluations of social life.

PART I

Modern Sociology

The four chapters in Part I provide an introduction and overview of modern sociology. Chapter 1 deals with the fundamental goals of sociology. Chapter 2 shows how and why a science of society has emerged in Western nations in the past few centuries and how it developed in nineteenth-century Europe. Chapter 3 deals with the early progress of twentieth-century sociology. Chapter 4 deals with developments that have influenced recent progress in the study of social situations of everyday life and social structures.

CHAPTER 1

The Importance of Sociology Today

This chapter shows sociology to be primarily an attempt by men of the Western world to find practical solutions to their social problems, which have become increasingly complex and difficult to solve as society has become increasingly complex and technological. This chapter also deals with the details of sociology's promise to provide men with scientific knowledge about their society that they can apply in solving their social problems. Specifically, sociology is shown to make three basic contributions to the solution of problems: (1) factual knowledge about society, (2) valid explanations of the relations among facts, and (3) predictions of future events so that problems may be anticipated.

The attempts to fulfill the promise of sociology involve important problems for sociology and potentially for society itself. We find that the promise can be fulfilled only if we concentrate first on providing objective scientific knowledge about society. But we must also pay increased attention to how practical applications of this knowledge are made. We must prevent the use of sociological knowledge to control men, or sociology may become a helpmate to those who wish to control others for their own purposes.

Never before has rapid change become the permanent condition of a society, purposefully sought and valued by large segments of the population. Consequently, no society has ever had to solve the problems produced by a permanent state of rapid change. In little more than half an average human lifetime, the technological revolution has produced the automobile age, the air age, the atomic age, the space age, the revolutions in communications, automation, and medicine, and other changes that have drastically affected our daily lives. In the Western world, the scientific and technological revolution has helped to eliminate some poverty, to eliminate plagues, to send men to the moon, and now through automation gives realistic hope of eliminating drudgery while producing greater wealth. But, at the same time, this revolution has helped to produce great gaps between the rich societies and the poor, and to pollute our environment and endanger the ecological balance of nature. It has also caused growing numbers to question the quality of our daily lives, has posed a growing threat of technological tyranny, has contributed to the atrocities of two world wars, and threatens to annihilate man through a nuclear holocaust.

The growing complexity and rate of change of our society make it increasingly difficult for us to know what is going on, and harder to understand the complex relations among the many changes. As C. Wright Mills has argued, the answers of common sense seem ever less adequate to deal with ever more complex problems (Mills, 1959).

It is no coincidence that sociology and the other major social sciences have developed in the Western world in direct proportion to the growing complexity and accelerating changes in our society. From its beginnings in the seventeenth century, the scientific study of man and society has been pursued and supported primarily because it promises a better understanding of man and society to solve the social problems caused by increasingly complex changes. While there are important reasons to doubt that this promise can be completely fulfilled, it remains an important justification for sociology and other social sciences. This promise has led sociology students to seek something beyond their common-sense understanding of man and society. For this reason it is important to begin our study of sociology with an analysis of the goals of sociology and the practical possibilities of attaining these goals.

THE PROMISE OF SOCIOLOGY

Although sociologists differ over the details of what sociology is and what it tries to do, there is general agreement that *sociology is the study of man and society that seeks to determine their general characteristics, especially as found in contemporary civilizations.* One of the basic goals of this science is to provide scientific knowledge that will help us solve our social problems better than if we relied entirely on our common-sense understanding. While sociology overlaps all the other social sciences these combined commitments make it unique among the social sciences and of unique importance to our society.

Sociology shares the commitment to creating scientific knowledge of man and society with most of economics, anthropology, psychology, and political science. However, the commitment of sociology to creating scientific knowledge of men and society is different from that of economics, psychology, and political science because they seek specialized forms of knowledge of man and society. Economics is exclusively concerned with economic arrangements and institutions; political science, with the study of power and political institutions. Psychology seeks scientific knowledge of man and of other animals but almost always abstracts individuals from their everyday social worlds and excludes consideration of the social factors important in determining what individuals are and what they do. Anthropology overlaps most with sociology in its goals and subject matter. In some ways, by including physical anthropology and archaeology within its boundaries, anthropology seeks a more universal knowledge of man than sociology normally does. Yet anthropology is very different from sociology in its almost exclusive concern with studying smaller and simpler societies.

Sociology is also different from the other social sciences in its basic commitment to creating scientific knowledge to help solve social problems. Some segments of psychology are concerned with solving individual problems, but these problems are usually abstracted from their social settings. Political science and economics have both become more concerned in recent years with such social problems as poverty and tyranny, but they remain largely concerned with their traditional subjects of how power and wealth are gotten, kept, and used. Traditionally, their aim has been more individualistic than that of sociology. Anthropology has become somewhat concerned with social problems in recent years, especially through "urban anthropology," but it remains the least problem-oriented of all the social sciences. In spite of the frequently important cross-fertilization of knowledge in the social sciences, sociology today is unique among them. If it is able to fulfill its commitment to providing general scientific knowledge of our society that can be used to find practical solutions to our growing social problems, sociology will also be of unique importance to our society.

SCIENTIFIC SOCIOLOGY AND APPLIED SOCIOLOGY

While sociology and the other social sciences are becoming increasingly significant in attempts to solve complex social problems, their commitment is to providing the knowledge necessary to solving those problems rather than direct solutions. It is especially important to recognize this fact today when people seeking immediate solutions to urgent problems demand that the social sciences should both provide knowledge and take direct political action in line with that knowledge.

The relationships among theoretical science, applied science, and practical action have become very complex in a world in which some forms of scientific knowledge have produced immense power. Before the nuclear age, the age of intercontinental missiles, and the age of threats to the ecological balance of nature, most natural scientists believed they could best serve the interests of all men by leaving most decisions concerning the use of their knowledge to the men of practical action, the political leaders. But, as the destructive power provided by scientific knowledge grew to proportions that few scientists would have believed possible before World War II, more scientists became committed to direct action to prevent the suicidal use of the power provided by their knowledge. Some of them, conscience-stricken by the use of their knowledge to build atomic weapons that threatened to destroy mankind, came to feel strongly that the interests of mankind demanded a more active participation of scientists in government policy making. The role of *scientific advocate* became an increasingly important one for natural scientists, especially after the example of the nuclear physicists who published their advocacy of armament controls in the *Bulletin of Atomic Scientists*.

Scientists today cannot rely entirely on political leaders to adequately evaluate the problems and dangers posed by the use of scientific knowledge. The responsibilities of scientists are very different in an age when their knowledge could be used by unwise or unscrupulous political leaders to produce mass destruction and to exploit millions. Natural scientists must now publicly advocate the ways in which their knowledge should be used, if they are to meet these responsibilities. The same holds true for social scientists insofar as their scientific knowledge poses the same kinds of problems. However, their knowledge does not now pose such problems and may not for decades to come.

For some time to come, the greatest task of sociology will be to fulfill its promise of providing scientific knowledge to solve our problems. The problems posed by responsible advocacy will grow as we accumulate such knowledge. Our primary concern must now be with developing our methods, findings, and theory. But this does not mean that our concern with fundamental issues must exclude the application of sociological knowledge to urgent problems.

There are many ways in which sociological knowledge today is more reliable than common-sense ideas. While applied knowledge is ultimately dependent on the development of more fundamental, or "pure," forms of scientific knowledge, it is possible to go further in developing applied sociological knowledge, because we have made more progress in developing our fundamental methods and knowledge than we have in applying that knowledge. This may be due to the frequent insistence on doing "sociology for its own sake," which many sociologists felt was necessary for achieving academic respectability in the United States. Now that this struggle has been won, sociologists are returning to their basic commitment, which requires more direct attention to developing applied sociological knowledge, for the development of fundamental knowledge does not guarantee the simultaneous development of applied knowledge. Applied knowledge considers the specific problems of practical action. In applying sociological knowledge to our social problems, we must keep in mind the nature of action directed at solving social problems in our democratic society. The consideration of practical political action brings us to the question of the relationship between sociological knowledge and the common-sense ideas that dominate thought in everyday life.

SOCIOLOGICAL KNOWLEDGE AND THE COMMON SENSE OF EVERYDAY LIFE

It was once common for sociologists to deride common-sense descriptions and explanations of human events. Recently, it has become apparent that sociology itself is partially based on common-sense understandings. As we shall see throughout this book, sociology's dependence on common sense is based on the fact that sociology is always fundamentally concerned with understanding what goes on in everyday life; however scientific we seek to make this understanding, it is necessarily founded on common-sense understandings of everyday life.

However, sociology as the science of man is different in crucial ways from common-sense theories of man and society. As a science of society, *sociology seeks a knowledge of society that is more objective than the practical thought of everyday life.*

In almost all situations of everyday life, we restrict our interest in understanding the situation to those details we see as important in "getting the job done" at the time. For example, a businessman may say that "You can't trust anyone because it's human nature to take all you can get," but his concern is not with human nature in general, but, rather, with the application of such an idea to his dealings with customers. His knowledge of human nature would be largely at the level of what he might call "rules of thumb," or knowledge to be used within the boundaries of a given situation. He would not be seeking a theory of human nature that could be used in all situations. He would not set out to systematically test his idea about the untrustworthiness of human beings, nor would he be likely to interest himself in any work of social science that did try to systematically test such an idea across many kinds of situations.

The interest of the sociologist in human nature is very different. His interest would be in the generalizability of such an idea about the trustworthiness of human beings, and he would be mainly concerned with testing any such generalization to see if it holds true in different situations. The sociologist, then, is seeking a transsituational knowledge of man and society, potentially useful in many different situations to many different individuals with different feelings, ideas, values, and goals. In this sense, sociologists have been said to be seeking a *value-free* knowledge of man and society.

In the early part of this century Max Weber, the most important of the German sociologists, wrote the classic statement on the need for commitment to providing a value-free sociology. In a period when German sociologists were under great pressure to commit their work entirely to direct involvement in social reform, including pressure from many student activists of their day, Weber argued that sociology and the other social sciences must resist such pressures if they are to be true to the goals of creating a science of society. He argued:

> It is said, and I agree, that politics is out of place in the lecture-room. It does not belong there on the part of the students. If, for instance, in the lecture-room of my former colleague Dietrich Schafer in Berlin, pacifist students were to surround his desk and make an uproar, I should deplore it just as much as I should deplore the uproar which anti-pacifist students are said to have made against Professor Forster, whose views in many ways are as remote as could be from mine. Neither does politics, however, belong in the lecture-room on the part of the docents [teachers], and when the docent is scientifically concerned with politics, it belongs there least of all.
>
> To take a practical political stand is one thing, and to analyze political structures and party positions is another . . . the prophet and the demagogue do not belong on the academic platform (Weber, 1970, pp. 52–53).

Many sociologists interpreted Weber's position as proposing that they study society without any value commitments, and they used Weber's arguments to support their position that sociology should remain aloof from the study of social problems and from attempts to create an applied sociology directly concerned with finding general solutions to social problems. But this was a misinterpretation of Weber's position. As Alvin Gouldner has argued (1970, p. 69), Weber knew that sociology inevitably involves some value assumptions. He was trying to keep political values out of the university to avoid the conflicts they would entail.

It has become increasingly clear to sociologists that it is not possible to study man and society scientifically without making some value commitments—at least implicitly. First, the commitment to creating a science of society is itself a value commitment, and science is necessarily governed by rules or values intended to assure truthful results from scientific work. Second, any scientist must make decisions about what to study and what methods to use, or not to use, that involve implicit value judgments about what is worthwhile and moral. For example, in the past several decades American sociologists have put immense effort into studying and explaining juvenile delinquency, while they have rarely studied crimes committed by businessmen, professionals, or politicians. An implicit value judgment is involved in such a nonrandom distribution of sociological effort. Third, while any scientist has a commitment to try to control the effects of his personal feelings, beliefs, and values on his research and analysis, it seems almost impossible that anyone studying society, which is so important to all of us, could eliminate all effects of his personal feelings, beliefs, and values about the subject.

It would, then, be unreasonable for sociologists to expect that they could ever eliminate all value commitments from their research and theory. Rather, what they can reasonably expect to do, and what most sociologists today try to do, is to *control* the effects of their personal feelings, ideas, and values. There are three major ways in which they do this. First, like all scientists, sociologists have organized their discipline to attempt to control these effects by training sociology students from the beginning to try to eliminate them from their work. That is, members of the discipline teach the need for such individual controls and punish those who deviate from the rule. Second, sociologists do not rely too heavily on such self-control, for they know how common deviations can be in any group. Instead, they seek to control effects of personal feelings, ideas, and values on sociological work by insisting that any research and theory be *public* and *repeatable*. The methods and findings must be reported, or they will not be accorded credibility, and no findings are accepted until they have been found true (or valid) by independent retest. The insistence that findings be public and repeatable is reinforced by the insistence on free competition and the training of students to be creative or original to make certain that any findings will be subject to intensive review and argument from competitors for the scarce commodity of prestige among fellow scientists. Third, unlike other sciences, sociology has come increasingly to try to control personal effects on findings through a form of self-analysis and self-criticism known as the *sociology of knowledge* and, more specifically, the *sociology of sociology* (see Insert Nos. 1 and 2). The sociology of knowledge seeks the implicit assumptions and involvements that lie behind any form of social knowledge. The sociology of sociology seeks the implicit assumptions of sociological investigations and findings. Both help sociologists to be aware of the effects of personal or cultural feelings, ideas, and values on their work as sociologists and thereby to better control these effects.

Just as any social controls are imperfect, sociologists have sometimes failed to control their personal feelings, beliefs, and values, with the result that biases have not been uncommon in sociological works. However, by progressively controlling the biases that come from the concrete, situational involvements of the researcher and theorist, sociological knowledge becomes more *transsituational,* applicable to more kinds of old and new situations, than can be expected of most common-sense social thought. This transsituational, objective nature of sociological knowledge makes it of crucial importance in attempts to solve social problems in our increasingly complex and changing society.

CONTRIBUTIONS OF SOCIOLOGY TO SOLVING AMERICA'S SOCIAL PROBLEMS

Scientific knowledge of man and society has become increasingly crucial in attempts to solve our social problems, primarily because of the growing complexity of our society. This complexity is due partly to the continuing pluralistic nature of American society. But it is also due to the accelerating pace of scientific, technological, and general social change, which makes knowledge ever more complex, throws individuals and groups into new situations they did not anticipate, casts up new groups overnight, and destroys the economic basis of existence of many old groups. This growing complexity has made it increasingly difficult for political leaders to have first-hand knowledge of the problems, their causes, the people they affect, and methods to solve them. This growing complexity has produced an inevitable increase in individuals' relative ignorance of our society, as true of political leaders as it is of anyone else.

This growth in ignorance has been made more important by an accompanying centralization of power, most obvious in the case of the federal government, which has taken over more and more power from state and local governments. In addition, businesses, educational institutions, and private groups have become increasingly centralized in recent decades, as

W. Lloyd Warner and his co-workers have found (1967, pp. 15–16). As decision making about social problems has become more centralized, it has become more difficult for decision makers to have first-hand knowledge of the relevant social facts. At the same time, their decisions affect growing numbers of people, while their inevitable lack of first-hand knowledge of local situations makes serious mistakes more likely.

The first contribution of sociology to solving social problems in our society, then, is the scientific information it provides on the many far-flung parts of our society and world. In a world in which knowledge of situations other than those at hand becomes ever more vital, the transsituational knowledge provided by a scientific sociology becomes ever more useful. A typical example of differences between sociological knowledge and common-sense knowledge, with bearing on social policy, will make this clear.

Our example comes from the long history of sociological studies of slums. We shall consider the problems of slums and urban renewal in greater detail in chapters 4 and 19. (At this time, the reader might want to read the section

---

INSERT NO. 1

On Robert W. Friedrichs' *A Sociology of Sociology*

According to Berger and Luckmann, any attempt to apply the sociology of knowledge to sociology itself represents an attempt to push the bus in which one is riding (1967). But Friedrichs' application of the sociology of knowledge to the discipline, *A Sociology of Sociology*, indicates that the attempt may not be so implausible.

Friedrichs' work applies the principles developed in Thomas Kuhn's *The Structure of Scientific Revolutions* to sociology. Kuhn, analyzing the history of science and the accumulation of knowledge that represents scientific "progress," points out that such knowledge does not build steadily in an evolutionary sense but, rather, develops through revolutionary changes in the basic assumptions or paradigms of scientific knowledge itself. Friedrichs applies this central concept to sociology, undertaking a massive inventory of sociological theory and research activity since the beginning of the discipline.

In the United States of the post–World War II era, according to Friedrichs, the major sociological paradigm was that of system, or structural functionalism, in which the equilibrating tendency of societies was stressed, rather than conflict between groups. The sociologist's self-image was that of "priest," the upholder of the status quo and of society's core values.

However, asserts Friedrichs, sociology today is witnessing a revolutionary change in fundamental paradigm and in the sociologist's conception of his role. The rising paradigm is that of conflict, and the current self-image of the

in Chapter 19 on "The Urban Crisis and the Continuing Failure of White Magic.") It has been a common belief in our society, and one widely shared by those making policy decisions concerning slum dwellers, that people who live in slums are highly "disorganized." This idea probably came in part from the appearance of disorder in the complex and noisy street lives of slum dwellers. Whatever its origin, it has had a great effect on public policies as justification for using a great deal of police power in the slums in an attempt to impose order from outside and for breaking up old slums with massive urban renewal projects. As long as sociologists felt that official statistics on crime and similar phenomena were reliable sources of information on such groups, they believed the common-sense theory of the disorganized slum and proposed theories of social disorganization to explain official rates of crime, suicide, and so on in slum areas (see Chapter 20). But, as sociologists developed more intensive participant-observer methods of studying the slum areas, they began to discover many forms of highly developed social organization in the slums. Herbert Gans was one of the

> sociologist is the prophet, the humanistic spokesman for creative social change, and the carefully objective research scientist. However, the conflict paradigm will never be fully accepted in sociology, says Friedrichs, because science deals ultimately with the problem of order.
>
> Friedrichs' theory of paradigms does not mean, of course, that all sociologists at any one time use the same kind of theories and hold the same kind of attitudes toward themselves and society. It indicates that in the sociological discipline, at any one time, certain major paradigms are most significant and bring sociologists the most professional acclaim and reward. In recognition of the variety of sociological competitors for contemporary paradigmatic status, Friedrichs analyzes the claims made by competing theories in this time of revolutionary alteration in the basic modes of sociological thought, from Marxism to phenomenology.
>
> Friedrichs speaks for a sociology that uses both system and conflict, priest and prophet, as conceptual modes and professional roles and concludes:
>
>> Although I have both revealed and admitted my support for the current reclamation of the prophetic mode, it does not mean that I would at the same time deny the priestly . . . although the one will appear dominant at one moment in sociology's history and the second at another, the prophetic and the priestly modes will continue in dialogue—as they do in the larger religious-philosophic life of our kind. If one would seek a term that would envelop both the active and passive, the liberating and the ordering, nature of our calling as sociologists, perhaps *witness* may do. The sociologist would be witness to the profoundly social dialogue that is man (1970, pp. 327–328).

first sociologists to make this point, after living in an inner city Boston area for an extended period (see Insert No. 3). Following Gans' work, Gerald Suttles' more detailed study of a slum area in Chicago found complex forms of social organization that are different in many ways from those found in most urban nonslum areas (see Insert No. 4). Other studies—for example, in Detroit and Indianapolis—have shown that the overall picture is variable. Some slums are more organized than others, and their inhabitants' feelings about living in the slums differ widely.

All this evidence makes it clear that any simple social policy based on the assumption that slums are socially disorganized is apt to cause more trouble than it can correct. Sociologists have argued that urban renewal projects that break up slums are likely to break up patterns of community organization that are vital in preventing forms of behavior defined by police and inhabitants as deviant. There is good reason to suspect that much well-

---

INSERT NO. 2

On Alvin W. Gouldner's *The Coming Crisis of Western Sociology*

While the morality promoted by conventional academic sociology has heretofore reserved the cutting edge of its scapel for its patient, the "subject," *The Coming Crisis of Western Sociology* is Alvin W. Gouldner's attempt to turn the sociological imagination upon the doctor. This attempt to construct "an historically informed sociology of social theory" is grounded in the author's conviction that the social theories of previous times no longer capture the existential realities and sentiments of those who have experienced the turbulence and conflict of recent decades. Gouldner's scholarly historical critique of American academic sociology (especially of the arcane thought of Talcott Parsons) combines with the author's promotion of a reflexive sociology. As conceived by Gouldner, this new sociology of sociology would regard the knowledge it purports to have about the world "out there" as being as problematic as conventional academic sociology has typically regarded the knowledge of its subjects—those thought less capable than the omniscient sociologist of knowing the real and the good. Reflexive sociology would regard as problematic the subject-object dichotomy, historically sacrosanct in Western rationalist thought; self-knowledge would be the *raison d'être* of its practitioners, a self-knowledge forged in personal involvement and a politically conscious practice.

Asserting that every social theory is a tacit theory of politics as well as a personal theory "inevitably expressing, coping, and infused with the personal experience of the individuals who author it," Gouldner analyzes the historical development of social theories since the time of St. Simon and Comte as im-

intended slum clearance, costing great amounts of tax money, has had the opposite result from that intended.

But providing reliable knowledge about our complex society and world is only the most basic, and the easiest, contribution of sociology to effective social policies. The second contribution is knowledge of the relations between the parts, the task of social theory, or what most people would see as determining the causes of problems, or explaining the social facts about them.

The determination of the facts and the explanations of the relations between these facts are more closely related to each other than our discussion so far might indicate, because sociologists rarely do field research without first having some theory about what to look for. This procedure is necessary, as the observations one might make are infinite, while time to make them is decidedly finite. But any theory is at least partially based on previous fac-

---

mersed in their "infrastructures"—the subtheoretical assumptions and sentiments taken for granted by the theorist and his colleagues working within a given intellectual milieu. From this perspective, social theories are conceived by Gouldner as efforts to remedy the meanings of the world of experience, attempts to impose a theoretical structure upon the existential world in order to make sense out of it and to control it more effectively. While more often used by men in power to conserve their own ideological interests, many social theories possess liberating as well as constraining potentials. However, he views most social theories to date as attempts to define social reality rather than to investigate it.

Added to Gouldner's critique of sociological theories and their uses is a more explicit political message. The author calls for the construction of a counterculture to oppose the prevailing absolutist definitions of personal reality in the "utilitarian culture" of contemporary technological societies, both East and West. Thus, while criticizing conventional academic sociology for its failure to examine the metaphysical assumptions upon which it rests (and to which it owes its recent respectability), Gouldner's reflexive sociology would be grounded in an absolutist opposition to those definitions. To oppose the power and influence achieved by the now respectable sociologists who are presenting themselves as the philosopher-kings of the "Welfare State," the practitioners of Gouldner's "new" sociology would promote the activist philosopher-serf, the streetfighter armed with a new subjectivist epistemology to guide his practical action. The scientific, absolute knowledge (or God) promised, but never delivered, by the positivists has led the author to conclude that the pain and uncertainty of *struggling* for objective knowledge in the social sciences is much less exhilarating than the action at the barricades (John M. Johnson).

tual investigations, producing a feedback system open to new experience that has not yet been incorporated into theory. In spite of this relationship between fact and theory, there is a difference in degree of reliability. Any proposed theoretical relation is certainly more risky, more subject to error, than the factual relationship it seeks to explain, which is why there is more

---

INSERT NO. 3

On Herbert J. Gans' *The Urban Villagers*

The Urban Villagers is "a report of a participant-observation study of an inner city Boston neighborhood called the West End, and, in particular, of the native-born Americans of Italian parentage who lived there amidst other ethnic groups." Gans refers to the West End as an "urban village" rather than a slum —an urban area in which European immigrants, and sometimes other minorities, try to adapt their nonurban institutions and cultures to the urban environment:

> Nor did the West End satisfy the social criteria that would have made it a slum. Residents with social and emotional problems, with behavior difficulties, and with criminal records could be found in the area, partially because of the low rents. This was especially true after 1950, when increasing vacancies attracted single transients, Gypsies, and "multi-problem" families. Such people obtained apartments in the West End because landlords could no longer afford to reject what they defined as "undesirable" tenants. The presence of such tenants helped to convince the community at large that the West End was a slum. Yet all this time the West End was also a major area of first settlement for newcomers without problems or criminal records: especially immigrants from Italy, from Displaced Persons camps in Europe, from rural New England, and from French Canada. Thus, the area had an important but unrecognized function in the city. Even so, the majority of West Enders were people who had lived there since before 1950. Many of them also had problems, especially those associated with low income and acculturation. But the problems of old residents and newcomers alike had not been created by the neighborhood. If anything, the stability of a large part of the population created a more desirable social climate for newcomers than existed in the other major area of first settlement in Boston, the South End (Gans, 1962, p. 316).

But the city planners did not make Gans' distinction between a socially disorganized slum and a relatively organized urban village. The West End was torn down between 1958 and 1960, just after Gans completed his year-long residence there.

argument among sociologists and between sociologists and others over the explanations of social facts than over the facts themselves. For this reason, valid social theory normally develops more slowly than reliable research findings. Yet the contribution of valid explanations of social facts is potentially of greater importance in solving social problems than the contribution of reliable social facts, especially in a complex society in which commonsense theories have trouble allowing for all possible important relations.

Providing scientific explanations of complex and problematic social phenomena, of the relationships between different facts about different social situations that pose problems for members of society, has been such a unique function of sociology in Western societies that some have mistaken it for the "sociological imagination." They have failed to see that the first concern of sociology must be with the facts of everyday social situations because the rest of sociology, and certainly the explanations of the relations between these situational facts, cannot be valid unless the facts on which they are based are valid. Nevertheless, some sociologists have seen that the explanations of the relations between situations is the greatest contribution the discipline can make to the solution of complex social problems.

C. Wright Mills has been the most influential authority to urge sociologists to concentrate on general descriptions and explanations of society to reveal the causes of social problems, especially as members of society experience these problems in their everyday lives without realizing their social origins (1959, p. 35). Mills argues that our situation demands the "sociological imagination," rather than sociological theory. The rapidity of change and the development of social problems makes practical action to solve them so vital that it is often impossible to wait for the development of theory that can be validated by scientific investigations. Part of what is demanded for practical action—especially at the highest level of action by central governments—is a general picture of what is going on throughout society and, indeed, throughout the world. This picture is necessary for the general planning that is increasingly essential for maintaining rational order in the massive operations of central governments. Sociologists and others must make use of what valid scientific information and theory they have at the time, but they must use it partly to construct more speculative ideas about what is going on in our society and how these patterns of events are related to what is going on in other societies and throughout the world. It is the construction of this more speculative picture which Mills has seen as the province of the sociological imagination.

Normally, sociologists talk about these "big pictures" of society in terms of *social structure* or *macrosociology*. While many have made the mistake of taking these broad generalizations as social facts, sociologists must make these *over*-generalizations if they are to use scientific information and theories in the solution of social problems. An excellent example is found in current policy considerations of the relation between race and poverty in the United States. The facts are diverse, as we shall see in Chapters 14 and 19. Any given study, like any given personal experience, could give one a false picture of what is going on. Any investigation of a particular everyday situation may prove highly unrepresentative. The *problem of representability*, that is, of seeing how a study of one part of society is related to the whole society, is one of the greatest problems of most studies of everyday life situations because, generally, such studies are done intensively rather than extensively. As a result, studies of everyday life situations must be put into the more general context of structural studies of our society that provide much less detail, but do give us an idea of the representativeness of the

---

INSERT NO. 4

On Gerald D. Suttles' *The Social Order of the Slum*

Gerald Suttles' study of a modern slum (1968) is done in the tradition of Chicago urban studies. Like most of the Chicago studies since the 1920s, and like William Foote Whyte's classic study of a Boston slum, *Street Corner Society* (1943), Suttles did this study by becoming a participant-observer in the everyday lives of its members. He lived in the area he called the Addams area, really the Near West Side of Chicago, for three years and through his daily contacts and more formal research work came to know its inhabitants intimately. His book is largely a description and analysis of the area "from the inside," of the way its members see the world and of how they act in their everyday lives.

The Near West Side fits all the standard stereotypes of a "slum." Its inhabitants are poor and crowded, its buildings dilapidated. It is still commonly known in Chicago as the old neighborhood of Al Capone and Frank "The Enforcer" Nitti. It has one of the highest official crime rates, including delinquency rates, in a city with a high crime rate. Among the citizens of Chicago, "It is also known that there are 'gangs' and that 'a lot happens on Taylor Street.' At night it is supposed to be dangerous and inhospitable to outsiders" (Suttles, 1968, p. 25). In short, the Addams area is a classic example of what outsiders who do not know an area see as a "highly disorganized" one.

However, through his intensive participant-observation of the everyday lives of its inhabitants, Suttles found that the social life of this slum area is about as organized as the lives of any group who live with each other over a long period of time. Judged by the "ideal" standards of American public life, the Addams residents are indeed "disreputable" and "untrustworthy." They are

findings. Someday it may prove possible to do enough systematically chosen studies of everyday life situations to derive our ideas of the structure of society entirely from such studies. In the case of the relation between race and poverty, structural studies would seek to determine what are the most probable relationships between the two throughout our society.

But structural analyses have failed to provide an additional factor of key importance in deciding what to do about social problems. Structural analyses have generally remained *static* pictures of our society, pictures of our society at one given time, rather than *dynamic* pictures, pictures of relationships between social facts over a number of time periods. Yet any plans concerning what to do must take into consideration the trends or changes in the

> poor and almost all of them are members of one of four ethnic and racial minorities: Italian, Negro, Mexican, and Puerto Rican. There is more use of physical force, especially on the part of gang boys, and many of its residents condone various forms of public deviance. But looking at the area in this way, from outside, gives one a misleading picture. The careful participant-observer discovers that the residents do not reject the moral standards of the wider society, the so-called public morality. Instead, they give their own emphases to it and put the particular moral edicts into the context of their own complex lives; they "observe" the public morality in their own way. In addition, he finds that they have other important ways of ordering their lives that go beyond the morality of the wider public to deal with the problems specific to their own complex situation. As Suttles concludes, "Seen in more holistic terms, the residents are bent on ordering local relations where the beliefs and evaluations of the wider society do not provide adequate guidelines for conduct" (1968, p. 4).
>
> Above all, residents of the Addams area find that they must live *with* members of three other ethnic and religious groups. They must find some way to get along with each other. If they were to try to order their lives in terms of any abstract set of morals, especially one imposed from outside, they would come into continual conflict with these other inhabitants. The attempt to live by abstract morals would create a war of all against all, rather than producing social order. In order to live together, the slum inhabitants must create values and social order in the context of their own specific, concrete situations. Suttles found that residents of the Addams area have created a social order based primarily on ethnicity and on territoriality. This allows them to live separated from each other culturally, in their own distinct ethnic cultures, while also living with each other in daily contact and dealing with the outside areas of the city in terms of the interests they share as members of the Addams area. It is a complex social order, and one involving a great deal of individual effort to deal with the practical problems faced, but not a "disorganized" world.

relations between particular facts, because we must know where we are going before we know how to intervene to produce the situations we want.

Providing such *predictive knowledge* about the relationships between social facts is the third purpose of sociology, which makes it of crucial importance today. As Robert Lynd long ago argued, in a rapidly changing society sociological knowledge that allows us to predict the directions changes are taking and will take becomes of vital importance in solving the problems and in changing conditions before the problems arise or before they become critical and intractable (Lynd, 1939, p. 38).

The rapid growth of urban riots in the United States in the 1960s presents us with an excellent example of the importance of being able to predict what will happen if the dominant trends of a period continue. The situation in the urban ghettos and the militancy of many young blacks were not sudden occurrences. They had been developing for decades as changes in the agricultural economy of the South, aspirations, and new opportunities produced immigration to northern and western cities where the new arrivals met discrimination in jobs and housing. A growing number of the newcomers and their children turned to various forms of political action to alleviate their situation, and some of these took on an increasingly militant orientation—the best known, that of the Black Muslims. Sociologists, continuing their practice of studying racial relations, did studies during this period which revealed such trends, but little notice was given to them and little action was taken to alleviate the situation. As Melvin Tumin has argued, much evidence revealed by sociological investigations could have been used to predict violence, had there been an interest in making such predictions (Tumin, 1970, p. 116).

It is not possible today to predict most social events from any social theory. The relative freedom of choice involved in human decisions in concrete situations leads us to expect that we shall never be able to predict many concrete events (see Chapter 4). Nevertheless, we can already predict some important short-run trends in society and make good estimates of how these trends will interact. A major reason that sociology has not contributed more by making such short-run predictions is that little effort has been devoted to them, partly because of the relative lack of attention paid to the application of sociological knowledge to social problems, but also because of a lack of appreciation of the difficulty of making social predictions.

Some sociologists have recently begun to correct this lack of effort. Daniel Bell, who directed the Committee on the Year 2000 and edited the volume *Toward the Year 2000*, has done the most in the United States, though the committee's work has thus far been greatly influenced by the pioneering work in Europe of Bertrand de Jouvenal and other futurists.

Much of this has consisted in exploring various kinds of predictions and the relative difficulties of each kind. Even such exploratory work gives us reason to believe that we can do better. In the short run, we can at least provide the kinds of *extrapolations* (or simple projections) from current trends that will provide valuable information.

OPPORTUNITIES AND PROBLEMS OF INVOLVEMENT FOR SOCIOLOGY

The growing involvement of sociologists in attempts to solve social problems will create opportunities for sociology, and many difficulties. We must be clear about these opportunities and difficulties so that we can manage our involvement in a way that will prove most beneficial to sociology and to society.

The main opportunity for the discipline will be the greater access to information about practical and political activities in our society. By participating more directly in political decision making, sociologists will learn first hand about matters they have rarely studied in depth, partly because it is so difficult to get access to politically touchy activities. This information will be most important for the development of applied sociology, but it will also affect the development of social theory in much the same way that practical applications of knowledge in the natural sciences affected their theories, especially in the early stages of their development.

But direct involvement, especially involvement that encourages commitment to the values implicit in attempts to solve social problems, always poses the danger of bias. The more directly involved the sociologist is, the harder it is for him to become aware of some of the ideas, beliefs, values, and feelings of the participants. He comes to take many of these for granted and fails to note their importance. The more involved the sociologist is, the more he is likely to identify with the goals of the organization and to come to see it as the members do, especially since they will exert pressures upon him to be loyal to their purposes and ideas. The danger of becoming a "booster" for the enterprise is far greater than if he were simply studying the activity.

Perhaps the best solution to these problems is to minimize the costs (or difficulties) while maximizing the profits (or opportunities). This would seem best done by avoiding any full-scale commitment of the individual sociologist or of the discipline as a whole to the practical activities of solving social problems. A middle-range strategy means becoming involved enough to understand the problems, but not so much that we become men of practical affairs rather than seekers of knowledge first and action second.

SOCIAL DANGERS OF INVOLVEMENT

Besides the problems for sociology posed by our growing involvement in attempts to solve social problems, at least two major dangers to our society could result from such involvement: (1) danger from the soulless technocrat who provides technical knowledge to his political master for use in controlling the people and (2) the closely related danger of a tyranny of experts. Each danger must be understood if we are to prevent them from becoming actualities.

Many sociologists who have studied social problems have been *technocratic*—that is, they have sought to provide information on social problems, as defined by political officials, which these officials can use to control the people they see as the causes of the problems. This alliance, which goes back to the origins of sociology in the nineteenth century, has led many sociologists of social problems to assume that the moral standards and beliefs of the middle-class groups are right and that anyone who deviates is a problem case who must be controlled. This outlook is what C. Wright Mills meant when he argued that the social pathologists, the sociologists studying social problems from the 1920s into the 1950s, made implicit assumptions that predetermined the nature of their work (1963, pp. 527–533). Analyses of such implicit value commitments have made sociologists more aware of them and more able to control them, but they continue in important ways today.

The danger of a *tyranny of experts* results from the opposite possibility that, instead of being faceless technocrats serving their political masters, sociologists and other social scientists could seek to impose their own values and beliefs on the officials and the public. This becomes possible as officials and the public come to believe that problems are too complex for them to understand and solve and that they must turn them all over to "experts." The experts may even decide that the public is so ignorant that it must be controlled for its own sake. The more likely form of tyrannical control is a more indirect one, which the perpetrators might not realize they are practicing. It is the form of control that comes from insisting on the validity of one's own ideas about how social problems can be solved, even when there is no reason to believe such a conclusion. Daniel Moynihan has given an excellent discussion of this imposition of one's own ideas on an area in which there was inadequate knowledge to reach certain conclusions. From his own experience with the poverty program during the Johnson years, Moynihan argued that the sociologists and other social scientists entrusted with mapping the strategy to end poverty refused to recognize the existence of important evidence that opposed their own pet ideas—refused, in fact, to "look at the data" (Moynihan, 1969, p. 1).

Some sociologists have argued that there is no threat of a tyranny of experts because social scientists do not have the knowledge to control society (see Waitzkin, 1967). But this faith assumes that control over behavior will flow directly from scientific knowledge. It assumes that, if there were already real scientific knowledge of human behavior, there would already be practical forms of scientific control over that behavior. Yet scientific knowledge does not lead directly to the power necessary for control. Knowledge of trajectories and rocket power did not assure space engineers they could send men to the moon. Vast resources were needed to put that knowledge to work, resources beyond their control as scientists. While gaining control over such social power is itself a subject studied by sociologists and may be partially controllable by those who have systematic knowledge of it, we cannot judge the practicality of sociological knowledge in general on the basis of effective control over social events.

We can know whether sociological knowledge is able to control social events and is thereby dangerous when used for the wrong purposes, only when it has been applied to actual problems by those who control the physical and social resources, those who have the power in society. Only then can we see if it works, just as we could see that rocket engineering works only after those with the power allocated resources to put men on the moon. In the past few decades, sociologists have become more important as advisors and administrators in the federal government. The dangers associated with such power are now growing.

Belief in the necessary impotence of sociology assumes that sociological knowledge in the future will remain the same as in the past. But progress in research and theory is accelerating. Also, sociologists in the past paid little attention to the development of applied sociological knowledge, whereas they are now paying ever more attention to applied sociology. It seems likely that the development of practical applications of sociological knowledge to social problems will now be rapid.

Scientific knowledge takes quantum leaps that invalidate simple projections of the future from the past. For example, molecular biology had few practical applications and thus few dangerous implications for society during many decades of its development, but the discovery of means for controlling hereditary traits through DNA changes that. The same must be expected of the social sciences. The most harmless-looking discipline today, the most abstract pastime of scholars, may become an angel of mercy tomorrow—or a Frankenstein.

But the dangers of using sociology to control human beings do not come entirely from those involved in applying valid sociological knowledge to society. They come as well from the use of sociology as a front to exploit the prestige of science and of the academic world to control society. In our society, science and technology have acquired vast prestige. "Scientific knowledge" becomes the ultimate test of truth, and the scientist becomes the folk hero. Diverse groups try to adopt the name of science or engineering to advance their causes—as with poultry scientists, dental technicians, or sanitation engineers. Science is used as a front to make the public see their activities as more important and deserving of higher pay and more power.

This pretense of scientific knowledge, often called "expertise," poses a threat. While those who wish to control our society may not have many social scientists to serve their purposes, they can often buy the help of a few or buy "scientific reports" that will support their position.

It is this use of social scientists that Loren Baritz has examined in his work on *The Servants of Power,* in which he has showed the ways in which social scientists have been used in industry by managers to control the workers:

> Through motivation studies, through counseling, through selection devices calculated to hire only certain types of people, through attitude surveys, communication, role-playing, and all the rest in their bag of schemes, social scientists slowly moved toward a science of behavior. Thus management was given a slick new approach to its problems of control. Authority gave way to manipulation, and workers could no longer be sure they were being exploited (Baritz, 1970, p. 154).

The assumption that the man of practical thought is wrong about the nature of reality, while only the scientist can know ultimate truth, is another all too common fallacy that lends itself to a tyrannical approach to controlling the common man. For if he is in disagreement with the scientist, surely he must be presumed to be wrong, even about those matters concerning his own well-being.

In the latter part of the nineteenth century and the early part of this century, this belief in the necessary superiority of science in determining what is right led many social thinkers, both those who looked primarily to science for their methods and those who looked primarily to philosophy or the humanities, to believe that they had created a "positive" or "positivistic" ethic that could determine what is morally and ethically right in a given situation by scientific means. This assumption that the superiority of science in determining objective knowledge about events holds true for values and goals has far-reaching implications of tyranny. Such an assumption might justify control of society by "scientific experts" who can determine what is desirable and undesirable for all the citizens of a society. However, there remain only a few extreme positivists such as B. F. Skinner, who has described the perfect tyranny of experts in *Walden II*.

There are two major reasons that the assumptions which would justify such a tyranny of experts are wrong. First, there are no grounds for believing that scientific thought and common-sense thought are of a different order.

We now find that science is based on the assumption of everyday, practical thought. Scientists, for example, make such unexamined, or "metaphysical," assumptions as: there exists out there a world independent of the mind of the scientist; ordinary perceptions can be counted on to provide evidence about that external world; the world any given individual experiences is the same for other individuals; it is possible for those individuals to communicate with each other in some reliable fashion about that external world; this communication may reliably take place partly in terms of common-sense languages; and so on. As Karl Popper, Thomas Kuhn, and other historians and philosophers of science have argued, the basic methods of science are necessarily determined in part by the nature of the practical, everyday involvements of the scientists themselves. There is, then, no reason to see a basic opposition between common sense and science. Science must be seen as partly determined by common sense, and as scientific thought also becomes a determinant *of* common sense, the two must be seen as interdependent. Their differences are matters of degree, which are no doubt important, but there is no justification for exaggerating them.

Second, while values can be illuminated by logical argument and while any applications of values to concrete situations must always be made in the light of factual considerations, values are relativistic and cannot be "determined" by scientific investigation. Values vary with cultures and individuals, and no scientific method can ultimately determine that one value is better than another, though science can determine which values are more viable in given situations. The sociologist can determine what values exist in a given group, analyze their relations to each other and to beliefs, and try to determine what effects they have on the actions of those who hold them. But in most situations he has no advantage over other members of society in saying which values are better than others.

While social scientists must go beyond common-sense considerations of social phenomena if they are to provide scientific knowledge to solve social problems, inevitably they remain partially grounded in common-sense considerations of those problems. And solutions to those problems must be sought within the constraints of democratic decisions about what is worthwhile and what is not.

The sociologist need not become a faceless technocrat providing information to any who choose to hire him. Rather, he must try to determine causes of problems and anticipate the problems that will arise, both of which he can do adequately only by going beyond the concerns of men in their everyday, practical lives (see Chapters 19 and 21). But, rather than trying to impose his ideas and conclusions about those problems and what he believes are the best possible solutions, he must seek to communicate these ideas to the public and to convince them through free argument and persuasion that his conclusions are right. He must, then, become a more active advocate (or "witness"), but never a tyrant seeking to impose his ideas by direct or indirect manipulation of power.

EVERYDAY LIFE SITUATIONS, SOCIAL STRUCTURES, AND SOCIAL PROBLEMS

The task of the sociologist in helping people solve social problems is made more difficult because the meanings of "social problems" and of "solutions" to those problems are partially determined by the decisions of members of our society (see Chapters 19 and 21). The dual role of the advocate-sociologist—partially directed by democratic decisions on values while at the same time remaining partially independent of those decisions so that he can try to persuade the public what decisions to make—means that the sociologist should allow the public to specify for him the problems he should try to solve while he tries to persuade the public that certain potential problems exist.

But this *sociological dilemma* is central to the nature of the sociological enterprise and the scientific enterprise. This dilemma results from the need to base sociology on the scientific study of everyday life situations while going beyond those studies to provide structural analyses of situations in the society as a whole.

Necessarily, sociology begins with an understanding of everyday life situations, and it can progress as a science only by developing more objective means of observing and analyzing those everyday life situations. What sociologists seek to do in order to gain a scientific understanding of the society is to determine the relations between different everyday life situations. In this way they get at the patternings or structurings of situations.

At the same time, the commitment of sociologists to providing scientific information and explanations that can be used in solving social problems may force them to extend their generalizations beyond the level justified by the evidence. Often, social problems involve large segments of society and are complex. But their urgency is such that we cannot always wait for highly reliable scientific information and theories. The urgency of the problems and their complex relationships to the many parts of our society, then, force us to develop analyses of the patterns of our society, *structural analyses*, that can be used in understanding and solving the problems even though they may not be based on sufficient evidence to be considered "hard science." We must sometimes leap ahead of our evidence in inferring structural relations among these situations. But we must then constantly revise our analyses of social structures in terms of further studies of everyday situations. Only in this way can sociology fulfill its dual promise of developing a science of man and helping to solve social problems of our society.

SUGGESTED READINGS

Baritz, Loren, *The Servants of Power: A History of the Uses of Social Science in American Industry*. Middletown: Wesleyan University Press, 1960.
> An account of the ways in which social scientists have been used by managers of industry in an attempt to control the workers.

Friedrichs, Robert W., *A Sociology of Sociology*. New York: The Free Press, 1970.
> A scholarly account of the historical development of sociology, and its present status in terms of its own concepts.

Gouldner, Alvin W., *The Coming Crisis of Western Sociology*. New York: Basic Books, 1970.
> This account of the historical development of sociology, from the Marxist perspective, is brilliant, thought-provoking, and polemical.

Liebow, Elliott, *Tally's Corner*. Boston: Little, Brown, 1967.
> A participant-observer study of unemployed blacks on a street corner in Washington, D.C. Liebow observed their interactions in many settings, from family life to sporadic employment situations.

Mills, C. Wright, *The Sociological Imagination*. New York: Oxford University Press, 1959.
> A fascinating and controversial analysis and indictment of contemporary sociological methods and theory.

Parsons, Talcott, *The Social System*. New York: The Free Press, 1951.
> One of the best known of the structural-functional analyses of society, Parsons' monumental work has had a profound influence on the progress of sociology in the twentieth century.

Suttles, Gerald D., *The Social Order of the Slum*. Chicago: University of Chicago Press, 1968.
> A participant-observer study of a slum community in the Chicago tradition, Suttles' analysis stresses the social organization underlying the apparent disorder of the slum.

CHAPTER 2

The Emergence of Modern Sociology

Individuals have always been concerned with understanding their societies, for they must have such understandings to act effectively. Attempts to create scientific knowledge of society go back centuries, but only in the last few centuries have these attempts become systematic in Western societies.

Because sociology, like any discipline, is so much influenced by the historical situations in which it is created, this chapter shows the major historical paths of development of basic ideas of sociology. It analyzes the nineteenth-century situation in which most of the major theoretical perspectives we still find in sociology were created, shows the specific kinds of research data used by sociologists in developing these perspectives, and analyzes the major perspectives. Four basic perspectives are related to modern sociology: positivism, organicism, Marxism, and historicism.

In this chapter we show how sociologists rejected the mechanistic theories of society, which did not consider the meaningful nature of social action, and how they slowly recognized that any valid theory of society must be a theory of meaningful action. This basic theme runs through modern sociology, as we see in Chapters 3 and 4. Because Chapter 2 deals with so many of the classical ideas, works, and figures in sociology, many subjects only touched upon in this chapter are elaborated in succeeding chapters.

Aristotle maintained that "man is the political animal." While many would deny that the quest for power or influence is a natural characteristic of man, few would deny the broader implication of this dictum, that man is the social animal who seeks to control his relations with his fellow men. This distinguishing characteristic of man, his commitment to society and to ordering his social world, is the primary concern of all sociology.

Man is so completely social, so concerned with other human beings and with himself in relation to them, that almost every aspect of his life is affected by his involvements in society. Even those parts of his life that at first might seem nonsocial are influenced by society. We are even concerned with dying "in the right way" and "at the right time."

Because all men have been concerned with managing their social existence, they have always had an interest in describing and explaining human action. Over the centuries, cultural groups accumulated complex commonsense ideas and theories about individuals and groups, and the members of these groups have used this common-sense knowledge to order their everyday lives and social relations. In this respect all men have been common-sense sociologists. Even in "primitive societies," anthropologists have often found complex theories of man and society developed by "primitive philosophers." It is little wonder that civilized men early turned their attention to developing and recording observations and explanations of human action. But scientific sociology developed slowly over many centuries.

EARLY SCIENTIFIC WORK ON SOCIETY

There have been two major periods of scientific sociology. The first was a relatively brief period in ancient Greece, which culminated in the work of Aristotle. The second began in the sixteenth century with the development of secular social thought.

The movement from common-sense social thought to more scientific social thought can be seen in the development of social theories from Plato to Aristotle. Though the philosophers were only one generation apart, there is a great difference in the ways they developed and tested their theories of society.

Plato's theories of society, presented primarily in his two important dialogues, *The Republic* and *The Laws*, were derived almost entirely from common-sense ideas. Presented largely in terms of mythical characters and events, they were influenced by Plato's own value commitments. Aristotle's writing is very different and bears striking similarities to modern works, especially in *The Politics*, his most important work. While Plato had made use of bits of historical and scholarly evidence to illustrate his major points, Aristotle made a systematic study of the constitutions of the Greek city-states and used this data to demonstrate the truth of his ideas.

Aristotle's work on society constituted the beginning of a scientific sociology, but an abortive beginning. The decline of Greek civilization, the failure of the Romans to develop fertile scientific work, and the almost complete lack of scientific attitude during the "Dark Ages" put an end to scientific social thought in Western societies for over fifteen hundred years. Almost all social thought during that period was dominated by theology. Modern scientific social thought began only with the secularization of social thought apparent in the famous work of Machiavelli in *The Prince* and of Hobbes in *Leviathan*. As was true of ancient Chinese, Indian, and Greek works, these writings and others like them were concerned with the problem of social order for the next few centuries. Each was interested in how rulers could most effectively use power to maintain social order and to keep themselves in power. Each was unconstrained by significant moral or theological considerations. Each made use of some evidence to support points but was not so objective or systematic as later, more scientific works. Basically, each made use of evidence from his own experience or from common-sense accounts of historical events, rather than attempting to draw information from more systematic, controlled observations. These first Western works of "social engineering" made a beginning in the development of scientific social thought.

The first systematic analyses of social data in the spirit of modern science were primarily designed to solve specific problems of society. These problems were defined for the early social scientists by their rulers, and the information they used to develop and test their theories was provided by the government, which further limited the possibility that they would extend their analyses to include the rulers. From the seventeenth century, a close alliance existed between the government officials who defined social problems and the social scientists who used official statistics to develop and test their theories of society. Only recently have sociologists realized how this alliance determined their theories of social problems.

NINETEENTH-CENTURY SOCIAL THOUGHT

Until recently, sociologists believed that the main contributions of the nineteenth century to the development of sociology were those of "grand theorists." The works of Saint-Simon, Auguste Comte, Herbert Spencer, Karl Marx, Emile Durkheim, and Max Weber were seen as the primary sources of sociological developments in this period. Their influence was believed to result from their generalizations about social man.

The theoretical works of these men had great influence on the development of sociology, especially on the broad perspectives of sociological theory. But the argument that sociology originated in grand theoretical statements is comparable to the argument that physics originated in the works of Sir Francis Bacon. Just as the works of Bacon were important in popularizing physics and other natural sciences in the seventeenth century, so were the works of Comte and Spencer important in popularizing sociology. But, just as one must distinguish between the actual empirical work of physics and the general proclamations of Bacon, so must one make a distinction between the empirical works of sociology in the nineteenth century and the theoretical statements of Comte and Spencer. As Durkheim argued in his introduction to *Suicide* in support of his own empirically based theoretical study of social phenomena:

> Sociology has been in vogue for some time. Today this word, little known and almost discredited a decade ago, is in common use. Representatives of the new science are increasing in number and there is something like a public feeling favorable to it. Much is expected of it. It must be confessed, however, that results up to the present time are not really proportionate to the number of publications nor the interest which they arouse. The progress of a science is proven by the progress toward solution of the problems it treats. It is said to be advancing when laws hitherto unknown are discovered, or when at least new facts are acquired modifying the formulation of these problems even though not furnishing a final solution. Unfortunately, there is good reason why sociology does not appear in this light, and this is because *the problems it proposes are not usually clear-cut. It is still in the stage of system-building and philosophical syntheses.* Instead of attempting to cast light on a limited portion of the social field, it prefers brilliant generalities reflecting all sorts of questions to definite treatment of any one. Such a method may indeed momentarily satisfy public curiosity by offering it so-called illumination on all sorts of subjects, but it can achieve nothing objective. Brief studies and hasty intuitions are not enough for the discovery of the laws of so complex a reality. And, above all, such large and abrupt generalizations are not capable of any sort of proof. All that is accomplished is the occasional citation of some favorable examples illustrative of the hypothesis considered, but an illustration is not a proof (Durkheim, 1951, p. 35).

The nineteenth century was an era of revolutions and social conflict within societies in Europe, just as the twentieth century has been an era of conflict between national societies in Europe and the rest of the world.

Because of these intranational conflicts, the nineteenth century was an era in which social thought in Europe was highly ideological. The social thinkers were concerned with developing arguments about society that supported the interests of some groups in society. The grand theories of nineteenth-century sociology, like many of the grand theories of twentieth-century sociology, were greatly influenced by this context of ideological argument and social conflict.

When we examine nineteenth-century social thought on the development of sociology, there seem to be four major streams: *positivism, organicism, Marxism,* and *historicism.* There were many variations of each and each had ties with the others, yet each was also distinctive and unified enough to warrant individual consideration. While each stream of thought was imbued by ideological considerations, each was also partly independent of ideology, at least at those points at which it influenced the development of the young science of sociology. Each had to take empirical evidence into consideration to justify its claim to be scientific. While empirical evidence can certainly be biased and manipulated, nevertheless it exerts constraints on theoretical ideas developed from it or tested by it. All four kinds of abstract sociological theorists shared methodological characteristics in the empirical evidence available to them for constructing and testing abstract ideas. Because the empirical evidence and those theoretical ideas that grew out of it were not subject to control by the ideological biases of the nineteenth-century sociologists, this shared empirical base had a longer-lasting effect on the development of sociology. First, we shall discuss the major forms of empirical data used by the nineteenth-century sociologists. Then we shall return to consider the major streams of abstract theory and their relations to contemporary sociology.

THE ORIGINS OF QUANTITATIVE SOCIOLOGY

By the nineteenth century, the natural sciences had achieved major triumphs in understanding the physical world, and they became the arbiters of knowledge. Science became a prestigious enterprise, especially the quantitative sciences such as physics, thermodynamics, and astronomy. Numbers came to be seen as the hallmark, the one true symbol, of scientific method and theory; and the prestige of these sciences was the more accentuated by the mystery of mathematical analyses in an age when few people knew more than basic arithmetic. Unquestioningly, many accepted Kelvin's dictum that measurement is the only source of knowledge.

Social thinkers were greatly affected by the spirit of science, especially by quantitative analyses of social data. Quantitative analyses offered them prestige and, they hoped, a sure way to defeat their opponents in disputes about the nature of society and social problems. This power was particularly valuable in the realm of social thought; commitments to competing theories ran deep, and in the nineteenth century the revolutionary conflicts in all European societies made such analyses extremely relevant. For example, Karl Marx went to great pains to develop quantitative "measures" of the basic variables in his theories, a fact disregarded by modern Marxists.

The nineteenth century witnessed the founding and growth of many kinds of quantitative theories of society, but the *mechanistic theorists* identified most closely with the quantitative theories of the natural sciences. The essential ideas of this school of thought have been described by Sorokin:

> The essential elements of the mechanistic interpretation of man's nature, behavior, and social activities were set forth long ago. Since the mechanistic school views all social phenomena as mere variations of physical phenomena, its essential characteristic is a monistic conception of the universe as a whole, including the universal application of all natural law, or unity of all its laws. For this reason potentially all the monistic conceptions of the world, and especially the materialistic monism, contained one of the substantial elements of the mechanistic school.
>
> Another element of the mechanistic interpretation of social phenomena, that was known also to the past, is the application of mathematics to their interpretation and a belief in the universality of quantitative regularities, or laws, in the dynamics of social, as of all other, processes (Sorokin, 1928, pp. 3–5).

The mechanists, then, saw nothing special about man and society. All that was necessary was to find the aspects of man and society directly analogous to natural forces such as gravity. Then they would plug the social variable into the formula for the physical forces and derive a prediction of what should happen in society. However, such simplistic procedures didn't work. Men refused to act like heavenly bodies, rocks, or atoms.

The spirit of the mechanistic theories has continued—with dwindling force—to the present, but the more simplistic theories of the mechanists were supplanted by the mathematical ideas of the *neopositivists* in the early part of our century. These theorists—led by George Lundberg, Stuart Dodd, William Ogburn, and F. Stuart Chapin—tried to find some simple mathematical formula, especially one with wide applicability to physical phenomena, that would predict social phenomena of many different kinds. They built theories on the assumption that social phenomena over time will follow the so-called S-curve—that is, they believed that such factors as population growth and social movements would start out slowly, accelerate, and then level off. If we could find the position of any given social phenomenon on the curve at a given time, we could then predict where we would be at any time in the future. By carefully choosing the social phenomena to which they applied this idea, they achieved some short-run success with it. But, eventually, their predictions foundered on social realities. For example, population growth in the United States in the 1920s followed their S-curve reasonably well, but the erratic drop in growth due to the Depression wrecked the theory, and the postwar baby boom made it a shambles.

The mechanists and neo-positivists made one crucial mistake in their approach to the study of man and society: they eliminated the factor that makes man distinct from any other animal and his society distinct from animal society—the meaningful nature of man's actions. Man does not have the complex patterns of reflexes and imprintings that lower animals use to determine their adaptive responses to life (see Chapter 5). Man must depend upon his rational capacities to develop symbolic meanings and to transmit them to succeeding generations, if he is to live in a world of many dangers that he is not otherwise equipped to overcome. *It is the complex social meanings man gives to a situation that determine how he will act in that situation.* If a policeman sees an unknown man holding a woman, he can decide how to act only by first deciding on the social meaning of that perceived situation. If he decides that it means "love making," he will probably do nothing. If, however, the woman calls for help, his response will be different. Yet anyone who did not know the meaning of the woman's words would not be able to see the "reason" for different actions in these two similar situations. It is not surprising that these theories failed to make adequate "sense" of human actions and were unable to predict what human beings would do in different situations. Any success they might have in the short run in predicting human actions would be due entirely to the fact that the meanings of the situations had not changed for the social actors. But any changes in the meanings of the situations, which are inevitable in human life, would make their theories irrelevant.

Even in the early nineteenth century most of those working to create the sciences of man realized that their theories would have to take into consideration the importance of social meanings in determining human actions. This seemed so obvious that often sociologists took these social meanings for granted. What they sought in their quantitative theories was to determine, analyze, and, if possible, predict the number of times any *significant meaningful situation* occurred. They focused their attention on the quantitative analysis and explanation of such socially meaningful phenomena as divorce, crime, and suicide.

Among the many kinds of quantitative social theories in the nineteenth century, a great deal of work was done on what were called social hygiene and moral statistics. Among the best of these works was Parent-Duchatalet's massive study of prostitution in Europe in the middle of the century, a work which remains the most extensive and meticulous statistical study of prostitution ever compiled. The "social Physicists" were important in their influence on later sociologists. The most influential of the social physicists was Adolphe Quetelet, a renowned statistician whose *Social Physics* stood as the most impressive quantitative work until Emile Durkheim's *Suicide*. Although Quetelet's work appeared to be totally mechanistic, like his early work in astronomy, it was rather a fine example of *moral statistics,* which derived its name from the work of De Guerry, beginning in 1828. The moral statisticians, who probably did more work than any other school of quantitative social theorists in the nineteenth century and whose works clearly had the most influence on later sociological theories, were primarily concerned with applying quantitative thought to socially meaningful phenomena for the purpose of solving what they saw as social problems. Their primary method was to analyze the official statistics on whatever aspects of social action officials saw as important. Most of their work was concerned with the relationships between such phenomena as divorce and crime or marriage and suicide. They hoped to determine what they called the "social rates" of such actions. A *social rate* was defined as the number of times a given action was committed for a given number of the population in a given time period. Sometimes they gave rates in terms of the number of actions for each 100,000 people in a given society in one year. Thus, to say that France had a suicide rate of 15 would mean the official statistics indicated that there were 15 suicides in one year for each 100,000 people in France. Having determined the social rates of various actions, they analyzed the statistical relationships among these rates, seeking to explain how one rate or set of rates was causing another rate or set of rates. In this fashion, they showed that the official rate of divorce was closely associated with the official rate of suicide, concluding that the more divorce, the more suicide, and that, consequently, divorce must be seen as one cause of suicide.

In the early works of the moral statisticians, there was still an emphasis on individual actions, and their explanations were often what today we would call more psychological than sociological. But they concluded that no psychological theory could explain the stability of social rates that they found for any one society. They found, for example, that each nation tended to have roughly the same suicide rate from one year to the next, while each nation's rate was distinctively different from the others. First, they tried to explain this stability in terms of individual actors, but they did not see how stable social rates could be caused by individuals assumed to be different from each other and free to choose their own actions. They concluded that something which was the same for the individuals within any one society was causing the same social rates for that society from year to year. Quetelet tried to explain stable rates in terms of an "average man" theory, arguing that a certain type of personality in each society produces a given probability of any action such as suicide in a given time period. But how would such a stable personality type occur? Increasingly, the moral statisticians moved toward the belief that something outside the individual must determine what he was and did. Deciding that the individual did not have free choice to formulate his actions, they theorized that the factor determining his actions must in some way be society. Henri Morselli, an important early sociologist, believed that other factors (for example, the phases of the moon) had some influence in determining suicide rates, but he concluded that society was the most important factor.

This history of analyses of social rates, or moral statistics, made it possible for Durkheim to write *Suicide* in 1897 (see Insert No. 5). Durkheim was convinced that society must be studied independently of individuals and that, therefore, sociology must be a scientific discipline independent of psychology, which saw the individual as the only reality and rarely paid attention to the social situations in which individuals were trapped. He had progressed toward this theory in his first two works, *The Division of Labor* and *The Rules of Sociological Method*. But in *Suicide* he made a strong

INSERT NO. 5

On Emile Durkheim's *Suicide*

Of Durkheim's four major works, *Suicide* has been the most influential among sociologists as a stimulus to further theory and research. Durkheim, like many of his contemporaries, was struck by the fact that the economic progress of newly industrialized societies seemed everywhere to be accompanied by a rise in suicide rates—clearly, an anomaly from the point of view of the popular utilitarian theory that the division of labor and economic progress would be accompanied by increasing personal "happiness." In *Suicide*, Durkheim made a systematic study of available statistical information on suicide rates in the Western world and related the variations in such rates to a whole series of characteristics of the populations. These variables included nationality, religion, age, sex, marital status, family size, place of residence, economic status, and variations in economic condition, as well as the seasons of the year and even the times of day when suicides occurred. He was careful to gather data from the broadest possible comparative range, using illustrative material from countries where suicide statistics were not kept.

In order to classify the "causes" of suicide in a sociological manner, Durkheim introduced a highly original scheme, built about the question of the individual's relation to the normative structuring of the society in which he lives. Characteristic of societies with very strong norms, according to Durkheim, is *altruistic suicide*, where the individual dies because he perceives that his death would be useful for or is prescribed by his social group.

argument for sociology as a separate discipline concerned with studying society as an independent level of reality:

> The individual is dominated by a moral reality greater than himself: namely, collective reality. When each people is seen to have its own suicide-rate, more constant than that of general mortality, that its growth is in accordance with a coefficient of acceleration characteristic of each society; when it appears that the variations through which it passes at different times of the day, month, year, merely reflect the rhythm of social life; and that marriage, divorce, the family, religious society, the army, etc., affect it in accordance with definite laws, some of which may even be numerically expressed—these states and institutions will no longer be regarded simply as characterless, ineffective ideological arrangements. Rather they will be felt to be real, living, active forces which, because of the way they determine the individual, prove their independence of him; which, if the individual enters as an element in the combination whence these forces ensue, at least control him once they are formed. Thus it will appear more clearly why sociology

In a society that is *anomic*, or has very weak social norms, the individual may commit *anomic suicide* because he is unable to discover what is expected of him or what he is supposed to want in his everyday life. Durkheim thought that the society in which he lived was becoming an anomic society, and many sociologists have followed this historical evaluation and described their society as anomic. Of all Durkheim's theories and concepts, that of *anomie* has been most used and modified by later sociologists.

Another type of suicide seen by Durkheim as characteristic of industrialized urban society was *egoistic suicide*. *Egoism*, in Durkheim's special sense, is a designation for what may be more generally called "institutionalized individualism," or pressure upon the individual to be an individual and not to conform to others' wishes. Eventually, the egoistic person may become so alienated that, unable to accept even the essential normative conditions of a stable system of organized personal freedom, he will commit egoistic suicide. The concept of egoism has received far less attention than that of anomie, but there are signs of a renewed interest in it. Durkheim also believed there was a fourth kind of suicide, *fatalistic suicide*, which consists of an "oversubmission" to society and is supposedly found in "primitive societies." But he never elaborated on this point.

Both his use of official statistics and the concepts contained in his typology have been extended, criticized, and modified by sociologists, especially in the last twenty years (see Douglas, 1967). The most important extension of Durkheim's theory is Merton's analysis of anomie and deviance. (1957) A complete listing of works stimulated or influenced by *Suicide* would be nearly impossible, since its contributions to the development of sociology have been so great.

can and must be objective, since it deals with realities as definite and substantial as those of the psychologist or the biologist (Durkheim, 1951, pp. 42–43).

Durkheim went further in his insistence that society is a separate level of reality than sociologists would go today. He committed the *fallacy of social realism*, the belief that "society" is not determined by individual ideas, feelings, and actions. Today, most sociologists would argue that only individuals "exist" and only individuals can have ideas, beliefs, and feelings. But they would also insist that Durkheim and the other early sociologists working on moral statistics were right in seeing that the social structures into which individuals are born, raised, and must act throughout their lives are important in partially determining what those individuals will be like and what they will do in specific situations.

Durkheim's acceptance of the fallacy of social realism was partly the fault of the statistical method he and the early moral statisticians used. The statistics on social rates, which came to them as disembodied numbers in official tabulations published by government agencies each year, tended to hide from them the individual realities that lay behind the numbers. The man in the street dealing with individual acts of crime or suicide tends to be so concerned with specific situations and events that he fails to see the general social patterns in such events. He is apt to commit *the fallacy of psychologism*, the belief that all phenomena are individually determined and isolated. He may fail to see that crimes and suicides are committed in distinctive ways in a given society and for distinctive reasons. Those early sociologists who looked only at disembodied numbers went to the opposite extreme. Fortunately, other forms of evidence were available to sociologists than the official statistics used by the moral statisticians to do studies of crime and suicide.

HISTORICAL EVIDENCE, CASE STUDIES, AND FIELD RESEARCH

In the early stages of the development of sociology, there was necessarily considerable reliance on the methods of "armchair sociology." As the early sociologists had relatively little scientific data to construct and test their theories, they relied on their own experience in society and on the current information available through newspapers and magazines; although sociologists are still dependent on their own common-sense experience in fundamental ways to find social meanings, their dependence on common-sense information decreases as more scientific research accumulates. But other important sources of research data were available to them—history, case studies, and field research.

History was probably the most important of these sources. The nineteenth century was a period of great historical research and analysis. Vast stores of historical data, called "primary source material," were uncovered and used by the growing numbers of historians. For the first time the histories of other cultures, especially of oriental societies, became available to Western scholars as sources of information.

In Germany, where in the nineteenth century the discipline of history reached its zenith, sociology grew directly out of history. This form of sociology consisted largely of an attempt to make history into a science by discovering basic patterns of history and trying to explain them in terms of some theory. The more grandiose theories became the "social philosophies" we have seen in the twentieth century, as men sought to understand human history in order to control it. One of the earliest was Marx's theory of class conflict, which he saw as basic in determining human history up to his own time and which he arrived at by using historical material. In our own day the works of Arnold Toynbee best represent this approach. The more meticulous theoretical works of this sort became what is called *historical sociology*. Almost all of Weber's influential works used historical material as the primary source of evidence.

Case studies, analyses of individuals in an attempt to get at their general properties, came to sociology from history. Historians had long used case studies as examples of general ideas. The sixteenth-century philosophical essays of Montaigne contain numerous uses of individual cases from historical sources. In the nineteenth century the use of case studies became more systematic and analytical. Historians developed the method of *analytic induction*, which consists of carefully analyzing a number of individual cases to infer general properties and causes. This method was used in studies of suicide and crime, such as the study of suicide notes by Brierre de Boismont in 1856. It continues to be important, especially in studies of deviance.

Field research, the most important research method for studying everyday life (see Chapter 4), came from a very different source. It began largely in the travelogue, which goes back to the semifabulous accounts by Herodotus of strange lands and peoples and includes the famous account of Marco Polo's travels. But, while the traveler wrote for pleasure, the basic idea of all field research is that you have to see for yourself if you want to know what is really going on. Field research in the social sciences is very much like the field observations of geologists, naturalists, and biologists, who had been doing observational studies of natural environments for centuries before social scientists did such work. By the seventeenth century, the practice of carefully observing social settings had become accepted. In the nineteenth century, the field research of Alexis de Tocqueville leading to his

Democracy in America paralleled the naturalistic field research of Charles Darwin who was working toward his history of evolution. Later in the century, Frederic Le Play and his followers carried out meticulous field research studies of family economies in European nations. Throughout this period, the early anthropologists were establishing the tradition of field research that has remained the dominant method of anthropological research. While Durkheim himself did no field research, his later works on religion (1961) and kinship (1967) were based on the reports of anthropological field researchers (see Insert No. 6).

POSITIVISM: THE SOCIOLOGY OF CONSENSUS

Positivism probably had more influence on the development of sociological theories in the nineteenth century than any of the other four major

---

INSERT NO. 6

Emile Durkheim

Emile Durkheim (1858–1917) is one of the founders of sociology, providing a point of reference even for those who do not accept his ideas. Born in Strasbourg, France, in 1887 he became the first French professor of sociology in Bordeaux. During his stay in Bordeaux he published three of his four major works, *The Division of Labor in Society*, *The Rules of Sociological Method*, and *Suicide*, and founded the influential journal *L'année sociologique*.

In 1902 Durkheim became professor of sociology and education at France's most distinguished university, the Sorbonne, in Paris. During the next ten years he was deeply involved in teaching and in activities centering around *L'année sociologique*, and he published several important articles. His fourth major work, *The Elementary Forms of the Religious Life*, appeared in 1912.

The most important of Durkheim's theoretical concepts was that of society as a real entity, different from the sum of its parts and exercising a constraining influence over its members. This constraint was accomplished both by society's laws and punishments and by the *conscience collective*—the system of norms and values held in common by members of the society. Later in his sociological career, Durkheim turned his attention to the question of socialization and education of children and to religion and modified his precious theory of the constraining nature of social rules. He developed the theory that members of society internalize various norms and values during the socialization process, so that society is maintained by the *internal* constraints of individuals, such as individual conscience and guilt, as well as by external constraints on members.

abstract theories of society. Many of the fundamental ideas developed by Auguste Comte, the principal founder of positivism, have remained basic to many abstract sociological theories up to the present (see Insert No. 7). Positivism was primarily the product of three dominant ideas in nineteenth-century Europe: that the progress of man had culminated in nineteenth-century European civilization, that science was both the ultimate expression of that progress and the means by which future progress could be assured and controlled, and that science must be used to solve social problems that were impeding progress. All three ideas are found in the utopian socialism of Henri de Saint-Simon (1760–1825). Saint-Simon was concerned with solving the urgent social problems he saw facing Europe, especially problems of political and economic inequality. He believed that it was necessary to create a positive science of human society comparable to the physical sciences to solve these problems. Auguste Comte (1798–1857) became secretary to Saint-Simon and worked as his collaborator from 1817 to 1823. Comte

---

In *The Division of Labor in Society*, Durkheim applied his theoretical view of society to the problem of order and social structure. In contemporary society the division of labor is complex and individuals are functionally interdependent for their economic survival: in these complex societies order is based on *organic solidarity*. In simpler societies, without this economic interdependence, individuals are bound together by many emotional ties, especially those of kinship: order is based on *mechanical solidarity*. In *Suicide*, Durkheim made his other major substantive contribution, his study of comparative rates and types of suicide.

Durkheim was concerned not only with theory and substantive problems, but also with methodology. His main methodological focus was on the means used by the social actor and by the sociologist to make sense of the world and on the differences between the two methods. He believed that the actor or member of a society makes sense of the world through common sense and that the sociologist must repudiate common sense and utilize a more scientific perspective in order to gain scientific knowledge of society. He felt that an essential tool of the scientific method in sociology was statistics since numbers seemed to him to be uncontaminated by nonscientific elements.

The importance of Durkheim's work lies in his creativity and his ability to synthesize various ideas about the nature of societies and individuals. He was one of the forerunners of a sociology based not only upon philosophical ideas but also upon a thorough and careful investigation of empirical evidence. Durkheim's ideas and concepts remain a fertile source of theory even today, and the empirical methods he used are still being developed and modified. Few other sociologists have contributed as much.

was greatly influenced by Saint-Simon's commitment to creating a science of society to solve social problems. Comte wrote voluminously but achieved little in his *Positive Philosophy* in the way of scientific analysis or demonstration. However, because of the temper of the times, his works became the basis for the widespread social movement of positivism and had great influence on the development of sociological theory.

Comte sought a true science of social phenomena, a "social physics" comparable to "celestial physics." But, as in the case of Quetelet and other students of *social physics* and *moral statistics,* Comte was no social mechanist. He believed that ideas were the dominant factor in human society. Accordingly, his first "law of human society" was that of the three *stages of progress.* He argued historical evidence shows that man's earliest thought was dominated by *theological* attitudes, then progressed to *metaphysical* attitudes, and finally to the *positive* (or scientific) attitudes.

Believing that any given period of society is dominated by one attitude,

---

INSERT NO. 7

Auguste Comte

Auguste Comte (1798–1857) was the French philosopher and sociologist who, in the 1838 edition of his *Cours de Philosophie Positive,* coined the term "sociologist." His family background was Catholic and upper class, but at the age of thirteen he abandoned the Catholic faith and, throughout his life, intellectually challenged the monarchical political ideas taken for granted by the French upper class at that time. In 1814 Comte entered the Ecole Polytechnique in Paris, then the lively center of progressive thought in France. The liberalism apparent in his writings at that time remained influential in his later work, although he became more conservative in later years.

From 1817 Comte was associated, by friendship and intellectual exchange, with the liberal Saint-Simon, and this association had a profound influence on his thinking. Comte's famous sociological theory of the three stages of society was derived from the "law of three stages" formulated by Saint-Simon. In later years, Comte became estranged from Saint-Simon, and denied that the great liberal had had any influence on his work.

Comte has been most remembered and most criticized by sociologists for his social evolutionist theory of the three stages of society, but his contribution to the sociological thought of that time went beyond this theory. He was particularly interested in solving what he saw as important social problems of his times and his sociological theory was basically oriented toward propounding solutions to those problems. Like many of these other sociologists,

Comte, not surprisingly, tended to see society as reasonably homogeneous. Comte focused his attention on basic *patterns of social action* and the relations between lesser patterns, or what sociologists came to call social structure or the *social system*. He paid more attention to explaining *social order*, the way in which the patterns of the social structure held together and moved together over time, than to the lack of patterning in so many parts of social life and the problems of social disorder or conflict. As a result of such focus, much recent work in sociology has had to work on repairing the biases against considering conflict built into sociological theory.

To Comte, social order was made possible only by a universal consensus in society. The combination of his belief in such a *consensus universalis* with his belief in the progressive evolution of human society led Comte to argue that there is a basic analogy between human society and biological organisms. His analogy of human society with biological organisms allied him with a group of social theorists who had vast influence on the development

like Durkheim and Marx, his solutions had as their fundamental character the reassertion of order in what appeared to be the monumental disorder of urbanizing society. Although the nature of his solution, religious positivism, is not accepted by contemporary sociologists, his interpretation of the problems, their history and possible solutions, contains a wealth of unexamined sociological theory.

A further conception first formulated by Comte was what we now call "cultural relativism." In an article published in Saint-Simon's journal *Industrie*, Comte asserted that moral ideas are relative—that is, they vary with different cultures and social systems. A conception taken for granted today among sociologists, this aroused considerable opposition, since the intellectuals of Comte's time tended to believe that norms are rooted either in divine revelation or in a general spiritual order, separate from social life and untouched by it.

Like many other famous men, Comte has been accused of allowing his personal life to affect his intellectual output. In 1826, at the age of twenty-eight, Comte had a nervous breakdown, probably associated with the dissolution of his relationship with Clotilde de Vaux. His "change" at that time from objective positivism to subjectivism has been attributed to this emotional crisis although, upon careful examination of all his work, this change appears to be more in the nature of a shift in focus than of a radical departure.

The meaning of Comte's subjectivism is closely associated with his positivistic approach. The meaning of his "subjective synthesis" is based on the assumption that "nature becomes conscious of itself in man" so that, as Comte put it, "man sums up in himself all the laws of the world." Therefore, "to one who has understood the full meaning of process, this 'subjective synthesis' will also be objective."

of sociology, the *social organicists,* who developed many of their ideas about the nature of human society from this analogy.

SOCIAL ORGANICISM

Society cannot be seen or touched, though we can perceive its physical manifestations, such as houses, roads, and cities. We can see individuals who make up society, the members of society. But society is not simply the sum of the individuals "in" it. Society is the relations between individuals and relations cannot be seen, only understood. But the intangible is difficult for us to understand and to communicate. Intangible relationships are easily subject to disagreement among those trying to understand them: not everyone can tell who is a member of society or who is not, or when he is "seeing" one society, many, or none. One consequence is that men have tried to understand society in terms of physical objects, and analogies between biological organisms and society have been particularly appealing.

The first highly developed organismic theory of society in the Western world was developed by Plato in *The Republic.* Plato tried to show that each part of the human body has a corresponding part in society. The head is analogous to the head of state, the rulers. Having drawn this analogy, he then analyzed society as one might analyze the human body. The rulers, the heads, are rightly given the function of running the rest of society, or the body politic, and are more important than mere stomachs, the farmers and other providers. Obviously, the organismic analogy can lead to many biases in the social analyses based on it.

Some early organismic theories classified society as one type of organism. Then the organismic theorists applied the principles of biology to society as the social mechanists had applied the principles of physical sciences to society. But these theories committed the same mistakes, especially that of failing to see the essentially meaningful nature of human social action.

The organismic theories that accepted human social action as basically meaningful and did not carry the analogy between society and organisms to the extreme of identifying the one with the other had a more lasting effect. The most important of these early theories was that proposed by Herbert Spencer (see Insert No. 8). Like Comte, Spencer believed in the inevitability of human progress, through an evolutionary process. Unlike Comte, Spencer saw evolution in organismic terms and in line with the developing biological theories of his day, as achieved by the free competition of individual organisms and societies. Spencer was a firm believer in the *laissez-faire* capitalism of nineteenth-century England and a firm supporter of the status quo.

Spencer's *social organicism* can be seen clearly in this summary of his analogy between society and biological organisms:

First, both society and organisms are distinguished from inorganic matter by visible growth during the greater part of their existence. A baby grows up to be a man; a tiny community becomes a metropolitan area; a small state becomes an empire.

Second, as both societies and organisms grow in size they also increase in complexity of structure. Here Spencer had in mind not so much the comparison of the development of a society with the growth of an individual

---

INSERT NO. 8

Herbert Spencer

Herbert Spencer (1820–1903) was born in Derby, England, into a family of Dissenters; he was educated at home by his father and an uncle, who wanted him to attend Cambridge. Spencer declined and at seventeen went to work for the London and Birmingham Railway, where he became interested in evolution through examining fossils taken from railroad cuts.

After leaving the railroad, Spencer became a subeditor of the *Economist* and launched himself on the writing career through which he became one of the leading figures in the intellectual revolution of the nineteenth century, playing an important role in the development of biology, psychology, sociology, and anthropology. He applied the theory of evolution to all these areas, defining the general process of evolution in the following terms: "Evolution is a change from a state of relatively indefinite, incoherent, homogeneity to a state of relatively definite, coherent heterogeneity."

Spencer's major areas of interest were synthesized in his *Synthetic Philosophy*, published between 1862 and 1896. His other works in sociology include *Descriptive Sociology* (1873–1934), a meticulous collection of cultural data taken from ethnographic and historical sources, and *The Study of Sociology* (1873), which he wrote partly to demonstrate that a science of society is possible.

Spencer was so frequently attacked for making the analogy between biological organisms and human society that he took pains to make clear the nature of the analogy: "Analogies . . . cannot be . . . of a visible or sensible kind; but can only be analogies between the systems, or methods, of organization. Such analogies as exist result from the one unquestionable community between the two organizations: *there is in both a mutual dependence of parts.*" As this statement illustrates, Spencer was not only an evolutionist but a functionalist, arguing that "there can be no true conception of a structure without a true conception of its function."

Spencer's work has had little direct influence on the development of sociology and today is rarely used as a source of theoretical ideas. But indirectly, through Durkheim and Radcliffe-Brown, Spencer's functional theories have had considerable influence on structural-functional theory, discussed later.

organism as the affinity of social development and the assumed evolutionary sequence of organic life.

Third, in societies and in organisms progressive differentiation of structure is accompanied by progressive differentiation of functions.

Fourth, evolution established for both societies and organisms differences in structure and function that make each other possible.

Fifth, just as a living organism may be regarded as a nation of units that live individually, so a nation of human beings may be regarded as an organism (Timasheff, 1961, p. 23).

Spencer's statement of the analogies between organisms and society contains the basic ideas of social organicism that later became part of the theory of society as a social system.

The idea that society is like an organism in its fundamental properties had a special allure for nineteenth-century social thinkers because it offered a ready explanation for society's ability to remain integrated while changing rapidly and becoming far more pluralistic. As we noted at the beginning of Chapter 1, sociology developed in part as a response to the rapid change and complexity that have characterized Western societies since the Industrial Revolution. Thus sociology, which took civilized society for its province and sought to deal with its problems, early developed a fundamental concern with social change and complexity. Most sociologists were concerned with explaining, and helping to maintain, the social order of their societies. Consequently, any analogy offering a simple and satisfying explanation of the ways in which change and complexity were related to social order was attractive to them. The organismic analogy was one.

The primary idea of the *organismic theory* was that society maintains its integral structure throughout its transformation into more complex forms just as a biological organism maintains its integral structure while developing into a more complex entity. Some saw the ideal analogy as that of plants and society. The plant is the same plant, as it grows from a tiny seed into an immense tree. The organic structure, or essential form, of the tree remains the same in spite of its increase in complexity. In the same way, they argued, French society retained its *social structure,* or its essential form, in spite of the increase in complexity resulting from the changes produced by the Industrial Revolution.

But what led society to maintain its social structure, its essential form, throughout these changes? Biological organisms were presumed to contain some substance that controlled their development and maintained the basic form. What comparable substance was there in human societies? The differences between societies of the same species made it clear that social structure could not be the result of biological substance, though some argued that structural differences between the societies of racial groups were the result of differences in the organic structure of the races. The fact that the structure was supposed to stay the same for one certain society but to differ from that of *other* societies convinced most of the sociologists that the social structure could not be the result of individual or personality factors, unless these were in some way controlled by external factors. Some sociologists, who thought these external factors must be physical, developed mechanistic theories, but most decided that these external factors must be social. In the nineteenth century, many saw these social factors as external to the individuals and, as did Durkheim, arrived at the fallacy of social realism, believing that society is independent of its individual members.

But by the twentieth century most sociologists, including Durkheim in his later works, had concluded that the external factor must be part of the individual members but independent of individual wills. They concluded that the factor had to be social meanings, but meanings not subject to the individual's own choice, or there would not be a resulting structure to the actions of individuals. *They concluded that the social meanings most important in maintaining the structure of society were social rules, especially the social values and laws of the society.* As Durkheim had said, "Social order is a moral order." This is equivalent to saying that social order is primarily the result of an order in the morals or values of a society. But how did there get to be an order to the morals of a society? How did the members come to share the same set of morals or values, as distinct from those shared by the members of another society? The answer was *socialization* and *social control,* the training of each new generation by the previous generation to hold the same values as the previous generation, followed by the use of control measures to make sure that individuals lived in accord with those values and that they taught those values to their own children.

The basic idea of the organismic theory of society, and of the later structural theories of society derived from it, is simple. Each individual born into a society is taught the values of his parents' generation. As those values become the determinants of his actions in society, his actions will be patterned or structured in the same way as his parents' actions. The same structure will be maintained across generations and throughout the society. Regardless of what situations the individuals face, they will continue to use those values to produce the same structure to their actions. Though society changes, its essential structure will remain the same.

By Durkheim's time, it was clear to sociologists that the organismic analogy and the social theories derived from it were too simplistic to adequately explain society. These theories failed to consider the basic differences between groups within a society and the conflicts between groups. Rather than trying to encompass all of society in one analogy or theory, sociologists became increasingly analytical in their approach, so much so that some historians of sociology have treated this later nineteenth-century period as one which saw the rise of *analytical sociology*. At that time we can see a move toward analyzing more detailed problems. The work of Tönnies, Durkheim, and others on the division of labor and social integration in Europe represented a move in this direction; and Durkheim's *Suicide* is specifically prefaced with a plea for more detailed studies of society. But organismic theories, including those elements in Durkheim's work, continued to exert influence. In the twentieth century, the fundamental ideas of the organismic theories were incorporated into the structural-functional theory of society (see Chapter 4).

MARXISM: THE SOCIOLOGY OF CONFLICT

Marxism has been one of the most important forces in social thought in the last century, yet until recently Marxism has had relatively little effect on sociological thought, partly because of the strong ideological commitments of Marx and his followers, which conflicted with the more conservative commitments of most nineteenth- and twentieth-century sociologists (see Insert No. 9). European sociologists in the nineteenth century were apt to be negatively influenced by Marx. Max Weber wrote some of his most important works, such as *The Protestant Ethic and The Spirit of Capitalism* (1958), partly in an attempt to show that materialistic theories such as Marx's were wrong. The influence of Marxist thought on American sociology has been less than on European sociology, probably because class conflicts are less developed and much more complex here. In recent years Marxism has had a growing influence on sociology, especially through the works of C. Wright Mills.

Much of Marx's thought was concerned with economic questions. For example, he argued that labor is the basis of all economic value, that labor in capitalist societies is inevitably maintained at the level of subsistence wages, that capitalists expropriate the *surplus product* (the difference between the subsistence wage paid labor and the price the product brings in the marketplace) from the workers. As sociologists have rarely interested themselves in economic questions of this sort, it is not surprising to find that this part of Marx's work has had little influence on sociological thought. The Marxist influence on sociology has been largely restricted to two basic ideas: that the *economic mode of production* is the basic determinant of social values, social thought, and social action and that class conflicts are the basic determinant of the kinds of social change that will occur in society.

The first key idea of Marxism, called his theory of *economic determinism,* is derived from his early commitment to the philosophical idea that all things are based on matter, that conscious thought itself is an aspect of the material motion of brain cells. To one who had accepted this belief in philosophical materialism, it seemed reasonable to expect that man's life and society would be determined by his economic activity, the way in which he dealt with the material or physical world.

Marx believed the crucial factor was the technological means of production. Whereas most other economists of his day focused their attention on the pricing mechanisms of the market, Marx saw such mechanisms as deriva-

---

INSERT NO. 9

Karl Marx

Karl Marx (1818–1883) was born into a professional family in the Prussian Rhineland. He received his doctorate in philosophy at the University of Jena at the age of twenty-three but was prevented from receiving a university appointment by his association with the Young Hegelians, a radical group critical of the Prussian government. Although Mark married into the aristocracy, his wife had no dowry, and the family was forced to live on the generosity of Marx's close friend Friedrich Engels.

Alienated from his parents and from Prussian society, Marx left his homeland at the age of twenty-five, to return only once for a brief visit, and in 1845 he renounced his Prussian citizenship. He lived in Paris and Brussels until in 1849 he moved to London, where he spent the rest of his life. His grave is in Highgate cemetery in London.

Marx's scholarly work is a mixture of scholarship and radical rhetoric, economics and sociology, history and philosophy. His best-known work, in which in collaboration with Engels he developed his conception of the relationship of man and history to the means of production, was the *Communist Manifesto* (1848). His other famous work, *Capital: a Critique of Political Economy* (published in several volumes between 1867 and 1879), carries out and elaborates the major ideas contained in the *Manifesto*, in a scholarly and systematic but still polemical style.

Marx contributed significantly to the first formulations of the sociology of knowledge with his conception that man's social being determines his consciousness. The concept of the alienation of modern man, worked out early in his career (now in a collection of his work published as the *Economic and Philosophic Manuscripts of 1844*), has been important for the development of the theories of *mass society* and *mass man*.

Many well-known sociologists have been political Marxists, and others have been political anti-Marxists, attempting to disprove various Marxist interpretations of society. But, for the majority of sociologists, Marxist writings have been valued as a source of new ideas about the relationship of man and his consciousness to his society, to be tested against contemporary evidence, not accepted or rejected on the basis of political bias.

tives of the more basic factor—the means of production. In this sense, he was putting economics into its social context and looking at economics as one would expect sociologists to do.

Marx saw the *class struggle* as derived from the economic determinism of the means of production. A class consisted of members of a society who had in common their relationship to the means of production and who consciously recognized this shared relationship as the basis for their action. Class struggle resulted because there always were a variety of class relationships to the means of production, and changes in the means of production led to changes in control over them. The class controlling the means of production would inevitably be faced with a new class arising to meet the demands of new means of production. Just as the European aristocrats had come into conflict with, and been deposed by, the bourgeoisie, who understood and controlled the new means of industrial production, so would the working class who manned the new machines inevitably come into conflict with and depose the bourgeoisie. Marx believed that the *proletariat,* the industrial workers, would revolt against the bourgeoisie and displace them.

Some aspects of his theory have not been confirmed by subsequent events in Western societies. Workers were not progressively "immiserized," made progressively worse off, as he had expected. Partly because of labor unions, the condition of workers improved. Second, instead of revolting against their masters, the workers increasingly became *petty bourgeoisie* themselves, so much so that many workers in America today are very conservative. Third, the bourgeoisie are being displaced today by technocrats, who have progressively taken over as managers of industry and then as government officials, rather than by workers. Fourth, the revolutions in the name of communism took place in the industrially backward nations where Marx least expected them. Of course, no social theory has yet achieved the kind of predictability that Marx assumed for his theory. But the fact that his theory was not wholly right does not make it wholly wrong.

The great contribution of Marx to modern sociology was his argument that *social conflict* is persistent and necessary in Western societies. His major error was in believing that social class is the only basic cause of such conflict. Marx was not the only social thinker to analyze social conflict, even in the nineteenth century, but, as we have seen, other major theorists were not concerned with conflict. The works of George Sorel on syndicalism and social conflict and of Gustave LeBon on crowd behavior and violence were certainly important. But Marx was the primary influence on twentieth-century sociologists concerned with analyzing social conflict, and Marx saw conflict as far more integral to society than did other analysts. While most sociologists were analyzing society in terms of the organismic analogy and searching for the lasting order and higher harmonies of society, Marx was analyzing the darker conflicts of society that have given rise to rebellion, revolution, and war in the twentieth century.

Marx's major influence has been on sociological studies of social class. As we see in Chapter 14, social class was for a long time one of the most important fields of sociological research and theory in America and Marx was the major stimulus to this work, though the American sociologists early found it necessary to go around most of his arguments in order to deal with complicated aspects of American social stratification.

Recently, there has been a resurgence in Marxist-oriented sociological research and theory, especially with reference to social policy and social action. This has been particularly true in Europe, where even major non-Marxist sociologists such as Ralf Dahrendorf (1959) have concentrated on the analysis of modern society in terms of the class conflicts that still play such an important part in European politics and general social life. It has also been true in the United States, especially under the influence of C. Wright Mills. The emphasis of modern Marxist sociologists, however, has been on the more subtle and complex aspects of class conflict, as they have sought to correct fundamental omissions in Marx's theories. Mills, for example, is probably best known for his argument that there exists a *power elite* in the United States that is of major importance in running the country at the top levels of business, government, and the military. The theory of the power elite is more complex than Marx's social class theory. Mills saw the power elite as consisting of complex and subtle relations among many different, but partially overlapping, groups (Mills, 1956, pp. 288–289; see also Insert No. 10).

In addition, Marx has had considerable effect on modern social thought through his influence on such social critics as Herbert Marcuse and Norman Birnbaum. These neo-Marxist thinkers argue that Marx was basically right, but that society and history are more complicated than he thought. In *One Dimensional Man* (1964), Marcuse argues that there is a "secret tyranny" in American society that exists precisely where Americans see themselves as most free:

> A comfortable, smooth, reasonable, democratic unfreedom prevails in advanced industrial civilization, a token of technical progress. Indeed, what could be more rational than the suppression of individuality in the mechanization of socially necessary but painful performances; the concentration of individual enterprises in more effective, more productive corporations; the regulation of free competition among unequally equipped economic subjects; the curtailment of prerogatives and national sovereignties which impede the international organization of resources (Marcuse, 1964, p. 3).

Most recent Marxist and neo-Marxist theories of society are attempts to revise or interpret Marx's theories in such a way that they will fit current social circumstances. Modern Marxists have appealed to what they call *false consciousness* to explain why those who are supposedly exploited and oppressed do not realize it, and why the rest of the citizens do not realize that the power elite have imposed a "comfortable tyranny" on them. False consciousness is defined as a failure to recognize the true nature of one's situation. While Marxist thought remains a dynamic force in modern social criticism, such ideas as false consciousness are not widely accepted. Young social critics have found such ideas untenable and have turned to new forms of radical social theory.

HISTORICISM: MAX WEBER

The study of history was seen as very important in the nineteenth century, which had great influence on the development of social thought. It is not surprising that history should have had a major effect on the evolution of ideas that have remained basic to sociological theory. In view of the dominance of German scholars in the development of history in this period,

---

INSERT NO. 10

C. Wright Mills

C. Wright Mills (1916–1962) was at his death a professor of sociology at Columbia University and one of the most controversial figures in American sociology. Shortly after his death, a series of essays, *The New Sociology*, was published in his honor. A central theme of these essays was that Mills exemplified that spirit of social concern which he saw as the fundamental duty of the sociologist—and which he felt was not fulfilled by the modern American sociological establishment.

He saw modern American sociology as, first of all, undirected toward the pressing social problems of his day, an issue which he dealt with in one of his most famous books, a collection of essays called *The Sociological Imagination* (1959). In this same collection, he criticized American sociologists for not using creative imagination in their work and for being preoccupied either with jargonistic Grand Theory or with minute and irrelevant statistical "problems," in fact, for having "abdicated" responsibility for relevant sociology: "The vehicle of their abdication is pretentious overelaboration of 'method' and 'theory'; the main reason for it is their lack of firm connection with substantive problems. . . . As practices, they may be understood as insuring that we do not learn too much about man and society—the first by formal and cloudy obscurantism, the second by formal and empty ingenuity" (Mills, 1959, p. 75).

Mills' best-known book, *The Power Elite* (1956), has been one of the most influential interpretations of the power structure in America. The main theory is summarized by Mills:

it is also not surprising that a German historian turned sociologist, Max Weber, should have been the major theorist of sociological historicism and probably the man most people in the field would today recognize as the most important sociologist.

The key idea of Weber's voluminous studies of society is simple: Social action is meaningful action and must be studied as meaningful action by any sociologist wishing to explain it. Throughout the nineteenth century, most sociologists had moved toward the recognition that social meanings are basic to all human social action and that sociologists would have to develop scientific means of analyzing those meanings if they were to develop valid theories to predict human action in real situations. But the fear of subjectivism and of looking unscientific in an age dominated by the prestige of scientific thought, combined with the difficulty of scientifically studying such phenomena as social meanings, prevented most sociologists from recognizing and accepting this idea. The importance of social meanings in de-

---

As the means of information and of power are centralized, some men come to occupy positions in American society from which . . . their decisions mightily affect the everyday worlds of ordinary men and women. . . . They need not merely "meet the demands of the day and hour;" in some part, they create these demands, and cause others to meet them.

Mills contrasts the power elite and the mass society—the powerful and the powerless, the politically active and the politically passive, the few and the many. The few, the elite, include not only those politically active in local and federal government, but also the top military, some celebrities, the families of "good" and "old" blood, the executives, the corporate rich, and the merely rich.

The power elite is not a single group, but it is unified and its unity is maintained by intermarriage, elite private schools, social clubs, cliques, and churches. By contract, mass society is formed of fragmented individuals, living in a largely urban society which lacks true community and substitutes the anesthesia of mass media for human communication.

Mills' method in tracing the development of the power elite and mass society is eclectic historical comparisons, on a macrosociological and philosophical basis. *The Power Elite* has been criticized by sociologists for lack of documentation but, along with his analysis of the American middle class, *White Collar*, it remains a vivid and imaginative portrayal of what Mills called the moral uneasiness of our times.

Mills thought that knowledge, properly used, could bring about the good society, and that if the good society was not yet here, it was primarily the fault of men of knowledge. This reminder alone is a great contribution to sociology.

termining social actions is so taken for granted at the concrete level at which we think and act in our everyday affairs that we tend not to recognize them or to see their importance in developing sociological theory.

Historians studying historical documents to determine what happened in history and why had to use common-sense understanding of human action to analyze actions described in the documents. In doing so, they arrived at a clearer understanding of the importance of social meanings in explaining social action than did the earlier sociologists, who were relying largely on data such as official statistics. Historians came to distinguish between what R. G. Collingwood called the external aspects of any action, or those that could be observed with the eyes, and the internal aspects, the meanings that could not be directly observed but could be inferred as taking place inside the head of the actor (Collingwood, 1956, p. 213).

Weber, following the lead of the historian Dilthey, was eventually able to formalize this idea of the essentially meaningful nature of human action. Because he saw it as fundamental to all social action, he defined sociology as the study of meaningful action:

> We shall call "action" (*Handeln*) any human attitude or activity (*Verhalten*) (no matter whether involving external or internal acts, failure to act or passive acquiescence) if and insofar as the actor or actors associate a subjective meaning (*Sinn*) with it (Weber, 1965, p. 328).

INSERT NO. 11

Max Weber

Max Weber (1864–1920) grew up in Germany in a home where intellectual interests were considered very important. Weber studied law, economics, and philosophy at the universities of Heidelberg, Göttingen, and Berlin, and took his bar examination in 1886. Although his poor health never permitted him to hold a permanent academic position, he served as a teacher of law at the University of Berlin and as a government consultant. Eventually, he became professor of economics at the universities of Freiburg and Heidelberg, but suffered a nervous breakdown in 1898 from which he never recovered sufficiently to return to teaching.

Incapacitated for four years, Weber resumed his scholarly activities in 1903 by becoming co-editor of the influential journal *Archiv fur Sozialwissenschaft*. In 1904 he began to publish his own scholarly work. From this time on he lived as a private scholar, mostly in the city of Heidelberg, returning only briefly to more formal academic work, in Vienna and Munich, in the years immediately preceding his death.

Weber's idea that social action is essentially meaningful action put him in conflict with the materialistic determinism of Marx. He disagreed with the mechanistic and materialistic ideas of Marx and other sociological thinkers in another respect. He did not argue that there was any one basic motive for human action, but he saw social action as motivated by many factors and guided by many ideas. While he believed that social values, or shared ideas about right and wrong, were basic in determining social actions, he also believed there were many values at work in any given society at any one time. This belief is clear in his discussion of *social legitimacy,* the value orientations used to justify one's social actions, especially the value orientations used to justify any exercise of authority in society. He stated that three major types of legitimacy could be seen at work in the history of Western societies: traditional legitimacy, charismatic legitimacy, and rational legitimacy (see chapters 13 and 16). But he believed that, while one form of legitimacy tends to be dominant at any time in a society, all can coexist and at times conflict with each other.

One of the guiding ideas in Weber's work was the belief that rational legitimacy and a general rationalizing of ideas and action has been taking place in all Western societies over the past several centuries, as can be seen clearly in his studies of religion, especially in his study of *The Protestant Ethic and the Spirit of Capitalism* (1958). This work shows the ways in which, he argued, social actions result from forces other than materialistic

> Weber had wide-ranging interests in sociology, from general theory and methodology to political and religious sociology. His most famous work is *The Protestant Ethic and the Spirit of Capitalism,* in which he developed the thesis that the development of capitalism in the Western world was associated with, and in part caused by, the economic incentives implicit in ascetic Protestantism. This theory has been the subject of much debate, especially among those who believe that the association between religion and the economy is the reverse—that capitalism results in changes in the religious sphere. Later, Weber continued his inquiry into the relationship of religious ideas and social organization with studies of Confucianism, Hinduism, Judaism, and Buddhism.
>
> Weber also did some work in political sociology that has been extended by later sociologists. He believed that the exercise of authority, the basis of political power, is a universal phenomenon and that there are three types of domination that characterize authority relations: charismatic (based on personal mystique), traditional, and legal (see chapters 13 and 16). He extended his discussion of legal authority relations into analyses of bureaucratic rules and relationships.
>
> Weber's work has been continuously influential throughout sociology. It has been particularly important since World War II in the development of symbolic interactionist and phenomenological theory (which we will discuss later).

ones. He stated that in Western societies Protestantism became a dominant motivation for "the spirit of capitalism" which, in turn, was a dominant motivation for the development of the modern industrialized economy and state (see also Chapter 12).

Weber's study of Protestantism and the spirit of capitalism reveals the method Weber used to study society. Because he believed meanings to be the primary determinants of individual actions and therefore felt the sociologist must be primarily concerned with discovering the meanings of situations to the actors he is analyzing, he sought to develop a method for determining social meanings. The method he developed is called *Verstehen* (understanding). The basic idea is that the sociologist must reconstruct a plausible meaning to connect the individual's actions—that is, the sociologist must infer from his observations of an individual's actions and statements what the internal or meaningful connection is among them. This method consisted of providing a plausible link between what an individual experienced in a given situation and what he did in that situation. Commonly, this link consisted of a plausible *motive*. For example, in his study of Protestantism and capitalism, Weber tried to show from studies of diaries and other sources a plausible link between a Protestant's beliefs and his worldly work as a capitalistic businessman.

Weber was not so much concerned with the plausible meaning for each individual's actions but, rather, with the plausible link for groups or societies, such as all Protestant societies. In order to analyze these social meanings he constructed what he called *ideal types*. Ideal types were not ideas or motives that he believed to exist in the minds of the social actors but the typifications of the actor's ideas that he or any other social analyst reconstructed from observations of the actor's actions and statements. The ideal types were supposed to be the center or average around which the actual ideas of the actors were found to fall, or toward which they tended.

As we examine them in our discussions of political authority (Chapter 12) and organizations (Chapter 16), Weber's works continue to have a major impact on sociological thought. His most lasting contribution is his argument that social meanings are the primary determinants of social action and his treatment of the problems in analyzing social meanings. There remain important problems in analyzing social meanings that sociologists have only recently begun to solve, but Weber's work forms the classic background in sociology for all studies and theories of everyday life.

THE END OF THE EUROPEAN ERA IN SOCIOLOGY

In the nineteenth century, sociology emerged as a scientific discipline. This period saw the development of the outlines of most theories proposed in the twentieth century. By the beginning of the century, sociologists had recognized the fundamental problems of their discipline and the nature of the answers that would later be found. They had learned that social actions are socially meaningful actions and that they must learn how to scientifically analyze the social meanings of actions to the actors. They came to see how little they knew and determined the outline of the answers to be sought.

Necessarily, this review of the major figures and theories in sociology in this period leaves out many ideas and sociologists. We have not considered, for example, the ideas of Vilfredo Pareto or those of Georg Simmel (see Insert Nos. 12 and 13). Although both are of interest in the history of social

---

INSERT NO. 12

Vilfredo Pareto

Vilfredo Pareto (1848–1923), an economist as well as a sociologist, was born in Paris of Italian parentage. He spent his early years in France, but his secondary and higher education took place in Italy. Partly because his intellectual interests were somewhat outside the main current of thought in Western Europe, he did not and does not have a reputation equal to that of Weber or Durkheim.

Pareto's sociology was much influenced by economics and mathematics; he defined the study of sociology as dealing with those aspects of social life not subsumed under economics. His main focus was on the difference between logical and nonlogical individual action, that which devises objectively suitable means to gain desired ends and that which does not. Society provides logical and nonlogical "guides to action" for individuals and constructs nonlogical "derivations," or arguments and assertions, to legitimate the nonlogical systems, which are then further bolstered by individuals' "residues" or nonlogical, emotional tendencies.

This was elaborated into a theory of society in Pareto's most famous work, *The Mind and Society: A Treatise on General Sociology*. In this work he described the "circulation of elites," the two ruling political classes of a society—the "lions" and the "foxes," the former activated by emotions or "residues" of commitment and tyranny and the latter by flexibility and adaptation. He argued that these two groups alternated historically in power, constantly overthrown and reinstated because of the weaknesses and strengths inherent in their residues.

Because of the unusual nature of Pareto's thought and because he has been considered a political conservative, his work has never received much systematic attention. His theoretical formulations are not as sophisticated as those of his contemporaries Weber and Durkheim, and he did not attempt to use or develop techniques of empirical research.

thought, neither has had a great effect on the central thrust of sociological theory and research. Pareto's central ideas were rarely made use of, partly because he made few contributions to the analysis of the socially meaningful nature of everyday social action or to the analysis of social structures. While some of Simmel's ideas are useful in analysis of everyday life, and some have been used in theories of social conflict, they too have had little impact.

All the great figures we have analyzed in presenting the classical tradition have been Europeans. The nineteenth century and the first decade of the 20th century was the great era of European sociology. There were antebellum (pre–Civil War) sociologists in the United States, but they were

---

INSERT NO. 13

Georg Simmel

Georg Simmel (1858–1918) was a German philosopher and sociologist who received his education at the University of Berlin and spent much of his life teaching there. He was not popular with his colleagues, partly because of his Jewish origin and his nonprofessorial brilliance, and he failed to attain a full professorship until the age of fifty-six, when he was called to a chair at the University of Strasbourg.

Sociology was only one of Simmel's many interests, and his productive period in this field lasted only about ten years. Simmel rejected the society-organism analogy popular at that time and concluded that society could be nothing more than the sum total of the interactions and interdependencies among individuals and that social unity is maintained by this functional interdependence. The study of sociology, for Simmel, was the study of subinstitutions or microsociological interactions—an unusual approach at that time. He regarded the intermixing of sociology and philosophy in macrosociology as not really sociology, and proposed that sociology should be closely rooted in empirical data, not dedicated to the formulation of large-scale laws and schemes of history and society. Later in his life he proposed a distinction between formal sociology—forms of interaction—and general sociology—the content of interaction—but he died never having made this distinction theoretically clear.

Simmel's sociological ideas are difficult to classify in terms of the intellectual movements current at the time. He was not a positivist, because he rejected the use of natural science models in disciplines dealing with man. His work attends both to the meanings of individuals' interactions and to the objectively perceived results of action. The only major modern sociologist to follow up Simmel's thinking explicitly is Lewis Coser, in *The Functions of Social Conflict* (1956).

applying European ideas to American society without making significant contributions of their own.

But, during World War I, a generation of French sociology students was killed in the trenches. And the German sociologists who were not killed were silenced in the rising tides of anarchy and Nazi tyranny that gripped Germany after World War I. Since World War II there has been a slow revival of sociology in the nations of Europe, especially in France, Germany, and Great Britain. But until recently the bulk of this sociology has been imitative of American research and theory. The creative work of twentieth-century sociology has been predominantly American, and it is to sociology in America that we now turn.

SUGGESTED READINGS

Birnbaum, Norman, *The Crisis of Industrial Society*. New York: Oxford University Press, 1969.
One of the most thoughtful works in the tradition of neo-Marxian sociology.

Coser, Lewis, *The Functions of Social Conflict*. New York: The Free Press, 1956.
The most significant contemporary study from the conflict perspective on society, Coser's book draws heavily on the work of Georg Simmel.

Durkheim, Emile. *Suicide*. New York: The Free Press, 1951.
Durkheim's famous and influential comparative study of suicide statistics.

Fromm, Erich, ed., *Marx's Concept of Man*. New York: Frederick Ungar, 1961.
A representative collection of Marx's writings on economic determinism, social class, alienation, and other themes.

Marcuse, Herbert, *One Dimensional Man*. Boston: Beacon, 1964.
This book, by the controversial professor of philosophy, takes as its topic the alienation of contemporary man from his work, others, and his inner nature.

Martindale, Don, *The Nature and Types of Sociological Theory*. Boston: Houghton Mifflin, 1960.
A thorough and scholarly overview of the major theorists and theories in sociology from its inception as a specific discipline.

Mills, C. Wright, *The Power Elite*. New York: Oxford University Press, 1956.
Mills' book—with its major thesis that America is ruled by an unelected elite of men in industry, government, and the military—has been an important source of theory development in political sociology.

Sorokin, Pitirim A., *Contemporary Sociological Theories*. New York: Harper, 1928.
A readable account of the state of sociological theory at that time.

Timasheff, Nicholas, *Sociological Theory: Its Nature and Growth.* New York: Random House, 1961.

A historical critique of the development of sociological theory, Timasheff's book is highly readable.

Weber, Max, *From Max Weber: Essays in Sociology.* New York: Oxford University Press, 1946.

Translated by Hans Gerth and C. Wright Mills, this collection of Weber's essays covers major aspects of his thought, from methodology to comparative religion.

Weber, Max, *The Protestant Ethic and the Spirit of Capitalism.* New York: Charles Scribners Sons, 1958.

Weber's best-known work traces the development of capitalism to the spread of the Puritan religion in the Western world.

CHAPTER 3

The Progress of Modern Sociology: Social Psychology, Small Groups, and Functionalism

This chapter concentrates on American sociology in the twentieth century. It is concerned with three broad areas: social psychology, small groups, and functionalism.

Social psychology consists primarily of the study of society's effects on individuals rather than of the individual's effects on society; it tends to see society as the cause and the individual as the effect. As with the study of small groups, the methods used are predominantly experimental, taking the individual out of his everyday life situations. The realism of everyday situations is sacrificed in favor of greater experimental control made possible by the laboratory situation. Functionalism has been more concerned with everyday situations, but it has concentrated on abstract analyses of the society as a whole and has not given much consideration to the problems of determining the meanings of actions to members of society.

Each major line of development in these three broad areas is presented here. We find sociologists moving toward greater consideration of the problem of meanings, the dominant concern of the following chapter.

EARLY AMERICAN SOCIOLOGY

There was little in nineteenth-century American sociology leading one to expect the discipline to achieve such extensive development in the twentieth century. Almost all American sociology of the nineteenth century was directly imitative of the work of the Europeans. The work of the antebellum sociologists in both the North and the South was heavily influenced by the works of Comte and of the moral statisticians. For example, in *Sociology for the South* and *Cannibals All*, George Fitzhugh compared all of Northern society with all of Southern society in terms of quantitative data and official social rates, such as crime rates and rates of education (Boorstin, 1953). Whereas the sociological ideas of these works are comparable to those found in the works of their European teachers, although less sophisticated, the Americans were even more concerned with *using* sociology to achieve their goals in society than the moral statisticians of Europe. Except for the technical analyses of population data that began at this time, these works had clearly political goals, though the authors often presented them as "defenses" of culture and truth. The Northerners used their data to show that Northern society, or "free society," was superior to Southern society: their data on social rates showed more education, higher incomes, more books, and less poverty in the North. The Southerners used the same kinds

---

INSERT NO. 14

William Graham Sumner

William Graham Sumner (1840–1910) was one of the founders of sociology in the United States. He graduated from Yale in 1863 and, after studying languages and theology in several European universities, returned to Yale to teach.

Before the early 1890s, Sumner was known as a brilliant economist and essayist, a polemical opponent of socialism, sentimental social movements, and big government. But, from the early 1890s on, he became increasingly interested in sociological research rather than in economics and polemics, and his public reputation waned correspondingly.

The first indicator of Sumner's interest in sociology came when he adopted Spencer's *The Study of Sociology* as a text in one of his classes, which is the basis for the claim that Sumner gave the first university course in sociology. Like Spencer, Sumner began to collect ethnographic material as data for his sociological theories. Sumner's first published work in sociology, *Folkways*

of data to show that Southern society, or "slave society," was superior to Northern society: their data on social rates showed more authors, less crime, and less insanity in the South.

This ante-bellum sociology had considerable influence in its day, without convincing many true believers to change their minds and without deflecting the nation from its rush to carnage. The war and its aftermath brought an end to this politicized sociology. Indeed, few sociologists in the twentieth century were even aware of its existence until Daniel Boorstin rediscovered it (1953). Instead, American sociology in the latter part of the nineteenth century, like European sociology and largely in response to developments in Europe, developed in two directions: public hygiene and public welfare studies of a partially statistical nature and abstract theorizing.

Like the Europeans, Americans who did studies of public hygiene and welfare were usually not identified as sociologists but did the kind of research, unencumbered by philosophy, that later generations of sociologists would see as more sociological than the highly philosophical works of those who called themselves sociologists. These hygienists' works were oriented toward solving social problems as defined by officials and other men of power. Their influence on American sociology was great, both in setting this tradition of research on problems and in developing quantitative research methods that were later used by sociologists to do surveys (see Chapter 10).

(1906), made history. He defined *folkways* as the customary acts of the group, analogous to the habits of the individual, rooted in the fundamental need of man for maintenance, protection, perpetuation, and security of the self.

Over time, folkways that are at first simply expedient tend to exert more and more pressure on people and appear to have a compulsive force of their own. These compulsive folkways, perceived by the group as in the public interest, Sumner termed *mores*. Sumner elaborated further on definitions of mores. Those laid down by society as ethical principles are *morals*, negative mores are *taboos*, and *laws* are those folkways and mores that are given the added "specific sanction of the group as it is organized politically." Both folkways and mores coalesce around social interests and institutions, such as sex and government. They are, like the institutions themselves, basically conservative yet constantly undergoing modification. Deviance from folkways is sanctioned by disapproval, whereas deviance from mores—especially laws—earns punishment.

Folkways ranks as one of the most influential works in American sociology. In addition to inventing the concepts of mores and folkways, Sumner coined the word *ethnocentrism*, and distinguished between *in-group* and *out-group*, elaborated in *The Science of Society*, published in 1927, seven years after his death. But *Folkways* remains his most insightful and stimulating work.

The early theorists had considerable influence on the development of American sociology and created the first university departments of sociology in the United States, which gave them control over the education of the first generation of Americans in this field. The three most important early American sociologists were primarily importers of European sociology to America.

William Graham Sumner was the one famous American sociologist who was completely committed to a form of *Social Darwinism*. Like all Social Darwinists, he agreed with Spencer's general ideas of organicism and evolutionism, and believed that evolutionary progress is the result of conflicts or competitive struggles between individuals and groups that lead to the survival of the fittest. The victory goes to the more powerful individuals and social groups, who are best able to run things in the best interests of all. It was this form of conflict theory, rather than Marxism, which influenced American social thought up to the 1930s, at which time this Darwinist idea gave way to more Marxian ideas in the wake of the depression. Today, Sumner is remembered by American sociologists primarily for his ideas about folkways and mores, rather than for his Darwinism (Insert No. 14).

Lester F. Ward was probably the most famous American sociologist of his day, but has been largely forgotten by modern sociology (Insert No. 15). His influence on the development of distinctively American sociological theories was great, primarily because of his modification of the organicist and evolutionist theories. He started by accepting Spencer's theories, but found it necessary to modify them to include the ways individuals can change evolution by willing their own actions in accord with what they believe to be their interests. This insistence on the importance of individual factors in affecting the development of society became basic to much of American sociology and distinguished it from European sociology. It was this idea that led to the development of *social psychology* in American sociology and psychology, and the theory that individuals act primarily in accord with what they see as their interests led to the emphasis on *motives* in these areas of study. While these emphases on individual factors are partly the result of common-sense ideas that Americans share about themselves and about social action, it was Ward who first analyzed their implications for sociological thought. Moreover, there is a direct line of influence from Ward to the Chicago tradition of American sociology.

Albion Small was one of the most influential American sociologists (see Insert No. 16), but has been little remembered. His thought was greatly influenced by Ward's sociology, especially by his emphasis on individual interests. His influence was primarily the result of his systematic introduction of European sociology to America and his position as the founder and chairman of the Department of Sociology at the University of Chicago, which became the dominant center of sociological research and theory in the United States up to the 1930s.

SOCIAL BEHAVIORISM: GROUP EFFECTS ON PERCEPTION AND COMMUNICATION

As we shall see in Chapter 4, field research and social interactionism are the traditions of sociological thought most remembered as the contributions of Chicago sociology. But there were many streams of thought at Chicago in the 1920s when the department was at its zenith. One was *behaviorism,* which we have since realized is in conflict with most of the other ideas of

INSERT NO. 15

Lester F. Ward

Lester Frank Ward (1841–1913) was eulogized at his death as the last of the giants of nineteenth-century sociology. Brought up in a farming community, the young Ward became convinced of the value of the education which he lacked and taught himself Greek, German, French, and Latin. After service in the Union Army during the Civil War, he attended night schools, and attained an M.A. in biology from the Columbian (now George Washington) University. He became interested in sociology and wrote a work entitled "Dynamic Sociology," published in 1883, containing his major ideas. His subsequent writings were either elaborations, clarifications, or (as in his *Outlines of Sociology,* 1898, and *A Textbook of Sociology,* 1905) condensations of his system of thought.

Ward was a positivist who believed in social evolution. His major idea was that the evolution of structures from the simplest to the most complex is the product of a struggle among forces unique to each of three stages: the genesis of matter, the genesis of organic forms of mind and finally of man, and the genesis of society. In his account of societal evolution, Ward introduced two concepts which have had a lasting influence in sociology. The first is that social forces are essentially *psychological* rather than transcendent or biological in nature; this idea has been of considerable importance in the development of social psychology. The second concept is that of *telesis,* which refers to the artificial or purposive selection society uses in the process of evolution in addition to processes of natural selection that society has in common with other phenomena. His utopia was a society in which government, as the instrument of social telesis, armed with sociological principles, would produce legislation to ensure maximum happiness for all.

During his lifetime, Ward was one of the most important American sociologists; he was elected first president of the new American Sociological Association in 1906. But his influence was confined mostly to his lifetime, partly because he had no interest in quantification, which has dominated American methodology and even theory from the 1920s to the present.

the Chicago school of sociology, but which often looked compatible in the early days.

Behaviorism was primarily the work of John B. Watson, a psychologist at the University of Chicago, who argued that any science of man must be concerned entirely with quantitatively predicting what can be observed with sense impressions—or, in other words, any internal phenomena must be banished from consideration. Behaviorism was a new kind of mechanism that denied the socially meaningful nature of human actions but did not try to explain those actions in terms of analogies with physical bodies or abstract mathematical formulas.

Because sociology has always been concerned with explaining human actions in the everyday world and because these actions are meaningful to the actors, behaviorism in the extreme form proposed by Watson has rarely been accepted by sociologists. But behaviorism as a method and an ideal has had great influence on the thought of some American sociologists. The

---

INSERT NO. 16

Albion Small

Like many American sociologists at the turn of the century, Albion Woodbury Small (1854–1926) was initially trained in theology, but this training had been broadened and secularized before he began to teach sociology. After graduating from an American Baptist college, he spent two years studying in Berlin and Leipzig and obtained a doctorate in 1889 from Johns Hopkins. During his years in Germany and at Johns Hopkins, Small became very interested in social welfare and planning and believed the major justification of sociology to lie in these areas.

In 1892 Small was appointed to the first chair of sociology in the United States, at the newly founded University of Chicago. There he built the first, and long the best, American department of sociology. With George E. Vincent, one of the first members of the department, he wrote the first sociology textbook, published in 1894. He also founded the *American Journal of Sociology*, which he edited for the next thirty years, in 1895. His best-known work, published in 1905, was *General Sociology*.

His sociological ideas exemplify a general trend of the early years of the twentieth century, away from attention to relatively static social structures and toward dynamic and functional analysis of social processes. During his lifetime, his interest shifted from analogies between organisms and society to the concept of the social process, especially as it is found in group activities. But Small is most remembered for his contributions to the establishment of sociology as a discipline, not for his intellectual contributions.

social behaviorists have tried to use highly operational or externally perceivable forms of data and quantitative means of analyzing that data. Generally, they have dealt only with visible or audible forms of behavior, which they quantified; and, while they implicitly dealt with meanings, they did not given explicit consideration to those meanings. Much of their work consists of trying to show that there is a quantitative relation between two or more perceivable sets of phenomena, as between a physical setting and verbal responses; but this early ideal has been progressively extended to consider less and less physically perceivable phenomena.

Social behaviorism is a form of social psychology. Whereas social psychology as a whole consists of studies that emphasize the relations between the individual and his social settings, social behaviorism studies these relations between the individual and his social setting in a behavioristic manner. An example of such social behaviorism, and the progress in understanding its advantages and problems, is found in the history of studies of the effects of social settings on perception.

The classical psychological approach to the study of perception gave no consideration to social setting. The human individual's perceptions were treated as the result of the relation between the organism and its physical environment. This approach failed to take account of how profoundly man's social setting affects almost everything he does and is. Recognizing this, many psychologists began to experiment with the effects of social settings on perception, which influenced the development of social psychology. Much of this work sprang from the common-sense recognition that members of different societies have different perceptual abilities, without differences in the organisms. For example, anthropologists have found that some Africans who are members of cattle-grazing societies are able to perceive differences in cattle at far greater distances than Western men can. One of the classic sets of experiments in this area, by Muzafer Sherif, demonstrated what he called the *autokinetic effect*. He was able to show that two individuals in a dark room will affect each other's perceptual judgments when there is no external basis for judgment. He demonstrated that a tiny stable point of light shown to an individual alone in a dark room will appear to move erratically. Next, he was able to show that lone individuals placed in this situation will develop some set of internal comparisons that they use to judge the apparent movements of the light. Finally, he showed that two or more individuals looking at the same light and trying to reach agreement about the movements of the light will affect each other's judgment about these movements. Sherif found that such groups of individuals established a norm with which to judge the movements of the light. Sherif believed this norm was an elementary form of all *social norms,* which are standards or criteria of judgments agreed upon and used by members of social groups to make evaluations. He argued that these norms tended to become *values,* which are prescribed norms or standards that members of a group morally demand that all members use in making their evaluations. In accord with this belief, he showed that once the norm had been established in a group observing the light, any individual who diverged in his judgments from the norm no longer influenced the others' judgments. Even the individual who had established himself as a leader in evaluating the movements was deposed from his leadership position if he diverged from the norm. In this sense, Sherif argued, the experiment showed how social values are established through group interactions and then become partially independent of individual factors. In his discussion of his results, we can see how social psychologists used laboratory experiments as the basis for generalizations about society:

> The experiments, then, constitute a study of the formation of a norm in a simple laboratory situation. They show in a simple way the basic psychological process involved in the establishment of social norms. They are an extension into the social field of a general psychological phenomenon that is found in perception and in many other psychological fields, namely, that our experience is organized around or modified by frames of reference participating as factors in any given stimulus situation.
>
> On the basis of this general principle considered in relation to our experimental results, we shall venture to generalize. The psychological basis of the established social norms, such as stereo-types, fashions, conventions, customs and values, is the formation of common frames of reference as a product of the contact of individuals. Once such frames of reference are established and incorporated in the individual, they enter as important factors to determine or modify his reactions to the situations that he will face later—social, and even non-social at times, especially if the stimulus field is not well structured (Sherif, 1947, pp. 85–86).

Social psychologists continued to study the effects of group involvement on such basic and seemingly psychological or organic responses as perception. They found that social interaction of any form does alter even such basic behavioral responses as perception. The research that followed such pioneers as Sherif showed that social influence on perception and other "psychological" behavior is greater than Sherif thought. There were two major lines of research leading to this conclusion. Social psychologists such as Leo Postman and Jerome Bruner have argued that the values of an individual, which they believed are learned from earlier social interaction, have important effects on perception. For example, values may produce *perceptual sensitization,* or a greater readiness to perceive, or they may lead to *perceptual defenses,* or a lower readiness to perceive. Other social psychologists, especially Solomon Asch (1952), tried to show that social interaction affects perception even when the individual has already established a *frame of reference* for his perceptions, that is, a set of standards in terms of which anything is judged, and even when the *stimulus field* is not ambiguous as the light was in Sherif's experiments on the autokinetic effect. For example, Asch stated that individuals will see the lengths of lines differently when a group in which they are involved tries to influence their perceptions by lying to them about the lengths of lines presented to them.

Experimental studies of the effects of social interaction on perception were later found to have weaknesses. Because, like all behavioristic studies, they concentrated on measuring the external responses of their subjects, without trying to determine why they were responding that way in that experimental situation, these early experiments greatly oversimplified the effects of social interaction on perception and thought. The succeeding history of the Asch experiments made this clear. Other social psychologists argued that Asch's subjects were not seeing the lengths of lines differently when they were subject to group evaluations of those lengths, but were lying to avoid conflict with the group. This criticism, which has a commonsense plausibility to it, led Asch to do more extensive experiments, including interviews with the subjects after the experiments, to see what had been going on "in their minds." He found that there were indeed a number of complex reasons that subjects acted the way they did. Once again, it had been found that the meanings of situations to the actors are basic determinants of what they choose to do and anyone who disregards these meanings will not understand the actors' actions.

Recognition of this weakness was one factor leading to the development of a new line of social psychological research on communication and mass communication in the 1940s and 1950s. The goals of this research were to determine the effects of messages on the behavior of individuals and to determine how and why these messages had such effects (see Chapters 11 and 12). Much of this research was concerned with consumer behavior and led to the conclusion that advertising messages cannot create the motivation to buy products but can affect which brand an individual will buy. In related research, Merton and his co-workers studied why individuals responded favorably to advertising by purchasing war bonds, or unfavorably by not purchasing them in the case of an appeal by Kate Smith during World War II. Many of these studies also tried to determine the reasons for the effects of messages other than advertisements or appeals. The most famous of these was the study by Hadley Cantril of the effects on behavior of Orson Welles' famous radio program on "The Invasion from Mars" (see Insert No. 17).

A second weakness of these early studies of the effects of group interaction on perception, one shared by later studies of communications, was that they concentrated on individual effects rather than examining how the interaction of individuals affects all their relations as members of a group. In order to study the effects of interaction on whole groups, while retaining the advantages of the experimental controls demanded by social behaviorism, sociologists developed experimental methods for studying small groups.

SMALL GROUP STUDIES

Sociologists have been concerned with studying small groups since the nineteenth-century research on families by LePlay and since Tönnies' theory of *Gemeinschaft und Gesellschaft* (see Insert No. 18). This interest was continued in the works of the Chicago sociologists of the 1920s and 1930s in their concern with *primary groups,* such as the family in which there is a high degree of interaction and emotional involvement, contrasted with *secondary groups,* in which there is low interaction and low emotional involvement, such as the classroom group. But the experimental studies of small groups as distinct little societies did not begin until the 1930s.

Much of the early experimental work on small groups consisted of trying

---

INSERT NO. 17

"The Invasion from Mars"

On the evening of October 30, 1938, thousands of Americans were terrified by a fictional radio broadcast by Orson Welles that described an invasion of the Earth by Martians. It has been estimated that at least a million of the six million people who heard the broadcast were upset by it. Some fled from their homes to escape death at the hands of the Martians, while others sought information from newspapers, summoned ambulances, telephoned warnings to friends, or prayed for deliverance.

This occurrence offered psychologists and sociologists a rare opportunity to study panic reactions of many kinds of people in a natural, rather than a laboratory, setting. One of the best-known studies to come out of the scare was that by Hadley Cantril and his associates, who interviewed 100 persons frightened by the broadcast to find out why this particular science-fiction broadcast had frightened them while others had not and why it frightened some individuals and not others.

The major factor in the program's impact was its extreme realism and dramatically convincing style. The "events" were reported in detail, proceeding gradually from the fairly credible to the more fantastic. Not only were the details realistic, they were backed up by "experts"—astronomers, scientists, army officers, and college professors. The radio itself was seen as a source of expert information about news and crises, and people had become accustomed to the interruption of regular programming by bulletins. Why the program

to determine the nature and causes of the patterns of relations among members of groups. The most influential work was done by J. L. Moreno on *sociometry*, which consisted primarily of studies of the patterns of choices (for friends, roommates) among members of groups (see Insert No. 19). Sociologists became concerned with the ways in which the members of small groups come to play *social roles* within the group—that is, ways in which individuals come to act in accord with certain stable expectations of other group members about how they will act. The study of social roles within groups and their effects on group actions became the focal point of most research on small groups, but many other factors were investigated by these researchers, such as the emotional effects on members of different kinds of interaction or the productivity of different kinds of groups in solving problems. Small group studies were influential in the later development of *psychodrama* or *sociodrama*, which consists of purposefully *playing roles* within small *groups* to achieve therapeutic goals, and sensitivity training groups (or T-groups), which are widely used to try to solve interper-

---

affected some people and not others had to do partially with the time of tuning in. Obviously, those who missed the initial announcement that the program was fictional were more likely to believe it than those who had been warned. Cantril classified listeners who tuned in late and at first believed the broadcast to be true into the following categories:

1. Those who regarded the broadcast as too incredible to be true and did not remain frightened.
2. Those who checked the broadcast against other information and learned that it was a play.
3. Those who tried to check against other information, but for various reasons were not convinced that the broadcast was not an authentic news report.
4. Those who made no attempt to check the broadcast or the event.

Cantril regarded the people in the last two categories as extremely suggestible and suggested four major reasons for their suggestibility: lack of education, lack of adequate standards of judgment to interpret a stimulus, lack of any standards of judgment to interpret a new stimulus, and the economic and social insecurity of the times which made the strangest phenomena seem plausible. Overall, those who were suggestible were not equipped with an adequate frame of reference within which to orient their everyday lives.

Finally, Cantril looked for reasons for the extreme nature of the invasion panic. He concluded that people were frightened because the threatened danger was so extreme, threatening their self, their loved ones, and their whole way of life.

sonal problems such as the inability of subordinates to tell their bosses what they really feel and think.

The students of small groups first used common-sense ideas about what constitutes a group. But their studies led them to conclude that certain properties are common to all small groups:

INSERT NO. 18

Ferdinand Tönnies

Ferdinand Tönnies (1855–1936) was brought up and educated in Germany and received his doctorate in philology at the University of Tübingen in 1877. Even then his interests had shifted to political philosophy and social problems and, because he came from a wealthy family, he was able to pursue postdoctoral research in these areas. From 1881 to 1916, Tönnies taught philosophy, economics, and statistics at the University of Kiel, Germany, and spent most of his time writing articles for academic and political journals. In 1921 he became professor emeritus of sociology at Kiel, and from 1909 to 1933 he was president of the German Sociological Society. But his public denunciation of Nazism and anti-Semitism in 1932 led to his dismissal from the university the next year. He died in 1936.

Tönnies' earliest and most famous work, *Gemeinschaft und Gesellschaft* (1887), established his reputation as a sociologist, although the work remained unknown outside a small group of scholars until after World War I. In this and later studies, Tönnies made use of empirical observational and statistical data, as well as historical material, since he realized that sociology must be rooted in the observation of phenomena. His main sociological interest was in groups, and he observed many—business associations, families, kin groups, neighborhoods, and religious sects. From these observations he developed his major concepts, *Gemeinschaft* (community) and *Gesellschaft* (association).

Gemeinschaft refers to a type of social group based on mutual sympathy, habit, or common belief, which the members belong to as an end-in-itself, having a barely conscious desire to be a part of the group that Tönnies called *Wesenwille*. *Gesellschaft*, on the other hand, indicates a group joined by the members because they see it as a means to an end—their will to join is *Kürwille* (rational and conscious will).

Tönnies' great contribution to sociology was his conceptualization of *Gemeinschaft-Wesenwille* and *Gesellschaft-Kürwille*. The concepts express a real difference in kinds of group and link structural and subjective aspects of society, thus foreshadowing the work of the phenomenologists. Although Tönnies' work was long neglected, it has now assumed a deserved prominence among sociologists.

There is no definite cutting point in the continuum between a collection of individuals, such as one might find waiting for a bus on a corner, and a fully organized "group." There is also no definite cutting point between the small, intimate, face-to-face groups and the large, formal group. For a collection of individuals to be considered a group there must be some interaction. In addition to the interaction of the members, four features of group life typically emerge as the group develops . . .

1. The members share one or more motives or goals which determine the direction in which the group will move.

2. The members develop a set of norms, which set the boundaries within which interpersonal relations may be established and activity carried on.

3. If interaction continues, a set of roles becomes stabilized and the new group becomes differentiated from other groups.

4. A network of interpersonal attraction develops on the basis of the "likes" and "dislikes" of members for one another.

There are then, in sum, five characteristics which differentiate the group from a collection of individuals. The members of the group are in interaction with one another. They share a common goal and set of norms, which give direction and limits to their activity. They also develop a set of roles and a network of interpersonal attraction, which serve to differentiate them from other groups.

Small groups include all those having from two up to about twenty members. However, even larger groups may be considered "small" if face-to-face interaction is possible, and collections of fewer than twenty individuals may actually include several smaller groups (Hare, 1962).

The number of studies of small groups runs into the thousands and hundreds of different subjects are investigated. But the essential features of this field are revealed in the famous series of studies and theory of R. F. Bales and his co-workers on what they call *interaction process analysis* (see Insert No. 40 in Chapter 10).

RECENT THEORIES OF SOCIAL BEHAVIORISM

Most of the theory developed in behavioristic social psychology, including the experimental study of small groups, has more bearing on psychology than on sociology. Most of these theories are concerned with the effects on individuals of their social situations and their social experiences, rather than with the nature and interdependent effects of interaction in natural social situations. This is not true of works by sociologists who have attempted to develop behavioristic theories of human interaction based on studies of small groups. Three recent works of considerable importance are *The Human Group* (1950) and *Social Behavior: Its Elementary Forms* (1961), by George C. Homans; and *Exchange and Power in Social Life* (1964), by Peter Blau. These works show the general strengths and weaknesses of social behaviorism.

In *The Human Group,* Homans used four earlier studies of natural groups, but his analysis of them was behavioristic. The early chapters of *The Human Group* state the need for systematic, detailed, and quantitative theories of human interaction. Choosing his data from the four earlier works on the basis of their detailed information about interaction, he then develops a theory of group interaction, which he believes goes far beyond the experimental studies of small groups. The theory first distinguishes between the *external system* of a group, those relations between the group and the larger society that lead the group members to interact with each other in any way, and the *internal system* of the group, those aspects of interaction that

---

INSERT NO. 19

Sociometry

The term *sociometry* has several meanings but, historically, the closest association is with the work of J. L. Moreno, particularly his analysis of interpersonal relations in *Who Shall Survive?* (1934). The purpose of sociometry is the analysis of data in interpersonal relations by means of the sociometric test, a questionnaire designed to elicit opinions from each member of a group about the other members. The member may be asked whom he would like to see as leader of the group or with whom he would or would not like to carry out a specified activity. The patterns of choice and rejection may be represented graphically in a sociogram, which uses symbols to designate persons and lines and arrows to show the presence and direction of choices. This sociogram illustrates a situation in which the subjects were asked to state their "best friends" in the group.

Although the earliest uses of sociograms were haphazard and untheoretical, a number of useful theoretical concepts have since been derived from them by Moreno and others. The simplest concepts are the *unchosen,* the person who receives no positive or negative choices (*D* in the diagram), and the *isolate,* who neither receives nor makes any (*P*). The opposite extreme is the *sociometric star,* who receives the highest number of positive choices, either on the basis of power—as a leader—or popularity—as a friend (*L*).

Relationships between people in the networks may also be characterized conceptually—for example, *mutual pairs* of positive choices (*M* and *S*). The description of relationships between persons is most intricate in the area of re-are specific outcomes of what goes on within the group. He concluded that the external system was especially important in determining the patterns of interaction that develop within a group, including the determination of whether a group has formed and who will be members. In a study of a small group in an electrical wiring room, certain patterns of interaction between the group members were determined by the job requirements set up by the employers. Homans shows that within the group there are mutually dependent relations among activities, interaction, and sentiment. The activities of the group determine what kinds of interaction will take place; the interactions produce both activities and sentiments, or feelings, between the interacting members; and the sentiments, in turn, lead to further activities and interactions. The most significant principle of his analysis concerns the relations between interaction and sentiment. He explains that any increase in interaction will produce a mutual increase in friendliness (positive senti-

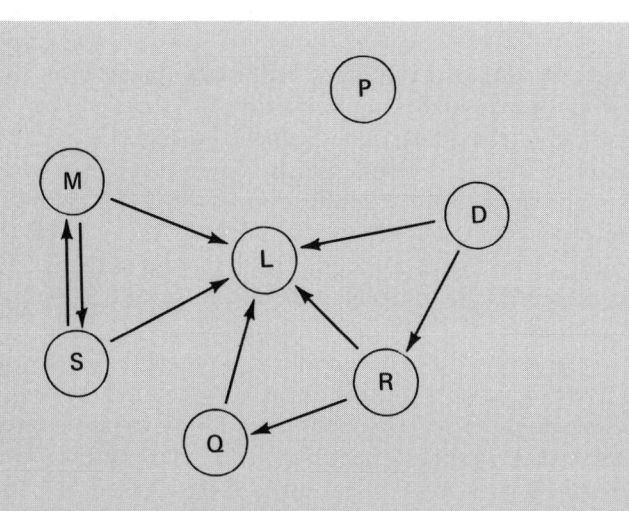

lational analysis, which involves both the calculation of all possible choices and rejections in a given situation and predictions of how the actual choices and rejections will be distributed.

Since its introduction, sociometric analysis has remained important in social psychology, enjoying its greatest popularity in the early 1950s. It has been used in many areas, including personality research, small group research, analysis of networks of communication and group structures, and special topics such as the reputational study of social status in the community and the study of segregation patterns.

ment) in those interacting and that an increase in friendliness will lead to an increase in interaction.

In *Social Behavior,* Homans shows the underlying reasons for these relations between friendliness and interaction. He explains all social interaction in terms of the behavioristic learning theory proposed by the psychologist B. F. Skinner. Homans argues that every human action is determined by its relative profitability to the actor: the actor seeks to increase his rewards and decrease his costs in his interactions with other actors. It is the difference between rewards and costs that constitutes the profit to any actor of his social action: Profits = Rewards − Costs.

The work of Peter Blau on *Exchange and Power in Social Life* (see Insert No. 20), though more limited in its goals than Homans' general theory, has also had considerable influence. These are representative of the best theoretical works of social behaviorism today. The obvious strength of social behaviorism is the high degree to which it fits the ideal of experimental science; this is the basic reason that some sociologists have continued to devote their energies to this form of endeavor, in spite of the earlier failures of the closely related social mechanists (see Chapter 2). There are at least three ways in which these works appear to fit the scientific ideal. First, by using small group experiments, such as those of Bales and his students, the behaviorists have achieved a high degree of experimental control over human actions, which they believe has constrained these actions enough to get simpler results than in studies of natural groups. Second, concentration on small groups has allowed them to get detailed information to use in developing theories. Third, the use of the behavioristic perspective has allowed them to develop specific theories that can be tested in small group settings.

There are weaknesses with behavioristic experimental data and theories that make the perspective questionable as an approach to analyzing human social action. First, the greatest supposed strength of social behaviorism is also its most important weakness, because of its failure to note how great the *uncertainty effect* is in most social experiments. When human beings are put into an experimental situation, the meanings of that situation are different for them from a natural social situation. As human beings act in any situation because of the meanings of that situation for them, they will act differently in an experimental situation from the way they would act in a natural situation. This means that the experimental situation becomes a determinant of what goes on in that situation and of the social action the behaviorists observe. The behaviorist might argue that his work is intended to be a study of experimental action, rather than of natural action. But this would condemn his work to irrelevance, as most sociologists are concerned with understanding what goes on in the natural social world, rather than with what goes on in strange experimental situations. Second, social behaviorists have the problem of *reductionism*; that is, they fail to consider ways in which social situations, especially the structures or patterns of situations, are important in determining what human beings do. Behaviorists take for granted the social situations in which individuals and small groups find themselves, but they cannot explain how those social situations arise for individuals and groups or how situations are structurally related to each other. Third, behaviorists have failed to adequately consider the problem of discovering the social meanings determining what the actors do. Unlike

---

INSERT NO. 20

On Peter M. Blau's *Exchange and Power in Social Life*

The aim of Peter M. Blau's *Exchange and Power in Social Life* (1964) is "to contribute to an understanding of social structure on the basis of an analysis of the social processes that govern the relations between individuals and groups." He attempts to generalize the social processes of the larger community from those which take place among individuals in their everyday lives and to bridge the gap between microsociological studies of small groups and grand macrosociological theories of society.

A central concept in the book is that of *emergent properties*, which are relationships between elements in a social structure that define the structure. *Social exchange* refers to the emergent properties in interpersonal relations and social interaction. *Social relations* are the joint product of the actions of interacting individuals, with the actions of each dependent on those of the other. The exchange situation begins with a *service*, for which the recipient is expected to express gratitude. If *gratitude* is expressed, this serves as a reward for the other, who is then induced to extend more services, and a mutual social bond is created. If he does not reciprocate or express gratitude, the recipient of a service is regarded as remiss, and the interaction is terminated.

For behavior to lead to social exchange, two conditions must be met that are characteristic of most social interaction. The behavior must be oriented toward ends that can be reached only through interaction, and it must be directed toward finding means to achieve those ends. Blau does not extend the concept to expressive interactions, such as rioting, or to interaction indulged in for its intrinsic enjoyability, such as lovemaking.

Power and authority are types of secondary, or more complex, large-scale and structural exchange. The exercise of power depends upon collective reactions such as legitimation and is threatened by other collective reactions of opposition. Legitimation, based on an evaluation of power as "fair," transforms power into authority and thereby into an important source of social organization, while opposition presupposes evaluations of unfairness and leads to social disorganization.

the mechanists, social behaviorists have made *meanings* the basic variables in their theories. In Homans' theories, *friendliness* (or, more generally, sentiments) and *profit* are internal states of the actors and, therefore, are meanings. But they have not considered how to go about determining that these meanings of the actors are determining their actions. Homans is not able to show that interaction is producing friendliness and that friendliness in turn produces more interaction. He simply asserts that this is the case. He does not see the problem of specifying (or operationalizing) such concepts as friendliness. All of us know from experience that it is difficult to know when we feel "love" for someone and that it is often impossible to be sure whether someone else feels friendliness or love for us. How could Homans have had a sure method of quantitatively measuring what we are feeling or thinking when we ourselves are not sure what we are feeling or thinking?

Social behaviorism made some advances over social mechanist theories, but it continued to suffer from some of the same problems. Though it continues to exert some influence in contemporary sociology, especially in some of the recent works on mathematical models and computer simulations of social interaction (see Chapters 10 and 17), its influence seems destined to wane.

SOCIAL SURVEYS AND SOCIAL ATTITUDES

A second broad area of social psychology is that of *attitude surveys*. Sociological studies of attitudes, almost always done through *questionnaires* (see Chapter 10), have made some significant progress over social behaviorism in dealing with social meanings and how they are involved in social action, but they have not solved all these problems.

The idea of social surveys is simple and goes back to early stages of sociology's development. As the name suggests, the basic purpose of a *survey* is to take a systematic and detailed look at society to determine what is going on in its different parts. Some of the earliest surveys in the nineteenth century were made of city data and consisted of little more than systematic presentations of certain information about the city—how many businesses, how many employees, and so on. Later, this kind of survey developed into the community study, which we consider in Chapter 4. But surveys, in the modern sense, are not generally collections of this sort. The purpose of the modern survey is to provide reliable information about some part of society that will be representative of what goes on throughout some specified part of the society. The survey sociologist is trying to get good information on a small part of the society that accurately represents the whole society or some large part of it. The idea is to reduce the amount of study necessary to determine what is going on in the whole society. It is of great practical value to be able to say what many members of society think or do by studying only a small number of them, say, 1,500. This is what survey analysis tries to do by studying intensively a *representative sample,* a carefully chosen small number that can be taken to represent the whole society or group (see Chapter 10).

One of the simplest and most common forms of social survey is the *opinion survey,* known as the *opinion poll.* The opinion survey measures what the members of society or some subgroup of society think about something. Though the opinion survey may be concerned with something as simple as "In your opinion, should everyone drink orange juice in the morning?", probably the best-known form today is the poll of voting opinions, which often consists of such simple questions as "Do you think President Nixon is doing a good, fair, or bad job as President?" The voting poll is a social survey in the strict sense—that is, it is an intensive study of the opinions of a small number of people (about 1,500), carefully chosen as representative of the entire population of the nation or some smaller governmental unit.

The word "opinion," however, is misleading. Sociologists were first interested in what people think about something because they believed that these thoughts would determine what these people would do. It was felt that the opinion someone had of how well the President was doing his job would tell us whether he would vote for the President in the next election. This was an oversimplification. Individuals have many different beliefs, feelings, and values (or social meanings) and they are interrelated. It is some combination (what we shall later call a *construction*) of these meanings in a given situation that determines what individuals do. Because sociologists were concerned with explaining and predicting what people would do, they were not concerned simply with distinct and possibly independent opinions, but with how they were all combined with feelings and other meanings to lead an individual to act in a certain way. This led to a concern with attitudes and the development of questionnaires intended to provide reliable attitude surveys.

The sociological idea of attitudes goes back at least to the work of W. I. Thomas and Florian Znaniecki on *The Polish Peasant* (see Insert No. 21). *Attitude* was defined as "a tendency to act" in a certain way. Although some studies of attitudes, especially that by Thomas and Znaniecki, analyzed the writings of members of society, today almost all such studies are done with the use of questionnaires, consisting of series of interrelated questions whose answers are believed to give a direct indication, an *index,* of an individual's attitudes. The *social index* (or social scale) consists of a set of questions related to each other in such a way that the answers will give a measure of how strong the attitude is and thus how strong the individuals' tendencies are to act in accord with that attitude. First, the sociologist must decide upon a definition of the attitude he wishes to measure. Then he must decide what questions will measure that attitude. Finally, he must administer the questionnaire and evaluate the results (see Chapter 10).

Strengths of the attitude surveys have made them widely used tools in modern sociology. First, they constitute progress over social mechanism or social behaviorism, as they are directly concerned with determining social meanings. Second, because they are aimed at producing findings representative of the whole society or some large group in society, they give more information about the larger society than the experimental studies of social behaviorism. Third, attitude surveys maintain controls over the

---

INSERT NO. 21

On W. I. Thomas and Florian Znaniecki's
The Polish Peasant in England and America

The Polish Peasant in England and America (1918–1920) is the monumental result of a collaboration between the American sociologist and social psychologist W. I. Thomas and the Polish sociologist Florian Znaniecki. This work was a monograph on a particular cultural group, but it also contained important methodological and theoretical insights.

In *The Polish Peasant,* the authors developed the idea that there are "four basic wishes," or attitudes, common to all men, which are partly biological and partly social in character: the desire for mastery, security, new experience, and recognition. These attitudes must be satisfied socially, and thus they function as an incentive to conformity and thereby as a means of social control. The idea of the "four wishes" was built into their "attitude-value" schema, designed to distinguish between attitudes and values, or what they perceived as the objective and subjective aspects of society. They defined a *value* as an objective datum, and an *attitude* as a motivational element in individual consciousness, such as one of the "four wishes."

During this study of the Polish peasant, Thomas and Znaniecki also became interested in and presented a new model of social change. The basis of the model is the idea of *social organization,* with behavior and norms generally congruent. At this stage, deviation is minor and isolated and is dealt with by a process of *social reorganization* or reaffirmation of norms and values. However, if deviation becomes frequent and widespread, *social disorganization* sets in, either through the general acceptance of new norms and values by the younger generation, through dissension among adults, or through both. Like many later sociologists, Thomas and Znaniecki felt that social disorganization was endemic in Western society.

methods of observation to help produce objective results. Fourth, results are quantitative, making it possible to compare groups in terms of the strengths of their attitudes.

But, while attitude surveys give some consideration to problems involved in determining social meanings, they do not see how fundamental the problems are. Most important, attitude surveys have been dependent on common-sense understandings of language, questioning, and answering, on which we lack adequate scientific studies. Second, as Irwin Deutscher (1966) and others have argued, sociologists who do attitude surveys have too often failed to show that the attitudes they measure lead to the actions they assume.

Often, people do not say what they "really think" or do what they "would really like to do." It has been found that individuals who express negative attitudes about having members of different racial groups move into their neighborhoods rarely do anything about it once such people move in. In fact, negative attitudes often change to more positive ones (Deutscher, 1966). Third, attitude studies often do not take into consideration factors such as power that tend to structure social action. For most kinds of social action everyone does not have an equal vote. For example, in hiring and firing only the decisions of a small group of people count, not those of a wide spectrum of society.

There are major problems with attitude studies that have not been solved and that limit their usefulness for sociology. As a rule of thumb, sociologists believe that any questionnaire survey will be more reliable the more it is concerned with simple and concrete activities rather than complex and abstract attitudes. For example, one can get more reliable results on a questionnaire concerning drinking orange juice, attending church, voting, or any other *self-report* of concrete activities, than on a questionnaire concerning sentiments of "friendship," "love," "prejudice," or any other complex social belief, value, or feeling. It is to be hoped that some of the problems can be solved but, until then, attitude studies will continue to be of primary importance as sources of practical information concerning social meanings and action that we must have to make effective social policies. Even here, however, sociologists seem to be moving toward the use of in-depth interviews that employ survey techniques other than questionnaires.

THE STRUCTURAL-FUNCTIONAL THEORY OF SOCIETY

As we have seen, with the exception of a few important behavioristic theories of social action, most social psychological work in sociology has been concerned with developing low-level theories about social action. But much work on attitudes and surveys has been directed at testing hypotheses derived from the general theory of society that had replaced the earlier organismic theories.

By the 1930s sociologists had abandoned earlier forms of the organismic analogy to adopt a more complex form of the organismic analogy, which we may call the *systems analogy*.

The earliest and most general form of sociological theory based on the systems analogy was the *functional theory of society*, often called the *structural-functional theory of society*. This perspective on society became dominant in American sociology in the 1930s and remained reasonably dominant through the 1960s, though opposition grew stronger throughout the 1950s.

The functional theory assumed the basic part of the organismic theories to be true. Functional theorists believed that they must be primarily concerned with getting at the structure of society in the same way organismic theorists did. But the functionalists were not involved simply with getting at the structure. Unlike the organismic theorists, who thought of society as being like a plant that opens up as it grows to reveal its structure, the functionalists thought of society as more like a physiological organism or system. They were concerned not only with getting at the structure of society or the way the parts were patterned or ordered, but also with the relations between the parts of society and the ways in which the parts affect each other to maintain the stability of society.

Functionalists were concerned with the ways in which the parts were related to each other, or interdependent. In this respect they were concerned not only with structural relations, such as the existence of a connecting link between two government agencies, but with the way in which the working of one part of society affects the working of other parts. They were interested in the *effects,* or the *functioning,* of each part on the whole society: for example, ways in which actions considered immoral or deviant affect society. Durkheim, some of whose earlier organismic ideas evolved into functionalism in his later works, argued that immoral actions have important effects on society that are rarely recognized by ordinary members of society. In fact, he argued that violations, by leading to punishments, dramatize the rules and serve the function of reinforcing them (Durkheim, 1962, pp. 11–12).

Following this lead, Robert K. Merton, one of the most important functionalists, argued that the corruption of political machines in American cities has unexpected effects on the city that, contrary to normal expectations, are conducive to the best interests of the whole society:

> *The functional deficiencies of the official structure generate an alternative (unofficial) structure (the political machine) to fulfill existing needs somewhat more effectively.* Whatever its specific historical origins, the political machine persists as an apparatus for satisfying otherwise unfulfilled needs of diverse groups in the population (Merton, 1957, p. 127).

When the effects of one part of social action were conducive to maintaining the established structure of the society, the operations of that part of society were called *eufunctional* for the society. When the effects of one part tended to destroy or change the established structure of society, the operations of that part were said to be *dysfunctional* for the society.

The early functional analogy between society and physiological organisms also led the functionalists to be concerned with the ways in which the parts of society function to maintain the *equilibrium* or *stability* of the whole society. They believed that when one part of society changes it not only affects other parts but also changes in a direction that will reduce the change in the whole system of society or return it to where it started. This is the equilibrium assumption of the functional theories and has an obvious analogy to the ways in which physiological systems, such as the human body, have built-in controls that work to maintain the system in a given state. As Talcott Parsons and his co-authors argued in their famous work *Toward a General Theory of Action* (1954), society tends to maintain its boundaries.

Probably the best known application of functionalism and of the equilibrium assumption was to deviance (see also Chapter 20). As we have already seen, Durkheim and Merton argued that certain forms of deviance can be eufunctional for the whole society, even if dysfunctional for those parts it most directly affects. But the functionalists have also argued that deviance is generally dysfunctional for society, that is, that deviance tends to produce changes in the basic patterns of society. Believing that such tendency in one part of society will affect other parts in such a way as to prevent basic changes in the patterns of society, the functionalists argued that deviance will produce counteractions that tend to reduce deviance and, thereby, prevent its producing basic changes in the patterns of society. These counteractions are the function of the institutions of social control, such as the police, who act to control the dysfunctional actions of juvenile delinquents.

But, given the general argument that society is like a system of interdependent parts that tend to remain in equilibrium, what did the functionalists believe constituted the crucial parts of society? While there are significant differences in the major functional theories on more specific points, they all agree with Durkheim's argument that "social order is a moral order." That is, they all assume that social values, or shared conceptions of right and wrong, are the basic determinants of social action. They all believe (1) that in some way individuals come to have shared values through *socialization practices* in childhood, (2) that these values are the primary determinants of what they will do in society, and (3) that, therefore, these social values constitute the structure of society—the bones of the social body on which all else must be built.

Functionalists argue that one of the basic ways in which values work to determine social action and, thence, social order is by determining the nature of *social roles*. Social roles are defined as the normatively prescribed patterns of interaction between socially defined actors. For example, "mother" and "son" are two basic social roles in any society. Each of the *role players*—that is, the mother and the son—is defined by society and given the name of "mother" or "son"; and each of the role players has normatively prescribed *rights* and *obligations* toward the other role player in this pair. The "mother" in our society would have the right to expect obedience from a young "son" and the young "son" would have the obligation of obeying; the "mother" would have the obligation to take care of the young "son" and the "son" would have the right to be taken care of by the "mother." Because these roles are normatively prescribed for the members of society and everyone is supposedly socialized to know and accept these normative prescriptions of the roles, each role player would expect the other role player to act in certain ways toward him when he acted in certain ways toward the other. For example, the mother would expect the son to obey when she gave him an order, and the son would expect the mother to

---

INSERT NO. 22

On Robin M. Williams' *American Society: A Sociological Interpretation*

Robin M. Williams' book *American Society: a Sociological Interpretation,* first published in 1951, is one of the best-known works in American sociology and an excellent example of the structural-functional school of sociological thought. A second edition appeared in 1962, incorporating many new empirical findings but retaining the same major theoretical ideas.

The analysis of American society in Williams' book is based on a theoretical division of society into *social structure* and *culture*. For Williams, culture is "social heredity—the total legacy of past human behavior effective in the present, representing the accumulation through generations of the artifacts, knowledges, beliefs, and values by which men deal with the world." Thus, the structural-functional study of culture overlaps at least definitionally with the fields of inquiry of phenomenological society—the sociology of everyday life and the sociology of knowledge.

Williams' definition of social structure is abstract and refined, drawing on physical analogies: "In a field of inquiry a 'structure' is a relatively fixed relationship between elements, parts or entities (as, e.g., the structure of a house, an animal, or a plant) containing gross, observable parts that maintain a fixed relationship to one another for an appreciable time." Williams gives no em-

punish him when he did not obey. In this sense, each role player's expectations are interdependent with the expectations of the other role player, so roles are said to produce *doubly contingent* expectations in the role players.

Role analysis has constituted a large part of the functional analyses of society. Many different aspects of role play have been distinguished and analyzed. An important part of this work has consisted of analyses of what Merton has called *role sets,* the combinations of roles that one normally finds in a society. Normally, a foreman in a factory plays both the role of leader, in his relations with his workers, and the role of subordinate, in his relations with the supervisors and executives above him. He has, then, a role set consisting here of both follower and leader. A great deal of role analysis, especially the analyses of role sets, has been concerned with *role strain* or *role conflict*—conflicts that arise either within a role, because of conflicts in the normative prescriptions for that role, or conflicts between different roles. The foreman, for example, is commonly given as the example of a man experiencing role strain because he must be both leader and follower in the same organization.

Besides making up role sets, roles are further elaborated into *organiza-*

---

pirical prescriptions for discovering or analyzing "structure" in the real world, although he does state that the existence of culture may be inferred from action. Using these twin concepts of social structure and culture, Williams goes on to define his other major concepts: institution, norm, value, role, status, deviance, integration, and change. Throughout his discussion, he implicitly defines American society as a working system of institutions (the family, government, education, law, economics, and religion) and discusses the norms and values "contained" in each from the perspective of conformity and deviance. Conformity to norms is regarded as functional for the *integration* of American society, and nonconformity or normlessness (anomie) as dysfunctional.

At the same time, Williams recognizes the existence of heterogeneity and value pluralism in American society, although he subordinates the ideas of pluralism and relativism to *fundamental consensus* and integration. As he states in his note on method, most of his illustrative and empirical material derives from macroscopic sources appropriate to macroscopic analysis; and, as we shall see throughout this volume, macroscopic sources (official statistics, political, sociological, legal, and governmental evaluations of American society) tend to be value-absolute and to take the perspective of the American middle class. Although other approaches have since been developed in American sociology, relying more on data from observations of everyday life, many aspects of Williams' book are still useful and valid. The best of any theoretical approach usually contains, because of thorough scholarship and the imagination of the individual sociologist, some furtherance of knowledge.

tions and *institutions*. Functional analyses of organizations, such as the Supreme Court of the United States, are done in terms of the roles that the functionalists say make up the organization. In the Supreme Court, for example, one would analyze the interdependent role relations between the Chief Justice, the Associate Justices, the Clerks, the attorneys pleading cases before the Court, and so on. The organization, in turn, is dealt with as part of a more general set of organizations called an institution. The Supreme Court would be seen as the dominant organization within the judicial institution of the United States. Institutions, in turn, are said to make up the overall social system. A simplified picture of the functional model of society, as presented in Figure 3-1, will illustrate this model. Much of this general functional model of society can be seen in Robin Williams' *American Society* (see Insert No. 22).

There are a number of strengths to the structural-functional theory of society. Functional theory saw the fundamental importance of social meanings in determining social actions. It brings together many important aspects of society in a systematic, general theory that serves to integrate and simplify our understandings of society and to stimulate specific research on society. It has obvious value in explaining social order in a relatively stable and simple society. It has generated many original ideas about social interaction that have led to productive research.

However, the weaknesses of functional theory have become increasingly clear in recent years. While functional theory had the merit of putting social meanings at the foundation of social theory and research, it failed to see how uncertain social meanings often are for members of society and how difficult it is for sociologists to determine what meanings are determining social actions. The functional idea that social values are the crucial determinant of social action now seems far too simple. (We see this in detail

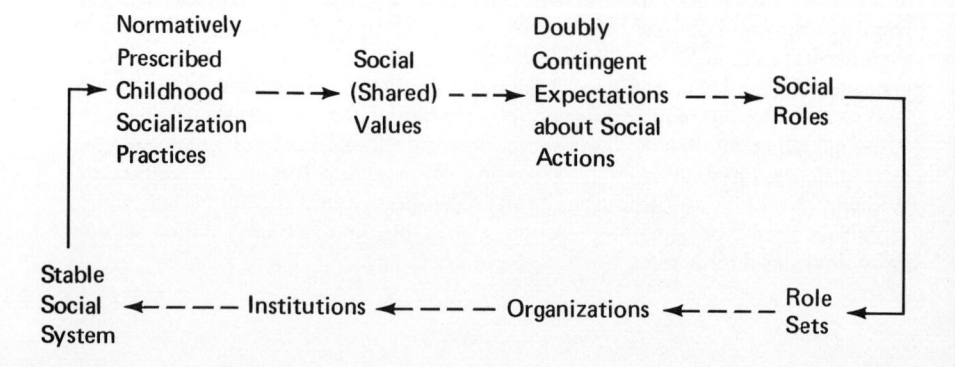

Figure 3-1. Simplified Picture of the Functional Model of Society

in Chapter 20.) For example, it overlooks the importance of beliefs about what is practical. By failing to see how uncertain social meanings may be for the members of society, such as how difficult it may be for an individual to decide what is right in a given situation, functional theory fails to see how much freedom individuals in our society have in deciding what meanings are appropriate to a given situation and how much freedom they have in deciding what to do in any given situation.

Many sociologists have come to believe that functional theory cannot adequately analyze our complex, pluralistic, changing, and conflictful Western societies. While functional theory has contributed many ideas of lasting importance, in recent years it has been increasingly challenged in theory and research by those forms of modern sociology that have developed out of symbolic interactionism and phenomenology.

SUGGESTED READINGS

Asch, Solomon E., *Social Psychology*. Englewood Cliffs, N.J.: Prentice-Hall, 1952.
   A classic formulation of behaviorist social psychology in research and theory.

Hare, A. Paul, *Handbook of Small Group Research*. New York: The Free Press, 1962.
   A readable summary of the major findings in small group research in social psychology.

Homans, George C., *The Human Group*. London: Routledge & Kegan Paul, 1950.

———, *Social Behavior: Its Elementary Forms*. Boston: Harcourt, Brace & World, 1961.
   Two books which cover the major theories of the social psychologist Homans, which have been highly significant in the contemporary development of social behaviorism.

Newcombe, Theodore M. et al., eds., *Readings in Social Psychology*. New York: Holt, Rinehart, 1955.
   Remains an excellent and representative collection of some of the most significant traditional social psychological research.

Parsons, Talcott and Edward A. Shils, eds., *Toward a General Theory of Action*. Cambridge: Harvard University Press, 1954.
   A collection of empirical studies performed from the functionalist perspective, and an introductory statement of the editors' theories of social action and of social, cultural, and personality systems.

CHAPTER 4

The Progress of Modern Sociology: Field Research, Interactionism, and Phenomenology

This chapter begins with the Chicago sociologists of the 1920s. Though their work preceded some of the work considered in Chapter 3, there is a direct link between the Chicago work and the sociology of everyday life. The Chicago sociologists were field researchers: they went out into the city of Chicago to observe everyday life much as naturalists go into the field to study animals (see also Chapter 5). Out of this research came modern methods of participant observation, with the sociologist participating in situations in order to observe the other participants and their meaningful actions.

From the 1920s on there has been steady progress among these sociologists in seeing and analyzing the problems of society. Increasingly, we have come to see the need to "maintain the integrity of the phenomena," and to determine the meanings of action from the standpoint of the actors; and we have developed our theory of social meanings and social actions in everyday life.

In the final section of this chapter we deal briefly with the most recent theoretical developments in this area of sociology, phenomenology and ethnomethodology (see also Chapter 11). While seeing these as valuable lines of research and theory, we find that much of this work has suffered from too little concern with objectivity and social order (see Chapters 20 and 21).

COMMUNITY STUDIES AND PARTICIPANT OBSERVATION

Though the acceptance of functional theory in American sociology grew steadily from the late 1930s into the late 1950s, there were always sociologists with very different ideas. One of the two most important groups was the *field research sociologists,* who concentrated on community studies and participant-observer studies of small natural groups. The other group of sociologists, which partially overlapped the field research group, was the *symbolic interactionists,* who saw meanings as more problematic than did the functionalists. The research and theoretical work of these groups constituted the main alternative to the theories of social systems proposed by the functionalists, and their work became a springboard for contemporary works challenging functionalism.

The field research sociologists argued that sociological research should be done in the same way early biologists, or naturalists, studied biology. Because of this similarity between what the field researchers did and what naturalists did, David Matza has called this *naturalistic or natural sociology* (1969). The emphasis of the field research sociologists was on going into the field to make direct observations of natural social phenomena rather than on experimental controls like the social psychologists' or on abstract theory like the functionalists; this method was developed primarily in the Department of Sociology at the University of Chicago in the 1920s. Many of the ideas of W. I. Thomas supported such research, and his own study of *Unadjusted Girls* was one of the early field studies. But Robert Park, who had been a newspaper reporter before he became a sociologist, was the dominant influence (see Insert No. 23).

Throughout the 1920s and 1930s the sociologists at Chicago made a number of field research studies of local groups, many of which remain classics. Many of these Chicago studies have been studied as urban sociology because they tried to show how the social disorganization of the city led to the kinds of deviant groups they often studied. However, as almost all these works included theoretical considerations with little direct bearing on the study of the city, their more general importance has also been recognized. Works such as Harvey W. Zorbaugh's classic study of *Gold Coast and Slum* and W. I. Wirth's study of *The Ghetto,* for example, were more important as contributions to studies of social stratification and ethnic relations than to the study of the city itself.

The field research studies of the Chicago sociologists have over the years developed two closely related types of analysis. Throughout the 1930s and into the 1950s, by far the largest stream of field research was that of *community studies,* studies of whole towns or cities, such as the classic study by the Lynds of *Middletown.* But in the 1950s such community studies were increasingly replaced by field research on organizations and other comparatively small natural groups. The basic field research methods, which we shall soon examine under the name of participant-observer methods, were the same for both types of study; some theoretical concerns of later field research were the same as those of the early Chicago sociologists.

Community studies were central to much of sociology from the 1920s to the 1950s. One of the basic concerns of community studies was with what Maurice Stein has called *The Eclipse of Community* (1960). Since the years immediately preceding the Civil War, the United States had been industrializing at an accelerating rate, producing an increasing movement of the population from the farms and towns to the cities. At the same time, industrialization was producing a continuous merging of businesses. As businesses came to affect ever more people and to cut across all local political boundaries, and as the government became more involved in governing such national and international enterprises, decisions affecting the work lives of

---

INSERT NO. 23

Robert E. Park

Robert Ezra Park (1864–1944) was a leading figure in the well-known University of Chicago school of Sociology. He grew up in a newly settled part of Minnesota, and in 1887 received a Bachelor of Philosophy degree from the University of Michigan. From 1886 to 1898 he worked as a newspaper reporter, but in 1899 he left the newspaper world to study psychology at Harvard. After receiving his M.A., he studied sociology under Simmel at Heidelberg and received his Ph.D. in 1904.

In 1914 Park joined the Department of Sociology at the University of Chicago, where he remained until he retired in 1929. Between 1929 and 1932 he traveled in the Orient and in Africa and guest lectured at the University of Hawaii and Yenching University in Peking. From 1936 until his death he lived and lectured at Fisk University, a Negro institution in Tennessee.

Parks first sociological interest, which continued throughout his life, was in the condition of the Negroes in the Southern states. Eventually, he came to see the mode of life of Southern whites and Negroes as an instance of a universal historical process whereby human nature and human communities take form through conflict followed by accommodation. The stage of accommodation produces a caste society which eventually changes into a class system.

citizens were more often made at the national level in Washington. America was becoming what the Civil War had assured she would become—a national union, rather than a decentralized confederacy of states and local areas. The old forms of important community membership—those of neighborhood, town, city, and state—were declining, and they were being replaced with membership in far wider and more national forms of community.

Though this process of centralization had been going on for many decades, most people were not aware of it until the 1920s, when it had progressed very far, or until the 1930s, when the Great Depression made it apparent to most people that jobs and food for most Americans were ultimately dependent on what happened in Washington, New York, and a few other financial and industrial centers. During this period, the field research sociologists became the documenters and analysts of the decline of the old forms of local community. This is shown graphically in the most famous community study, the analysis of Middletown by the Lynds.

The first (1930) study done by the Lynds of *Middletown* (actually Muncie, Indiana) covered the time span from 1890 to 1924 and was concerned with the effects of industrialization on a small American town. In

---

Park's major work, in collaboration with Ernest W. Burgess, was his *Introduction to the Science of Sociology* (1921). The book combined philosophical, scientific, and literary documents and general and theoretical formulations used in the study of group life social interaction.

According to Park and Burgess, social attitudes (tendencies to act), through interaction, constitute the basic social forces. Social forces may be informal (for example, folkways, custom, public opinion) or institutionalized (law, the state), and the interaction based on these forces takes four typical forms: competition, conflict, accommodation, and assimilation. The main tendency of social forces and interaction is the preservation of the status quo, but they are also the source of social change.

For years, the *Introduction* had few effective competitors in university classes all over the United States. His later, wide-ranging works included *The Immigrant Press and Its Control* (1922) and the *Collected Papers*, which elaborated, in several volumes, Park's theories on race, culture, collective behavior, the newspapers, and urban ecology.

His participant-observer work on urban ecology was, with his textbook, Park's major legacy to sociology. Park and his student, R. D. McKenzie, coined the term *human ecology*, and some of Park's students in the field—including Clifford Shaw, Harvey W. Zorbaugh, M. Thrasher, and Ernest R. Mowrer—went on to become well-known sociologists. Park trained his students in the methods of participant-observer research.

1890, Middletown had a small, native-born population, and a stable two-class society of craftsmen and businessmen. But by 1924, although it was still small and fairly homogeneous, the society had been transformed by industrialization.

The Lynds studied six areas of life in Middletown: work, homemaking, the socialization and education of the young, use of leisure, religious practices, and community activities. They found that the major economic change, industrialization, had profoundly affected all these areas. The old society of craftsmen had disintegrated, replaced by a society of unskilled workers whose life centered on consumption. The only status model for people to aspire to, by 1924, was that of the conspicuously spending businessmen, as there was no longer any status attached to craftsmanship or production.

Community activities, education, religion, and the family were all transformed by the change in production and consumption patterns. Residence patterns shifted and the old craft associations broke up; there was less sense of community in 1924 than in 1890. This process was intensified by the increasing delocalization of production and of consumption standards. Absentee factory owners further diminished the autonomy and sense of community of the town.

The second study of Middletown by the Lynds, *Middletown in Transition* (1937), examined the effects of the Depression on the areas covered in their first book. They found Middletown in 1935 to be a place both very similar to and very different from Middletown in 1924. The changes consequent upon industrialization—the lessening of community, the increasing complexity of the class structure, and the basing of status on consumption rather than production—were still in progress, despite the drastic curtailment in jobs and salaries. (Middletown was less affected than neighboring towns by the Depression, as its major industry was a household necessity, glass jars.)

Education and religion continued to become more diversified and nationally oriented, while the trend continued toward leisure activity based on the mass media rather than on community and family interaction. The areas of life most specifically affected by the Depression were work and the family. Mass unemployment had a disastrous effect on family relations, as men were not able to support their families or retain their pride.

But, overall, there were no profound changes of values or norms in Middletown in transition. The old ideas, so useful in times of economic boom, were still bandied about, despite their inapplicability: "initiative," "independence," "free enterprise." People spoke of the Depression as an interruption to be waited out rather than a profound change and, although they were no longer secure in a world that seemed simple, took refuge from complexity in the old simplicities, the old customs, and the old ways.

The second most influential community study, in some ways more intensive than *Middletown*, was done by W. Lloyd Warner on Yankee City in the 1930s and led to a series of important sociological works (1963). In general, Warner and his co-workers found the same process at work in Yankee City (Newburyport, Mass.) that the Lynds had found in Middletown. Industrialization had led to important changes in the lives of the residents, stemming from automation, extension of markets, and the separation of ownership and control. The economy of Yankee City revolved around shoemaking but, during the process of industrialization, family-centered craft production had become mass factory production. The market had expanded from local to national and even international scope, and the major businesses were owned by people not concerned with the local community.

Like Middletown, Yankee City had undergone a change from an autonomous local community to a less autonomous, more associational entity, which based status on the acquisition of material goods. The coming of the Depression made such acquisition difficult and resulted in considerable conflict between factory workers and owners, whom the workers resented for their relative security. In just one generation, the community of interest between the two classes had been almost entirely destroyed, and the community was increasingly less a community.

Many other community studies followed these classics and their conclusions were similar. But in the late 1950s and the 1960s many sociologists began to question these earlier conclusions. Community studies stimulated by recent developments in interactional theory (see the next section) have tried to show that earlier studies overlooked many basic sources of community because they did not concentrate sufficiently on the everyday lives of the people but looked too much at their so-called institutions, or lack of institutions. However, it cannot be charged that the earlier studies failed to gather first-hand data on their subjects. In fact, Robert Lynd had made an excellent contrast between his in-depth studies and the "surface" work in attitude "surveys" and other forms of surveys:

> In the present instance . . . the investigator is critical of the type of research that throws its net too broadly, as does the general "survey." By and large, social research seems to him to make larger gains by digging vertically rather than by raking together the top-soil horizontally; and a disproportionate amount of energy in current social research appears to him to be going into the latter sort of work (Lynd, 1930, p. ix).

All the sociologists who did community studies used the in-depth "case study" method, and all participated in the everyday lives of the people in order to observe their natural interaction. That is, they all made use of some degree of *participant-observer methods,* involving the participation of the researcher in the natural social events of everyday life for the purpose of observing those events.

But it is also true that the earlier community studies concentrated far more on external facts, such as the number of businesses or the number of people in different types of jobs. The more recent community studies, partly because of the growing influence of the theories of symbolic interactionism, concentrated more directly on determining the meaning of these external social facts to members of society, for they were convinced that it was the *meanings* of these facts to the individuals being studied that determined what would be their *effects* on the social actions of the individuals. Moreover, they were increasingly convinced that the meanings the sociologists might expect to find on the basis of their own experience were often not the ones found by careful participant-observer studies of everyday life.

In one sense, these new community studies were more intensive or deeper than the earlier studies: they went further in the direction approved by Lynd and the others. Because of this basis and the limitations of time and research funds, these later studies follow the tradition of participant-observer

INSERT NO. 24

On William Foote Whyte's *Street Corner Society*

William Foote Whyte's *Street Corner Society* (1943) is a participant-observer study of a long-established Italian slum in Boston, "Cornerville." Whyte found that Cornerville was not a disorganized area and that it had both well-structured relations with the outer city and its own control and "rackets" systems. His findings were in contrast to the middle-class view of the slum, which sociologists had often accepted, as disorganized, cut off from, and at war with the agents of social control.

The main focus of the study is a comparison of two male gangs—the Nortons, led by "Doc," and the Cornerville Community Club, led by "Chick." Through this comparison, Whyte illustrates two possible modes of life adaptation open to the slum dwellers. The Nortons are a group which by and large accept the norms of the community and represent slum-dwelling stability, whereas the Cornerville Community Club, which has some college-educated members, has as its goal the upward mobility of its members out of the slum. To express this difference in orientation, Whyte calls the members of the Nortons "corner boys," a name descriptive of their habit of "hanging out" on corners, and members of the Cornerville Community Club "college boys."

The differences between the gangs are varied and numerous. While the corner boys reject the settlement house, the college boys utilize it, so that the house comes to be of service to those headed out of the neighborhood, not to those staying in it. The corner boys have rejected schooling and the future

(p-o) studies of single groups. These p-o studies of groups go back to the classic works of Chicago sociologists, but they were greatly influenced by the far more intensive study of Doc's Corner Boys reported in William Foote Whyte's famous book on *Street Corner Society* (1943) (see Insert No. 24). By participating in the life of the boys of Cornerville for three years, Whyte showed that the people of Cornerville had deep personal ties and a "sense of community" that one could not adequately observe without participating in their everyday life. Rather than a lack of social organization and community postulated by so many earlier critics of slum life, Whyte found intricate and varied forms of social organization and community, from the highly organized gangs up to the complex hierarchical political machines that ran the city.

In the 1950s Herbert Gans carried this argument further in his book *The Urban Villagers* (see Insert No. 3). Living in a similar "slum" area in the same city, Boston, and participating in the life of the people, Gans also

---

orientation it entails, and the college boys have accepted it. Doc, the leader of the Nortons, enters and finally withdraws from formal politics. But Chick succeeds in getting into the group of politicians who form a liaison between the slum and the city and state governments, as the Cornerville Club is the major avenue to politics and the "rackets."

Whyte focuses on the similarities between the gangs as well as on the differences. They are both essential agencies for the integration of their members to Cornerville life and, therefore, they are both socialization milieux. Both prepare their members for life careers, although in different ways and with different goals.

In addition to his comparison of the gangs, Whyte analyzes the role of the police in the area. One of the major industries in Cornerville is the rackets, or illegal gambling operations, and local racketeers are both wealthy and respected. The Cornerville police willingly cooperate with the racketeers, interfering with them only when strictly necessary. There is also an overlap between the personnel of the rackets and the political system, both functionally dependent on the gangs for support.

Whyte's method was that of participant observation. He lived in Cornerville for three years and obtained the trust of the gang leaders and of most residents, as well as of the police, politicians, and racketeers. He was allowed to participate in community activities and gained quasi-membership status. At the same time, he brought considerable sociological insight and imagination to this study, supplementing observation with meticulous analysis of everyday life situations. Without such participation, it is doubtful that he would have been able to understand the basic organization underlying the apparent disorganization of the slum.

discovered close and complex personal ties among the inhabitants of the area that did produce a real sense of community in the people, involving an identification with their neighborhood. In the 1960s Gerald Suttles reported probably the most intensive of all studies of slum areas in his book, *The Social Order of the Slum* (1968). He found that there was indeed a "moral order" of the slum, involving deep personal relations and a sense of community. This moral order was different from that of the typical middle-class neighborhood, or so sociologists have surmised without studying middle-class neighborhoods; but both the moral order and the sense of community were strong. At about the same time, Jane Jacobs extended this argument to the whole city in her famous book *The Death and Life of Great American Cities,* contending that urban populations that may appear to outsiders to be disorganized and lacking in community life may actually have intricate webs of personal relations and deep identifications with their local neighborhoods. Slightly later, Gans did another study of community life, this time in a famous middle-class suburb, that had often been used as a perfect example of a modern "soulless" suburb. In *The Levittowners* (Insert No. 25), he reported findings very similar to those in *The Urban Villagers,* but they dealt with a far more affluent and educated population (see Insert No. 3).

While participant-observer studies of neighborhoods continue to be important, for answering questions bearing on such basic issues as the quality of life they have become unusual. Modern methods demand too much intensive participation to allow any one investigator or any small team of investigators to adequately study more than a single group of moderate size, and methods of combining the work of large teams of researchers have not yet been developed well enough to overcome this difficulty. Consequently, the great majority of these studies in the past twenty years have been done on reasonably small natural groups, especially on organizations. (One of the most famous participant-observer studies of organizations, Alvin Gouldner's study of a gypsum factory, is presented in some detail in Chapter 16.)

Mistakenly, many of the early works on organizations took the *formal structure* of the organizations, their "organizational plans" showing the prescribed role relations among all members of the organization, as the focus of their analysis (see Chapter 16). But it quickly became evident to these students of business organizations that even the clearest picture of an organization's formal structure gave little idea how it operates in practice (see Chapter 16). Just as an abstract picture of social structure (or the "social system") will not allow one to understand and predict how people really act in everyday life, so an abstract picture of an organization will not allow us to understand and predict how its members actually do their work within the organization. The formal structure can be significant in understanding how people operate in daily life only to the extent that its meanings lead the members to act in certain ways; once again, it appears that it is the meanings of situations to the people involved that we have to discover.

Students of organizations tried to compensate for the inadequacies of formal structure by arguing that group members make use of *informal structures* or *informal practices* to supplement the formally prescribed roles of the formal structure (see Chapter 16). But this was merely a roundabout way of saying that the formal roles prescribed by any organizational plan must be meaningfully interpreted by organization members in concrete

---

INSERT NO. 25

On Herbert J. Gans' *The Levittowners*

Herbert J. Gans' study of Levittown, a suburban community in New Jersey, is an in-depth participant-observer investigation into the nature of suburbia in America between 1958 and 1962. As Gans says, suburbia has been "maligned" by sociologists for social disorganization and discontent, much as the slums were "maligned" by sociologists of earlier times.

Gans says of Levittown:

> I began this study with four questions, the answers to which can be generalized to new towns and suburbs all over America.
> *First* . . . New towns are ultimately old communities on new land, culturally not significantly different from suburban subdivisions and urban neighborhoods inhabited by the same kinds of people, and politically much like other small American towns. . . .
> *Second,* most new suburbanites are pleased with the community that develops; they enjoy the house and outdoor living and take pleasure from the large supply of compatible people, without experiencing the boredom or malaise ascribed to suburban homogeneity. . . .
> *Third,* the sources or causes of change are not to be found in suburbia per se, but in the new house, the opportunity for home ownership, and above all, the population mix. . . .
> *Fourth,* the politics of a new suburb is no more distinctive than the rest of its life (Gans, 1967, pp. 408–410).

Gans makes the further point that the difficulties and problems of life in Levittown are not unique to the area, nor to suburbs in general, but are much the same as those in places all over America—familial and governmental financial problems, imperfect provision of public transportation and services, and less tangible matters such as the inability of people to cope with life in a pluralistic society. In the final analysis, as Gans sees it, "The strengths and weaknesses of Levittown are those of many American communities, and the Levittowners closely resemble other young middle class Americans."

situations and that one must know these interpretations to know the effects on their actions. More recent studies, especially the work by Melville Dalton on *Men Who Manage* (1959), have shown that these unformalized meanings and practices are of crucial importance to members of organizations in getting their work done effectively. In fact, Dalton found that even seemingly clear formal arrangements may be highly misleading. The prescribed salary for each position in the organization may seriously understate the financial rewards received by the individual holding that position, because there are many forms of side payments, including payments that outsiders might regard as forms of deviance or "theft." Dalton has argued that the meanings of such concepts as "theft" are very problematic in such organizations:

> Use of materials and services for personal ends, individual or group, is, of course, officially forbidden, for in both plant theory and popular usage this is *theft*. But our concern to pinpoint the informal phases of administration where possible requires scrutiny of this generally known but taboo subject. . . .
> As theft requires more ingenuity, becomes larger in amount, and is committed by more distinguished persons . . . its character is correspondingly softened by such velvety terms as *misappropriation, embezzlement,* and *peculation,* which often require special libraries to define. . . .
> Always there are genuine transitional nuances, with debatable margins, between covert internal theft and tacit inducement or reward (Dalton, 1959, pp. 194–195).

The idea that organizations have some highly formalized structure of prescribed roles for members that tell them how to interact with each other in accomplishing the job is now seen as an oversimplification that has led to many misconceptions. It may even be that the formal structure is something used primarily to convince outsiders that the organization is more organized or more rationally structured than the insiders know to be the case. It now seems apparent that we have to look at formalizations of organizational structure as something the group members *make use of* in carrying out their everyday actions, rather than as something that tells us what is happening in the organization. Organizing the activities of human beings is extremely complex and problematic, as anyone knows who has ever tried to set up an organization or keep one running effectively. As any executive might point out, the ulcers don't come from living in a clear and simple world run by an organization chart (see also Chapter 20).

The participant-observer studies of organized human activities that concern us most have recognized the complex and problematic nature of action within organizations, just as they recognize the similar nature of action outside organizations. As a result, these studies are concerned first and foremost with determining the meanings of things to members of the organization. But, at the same time, they are concerned with group meanings and interactions, rather than with meanings and actions that might be peculiar to one or a few individuals. For this reason, they try to determine those meanings generally shared by members of the organization or group, especially the shared meanings relevant to their shared patterns of activities. These shared group meanings that tie together or "make sense out of" what people do as a group are what Howard Becker and his co-workers have called *group perspectives*. For example, in their study of college students reported in *Making the Grade,* they found that a crucial group perspective of college students was "making the grade" or making a passing grade-point average rather than trying to get the best possible grades or some other goal. Understanding this goal made it possible to understand a great deal of what they did, what their professors did, and so on (Becker et al., 1968).

These recent participant-observer studies of organizations and groups are fundamentally concerned with determining the complex and problematic nature of the meanings of things to the social actors. Moreover, they make use of the method—participant observation of the natural social activities of everyday life—that seems to enable us to determine meanings of phenomena to members of society in the most objective manner. Like any method and theory, however, it has certain weaknesses. First, most forms of participant observation have relied exclusively on the participation of one or a few individuals. It was not possible for them to show others directly what they reported, as so much was dependent on their memories and their own experience as participants. Recordings, where possible, have helped. The use of replications, studies of comparable groups by different individuals, should enable us to increase understanding, but such work has rarely been done. Second, although these studies give us reliable information in depth about social action, they give us only limited views of the whole society. We get a clear and detailed look into one segment of society, but how do we know whether other segments of society, even groups of the same type, will be the same? Participant-observer studies have rarely given us any clear idea of how representative their findings are or sufficient information on enough groups to enable us to make any reliable inferences about social structure. This tends to lead those using p-o methods to concentrate almost exclusively on social situations of limited scope and to overlook the practical necessity of reliably determining social structure. As we shall see, this has remained the problem of more recent theoretical developments in sociology (see Douglas, 1970f).

SYMBOLIC INTERACTIONISM AND EVERYDAY LIFE

We shall be considering interactionist theory (or symbolic interactionism) and studies of everyday life more closely throughout the rest of this book (especially in Chapters 8, 9, and 20). But it is important here to see the general ideas of this tradition of thought and its relation to other major traditions of thought in sociology.

The two early figures in the development of interactionist theory were Charles H. Cooley and George Herbert Mead (see Chapter 8 and Insert Nos. 26 and 27). They did most of their work at about the same time, and their basic ideas are so similar that it is difficult to distinguish between them. Cooley's work, however, is somewhat more empirical, less general and philosophical, than Mead's work. Cooley's work is more specifically concerned with the development of the social self and very likely had an effect on Mead's development of more general ideas along the same lines.

For both Cooley and Mead *the mind, or consciousness, and self of the individual human organism are the direct result of social interaction.* The human self, as known to the individual and to others, is seen as fundamentally social in nature. But they did not believe in some form of sociologism comparable to Durkheim's early belief that society is separate from and independent of the individual members of society. On the contrary, they

---

INSERT NO. 26

Charles H. Cooley

Charles Horton Cooley (1864–1929) was born in Ann Arbor, Michigan, and spent almost his entire life there. He studied to be an engineer at the University of Michigan, but when he was twenty-eight he accepted a research position in the Bureau of the Census, which was the start of his career in sociology. He took his Ph.D. in 1898, with economics as a major and sociology as a minor.

There are two principal themes in Cooley's great trilogy, *Human Nature and the Social Order* (1902), *Social Organization* (1909), and *Social Process* (1918). One is his organic view of society, the other is the central role he gave to mind.

Cooley limited his interpretation of the organic nature of society to the idea that all aspects of the life of the individual and of the society are interrelated. Cooley's organicism was also dynamic: he saw social life as a "tentative process," or a dialectical drama of changing roles and relationships.

The second principal theme in Cooley's work is that the essence of social life is its mental character and that the locus of all interaction is the mind. Persons and groups exist for each other only as they are conceived in each other's minds, and their interaction takes place only within the mind. The history of a language and of a human being are equally instances of mind in process.

believed that society consists of nothing more than its individual members and that the selves of individuals are the end results of interaction with other individuals in society. In this sense, their works are *social psychological* (or psychosocial) in the most complete sense: that is, they see the individual and society as completely interdependent, neither one dominating or taking precedence over the other. It is this viewpoint that leads Norman Denzin to be equally concerned with "individual freedom" and "social constraint" (see his Chapter 8 on interactionism).

Social symbols of the linguistic categories ("father," "mother," "good," "bad," and the like) are seen as the basis of all mind activity or consciousness, and necessarily as the basis of social communication. Society or social interaction, therefore, is seen as a symbolic reality. While the symbolic interactionists have been very concerned with morals or values, they view society as a symbolic phenomenon far more generally than did Durkheim when he argued that society is a moral phenomenon. In a general sense, the symbolic interactionists were the first American sociologists to argue, as Weber had done in Europe, that society must be studied by sociologists in

---

Cooley also developed a theory of the formation of the self. He thought that the sense of self arises partly from experience, and partly from imagining others' conceptions of oneself. He stressed that the person tends to accept the view of himself held by those whom he admires, an idea eventually developed into the theory of *reference groups*. He conceived the self as a social mind, socialized into his society through primary group interactions.

Cooley's conception of social structure was tied to his analysis of primary group relations. He theorized that the social mind is molded in childhood primary groups—the family, the peer group, the neighborhood. From the primary group experience comes the basic orientation of the larger social structure, as well as the individual's fundamental social mind, so that beneath cultural and personal differences around the world there is a common human nature formed by common experiences in primary groups.

Cooley's work has been criticized on several grounds. Mead, for example, saw mind developing from communication, where Cooley saw communication developing from mind. While more empirical than Mead's, Cooley's work was also criticized by others as not empirical enough.

Despite these criticisms, Cooley's work stands as a monumental achievement. His treatment of social classes, for example, was superior to anything in the American sociological literature at that time, and his work on the individual's sense of self and on primary groups was pioneering and remains basic to much of the later research in these areas. Cooley did not create a system of sociology, but he greatly enriched the discipline.

terms of the social meanings communicated by its members. There is a direct line of influence from this hypothesis of the earliest symbolic interactionists to the most recent theoretical developments in sociology.

The self is seen as what Cooley called a *looking-glass self;* that is, the self of each individual is the result of the infant's interaction with others who provide the meanings of his self through their responses to him. Both Cooley and Mead argued that the child acts toward others in terms of preverbal gestures, which are then responded to by adults in terms of social signs and symbols. In time, these symbols communicated to him in response to his own acts or gestures are taken by him to be representations of what his self must be. In other words, *the self of the individual is socially defined in terms of the social symbols.* The development of this looking-glass self, or coming to see himself as others see him, is accomplished largely through *role taking,* that is, through "playing at" the roles of the *significant others* interacting with him, especially the roles of "mother" and "father."

Cooley argued that there are three basic elements to the self. First, there is the individual's imagination or understanding of what his *appearance* is to others. Second, there is his understanding or imagination of the *judgments* others will make of that apparent self. Third, there is his *response* to

---

INSERT NO. 27

George Herbert Mead

George Herbert Mead (1863–1931) was a philosopher and sociologist who taught at the University of Chicago from 1893 until the time of his death. Throughout his life he developed his theories best while engaged in oral discourse with students. His major essays and articles are collected in *Mind, Self and Society* (1934), edited by Charles W. Morris.

In terms of the philosophies current at the time he lived, Mead was a pragmatist. *Pragmatism* represented an attempt to reformulate conceptions of man in terms of the then revolutionary scientific method and evolutionary theory. Mead viewed evolution as the process of meeting and solving problems, and scientific method as the conscious application of evolutionary theory. He contended that man's place high on the evolutionary scale was dependent on language, a form of interaction that evolves among human beings as they meet the exigencies of living in groups and gives rise to the human attributes of thinking in abstractions, self-consciousness, and purposive and moral conduct.

For Mead, society is an ongoing process consisting of *social acts,* which are interactions based on the needs and cooperation of the individuals taking part. Interaction is made possible by *role taking,* the ability of each interactant to visualize his own performance from the standpoint of the others. In

these imagined judgments. The socially derived symbolic meanings of the self then become a basic determinant of an individual's actions, in the beginning through direct interactions of the child with his significant others. But, as he learns their typical symbolic meanings for his actions, he is increasingly able to imagine what they will say or think about anything he might do. Moreover, he comes increasingly to think not only about what certain individuals such as "mother" and "father" will say or think but also about what the *generalized other,* or the typical member of society, will say or think about his actions.

But the meanings of the self represent only one of the basic ways in which society affects his actions. Society not only "defines" his self for him, but gives symbolic meanings to the acts he performs and the situations in which he performs them; that is, society also defines the situations he faces. The definition of the self and of the situation in terms of social symbols means that society must have a great influence on his actions. We can see in Figure 4–1 that there is a feedback relation between acts and meanings in society. That is, the acts lead to socially imputed (or given) meanings of the self and of the acts and the situations in which the acts occur, which, in turn, lead to further actions, and so on.

---

highly institutionalized interactions, collaboration is facilitated insofar as the participants share a common perspective; each takes the role of the generalized other. The basis of understanding society is an analysis of meaning, which for the pragmatists is a property of the interaction rather than of the interactants.

Mead is best known for this theory of the self. The *self* is created by the person's making an object or picture of himself through role taking, reviewing his intended conduct from the standpoint of those with whom he is situationally involved. Mead's analysis of the self is made extremely complex by the fact that he used the term to designate three different referents: (1) the perceptual object formed of oneself in a particular situation, (2) the process of self-control, and (3) one's personality. Voluntary conduct, for Mead, is constructed through a sequence of adjustments in which a person responds to himself as well as to the rest of his perceptual field. To study this process, Mead proposed the concepts of the "I" and the "Me." The "Me" is the object one forms of oneself from the conventional or societal standpoint, and the "I" is the unique individual's reaction to the situation as he perceives it.

Many ideas Mead developed at the turn of the century are now widely accepted in social psychology—for example, his concept of *reference groups,* those groups toward which the individual orients his actions. Because of the congruence of Mead's views with current trends, it seems likely that increasing attention will be directed to his work. Many implications of his position still remain to be explored.

Figure 4-1. Symbolic Interactionist Model of Social Action

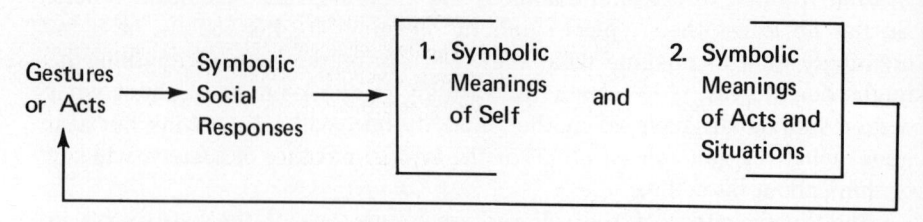

Gestures or Acts → Symbolic Social Responses → 1. Symbolic Meanings of Self and 2. Symbolic Meanings of Acts and Situations

In this simplest form, the model would seem to lead to a complete determination by society of the individual's meanings and, thence, of his actions. But, obviously, this is not what happens. As Cooley and Mead argued, there is not a complete identification of the individual self with the social definitions of the self. They believed that the social definitions of the self come to be seen by the individual as an object, or an *objective self,* which the individual looks at in the way others in the society might look at it. This objective self is what they called the "Me." But there is always a *subjective self,* an "I," which is independent of this "Me" in some way and which observes and judges this objective "Me." Necessarily, it is this subjective self that always stands outside society to some degree and that is the ultimate determinant of the choice of actions in any concrete situation. This subjective self is the source of freedom of action, or free choice in human action.

This subjective self acts partly independently of the symbolic meanings given to the individual's acts by others. This subjective self at times stands firmly, defiantly, or heroically against all attempts by members of society to make the individual believe something or do something. This subjective self decides how to put together or interpret the many differing meanings given the individual and his acts by various members of society; that is, the subjective self constructs the concrete meanings that the individual accepts as true for concrete situations, rather than simply receiving "what someone else says is true." His construction of meanings is, of course, greatly influenced by the social interactions between the individual and other members of society, but to an important degree it is the free choice of the individual. This is apparent when we look at the terrible arguments in society over the meanings of things, over what is "right" and "wrong" in a given situation, what "should be done," what is the "real truth," and so on. This subjective self, partly independent of the social situations and partly independent of the objective selves of the individuals, makes possible *the social construction of meanings.* This concept was first analyzed by Herbert Blumer (1969) and other interactionists and was later developed much further by the phenomenologists we shall consider in the next section.

It is this capacity of the individual to construct his own meanings for situations and to choose his own path of action that constitutes the foundation for the *dramaturgical analysis of everyday life* that has developed out of the interactionist theories (see Chapter 9). The dramaturgical analysis of everyday life begins with the assumption that there is a close analogy between the way individuals act in daily life and the way actors act on the stage. In this sense, the dramaturgists take seriously the Shakespearean line that "all the world's a stage" and try to analyze everyday life scientifically in terms of actors playing their roles.

But this does not mean that the dramaturgists share the functionalists' view of role play as determined by the values of the society. On the contrary, the dramaturgists also assume that, normally, social action is partly *rhetorical*. They agree with the interactionists and the later phenomenologists that the meanings of concrete situations are not given to actors by society but must be constructed by them for the situations they face. Then they add the proposition that social actors construct these meanings for other individuals, or present meanings to them, in such a way as to convince those others to do what the actor believes they should do in order for him to achieve his own goals. Social communications are seen as determined by the *social strategies* the actors use to get what they want from other people. This is seen clearly in the dramaturgical argument of Kenneth Burke in *A Rhetoric of Motives* (1950) that the motives an individual imputes to his own actions when explaining them to others are intended to *convince* them that he is right in his actions.

The dramaturgical sociologists have been primarily concerned with a special form of rhetoric. They have been involved with the *rhetorical presentations of self-images* by social actors to other actors. This is seen in the title of the most famous dramaturgical work, Erving Goffman's *The Presentation of Self in Everyday Life* (1959). In this famous work, Goffman argues that to some degree each social actor is always trying to *manage* the appearances he presents or the information he makes available about himself to other people so that they will have a certain (favorable) image of him (see also Chapter 9).

Interactionism went far beyond earlier sociological theories in recognizing that social meanings are the fundamental determinants of social action and that actions are determined by the meanings which the actors themselves construct for the concrete situations they face. It was this development, combined with the growing realization that experimental situations such as small group experiments and questionnaires tend to partially determine what people say and do, that led sociologists to recognize that they must be concerned, first of all, with determining how individuals construct meanings and act in everyday (or natural) situations. While the interactionist and the dramaturgical analysis of everyday life continue to contribute greatly to our understanding of meanings and actions, they have concentrated on the selves of the actors, rather than on other fundamental properties of social meanings and interaction. Because of this focus, the interactionist and dramaturgical theories can be seen as special theories of the more general phenomenological theories in sociology.

PHENOMENOLOGY, ETHNOMETHODOLOGY, AND EXISTENTIALISM

Increasing recognition among sociologists that social meanings are the fundamental determinants of social action, that these meanings are highly complex and problematic, and that they must be determined from studies of everyday life situations has led to the rapid growth of *phenomenological sociology*. As the name suggests, phenomenological sociology has been greatly influenced by philosophical phenomenology, which developed over the last century and a half, receiving its greatest stimulus from the work of Edmund Husserl and Alfred Schutz in the early part of this century (see Insert Nos. 28 and 29). However, unlike phenomenological philosophy, which relies almost exclusively on the experiences and introspective analysis of the philosopher to get at the nature of social experience, the phenomeno-

---

INSERT NO. 28

Edmund Husserl

Edmund Gustav Albrecht Husserl (1859–1938) was born in Austrian Moravia (now part of Czechoslovakia), the son of a prosperous merchant. He was educated in Vienna, Leipzig, and Berlin and, after studying mathematics and astronomy, he became interested in philosophy. In 1882 he took his doctorate in philosophy at Vienna University. From 1887 to 1901 Husserl taught at the University of Halle and the University of Göttingen. In 1916 he moved to the University of Freiburg, from which he retired in 1929.

The major influences on Husserl's early work in philosophy were the logician Bernard Bolzano and the philosopher-priest Franz Brentano. In 1900 and 1901 he published the two volumes of his *Logische Untersuchungen*, containing a brilliant extension of a vital concept he owed to Brentano, the idea of intentionality, which Husserl regarded as the major source of scientific data. Husserl further developed his phenomenology in *The Phenomenology of Internal Time-Consciousness* (1904–1905) and *Die Idee der Phänomenologie* (1907), asserting that sense data construct appearances, appearances construct

logical sociologist is concerned with discovering the nature of social reality through participant-observer research or field research.

All phenomenological sociologists are committed, first of all, to *maintaining the integrity of the phenomena.* This means determining and describing the actual (natural) experience of everyday life in all its fundamental properties. The basic goal of maintaining the integrity of the phenomena is stated in simpler terms as trying to see it the way the social actor ("the man in the street") sees it. Conventional sociology commonly assumed that the sociologist knows what the meanings of things are to the normal social actor. Normally, sociologists did not foresee any problems in determining the social meanings of things for the social actors. For example, some of the functionalists have assumed that they know the values of Americans without further studies. The phenomenological sociologist does not make such assumptions. He expects that the problem of determining what things mean to the social actors will be difficult. The phenomenological sociologist also sees it as completely normal that the social actors themselves may find it hard to decide on the "right meanings" of things in everyday life. It is common for members of our society to experience great uncertainty about what is right and wrong in a given situation. They must "worry" about things, "try to figure out the truth," "try to figure out what should be done in this situation," and so on. A person may worry all night over whether he "said the right thing" or over "what she really meant by that."

---

things, and perception and imagination construct identities. He felt that only by building from rigorous observation of meanings and identities, grasped intuitively, can the sciences be provided with an objective basis.

Husserl's later work included *Ideen zu einer reinen Phänomenologie und phänomenologischen Philosophie,* and *Formale und transzendentale Logik* (1929), which dealt with the problem of intersubjectivity, in which Husserl may have become interested through the influence of his leading pupil and chosen successor, Martin Heidegger. During these later years, Husserl developed an existentialist theme that was finally expressed in *Die Krisis der europaischen Wissenschaften und die transzendentale Phänomenologie,* published posthumously. The "crisis" of the title refers to the widening gap between modern science, which grows progressively more abstract and technical, and the *Lebeswelt,* or universe of meaning, within which each individual lives and within which science itself is ultimately founded.

Husserl's influence on sociology has been indirect, neither so pervasive nor so profound as it might have been. In the United States his influence has been almost negligible, until the very recent revival of interest in the historical roots of the new phenomenology. His work is likely to be read more widely by future sociologists.

Normally, the social actor in everyday life takes what the phenomenologists call the *natural stance* toward everyday life—that is, he takes for granted the reality of his everyday life and its typical social meanings.

As Husserl said,

> I find continually present and standing over against me the one spatiotemporal fact-world to which I myself belong, as do all other men found in it and related in the same way to it. This "fact-world" as the word already tells us, I find *to be out there,* and also *take it just as it gives itself to me as something that exists out there.* All doubting and rejecting of the data of

---

INSERT NO. 29

Alfred Schutz

Alfred Schutz (1899–1959) was born in Austria, studied at the University of Vienna, and from 1939 until his death lived in New York City, where he was professor of philosophy and sociology at the New School for Social Research. His principal theoretical work consisted of the application of Edmund Husserl's phenomenology to the problems of social reality, while his major methodological contribution was an attempt to relate phenomenological concepts to the sociology of Max Weber.

Schutz believed that the major problem for sociology is the study of the everyday world, of the common-sense reality that each individual shares with his fellow men in a taken-for-granted manner. All his writings, beginning with his best-known work *The Phenomenology of the Social World* (1932), take the reality of everyday life as a point of departure and as a subject for detailed examination.

Schutz conceived of man, or Ego, as constructed through everyday life interactions with others, or Alter Egos. Man is understood as a being who presents himself to others, takes his place in the social world, and knows himself only through others and only in a partial and fragmentary way. The action of Ego can be understood by Alter Egos only by grasping the meanings which the Ego gives to his actions, by understanding what they mean to him. This comprehension comes about through *verstehen,* or insight, which has both common-sense and sociological aspects.

Schutz's work has affinities with the thought of Max Weber, Husserl, Simmel, Cooley, Thomas, and Mead, but it was Schutz's distinctive achievement to center on the idea of action instead of the traditional theme of perception, and to approach both action and actor by way of the typifications of common-sense life. In the last decade, Schutz's work has aroused increasing interest among sociologists interested in phenomenology and the analysis of everyday life.

the natural world leaves standing the *general thesis* of *the natural standpoint.* "The" world is as fact-world always there; at the most it is at odd points "other" than I supposed, this or that under such names as "illusion," "hallucination," and the like, must be struck *out of it,* so to speak; but the "it" remains ever, in the sense of the general thesis, a world that has its being out there (quoted in Natanson, 1962, pp. 34–44).

Some sociologists seek to apply sociology from this natural standpoint of everyday life. This phenomenological sociology is what David Matza has called natural or naturalistic sociology (Matza, 1969). But the great majority of phenomenological sociologists do not try to do sociology from the standpoint of the everyday social actor, for they believe this turns the discipline into a form of common-sense thinking. They agree that we can get at the meanings of things to the social actors only by participating in their daily lives to experience the meanings they experience, but they also believe that as sociologists they must take the *theoretic stance* toward everyday life. That is, they believe the sociologist must not simply describe and analyze everyday experience from a common-sense standpoint, but must objectively observe and analyze that experience to turn it into scientific data to be used in constructing and testing scientific theories of everyday life. In this sense, the sociologists are seeking to do what the phenomenological philosophers before them called *reducing* everyday life (also called *epoché* by Husserl), which consists of analyzing everyday experience to get at its fundamental properties. The man acting from common sense in everyday life—that is, the man taking the natural stance toward everyday life—is not concerned with analyzing the fundamental properties of that everyday life but with the practical problems he faces in achieving his goals. As a scientist, however, the sociologist is most concerned with determining the fundamental properties of everyday life, though, as we saw in Chapter 1, he then wants to turn this understanding to practical uses. Because his orientation is primarily directed toward determining the fundamental properties of everyday life, the sociologist is said to be taking the theoretic stance toward everyday life and, therefore, is doing something very different from the man of common sense, even when both may be talking about the same everyday phenomena.

Phenomenological sociologists have directed their attention to a broad spectrum of social life—from studies of horse racing to studies of a suicide prevention center. Inevitably, there is a mass of detail in these studies that we cannot consider here. But, increasingly, these studies are directed toward investigating properties of everyday life which these sociologists agree are the fundamental properties of all social existence.

The construction of social meanings and social order. The phenomenological sociologists have come to see the constructive work in everyday life as fundamental. Because social meanings are problematic or uncertain for members of society, the members must go about constructing meanings for their situations which they and the other actors will see as plausible or rational, hence acceptable as a basis for their common actions. Because this construction of plausible or rational meanings in everyday life is so basic, Berger and Luckmann (1967) concentrated their major work in phenomenological sociology, *The Social Construction of Reality,* on the sociology of (common-sense) knowledge (see Insert No. 30). They defined this common-sense knowledge as the foundation of everyday life:

> The world of everyday life is not only taken for granted as reality by the ordinary members of society in the objectively meaningful conduct of their lives. It is a world that originates in their thoughts and actions, and is maintained as real by them (Berger and Luckmann, 1967, pp. 18–19).

As Berger and Luckmann saw, members of society use this common-sense knowledge in everyday life to construct the socially shared sense of reality —of what exists and what is true. It is the general necessity to construct meanings plausible or rational for other members involved in the social action—rather than simply rational to himself—that leads the individual to act in a manner conducive to constructing social order. It is this fundamental social necessity to be plausible or rational that makes social order possible. It is for this reason that the study of the ways members of society demonstrate to each other that their actions are (common-sensically) rational is so basic to the phenomenological studies of society. The importance of the study of the forms of rationality in everyday, common-sense activities is seen in the definition of ethnomethodology proposed by Harold Garfinkel: the investigation of the ways members of society construct for each other the rational properties of their everyday lives (Garfinkel, 1967).

The importance of practicality in common sense. Investigations of the properties of common-sense rationality (as in Garfinkel, 1967) show them to be different in important respects from the scientific and philosophical models of rationality that some individuals try to impose on everyday life. When we study what the members of our society consider plausible, sensible, or rational in everyday life, we find that they consider practicality of overriding importance. Regardless of how idealistic, logical, or scientific something might seem, it is regarded as stupid, irrational, insane, and so on, if it does not meet the requirements of practicality when applied to everyday life. This is why one of the most common and most damning criticisms of any idea in our society is that "It might sound good in theory, but it isn't practical" or "I agree with the ideal, but it won't work."

But when is something seen as "practical"? The best answer seems to be when it is seen as useful for achieving the purposes in the situation-at-hand. The *situation-at-hand* is the situation in which the actors are involved at the time they are trying to construct meanings.

The overriding importance of the situation-at-hand in determining the nature of social interaction is apparent in any study of everyday life. As Goffman argued, much of face-to-face interaction is governed by the unspoken *rule of the integrity of the situation-at-hand,* which he referred to as the integrity of the *encounter.* Whenever two or more people are in each other's presence, so that each is presumed by the other to engage the other's attention, each is normatively or morally bound to take the other into consideration in deciding what to do in that situation. Information about the past, about other situations, or about the future is relevant in deciding what to do in the present situation; but it must be dealt with in such a way as to maintain the integrity of the present situation. As Goffman further argued, this rule of the integrity of the situation-at-hand involves each actor's helping the other actor to perform properly in that situation, or to perform in such a way that the situation will not become untenable to the participants, helping to maintain the appearance of the adequacy of the other participant's performance (Goffman, 1959).

In this sense, any encounter is a cooperative effort that must be supported by all participants if it is not to be destroyed. We can see individuals acting in such a way as to support the performances of others in any situation. For example, it is common for us to help out the other actors by providing justifications for their actions when those actions might be interpreted negatively by others. An instance of this would be someone saying, "Yes, what you really mean here is . . ." We support others' performances by not pointing out evidence from past situations that contradicts their present performances. The rule of the integrity of the situation, like any rule, is sometimes violated, either accidentally or purposefully. If we want to show someone our contempt for them, we can "pass them by without a word," or we can be "curt," "short," "cold," and so on. This shows that we are not acting to maintain the integrity of the situation-at-hand, and thus not acting with proper deference to the integrity of the other actors in that encounter. We deny the integrity of that person, and his sense of self-worth is thereby supposed to be injured. If we are in an argument with someone, we may try to show that what he is saying now "doesn't square with what he said last week," or, if we wish to hurt him even more, we may try to get him to do something "out of place" ("gauche"), something that violates the integrity of the situation. If such stratagems are successful, the individual shown to be acting improperly will feel embarrassment or shame. When extreme, such embarrassment may lead to the destruction of the situation-at-hand, which Goffman called *flooding out* the encounter. But these violations and their sometimes extreme conse-

INSERT NO. 30

On Peter L. Berger and Thomas Luckmann's
The Social Construction of Reality

The Social Construction of Reality (1967) by Berger and Luckmann is one of the most significant books in the sociology of knowledge and of everyday life to appear since World War II. The basic premise of the book is that "reality is socially constructed and that the sociology of knowledge must analyze the processes in which this occurs." To Berger and Luckmann, *knowledge* refers not only to theorizing and ideologies but also to the structure of the common-sense world of everyday life.

The central focus of the sociology of knowledge is, then, the reality of everyday life, perceived by the individual as objectified or existing over and above himself. It is apprehended through the natural attitude or common-sense consciousness shared with others through language. The reality of everyday life is divided into routine, taken-for-granted reality and problems, always conceived as transitional interruptions to the normal and "more real" routine.

Reality is shared with others primarily in face-to-face interaction, which is the basic type of social interaction. The others are dealt with by means of typifications, such as "a man," "a European," "a buyer," "a jovial type," which may be modified during the interaction. The activities of the self and others in interaction tend to become habitualized or generalized from one face-to-face situation to others, and their meanings routinized.

Berger and Luckmann link the sociology of everyday life with social systems theory by means of the concept of *institutionalization*, which "occurs whenever there is a reciprocal typification of habitualized actions by types of actors" (p. 51). Institutions control human conduct by designating specific types of proper actions and *roles*, and who are to perform these actions. As an example, the institution of the family controls sexual behavior by specifying that certain people will be allowed to have sexual relations with certain other people who play roles, such as "man," "woman," "wife," "child," and under certain circumstances. Like the world of everyday reality, institutions appear to have an objective reality and validity of their own, independent of human consciousness, although phenomenologically they are products of that consciousness.

Because the institutionalized world has to be transmitted to the next generation as objective reality, it must be *legitimated*—explained and justified. Legitimation takes place through language, itself a type of rudimentary incipient legitimation. Other more complex kinds of legitimation are embodied in theoretical maxims specifying rules of conduct and in tales of conduct and correct behavior—legends, folk songs, and myths. Finally, institutions may be legitimated by symbolic universes or grand rationalizations of all aspects of the society, which draw upon realities perceived as outside everyday life. For example, American institutions are sometimes justified, as a whole, with reference to the Christian religion.

In a pluralistic society such as the United States, however, competing universes of meaning may be legitimated by different or competing symbolic universes, so that there is always the problem of emigration from any one universe. Two major devices are used to keep people within this universe: therapy and nihilation.

Therapy involves a conception of individual deviance, a collection of diagnostic concepts, and a specification of cure. In a heterosexual society, for example, there is a theory of homosexual deviance, a specification of how to diagnose the homosexual condition, and various theories of how to cure the condition—and the reverse would be true for a homosexual society.

Therapy is used to keep everyone within the universe, while nihilation is used to refute everything outside the universe by denying its reality. The process of *nihilation* is described by Berger and Luckmann:

> Our homosexual theoreticians may argue that all men are by nature homosexual. (Heterosexuals) who deny this . . . are denying their own nature. Deep down within themselves, they know that this is so. One need, therefore, only search their statements carefully to discover the defensiveness and bad faith of their position. Whatever they say in this matter can thus be translated into an affirmation of the homosexual universe, which they ostensibly negate.

The individual comes to accept legitimated institutions and everyday reality through the process of *socialization,* the mechanism by which he becomes a self and a member of society. Primary or childhood socialization is more significant for the individual than secondary, which is modeled on it, as primary socialization teaches the child to generalize abstract roles and typifications from concrete situations. This abstraction from the concrete situation of significant others—usually parents and other kin—is called the generalized other, the internalization of society and its objective reality. Subjective reality and objective reality, self and society, are thus maintained by each other within individual consciousness.

Berger and Luckmann's analysis provides important theoretical bridges between social psychology and social theory and between phenomenological and structural-functional sociology. Owing much to the work of Schutz, Durkheim, Max Scheler, Weber, and Marx, among others, *The Social Construction of Reality* is a scholarly and original contribution to the theory of knowledge.

quences show that the rule of the integrity of the situation-at-hand does indeed exist and that it is very important.

The practicalities of rule use. The overriding importance of the situation-at-hand in determining the construction of shared meanings and actions in the situation is also seen in the interpretations of the meanings of rules for any given situation. Whereas rules are generally presented in an absolute sense ("Thou shalt not . . ."), as if any violation should lead to automatic punishment of the offender, in fact they are always interpreted in the light of the situation-at-hand. They are interpreted in the context of other rules seen to be relevant to that situation as well. Rules are interpreted in terms of what seems practical in the situation-at-hand (see also Chapter 20).

Excellent examples are found in all situations, but they are especially apparent in police work, perhaps because most people least expect to find practical constraints operative in police enforcement of rules. In fact, police work is so largely determined by practical problems of everyday work situations that criminologists have come to believe we should analyze police work primarily in terms of their attempts to deal with those practical problems, or what Peter Manning has called "police trouble," rather than in terms of their attempts to enforce rules. In most situations the police choose not to enforce the rules they observe to be violated, for the simple reason that any attempt to enforce most of the rules would be impossible. This is most apparent in the extreme situations in which there are so many violations and so few police that the police admit that it is practically impossible to enforce the rules at all, as in riots or when a great number of some public group are violating the rules. One well-publicized example of this occurred at the Woodstock festival. Illegal drugs were used in plain view by almost all those at the festival but the universality of the violation, combined with the relatively few police present, led to an almost total lack of enforcement of the stringent laws against their use, in spite of the fact that police commonly enforce the drug laws very punitively when only a few individuals are present. But rules, including the legal rules, are interpreted in the context of practical considerations as a matter of routine, as well as in such extreme situations (see Bittner, 1967).

The contextual determination of meanings. Another fundamental principle closely related to the principle of the integrity of the situation is that of the *contextual determination of meanings,* which states that the meanings of anything (statements, grunts, acts, gestures) are determined for the participants by the context in which they occur. The contextual determination of meanings has been investigated primarily in terms of those parts of any situation *taken for granted* (not spoken about directly) by the social actors, but which must be understood as relevant by anyone who wants to grasp the meanings the way the social actors themselves do.

Field Research, Interactionism, and Phenomenology 113

The most obvious instances of the contextual determination of meanings are found in everyday conversations. The simplest kind is a linguistic one with which everyone is acquainted. The word *ear*, for example, can refer to either the ear on your head or an ear of corn. Only the context in which the word is used allows you to determine the intended meaning. Garfinkel has given excellent examples of the contextual determination of meanings in his analysis of an everyday conversation between a husband and wife about a shopping trip:

Husband:	*Dana succeeded in putting a penny in a parking meter today without being picked up.*	*This afternoon as I was bringing Dana, our four year old son, home from the nursery school, he succeeded in reaching high enough to put a penny in a parking meter when we parked in a meter parking zone, whereas before he has always had to be picked up to reach that high.*
Wife:	*Did you take him to the record store?*	*Since he put a penny in a meter that means that you stopped while he was with you. I know that you stopped at the record store either on the way to get him or on the way back. Was it on the way back, so that he was with you or did you stop there on the way to get him and somewhere else on the way back?*
Husband:	*No, to the shoe repair shop.*	*No, I stopped at the record store on the way to get him and stopped at the shoe repair shop on the way home when he was with me.*
Wife:	*What for?*	*I know of one reason why you might have stopped at the repair shop. Why did you in fact?*
Husband:	*I got some new shoe laces for my shoes.*	*As you will remember I broke a shoe lace on one of my brown oxfords the other day so I stopped to get some new laces.*

Wife: *Your loafers need new heels badly.*

Something else you could have gotten that I was thinking of. You could have taken in your black loafers which need heels badly. You'd better get them taken care of pretty soon. (Garfinkel, 1967, pp. 38–39.)

Garfinkel (1964) and others have considered the contextural determination of meanings so basic to the study of all social action that they have made it the primary focus of their ethnomethodological studies. But they have used the terms *indexicality* and *reflexivity*, rather than "contextuality," to refer to the effects of context on meanings. Garfinkel and his co-workers have tried to show that most activities in organizations such as mental hospitals are highly indexical or reflexive; ordinarily, the activities taking place in such organizations can be understood as members understand them only if one knows the context in which members perform those activities. The members generally understand this context so well that they come to take it for granted in their everyday communications; the sociologist cannot know the everyday meanings of things to these social actors without taking part sufficiently in their everyday situations to learn that context. An excellent example of this requirement comes from a study done by Garfinkel and Bittner of psychiatric records. Commonly, sociologists have either used such records or criticized them without considering the practical context in which members of the hospitals constructed the records and in what context they expected other members of that hospital or outsiders to use those records. As a result, Garfinkel and Bittner argue, the sociologists do not understand the meanings of the records the way members of the organizations do. Only by putting the records in the context of their practical use in everyday life can we see what they mean to the members—and only by coming to understand what they mean to the members in their everyday lives can we develop valid theories of social action (Garfinkel, 1967).

CONCLUSION

The phenomenological sociologies of everyday life have made fundamental contributions to our scientific understanding of man and society, altering earlier sociological theories. But, as we see in Chapters 20 and 21, there is reason to believe we have seen only the first important contributions from this new perspective.

At the same time, weaknesses are apparent in this work. Too many of the phenomenological sociologists have failed to consider the problems of objectivity in their research and the important (structural) relations among the situations of everyday life. We must do much more work on the ways members of society *construct order* (or structure) among their everyday social situations. By doing this, we will further a synthesis between the situational and structural perspectives on society which constitutes the essential theme of this book.

SUGGESTED READINGS

Berger, Peter and Thomas Luckmann, *The Social Construction of Reality*. New York: Doubleday, 1967.
> This is a very readable presentation of the basic ideas of phenomenological sociology, especially as developed by Alfred Schutz. It serves as a good introduction to the field.

Cicourel, Aaron, *Method and Measurement in Sociology*. New York: The Free Press, 1964.
> This is an excellent critique of the classic methods of measuring social phenomena and shows the basic reasons for the development of the phenomenological sociologies. It is clear but not easy reading.

Dalton, Melville, *Men Who Manage*. New York: Wiley, 1964.
> Dalton's study of three large chemical plants is a classic study of organizations. It is based on intense participant observation in the plants.

Douglas, Jack D., *American Social Order*. New York: The Free Press, 1971.
> This work criticizes the classical tradition in sociology, synthesizes the basic principles of phenomenological sociology, and attempts a phenomenological explanation of social order in America today.

Garfinkel, Harold, *Studies in Ethnomethodology*. Englewood Cliffs, N.J.: Prentice-Hall, 1967.
> This is probably the most important work in ethnomethodology, but the extreme difficulty of reading it makes it useful only to the most careful reader.

Schutz, Alfred, *The Collected Works of Alfred Schutz*, Vols. I–III, ed. Maurice Natanson. The Hague: Martinus Nijhoff, 1962.
> Those who want to go more deeply into Schutz's phenomenological theories will want to read the major essays in these volumes. They are sometimes complex but always clear.

Thrasher, Frederick, *The Gang*. Chicago: University of Chicago Press, 1928.
> This reprint of the classic study of 1,313 gangs by Frederick Thrasher serves as an excellent example of the field studies done at Chicago in the 1920s.

Warner, W. Lloyd and Paul S. Lunt, *The Social Life of a Modern Community*. New Haven: Yale University Press, 1941.
> This is one part of the field research studies done by W. Lloyd Warner and his associates of Yankee City, a town in New England undergoing basic changes in the twentieth century.

PART II

The Development of Man and Society

Provided with the overview of sociology in Part I, we now begin to study in detail the origin of man and society. Chapter 5 considers the relationship between animal social behavior and human social behavior and its implications for studies of human society. Chapter 6 deals with sex and love relations forming the basis of human reproduction and the family. Part II prepares us for the systematic analysis of social situations in Part III, which begins in Chapter 7 with consideration of socialization issues in terms of teaching and learning to become a member of society.

CHAPTER 5

The Biological Bases of Human Society

Man's biological nature has great influence on his individual and social life. Though we are not sure of the exact relations, our biological constitution is a common constraint on human societies. Increasingly, sociologists have become interested in the study of man as a biological organism.

We cannot separate man from his cultural heritage to determine what is cultural and what is biological, but we can study the social behavior of animals related to us, especially primates, to determine the ways in which such social behavior is dependent on our primate biology and independent of our abilities as the only symbol-using animal. To make this distinction is a basic goal of this chapter.

The last part of the chapter deals with the learned, cultural aspects of animal social behavior, especially those aspects related to family life, such as the relationship between mother and offspring. This final section leads to Chapter 6, which considers one biologically based form of human social life: sex and the family.

Other than the fact that man himself is an animal, why should sociologists be interested in animal studies? What is the importance of such work to humans? There are at least four answers to this question (Zajonc, 1969).

First, given phenomena may be difficult or impossible to study in self-aware human subjects. Human beings may want to be "good" subjects (Orne, 1962), acting in ways they think will help the investigator prove his hypothesis, rather than as they would if not under investigation. This is the problem of *reactivity*, or the uncertainty effect, the possibility of observing behavior that is a function of its being observed. Reactivity is a particularly acute problem in experimental studies of human social behavior, where the subjects are self-aware and able to construct conduct in terms of their awareness of themselves. There is no evidence that animals have a similar self-awareness.

A second reason is also methodological. We can neither interview animals nor give them questionnaires. Thus, we must *observe* them to see what they actually do, rather than study what they report that they will do or did do. Data about animal social behavior and organization comes from real situations, not verbally created, hypothetical constructions in which subjects' reports are taken "as if" (Vahinger, 1927) they stood for past or future actions.

Third, in handling data on animals, it should not be so tempting as with humans to interpret social behavior from the standpoint of our own experience. For instance, whether sociologist or man-in-the-street, our own biography will not ordinarily provide schema readymade for human-based interpretation of wolfpack social organization, though it might influence us more in studies of such human-like phenomena as mother-offspring relationships.

At the same time, we must be wary of the pitfalls of *anthropomorphism* and *zoomorphism* (Lastrucci, 1963, pp. 211–212). The anthropomorphic assumption involves the attribution of human characteristics to nonhuman life; the zoomorphic assumption involves the attribution of animal characteristics to man. Zoomorphism has been especially tempting to social analysts in recent years (see Insert No. 31, "pop ethology").

A related issue concerns homologies and analogies, both also implying parallels. *Homology* refers to a *structural similarity,* a correspondence or identity of properties, but not necessarily of function. *Analogy* refers to a functional similarity, a correspondence or identity of uses or consequences, not necessarily of structure. Thus, the former term refers to fundamental similarity, usually what is searched for, and the latter to surface resemblance.

The difference between the two is central to any search for relationships between animals and man and one source, if not the major source, of the confusion and obscurantism that typically plague such efforts. Because apparent similarities may hide structural differences and apparent differences may obscure structural identities, it may be advisable to deemphasize the search for human-animal homologies or analogies.

Forms of human or animal social behavior and organization may best be considered as *protologues,* new models of social life. To the extent that we know the structure or function at one level, animal or human, we have a testable hypothesis at the other level. Thus, even if given forms are not homologous, being innate in animals but learned in man, comparison is still important. How animals biologically solve problems of their environment may teach "learning man" something of value vis-à-vis his own problems.

INSERT NO. 31

Pop Ethology

Originally, the term *ethology* referred to the interpretation of character by the study of gesture. Now it refers to the observational study of animal behavior, such observations to be free of inference about internal states, including behaviors adaptive to species survival, acquired by evolution. Ethology is concerned with the evolution of *innate behavior,* those instinctive activities that aid (species) members in coping with their environment.

In recent years ethological work has been popularized, frequently by its own scholarly practitioners. One of the most well-known ethologists, working both sides of the street, has been Konrad Lorenz. His popular works include *King Solomon's Ring* (1952) and the controversial *On Aggression* (1966). Other well-received books include Robert Ardrey's *African Genesis* (1961) and *The Territorial Imperative* (1968), Lionel Tiger's *Men in Groups* (1969), and Desmond Morris' *The Naked Ape* (1969).

Though they vary their emphasis, the pop ethologists seem to share a set of assumptions:

A basic assumption of most social scientific considerations of animals is that there are continuities between human and animal behavior and organization, both in terms of antecedents and consequences. Whether these continuities exist is still more a matter of opinion, persuasion, and conjecture than established fact (Zajonc, 1969, p. 3). It will probably not be answered on a yes-or-no basis, but in terms of how much continuity or discontinuity prevails.

ANIMAL STUDY: PERSPECTIVES AND METHODS

Most studies of animal social behavior and organization fall into one of two camps: the *hereditarians* or the *environmentalists*, those emphasizing the structure of animals and those concerned with their situation. The first group is usually thought of as involving *comparative psychology*, the latter *ethology*. To contrast the two involves oversimplification of particular cases but provides a clarity of differences otherwise difficult to discern.

The *comparativists* have come primarily form North America. Academically, their training has been in psychology, and their explanations of variation have emphasized learning and stimulus-response models. The animals they have studied have usually been mammals—often rats—per-

---

1. That man's behavioral repertoire includes genetically determined patterns, that is, instinctive behaviors; and that the doctrine of instincts applies equally to all species—dogs, bird, fish, man, and what-have-you.

2. That in many ways humans are nastier than other beasts—for example, more aggressive. Ardrey has called man a "killer ape" (1961).

3. That, therefore, man's potential for brutality is natural—an innate and irrevocable part of his basic nature.

Thus, Lorenz asserts man's biologically based aggressive nature (1966), to which Ardrey (1968) adds aggressiveness due to the defense of territory; Tiger (1969) asserts that a biologically based propensity of males to bond with one another leads to their organizational superiority over women; and Morris (1969) obliterates distinction among primates by terming man "The Naked Ape." "Pop ethology" owes much of its success to the appeal of such simplified explanations of human problems, the prose ability of writers in this *genre*, and their ability to ignore negative evidence and alternative explanations. We discuss these questions below.

forming experimental tasks such as maze learning. Their goal has been to derive general laws, applicable to all species, especially to mammals.

The ethologists have been primarily Europeans, with academic backgrounds in zoology. In theory, at least, their animal subjects are free-ranging rather than experimentally cooped up—often birds, insects, and fish (aquariums being more nearly normal environments than cages). Their method is naturalistic observation and close analysis. Experiments, if used, are done in the field rather than in the laboratory. The ethologists' emphasis has been on innate characteristics and the *evolution of behavior,* especially those behaviors that are species-specific adaptations to environmental pressures—that is, manifested by a particular species as a response to its typical habitat.

As, ordinarily, the studies of ethologists involve free-ranging animals, such examinations should consider their social nature, a part of the animal's natural life space. The comparativists may or may not include social variables in their experiments. Thus, ethology may appear to be of greater relevance to sociology than the work of the comparativists.

THE ETHOLOGICAL MODEL

Ethology is interested in those regularized lines of behavior called *fixed-action patterns* (FAPs) that may be structurally determined—that is, biologically programmed in the organism as adaptive mechanisms known as *innate-releasing mechanisms* (IRMs), and the stimuli or cues (*releasers*) that lead to production of these behaviors. Most simply, the ethological model postulates that

The Releaser (R) Cues the *Innate-Releasing Mechanism* (IRM), Producing the Associated *Fixed-Action-Pattern* (FAP) Response

R ⟶ IRM ⟶ FAP

Often, the releaser is a characteristic of a *conspecific,* a species-other, that is, another member of the same species. When this is the case, the releaser is a communication, a message from one member eliciting a predictable behavior from the other. In the language of ethology, the releaser and response make up a *ritualized* relationship (Huxley, 1966), frequently involving behaviors that "stand for" something else—for example, gestures of aggression and submission that allow symbolic fighting, winning, and losing. These ritualized *display behaviors* are important devices in the maintenance of animal social order and function in ways analogous to the symbolic dramas reaffirming the order of human social life (on human society as drama, see Hugh Duncan, 1962, 1968).

Although it pays lip-service to the necessity of observing infrahumans in their natural habitat, much ethological literature in fact involves the study of animals in captivity, particularly when experimentation is involved. The major experimental strategy employed by the ethologist is the *deprivation experiment*, a basic tool in the attempt to demonstrate that a particular species-specific behavior pattern (FAP) is an innate or structurally determined function of an IRM, rather than a learned-action sequence. In these studies the animal, typically isolated from other members of its species, is deprived of a specified form of experience, contact with an hypothesized releaser. Later, it is put in a situation (including the appropriate releaser) where the behavior pattern (FAP) under study would be a normal response. The appearance of the fixed-action pattern in the presence of the previously unexperienced releaser is taken as evidence of behavioral causality by an innate-releasing mechanism, as deprivation is assumed to have negated the possibility of learning. For intraspecies social behavior, releasers are communicable characteristics of other members leading to ritualized behavior sequences, including aggression. Their view that aggression is natural has drawn ethologists both their widest audience and their most extreme criticism.

ETHOLOGY AND AGGRESSION

This issue has led to the heaviest barrage of criticism of ethology, especially of Konrad Lorenz's *On Aggression*, a book whose important and frightening thesis is so widely read that it merits specific comment. Most of the following discussion applies also to Lorenz's intellectual disciple, Robert Ardrey, who has added the hypothesis of an innate defense of territory to the basic conceptual model (see Ardrey, 1968).

AGGRESSION

The basic thesis of Lorenz's book is simple: Human (intraspecies) aggression is innate; there is a basic, structured propensity within persons (and/or groups) to fight and to try to harm or destroy one another. In popularity, this view bids well to replace an earlier orthodoxy of innate aggression, that of Freud. The evidence for Lorenz's assertion is extrapolated from data on infrahuman species—specifically, some selected nonhumans.

A major thrust in Lorenz's argument is that, according to animal examples, intraspecies aggression is functional or adaptive to survival. The positive benefits of such conflict are "survival of the fittest" and thus a stronger breeding population. Aggressive behavior is seen as a special case of Wynne-Edwards' more general thesis (1962) that all animal social organization is basically an adaptation toward optimal distributions of population size and spatial dispersion.

In the long run, according to Lorenz, aggression is "healthy," if not for individual species members—for example, losers—at least for the species as a whole. By inference, if not explicit writ, human fighting, wars, and the like are "natural." The Hobbesian notion of the natural condition of man as "mean and brutish," of humanity as naturally involved in a "war of all against all," is given biological justification.

It might be argued that, even if Lorenz's interpretation is correct, it should be ignored because of its tacit encouragement of activities that we consider negative, such as the taking of another's life. However, according to other data, a review of Lorenz's argument suggests that his assertion of innate aggression is not correct. Although there is no need here for point-by-point analysis of his evidence, we present a brief review.

Criticisms of Lorenz's view of aggression center on two major questions: 1. What is the quality of Lorenz's evidence that aggression is innate rather than learned, even among nonhumans? Is his evidence valid, nonselective, or biased? What of his interpretations? 2. Does his argument, based upon animals, apply equally to man?

1. Data contradicting the assumption that aggression is automatically functional has been presented by S. A. Barnett (1967), who has also noted that much animal behavior taken to be aggressive is actually symbolic display that functions to minimize aggressive incidents. The easy employment of selective or biased evidence and instinct-based explanations has been discussed by Schneirla (1968), who contrasts them with the more difficult-to-demonstrate but empirically valid explanations based upon learning (see also Holloway, 1967). His argument is a capsule illustration of the old English proverb, "Let him make use of instinct, who cannot make use of reasoning." A similar critique has been made by John Paul Scott (1967) and others. In sum, Lorenz's work is open to argument on the first question.

2. Among others, Gorer (1967a, 1967b), Leach (1966), Stewart (1968), and Beatty (1968) have marshalled extensive anthropological documentation of nonaggressive human cultures. However, to demonstrate that aggression is not a fundamental human-animal continuity does not mean there are not other continuities.

The definitive answer to the continuities question is not at hand; it is still open to conjecture, speculation, opinion, and persuasion.

AGGRESSION AND THE DEPRIVATION EXPERIMENTS

Much evidence rallied in support of aggression-as-innate comes indirectly from deprivation experiments. However, whatever releaser stimulus is explicitly and experimentally excluded from the animal's experience, there is always a second implicit deprivation: that of living in a natural habitat. The experimental laboratory is an unnatural environment, often crowded, restricting movement, dictating body rhythms through artificial lighting devices and feeding schedules. The animal in a deprivation experiment is deprived of its ordinary life situation. And it is in captivity that nondomesticated animals are most likely to behave aggressively toward conspecifics. Aggression in captivity seems heightened when coupled with crowding, sometimes taking the extreme form of cannibalism (for an overview see K. R. L. Hall, 1966). If aggression is a fixed-action pattern, it is one for which the releaser (captivity and crowding) is foreign to the animals' habitat. Evolutionary adaptations do not occur before the fact for contingencies not yet a part of the environment, but represent selective increases in survival potential to problems; no survival advantage leads to selective breeding for adaptation, merely potential to rise above environmental exigencies such as conditions of captivity.

Although, in the long run, captive populations may breed selectively in terms of adaptation to captivity, ethologists involved in deprivation experiments infrequently use animals drawn from such populations. Compared to his wild cousin, the *Rattus rattus*, the *Rattus norvegicus* bred for the laboratory is much tamer, less fearful, and less aggressive. For *norvegicus*, any aggressive response is due to the situation; it is nonaggression that is basically structured (on *R. norvegicus* compared to *R. rattus*, see S. A. Barnett, 1963).

Although such findings may shed light upon captive animals in particular, they tell us nothing about noncaptive animals in general and thus provide a poor base for making comparisons about humans in general. Although captive animals might provide insight into the situation of captive persons— for example, in jails—such a modest goal is not Lorenz's intent.

PRIMATES AND AGGRESSION

The interdisciplinary study of primates has drawn from both traditions, the hereditarian-comparativist and the environmental-ethologist, using both experimentation and naturalistic observation. Primatology draws upon the academic background of zoologists, psychologists, physiologists, and anthropologists interested in the phylogenetic relationships of man. The most frequent attempts to relate man and animals are found in this field.

Man and the apes, most often compared with one another, are both primates, phylogenetically more closely related to each other than to any other living species. Thus, if human aggression were innate, there should also be evidence of the innateness of such behavior among primates. The earliest primate studies, done fifty years ago, did indeed support the notion that some primates were innately aggressive—particularly the hypothesis that the anatomically advanced Old World monkeys were more given to high levels of aggressive behavior, rigid dominance orders, and the persecution of social isolates than the anatomically simpler New World monkeys. From this evidence, human aggression was inferred to be a natural evolutionary advance.

The available data supported these notions because the Old World monkeys were groups in captivity—typically, zoos—while the New World monkeys were in free-ranging groups, normally in their natural ecological niches (Russell and Russell, 1968). As the data—especially the naturalistic observation of primates in the wild—has accumulated, it has become clear that the "natural state" of primates is not aggressive, but overwhelmingly peaceful and nonaggressive. Where intraspecies aggression does occur, it is typically associated with a particular condition—crowding. In the wild, crowding results from either population growth in excess of increase in food and space resources or from a depletion of these resources without a concomitant reduction in population size. In either case, the primate population exceeds its ecological provisions.

The paradigm case of such conditions is zoo life, where crowding is permanent; it is here that aggression appears innate. All primates will behave aggressively in some conditions and nonaggressively in others. In normal ecological situations the latter is the normal behavior pattern; in abnormal ecologies the abnormal response of aggression becomes normal.

In summary, paraphrasing the language of ethology, we may say about primates (if not animals in general) that the evidence so far suggests that aggression is a situated-action pattern, not a fixed-action pattern; it is not innate but incipient. It may be biologically based—as are cancer, dwarfism, and the like in human beings—but is not a species-wide, basic structured characteristic of the population as a whole.

ANIMALS AND CULTURE

Data on primates raise questions about animals and the possibility of the presence of culture at the infrahuman level, questions ordinarily answered by sociologists with an *a priori* negative. We would suggest that the issue is worth more discussion.

First, what is culture? In their critical review of the usage of the term *culture* by social scientists, Kroeber and Kluckhohn isolated several dimensions frequently employed in its varied definitions. Among them are normative codes or rules, transmission of information through learning, shared habits, and utilization of symbols, this last a particular favorite of sociologists for differentiating humans from infrahumans.

DOMINANCE HIERARCHIES AND PRIMATE COMMUNICATION

The very existence of dominance hierarchies quickly disposes of the idea that three of these criteria might be humanly unique and that therefore culture is uniquely human. Dominance orders are (1) normative or rule-bounded status rankings; that is, they specify which members of a group (not a species) should interact with which other members and in what way (as superiors, equals, or inferiors); (2) learned and subject to modification, unlearning, and new learning as the group order changes over time; and (3) collectively held habituated responses, such as group submission to the leader.

Because sociologists, especially the symbolic interactionists, have emphasized the symbolic nature of human culture, contrasted explicitly or implicitly with the lack of symbols ascribed to nonhuman organisms, this issue is worthy of discussion (see also Chapter 8). Attempts to teach animals, particularly primates, to utilize human language have met with little success. In part, this failure has been due to physiological structure.

A new challenge to this established orthodoxy has recently appeared in Washoe, a "talking" chimpanzee. Washoe's talking does not involve vocalization, a process for which chimps are poorly equipped morphologically, but the *sign language* employed by deaf human beings. Taught by the Gardners, two experimental psychologists at the University of Nevada at Reno, Washoe has a vocabulary of some 160 words. In contrast, attempts to teach chimps to produce words vocally have never resulted in more than a handful of recognizable utterances. Further, Washoe is able to combine words; to invent and construct volitional, situationally appropriate sentences of two and sometimes more words (see *Simian*, The Simian Society of America, November 1969).

Washoe's proven ability to learn arbitrary symbols and to combine them in arbitrary but meaningful ways is the closest a nonhuman has yet come to producing the conversational aspects of human language. The real test will come when it is determined whether or not Washoe, or an animal similarly trained, can subsequently train another animal and thus transmit symbolic culture.

The presence of infrahuman communication and forms of organization such as *hierarchy* (rule-specific rather than biologically specific responses to members and collectively patterned reactions toward other group members) forcefully asserts man's continuity with nonman. While the conceptual tools, let alone the details, are not entirely clear, it seems that culture is not limited to humans alone. The question is no longer whether culture among infrahumans exists, but in which animals, how much, and in what forms (where, to what extent), and vis-à-vis what areas of social behavior and organization?

CULTURE AND ADAPTATION

Sociology's rejection of all but a human focus has led to a stereotyped view of animal behavior and organization as completely instinctual. By extension, it was assumed that instinctual explanations are totally inappropriate to unique, distinctive man.

A more moderate view might suggest that, even if human conduct is not biologically determined in the specifics, it might be so determined in terms of its possible range of responses—the alternatives available. Certainly, many factors biologically determined in animal social behavior and organization are culturally determined in man, but within a biologically defined range. Thus, humans may have no children, a few children, or many—but no more than an approximately 280-day gestation period allows. Much human culture functions to perform tasks and to create, establish, and maintain relationships; in general, to do things which are accomplished in other species more by biology and less by culture.

Man is the least functionally specific of all animals: he has no species-specific environment to which he is biologically adapted and no natural ecological niche. Man is specialized, through culture, in diversification and adaptability to the exigencies of life. Culture, being created, is more flexible than are biologically determined, biologically specific environmental responses. Man can invent where biology must mutate.

It is too simple to say that man's social behavior and organization is culturally determined and that of animals is biologically determined. For both man and animals, biology and culture set a range of possible responses. This is not to assert that all animals have culture, but to contradict the more frequent assumption that no animals do.

PRIMATES REVISITED—STRUCTURES AND SITUATIONS

Only in the last decade or so have we been able to gather much in the way of observational studies on nonhuman primates—phylogenetically and morphologically, the animals most like man—in free ranging, natural environments. The earliest of these studies attempted to derive generalizations about such animals as gorillas from the observation of a single social group (a band or troop). These pioneering studies of naturally situated groups and their social behavior and organization were searched for phylogenetic relationships (evolutionary continuities) with man and/or his ancestors. As such studies have accumulated, their collective findings have seriously challenged assumptions about behavioral and organizational homogeneity *within species* and about similarities *between species* within the primate order, and thus assumptions about the particulars of phylogenetic continuity.

The collective evidence shows that the ecological environment of free-ranging primates is such a strong and pervasive influence on their social behavior and organization that their social systems are poor indicators of the more basic phylogenetic relationships. Differences within species may be great, given ecological variation; and commonalities between species may be great, given ecological similarity. Thus, group cohesiveness is high among the *Gorilla gorilla* (studied by Schaller, 1963), but low among the closely related *Pan troglodytes* (Reynolds and Reynolds, 1965); the social organization of baboons is considerably different for the *Papio hamadryas* than the *Papio ursinus* (K. R. L. Hall, 1966). Populations may vary even within the same species. Thus, the male *Papio anubis* baboons observed in a Uganda forest by Rowell (1967) showed no evidence of a dominance hierarchy, while those in a Kenya savannah had a regular, linear hierarchy (K. R. L. Hall, 1966 and DeVore, 1965). Although a species may have a biologically determined predisposition toward certain behavioral and organizational forms, the environment may predominate in the determination of its members' social life. (For a general discussion, see Schaller and Lowther, 1969.)

The study of nonhuman primates has been based on evolutionary, phylogenetic grounds; it seeks the clues their social behavior and organization might provide about early man, if not man in general. And on phylogenetic grounds the choice has been a sound one, but not ecologically. Although some baboons (K. R. L. Hall, 1966) and chimpanzees (Goodall, 1965) have been observed to kill smaller animals and eat their meat, all nonhuman primates are basically vegetarians, not carnivorous like man. For over a million years developing man has been hunting and scavenging for meat, not adapting to life as a plant-eating group member like other primates. The fossil evidence also suggests that man has a longer evolutionary history than some monkeys and apes. Thus, it might make more logic to look for clues about their social life by observing humans.

As man is a carnivore as well as a primate, it may make as much sense to look at the social life of carnivores (and omnivores, too) as to look at the social life of primates. It has been hypothesized that the selective pressures leading to the social systems exhibited by carnivores may tell us as much about man as about the phylogenetically more related primates. Social carnivores include wolves, hyenas, jackals, lions, and wild dogs, as well as man.

A review of data (Schaller and Lowther, 1969, p. 336) indicates that, like primates, carnivores show both within-species and between-species variation in their social behavior and its organization. Differences are in dominance orders, territoriality and land tenure, and interspecies aggression. However, some practices appear common to most species—for example, cooperation in hunting and the sharing of spoils. The authors conclude, however, by questioning the assumption that a single social system was common to all early men or that all populations were similarly organized. They are not now—either among various human populations or those comprised of infrahumans—and may never have been.

Still, to suggest that situational variables always overpower species-associated structural ones might prevent generalization, save at a level of abstraction so high as to be programmatically useless ("animal offspring have some relationship with their mothers during infancy"). Instead, we would suggest an adaptation of Zajonc's (1969, p. 4) strategy for cross-species generalization to the data on primates: Let us assume that each theoretical or empirical generalization about primates, unless we know otherwise, applies generally to all nonhuman species and perhaps (either homologously or analogously) to man.

SOCIAL BEHAVIOR AND ORGANIZATION:
SOME BASIC CONCEPTS OF TERRITORIALITY

Most social animals live in groups which occupy a territory, a space they treat as home. Territoriality refers to those behaviors by which an animal or a group of animals lays claim to an area and defends it against invasion by others (K. R. L. Hall, 1966, p. 7). A major function of such activity is to regulate population density, according to the Wynne-Edwards thesis. Further, territoriality assists social organization by allocating space for various activities—places to learn, to hide, to do things. By "bracketing" members, territories tend to keep them within communicating distance of one another.

Individual territories, on the other hand, provide *withdrawal niches,* animal equivalents of human private places, where individuals may be alone. Individual territories are both causes and consequences of dominance orders. Inability to establish or defend a territory results in a low dominance position that will lead to little or no territory being allocated by other members. This lack reinforces the low dominance in breeding selection, because mating and protection of the young are both facilitated by territory. Thus, the following basic odds on success have been given for the male stickleback fish who guards the nest:

> (1) The male who has settled into his nest longer overcomes the newer settler; (2) a male with a nest overcomes one without; (3) one who looks after his nest well overcomes one who looks after it badly; [and] (4) the owner of a nest with eggs overcomes the owner of a nest without eggs (Portman, 1961, p. 198).

Such social behavior should be distinguished from aggression. These actions are basically *defensive* rather than offensive, an important distinction sometimes glossed over.

Ardrey, in his book *The Territorial Imperative* (1968), has argued that the tendency to defend territory is innate for both animals and man. Yet man's closest relatives, the nonhuman primates, have no permanent personal territories, only temporary collective ones as they wander about. When temporary collective territories are defended, the extent of defense is directly related to the rigidity of the group structure. Chimpanzees (phylogenetically nearest to man) do not defend territory, nor do their groups have fixed membership (Goodall, 1965). In addition to behavior associated with territories, which are fixed, most animals also employ *spacing mechanisms,* vis-à-vis both intraspecies and interspecies others, involving imaginary boundaries surrounding the individual animal. Although territory or location and spacing is a constant in human (and infrahuman) life, as everyone is physically and socially located in space (and time), it has received relatively little examination by students of man's social conduct.

DOMINANCE ORDER

Dominance order, roughly, is to animals what social stratification is to man; sometimes, ignoring solidarity, it is erroneously thought to be the only principle of social organization among animals (Tinbergen, 1953, p. 71). *Dominance* refers to the differentiating hierarchical position of an animal within a group of conspecifics and is found in all classes of vertebrates (Hebb and Thompson, 1954).

Associated with dominance in animals is privilege—the higher the dominance position, the greater the privilege. For animals, in general, dominance determines feeding opportunities and satisfactions, mating chances, and territory. The last, however, is partly a function of the first two—a place to feed and mate. Generally, dominance is associated with sex—males usually ranking above females, although there are sometimes separate orders for each sex—strength, and therefore maturation.

Pecking orders among barnyard hens were first described by Schjelderup-Ebbe (1935). He found that, although the chickens pecked at one another a great deal, their behavior was not random but rigidly structured. In each interchange one chicken would peck at the other, while the other submitted to being pecked. The pecking chicken was dominant over the other. Each *dyad* or pair of chickens had such a patterned relationship, and the entire flock was hierarchically ordered.

Is Pecked
(Subordinate)   Pecks At (Dominant)

	A	B	C	D
A	—	No	No	No
B	Yes	—	No	No
C	Yes	Yes	—	No
D	Yes	Yes	Yes	—

Not all dominance hierarchies are so rigid. Goats, for instance, have orders relatively well crystallized at the top and bottom, with a relatively fluid middle membership. The attempt to correlate dominance and leadership among goats has failed completely, the association between the two being what chance rather than common sense would suggest (John Paul Scott, 1958, p. 172). For baboons (K. R. L. Hall, 1966 and DeVore, 1965; Kummer, 1968), chimpanzees (Goodall, 1965), and gorillas (Schaller, 1963), however, the two have been found to coincide. In such cases we may look at dominance orders as forms of political organization.

Any group of animals whose members can fight with one another may establish a dominance structure. Its rigidity is a function of environment and abundance of resources such as food and space. Generally, the less of these commodities, the more definite the hierarchy. Thus, dominance orders do not disappear in captivity, as do many other forms of social behavior and organization; in fact, they are strengthened and even created in animals not naturally organized in hierarchies.

Logically, the size of a dominance-ordered social group would seem dependent on the species-specific ability of members to recognize one another and to associate a hierarchial position with that recognition.

Roger Brown has observed that human members of such an order—for example, a military contingent—typically learn all the relationships involved. As he suggests:

> Suppose, for example, that the individual is C and the total order is A, B, C, D, E. Person C would, by observation of who salutes whom, learn the position of each relative to each other one (1965, p. 17).

Such an individual could know dyadic relationships—for example, who is dominant between *A* and *B*—of which he is only an observer and not a member. It has not been positively determined whether animals in dominance orders possess this kind of knowledge.

In a sense, position in a dominance order appears to be almost hereditary. Strength—if not genetically fixed, at least genetically limited—is highly correlated with dominance position. Position is also determined by drive strength and self-assurance, conditioned by early social experience. Conditioning is extremely important in rigidly ordered systems such as those of baboons and macaques, the most hierarchically organized of the primate groups. Among the baboons and macaques, each mother is located in the female dominance order. Her position determines how she is treated by other members of the group and, therefore, the kind of social environment in which her offspring will grow up.

Low-ranking mothers are most likely to be anxious and tense, subject to threat display and attack, and lacking in resource control. In such an atmosphere, the young are likely to adopt the perspective and behaviors of the mother.

> They grow up afflicted with a sense of inferiority. They lack the style, the manner, the habit and attitude of the domineering animal; and, as if these drawbacks were not enough, they also lack entree to the dominant group (Eimerl and DeVore, 1965, p. 112).

High-ranking mothers are surrounded—as are their offspring—by other dominants. These young learn gestures and displays of confidence and control, the behavior of a superior. Such behavior is recognized and responded to by other members in ways that affirm and support dominance. In other words, through social heredity, the dominance is perpetuated and potential mobility is minimized.

MOTHERS, OTHERS, AND THEIR YOUNG—
AFFILIATION AND INTERACTION

Dominance orders express power and social differentiation; similarly, another fundamental axis of social life, *solidarity,* is expressed through affiliation (Roger Brown and Gilman, 1960; Roger Brown, 1965). *Affiliation* as a motive refers to a desire to associate with or be in the presence of another member of one's group; the presence of others is rewarding. As we shall stress in the next two chapters, for people, this kind of motive and experience appears universal (Schachter, 1959), possessing survival value for the species. Affiliation has a similar function for infrahumans, bringing members together so that adaptive forms of social behavior and organization can evolve. In this sense, affiliation may be conceived of as the primordial motivation of social life (see also Slater, 1963). [The fundamental importance of affiliation in human society is stressed in the next two chapters. Ed.]

It has been frequently observed that, among primates and other species,

INSERT NO. 32

Monkey Mothers and Monkey Others: The Experiments of the Harlows

Widely known studies of primate affiliation and socialization have been done by the Harlows, Harry and Margaret. Their research is concerned with the social relationships of the young with their mothers and with their peers and the consequences for affiliative behaviors. Though the Harlows speak of "love," we shall restrict our discussion to the idea of affiliation.

Like human beings, monkeys and apes rarely bear more than one offspring at a time. Twins occur about once in every one hundred completed pregnancies, and triplets once in every eight thousand. This may be an adaptation to transportation requirements: as a mother travels about all day from feeding area to area, she can carry only one infant if her limbs are to be free for movement. The infant clings to the mother, hanging on to her hair, either in front or in back.

The Harlows asked why the infant clings so closely to its mother. To answer in terms of survival misses the point. The question is what reward is experienced by the infant who clings? Man doesn't eat because eating is adaptive behavior; he eats because eating satisfies his hunger. The effort to find the immediate satisfaction from clinging resulted in the now famous experiments with the wire-monkey mothers, Harlow's "surrogate mothers" (1959, 1962).

Infant rhesus macaques, separated from their real mothers, were presented with a choice of surrogates. In a separate cage for each monkey were two wire-monkey mothers, a mesh body with a wooden head and an artificial breast. Half of these surrogates provided milk, half were covered with an imitation monkey's coat made of terry cloth. There were four types of surrogate:

1. No terry-cloth coat; no milk provided.

2. No terry-cloth coat; milk provided.

3. Terry-cloth coat; no milk provided.

4. Terry-cloth coat; milk provided.

In each cage, then, the infant would find two mothers, one covered, one with milk. Harlow, waiting, watched to see how the infants would behave toward the dummies.

They could have ignored them, going to them only to feed. They could have affiliated with the milk provider—which they should have done if suckling were the basic mother-child bond. All the infants, including those who fed from an uncovered mother, preferred the covered one. To the terry-cloth-coated wire-mother monkey they would cling and huddle; this affiliative behavior would go on for hours at a time. The milk provider was rewarding only at times of hunger; at other times the covered mother was preferred. In other words, affiliation appeared to be a more dominant orientation than the biological drive of hunger.

For the infant, then, the mother-offspring bond is primarily the social one of affiliation, not the physiological one of food provision: hugging and clinging is more rewarding than suckling. Naturally, outside of the laboratory, infants can get *both* from the mother, hugging and suckling, so that each reward contributes to the intensity of this basic social bond. In fact, this dyad is so basic that some evolutionary views of society stress the mother-offspring bond as the central, innately determined, primate social relationship (see Service, 1962).

But what is the role of the monkey's nonmother others? After all, Harlow deprived the rhesus, housed in individual cages, of all social contact. What of chances to interact with others?

To answer this, the Harlows (1965) raised some monkeys in complete social isolation from birth on and some others in sight of, but not in contact with, other monkeys. Later, varying the length of isolation, they brought them into contact with other monkeys.

The results can be categorized into two phases—caged and postcage behavior. For both periods the behaviors of the completely isolated were more "pathological" then those able to sight others; but the difference was one of degree, not of kind. While still caged, some sat and stared blankly into space; others wrapped their arms around themselves, rocking and swaying by the hour; and some, frightened when approached by humans, would tear, chew, or pinch their own bodies until raw and bleeding. In humans such behaviors are usually categorized as extremely neurotic, if not psychotic (for similar effects of social isolation on human children, see Davis, 1940, 1947, 1949, pp. 204–208).

The postcage behavior of the young isolates was no less bizarre. Those completely isolated were unable to affiliate or successfully interact with others. Those who had experienced visual contact were able to interact with others, but only to fight and behave aggressively; for instance, they were unable to copulate successfully. They could not handle the social requisites of the biology of sex. The drive may be biological, but even minimal proficiency would seem to require the experience of interaction with peers.

Although the Harlow experiments do not conclusively demonstrate whether mothers or others are more important in the development of affiliation, the infrastructure of social behavior and organization, they do show that both are crucial to this process. Probably, contact with both mothers and others is necessary for the development of affiliation, but neither mother-contact or other-contact is of itself sufficient.

members leaving or expelled from a group are usually unable to survive by themselves (Hafez, 1962). The early evolutionary sociologist Spencer, therefore, argued that affiliation tendencies formed the biological basis of morality: survival required social cooperation, meaning rule-following, which in turn rested upon affiliation. Certainly, affiliation suggests the origin of social behavior and organization (see Insert No. 32).

Among the phylogenetically near-human primates, affiliation develops within the context of mother-offspring interaction and play with age-mates, in four stages: (1) a reflex stage, during which infants maintain close physical *proximity* to others; (2) an *exploratory* stage during which there is oral and manual examinations of all objects in the environment, but especially of other animals from whom responses are sought; (3) a period of rough-and-tumble *play*, particularly with other young; and (4) an *aggressive play* stage in which relationships between the young crystallize into the hierarchy of dominant-subordinate pairs.

Typical forms of affiliative behaviors include grooming, greeting, play, cooperation, and sympathy. The communicative mechanisms involved in these kinds of interaction are visual, auditory, tactile, and olfactory (Argyle, 1969).

CONCLUSION

Animal social behavior and organization involve dominance and submission, hierarchical order, consumption of territory and production of meanings associated with it, affiliation, interaction, and communication. Their cultural qualities, if recognized, may augment more traditional, biological modes of analysis. The preceding analysis is selective and involves characteristics shared by human animals. Instead of assuming that these characteristics are innate, a wiser course would be to treat it as a possibility.

There is a question of homology and analogy: by treating animals as protologues, in a sense we beg this issue, but whatever the parallels may be between infrahuman and human social behavior and organization, the former make up a reservoir of insights (Bruyn, 1966, pp. 32–40) for the sociologically trained student. They provide models for the generation of testable hypotheses, even if all turn out to be straw men to be knocked down. It is no less important to discover what, empirically, is invalid than to find what is correct. For instance, what conduct do we bestow upon ourselves and upon others to establish, maintain, or alter our status or theirs?

In recent years ethologists have raised the level of their analysis phylogenetically. Formerly concerned with birds and fish, ethologists are turning their attention to primates, including man (Morris, ed., 1967). At the same time, primatologists have turned to primate life in the wild. Perhaps it is time for sociology to seek a similar reorientation. A genuine comparative sociology would not be merely intersocietal and international, but interspecies. And, if the conceptual equipment of animal studies may be of use for the analysis of human social life, the reverse is also worth consideration: the explanation of animal social behavior and organization may require a more genuinely sociological analysis, rather than the biologically based one it has received.

Thus, the student wishing to move from animals to humans might read an ethnographic description of human social life like Carey's *The College Drug Scene* (1968) and attempt to account for the findings in terms of concepts like affiliation or dominance, drawn from the analysis of infrahumans. Alternatively, moving the other way, he might ask himself how the conceptual tools of human sociology might help him make sense of such "animal ethnographies" as Schaller's *The Mountain Gorilla* (1963). We cannot argue that human social life is biologically structured, but neither can we claim that all animal social life is so determined. As the data accumulate, it is becoming more evident that infrahuman social behavior and organization are functions of the situations of their lives, ecological and cultural, not of the biologically given physiological-anatomical structure of their bodies (as discussed further in Chapter 4). If this is less so for infrahumans than humans, it is a matter of degree rather than kind—not a denial but a ratification of animal-human continuities.

SUGGESTED READINGS

Argyle, Michael, "The Biological and Cultural Roots of Interaction," in his book *Social Interaction*. London: Methuen, 1969, pp. 25–90.

> Looks at basic forms of social behavior common to human and nonhuman primates.

DeVore, Irven, ed., *Primate Behavior: Field Studies of Monkeys and Apes*. New York: Holt, Rinehart, & Winston, 1965.

> A collection of papers on free-ranging nonhuman primates. Topics include both types of behavior—for example, communication—compared on an interspecies basis and intraspecies investigations of a range of member behaviors (that of macaques, gorillas, lemurs, and others).

Hafez, E. S. E., *The Behavior of Domestic Animals*. London: Bailliere, Tindall & Cox, 1962.

> Contains papers on fundamentals of behavior as well as studies of particular domestic animals. The latter include selections on cats, dogs, rabbits, cattle, sheep and goats, horses, swine, as well as chickens, turkeys, and ducks.

Hebb, D. O., and W. R. Thompson, "The Social Significance of Animal Studies," in Lindzey, Gardner, and Elliott Aronson, eds., *The Handbook of Social Psychology*, 2nd ed. Reading, Mass.: Addison-Wesley, 1968, II, 729–774.

A discussion of animal studies and their utility for the understanding of human conduct. See also J. P. Scott, "The Social Psychology of Infrahuman Animals," in IV, 611–642.

Lilly, John C., *Man and Dolphin*. Garden City, N.Y.: Doubleday, 1961.

A fascinating discussion of the author's thesis concerning the possibilities of interspecies communication. The author presents data which make a forceful (if not completely persuasive) case in the affirmative.

McFarland, David, and Jill McFarland, *An Introduction to the Study of Behavior*. Oxford: Basil Blackwell, 1970.

A primer on the ethological perspective and method; broader than most ethological approaches, this explicitly considers the ethology of human behavior.

McGill, Thomas E., *Readings in Animal Behavior*. New York: Holt, Rinehart & Winston, 1965.

A collection of readings including some theory and a variety of research methods (for example, comparative, ethological). Also includes suggestions for a basic library in animal behavior.

Morris, Desmond, ed., *Primate Ethology*. London: Weidenfeld & Nicolson (also Chicago: Aldine), 1967.

Includes reviews of the literature and empirical studies—from an ethological perspective—on a variety of primate behavioral phenomena including grooming, facial displays, play, communication, and social interaction in a nursery school setting.

Schaller, George B., *The Mountain Gorilla: Ecology and Behavior*. Chicago: University of Chicago Press, 1963.

A study of free-ranging gorillas in natural habitats. Observational data on both individual and social behavior and social organization; the closest thing to an "animal ethnography."

Zajonic, Robert B., *Animal Social Psychology*. New York: John Wiley, 1969.

A collection of papers illustrating experimental work, organized in terms of social processes shared with humans: affiliation, cooperation and competition, aggression, and dominance.

Masters, William H. and Virginia E. Johnson, *Human Sexual Response*. Boston: Little, Brown, Company, Inc., 1966.

> As Kinsey's study represented the pioneering breakthrough of studying human sexual behavior by means of interviewing, this study represents the breakthrough of studying human sexual behavior by means of observing. Human subjects were wired for sound and photographed during coitus. Special attention was given to masturbating women who used a plastic penis with an inbuilt camera that recorded internal changes. This study is controversial.

O'Neill, William L., *Divorce in the Progressive Era*. New Haven: Yale University Press, 1967.

> Focusing on the period of 1890 to 1920, O'Neill analyzes the controversy over divorce, when divorce was as bitter an issue as slavery, polygyny, and the women's rights movement. The view is presented that divorce has strengthened, rather than weakened, the American family.

PART III

The Analysis of Social Situations: The Sociology of Everyday Life

Part I dealt with questions concerning social situations of everyday lives. This part presents a more detailed analysis of everyday situations and their relation to social structures. Chapter 7 shows how the child, the offspring of love and sex analyzed in Chapter 6, becomes a socialized member of society; systematically, it develops concepts and theories that run through Parts III, IV, and V. Chapter 8 deals with the nature of and relation between social situations and social structures and shows how they are related to the issue of individual freedom versus social constraint, underlying many of our later discussions of social problems. Chapter 9 examines details of the dramaturgical analysis of everyday situations, especially as developed by Erving Goffman. Chapter 10 considers the purposes and problems of sociological research on which any such theories are built. This part introduces the more detailed consideration in Part IV of the ways that members of society construct meanings and actions.

CHAPTER 7

Socialization

The last chapter was concerned with sex, love, procreation, and basic family relations. The child coming from these biologically based relationships must develop into an adequate member of society. This is the goal of the socialization processes from infancy to death. In this chapter we will consider processes.

Previously, sociologists believed that the social uses of rules were unproblematic; hence, they tended to look at socialization as learning society's dominant rules and expecting patterns of action in accord with those rules. If the individual learned these rules and acted in accord with them, he was said to be "successfully socialized"; if not, he was "inadequately socialized," a state used to explain deviance and social disorder. Sociologists now recognize what beleaguered parents have always known: development and learning involve deep and persistent conflicts.

The problems of socialization begin with the interaction between parents and children, but they are continued in our society in systems of formal education. This chapter begins with a consideration of the earliest, informal socialization processes and proceeds to the more formal ones.

Socialization, in the most general sense, is the process through which individuals acquire the social knowledge and skills necessary to enable them to interact with others. This process lasts throughout the individual's life. Children are born socially incompetent, a fact which all societies recognize, yet somehow they manage to develop into socially competent adults. This chapter will explore the nature of social competence and how it is acquired.

Socialization is also part of the process through which individuals locate themselves in society. Through the various agencies of socialization—such as the family, the peer group, and the educational system—individuals acquire membership in the various groups making up society. These include racial and ethnic groups, occupational and income groups, and political groups. This chapter, then, shall also explore the agencies of socialization and the role they play for an individual locating himself within society. We will begin our exploration by examining several theoretical issues involved in the study of socialization.

The study of the socialization process is a central concern of sociology for three reasons. The first two reasons, stated above, are that it is important to know (1) what individuals must acquire to be socially competent and how they acquire that competence, and (2) what effects agencies of socialization have on a child's life.

The third reason is that the study of socialization provides a partial answer to sociology's most basic question: How is social order possible? All theories of social order are based on either an implicit or explicit theory of socialization. No matter how one explains the phenomena of social order, there is always the assumption that men must acquire some type of social knowledge and social skill. By articulating what this knowledge and skill is and how it is acquired, sociologists specify some of the conditions for social order.

Furthermore, all theories of social order and socialization are based on some implicit or explicit conceptualization of the nature of human nature. How a sociologist accounts for the process of socialization and the conditions of social order is dependent on his conception of whether social behavior is produced as a result of human nature being free or determined, social or antisocial, creative or destructive. The relationship between theories of human nature, theories of socialization, and theories of social order can be seen clearly if we compare an *absolutist* sociology with an *existential* sociology (see Chapter 4).

Absolutist sociologists such as Talcott Parsons conceive human nature to be determined. Man's behavior is determined by society. Borrowing from Freud and Durkheim, Parsons views socialization as the "internalization" of society's rules, values, and motivations, controlling man's biological urges and providing him with a "blueprint for behavior" (Parsons, 1951; Durkheim, 1951; Freud, 1961). Social order is possible to the extent that we share a common fund of knowledge, to the extent that there is *consensus*. In Parsons' model social order may be viewed as a play, in which each actor has a script to follow and everyone knows everyone else's lines well enough to produce the drama as intended. In a sense, the play transcends any of the actors for, if they have the script, many people can produce the same drama and play the same roles.

Following this analogy, Parsons believes the part each of us plays is determined by our social position within the society. The sociological term for social position is *social status* and it refers to the formal categories of socially relevant attributes by which individuals may be identified. Race, religion, income group, sex, and occupation are examples of social statuses to which an individual may belong. Status may be either achieved or ascribed. *Achieved* statuses are those social positions acquired intentionally by the individual. They include such things as educational degrees, job titles, and marital identities. *Ascribed* statuses are those social positions acquired either through birth or motivation. They include race, sex, age, and ethnic and family background.

In a play, one performs a part by following a script. Similarly, for Parsons, behavior within a particular status is governed by a set of rules, called *norms*, much like the script of the play. By following the norms of a given status, individuals produce social behavior appropriate to that status. This behavior is the *role*. Not only do we learn our own roles, but we also learn the roles of the others we interact with, or at least enough so that we know what to expect from them.

For Parsons, deviance and a breakdown in the social order occurs when members fail to properly internalize the norms appropriate to their status or are prevented from properly playing their role due to some defect in the social system. Clearly, for Parsons' model, a key to the problem of social order is contained in the socialization process. The possibility for order exists to the extent that children internalize the shared norms of society.

Unfortunately, there are serious flaws in this model of social order. First, as Dennis Wrong points out, absolutist models such as Parsons' provide sociology with *"an over socialized concept of man"* (ASR, XXVI). In Parsons' model, man is determined by society, an actor following a predetermined script. There is no room for the uniqueness and individuality that characterize human interaction. Wrong points out that sociology must also take into account the side of man that is "unsocialized." Human beings act out of individual as well as shared motives. They perceive the world from the point of view of their own life experiences as well as from that of shared social experiences. For a theory of socialization and social order to be adequate, it must take into account both the socialized and unsocialized sides of man, for *both* have important consequences in the production of society.

A second major flaw in Parsons' absolutist model of socialization is that it ignores the *problematic* and *situated* nature of meaning. Parsons' model assumes that the meanings of things in the world are the same for all members of a society. This consensus is possible because of the socialization process. For absolutist sociology, meanings are *transsituational* and *nonproblematic*. They are said to be transsituational because absolutist sociology conceives meaning as shared by individuals *prior to* and not affected by their interaction with each other, and thus transcending situations. Meanings are nonproblematic for absolutist sociology because everyone shares the same meanings.

American society, however, is not characterized by such a consensus of shared meanings. American society is pluralistic. It is made up of subcultures, many of which have their own unique realities and meanings. Further, within each subculture exists a world of multiple realities, for individuals often produce behavior and interpret the world because of their own unique life experiences and intentions. Individuals may share some meanings prior to interacting because they are members of the same society or belong to the same subculture. But, just as often, individuals interact with persons they have never met before, who have different life experiences and perceptions, and who come from different subcultural environments. In such cases there may be little or no prior sharing of meanings. Meanings and interaction are then problematic for the individual.

Since, often, individuals do not share meanings prior to their interaction with each other, how is it possible for them to understand each other? The solution to this problem lies in the fact that shared meanings emerge through the process of interaction. This is what is meant by the situated nature of meaning. Each encounter between human beings develops its own set of meanings tied to that encounter. In most cases, individuals come to understand each other, not by a prior sharing of meaning, as is the case for absolutist sociology, but through the unfolding of the situation. As a situation progresses, shared meanings emerge as individuals define, interpret, and redefine objects and events in the situation. Existential sociology seeks to provide an alternative to absolutist sociology by (1) avoiding an oversocialized conception of man and (2) by recognizing the problematic and situated nature of meaning in the social world.

Existential sociology locates the heart of human nature in man's need for meaning. Man needs a meaningful world, for without meaning man soon perishes. For meaning to exist, the world must have the following characteristics: (1) it must have value, it must be able to produce both pleasant and unpleasant stimulations; (2) it must be predictable. Man must be able to recognize patterns, to see the world as sensible and familiar. At the same time the world cannot be too predictable, for too high a predictability will produce boredom and a fatalistic orientation to life, which may be as destructive as too little predictability; (3) it must be "manipulatable." Man must be able to exert an effect on his environment, obtaining goals and producing changes in the world around him; and (4) following from the first three, man must be able to create a world within which he has self-esteem. He must be able to see his role in the world as a positive, creative one, in which he feels a sense of belonging and purpose. Thus, for the world to be meaningful, it must allow for both permanence and change, security and adventure (for a similar formulation, see Thomas, 1923).

Existential sociology recognizes, however, that the world is *absurd*. By using the word "absurd" to describe the world, existential sociologists refer to the fact that "the world is essentially without meaning" (Lyman and Scott, 1970). This *does not* mean, though, that men experience the world as meaningless or absurd. When existential sociologists refer to the world as absurd, they mean that the world does not create meaning for man. If man is to experience the world as meaningful, he must create that meaning himself.

It is in the context of social interaction that man obtains most of his meaning and accomplishes most of his goals. However, in contrast to absolutist sociology, which sees the social system creating and determining man's behavior, existential sociology sees man as creating the social world and the meaning in it. Through each social interaction individuals construct social reality. Because man creates meaning in the world, existential sociology recognizes the potential for human freedom. Men may choose either to construct their own unique reality or share in the realities created by others. This potential freedom does not mean, however, that individuals have complete control over their social destiny. Most human beings drift between the ideal poles of absolute freedom and absolute determinism (Matza, 1969).

The drift between freedom and determinism occurs because no man is ever completely controlled by others nor is any man ever completely able to control others. Human beings accomplish goals and create a meaningful world through interaction with one another. The amount of control an individual has over the meanings created determines the amount of freedom he has in the interaction. Control over interaction is dependent on many factors; the two most important are (1) how competent and skillful a person is at interaction, and (2) how much power an individual can bring to bear to make his definition of reality stick (Lyman and Scott, 1970). The amount of freedom any individual has varies from situation to situation, depending on how much competence and power he has in that situation.

Existential sociology recognizes that, because no individual is absolutely free, there may be factors which determine that individual's life. The lives of children are far more determined than the lives of adults because children are not as competent and have less power in interaction. It is, therefore, not at all inappropriate to talk about factors which may determine aspects of a child's life, as this chapter will do in the section on the agencies of socialization. Existential sociology differs from absolutist sociology, which holds what seems to be a similar position, in that existential sociology recognizes the problematic nature of determining influences. Eventually, children acquire adult competence and power. Many early influences of parents and teachers may disappear as the individual encounters new situations. However, other influences of parents and teachers, particularly when the biological development of the individual is involved, may affect the person throughout his life. Existential sociology seeks to describe possible ways environments may influence children, but it recognizes that the relationship between the individual and the environment is always the result of an active social construction that may be subject to change.

Because existential sociology recognizes the potential for individual freedom in interaction, it avoids a deterministic and oversocialized concept of man. Furthermore, because existential sociology locates the construction of meaning and social reality in the interaction process, it recognizes the situated and problematic nature of meanings.

In contrast to absolutist sociology, which conceives socialization as the internalization of norms determining behavior and producing consensus, existential sociology conceives socialization as the acquisition of the ability to create meanings that can be understood by others and the ability to understand meanings created by others, within the context of social interaction. Furthermore, this ability to understand and to be understood is not dependent on the existence of a prior sharing of consensus of meanings, though there may be such a prior sharing.

It should now be clear how the sociologist's conception of the nature of human nature determines how he views the nature of social order and the socialization process. In this chapter we shall take an existential view of the nature of human nature, social order, and the socialization process. We will explore some of the abilities children must acquire to create and understand social meanings and how they acquire those abilities.

Theories of socialization not only make assumptions about the nature of human nature; they also make assumptions about the nature of the human mind. In studying socialization, there have been two major approaches used in accounting for the nature of the development of the mind. The first is the *empirical* approach, which conceives the human mind as a "tabula rasa," a blank slate, upon which experience writes. According to the empiricists, socialization is a process of learning, in which the individual develops his social competence through experience. The empiricists stress the uniqueness

---

INSERT NO. 35

Noam Chomsky

Noam Chomsky (1928–   ) is an American linguist and founder of one of the major revolutions in linguistic theory. His conceptions of mind have produced a new era in the analysis of language and meaning. Chomsky received his Ph.D. from the University of Pennsylvania in 1955 and since then has taught at the Massachusetts Institute of Technology, where he now holds the Ferrari P. Ward Chair of Modern Languages and Linguistics.

Linguistics is the scientific study of languages. Traditionally, linguistics was confined to the description of natural languages and the discovery of methods for developing these descriptions. Interest in the acquisition and production of language was secondary and when traditional linguists, such as Bloomfield, did approach these problems they did so from the point of view of *behaviorism* (Bloomfield, 1933). Behaviorism, an empirical approach, holds that language is learned. The production of language is dependent on the individual receiving the correct stimulus to produce the learned response. Thus a child learns the name of an object, then later, when that object (the stimulus) is presented, he repeats the name (the response). A behavioristic approach to language is interested in producing cause-and-effect statements by describing the stimulus conditions which elicit the various responses. Because each culture that produced language is unique, behaviorists argue that each language is unique and, therefore, linguistics must study that uniqueness. It is to this traditional behavioristic conception of language that Chomsky reacted when he formulated his linguistic theories.

Chomsky begins by criticizing behaviorism on two grounds. First, learning theory cannot account for how a finite number of sounds and grammatical rules can generate an infinite possible number of sentences. For, if the only thing we know about language is what we have learned, new situations and communication within them would be impossible. Behaviorism does not allow for "creativity." Children and adults can generate and understand sentences they have never heard before. Second, by dealing only with observable behavior—the speech and the conditions under which it is produced—behaviorism ignores the underlying structures that generate language and make understanding possible. It is only by understanding these underlying structures that we come to understand language. As an alternative to the empirical approach of behaviorism, Chomsky proposes a *rationalistic* orientation that conceives language and

of each language and culture, for they are produced by a unique history and environment. Thus, what interests the empiricist is how and what children are taught.

The second major approach to development is called *rationalism*. Rationalism conceives the human mind as an active, organizing mechanism

understanding as generated from innate structures of the mind. Thus, linguistics should be interested in discovering these innate mechanisms that produce language. Because the structural foundations for language are innate and biological, all human beings share the same underlying ability to produce language. Therefore, Chomsky conceives all languages as having the same basic structure, that is, these structures are *universal*.

Chomsky defines linguistic *competence* as the ability to "produce" and "understand" an infinite number of sentences, recognized as correct or incorrect by any native speaker-hearer, from a finite number of words, rules, and sounds. He contrasts this with *performance*, which is the actual speech produced. Performance may or may not reflect competence. Children can produce speech, yet they may not be able to understand what they are saying. By the same token, competent adults will make mistakes in performance due to errors in memory, attention, or other cognitive components. In order for a child to become a "linguistically competent adult," he must not only be able to perform, but he must develop the underlying competences that will generate those performances and allow him to "understand" performances generated by others.

Competence is located in what Chomsky calls the "deep structure." As native speaker-hearers, we are "unaware" that we are using the rules of the *deep structure*. When we produce sentences we don't think of what we must do to generate them, we just do it, and if someone asks us how we produced those sentences, we would be unable to tell them. What we are aware of is the produced sentence, or what Chomsky calls the "surface structure." The *surface structure* is generated by the deep structure. Languages differ in their surface structure, that is, they appear different, but for Chomsky all languages are generated from the same competences and therefore have the same deep structures.

To date, Chomsky's impact on sociology has been slight, and the sociologists who know his work tend to be critical of the heavy emphasis he places on grammatical structure and the unproblematic nature of meanings. But, with the increasing interest in linguistics in existential and phenomenological sociology, an understanding of Chomsky will become of major importance. As the reader will see, this chapter relies heavily on the concepts of deep structure/surface structure and competence/performance in its analysis of socialization. Among Chomsky's major works are the following: *Aspects of the Theory of Syntax* (1965); *Language and Mind* (1968); and a "Review of B. F. Skinner's Verbal Behavior" (1959). For an excellent secondary source, see *Noam Chomsky* by Lyons (1970).

with its own unique features independent of the world. Thus, instead of the world imposing reality on the mind as in empiricism, rationalism holds that the mind organizes and produces the reality we perceive. The rationalists stress the universals of language and culture that all human beings share because they belong to the same species and share the same mental structures. For rationalism, socialization becomes the study of how the mind develops to produce adult competence. A rationalist approach to socialization describes the structural preconditions of the mind that must exist before particular types of behavior can emerge. These structural preconditions develop in a sequence of stages. An individual must complete development at a lower stage before he can go on to a higher stage.

The positions of rationalism and empiricism are polar extremes. In practice, one finds more of a blending of the two positions, with one position or the other dominating the point of view. For example, in the radical behaviorism of B. F. Skinner, one of the most empirical theories of development, one finds Skinner recognizing that the mind plays a role in organizing experience but holding that the role of experience is far more critical and that the focus of investigation should be on learning (Skinner, 1957). Noam Chomsky (see Insert No. 35), on the other hand, believes that central in development is the "unfolding" of the mind's innate character. For Chomsky the structure of language is innate, but it takes a specific learned language to activate this structure. Chomsky recognizes the role of learning but emphasizes the innate character of mind.

Between the more polar positions of Skinner and Chomsky lies the work of Jean Piaget (see Insert No. 36). Piaget stresses the importance of the interaction of the environment and the innate characteristics of the individual. One cannot be separated from the other. Central in most such positions is the notion of "critical period" (Roger Brown, 1965, pp. 32–37). A *critical period* in development occurs when an individual is especially sensitive to an environmental influence. This sensitivity is the result of emergence of an innate structure. If, during this critical period, the individual does not receive enough of the appropriate type of stimulation, his development will be arrested or distorted from that period on. By the same token, during a critical period, if an individual receives an optimal amount of stimulation his development may be accelerated.

In this chapter we will follow a modified rationalism, similar to Piaget's, stressing the interaction between the innate structure of the mind and the world of experience. By accepting a modified rationalism, however, we assume a fundamental difference between adult and childhood socialization. The normative approach, discussed earlier, fails to make this distinction for, in assuming socialization is the learning of a set of rule systems, adult socialization becomes an extension of childhood socialization (learning more rules). On the other hand, a modified rationalism takes into account the fact that a child lacks the innate structural competences underlying adult interaction and, therefore, views how and what a child learns as different from how and what an adult learns.

THE CHILD'S ACQUISITION OF INTERACTIONAL COMPETENCE

For a human being to be competent in social interaction, he must make his behavior understood and be able to understand the behavior of others. Not only must he be able to communicate in situations where he knows the people and shares the same history and values, he must also be able to communicate with people he has never met and with whom he may share little or nothing other than perhaps, in some loose sense, language.

When human beings enter a situation, they do so with some expectation of what is going to occur. This is based on their *definition of the situation* and what they expect will be the other person's definition of the situation. Since individuals are rarely able to explicitly state their intentions, they must rely on others' interpretations of their presentations of self. Similarly, to discover what others are trying to communicate, individuals must be able to typify or classify the behavior of others as meaningful and representative of some underlying purpose. Thus, when a self is presented in interaction, it is presented vis-à-vis what the actor thinks others will take as representative of what he is trying to communicate. As the interaction proceeds, each actor discovers how well his typifications of his own behavior and others' behavior are working. Since each human being is unique, with his own motives, intentions, and perceptions, and since much of interaction is left up to what is "implied," human beings are never fully able to typify or make predictable the behavior of the other. Thus the self, the meaning of the presented language, and the typification of the other are in constant flux. Moreover, as we act vis-à-vis one another we revise the self, the meanings presented, and the typification of the other to meet changing perceptions, expectations, and situational contingencies. This process gives interaction its unique and emergent character (for elaboration, see Chapters 8 and 9).

When a child acquires the competence to interact, he acquires the ability to generate and understand a potentially infinite number of behaviors from a finite set of typifications or categories. Much like Chomsky's deep structure (see Insert No. 35), the interactional competences generate surface structure and performance; that is, they are responsible for how we choose to present ourselves and our behavior and how we interpret the self and behavior of others. During an interaction we are unaware of using these structures, yet they are so important that, not only do they provide the foundations for interaction, they are also building blocks for the development of language, the self, and the ability to construct a meaningful world—the substance of interaction.

Interactional competence is founded on three *analytically distinct but mutually inclusive cognitive structures.* They are (1) reflexivity; (2) typification devices; and (3) interpretive procedures. *Reflexivity* refers to the mind's ability to recall the past, be aware of the present, and project a hypothetical future. *Typification* is the ability to form categories for the classification, identification, recognition, and understanding of experience. It is dependent on the mind's ability to recognize patterns and extract their distinctive features and organize new and old experience around these "typical properties."

INSERT NO. 36

Jean Piaget

Jean Piaget (1896–   ) is a Swiss psychologist and perhaps the foremost contributor in the world to the study of intellectual development in children. Piaget published his first scientific paper at the age of ten and in 1918 received his doctorate in the natural sciences at the University of Neuchâtel. Early in his career he worked at the Binet laboratory in Paris (where the first "scientific" intelligence tests were developed) and soon became interested in the methods of thinking used by children of various ages. In 1921 he accepted a position at the Institute of Educational Science in Geneva; currently, he is co-director as well as a professor of psychology at the University of Geneva and founder of the Center for the Study of Genetic Epistemology.

Piaget describes his work as "genetic epistemology" (the study of the origins of knowledge). Genetic epistemology is essentially an experimental philosophy which seeks to answer questions through the development study of the child. Piaget's theory, in the most general sense, is that mental development occurs in stages. These stages have the following characteristics: (1) each stage represents a *qualitative* difference in children's modes of thinking; (2) these different modes of thought form an *invariant sequence* in development. While cultural factors may speed up, slow down, or stop development, they do not change the sequence; (3) each stage represents a *structural whole;* that is, each stage represents an underlying thought organization transcending the specific situations in which it is found; (4) stages are universal for all people in all cultures; and (5) stages are *hierarchical integrations.* Higher stages displace or reintegrate structures found at lower stages. The motivation for the higher stages to replace lower stages is that of *subject-object equilibration.*

Mental growth is governed by a continual activity aimed at balancing the intrusions of the social and physical environment with the organism's need to conserve the structural systems inherent in the mind. Mental growth is determined by three major sets of factors: (1) maturation of mental structures; (2) physical experience; and (3) social experience. The principle of equilibration regulating the interaction of maturational and environmental influences is

Socialization 179

The *interpretive procedures* describe some properties of the mind necessary to enable human beings to construct and interpret social interaction. They are founded on the mind's ability to categorize or typify and engage in reflexive activity; that is, recall the past and project a future. The interpretive procedures include such features as (from Cicourel, 1970):

1. *The reciprocity of perspectives.* This refers to the human being's ability to idealize the interchangeability of standpoints, whereby the participants both take for granted that each would see the world in the way the

essentially dialectical in nature. At each level of development are two poles of activity: (1) changes in the organism's structure in response to environmental intrusion; Piaget calls this *accommodation*; and (2) changes in the intruding stimuli due to the existing structure; Piaget calls this *assimilation*. In other words, both structure and stimuli change in order to conserve the integrity of the system. As each new level of equilibrium is reached, it prepares the way for a new disequalibrium by providing the child with new forms of information and new possibilities of contradiction. Thus, Piaget's system is *not* a static one but always mobile and open. Progress from stage to stage is one of increasingly differentiated and integrated structures which handle the developing worlds of mind and environment.

Piaget's method is to make observations in natural settings and under experimental laboratory conditions. In both cases he uses a semiclinical interview, a form of nondirective inquiry, centered about a verbal or practical issue. The child is given a problem to solve or a task to complete and is then asked questions about what he has done. From his research, lasting over the last fifty years, Piaget has isolated at least four stages of development (the number varies depending on which of his works you read). These are the *sensory-motor stage*, the *preoperational stage*, the *concretely operational stage*, and the *formally operational stage*. These stages will be explored in the main body of the chapter.

Though today there is a great deal of controversy over the validity of Piaget's theory and methods, most of the results, even those done cross-culturally, seem to confirm his findings—with one exception. The nature and sequence of the stages holds up, but the age groupings have a high degree of variance and seem very much culture-dependent (Roger Brown, 1965, pp. 197–246; Mischel, 1971). Piaget's work has had an important influence in child psychology, social psychology, and linguistics and has been of interest to existential and phenomenological sociology. The following are some of his major works: *The Growth of Logical Thinking from Childhood to Adolescence* (1958); *The Moral Judgment of the Child* (1932); *The Language and Thought of the Child* (1952); *The Construction of Reality in the Child* (1954). For a general overview of Piaget's work, see *The Psychology of the Child* by Piaget and Inhelder (1969); and *The Developmental Psychology of Jean Piaget* by Flavell (1963).

other did if they were to exchange places; that, until further notice, both assume that each is interpreting objects in the environment in the same manner for the situation at hand. People assume that their conversation will be recognized as features of a world known in common and taken for granted, until shown otherwise.

2. *The et cetera assumption.* The nature of interaction is such that people often have to "fill in" for the time being to make a situation or utterance meaningful. Things may not be clear, obvious, or meaningful, so they "let it pass" with the hope that in the future course of the conversation it will become clear.

3. *Retrospective-prospective sense of occurrence.* Routine interaction depends upon people waiting for later events in order to decide what was intended before. This enables them to maintain a sense of structure and understanding during the exchange of letting the past clarify the present or the present clarify the past.

4. *Glossing.* This refers to the fact that people recognize and understand each other as concertedly meaning differently than they can say in so many words. Because language is a typification of a unique world and must leave out some essential features of that world, people recognize that we mean more or differently than the words we use. Words are a gloss for the detail we expect others to know and fill in.

5. *Indexicality.* The meaning of words and behavior are bound to the situation in which they occur. Words and behavior "index" (hence indexicality) some shared or common feature of the situation or environment. When removed from that context, they acquire a different meaning and may cause confusion, if not elaborated.

The level and character of the child's interactional competence is dependent on his general level or stage of cognitive development. Piaget (see Insert No. 36) has isolated four stages of cognitive development. The first stage is what Piaget calls the period of *sensory-motor intelligence.* It lasts from birth to approximately the age of two years. This period is characterized primarily by movement from a world in which the child is unable to differentiate things around him from himself (Piaget calls this egocentrism) to a world with a relative differentiation of self and objects, in which both are objectified in terms of spatial-temporal locations. During this period the child discovers that he is an active agent of the world, that he has a body, and that this body is not the center of the universe. He notices the results of his actions and develops categories of the object, space, time, and causality.

The second period is that of *preoperational intelligence.* It lasts from approximately two to seven years of age. During this period the child acquires the beginnings of thought and language. At first, this language is egocentric; the child is unable to separate his point of view from others'. Children of this age have trouble cooperating in games and communicating their ideas, for they see things only their way. With the development of language and thought, the child is able to internalize action; that is, he can manipulate the world through "mental experiments." The child categorizes the social and physical world, but these categorizations tend to be based heavily on perception and imagery. For example, in one experiment done by Piaget, children were shown a glass of water. The same amount of water is then poured into another glass of the same size and shape and the children are asked which glass has more water in it. Most of the children said both glasses contained the same amount. Then the experimenter poured the same amount of water into a taller, thinner glass and asked the children to compare all three glasses. Most children under the age of seven said the taller, thinner glass had more water in it, though in reality it had the same amount. Thus, children under seven were unable to *conserve quantity* from one container to another.

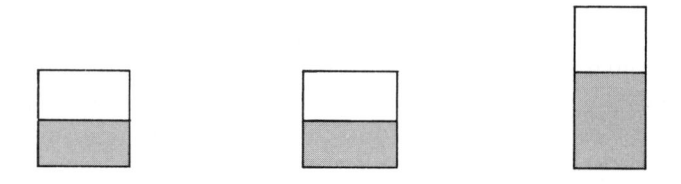

What the preoperational child lacks is operations. His categorizations are *not* based on features that transcend the situations and therefore, when operated on, do not allow for the conservation of the categorical qualities.

In the third period, called the *concretely operational intelligence*, lasting from approximately seven to eleven years of age, the child develops the ability to conserve the categorical qualities; he couldn't do this in the preoperational stage. Thus, he is able to determine that the taller, narrower container holds the same amount of water as the two shorter, fatter ones. Egocentric language disappears and the child is able to comprehend the point of view of the other and engage in cooperative activity. He is able to engage in games with rules and follow them.

The final stage, that of *formally operational intelligence*, occurs from eleven years of age onward. The child, now adolescent, develops the ability to engage in the highly abstract and symbolic thought of adulthood. Formally operational intelligence is characterized by hypothetical-deductive logic, in which the possibility of each situation is its most important feature rather than the concrete reality comprising it. In adolescence we see the beginning of interest in not what is, but what could be. Thus, the categories formed during this period are no longer concrete groupings but complex networks of lattices and groups founded on conditionals and abstract qualities. For Piaget, adolescence is the period for questioning, doubt, and exploration, in which for the first time we develop the ability to conceive the infinite possibilities open to us.

The effect the level of cognitive development has on the child's acquisition of interactional competence can be most clearly seen if we examine three of the "building blocks" that form the foundations of interaction. These building blocks are (1) the child's ability to use language; (2) the child's ability to construct moral meanings; and (3) the child's ability to construct the self.

LANGUAGE

Language is the major media of social interaction. It is, in part, through the use of language that individuals come to share meanings. Not only does language allow individuals to share meanings; it also plays a major role in how individuals organize and create reality. Perhaps one way of describing language is to see it as a series of categories. With these categories individuals are able to identify objects and construct realities. Human languages contain only a finite number of categories, yet, because of the unique and emergent nature of the social world, these finite categories must produce and understand an infinite possible number of events. The ability to use language, then, becomes a subset of interactional competence, the general ability to understand and construct an infinite number of behaviors from a finite set of rules and categories. Thus, the child's acquisition of language is dependent on his acquisition of the reflexive mind, the ability to typify, and the interpretive procedures.

Language categories are perhaps the most complex of the typification devices. In development, language categories are increasingly *differentiated, integrated,* and *abstract. After the first year the child begins to form the first words.* These are global categories that may include ten or more seemingly unrelated items, such that "da da" may refer to anything the child likes, including the father (Ervin-Tripp, 1966, p. 60). The child learns to discriminate more and more distinctive features of sounds making up language as well as form more distinctive categories (Roger Brown, 1965, pp. 246–306). This early development is highly correlated with the child's ability to move about, explore, and manipulate the world (Lenneberg, 1964). Some time during the second year children begin to construct two-word phrases and by the age of thirty-six months some are so far advanced as to produce all major varieties of English simple sentences up to a length of ten or eleven words (Roger Brown, 1965, pp. 246–306).

During the preoperational period, language is characterized by two features:

1. *The reliance on highly concrete, situationally embedded criteria for*

the definition of categories. This means that the child will often take the definition or meaning of something from its situationally specific properties, rather than from its transsituational properties. He will then overgeneralize these situationally specific properties to new situations. For example, a humorous result from a three-year-old: "The Ostrich is a Giraffe-bird," and "Can't you see? I'm barefoot all over" (Chukousky, 1971). In the case of the "Giraffe-bird," the child recognizes the similarity between the giraffe and the ostrich, in that they both have long necks. However, the child overgeneralizes from the specific context in which he learned the word "giraffe," and uses this word to express the concept of long-neckedness. The example in the category is confused with the category itself. Similarly, in the case of "barefoot," the instance becomes the category.

Because preoperational children rely on highly concrete, situationally embedded criteria for definition of categories, the categories they form lack a constant dimension of similarity. Rather than develop categories based on criteria which all members of that category share, preoperational children form what Vigotsky calls a *chain complex* (Vigotsky in Roger Brown, 1965). A chain complex is like a rope, made up of many short fibers, none running the length of the rope; short-run similarities link subsets of the total set but there is no similarity linking each with each (Roger Brown, 1965).

The nature of the chain complex is illustrated in a study by Bruner and Olver (reported in Roger Brown, 1965). Bruner and Olver presented children with a pair of objects such as a banana and a peach and then asked the children how the two objects were alike. Then additional objects were added and the children were asked to find a quality common to all. The children were unable to connect all the objects, so they formed chain complexes like "banana and peach are yellow; peach and potato are round; potato and meat are served together."

Adult categories are also characterized by chain complexes, as we shall see when we explore the concept of "family resemblances." There is one important difference, however. The qualities used by adults to organize categories are extremely abstract and well integrated. They tend to encompass a large variety of objects and events within the framework of a single quality.

2. *The development and use of children's interpretive procedures.* During the preoperational period the child begins to make greater use of his interpretive procedures, such as the reciprocity of perspectives, indexicality, and the retrospective-prospective sense of occurrence. He does not use them, however, in the same way adults do. Children's interpretive procedures are characterized by the same situational overgeneralization that characterizes their use of categories. Because of the egocentrism of the preoperational period, children tend to see the world only from their point of view. Thus the reciprocity of perspectives never becomes a problem for them, for they

CORRELATION OF MOTOR AND LANGUAGE DEVELOPMENT

Age (Years)	Motor Milestones	Language Milestones
0.5	Sits using hands for support; unilateral reaching	Cooing sounds change to babbling by introduction of consonantal sounds
1	Stands: walks when held by hand	Syllabic reduplication; signs of understanding some word; applies some sounds regularly to signify persons or objects, that is, the first words
1.5	Prehension and release fully developed; gait propulsive; creeps down stairs backward	Repertoire of 3 to 50 words not joined in phrases, trains of sounds and intonation patterns resembling discourse, good progress in understanding
2	Runs (with falls); walks stairs with one foot forward only	More than 50 words; two-word phrases most common; more interest in verbal communication; no more babbling
2.5	Jumps with both feet; stands on one foot for 1 second; builds tower of six cubes	Every day new words; utterances of three and more words; seems to understand almost everything said to him; still many grammatical deviations
3	Tiptoes 3 yards (2.7 meters); walks stairs with alternating feet; jumps 0.9 meters	Vocabulary of some 1,000 words; about 80% intelligibility; grammar of utterances close approximation to colloquial adult; syntax mistakes fewer in variety, systematic, predictable
4.5	Jumps over rope; hops on one foot; walks on line	Language well established; grammatical anomalies restricted either to unusual constructions or to the more literate aspects of discourse

always assume that they are understood. Preoperational children fail to recognize situations in which the reciprocity of perspectives may be problematic because they overgeneralize their point of view.

The property of indexicality is also overgeneralized during the preoperational period. Children learn very early that one word may be used to describe a variety of situations. This is possible because of the property of indexicality, the ability to let a word's meaning be provided by the situation in which it is used. Thus, the word indexes the situation. Adults use indexical or telegraphic speech all the time, but are sensitive to its problematic nature. For example, if Smith says to Jones, "Get me the thing over there," and Jones is in the other room, it is likely that there will be some confusion. Jones will have no idea what Smith is "indexing" by the word *thing* because he does not share the same situation. Smith would be much more likely, under these circumstances, to ask Jones, "Get me the hammer over there," the meaning of the word hammer being much *less* situationally bound. Preoperational children remain insensitive to this problem and will use indexical speech even when it is difficult to discover what the word is indexing.

Parents often reinforce this practice by correctly discovering what the child means. However, a good deal of parents' time is also spent teaching the child to use a more elaborate or normal form of speech. Consider for a moment the *reduction-expansion cycle* in the adult-child interaction of a two-year-old child (Roger Brown, 1965, pp. 246–306). The child produces the utterance "Eve lunch." The mother must decide how to expand this utterance into an understandable phrase. Does "Eve lunch" mean Eve wants lunch, Eve is eating lunch, Eve had lunch? To figure out what lunch refers to, the mother must rely on the situational context at hand. Then she expands the utterance to "Eve is having lunch," which the child reduces again to "Eve lunch." The child uses the category lunch to handle the whole situation, and thus provides an overgeneralization. In her expansion, the mother is attempting to teach the child to make finer discriminations in her categories so that they are not so situationally bound. She is trying to teach the child a *normal adult form* that can be communicated to others. The child is developing the ability to use interpretive procedures. Because of the success of her telegraphic speech, she learns that she can assume the reciprocity of perspectives and that language is indexical.

During the period of concretely operational intelligence, the child develops the ability to construct increasingly differentiated language categories. Reduced and telegraphic speech, relatively undifferentiated, decreases. So, where the preoperational child may utter the word "lunch" to describe the fact that she is hungry, the concretely operational child will say, "I want lunch."

The categories of the concretely operational child are based more on the transsituational features of objects and events defining those categories. Mistakes involving the overgeneralization of a situationally bound property, which occurs during the preoperational period, decrease. Thus, during the concretely operational period, the child is less likely to make such confusions as "I'm barefoot all over."

The concretely operational child is able to construct and understand distinctive features of increasingly abstract categories that allow him to integrate a variety of phenomena. Categories based on the "chaining" of *concrete* qualities of objects and events begin to disappear, in favor of using the more *abstract* qualities of objects and events. The chain complexes become more integrated and, because abstract qualities are more inclusive than concrete qualities, fewer distinctive features are needed to form a chain. The major difference between categories formed during the concretely operational period and adult categories is the level of complexity, abstraction, and integration. Adult categories are more complex, abstract, and integrated.

The formulation of categories during the concretely operational period makes increasing use of the mind's reflexive properties. To make finer discriminations about the world, the child must constantly utilize his ability to reconstruct the past with new things he has learned. Because the child's categories are more abstract and discriminating, he must increasingly use his ability to project a hypothetical future. Often, the category into which an object or event will be placed is now problematic for him. He is beginning to recognize several possibilities open for how he will define that object or event. Thus the child projects in his mind the possible alternatives available to him, given the situation at hand. As a situation progresses, he may then use the meanings he has projected as the basis for his understanding. Though we see an increasing use of the mind's reflexive properties during the period of concretely operational intelligence, adult reflexivity does not emerge until the formal operational period.

The increased complexity and abstraction of the child's categories and their dependence on the reflexive properties of the mind are, in part, reflected in the decline of the egocentric language of the preoperational period. Concretely operational children begin to recognize that often others may not understand what they say and that the meanings they use may be problematic; thus, they learn to recognize the conditions under which they must suspend, in part, the reciprocity of perspectives.

The decline in egocentrism is marked by the fact that children take into account the point of view of other persons with whom they are interacting. In choosing what category to use in describing an object or event, concretely operational children consider what they think is the other person's ability to understand, with less of a tendency to overgeneralize the indexical properties of language. They begin to use an elaborated norm adult form, less contextually bound than the preoperational telegraphic speech.

Adult language competence emerges during the formal operational period. The categorical structures of the formal operational period are more differentiated, integrated, and abstract than those of the concretely operational period. This new level of integration and abstraction provides a foundation for the construction and recognition of transsituational qualities of categories that can encompass a greater variety of phenomena than those of the concretely operational period. These transsituational features of a category form the "kernel" meaning of that category. The kernel meaning of a category gives that category its essence and makes it different from all other categories. These kernel meanings are so abstract, however, that individuals can talk about them only in relation to a specific object or event which the meaning helps define.

To illustrate this rather complex point let us consider the meaning of the word "game." There is the game of football, war games, the game of love, and a card game. What makes all these things games? What do war, football, love, and cards have in common? Well, first, you could say that all involve competition, fixed rules, winners and losers, strategies, and lack of serious commitment. Yet, if we look closely, people may or may not take these games seriously; there is evidence that they do both. Some games are cooperative rather than competitive without winners, losers, or strategies. Games like the game of love have no fixed rules. What, then, makes all these things games?

The philosopher Wittgenstein uses the term "family resemblance" to characterize the basic organizing principle of adult categorization (1958). War games may be like football in that they are strategic and competitive. Football may be like cards in that it is not serious and has fixed rules. War games may be like love in that they are serious but have no rules. Thus, love is related to war and war is related to football and football is related to cards. Love and cards are related only through a chain of other particulars in the category. "Game" can be given no specific meaning other than the one it acquires through its use in interaction; yet it is a recognizable general category used to organize reality. It maintains this feature through the existence of family resemblances which provide the kernel meaning.

Through adult interpretive procedures, individuals are able to recognize meanings as situationally specific and unique and yet, at the same time, as belonging to a familiar category. Some properties of the interpretive procedures that allow individuals to see unique particulars as members of a category are the et cetera assumption, the retrospective-prospective sense of occurrence, glossing, and indexicality. The et cetera assumption allows individuals to tolerate a high degree of ambiguity by letting them assume that things will become clear as the world unfolds. The retrospective-prospective sense of occurrence gives individuals the ability to make the necessary discriminations in placing objects and events into their proper categories. It does this by letting them reconstruct the past as they obtain new information and use past information to understand the present. Glossing and indexicality provide individuals with the ability to extract transsituational features of objects and events and at the same time to recognize their situated embeddedness. They do this by letting the label of the category stand for both the unique and general simultaneously. For example, the use of the word "game" is always a gloss, indexing the particular situation in which the word emerges. At the same time, by using the category "game" to describe a particular situation, claims are made about properties of that situation which it shares with other situations labeled "game."

Just as we may use the concept of family resemblance to analyze the organization of a single individual's typification system, we may also use this concept to analyze the relationship of the typification systems operating between individuals. As members of a society, individuals share a common language, to some extent. This means there is a sharing of categories and of the labels identifying those categories. Though individuals may share a language, this does not mean they share meanings prior to interaction. Again, let us use the example of the meaning of the word "game." My categorization of gameness may not overlap your categorization of gameness, just as a game of cards and a game of love do not overlap. We share the label "game" but it may have different meanings for each of us. However, if we were to come together in a social interaction and one of us were to use the word "game" within the context of that interaction, chances are we would understand one another. This understanding would be possible because, though our categories of game do not overlap, they will share some common properties. Through interpretive procedures, we will discover those common properties by the specific context in which we use the word "game." If we are unable to find any properties in common, we may either wait and see if we can figure out what properties each of us are using or we may ask each other to define "game."

Our typifications help get us started in the interaction and provide us with an overall general sense of understanding that is good enough, for most practical purposes, but we are tied *without remedy* to the use of the mind's reflexive properties and the interpretive procedures to gain intersubjective understanding and create social order vis-à-vis interaction.

MORALITY

Morality provides us with standards of what is right and wrong, good and bad, what one should and should not do. As Goffman has noted, one must always appear as a person worthy of the trust and respect interaction affords (1959). Thus, the presentation of self and the perception of the other are always implicitly if not explicitly organized around some critical judgment about what is morally appropriate for the situation at hand. Moral meanings are also central to our conception of self and self-esteem. For the world to remain a meaningful place, one must see his behavior as morally justified under the circumstances. Moral meanings provide us with a set of typifications whereby we can account to ourselves and to others that our actions are necessary and justified.

From a finite set of rules about morality, the child must be able to apply them to an infinite number of situations. This ability is dependent on the acquisition of cognitive structures that can contain particular types of moral thought and a set of interpretive procedures to govern their use.

Kohlberg has isolated three levels of moral development that correspond in sequence to Piaget's preoperational, concrete operational, and formal operational stages (1969). These are as follows:

1. *The premoral level.* At this stage of development, moral value resides in external, quasi-physical happenings, in bad acts, or in quasi-physical needs rather than in persons or standards. This level is characterized by an egocentric orientation that slowly shifts from the avoidance of punishment and deference to power to a utilitarian ethic where right action is what satisfies one's needs and sometimes the needs of others.

2. *The conventional moral level.* At this level, moral value resides in performing that which maintains conventional order and the expectations of others. This level is characterized by a "good boy" orientation toward approval, and to pleasing and helping others. There is an idealization of the "typical images of the majority" providing the standard for conformity. This orientation is transformed into "do your duty" and show respect for authority by maintaining the given social order for its own sake. There is a high regard for the earned expectations of others.

3. *The principled moral level.* At this level, moral value resides in conformity by the self to shared or shareable standards, rights, or duties. This level is characterized by a contractual legalistic orientation. There is recognition of an arbitrary element or starting point in rules or expectations for the sake of agreement. Duty is defined in terms of contract, general avoidance of violation of will or rights of others, and majority will and welfare. This orientation is transformed into one based on conscience and principle; it is directed not only to social rules but to principles of choice involving appeal to logical universality and consistency, as well as to conscience as a directing agent and to mutual respect and trust.

The ability to conceptualize morality at these levels does not guarantee its production. In fact, research indicates that the production of moral behavior is *highly situationally specific.* In the now classic study of "The Character Education Inquiry," by Hartshorne and May, some eleven thousand preadolescent children were given opportunities to lie, cheat, and steal in a variety of settings in classrooms, at home, in athletic contests, and in party games (1928–1930). It was found that morality was situationally determined. There was low predictability associated with cheating in one situation and cheating in another. Even in very closely related circumstances children were likely to be inconsistent; the child who cheated on an arithmetic test as often as not failed to cheat on a spelling test. Further, Hartshorne and May found no significant relationship between behavior tests of honesty and exposure to Sunday school, scouts, or the special character education classes.

A study by Havighurst and Taba found no significant correlation between resistance to cheating and stated belief in the badness of cheating or stated unwillingness to cheat (1949).

All studies of the effects of parental discipline and training techniques show little or no relationship to the development of moral character in children (Kohlberg, 1969, p. 469). What can we say, then, about the development of morality and moral meanings?

First, the type of moral typifications the child will develop are based on his level of cognitive development. To teach a preoperational child about the abstract rights of man would do little good. Second, the direction of moral awareness goes from egocentric relations to social relations to the unique existential relation man has with himself and others. Third, no matter at what level of development, the enactment of moral behavior is situationally specific, reliant on reflexivity of mind and interpretive procedures for its production. Moral meanings, like other meanings, are based on an interaction of a general typification and the unique demands of the situation.

THE SELF

Perhaps the self can best be described as the individual's typifications of himself. From an individual's classifications of his behavior, he comes to see himself as good or bad, smart or dumb, successful or unsuccessful, handsome or ugly. The sources of the typifications an individual uses to construct the self are that individual's interactions with the world. Most self-typifications are social and arise out of social interaction. In the formulation of these classifications, not only do individuals classify their own reactions to their behavior, they also classify others' reactions to their behavior.

The typifications of the self are the basis for the individual's presentation of self to others and to himself. Not only do individuals use the concepts of self to classify their behavior, they also use these concepts of self to generate their public identities. If I see myself as a happy person, I will try to generate information to others so that they will have a similar perception of me (for elaboration, see Chapter 8).

Reflexivity, typification, and the interpretive procedures form the foundations of the self by allowing us to be aware of our existence, discover continuity in our behavior, and make that behavior sensible. The reflexive properties of the mind allow the individual awareness of himself by giving him the ability to consciously reflect on his behavior and the world in which he produced that behavior. Because individuals can consciously remember what they do, they are able to categorize their behavior as representing something meaningful. As individuals act, they are constantly finding out new things about themselves. Because of the mind's reflexive properties, individuals are able to incorporate this new information into their old concepts of self and see continuity in their behavior. However, this process may also produce a reinterpretation of past behavior, and may cause a change in the concept of self.

The reflexive properties of the mind also provide grounds for the presentation of self to others. If I am to present myself to the world as a happy person, I must be able to decide what behaviors will be interpreted as "happy" behaviors by others. Individuals must project hypothetical situations in which they try out many self-presentations.

These hypothetical self-presentations may be addressed to a specific imagined other, such as a friend, or to a generalized other representing no one in particular and everyone in general. The imagined other is an idealization of how that specific person or people in general tend to react in a particular situation. Further, the hypothetical situation is an idealization containing only those aspects of the situation relevant for the problem at hand. From these imagined presentations, behavior is chosen which seems to best represent the meaning of self to be conveyed, given the situation and the other person.

The child, however, is not born with a self that displays all these abilities. The self must develop through maturation of the mind and interaction with the world. The development of the self is a continual process throughout the individual's life. The nature of the self developed by the child is to a large degree dependent on the child's level of cognitive development.

During the sensory-motor period of development, the child is at first unable to differentiate himself from his environment. Gradually, through the manipulation of the world around him, he discovers that he is an object like other objects and not the center of the world. His conception of self is based on his ability to manipulate objects both human and nonhuman in the physical world. During this period, the self is primarily biological.

In the period of preoperational intelligence, the child recognizes humans as a special class different from other objects, and sees that he belongs to this special class. His sense of self becomes more dependent on how he makes out in interaction with other people. The child's orientation during this period is still egocentric, however. He is concerned only with getting people to react in the way he wishes. Thus, the child's concept of self is still very dependent on getting his way.

The self of the preoperational period is highly situational. How the child sees himself is dependent on what he is doing. There is little use of the reflexive properties of mind to provide a transsituational concept of self. Further, children do not find their presentations of self problematic during this period. They assume that everyone sees them as they see themselves, and have difficulty understanding when things occur otherwise.

During the period of concretely operational intelligence, the child's concept of self becomes almost totally dependent on *how* others react to him. He is no longer solely interested in getting his way. His feeling about himself is largely based on his perception of how others react to his behavior and how they perceive his reactions to theirs. Do they treat him as a person who is enjoyable to have around, socially attractive and intelligent, or is he treated as unpleasant, stupid, and ugly?

The self, during the period of concretely operational intelligence, makes increasing use of the interpretive procedures. The child is able to extract particular aspects of his behavior from situations and integrate them with other aspects of his behavior. Thus, he is able to see continuity in what he does, by reflecting on and integrating situational particulars within the framework of an overall category. A transsituational self begins to emerge, less embedded in particular situations.

Because other people are now important to how an individual thinks about himself, individuals become sensitive to their presentations of self. Often, during the period of concretely operational intelligence, a child will consider how his behavior will look to others. Thus, he uses his ability to project a hypothetical future to decide which actions will make the best impression.

Finally, in the formally operational period, the person begins to develop an existential concept of self that typifies his unique relationship with himself, others, and the world as a whole. This self is characterized by an abstract integration and reformulation of the biological and social selves, and ultimately comes to grips with the meaning of existence and the value of life.

The development of the adult self is characterized by two properties not developed during the concretely operational period. The first is the level of abstraction and integration of the self. Adult categories of the self, like those of language, are organized around family resemblances. These resemblances allow the individual to incorporate increasing amounts of information as relevant to the discovery of who he is. The individual is more aware of himself and of his relations with others. This increased awareness, combined with the level of abstraction characterizing the adult self, however, may produce a periodic crisis of identity.

The second property of the adult self, then, is that the self may be problematic for the individual. The formally operational period is characterized by a search for the possibility within each situation. Because the adolescent recognizes the many possible selves he may choose from and the many different ways people react to the selves that he presents, he may ask the question, Which one am I? Intuitively, he feels that there is a self which uniquely represents him but, whenever he tries to discover this self, he can only see himself in a particular situation, presenting a self embedded in that situation. The intuitive recognition of a unified self but the inability to articulate it occurs, if you will remember our discussion of language, because categories based on family resemblances are recognized only through their use in particular situations.

The crisis of identity passes as the individual settles on those selves that he can integrate, and that are the most positive and consistent for him. The social nature of the self, however, ensures that the self will always be problematic to some degree for, as we interact with others, we will reflect on our presentations of self and the others' reactions to those presentations. Thus the door is left open for change and questioning.

AGENCIES OF SOCIALIZATION

We are now going to shift the focus of the chapter. In the previous section we explored some factors involved in the child's acquisition of interactional competence, such as the development of the interpretive procedures and the ability to typify. In this section, we are going to explore some agencies in society that provide the environments in which interactional competence emerges. In contrast to the level of analysis in the previous section, which stressed the universal features of cognitive development, this section will stress the specific effect environmental influences have on children and how these influences can affect the child's life chances.

There are four major agencies in American society that socialize children: the family, the peer group, the mass media, and the educational system. Each provides the child with a different set of abilities and contact with each may have a profound effect on how the child develops and locates himself within society. It is, however, necessary to clarify one point. An individual's behavior is not determined by his early family relations, his peer group, the mass media, or the educational system. *This is not to say* that each of these agencies *may not* have a profound effect on how individuals behave and locate themselves within society. What we *are* saying is that the effect the agencies of socialization have on an individual is always problematic. Some individuals may be influenced very little by their experience with their family, while for other individuals the family is the major source of influence. The same may be true of the peer group, mass media, and educational system. The effect of these agencies must be specified for each individual human being. This section will attempt to explore some possible influences the agencies of socialization may have on an individual's behavior and how he is able to locate himself within society.

The Family

Because the human infant is born both physically and socially incompetent, there is a prolonged period in which the child is totally dependent on others for satisfaction of his most basic needs. There is strong evidence to suggest that it is not enough to satisfy the child's physical needs for food and a warm, dry, clean environment, but his existential needs must also be met. Thus, even at several months of age, the child's world must be meaningful. He must have stability and change, security and adventure, and most of all self-esteem. The child's physical and existential growth is subject to critical periods. If the child's needs are not sufficiently met by either the correct amount or the right types of satiating agents, his growth may be permanently damaged.

Spitz, in his classic studies, found that babies in institutions such as orphanages had massively retarded scores in all measures of physical and mental growth (1959). Further, there was an extremely high rate of death from all causes. Though the children received proper nutritional and medical care, their environment was characterized by an extreme lack of human contact and attention. The children had little or no opportunity to explore their environment or receive new stimulation. Spitz believed that this lack of attention results in an infant disease called *marasmus* (literally, a listless withering away into death). According to Spitz, babies separated in about the middle of their first year from their mothers suffer depression and frequently go on to develop serious mental and physical disease.

In an attempt to discover why the marasmus effect occurred, the Harlows have done a series of experiments with primates (Harlow, 1961, 1963; Harlow and Harlow, 1965). Primates were used to avoid permanently damaging human children from the effects of social deprivation. Monkeys and apes belong to the same order as man and therefore share many of the same biological and social characteristics, particularly during infancy. Because of these similarities, it is often possible to extrapolate from primate behavior to human behavior. The Harlows discovered three major aspects of early social deprivation.

First, the *actual physical contact with another member of the species is central for normal development.* In rhesus monkeys contact and feeding responses are both important, but contact seems to be far more important. Nursing does not appear to be part of the affectional developmental process. Contact seems necessary to provide enough security to allow explorative behavior of new and fear-producing stimuli to occur.

Second, for normal social development in primates, there must be interaction with competent adults. It appears that early mother-infant association stimulates the formation and differentiation of facial and probably total bodily expressions that subsequently facilitate positive social interaction. In one study, two infant monkeys were raised together without a mother. The monkey infants placed together at birth clung to each other in a side-by-side position through adulthood and never developed any social play.

Third, the effect of social deprivation is dependent on the length of time it lasted, and whether it was total or partial. In partial social deprivation, monkeys were raised in empty cages without mothers and with only visual and auditory contact with other animals, so that they could have the possibility of imitating. In total social deprivation, the monkeys were raised in metal boxes receiving only light and piped-in noises to minimize sensory deprivation. The findings were that: (1) with three months' total deprivation, release leaves infants in shock (much like that of autistic children). If they survive this shock, they rapidly develop effective social relations with peers and total recovery is possible; (2) with six months' partial deprivation, social competences are permanently impaired but not destroyed; (3) with six or twelve months' total deprivation, the monkeys are totally and permanently unable to interact socially. Learning abilities are not impaired.

If we extrapolate from these studies to human infants, it seems that, for the normal development of interactional competence and a meaningful world, the child needs close affectionate contact with members of its own species. In American society this task is usually taken on by the family; in other societies, this may not always be the case. In the Israeli kibbutz, where children are reared communally, normal development occurs without the family (Spiro, 1965). Thus, the family is not essential for wholesome growth. To develop normally, children must have the stability and security provided by human contact and an environment that stimulates growth. Most adult human beings can provide these features for children.

During early childhood, the family is a major source of models for the child to imitate. Most social learning, both for adults and children, is through imitation rather than through direct teaching. The child, by watching adults, is able to typify and categorize things he does not experience directly. By learning in this fashion, children can elaborate their own direct experiences and develop a vast behavioral repertoire very quickly. Children imitate parents' language, values, goals, morality, and general behavior since such behavior allows the child to control his environment by making it a stable but interesting place.

Many factors determine whether a child will imitate the behavior of a model, but three factors seem most important. They are: (1) the level of cognitive development obtained by the child. For example, a child at the level of preoperational intelligence will be unable to imitate behavior that requires concretely operational intelligence; (2) the success of the model in obtaining his desired goal; and (3) the reinforcement consequence of obtaining that goal for the model (Bandura and Walters, 1963). Children often imitate people they do not like, but who are successful in manipulating the world in a way that the child also wishes to emulate (Bandura and Walters, 1963).

The stability of the typifications formed through imitation are subject to constant flux with new experiences. Thus, the typifications learned from the parents are open to change as the child encounters new spheres of influence. It was discovered that children and young adults are no more like their parents in level of morality or of masculinity-femininity than they are like a random parental individual of the same social class (Terman and Miles, 1936; Mussen and Rutherford, 1963). The presence of a same-sex parent is not necessary for normal moral or psychosexual development. Children in Israeli kibbutzes and children from father-absent households are little different from children of intact families (Terman and Miles, 1936; Maccoby, 1966). These findings suggest that particular imitation or good parent relations are not necessary for normal social development. But some findings suggest bad relations with parents are retarding or disrupting such development. Intact families with strong marital conflict or extremely unstable parents produced children with social problems more than did conflict-free, father-absent, or "good parent" homes (Glueck and Glueck, 1950; McCord et al., 1962). These studies suggest that the stability and security a family can provide have a far more lasting effect on the individual than the interactional typifications it produces. The apparent lack of effect parents exhibit on producing stable behaviors in children is due to: (1) the encroachment of the formal educational system; (2) the mass media, particularly television; and (3) the effects of peer influence. These three institutions are in constant competition with the family.

Perhaps the most important effect the family has on a child is the role it plays in locating the child in society. Most families do not exist in social isolation, but in an ecology of large social relationships. Members of families belong to religious organizations, racial and ethnic groups, political parties, economic hierarchies, and social classes. As members of a family, children often acquire automatic membership in many of the status groups occupied by the parents. Membership in these ascribed statuses, acquired from the family, is perhaps the most important of the family legacies to the child.

In a study quoted earlier, it was discovered that children were no more like their parents in levels of morality or of masculinity-femininity than they are like a random parental individual of the same social class. But we go on to discover that children are much more like random parents of their own *social class* than they are like random parents of other social classes. Thus, membership in ascribed status groups may have a more profound effect on the child's behavior than his relationship with his parents.

Membership in status groups acquired through the family may or may not last throughout the child's life, depending on the career contingencies he experiences with peers, the educational system, the military, employers, and so on. Their importance must not be underemphasized, though, for often they are the grounds for the direction the child is "tracked" within the social system. *Tracks* are the career paths leading to social positions. Often, there are many tracks leading to any given position. Along each track are many points to switch and get on a different career path. The track an individual is on and whether he stays on it or not is dependent on some factors which the individual can control and others which he cannot control.

A child's name, color of his skin, the way he uses language and behaves often determine what advantages or disadvantages he will have within society's institutions. Because some of the earliest typifications he learns to present himself with and make sense of the world with are developed from his subcultural environment, the child is often labeled and channeled into positions based on that label by the "gatekeepers" of our social institutions. *Gatekeepers* are those persons or institutions that allow or prevent individuals from entering or continuing on various tracks. The label given a child is often based on his performance rather than on his competence. Because this society's gatekeepers are dominated by the middle class, they reward middle-class performances. Parents in minority subcultures who wish to assimilate often recognize this fact and attempt to remove stigmatizing aspects of their lives. Thus it is not uncommon to find families changing their name, teaching their children what they think are middle-class ideals, and not practicing those customs that identify them as belonging to a particular subculture.

But, just as often, minorities and subcultures do not want to give up their unique identities and, besides, it is very difficult to change the color of your skin and the total way you and your children talk and think. Thus, children from subcultural minorities are often "tracked" into various programs that may limit their future opportunities and prevent them from acquiring the needed performance abilities it takes to be successful in America today.

This process is graphically illustrated in the consequences of children's language performance. In a study by Bernstein, significant social-class variations in the performance of language were discovered (1962a, 1962b, 1964). He suggests a contrast between restricted and elaborated codes. *Restricted codes* arise in close communication networks where assumptions are familiar and communication is more likely to be solidarity supporting, such as in families, closed friendship groups, ethnic and subcultural minorities, and the working classes. *Elaborated codes* appear when there is a need for specification of meaning, as in interaction with strangers. The middle class uses both forms (code-switching), being less closed in its communication patterns and needing elaborated codes in its occupational performances, because most middle-class and professional occupations involve meeting a variety of strangers each day. These class differences, the middle class using more elaborate speech and the lower class using more restricted speech, can be found among children as young as five and between the ages of twelve and fifteen these differences increase in both amount and number.

This differential performance in language accounts, in part, for why lower-class children are often labeled as less intelligent or culturally deprived by teachers and psychologists when they enter the public schools. For example, Jensen has argued that intelligence is genetic and that, among other things, blacks have a lower intelligence than whites (1969, pp. 449–483). He measured the children's intelligence by what he claimed were *"culture free"* tests, that is, tests that did not represent differences due to subcultural origins but, rather, due to the gene pool from which the individual comes. Jensen showed children pictures of objects and then, from fixed-choice labels, asked the children to give the object the label that the child thought corresponded. He also had children engage in tasks involving logic and reasoning abilities. In a followup of Jensen's study, it was discovered that the tests were biased in favor of middle-class language and typifications (Cicourel, 1971). Jensen was measuring performance rather than competence. For example, in retesting children who received incorrect scores on problem-solving tasks it was discovered that, independent of whether a child answered incorrectly or not, all used the same basic reasoning process and differing were the typifications used to identify elements. Thus, following from how each child typified the situation, his answer was logical and made sense. The test was biased in that correct answers were dependent on knowing middle-class elaborated categories. Further examination showed that in the picture-label placement tests, children's incorrect answers were due either to the fact that they had never seen the object presented or didn't understand the label. Thus, when a picture of a pair of scissors was presented, the correct label to correspond was the word "shears." Upon interviewing children who missed the question, many knew what the scissors were and what they were used for, but could only label them as the things "mommy" uses to cut with, or as scissors or cutters. Again, the test was biased toward children with highly elaborated, specific, and formal speech. Children were separated as to their performance rather than their competence and this performance was dependent on cultural rather than genetic determinants. If we consider that "intelligence" tests of this sort are used to decide a child's status in the educational system, it is no wonder children from cultural minorities are often labeled as deprived or less intelligent and processed on the basis of this label.

The Mass Media—Television

Our knowledge of the effects television has on the socialization process is rather slim at this point in time. We know next to nothing about the effects television may have on the development of cognitive structures or how profound is its effect on behavior. Many studies quoted in this section are by now out of date, with replacement not forthcoming. However, there are several things we can say about television watching.

We do know that television watching occupies a great deal of the child's time in America. From ages three through sixteen, the average American child spends about one sixth of his waking hours watching television, somewhat more than he devotes to school during these years, when one considers weekends and vacations. In terms of hours spent, television watching reaches its peak at the age when the child is in the sixth through the eighth grades in school. Older children, during adolescence, spend more time with one another and television viewing drops off somewhat.

Much of children's viewing time is devoted to "adult" programs. In the first grade, 40 percent of viewing time is spent in programs not intended primarily for children, and by the sixth grade this figure is nearly 80 percent. Favorite programs are "westerns" and situation comedies, with crime programs emerging as favorites by the eighth-grade level (Schramm, Lyle, and Parker, 1961).

What is the effect of this television watching? There is some evidence that children who watch a lot of television learn to rely more on stereotypes of the various groups presented by the media (Baily, 1959). Perhaps a reason for this is that the organization and presentation of characters on television is highly typified and normalized. Because there is no opportunity for interaction with the television character, one knows him only as an abstraction. To date, we have no evidence on how this affects interpersonal relations.

We know that some children may transfer what they have learned from television to real situations. Bandura and Walters have discovered that exposure to violence on television may make some children less inhibited for some time, particularly in similar situations, in their expression of violent and aggressive behavior. Not only that, but their data revealed that aggressive models are highly influential not only in reducing children's inhibitions over aggression but also in shaping the form of their behavior. Many children who observed the aggressive models displayed a great number of precisely imitative aggressive acts (Bandura and Walters, 1963). Bandura and Walters, however, are careful to point out that many factors determine whether a child will imitate a television model. These factors, some mentioned earlier, include: (1) the child's level of cognitive development; (2) the success of the model in obtaining his desired goal; (3) the reinforcement consequences of obtaining that goal for the model; (4) the reinforcement consequences for the child if he imitates the model's behavior; and (5) the degree of similarity between the situation of the model and that of the child. For example, in a home where aggressive behavior is not reinforced, the chances that a child will imitate an aggressive model are far less than if the child is in a home where he is reinforced for aggression. Further, it seems unlikely that there will be much similarity between the fantasy world of television and the real world the child encounters. Nevertheless, we cannot ignore the possible effects of television on the socialization process.

If television affects the behavior of children who watch it, what is the nature of the typifications developed from watching television? Himmelweit and her colleagues approach this question through a content analysis of a sample of television shows (Himmelweit et al., 1958). They found the values remarkably consistent from show to show. The world of television drama tends to be that of upper-middle-class urban and suburban society emphasizing the values and traditions of this class. The occupations of people of this social level are depicted as worthwhile, while manual labor is presented as uninteresting. Violence is characterized as an inevitable part of American life with good people often resorting to it. How much of this system of values "rubs off" on the young viewer? These investigators found that in some instances it affected their wishful fantasies about occupations and their beliefs concerning the factors making for personal success. It increased their attention to the cues of status. Children who viewed television were more likely to believe, for example, that "you can tell how important a man is from the way he is dressed." Again, this supports the thesis that television watching produces greater reliance on stereotypes. But more evidence is needed.

Future research should be addressed to the following areas: (1) the now outdated studies of how much time children devote to television watching and what programs they watch must be updated; (2) the effects television has on cognitive development must be explored. What is the relationship between the child's level of cognitive development and the effect television has on his behavior? Does the medium of television affect the way children think and process information? (3) the effects of television on different subcultures must be explored. If the United States, as a society, is composed of many subcultures with different language styles, meanings, perceptions, and values, is the mass media of television breaking down the boundaries of these subcultures by providing children with a common culture and speech community? These questions and many more wait to be answered.

The Peer Group

As the child enters the period of concretely operational intelligence, his egocentric language disappears and he is able to comprehend the point of view of the other and engage in cooperative activity. Thus, he enters a period in which the influence of others is extremely important to his development. The peer group is second only to the parents in socializing the child. It is probably more powerful in socialization than are teachers (Berenda, 1950). Parents and peer group seem to exert almost equal importance, by the time children are well into adolescence, in rather important life decisions such as whether or not to continue education beyond high school (James S. Coleman, 1961).

As the child acquires interaction competence he develops social typifications based on his experience with others. He learns to typify his social behavior, engage in covert role rehearsal where he projects a generalized or idealized other to which he addresses his own behavioral presentation. He learns how to react to others' reactions to his presentations as well as how to react to their presentations (see Chapters 8 and 9). The peer group is essential to this process, for it provides the developing child with a broad range of behaviors to react to as well as a variety of responses to his own behavior (Ausubel et al., 1952). The peer group supplies important confirmation-disconfirmation of self-judgments of competence and self-esteem although the foundation of these is probably more influenced by the family (Peck and Havighurst, 1960). Until about adolescence for girls and probably into adolescence for boys, the same-sex peer group is the principal arena within which the child develops his peer-influenced socialization. It is

school system, whether or not the child is prepared for advancement to the next class, has led to many serious problems. Not the least of these is the possibility of going through the public educational system, graduating from high school, and still being unable to read. At present, 24 million Americans eighteen years of age and older have never learned the basic skills of reading, writing, and arithmetic and are functionally illiterate. In addition, 8 to 12 million children now in school have such serious reading problems that they are likely to remain functionally illiterate.

It is primarily America's minorities—the blacks, Chicanos, Puerto Ricans, Asians, and "poor whites"—who constitute these statistics. The standardizing curricula fails to recognize ethnic and subcultural differences in performance, values, meanings, and life styles, thus systematically excluding minorities from equal participation within the system. Most school curricula are based on white middle-class values, skills, language, and educational goals. A study by Spady indicates that, over the last forty years, admission and graduation rates for lower strata boys, with respect to their relative chances of beginning and completing college, compared to the sons of college-educated fathers, have diminished (1967, pp. 273–286). Social class more than academic ability influences who attends and graduates from college (Sewall and Shah, 1967; J. S. Coleman and E. Q. Campbell, 1966). The process whereby miniorities and subcultural groups become excluded is complex and varied but the following trends seem to emerge and most are in one way or another related to the standardizing of education:

1 As noted, the educational system contains "gatekeepers" whose task is to track" students entering the system into programs best suited to their abilities and allowing the system to maintain its standards. The measures used to judge these abilities are based on the child's performance rather than his competence. Because these measures favor white upper-middle-class performance, ethnic and subcultural minorities may be placed at a disadvantage and therefore may do worse than their middle-class contemporaries. Thus, at a very young age, perhaps even from the beginnings of their educational career, many minority children may be unjustly labeled as "retarded," "slow learners," and "culturally disadvantaged." Often, they are placed in special classes and, as several studies have shown, receive a disastrous education because teachers expect little from them and do not try to provide motivation for achievement or even an interesting class (Rosenthal and Jacobson, 1968; Kozol, 1967; Kohl, 1967). Further, many minority children who enter regular classes must often learn not only what is taught in the class, but also performing abilities that go along with that learning, such as a middle-class vocabulary and set of typifications. Again, this places them at a disadvantage when competing with middle-class children who already have such skills.

2. A standardized curriculum assumes that all schools can provide the same quality of education so that, as children from different primary

schools come to a secondary school, they are equally well prepared. Unfortunately, this is a myth. Many ghetto schools are inferior and their students acquire inferior educations (Kozol, 1967; Holt, 1967; Kohl, 1967). Basically, this has to do with funding and resources; ghetto and rural schools do not get as much money as do the predominantly middle-class schools. The United States is perhaps the only large industrialized nation in the world in which education is not centralized and federalized. Each state—in fact, each local school district—has its own administration and rules and relies for its survival upon raising sufficient funds through local school bond issues. This has frequently led to inadequate funding of local public education and sometimes to the total elimination of public education on a local level because of inadequate funding.

3. It has also been discovered that, because the family and peer group exert a strong influence upon promoting student aspirations and support for pursuing established educational goals, many minority students do not go on to higher education. In part, this is due to the different values and perceptions placed on education; in part, it is due to the influence of the family in directing the child's career. "Gatekeepers" such as teachers and counselors are far more inclined to follow the wishes of a white middle-class parent who wants his child to take a college prep course than of a black lower-class parent who wishes the same thing (Ellis and Lane, 1963).

4. Other studies have shown that many minority students and parents are alienated from the educational decision-making centers and have been denied a meaningful role in their educational destiny (N. Kerr, 1964; Howard Becker, 1953; Moeller, 1964). Usually, for example, the state decides which textbooks are to be used at each class level in order to standardize education and to socialize the child into the expectations and dictates of existing "core values." Thus, in a black ghetto school there may be no books on black culture or history. The teacher's efforts to subvert the goal of providing white middle-class core values in order to better serve the child's educational needs can lead to reprimands and/or dismissals. Parents' attempts to remedy the situation are often rewarded only with failure and frustration.

5. In order to provide a stimulating and rewarding educational experience for many children from ethnic and minority subcultures, as well as for white middle-class children, it is necessary to have teachers who can provide and share relevant life experience. It is very difficult for a white middle-class woman to teach a young black male in the ghetto. This brings up the question: Who are the authorized persons in positions of power vis-à-vis those being socialized and what are the consequent outcomes of this structuring? Many persons without teaching credentials—for example, lay persons without the stipulated qualifications—are able both to teach and to contribute something to the educational experience that credentialed persons cannot. The diaries, autobiographies, and other verbatim accounts of prostitutes, Indian chiefs, suicides, revolutionaries, peasants, and mystics

are examples of what noncredentialed persons with special skills or experiences not usually held by credentialed persons can contribute. The revelation of these special skills and experiences is, in turn, important for a better understanding of history and the current structure of society.

For one of the above reasons, or others, the educational careers of many ethnic and subcultural minority children are cut short because of a lack of credentials which the system denies them.

One needs the proper credentials to qualify for the status of college student—usually including a high school diploma, a certain standing in one's graduating class, a special high school curriculum, and a high level of performance on college entrance exams. Just as noncredentialed persons are excluded from the status of teacher, noncredentialed students are excluded from access to advanced student status. Cicourel and Kitsuse have noted how student deficiencies in these areas work to orient the careers of high school students in such a way as to exclude them from being seen by screening personnel as college material (1962, pp. 124–135). This is not only unfortunate for the student but for society as well. Such an attitude has an adverse effect upon society's attempts to provide for a "conservation of brain power." And, what is worse, it may seriously affect one's "life chances." Consider the following figures: a study of 417 migratory workers (402 white, 15 Spanish-American) showed that 18 percent had less than four years of schooling and only 5 percent had finished high school (Manis, 1959, p. 31). In contrast to migratory workers, another study indicates that 80 percent of wealthy suburban high school pupils go to college (Conant, 1961, p. 144). These statistics take on a special importance when we relate level of education to level of income. In 1958 the distribution of average incomes for American males between the ages of 45 and 54 was as follows (Herman Miller, 1960, pp. 962–986):

Some elementary schooling	$ 3,008
Complete elementary school	4,337
Some high school	4,864
Complete high school	6,295
Some college	8,682
Complete college	12,269

A NOTE ON ADULT SOCIALIZATION

This chapter has concentrated mainly on the socialization of the child. It has done so for two reasons: (1) the study of the child's acquisition of interactional competence tells us more than how children develop into adults; it tells us also about the nature of social order by making competence problematic; and (2) the success an individual has within the social world is to some degree dependent on childhood experience and opportunities.

By middle to late adolescence most individuals have acquired adult interactional competencies. This does not mean that we stop developing. Our old typification structures keep receiving and organizing new information, providing them with constant elaboration as we have new experiences. We also become "tracked" into new jobs, social circles, and life contingencies such as marriage and a family. Each new career requires us to form new typification structures which integrate with our old ones. Yet, within the midst of all this change, there is a constant struggle to maintain congruency and stability of those core typifications that form the inner self and existential vision of the world. Activities by the individual that contribute to this stability include the following: (1) selective perception of the behavior of others and his own, guaranteeing, in part, that he does not perceive inconsistent experiences; (2) selectively interacting with persons who behave congruently toward him; (3) positively evaluating persons who have congruent behavior toward him; (4) evaluating most highly the aspects of self that he perceives as congruent with the behavior of significant others; and (5) evoking congruent responses from others through presenting himself in an appropriate manner or through casting the other in a congruent role (Secord and Backman, 1964). Through these procedures, the individual is able to maintain enough stability to produce self-esteem and to be the carrier and transmitter of his subcultural and individual typifications, providing him with a degree of existential security.

Unfortunately for some human beings, a set of social institutions exist that can destroy this existential security and the inner self and vision of the world that goes with it and resocialize a new one. Goffman has called them *total institutions,* which he defines as "a place of residence and work where a large number of like situated individuals, cut off from the wider society for an appreciable period of time, together lead an enclosed formally administered round of life" (1961a). Such places include prisons, army training camps, naval vessels, boarding schools, monasteries, mental hospitals, and old folks' homes. One major task performed by most total institutions is to either totally or partially resocialize the inmates under its control. By systematically destroying the individual's old system of typifications—including the self-concept, moral and political categories, and expectations about the world—the institution is able to tear down the old identity and build a new one. The degree of success the total institution has in reforming the typification system is dependent upon the amount of control it can exert. Often, the institution is successful in destruction of the old self, but is unable to create the intended new self. For the most part, this is due to the development of an *underlife* by the inmates. This underlife is not recognized or created by the institution, but is formed by the inmates because the "ideal-self-to-be-acquired," projected by the institution, is often highly objectionable and because everyday life in the institution provides little opportunity for security. Thus, in the case of a prison or a mental hospital, the underlife provides inmates with a source of existential security, whereby they can gain some self-esteem and stability. In the total institutions with enough control and power to prevent the formation of an underlife, the resocialization process may be complete.

One such example was recorded by Schein in his study of brainwashing techniques used by Red China during the Korean War (Schein et al., 1961). He discovered that the resocialization of typification structures underwent three distinct phases. The first phase he labeled "unfreezing." *Unfreezing* involved the total isolation and control of the individual. In this environment the normal stability-producing devices mentioned earlier are denied. There is constant condemnation and punishment for use of the old typification system. Responses to the individual's behaviors are inconsistent, contradictory, and senseless, destroying the ability to successfully employ interpretive procedures, such as the reciprocity of perspectives or the retrospective-prospective sense of occurrence. The meaningfulness of the world, the self, and social interaction is destroyed and the individual is led to the point of mental collapse. Then the second phase starts. Schein labeled this phase "changing." During this period the individual is exposed to various role models that exhibit the desired behaviors to be imitated. In the final phase, labeled "refreezing," the individual is given the opportunity to practice his new behaviors and elaborate on their typical properties. What is necessary during this period is community consensus and an intensification of peer group pressure and support for the new identity. As with most typification systems, there is evidence to suggest that the typifications acquired under "coercive persuasion" must be constantly reinforced or they will disappear. One encouraging note emerges from these studies. Of all the prisoners subjected to "brainwashing," few changed their belief systems. Man's will to freedom can transcend his dependence on the social world for the construction of meaning.

SUGGESTED READINGS

Becker, Howard S., Blanche Geer, and Everett Hughes, *Making the Grade*. New York: John Wiley, 1968.
> A participant-observer study of how students maintain their desired grade point averages while also maintaining a nonacademic life.

Brown, Roger, *Social Psychology*. New York: The Free Press, 1965.
> Contains a highly readable yet extensive review and introduction to the social psychology of language and intelligence. This book is recommended as an excellent outside source for the beginning student as well as for the professional sociologist.

Cicourel, Aaron and John Kitsuse, *The Educational Decision-Makers*. Indianapolis: Bobbs-Merrill, 1963.

An excellent account of the factors involved in deciding the direction of a student's educational career.

Douglas, Jack ed., *Understanding Everyday Life*. Chicago: Aldine, 1970.

Essays in this book provide a nice account of the theoretical position of existential and phenomenological sociology upon which much of this chapter is based. This book is, however, very difficult for the beginning student.

Goslin, David, ed., *Handbook of Socialization Theory and Research*. Chicago: Rand McNally, 1969.

Contains chapters on all the major areas of theory and research. Very much up to date. May have a bit too much detail, though, for the beginning student.

Herndon, James, *The Way It Spozed to Be*. New York: Simon & Schuster, 1968.

A lively account, using documents written by the students, of teaching and learning in a secondary school class for students of low educational attainment.

Hoffman, Martin and Lois Hoffman, eds., *Review of Child Development Research*, I, II. New York: Russell Sage Foundation, 1964.

Fine review of major studies done in such areas as language, peer groups, and the effects of mass media. Easily understood for the beginning student but contains little theory.

Kohl, Herbert, *36 Children*. New York: New American Library, 1967.

A teacher's account of his class for underprivileged children.

Kozol, Jonathan, *Death at an Early Age*. Boston: Houghton Mifflin, 1967.

Kozol's account of a slum school in Boston focuses on teacher inadequacy and the problems of racial segregation and prejudice.

CHAPTER 8

Self and Society

This chapter carries forward the analysis begun in the Introduction, starting with the question common to all sociology, How is society possible? or, How do the members of society accomplish society? Then it considers in detail two answers sociologists have given. Structural-functional analysis explains social order as the result of shared rules and other social meanings. Interactionists explain social order as the result of the social meanings that individuals construct in their everyday situations. This chapter sets forth the relation between the social situations of individual actors and the social structures of society.

Much of the chapter is concerned with development of the self. The preceding chapter was primarily involved with the effects of society, especially through the family and peers, on development of the self. This chapter goes further, considering the interdependencies of self and society, both how the society constrains the self and how the self is free to construct society.

HOW IS SOCIETY POSSIBLE?

Sociologists have long asked, "How is society possible?" (Simmel, 1910, pp. 373–391). Typically, answers to this question have taken one of two forms. Some find an explanation in structural elements of society, such as roles, rules, languages, statuses, or systems of social control. In this view, termed *structural functionalism,* society is possible because individuals internalize relevant values and prescriptions for action through the process of socialization. Having internalized these values, the individual becomes a self-regulating actor who plays out his roles in socially useful and acceptable ways. Society exists because it makes individuals act in appropriate, structured fashions. According to the structural school, whose thought will be elaborated shortly, explanations are to be sought in social elements and features external to the individual.

From another perspective, termed *symbolic interactionism,* society is made possible by the interactions between and among its members. Society is no more and no less than what its members bring to it. It becomes a cooperative concern, an ongoing moral and social order created and sustained through the interaction process in concrete situations of everyday life. This chapter reviews these two traditions and suggests points of synthesis, although it must be recognized that there exists no completely unified theory of society.

THE FUNCTIONAL PERSPECTIVE

A basic assumption of functionalism is that human behavior can be analyzed from the standpoint of larger systems. The behavior of any element within a system is determined by that system's relationship to other systems. As we saw in Chapter 3, a clear biological analogy is employed in such studies.

For Durkheim (1933, 1958), the use of the biological metaphor and unit of analysis was clear (Stone and Farberman, 1967, pp. 149–164). A function represented the correspondence between an institution and the needs of the social organism. The division of labor in society, he argued, served as principal source of cohesion needed for the society's survival. Similarly, Radcliffe-Brown later assumed there are conditions that must be met for the continued existence of any social system, just as there are necessary conditions for the biological organism to survive. Hence, these early functionalists attempted to explain a social event by examining its function within a larger system.

Durkheim's early works provided a method of implementing the functional model. His perspective took as a central hypothesis the presence of *social facts* existing over and above any individual. These facts (for example, rates of suicide) could be discerned and analyzed sociologically and without reference to the personalities of actors (individual suicides). Because the sociologist could not bring social facts under experimental control, as could the psychologist, he was forced to engage in comparative studies. Thus, communities and even entire societies were to be analyzed in terms of such dimensions as their legal systems, density of population, patterns and types of religion.

Malinowski (1945) expressed the functional model through several postulates. The first held that all societies represent a *functional unity*. The second, the postulate of *universal functionalism*, assumed that all actions within a system had to fulfill some function. By definition, the postulate of functional indispensability stated that all functions filled a function that had to be filled. In a statement anticipating formulations by Robert K. Merton (1957), Malinowski also stated that a single unit within a system could have more than one function.

Malinowski's statements, which, according to Martindale (1960, p. 458), laid the foundations of a functional theory of culture, included the following points. All humans have the need for food, reproduction, and shelter. All human drives are physiological, but they become socially restructured through culture. Man never acts alone; he organizes his activity into systems such as the family or the economy. Language is the major facilitating component of this organizing activity. Because man's basic biological needs are culturally restructured, culture imposes secondary imperatives on man, leading to an emphasis in all societies upon systems of production, distribution, and consumption (analogs to the needs of food, reproduction, and shelter). In the end, the basic unit of analysis becomes these institutions or systems which translate man's biological needs into patterns of social conduct. Malinowski produced a tightly knit scheme which, while focusing attention on man's basic biological needs, placed social explanations in cultural and social systems, all external to the individual.

Malinowski's version of functionalism, emphasizing the integrative features of social systems, resembles recent statements by Talcott Parsons (1968a, 1968b). Perhaps more than any contemporary theorist, Parsons has given the greatest attention to our opening question (see also Blumer, 1969). To Parsons, society is possible because it is capable of transcending the lives of its members. By socializing and recruiting its members in special ways, society is able to meet its functional prerequisites; it becomes a self-contained system operating beyond the lives and activities of any of its members or subsystems.

Because the focus of this chapter is on the relationship between self and society, it is important to review Parsons' view of what he calls the *personality system* and the *social system*. The basic analytic category for Parsons is the social system, in which the cultural, personality, and behavioral systems are integrated. The personality system represents the interconnections of the actor's various activities into an organization of needs and dispositions. The minimal social system (the social relationship) becomes the intersection of two personality systems, in which the actors are taking account of one another. This is based on mutual need gratification and the complementarity of expectations and rewards; each actor meets needs of the other.

The basic question now reappears as: "How does the social system transform behavioral and personality systems into the larger network of interpenetrating systems?" It does so through the process of socialization, which for Parsons is displayed in a complex learning process. Socialization (Parsons, 1968a) proceeds by differentiation. Beginning with the smallest dyadic structure, the mother and the infant, socializing agents become progressively more complex and specialized in their demands and expectations. The nuclear family, the school, and peer groupings in turn layer new socialization demands so that a process of upgrading may be observed. The child is expected to learn and allowed to perform new roles in groupings that formerly excluded him. The child's *identity* represents the progressively differentiated meanings of self that he acquires through social interaction at each stage of socialization. For Parsons, identity is the most developed and stable aspect of personality, and it represents an individual's normative links with society.

The functionalists make the following link between self and society: the self, as such, hides behind roles, personality need dispositions, expectations of others, and even one's own identity. The self is an irrelevant concept in the functionalist scheme, because it is obscured by these other factors.

Each of the functionalists offered a general or formal theory of self and society in addition to a theory of society and its operations. Yet their schemes suffer from two basic problems. First, they rest on concepts lacking clear real-world referents, making it difficult to subject their formulations to tests. Second, they employ the concepts of *need* or *drive*, which are rejected by growing numbers of scientists. The *oversocialized view of man* presented in the functional scheme leaves the self ever removed from social experience (Wrong, 1961, pp. 184–193), so that free human action appears to be a mere delusion.

SOCIAL MEANINGS: THE PERSPECTIVE OF MAX WEBER

To Max Weber (1947), the central data of sociology were social meanings, not social facts such as Durkheim stressed (see also Insert No. 11). An acceptable causal hypothesis for Weber existed only after the sociological observer interpreted a line of action from the perspective of the meanings to individuals he was studying. His basic point of analysis was social action, not the system. But Weber was not interested in action *per se*. His concern was with recurrent patterns of interaction, those situations in which individuals came together for the purpose of accomplishing a joint task. The key concept here was the *social relationship,* which referred to any joint action where a "plurality of actors took each other into account where the probability of future interaction was high" (Weber, 1947, p. 118). When relationships became stabilized over time, so that one or more participants felt a legitimate order, the grounds for *corporate group* conduct were created. The key feature of corporate groups was the belief that uniform action could be upheld by vested authority. In their most developed forms, corporate groups could be described as large-scale bureaucracies, within which were fixed rules of entry and exit. The modern university is a case in point. Specific territories, often legally controlled, would be observed. A hierarchy of control and authority would be recognized, and people would have careers within these structures. Division of labor and stable patterns of recruitment would be created.

People were linked to corporate groups, bureaucracies, and social relationships through their *interactive roles* or *vocations.* Individuals in Weber's scheme developed their own, often highly personal, definitions of their positions within these interactional structures, basing them on past experiences with other persons. Change in the organization relied on the fact that the fit between individuals and social organization was never straightforward. When behavior became stabilized, concomitant stabilization in power and authority would be observed.

All recurrent interactions rested, in Weber's scheme, on legitimations of power. *Legitimation* could be achieved by one of three forms: rationality, charisma, or tradition. Change is created in those situations where conflict surrounds the mode of legitimation. Since every individual tends to define his relationships to others in slightly different ways, change is a constant feature of social life.

Weber's scheme offers two essential features for an understanding of self and society. First, his recognition that social action could take several forms suggests that most theories of motivation are inadequate because they deal with only one kind of motive. Action can be justified on many different grounds, and to understand this the observer must enter his subject's world. Weber's model demands such entrance. Second, his model recognizes change and negotiation as central features of everyday life. Nonetheless, Weber fails to discuss the self in any precise terms, so we must turn to several others—Simmel, Cooley, and Mead—for a more elaborate theory of the relationship between self and society.

GROUP AFFILIATION: THE PERSPECTIVE OF GEORG SIMMEL

Georg Simmel contributed three essential features to an interactionist conception of society (see also Insert No. 13; for references, see Coser, ed., 1965; Kurt Wolff, ed., 1950, 1959; Spykman, 1966).

First, he offered the most succinct view of *formal sociology* as a method and goal of the discipline. The task of sociology, he argued, was to uncover the myriad patterns of affiliation and interaction that brought and held a society and its members together. Simmel's position forces the analyst to compare dissimilar social forms and to uncover the similarities in these forms (theater audiences and labor movements, art and political history, churches and social groups).

Second, he held that society was no more and no less than the interactions among its members. Society was conceived in terms of overlapping and concentric social circles. Each individual, each self, was unique for Simmel, a point later stressed by Mead. The individual viewed the world from the perspectives offered by his social relationships; one person's patterns of group affiliations would never be duplicated by another. Though several people might belong to the same groups, they were likely to view those groups (and themselves) differently because they held a different orientation toward them.

Each individual enters society through a web of circumstances and relationships that are initially undifferentiated. The self develops only out of interaction. The individual becomes more differentiated as he becomes involved in more and larger circles of interaction. This resembles Parsons' theory of socialization, but Simmel recognized more the possibility of conflict it implied. He noted the cardinal feature of modern society: Every individual is a member of multiple groups, relationships, and social circles. These affiliations may be in conflict, but this fact alone gives the individual multiple perspectives on life. The self develops from such perspectives and conflicts. As the person leaves his primary groups and enters the secondary affiliations of the occupational, political, and educational worlds, he begins to lose the security and intimacy of the primary group. With this loss of security comes a sense of ambiguity, even though the individual acquires greater freedom to become what he wants. Although external and internal conflicts can arise during this transition, which takes a lifetime, the personality can be strengthened; the confrontation of conflict can have positive functions for the self. Individuals tend to order their group affiliations, placing some above others in priority and importance, so that the self finds its place in these groups and their ordering (Kuhn and McPartland, 1954, pp. 68–76).

Third, Simmel observed that the individual tends to form and play out his relationships to society within his own small worlds of social interaction. There was no such thing as *a society* for Simmel; there were only social circles and social relationships. Furthermore, in their unserious moments, individuals reconstruct the troublesome features of their daily affiliations with the outside world (Theodore Mills, 1965, pp. 157–170). In times of stress and crisis, play would overcome the serious pursuit of daily affairs. Thus cocktail parties, trips to the beach, theater, or conventions all revealed problematic elements of more serious daily life.

Simmel's emphasis was on what people do when they associate with each other. His scheme was grounded in these observations; yet he too did not satisfactorily structure the nature of the self and its various relationships with society. If a single flaw runs through the statements of Weber and Simmel, it is a failure to indicate clearly the nature of the symbolic and psychological relationships between the individual and society. Although both theorists emphasized the interactional quality of social life, neither elaborated the processes producing this phenomenon.

THE GENESIS OF THE SELF

Cooley and Mead established the important point that society and the individual were two aspects of the same process. Society existed for Cooley in the self and its conversations with others, imagined and real. Cooley opened the way for the first systematic study of self and society. The self arose out of the socialization process within primary groups, characterized by intimate personal interactions. The individual felt a sense of solidarity and "we-ness" with these groups, which were *primary* in the sense that they gave the individual his earliest and most complete experiences in the social order. Here the self was formed and shaped—as were ideals, standards, and norms—leaving the individual with a permanent sense of self. These groups, in the words of Manford Kuhn (1964, pp. 5–21), constituted the individual's *orientational others*, to whom he was fully committed emotionally and psychologically. These others gave him his general vocabulary, his basic concepts and categories. He was in most constant interaction with them and, in problematic situations, he relied on their perspectives. In short, these primary others gave the self-conception its basic shape and content. These orientational or primary others change during the life cycle; they are likely to be one's parents in early childhood and spouses or friends in mid-adulthood.

The self, for Cooley and Mead, arose out of communication (Cooley, 1908, pp. 337–357; George Mead, 1934). Without language, no self will develop. The human organism was unique because it possessed the ability to manipulate symbols in a self-conscious fashion. The self developed in linguistic phases grounded in the child's ability to make self-references. Unless a child could distinguish itself from other objects, no self would appear. As Bain (1936, pp. 767–775) and others have since shown, by the age of two the child has acquired a sufficient vocabulary to make self-designations (Denzin, 1970c, 1970d, 1971).

Cooley's conception of the self stressed three processes: the presentation of a self, the interpretation of the other's reaction to that presentation, and an emotional response to that interpretation. The self arose out of the interaction process; it represented both a structure and a process. The self was neither a stable set of attitudes nor an ephemeral interactional production.

For Mead (1934), the self developed through a single three-step process: the play, the game, and the generalized-other phases. Each phase was characterized by the child's increased ability to become an object of his own conduct. The self emerged as a well-developed object only after the individual could view his own behavior from the perspective of multiple others.

A basic feature of Mead's, and later Blumer's (1969), perspective is emphasis on the terms interaction and self. Human behavior cannot be catalogued under such terms as need, drive, impulse, cultural demand, or role prescription. Man acts only in terms of the things he perceives and of which he takes account. Interactions between self and other represent the central data of sociology. Mead's perspective forces investigators to recognize that human activity is an emergent affair. Here lies the profound meaning of the term *interaction*: behavior cannot be reduced to the constituent lines of action of isolated individuals because it consists of the reciprocal, shaping impact of individuals upon one another. The *joint action* (Blumer, 1966, pp. 535–544), the joining of two lines of action into an interactional sequence, represents the basic fact of human group life. Society exists because human beings possess the ability to take one another's roles and to self-consciously direct their conduct on the basis of these interpretations. The *self* becomes both an object and a process in this framework. On occasions best seen during ritual encounters, such as games, the individual treats his own self as he would other objects in the environment. But on the important occasions the self is a process; it is a continuous series of declarations and indications made to others.

In the Mead-Blumer scheme, self and society are linked in a way no other interactionist has achieved. Social structure emerges out of the interaction process and becomes, in Mead's model, stable ways of thinking and acting toward a common body of objects. Language, object, joint action, and self are the major conceptual tools of this perspective.

There is no need for detailed discussion of the methodology implied in this scheme (Blumer, 1969, pp. 1–60; Denzin, 1970b). It calls for a direct confrontation of the empirical world by the investigator. He must enter the spheres of interaction held by his subjects, take their roles, learn their languages, and fit their perspectives to the social order; he must become a participant-observer (see Chapter 4). He must ground his theories in these experiences; a theory which fails to grasp the interactional quality of human life ends by explaining nothing.

With Mead and Blumer, the ground is laid for the systematic development of a theory of self and society. The processes by which selves develop, change, and take on others' views are given. The structural features of society are placed in perspective; they are objects created by human beings relevant only to the extent that human beings take them into account.

Note a curious parallel between the functional and the interactional models. Both assume a social order that precedes the life of any individual.

But the conception of this order sets the two perspectives far apart. For Parsons, human beings are made to fit into that order by the socialization process. If socialization is successful, little change in society is observed; the roles are perfectly played. For Mead and Blumer, every generation—indeed, every self—possesses the ability to remake its society. The individual is free to create society (Strauss, 1959). Continuity over time arises only out of consensus, and society emerges as a continuous production of interacting selves consensually taking one another into account.

SELVES AND SOCIETY: ASPECTS OF THE CONSTRUCTION OF SOCIAL REALITY

Social reality does not exist until it is conceptualized. The bare requirements are two: first, human beings possess the ability to self-consciously manipulate symbols, and there are symbols or languages that can be learned, modified, and taken into the self; second, the human being is able to take the role or position of his own activity; he can ponder his own thoughts and conduct and make them objects to act on and toward.

Social reality comes into existence because men can take their own roles, as well as those of others. In taking the other's perspective, they shape their own images of self. Thus, the link between self and society is lodged in the "self and other taking process" that requires only language and self-conscious activity.

The Interaction Process

First, the interaction process is always situated by time and place. (Even when a person imagines the perspective of another person, he does so within a specified temporal and situational locale.) Second, interaction is *joint*, representing more than the sum of individual lines of action. It is often an emergent and reciprocal event. When two persons walk into a room, the behavior that follows can not be attributed solely to the thoughts and intentions they bring with them. In the process of judging the character of another's activity, each individual is forced to reevaluate his own intentions. Each gesture and utterance of the other calls forth reactions that could not have been completely anticipated before the interaction began. Third, interaction is partially rule-directed (see Chapter 20). Certain standards and properties are recognized and taken account of by interacting selves. Often followed because of ritual or custom, these rules give a partially predictable shape to the interaction process.

We may distinguish three categories of such rules (Denzin, 1970d).

First are the *rules of etiquette*, or civil propriety, which exist primarily to protect the ceremonious occasions of interaction (Goffman, 1961b). They include such prescriptions as how to introduce oneself to a stranger, what clothes to wear to the theater, how to request food at dinner, how to take leave of a host after a sociable gathering. In part, as the term implies, they exist to keep selves civil and apart from one another, and their use protects interactants from embarrassment.

Second are *civil-legal rules* that function to protect objects and their owners. Upheld by courts of law or professional bodies, these rules find their way into books of ethics and law, unlike the etiquette rules which are in books of manners and polite conduct. Civil-legal rules include curfew laws and proscriptions regarding violence to people.

Third are those rules, here called *relational*, which express the distinctly personal elements of recurrent interactions. Seldom if ever written down or codified, these rules govern how selves are to interact within the tightly drawn moral orders of the relationship and the social group. Relational rules redefine and frequently make irrelevant civil-legal and polite interactional standards. Examples can be found in organizations that sanction white-collar crime, or within juvenile gangs that make a theft a way of life. In short, wherever recurrent interactions are observed, relational rules will be found.

Relational rules cover such matters as how selves are defined and presented, how knowledge is controlled and given off, how work is accomplished, how emotion and affect are displayed, and how one is to act when not with his relational partners. Such rules are neither personally nor situationally abstract. They have relevance only within specific relationships and specific situations. The difference in conduct of husband and wife when alone and when in the presence of outsiders illustrates this feature of the relational rule. In the development and application of these rules, society is made real within the relationship. Even though general societal norms or laws may be violated, they are replaced with another set of standards that permit orderly and permissible public conduct (Denzin, forthcoming).

Forms of Joint Action: Encounters and Social Relationships

It is possible to distinguish several forms of joint action, each varying in terms of the dominant rules governing conduct. Other variables of joint action include situational locations, length of time spent, and the nature of the involvement and commitment displayed by members. In a very general sense, the sum of the joint actions within a society at any moment represents what that society is to its members. For present purposes, only two forms will be discussed.

First are *encounters* (Goffman, 1961b), consisting of any action sequence that arises because of the presence of people. Cognitive, visual, and physical alignment of behavior will be observed, as in a social game or in the crowding of people into an elevator. Encounters are of several types. Some remain *unfocused,* such as those in elevators or at street corners. Some are *focused,* in which the basic features of coordinated action are displayed for a specific length of time, such as dinner parties or clerk-customer interactions. Some are *multifocused,* with simultaneous interactions. Smoking a cigarette and driving an auto while conversing with a passenger and talking on the telephone while gesturing to another person in the room are examples.

Each form of encounter rests predominantly on polite interactional rules. Each has demands peculiar to it, including how the eyes are employed, how one takes leave of the others, and what language one uses. The basic feature of all three types is that they have no life beyond the period of interaction. They are ephemeral sequences, the effects of which are usually minimal. They do not fill up the significant moments in anyone's lifetime. That society provides the setting for such encounters in no way suggests that they represent all of what society is for its members.

In a fourth type of encounter, *encounters of significance,* something important to the self happens. Often grounded initially in civil-legal or polite interactional rules, these encounters lay the foundation for subsequent interactions. Police-juvenile encounters, witnessing a birth, participating in a marriage, taking an exam, or being interviewed for a job are all encounters of potential significance.

The defining feature of these interactions is the ability of participants to carry away from the episode some sense of what has transpired and some sense of their fellow participants. If reconstructions of the event cannot be called forth after a length of time, an encounter of significance has not occurred.

These episodes present the possibility that important and valued aspects of the self will have been translated into the memories of each interactant. Encounters of significance produce, or make way for, the process of *self-lodging,* translation of the self into the interaction process. The individual successfully establishes and communicates who he is with respect to the encounter, and this communication has an effect on others. They are able to carry away images of him and he, in turn, carries away images of them. As a consequence, the encounter begins to take on a life of its own; its effects transcend the immediate episode.

In this way, a structure to the everyday round of activity begins to appear. Individuals seek out settings where the self has been lodged or where there is a high probability that such an event will occur, developing the second major form of joint action, *social relationships.* A relationship exists between two or more persons when they engage in recurrent forms of symbolic interaction. Each takes the role of the other and converses with that person, even when out of his immediate presence. The other comes to exist in imaginings of him. In this way, Cooley's dictum is realized: Society as we know it does exist in our imagination.

Human beings can become involved in two basic types of relationships, with absent others or present others. In the case of an absent other, recurrent symbolic interactions, "interior conversations," occur between the self and an other who is not physically present. Conversations with "higher beings," deceased spouses, symbolic heroes, or distant friends involve such relationships. Such interactions constitute a large part of some humans' daily activity. When the other is physically present—as in marital, work, and sociable relationships—the views of the other come out of daily confrontations with him. He is there to converse, argue, and present his side of the picture. Society exists in both kinds of these relationships. This is the world as the individual knows it.

Relationships may also be distinguished by their temporal and spatial dimensions, as well as by the degree of involvement and commitment displayed by each participant. Thus, there are *situationally specific relationships,* as in customer-clerk, employer-employee, and teacher-pupil transactions. Others are short-term, as between co-passengers on an airplane, members of a class, or participants in a small group experiment. The relationships forming the primary substance of society are intimate, long lasting, and situationally irrelevant. I call these *relationships of substance.* They are seen in marriages, long-standing friendships, and work relationships of several years.

Relationships provide the setting for relational rules of conduct. When two or more persons construct their own relationship, they do so with specific rules on the nature of their selves, how they will display affection, how they will accomplish work, how they will give off knowledge to outsiders, and how they will act when out of one another's presence. Thus, relationships are morally bounded units of interaction.

The Construction of Relationships of Substance: Lindesmith and Becker

A number of models have been offered to explain the creation of relationships (see Chambliss, 1965, pp. 370–380; and Litwak and Szeleny, 1969, pp. 465–481, for reviews). Alternatively stressing such factors as the complementarity of needs, propinquity, agreement on fundamental issues, fulfillment of self-gratification, or reciprocation of rewards, these formulations have failed to offer any systematic explanation of how and why relationships are created. While Chambliss (1965, pp. 370–380) has offered a formulation that stresses the perceived effectiveness of interactive sequences, his model fails to account adequately for links between the self and its choice of others. Nor does he discuss relationships with absent others.

The following perspective borrows in substance from the research of Lindesmith (1947, 1968) and Howard Becker (1953, pp. 235–242; 1955, pp. 35–44) on drug use, which suggests that a chain of events has to be followed if a person is to become an opiate addict or a marihuana user. An individual has to learn how to act toward the drug, to define experiences with the drug as pleasurable, how to create such experiences, and to define the absence of those experiences as negative. A person *becomes* a user through the process of *being* a user. The individual must actively construct his self around drug objects and learn new meanings for both his self and the drug. No single event—such as exposure to the drug, definitions of the experience in favorable terms, or rewarding reactions from significant others—will produce addiction or habituation. A series of necessary conditions produce the final outcome. The same conclusion must be reached regarding the creation of friendships and enduring social relationships. No single event will produce a relationship of substance.

These remarks anticipate the necessary conditions for understanding social relationships. Self-conscious selves must be present, encounters of significance must be produced, and self-lodging must occur. Clearly, however, these three conditions alone will not produce relationships. Persons have many encounters of significance that do not end in relationships. Imagined thoughts of a symbolic leader, moments of infatuation with members of the opposite sex, and praise from a respected other are examples. In each of these situations the self is shaped, but only for a moment or a few days. The other person seldom reciprocates in such a way that an enduring face-to-face relationship is created

The question focuses on the *reciprocated relationship of substance*, but we must note a final point before presenting the chain of necessary events. Individuals develop and employ a vocabulary of meanings and evaluations leading them to designate certain categories of persons as potentially acceptable or unacceptable relational partners. Commonly linked to location in the age-sex-educational-occupational structures of society, these vocabularies vary by current relational statuses as well. Married men face written and unwritten sanctions for violating the contract of marriage. Ph.D.'s may look down on those who are not as well educated. Drug users look askance at nonusers. These *rules of acceptance* describe an important aspect of human behavior. At any moment, any individual judges himself open to a very small set of others. Paradoxically, the choice of marrying, making love to, or forming an occupational contract with one person never excludes the possibility that another individual would have fit the perceived requirements for the relationship. I am not suggesting that human interactions can repeatedly be achieved with interchangeable sets of individuals. After self-lodging and encounters of significance, a change of relationships becomes impossible—at least, for many people. This is the existential question: How does a man select a finite set of others in terms of which he may live his life?

An enduring, reciprocated relationship of substance will not develop unless the following conditions are present. First, the individual must come in contact with another who fits his present rules of acceptance. Both people must be open for interaction and willing to communicate important features of their selves. Second, these conditions must produce a situation of self-lodging; unless self-lodging occurs, future interactions are unlikely. Each, then, must carry away images of the other from the encounter which are couched in favorable and acceptable terms. The individuals must see themselves as persons who can have a relationship, which demands a consideration of such essentials as time and situations for interaction. Further, if each person is already located in a relational network, the imagined reactions of other persons to the new relationship have to be judged. Each must be willing and able to set aside time for future meetings. A series of interior conversations with and about the other must occur. The individual must see, finally, that the experience with the other in question is unique; so unique, pleasurable, and acceptable that future interactions with him (or her) are necessary for that perceived experienced to be recreated. Similar thoughts, reactions, and definitions must evolve for both parties; if not, it is a one-sided relationship.

If this chain of events occurs, there are grounds for a reciprocated relationship of substance. New selves and a new relational order are created. Rules specific to each self come into being, and the relationship now begins to exist beyond the specific interactions of either party. It comes to live in their imaginations and is recreated every time they meet. It is important to note that these formulations describe intimate relationships. Although I am convinced that similar processes operate in the construction of more fleeting relationships, such as casual friendships, further treatment of variations is not necessary here.

Social Relationships: A Summary

Stated in summary, the formulation predicts the following relationships:

1. Encounters of significance will be produced only between interacting selves who fit one another's rules of acceptance.

2. Self-lodging will occur only when interacting selves emerge from encounters of significance with favorable definitions of one another and see each other as unique.

3. Future encounters will be planned only if both parties define their previous interactions in favorable terms and judge that these experiences can be created only with the other individual.

4. Future encounters must be timed and arranged, and favorable definitions and expanded self-lodging must continue.

5. A reciprocated relationship of substance will evolve if these conditions have been met.

Systematic consideration of this model awaits further research, which must be conducted at each point in the chain, preferably longitudinally with the same set of individuals. Several strategic points of research can be noted. One valuable source of data would be the study of individuals who have been taken out of permanent relationships, as in such groups as Alcoholics Anonymous and Parents Alone. In the latter group, marital partners have dissolved their relationship and are left with the remnants of their previous experiences. In their efforts to make a new life, they are forced to reevaluate their previous selves and their long-taken-for-granted rules of interaction; they must decide whether a new person can be found to fill the gap left by the previous "implicated other." There are few studies of such groups (for a partial exception see Weiss, 1969, pp. 36–43).

Social Relationships: Interaction and Social Structure

Social relationships constitute tightly drawn moral orders. Unique conceptions of self and other exist within them, and these conceptions are continually changing (Gregory Stone, 1962, pp. 86–118). Relationships are *negotiated orders*; they are created and maintained in a shifting but orderly process (see Strauss, Schatzman, Bucher, Ehrlich, Sabshin, 1963, pp. 147–169; 1964, pp. 292–315; and Glaser and Strauss, 1968, pp. 239–242, for comments on the negotiated features of organizational life). The rules of interaction, the definitions given selves, the social objects, and the conceptions of the relationship undergo continual change.

It is now possible to show how social structure emerges out of interaction, a point made long ago by Wirth (1939, pp. 965–979) and more recently elaborated by Strauss and associates (1968). Wirth's argument was straightforward and has furnished the underlying thesis for this chapter. Social structure, of whatever form, is created by individuals constructing ongoing lines of action into meaningful and regularized patterns. Social organization—and society, more generally—exists whenever a number of persons enter into reciprocal relations with one another. Thus, the focus of sociology becomes the examination of interpersonal conduct, social relationships, and patterns of interaction. Znaniecki (1939, pp. 799–811) spelled this out in his conceptualization of the social group, which he saw as a system of interconnecting relationships experienced by interacting individuals. Those who participate in groups bring part of themselves into the emergent group structure, and the group becomes their product. Each person lends a portion of himself to the situation, and each member shapes the actions and thoughts of every other member. The structure produced exists only so long as the participating individuals take it, and one another, into account. Group life is negotiated because the basis of coordinated action is continually shifting. New situations and the entry of new members produce changes in the underlying order of the group. New meanings have to be forged and old definitions reworked so that ongoing and coordinated action can persist.

Group life takes on moral overtones. Durkheim stressed that human beings become sacred and valued objects to one another. As a result, special rules are built up to honor and protect this moral object called the self. Relational rules, in part, reflect this moral aspect of human group life. Selves are accorded very special statuses and can be approached only in certain ways (Goffman, 1956, pp. 473–502).

Because relationships and groups become regularized moral orders, each individual has a *moral career* through his social circles. The self is continually changing in conception, emphasis, and organization as the person progresses from group to group, relationship to relationship, or even as he moves through single relationships. Changes in the self are fundamental alterations in the nature of the individual and in his moral values. To be married seven years is to make the self different from what it was after one year of marriage; a different set of meanings and definitions characterize the self at each point in its many moral careers. The individual is never the same; each experience can change his conception of who he is (Strauss, 1959, p. 92).

As Simmel noted, every individual simultaneously plays out many careers. In any modern society, a fundamental problem for every person is to organize his many moral careers into some orderly pattern. Every interaction sequence requires the fitting of diverse careers and conceptions of self into a coordinated whole. A problematic feature of everyday life, reflected in the term *mixed awareness context,* emerges every time people come together (Glaser and Strauss, 1964, pp. 669–679). An awareness context is what each individual knows about another in an interactional situation. The task of each interactant—at least, in early encounters with strangers—is to sort out conceptions and definitions appropriate to the behavior at hand. Because every person enters every situation with a different moral career, the negotiation of meaning is always problematic.

This problematic feature of encounters with strangers tends to lead every individual to search out, help create, and become a part of stable patterns of interaction.

Freedom and Constraint: The Existential Problem

Individual relationships, groups, and organizations present special problems for their members. Although a sense of satisfaction may be achieved once one becomes a member of a stable moral order, often a tension emerges that finds its locus in the very order of everyday life for which all persons search. Group life is characterized by recurrent tensions between predictability and change. The very structures that the individual creates, best seen in his intimate relationships, can rise up to destroy the individuality he seeks. Marriage, for example, affords regular sexual outlet, predictable meals, comfortable situations, and a close associate for interaction. Yet stabilizing these aspects of life, choosing to live inside certain moral orders, by definition and commitment, excludes other experiences. To commit one's self to a relationship means to live in terms of the demands and rules one has created with his relational partner.

The existential problem is twofold. On the one hand, the individual has to select and make his moral orders and, on the other, he must learn to play by the rules he has fundamentally helped to shape.

The first problem is confounded, at least in our society, by the fact that, initially, all moral orders and all individuals are not different. Their uniqueness emerges only after we enter into relationships. This feature gives the human condition an unavoidable political complexion: the choice of a moral order or a significant other is a political decision. It involves the commitment of resources, time, and selves to one enterprise and not another.

All of us, then, create our own fate; we determine who we are and who we are going to become. This places a large burden on every self. Necessarily a moral object, each self carries the burden of past experience upon his shoulders. Much as Conrad's *Lord Jim* and Hesse's *Demian*, each individual must continually confront the fact that he is what he has made himself.

This feature of everyday life produces the continual attempts of men to break out of their interactional routines. Moments of unserious activity are regularly scheduled to permit the loss of self. Dinner parties, trips to the beach and the bar and the fancy restaurant, the use of intoxicants and stimulants, all represent these moments. In these fleeting episodes, the self becomes what the situation permits: the individual drops the cares of the day and relaxes. These actions serve two functions. First, the predictable features of everyday life are removed as change and unpredictability rein; relaxed, the self now confronts the world of responsibility with renewed vigor. Second, these moments of unseriousness furnish the basis for new experience within the stable structure of everyday life. New selves can be tried out, new objects can be brought in, and old selves can be reevaluated. Once again, the emergent quality of group life appears.

The Self and Socialization

Beginning with the question of how society is possible, I have discussed how society emerges out of the interactions of its members. Society in the singular was replaced with the proposition that many little societies or moral orders make up what society is for its members. Individuals create and play out their social lives within relationships and groups. The structures of relations must be constructed by individuals through their interactions in everyday situations.

I have presented a *perspective* on self and society, a way of examining the problem. It is basically a humanistic conception of the social enterprise which stresses the individual's role in determining his own fate.

An important unanswered question in this view of self and society is how socialization is organized and routinized within the social structure. Too little is known about this process. The study of how selves are created and changed, at every point in the age cycle, is one of the most crucial questions confronting sociology.

SUGGESTED READINGS

Cooley, Charles Horton, *Human Nature and the Social Order*. New York: Charles Scribner's Sons, 1922.
> A theoretical statement by one of the major symbolic interactionists of the early twentieth century.

Coser, Lewis, ed., *Georg Simmel*. Englewood Cliffs, N.J.: Prentice-Hall, 1965.
> This contemporary collection of essays concerning the thought of Georg Simmel focuses on his theory of social conflict and of the nature of social action.

Denzin, Norman K., *Intimate Interactions: Aspects of the Moral Order*. Chicago: Aldine, forthcoming.
> Denzin analyzes intimate interaction as an aspect of society's moral order.

Goffman, Erving, *Encounters: Two Studies in the Sociology of Interaction*. Indianapolis: Bobbs-Merrill, 1961.
> Goffman analyzes encounters between individuals in both focused and unfocused contexts, using the dramaturgical perspective. A highly readable and thought-provoking book.

Lyman, Stanford M. and Marvin Scott, *A Sociology of the Absurd*. New York: Appleton-Century-Crofts, 1970.
> The sociology of the absurd is a new theoretical approach to sociology, emphasizing phenomenology and existentialism and rejecting functionalist thought. A penetrating and lively presentation.

Malinowski, Bronislaw, *Coral Gardens and Their Magic*. New York: American Books, 1935.
> As early presentation of anthropological functionalism, Malinowski's works had considerable influence on later anthropology and sociology.

Radcliffe-Brown, A. R., *Structure and Function in Primitive Society*. New York: Free Press, 1952.
> Along with Malinowski, the work of Radcliffe-Brown was seminal in the development of structural-functional theory in the social sciences.

CHAPTER 9

The Sociology of Everyday Life

This chapter begins with the argument that sociology must analyze the social meanings constructed by the members of society through their everyday interactions. Then, in a systematic analysis of the works of Erving Goffman, it shows how the self-presentation of individuals in everyday life is central to understanding interaction processes.

Situations, especially encounters, are basic to this analysis. Individuals make use of many ideas about situations, such as "front and back regions," to try to construct their self-images effectively. By building one self-image rather than another, they try to control how other individuals will act toward them. Consequently, self-presentation, the construction of self-images, is basic to all social interaction.

The dramaturgical approach sees human reality as symbolic and meaningful; and this chapter draws some inferences from this approach for our understanding of man and society.

In the next chapter we examine research methods used to determine social meanings and social actions. The interactionist and dramaturgical perspective developed in Chapters 8 and 9 will be used to deal with other subjects throughout this book, such as in our consideration of political strategies in Chapter 13.

Everyday life means to the sociologist just what it sounds like to you—the common, ordinary activities in which people routinely engage. As man goes about his daily life, ordinarily, he does not question the fundamental order or structure of his world. The fundamental aspects of his life are the "givens," the unquestionables of everyday life, within which he lives and from which he constructs his social reality. Usually, he accepts the form and content of interaction as something to be taken for granted, as self-evident because "life is like that," "bosses are like that," "women are like that," "the rich are like that," "Blacks are like that" (see Chapter 4).

If the sociologist is to understand the fundamentals of human interaction, he must question those fundamentals, taking them apart (*reducing* them) and putting them together again in some analytical form that he can examine and communicate to others so that they too will develop a broader understanding of concepts they have accepted almost unquestioningly (Ichheiser, 1970). This is where the sociology of everyday life comes in. It is an attempt to understand man's routine, ordinary, everyday interaction, his common ways of living and dealing with others. We shall summarize the analysis of the foremost contemporary sociologist of everyday life, Erving Goffman, especially his major book, *The Presentation of Self in Everyday Life*. In doing so, we also present applications of his thought made by other sociologists.

IMPRESSION MANAGEMENT

Goffman analyzes what he calls "the art of *impression management*," the techniques that people use to control the impressions others receive. The model he utilizes is the *dramaturgical* model, the model of the theater. Using this model, Goffman analyzes the ways an individual in ordinary situations "presents himself and his activity to others, the ways in which he guides and controls the impression they form of him, and the kinds of things he may and may not do while sustaining his performance before them" (Goffman, 1959, p. xi). This dramaturgical model presents a coherent framework for viewing everyday life, providing the reader with a different perspective on his everyday world.

When someone comes into the presence of another person, he tries to gather information about the other because this personal data helps him know what to expect of the interaction. Information about the other's attitudes, social class, occupation, background, and mood serves as a guide for action. This information is gathered from the other individual's conduct, his appearance, the social setting, and what the individual says about himself. By means of these *sign-vehicles* that communicate information to others, the observer presumes to know what the other is like.

In this dramaturgical analysis of impression management, life is an "information game." We all try to become expert players of this game; by means of skillful impression management, we try to control others' impressions of us. The basic premise in this analysis is that we dexterously manipulate a whole system of sign-vehicles, using such factors as clothing, manners, the way we speak, whom we're seen with, as well as what we allow or do not allow others to see us do, in order to make others' ideas of us compatible with our image of ourselves (our *self-concept*).

Take the following example of Preedy, the vacationing Englishman:

> But in any case he took care to avoid catching anyone's eye. First of all, he had to make it clear to those potential companions of his holiday that they were of no concern to him whatsoever. He stared through them, round them, over them—eyes lost in space. The beach might have been empty. If by chance a ball was thrown his way, he looked surprised; then let a smile of amusement lighten his face (Kindly Preedy), looked round dazed to see that there *were* people on the beach, tossed it back with a smile to himself and not a smile *at* the people, and then resumed carelessly his nonchalant survey of space.
>
> But it was time to institute a little parade, the parade of the Ideal Preedy. By devious handlings he gave any who wanted to look a chance to see the title of his book—a Spanish translation of Homer, classic thus, but not daring, cosmopolitan too—and then gathered together his beach-wrap and bag into a neat sand-resistant pile (Methodical and Sensible Preedy), rose slowly to stretch at ease his huge frame (Big-Cat Preedy), and tossed aside his sandals (Carefree Preedy, after all) (Sansom, 1956).

In this dramaturgical approach to understanding everyday life, it is assumed that the individual expresses himself in a way designed to impress others around him. There are two kinds of expressions: *expressions given*, sign-vehicles used purposely in order to convey certain information to others, and *expressions given off*, information communicated unintentionally (Goffman, 1959, pp. 1–2). Because people know that an individual is likely to present himself in a favorable light and that he will manipulate symbols to do so, they may frequently use the expressions he gives off as a check upon what he is communicating about himself. "Expressions given" are presumed to be under the control of the individual, while "expressions given off" are relatively spontaneous expressive behaviors that are less controllable.

At the same time that we are trying to manage others' impressions of us, we are well aware that others are trying to control our impression of them. We know that others are also well versed in the art of impression management, and we know how to read or interpret the sign-vehicles by which they are communicating information to us. Because we know that they are attempting to manage our information about them, we do not accept everything at face value but try to interpret the meaning of their "sign activity." We assume there is some "real" meaning behind the signs they are communicating. "Managed news" is, according to this analysis, a fundamental fact of life in society.

A common way of attempting to get at the real meaning of others is to check on how well expressions given off match expressions given. Since we assume expressions given off are less under the control of the actor, we also assume they tell us more about the "reality" of the actor in some particular situation. Expressions given off used for such validity checks include nervousness, the way someone looks when he thinks himself unobserved, signs of embarrassment, stuttering, gaffes, and unintended gestures. Thus, if a boy is telling a girl that he loves her, how beautiful she is, what a wonderful feeling he has for her, and he is speaking with a sincere tone to his voice, is the proper distance from her (very close), and is looking at her in the way that we have come to associate with such statements, but at this moment a shapely lass passes by and he forgets himself and looks after her retreating figure, his girlfriend is unlikely to accept his statements. What the boy said and the way he said it are examples of expressions given, while his unanticipated glance was thought by his girlfriend not to be so much under his control and is an example of an expression given off. In the information game, because people know that others use this validity check, they try to control the expressions they give off, making them match the expressions they give, in order to better manage a desired impression.

Not only do people seek, reveal, and conceal information in *encounters* (face-to-face interaction), but in this information game of impression management they ordinarily accept the expressions or definitions that others give of themselves. The participants in encounters are expected to cooperate with each other in maintaining a group definition of the situation by (1) suppressing immediate feelings, (2) offering a view of the situation that is acceptable to others, (3) concealing their own immediate wants, and (4) asserting group values. Additionally, (5) each participant is allowed to give his own definition of the situation when it comes to irrelevant personal matters, (6) each is expected to agree with others on the purpose of the interaction (for example, issues to be discussed), and (7) each is expected to avoid open conflict (Goffman, 1959, pp. 9–10).

These seven basic assumptions of nonconflictual encounters summarize the "working consensus" of interaction. The actual content of the working consensus varies from situation to situation but, generally, these assumptions remain the same. For example, the amount of feeling we are allowed to express varies from situation to situation, as does the degree to which we must conceal our personal wants, assert group values, or avoid conflict. This drastic varying of content becomes apparent when we compare interaction in a formal setting, such as a church or classroom, with that in an informal setting, such as relaxing at home with one's family or attending a drive-in movie. Adequately understanding encounters includes examining these seven basic characteristics and being able to specify in what way and to what degree they are present.

Just as an actor can mess up his performance on the stage, making other actors and the audience conclude that his performance is inadequate, so the performance of an actor on the stage of life can be *discredited*. When disruptive events occur that discredit or contradict the self projected by an individual, it tends to bring the interaction itself to a "confused and embarrassed halt" (Goffman, 1959, p. 12). The participants feel embarrassed, shamed, or ill at ease because some assumptions upon which they were accepting the performance are demonstrated to be untenable. The illustration of the young man who let his eyes stray is an example of a *discredited self*. Similarly, take the case of a young man sweet-talking a girl in a university cafeteria:

> The male was extremely engrossed in the conversation, and the girl he was talking to was correspondingly flattered by his attention and "caught up" in the interaction. In the midst of his flirtation, and just as he was asking her to go out with him, his "friend" walked up to the table and said, "Hi, Bob. How's the wife?"

Since a performance can be disrupted at any time by discreditations or by some violation of the working consensus, precautions are taken by participants to prevent these disruptions. Such precautions safeguard the impressions that individuals are attempting to manage in the encounter. In any encounter preventive practices are utilized. These preventive practices are of two types: *defensive practices,* the strategies an individual uses to protect his own projected definitions, and *protective practices,* such as tact, the strategies used to protect the projected definitions of others (Goffman, 1959, pp. 13–14).

Regions

Just as theatrical performances have a stage, so everyday life performances are staged. In his analysis, Goffman divides the world into *regions,* places "bounded to some degree by barriers to perception" (1959, p. 106). In the United States, with its relatively indoor society, performances are usually given in highly bounded regions marked off visually and aurally. Sometimes the performances are fixed, as with the typical professor before his typical class, but they are sometimes mobile, as with the tiny clusters of performers at a party.

The place where the audience is found and a performance delivered is known as *frontstage*. Frontstage is not fixed, but mobile; it exists wherever an audience is present and a performance is given. Thus frontstage can be formal and fixed, such as church, or fluid and mobile, such as a cocktail party whose actors move throughout the room. With cocktail parties there are many simultaneous performances and, accordingly, several simultaneous frontstages. In our home, frontstage is usually the living room.

Backstages are regions usually inaccessible to the audience, where performers can be offguard with other actors and prepare for their next per-

---

INSERT NO. 37

The Beauty Parlor as Backstage by Carol A. B. Warren

Backstage, according to Goffman, is a geographical area where individuals violate the performances they put on elsewhere: "A back region or backstage may be defined as a place, relative to a given performance, where the impression fostered by the performance is knowingly contradicted as a matter of course" (Goffman, 1959, p. 112). The woman's beauty parlor is a unique instance of backstage as, in a sense, it is a backstage to performances put on elsewhere in everyday life.

The function of beauty parlors is to create, maintain, and alter women's appearance. Appearance is, in our society, a significant aspect of interaction in everyday life, as individuals, especially strangers, tend to be typified in terms of their appearance and manner (men with long hair and bare feet are labeled "hippies" by many people). Appearance and manner together create the individual's situational front which, combined with his situational performances, is the presentation of self.

Others react to individuals (especially strange individuals) on the basis of the contextual situation and the presentation of self. As a key aspect of this presentation, appearance—especially clothing, hairstyle, and makeup—serves to express not only the individual's self-image but also his expectations of how others will react to him. Different personal styles express different reference group orientations and different self-typifications.

This means, often, that individuals change their appearance and front as they change groups. A woman may wish to appear "conservative" in appearance when seeking employment in a bank, but more "hip" when she is interacting with student friends. For some, beauty parlors serve as backstage where relatively permanent transformations of self take place; for others, they are backstage for relatively transitory and situational changes.

For the average client, the beauty parlor serves as an arena for the weekly maintenance of hair (sometimes of makeup and manicure) with respect to cleanliness and style. In fewer, but still many, cases the client also visits the beauty parlor regularly to maintain a different hair color—to cover brown with blonde or gray with red. In still fewer cases, the beauty parlor serves as an arena for the transformation of appearance through change of hair color, with the initial step representing a long-term commitment to a new self-presentation.

formance. The beauty parlor provides an excellent example of the use of front regions and back regions (see Insert No. 37). In analyzing our homes, we may think of the bathroom as backstage because an audience is usually not tolerated, one can relax (albeit by onself) and prepare oneself for coming performances by applying makeup, costuming, and, in general, sprucing

> These activities tend to assume a ritualized and symbolic character. Frequently, the change of hair color represents a commitment to current standards of feminine beauty or a desire to conceal the signs of aging—both ritual commitments in our cosmetic society. The weekly visit to the beauty parlor to maintain hairstyle represents an accommodation to the smooth course of everyday life, broken into only by important festivals that signal ritual changes in appearance—hair is done more elaborately for a ball, and makeup may be toned down for a funeral.
>
> Beauty parlors are backstage to life in a related but more unexpected sense. The physically backstage aspects of the area function to promote an atmosphere of psychic backstage, making hairdressers function for their clients as semi-psychiatrists or confessors as well as appearance-maintainers. It is well-known beauty parlor lore, taught to novices in beauty school by written and verbal instruction, that hairdressers are required to listen sympathetically to details of their clients' private lives.
>
> So far we have focused on the beauty parlor as a backstage from the perspective of the customer. Of course, for the stylists, beauty parlors are frontstage regions where they are expected to keep up their own appearance and self-presentation while demolishing and reconstructing their customers'. Therefore, beauty parlors have a backstage region, cut off physically from the customers' sight, where the operators can relax, make jokes about their clients, and mix the products that will go into the customers' hair. In their backstage region, the operators can let fall the impression of infallibility they are required to maintain in front of clients and seek aid and advice from colleagues.
>
> Customers can relax out of role in only one "backstage to backstage" region in the beauty parlor—the washroom. Here the customer can engage in the one action most taboo in the salon—rearranging hair that has just been arranged by the operator, provided the changes are not too obvious. Or she may give her hairdo a much closer scrutiny than is legitimate within the salon.
>
> The beauty parlor is a kind of backstage to life, where women create and maintain their appearances for frontstage regions of everyday life. Even within the beauty parlor, customers are frontstage with reference to their operators, so that they need a backstage region where they can relax out of the role of customer, just as the operators need a backstage region where they can drift out of role. Finally, the beauty parlor functions as a sort of backstage to the problems of everyday life, in much the same way as a psychiatrist's office.

up one's appearance. Sometimes stages are reversible, and a backstage region at one time will be frontstage at another time. A common example is a home with no dining room. The kitchen is frequently backstage, a place in which meals are prepared to be served in frontstage, the dining room. When there is no dining room and the guests dine in the kitchen, the kitchen is transformed from backstage to frontstage. Removing this major backstage leads to complications for the hostess as her ordinary backstage behavior, food preparation, now becomes part of her onstage performance. This complication is frequently handled by having her team performer, her husband, entertain guests in the living room while the hostess, after making a quick stage appearance at the front door, exits with an apology and busily engages in backstage activities in the kitchen. This technique of insulation is usually successful and, by sequencing the activities through a cooperative team performance, the backstage work is out of the way by the time the kitchen becomes frontstage.

Personal Front

Cultural sayings or maxims frequently possess much sociological wisdom. The adage "Put your best foot forward" might be interpreted sociologically as "Put your best self forward." We have various ideas about our self and are concerned with influencing other's perceptions of us. As we act in different scenes, as we interact on different occasions or situations, we attempt to present our most acceptable self. We do this through the disciplined management of our *personal front,* by maneuvering and manipulating our appearance and manner. We meet others' expectations by presenting ourselves in the right clothing, makeup, hairdo, and other surface decorations on our person (Goffman, 1963, p. 25). Through sustained control, we try to keep our personal front properly arranged during an encounter. If we fail to do so, it is likely to be taken as a sign that we do not have a proper regard for the other actors in that setting.

Once one is acting in a scene, it is ordinarily difficult to check on how one's personal front is holding together. For this reason, we have set aside certain islands of privacy where the front can be examined and, if necessary, put together for further presentation of the self in some interaction yet to unfold. Restrooms are perhaps the best example of such places. It may be significant that they are called "rest" rooms, indicating a respite from the strain of self-presentation.

Our interactions are ordinarily sequenced; that is, one scene follows the other. This sequencing of interactions, by structuring time between activities—such as between school classes or between meetings with business clients—frequently provides the opportunity for an actor to check out his personal front. Because our personal front is an integral part of our presentation of self, we are concerned that there is no discrepancy between it and the impression we desire to manage, and during such times a woman might fleetingly check her makeup as she passes a hallway mirror, or a man might glance downward to make certain that his fly is still zipped.

A usual requirement of everyday interaction in American society is that we conceal the physical signs of our sexual capacities. For example, a man who has been necking in a car with his girlfriend will at times be unprepared to get out of the car to interact in a different scene with different role requirements because, if he is to meet this expectation of concealment, it may be necessary for him to wait for partial detumescence before exiting. His girl is more easily adaptable to such a scene change. Male high school students, who are probably most plagued with this problem, have been known to feign ignorance when called upon in class to avoid the possibility of offense and embarrassment that would result from walking to the blackboard in full view of everyone.

To conceal sexual capacities, our females are taught "limb discipline" at a very young age. Little girls are told to sit with their knees together, not to let their underwear show, and how to "correctly" bend over while retrieving objects. After growing up, they are concerned not to expose their upper thighs and underclothing. They are not allowed the luxury of relaxed sitting but must be constantly vigilant in self-control. Frequently, especially in an age of miniskirts, they "take the extra precaution of employing a protective cover, by either crossing the legs or covering the crotch with a newspaper or books" (Goffman, 1963, p. 26).

Balanced against the requirement of concealing one's sexual capacity is the expectation that we also demonstrate such capacity. For example, we are expected to wear clothing that easily identifies us as a member of a particular sex. (My prediction is that current developments in unisex clothing will merely become an interesting historical footnote.) Men are allowed to wear clothing that suggests virility, using leather and Western-style clothing (Popplestone, 1966); and, although women are permitted to wear clothing that suggests seductiveness, the amount of décolletage is strictly circumscribed. There is a tension between the degree of tolerable expression of seductiveness and virility and the expectation concerning concealment of sexual capacity. Women frequently find themselves in a bind because of these two mutually incompatible expectations. They must show themselves to be pure and untouchable and at the same time sexually available—at least for a potential spouse. If a woman goes too far in one direction, she runs the risk of being labeled prudish, and if she goes too far in the other, she risks being labeled "easy."

Society has well-defined expectations and rules regarding the permissibility of body exposure. In order to understand our attitudes toward body exposure, Goffman suggests that, instead of considering either the amount or parts of the body exposed, we examine the situations in which differential exposure occurs. As the occasion (scene) changes, we are required to show proper regard for the demands of each occasion—that is, we must show appropriate involvement for the situation. Nudity is permitted in a nudist colony or for the model in an art class because it shows proper regard for the demands of the occasion. For a woman to wear a slip on these occasions, although more of her body would be covered, would be considered improper. The role demands nudity, and to appear half clothed would be out of role. Because of this, ordinarily, the art class model who poses *au naturel* does not undress in front of the class; if she did, she would be out of role. Undressing before the class would be suggestive of a role other than that of model. Wearing only a robe, however, which is removed with a single motion, eliminates this awkward transition. (Goffman, 1963, pp. 211–213).

Self-Identities and Personal Fronts

Clothing, a very ordinary part of the everyday world, is a subject of sociological study. Following the dramaturgical model, we conclude that it is not accidental that you are wearing the clothing you have on right now. You have a particular idea about yourself, about who and what you are, and by means of clothing you communicate to others some aspect of this conception of self. When you are shopping for clothing, certain clothing makes you feel comfortable, as though it reflects the "real" you, some clothing makes you somewhat uncomfortable, and other clothing is so contrary to the way you feel about yourself that you "wouldn't be caught dead" in it. The clothing that makes you feel comfortable matches in some way an idea you have of who you are, of your feeling of self. When a person feels that certain clothing brings out the "real me," he feels the clothing matches some integral idea of the self.

Clothing not only communicates something about the self to others and to the wearer, but it is also a costume. Clothing helps establish and communicate social identity, and it changes as the scene changes. Just as the costume an actor wears on stage is meant to convey meaning about the social identity of that actor, so it is with all of us. By means of our clothing, we tell others something about our social identity. Through clothing, we forcefully claim membership in a particular sexual grouping, figuratively shouting out, "I am male!" or "I am female!" We want no one to mistake that social status. As on the stage, by means of clothing we communicate our other social statuses such as age, occupation, and relative wealth.

It is necessary to establish gender in social transactions because our vocabularies are sexually distinguished; we have languages for males only, languages for females only, and languages used "to communicate across the barriers of gender" (Stone, 1962, p. 90). It is seldom that we need inquire about the gender of another person whom we encounter because we communicate gender through personal front or appearance.

We receive identity, or determine who we are, through where we are *socially situated;* identity comes through participation or membership in social relations. Having learned our identity, we announce it to others, hoping they will accept it. When our announcement of identity and the acceptance of identity match, this identity becomes permanently rooted in the self. Clothing is a major means for an individual to make such announcements of the self and to mark the identities of others, serving as cues for interaction. Because of this announcement via clothing, we know what is expected of us in a particular interaction situation. Thus, the policeman's uniform announces an identity nonverbally, giving us cues for action (Stone, 1962, pp. 93–94).

Just as costumes change on the stage as scenes change, so we change our clothing to match the routinely changing scenes of our everyday life, such as work, church, and recreation. As we are called upon to present the self differently on different occasions, we change our clothing to match varying presentations of self. To demonstrate to others (and probably to ourselves) that we are industrious workers, we wear clothing designed to communicate that impression, such as a business suit or a company uniform. To demonstrate that we are ready to relax, we might wear golfing shoes, bowling shoes, tennis shoes, sandals, or sneakers. We don't usually communicate our role intentions quite as overtly as the one-day-a-month backyard barbecue expert who puts on a chef's hat and a bibbed apron imprinted "Watch me cook!" or the bowler who dons a tee shirt with "Butterby's Bowling Buffs" emblazoned on the back, but we do communicate through clothing, as a routine part of our everyday life, both role intentions and ideas of the self.

Sometimes the scenes we are called upon to play require the donning of clothing that indicates specific identity. Such group costumes or uniforms permit the wearer to partake of a group identity, to merge or connect his self with that of the group. The uniform reminds both the wearer and others of the wearer's identity. When someone puts on a uniform, we assume that it serves to signify that the wearer will be interacting within the framework of the meaning of that uniform—that the wearer of a policeman's uniform will enforce the law; that the wearer of a meter reader's uniform will read meters; and that the wearer of a clerical collar will not be seductive or drunk in public. Uniforms, like names and other items of clothing, give identity to the wearer and provide interaction cues for others.

Besides marking the self-concept, social identity, and scene changes, clothing designates status change. Frequently, names and clothing match to designate status changes; as, for example, "Freddy" undergoes a change to "Fred" to "Frederick" to "Mr. Smith," so his clothing changes from rompers to high school letter jackets to suits. Thus, clothing, along with terms of address, helps validate changing statuses. It is even possible for clothing to replace an individual's name (Stone, 1962, p. 95). This happens with a person who exhibits little variety in his dress so that, although people do not know him personally, his dress functions in place of a name. This replacement applies not only to clothing but to other objects associated with an individual; thus, when cabbies do not know the name of a particular driver, they may refer to him by the number of his cab, calling him "Number 82." Sometimes the cab number becomes so associated with an individual that drivers prefer to designate him by the number of his cab even when they know his name.

In order to maintain our appearance, we use what Goffman calls *identity kits*, "consisting of cosmetic and clothing supplies, tools for applying, arranging and repairing them," and "access to decoration specialists, such as barbers and clothiers" (1961a, p. 10). If one wants to change identity, manipulating the identity kit is one way to do so. This strategy is often used by *total institutions* attempting to control their members—such as mental hospitals, armies, prisons, and monasteries. They attempt to create a new identity for those joining; in so doing, they first try to obliterate the individual's previous identity. Such institutions remove the identity kit the individual brings with him, replacing it with a kit more in keeping with the institution's definition as to its membership. For example, prostitutes have a particular idea about their selves that they support through choice of wearing apparel. In prison, part of "rehabilitation" is a drastic change in identity kit. This can be an upsetting experience:

> There are only a few of them (officers) on duty, and each one has her own rigidly defined function.
> First, there is the shower officer who forces them to undress, takes their own clothes away, sees to it that they take showers and get their prison clothes—one pair of black oxfords with cuban heels, two pairs of much-mended ankle socks, three cotton dresses, two cotton slips, two pairs of panties, and a couple of bras. Practically all the bras are flat and useless. No corsets or girdles are issued.
> There is not a sadder sight than some of the obese prisoners who if nothing else, have been managing to keep themselves looking decent on the outside, confronted by the first sight of themselves in prison issue.
> "I always knew I wasn't much," Molly Sands, a two-hundred-pound streetwalker in her early forties, says. "But now, every time I look down at myself, I think I'm less than nothing" (Murtagh and Harris, 1957, p. 281).

In addition to appearance, there is a second part of personal front, *manner*, the indication an actor gives of how he will play his part on a particular occasion (Goffman, 1959, p. 24). (See Insert No. 38.) One's manner is part of the presentation of self in everyday life that further indicates to others how they should react to the performance. By our manner we indicate our moods and feelings, communicating to others how they should adjust their behavior.

In certain types of interactions, the manner of a performer can play a fairly insignificant role because the encounter has an anonymous character; the interaction is not based on *personal identity*, who the individual is (Mary or George), but on *social identity*, the role or part that the individual plays. For example, if we wish to purchase something from a sales clerk in a metropolitan area, the major characteristic of that person concerning us is whether he is, in fact, a sales clerk and whether he is available at the time to fulfill the role of sales clerk. In such cases, manner is definitely secondary and it is not our concern whether George the clerk is undergoing personal problems that have made him sad. The relevance for the encounter is that the role be played, and that the player is available to exchange our money for his goods.

When we are dealing with others on a personal level, however, we are interested in aspects of manner such as moods. Frequently, we will inquire how others feel at the beginning of our interaction with them because this will indicate the manner of the ensuing interaction; it will tell us how the person is going to act in the situation and serve as a cue card for the way we should interact with him. As Stone (1962, p. 97) has put it:

> In a certain sense, interpersonal relations demand that the *moods* of the participants be established (as well as their names or nicknames) prior to the initiation of discursive phases in the transaction: that "Joe" or "Jane" is mad or sad will have definite consequences for the talk with "Jim" or "Joan."

It makes quite a difference for the ensuing interaction if to our question "How do you feel?" someone replies, "Not too good. My father just passed away." Only a most insensitive person would not adjust his interaction on the basis of this knowledge.

Mental Illness and Dramaturgy

Having one's personal front under control and appropriately varying the presentation of self from situation to situation is such an essential part of man's life in society, expected of any socialized member of society, that lack of control over the personal front or inappropriate presentation of self is sometimes taken to be a sign of mental illness.

We have pejorative terms for behaviors that violate our more serious expectations, such as "drunk" for those who violate our expectations of usual sobriety, "criminal" for those who violate our expectations of law conformance, "tattletale" for those who violate our expectations of in-group solidarity, and "informer" or "spy" for those who do the same in more serious situations. When we don't have a specific word to apply to violations of behavioral expectations—especially violations of routine and foundational aspects of interaction—we are likely to apply such terms as "nuts," "loony," "bats in his belfry," "bananas," "weird," "odd-ball," or "mentally ill." Such persons have violated our basic expectations of behavior so that we assume that any adequately socialized member of society will conform to them. For example, we assume that one should not have his finger stuck up his nose while talking to other people. If someone persists in keeping his little finger inserted up his nostril we are likely, in the absence of an explanation that

INSERT NO. 38

Self-Presentations of Homosexuals by Carol A. B. Warren

The study of self-presentation among homosexuals involves the analysis of how stigmatized individuals manage their identities in different "worlds"—at work, with homosexual friends, and among their families or heterosexual friends —during everyday interaction. The presentation of self has two elements: front, subdivided into appearance and manner, and performance (or behavior).

Most homosexuals have the problem of changing their performance to suit different situations in their different worlds. For example, at work a businessman may wish to present himself as a heterosexual, and will invent fictional dates with girls, while with homosexual friends he drops this pretense. Further, in his interactions with his family, he may mention neither fictional girls nor real men—he may not mention his sexual life at all. "John," in a taped interview, illustrates three alternative presentations of self for a stigmatized homosexual:

> I was always just scared to death that my family was going to find out, and I would go to any lengths not to have them. I think I am starting to adjust myself where—I've gotten the attitude now if it happens it's going to happen; we're just going to have to sit down and discuss it, and I'm not going to worry about it. . . . I used to always, er, date the girls from the office, always trying to put up a pretense. I always made sure that my family, you know, knew who I was going out with. Now I don't particularly do it, er, and generally, er, it can be . . . so many people, you know, in—in this life will never refer to two men together to their parents—er—constantly, and I do now. I'm either, you know, talking about Roger and Sam, or Dean and Bob, or something like this, and if it's girls, they're generally two girls' names involved, and I'm never speaking now, er, as, er, Mildred and Rex or something like this.

John's comment illustrates how homosexuals may construct—mentally and outside of actual events—three possible performances for homosexuals in the world of parents. One alternative, a performance of heterosexuality, was under-

would legitimate this behavior (such as stopping a nosebleed), to call him a "crackpot."

In this view, mental illness is a violation of the fundamental behavior patterns of our society. Offenders have violated basic expectations of human interaction, and to this category we apply a catch-all term such as "mental illness." As we have no specific label that means "one-who-keeps-his-finger-in-his-nose-all-day-long"—or for those who hear voices, see visions, make up their own language, wear inappropriate clothing, continually say the inappropriate thing, laugh boisterously when no one else is laughing, weep

---

taken by John in the past, and involved presentation of a maximum of misleading antistigmatizing activities (dating girls) to the parents. Another, apparently taking place in the present, is more neutral, and involves for John (1) not directly telling the parents about his homosexuality, (2) not inventing or distorting details of his life tangential to his homosexuality, and (3) minimizing stigma-linked stimuli presented to the parents.

John's third alternative (in the speculative future), presenting himself to his parents as a homosexual, involves blending two of his worlds—the family and his homosexual world—through making his stigmatized identity known in the family. *Blending* occurs when the world, learning about the stigma, accepts it as part of the homosexual's identity and does not negate or ignore it. One example of negating nonblending occurred to two of my research subjects, brothers, who told their mother about their homosexuality. The mother refused to define her sons as homosexual, forgot their revelation, and required them to continue their neutral self-presentations.

Presentations of self are composed not only of performances, but also of fronts (appearance and manner). There are often differences in the fronts, as well as the performances, which homosexuals use in their different worlds. For example, the businessman at work may be careful to dress in a conservative manner (appearance) and hold his cigarette in a masculine fashion (manner), but among his homosexual friends he may wear see-through flowered shirts and use a cigarette holder. Many homosexuals refer to changes in self-presentation in the homosexual world as "letting down their hair," indicating the more comfortable environment that reinforcing others present over possibly hostile others.

It is evident that this type of problem—theorizing in advance about possible presentations of self, and being required to perform misleadingly—occurs dramatically when the individual perceives himself as possessing a stigma which must be kept secret from some of the worlds within which he lives. In our society, the homosexual is stigmatized in almost every group other than the homosexual one; other stigmatized groups include criminals, the mentally ill, Communists, and drug addicts. But self-presentations are carried out by all of us in our everyday lives, in a more rudimentary fashion, as we adapt to changing groups and contexts.

when there appears nothing to cry about, or insist on staying in bed all day long—we assign to such persons the catch-all label of mental illness.

The mentally ill, then, are persons who give inappropriate performances for others. They do not present the self in the accepted or anticipated manner. Instead, they exhibit behavior considered inappropriate, playing the wrong role at the right time or the right role at the wrong time. They do not satisfy the fundamental role expectations attached to their societal status, and others react to them with a "there's-something-wrong-in-his-head" attitude. The homosexual is such an inappropriate role player in our society and many Americans, feeling that the homosexual is playing the wrong sex role, attribute it to something wrong inside his head.

To behavior considered inappropriate, in other words, some corresponding mental state is posited. Our examples illustrate violations of expectations concerning such basic matters as one's nose and "proper" sexual partners, but almost any behavior that violates the assumptions underlying interaction can be taken as a sign of actual or impending mental illness. If people engage in such disparate behaviors as wetting the bed, urinating in public, refusing to work, going nude in public, not supporting their family, remaining unmarried, or living alone in a remote or isolated area, they are violating fundamental expectations regarding continence, privacy of bodily functions, ambition, modesty, familial obligations, marital status, and association. For each of these, both the "mental experts" and common man can find something wrong with the "mind," for which the violator must be "straightened out." It is important to note that these are culturally bound expectations, with assumptions concerning these behaviors differing from culture to culture and even within our own culture over time. At one time in this country, it was necessary only that a woman disagree with her husband to be, on the husband's complaint, locked up in a "mental" hospital (Packard, 1868).

Personal front is important in this context because taking care of one's appearance and paying attention to personal hygiene are accepted as basic to interaction in our society. To neglect one's personal appearance and hygiene is to run the risk of being thought mentally sick by others (Goffman, 1963), although we are apt to apply the term "eccentric" if the violator is wealthy.

It is easy to make pejorative ascriptions of mental illness to an individual who makes unacceptable or disapproved changes in his characteristic personal front, but it becomes increasingly difficult to do so when such changes are effected by large numbers. Thus, if John as an individual stops bathing and lets his hair and beard grow, it is easy to define him as "sick" on the basis of his violations of basic assumptions of personal front concerning hairstyle and hygiene, and to conclude that "something is wrong with his head" and he needs a "head shrinker." It is more difficult to ascribe this label to a group phenomenon, however, and if John joins a group with a similar style, he is more likely to escape the label. Although in such cases this label will be applied by some people ("All hippies are sick"), it is more difficult to make it stick. While a psychiatrist might be eager to talk to John when his parents complain about his individualistic behavior, and even to agree with their diagnosis of mental sickness if he shares their middle-class view of hygiene and appearance, he might be less likely to look for some internal mental malignancy as the cause of a mass phenomenon such as hippy-ness.

It is not the behavior that determines whether someone will be called "mentally ill." There is no particular behavior that automatically summons forth from people throughout the world the response, "He is mentally ill." Rather, as each culture differs in its expectations of interaction, it applies labels such as "good" or "bizarre" in different ways. As a result, in one culture some behavior, such as hearing voices, will be defined as a mental quirk for which the person should be locked behind bars until cured, while in another culture, as with the Plains Indians, hearing voices will be taken as a sign of a visit from the gods and the person will be assigned a position of authority, perhaps that of *shaman,* a sort of combined doctor and priest (Lowie, 1954, pp. 161–164). It is not the behavior itself that determines whether one will be labeled "mentally ill" and treated suspiciously; it is the societal reaction to the behavior (Howard Becker, 1963), dependent, in part, on the way labels are used in a culture.

Team Performances

In many situations in everyday life, it is not a single individual who is presenting a self before an audience, but two or more individuals who are cooperating in delivering a unified performance. Such *team performances* are given, for example, when a doctor and a nurse dramaturgically "desexualize" a vaginal examination.

In our culture we have defined vaginal examinations as something necessary for women. Yet we have also defined exposing the genital area as something problematic, socializing our females into rigorous norms concerning the covering of specified areas of their bodies, making the vaginal examination an activity frequently conflictual and fear-laden for our females. Additionally, a male doctor usually performs the examination. Because of this threatening aspect of of structured genital exposure, the actors stage the performance in such a way that they avoid even the hint of sexuality. How is the interaction designed or structured so that the examination of the vagina will be defined as nonsexual? A study based on twelve to fourteen thousand examinations (Henslin and Biggs, forthcoming) concluded that it is accomplished by dividing the examination into five distinct scenes, each contributing to the overall performance and to the removal of sexuality.

In the first scene the patient is fully clothed, and the doctor deals with her as a "full person"; that is, he extends her the courtesies of middle-class verbal interaction, such as saying "hello" as he enters the room. In addition to inquiring about her medical problems, he may ask her about nonmedical personal matters. Before leaving the room, he announces via intercom that he wants to do a pelvic on the patient.

In the second scene the nurse enters the room and prepares the patient, helping her undress and positioning her on the examination table. The doctor's absence at this time is not irrelevant in the light of our cultural meanings of undressing. By absenting himself, the doctor is removing any suggestion that a strip-tease is being performed for his benefit or that he is receiving any untoward pleasure from his work.

In view of what we said earlier about the meaning of clothing for identification, it is interesting that the patient faces the problem of what to do with her underclothing. Not only can a person come to be identified by a particular type of clothing, but clothing can come to be identified with a specific part of the body. In this case, panties symbolize the genital area and, though the patient is about to expose herself for examination, she is concerned about concealing the symbol of this part of her body. Her favorite hiding place is usually her purse, although some patients cover their panties with coats, sweaters, magazines, or even their own body. Only rarely are panties left exposed in the room.

After the patient is positioned on the examination table, the nurse uses a drape sheet to further eliminate sexuality. By covering the patient's legs but leaving her pubic area exposed, the drape sheet sets the pubic area apart from the rest of the person. Its purpose is not to cover the pubic region but, rather, to desexualize the person, setting the pubic area apart so that the doctor can view it as an object isolated from the rest of the body. From her prone position, if the patient looks at her body, she cannot see the exposed area. The drape sheet hides her pubic area from herself while exposing it to the doctor.

When the doctor arrives for the examination, the third scene, he seats himself on a low stool from which he does not see even the patient's head. He need not deal with a person, just with the exposed genitalia marked off by the drape sheet. The patient has become an object; she has been depersonalized and desexualized through dramaturgical techniques. The goal of removing sexuality from the interaction has been accomplished through the skillful manipulation of props and scenery and through the team performance of the doctor and nurse.

Interestingly, the patient also becomes a part of the team, playing the role of object. Usually, she avoids eye contact with the doctor, and he with her, and she does not object when the doctor treats her as a *nonperson,* as an object. During this scene, the doctor may carry on a conversation with his nurse as if the patient were not present as, in the dramaturgical sense, she is not. During one examination, the doctor said to the nurse:

> "Hank and I really caught some good-sized fish while we were on vacation. He really enjoyed himself." He then looked at his "work" and announced, "Cervix looks good; no inflammation—everything appears fine down here" (Henslin and Biggs, forthcoming, p. 264).

In the fourth scene the patient undergoes a demetamorphosis, dramaturgically changing from vaginal object to person. After the doctor leaves, she dresses and makes use of her "identity kit" to make her self once again presentable for her other roles. During this scene the patient may indicate by her comments that she is ready to be treated again as a person, not as an object. By reasserting the self in conversation about personal matters, she shows she is reentering "personhood." In the last scene the doctor makes his final entrance, and interaction between doctor and patient is once more on the full-person level, with observance of the usual middle-class amenities.

The success of the definition of nonsexuality in the vaginal examination depends on sequenced interaction and team performance. Team performances depend on two basic components to bind members of the team together, *reciprocal dependence* (each team member depends upon the other not to disrupt a performance by inappropriate conduct) and *reciprocal familiarity* (each team member knows that the other team members know the secrets of the performance). Because each team member is "in the know," the same front or impressions given to an audience cannot be maintained before the members. This "familiarity" binds the team members together in "guilty knowledge" (Goffman, 1959, pp. 79–83). The purpose of a team's performance is to present some sustained definition of the situation. As such, public disagreement must be avoided because it not only may make them unable to perform, but may cast doubt upon the definition of reality they are offering.

The unity of a team performance is illustrated when a team member makes a mistake in the presence of an audience and the other team members ignore the mistake; to call him down would be to question the solidarity of the members, on which the performance is predicated. However, it is quite another matter when the audience has departed.

For a team to sustain the impression that it wants to make, teammates must be careful not to betray its secrets. This obligation is called *dramaturgical loyalty*. Every team must shield its secrets from others if it is to give a good performance, secrets having to do with disagreements between team members, rivalries with other teams, incompatible activities by team members between performances, or family skeletons. If leaked to a rival team, these secrets could be utilized to the disadvantage of the first team. If revealed to an audience, they could cast doubt upon the performance. Two major defenses to prevent a breach of dramaturgical loyalty are to cultivate solidarity among team members and to change audiences periodically, preventing emotional ties between team members and audience.

For good performance, it is also required that the team members practice *dramaturgical discipline,* the ability to maintain their performance while dealing with any unanticipated problems during the course of the performance. To do this, each team member must demonstrate to his audience that he is caught up in his performance, that he is spontaneous and uncalculating, yet remain aloof to the extent that he can handle problems that might arise. He must not get carried away with his performance to the extent that he can't summon presence of mind when necessary to deal with disruptions (Goffman, 1959, pp. 212-216).

Appearing Versus Being: Performance Versus Reality

Goffman's dramaturgical analysis emphasizes that human behavior is not simply the manifestation of personality, of an inner character, but, rather, an intricate exchange of symbols and meanings. Goffman emphasizes the symbolic nature of human interaction, the exchange of meaning between people through symbols. He says that behavior is a symbol of what is exchanged between actors. The emphasis is on man as a symbol manipulator living in a world of symbols, with man's behavior composed of those symbols. Goffman's work is an attempt to lay bare the nature of those symbols to demonstrate what man is communicating to man as he interacts within the everyday situation. He is in the tradition of the *symbolic interactionists,* following the foundations laid by such men as Charles H. Cooley and George Herbert Mead (see Insert Nos. 26 and 27).

When man acts, he is not merely reacting to his situation, but communicating to others through his behavior. There are two simultaneous aspects of man's behavior, what he does and the meaning of his behavior. Hanging out the wash seems very simple behavior. When we look more closely, we find a meaning to the behavior; the housewife is playing a scene to an unseen audience. As she hangs out her wash, she has in mind that others will see her wash and what they might think of her and her family (Klietsch, 1965).

We might say that behavior is both *instrumental* (designed to accomplish some goal) and *expressive* (having a symbolic value). The sociologist, concerned with understanding as much as he can, is interested in both aspects of human behavior: what the behavior looks like and its meaning, or symbolic nature, for the participants. He wants to determine what definitions or impressions are managed or sustained by behavior. He looks beyond the behavior to ferret out its meaning for the performers. One value of Goffman's work is that he sensitizes the reader to "look behind the scenes" to find "reality."

This aspect of Goffman's work is somewhat disturbing; reality is not in what first meets the eye (the behavior), but in the symbolic nature of that behavior. One looks behind the behavior to find the symbol, or the meaning of the behavior, but what does one find behind the symbol? The alarming possibility is that nothing is there except another symbol of some sort, and if one removes that symbol, one is left facing another symbol. And if one continues stripping away these layers of symbols, perhaps nothing is left beyond the symbols except a biological organism. Is there not more to man than this? Goffman would seem to think not.

Goffman's genius lies in his ability to demonstrate the pervasiveness of the symbolic nature of man, that man is always manipulating symbols, or managing impressions, for the benefit of both others and himself. To put it another way: If we are all playing parts in various scenes on the stage of life, isn't everything just a fake? Doesn't this model of human behavior lead us to conclude that everything is "play-acted"? Something about this analysis of human behavior does not sit right. From our own experience, we know there is a difference between appearance and reality, between appearing to be something and actually being something. There is a world of difference between a man who *appears to be* a doctor and a man who *is* a doctor. Is all of life acting? Are there not major differences between being friendly and acting like a friend? Is there not a difference between being a lover in love and acting like a lover? Certainly, one can appear to others to be a friend and not actually be a friend, but is there not a basic difference between the two?

One sociologist, commenting on this problem, said that according to Goffman the impressions that man manages

> . . . are all that man *is* as a social being. Strip these away and we have dehumanized man. Conversely, cloak man with those fragile devices that permit him to maintain an impression before others and we have given him the shaky essence of his humanity. This perspective reduces humanity to an act or performance; moreover, it is a performance based on dreadfully flimsy devices (Cuzzort, 1969, p. 175).

Goffman also recognizes this problem, and as the solution he points to what he calls a *performing self*. The performing self is the one who wears the mask and puts on the character and performs for others (Goffman, 1959, p. 235). Unfortunately, this proposed explanation does not offer us a solution. Although the self is viewed as putting on the performance, the "reality" that supposedly underlies the presentation and from which the character or dramatic self arises, the performing self, also rises out of the performance! Although Goffman perceives the dilemma, he has proposed no solution.

Goffman (1959, p. 254) says that he does not expect his dramaturgical model to explain all of life, but that his model of the stage is a scaffold and not the structure itself. This scaffold is not the substance but an attempt at explaining what happens when people interact in one another's immediate physical presence, how they maintain definitions of the situation, and how they sustain this definition in the face of potential disruptions.

In following the dramaturgical perspective, we find that sincerity is a part of role playing, a quality structured into performances. If performances are to be convincing, the audience must believe that the actors are sincere. Thus, as we learn to play a role, we learn to believe in that role; the role becomes a part of us and we learn to project it convincingly to others.

It may be that all the world is not a stage, as Goffman reluctantly admits, but he quickly adds that the crucial ways in which it is not a stage are not easy to specify. He states that ordinary interaction "is itself put together as a scene is put together, by the exchange of dramatically inflated actions, counteractions, and terminating replies" (1959, p. 72). What if the difference is that the actor on the stage recognizes that he is merely playing a role to convince an audience while we, doing the same thing, do not recognize the contrivance of our performance? What if the difference is merely one of awareness? Is there more to man than his roles?

SUGGESTED READINGS

Cavan, Sherri, *Liquor License: An Ethnography of Bar Behavior*. Chicago: Aldine, 1966.

> This monograph analyzes behavior in bars. Through participant observation, Cavan presents a detailed study of the routines of barroom interaction. She not only describes what happens, but also analyzes the patterns underlying these commonly occurring but seldom analyzed interactions.

Goffman, Erving, *The Presentation of Self in Everyday Life*. Garden City, N.Y.: Doubleday Anchor Books, 1959.

> This is a seminal work on the analysis of everyday life. Goffman develops a dramaturgical model to explain or interpret the ways in which people present the self in ordinary situations. It is "must" reading for this area of sociology.

Hall, Edward T., *The Silent Language*. Greenwich, Conn.: Fawcett Publications, 1959.

> By analyzing common cultural elements as they occur cross-culturally, this book gives a different perspective on our own culture. Hall focuses on such aspects of everyday life as communication, time, and space. Many of the taken-for-granted rules that control our daily behavior, that are so pervasive that we are frequently unaware of their influence on us, become visible and more readily understandable through this book.

Ichheiser, Gustav, *Appearances and Realities*. San Francisco: Jossey-Bass, 1970.

> Ichheiser makes a strong case for greater attention by social scientists to man's ordinary interactions and to the analytic penetration of presuppositions on which they are based. By examining the obvious, by making explicit what we usually take for granted, we can uneath our biases in judgment and better understand human interaction.

Murtagh, John M. and Sara Harris, *Cast the First Stone*. New York: McGraw-Hill, 1957.

> This book consists of case studies of prostitutes and pimps, with suggestions for legal change. Although sometimes overly psychiatric in its approach, it presents good ethnographic data that is not only interesting but yields much insight into both the process of becoming a prostitute and the life of one.

Schutz, Alfred, *The Phenomenology of the Social World*. Evanston: Northwestern University Press, 1967.

> In this work, Schutz raises questions about the nature of the social sciences. Dealing with such problems as objectivity versus subjectivity, Schutz makes a case for the method of the social sciences to match the object of social scientific study—humans. He emphasizes understanding man as a symbolic actor, rather than quantification of his acts or characteristics.

Szasz, Thomas S., *The Manufacture of Madness: A Comparative Study of the Inquisition and the Mental Health Movement*. New York: Harper & Row, 1970.

> Szasz argues convincingly that our contemporary mental health movement is not only analogous to the Inquisition, but a direct outgrowth and continuation of the Inquisition. He emphasizes that social scientists should understand man as a symbolic actor, rather than quantifying his acts or characteristics.

CHAPTER 10

Purposes and Problems of Social Research

Any theory can be only as valid as the research on which it is built and which is used to test it. In Chapters 1 and 4 we saw that sociologists are aware that research methods are less reliable than they once thought, an idea developed in this chapter. The research methods of historical analysis, participant observation, experimental group studies, social psychology, surveys, and questionnaires are shown to be more or less valid for various purposes. For example, participant-observer methods are involved, either formally or informally, in almost any research because the researcher uses common-sense knowledge gained from everyday participation in the culture to communicate with the people he is studying. The more specialized techniques such as questionnaires can be used to study special topics, especially those that involve few problematic meanings.

The researcher must choose his method carefully to minimize the problems in obtaining valid data. We find this concern with research methods, both implicit and explicit, in every chapter of this book.

Once it was easy to write about the purposes and problems of research in sociology. The central purpose of research was to provide scientific evidence that would support or refute hypotheses about social life. The problems of research were minor annoyances that arose when one tried to apply the scientific method to social behavior, annoyances that would disappear as we learned more about using the methods of science in this area. This comfortable view is passing. "Annoyances" that detract from the claim that sociology is scientific stubbornly refuse to go away.

I will describe some current controversies as I outline the various research methods used in sociology. I will try to be objective, but the reader should know that I doubt that these annoyances will go away; hence I am "objective" on that side.

A BRIEF DESCRIPTION OF THE SCIENTIFIC METHOD

Sociology calls itself a science and, to deserve the title, must use the scientific method. Though we shall see a need to expand our view of science, the scientific method is a content-free procedure for discovering laws of the form "X caused Y" that are generally true in the natural world. Being content-free, the same procedure can be applied in many parts of the natural world—in our case, to the social world. The scientist proposes a hypothesis about some aspect of his field of study, an idea about how something in his field might work. He puts his idea into the form of a statement that can be tested empirically (and may be found false), and he collects evidence to make a test. If the evidence supports the hypothesis, the hypothesis has passed the first test on the road from proposal to law. If the evidence does not support the hypothesis, the investigator must go back and rethink his problem. If he discovers a flaw in his reasoning, he may propose a corrected hypothesis and start the process again.

In simplest form, a hypothesis is an assertion that two factors, X and Y, are associated with one another. That means that when X occurs, so does

Y, and when X does not occur, neither does Y. If these assertions are found true in all cases, the investigator can then infer that X causes Y, or Y causes X, or that X and Y are caused by an unknown third factor. Further, if he knows that X precedes Y in time, he can then often infer that X is the cause and Y the effect. But, unfortunately, it is a long way in sociology between the hypothesis that X and Y are associated and the law that X causes Y.

The discovery of laws has largely eluded sociology. For example, wealth is known to be associated with high social status, but does wealth cause high social status? For almost every hypothesis studied in sociology, there are cases that confirm it and cases that do not confirm it. Most persons of great wealth also have high social status, but some have low social status. Most persons of little wealth have low social status, but some have high social status. The same direction of causation may not apply to all persons. There are persons for whom it is plausible to say that high social status causes wealth; "poor relations" in a "good" family may use family contacts to obtain business opportunities that lead to wealth.

The most difficult problem to overcome in searching for laws in sociology is the problem of multiple contributing causes. It is rare to find a single cause for a social phenomenon. Rather, the phenomenon occurs when a series of conditions are met. Our newly wealthy friend will achieve high social status if his money is "clean," not the product of criminal activities; if he spends substantial amounts of it, rather than hiding it in a mattress; and if he meets certain standards of etiquette.

The general methods for establishing causation were first laid down by John Stuart Mill (1843). Three of his four methods are most relevant to sociology, the method of *agreement,* the method of *difference,* and the method of *concomitant variations* (see Insert No. 39).

METHODS OF SOCIOLOGY

The student should be familiar with four common research methods used in sociology: analyzing existing records, observation, survey analysis and interviewing, and testing hypotheses. These methods are not used to discover hypotheses; they apply when the hypothesis is ready to be tested.

How does the investigator discover a hypothesis? He thinks of a likely possibility. How he gets the idea is hard to say. Someone may suggest it to him; he may come upon it inductively while analyzing some data; he may discover it deductively by deriving it from some theory; or it may come "out of the blue." Discovery remains an unexamined part of the investigator's methods. One could propose an endless number of hypotheses once he has the idea of an association in mind. Just assume that any two factors or variables imaginable are associated, and then proceed to test that hypothesis. But many proposals developed in such a mechanical manner would duplicate ideas already tried; others would be nonsensical; still others would be minor variants of ideas previously attempted. The good hypothesis, one that will add something really new to sociology, is hard to discover and there is no way we can teach anyone to do this creative task. Let us turn, then, to the four methods for testing hypotheses. I present them in order, from the method with least control over the events under study to the method with greatest control over them.

Analyzing Existing Records

Historical questions are generally treated by the method of analyzing existing records. Questions about the past are studied by examining documents pertinent to the events under consideration—such as diaries, letters, government records, and newspapers. Obviously, the further back into history he inquires, the less control the sociologist can exercise in studying the question. The authors of his sources may not have been careful or objective on the point of interest to us; the accuracy of their information is unknown. If we are interested in sociological questions that pertain to earlier periods, we are at the mercy of whatever documentation has survived from that period to the present, in original form or through the eyes of later commentators.

How would the sociologist study questions of the past? Assume that the investigator wants to know whether the men of ancient Greece adopted the occupations of their fathers. If he is lucky, someone has already tried to answer this question, and he has the task of assessing the quality of the earlier person's work. That is unlikely, and it is also unlikely that he will find original survey materials on this question. He will be forced to answer it by examining surviving documents for material pertaining to the occupations of son and father. The sociologist will have to invent a plausible reconstruction of ancient Greek social structure to fill in the fragments; then he can try to see what answer to his question is consistent with his reconstruction.

The necessity for reconstruction is seen most clearly in a historical situation like this one, but it occurs in all sociological research. No matter how much information the sociologist has, he never has enough, and therefore he has to reconstruct large parts of the social world of the persons under study to make sense of his data. Most sociologists are not attentive enough to this reconstruction process. They fill in gaps in a common-sense way, without noticing their assumptions.

The reconstruction process is vital to the research. The better it is, the more illuminating will be the research conclusions. Yet no one knows much about that process. It belongs to the "discovery" aspect of method, and methods of discovery are not well understood. The investigator cannot describe the process, which remains uncontrolled.

Our student of history will have all the researchers' problems in testing hypotheses on present-day evidence, with fewer possibilities for corroboration, as the student of the past cannot return to the scene to collect additional evidence.

Content analysis is one approach to data based on documents. Ordinarily, the communication is in written or printed form, such as newspaper editorials or scripts of radio broadcasts. Bernard Berelson defines content analysis as follows: "Content analysis is a research technique for the objec-

---

INSERT NO. 39

John Stuart Mill's Methods for Establishing Causation

J. S. Mill stated four methods for establishing causation. The *method of agreement* sounds simple enough:

> If two or more instances of the phenomenon under investigation have only one circumstance in common, the circumstance in which alone all the instances agree is the cause (or effect) of the given phenomenon (Madge, 1965, p. 53).

The problem is that the investigator has to guess the common element that is the cause, when there may be more than one element in common and more than one cause for the effect in question.

The *method of difference* underlies experimental investigations, as can be seen from the following statement:

> If an instance in which the phenomenon under investigation occurs, and an instance in which it does not occur, have every circumstance in common save one, that one occurring only in the former; the circumstance in which alone the two instances differ is the effect, or the cause, or an indispensable part of the cause of the phenomenon (Madge, 1965, p. 53).

The sense of this method is that you experiment, trying to produce or reproduce a given phenomenon. If you find that when X is present, Y occurs, and that when X is not present, Y does not occur, then you have strong evidence that X is the cause of Y, or is at least a part of the cause of Y.

The two methods were joined together by Mill to create a nonexperimental analogue to the method of difference, the *joint method of agreement and difference*, which underlies much of survey research today.

tive, systematic, and quantitative description of the manifest content of communication" (1954, p. 485).

The aim of the method is to discover if certain themes of interest to the investigator are present in a particular set of documents, or how the themes of one set of documents differ from the themes of another set. *Themes* range from abstract concepts such as liberalism to particular words, the presence or absence of which might help to prove that A wrote the document and not B.

Lowenthal (1956) analyzed the biographies appearing in two popular magazines, *The Saturday Evening Post* and *Collier's,* in four different time

> If two or more instances in which the phenomenon occurs have only one circumstance in common, while two or more instances in which it does not occur have nothing in common save the absence of that circumstance, the circumstance in which alone the two sets of instances differ is the effect, or the cause, or an indispensable part of the cause, of the phenomenon (Madge, 1965, p. 54).

This method appears identical to the method of difference, at first reading, but the sense of experimentally produced phenomena is absent. After-the-fact investigations are included, as they often occur in survey work. For example, the hypothesis that college-educated persons are middle class and non-college-educated persons are working class has some support from surveys. The findings are arrived at by using the method of agreement twice—once for middle-class persons, finding college education in a large percentage of cases, and then for working-class persons, finding a lack of college education in a large percentage of cases. The method is inferior to the method of experimentation because the "experiment" has been completed by the time the survey man arrives on the scene. Therefore, he has no chance to control the conditions of the "experiment," thereby ruling out other possible causative factors.

I mention the *method of concomitant variations* only to raise and then dispose of problems of measurement.

> Whatever phenomenon varies in any manner whenever another phenomenon varies in some particular manner, is either a cause or an effect of that phenomenon, or is connected with it through some fact of causation (Madge, 1965, p. 56).

For example, amount of income varies directly with degree of education. Both income and education have many gradations, not simply presence or absence. In both cases the gradations can be assigned a series of increasing numbers, and we then say that we have measured income and education. Causation is confirmed, ultimately, by testing hypotheses in many situations. In this chapter I will describe the various ways of testing a given hypothesis that are common in sociology.

periods, 1901–1914, 1922–1930, 1930–1934, and 1940–1941. According to occupation, he classified the subjects into three categories: politics, business and professions, and entertainment. He found that the percentage of men in these biographies who were in politics, business, or the professions declined sharply from the 1901–1914 period to the 1940–1941 period, while the percentage of entertainers increased sharply. The percentage of entertainers working in the serious arts—defined as literature, fine arts, music, dance, and theater—declined from 77 percent in 1901–1914 to 9 percent in 1940–1941, while the percentage of less serious entertainers such as sports figures or nightclub singers increased. Lowenthal concluded that there had been a dramatic shift in the American reader's interest from the "agents and methods of social production," as seen in biographies of politicians, businessmen, and professional men, to the "agents and methods of social and individual consumption," as seen in the biographies of entertainers in the less serious arts.

Virtually all scientific research is conducted by analyzing documents. The observer, the survey man, and the experimenter also draw conclusions from documents they generated in the past. Social events are ephemeral. All that remains is the physical impact of such events or the record kept by some observer. Investigators cannot conduct a serious analysis as the events are going on but must reflect upon records, the tangible evidence of the event. Thus, the historian's problems are problems of the sociologist. It is not simply that some person in ancient Greece wrote a book biased in unknown ways, but that the sociologist himself, as generator of his own "historical" documents, may also bias them.

Methods of Observation

The journalist's inclusive question: "Who did what to whom, when, how, and where?" best expresses the investigator's interest when he uses the methods of observation. He is interested—at least as a first step—in recording certain events as factually as possible, just as a newspaperman is interested in reporting a story. The observer tries to watch the events take place, rather than reconstruct them from others' accounts. If the events have already occurred, the observer is involved in problems of testimony, and the difficulties are much the same as discussed under the method of analyzing documents: How complete is the testimony? How accurate is it?

Weick (1968) defines observation as follows: "An observational method is defined as the selection, provocation, recording, and encoding of that set of behaviors and settings concerning organisms 'in situ' which is consistent with empirical aims." The crucial term is *in situ*, which means that the sociologist goes to where the action is, rather than trying to bring it into his laboratory.

Sociologists divide observation into two kinds: participant observation and nonparticipant observation. In participant observation, the sociologist takes part in the social events he is studying, either with or without the knowledge of the other participants. In nonparticipant observation, the sociologist arranges to observe the events in which he is interested without very much involvement. The anthropologist doing an ethnography of a primitive tribe falls in the latter category, because he tends to participate little in the life of the people he is observing (see Chapter 4).

The disadvantage is that only one setting is studied, and therefore no hypothesis pertinent to other settings can be adequately tested. The advantage is that a single major counterexample to a hypothesis uncovered by such a study forces a reconsideration of the adequacy of the hypothesis.

The nonparticipant observer takes less part in activities than does the participant-observer. But, ordinarily, he must play some part in the activities, as he cannot usually observe without his presence being known. Thus, typically, he takes the role of a marginal person of some kind—a writer, a researcher, a visitor, and so on. He influences the performers' activities to the extent that their behavior is different from what it would be if he were not present. He need not do anything but stand around; but knowing he is observing may change the behavior that he came to see. Worse, he cannot know if this is true unless he already has a lot of information about the performers. The nonparticipant observer does not escape influencing the persons he wants to observe; therefore, this method differs only in degree from that of participant observation.

One method fitting into this category is Bales' laboratory method for studying small groups of persons engaged in conversation (Bales, 1950). The central feature is interaction process analysis (see Insert No. 40).

There are many problems with interaction process analysis. As carried on in an experimental setting, it may have few points of similarity with group behavior outside the laboratory. Observers may not see or hear all ongoing behavior, even with the complex machinery often used to record it. The categories used by the observers are arbitrary but all instances of behavior, whether they fit or not, will be forced to conform to these categories. However, the method can be valuable when these problems are carefully weighed, because it can answer questions that cannot be answered in another way, questions that demand a continuous monitoring of someone's behavior over a period of time (Strodtbeck and Mann, 1956).

SURVEY ANALYSIS AND INTERVIEWING

This section includes two related methods, survey analysis and interviewing. Each method collects information by asking questions of respondents. Survey analysis appears the more scientific, with its carefully selected samples, trained interviewers, and neat statistical tabulations; interviewing is looser, more concerned with what the problem is about than with scientific precision. Survey analysis tries to settle issues while interviewing tries to illuminate issues. Settling and illuminating are somewhat contradictory goals, and it is impossible to synthesize an ideal survey-interviewing method from the two separate techniques.

The survey method is the dominant method in sociology. Many more surveys are carried out by sociologists than historical studies, observational studies, and experiments put together. The reason is clear. The only inexpensive way to collect information about an institution, an organization, or a group, particularly if it is large, is to survey some or all of the persons who are processed by it or members of it. Historical records don't deal satisfactorily with present events; observation is limited to small numbers of persons; and experiments are also limited to small numbers, often in the artificial laboratory setting.

To attain a sense of conducting a piece of research from beginning to end, consider a hypothetical survey as it might be carried out over time.

INSERT NO. 40

Interaction Process Analysis by Robert Freed Bales

Interaction process analysis is an observational method for the study of the social and emotional behavior of individuals in small groups—their approach to problem solving, their roles and status structure, and changes in these over time. The process was introduced by Robert Freed Bales in 1950 in his *Interaction Process Analysis*. Although there are several ways of using this type of analysis in experimental studies, the best known is that used by Bales.

Interaction process analysis is a systematic, empirical, and quantitative method of analyzing the form, not the content, of interaction. Each person's behavior in the group, verbal and nonverbal, is reviewed from behind a one-way mirror by a trained observer, and each instance of behavior is classified into one of the following twelve categories:

1. shows solidarity
2. shows tension release
3. agrees
4. gives suggestion
5. gives opinion

Suppose the investigator asks: "Do sons take up the occupations of their fathers?" (Rogoff, 1953). The first step is to put the question into testable hypothesis form. The most obvious hypothesis is the following: "All sons take up the occupations of their fathers." But this we know from personal experience to be false. Any single counterexample falsifies an "all" statement, and we know that some sons don't take up their fathers' occupations.

However, the weaker hypothesis, "there will be a tendency for sons to take up the occupations of their fathers," could be true. This statement is a "some" statement; it has the form "Some sons take the occupations of their fathers," and can't be refuted by a single counterexample. But the "some" form is not an adequate translation of the "there will be a tendency" hypothesis. The word "tendency" implies a comparison that can more accurately be translated by the following statement of the hypothesis: "A larger proportion of sons will be found in their fathers' occupations than would be expected if sons selected occupations randomly." In this form there is a hypothesis to test. It is not obvious whether this statement is true or false.

6. gives orientation
7. asks for orientation
8. asks for opinion
9. asks for suggestion
10. disagrees
11. shows tension
12. shows antagonism

The forms of interaction are, according to Bales, grounded in three fundamental dimensions of social evaluation, or three ways in which one person may view another in a group setting: his power or dominance; the feelings, pleasant or unpleasant, aroused by him; and his value in the achievement of group goals. This conception has been used as a starting point for the classification of the functional problems of small groups, which are four in number: adaptation, integration, instrumentality, and expression.

The twelve forms of interaction and the three fundamental bases of social evaluation may be used to classify the behavior of each individual in the group, in what is called an *interaction profile*. Similarly, the number of acts addressed by each individual in a group to each other individual and to the group as a whole may be tabulated into an *interaction matrix*, and analyzed according to the power structure, values, and emotions of the group.

Testing Hypotheses

The next step is to test the proposal. Abstractly, we know this means collecting cases until we establish the truth or falsity of the hypothesis. How would we go about that? This process is called *operationalization* of the hypothesis.

As we must collect evidence on sons and fathers, we must first know what constitute a "son" and a "father." Shall adopted sons be classed with sons or excluded from analysis? Shall stepfathers and guardians be classed with fathers or excluded from analysis? Another set of problems surrounds the concept "occupation." We think of an occupation as work that a man does regularly for which he gets paid. How about self-employed businessmen? How about men who do not work, either because they are wealthy or because they are on relief and can't find work? Shall we call "playboy" and "on relief" occupations?

Another problem arises because many sons and fathers do not stay in the same occupation for their entire lives. Shall we decide to base our test on the son's first occupation and compare it with his father's present occupation? That sounds sensible. But what if he has been a paperboy for years? Shall we count that as his first occupation?

We find ourselves facing a complicated problem of definition. What is a son? What is a father? What is an occupation? There will always be puzzling cases that we did not anticipate and that we will not be sure how to handle.

Assume that we evolve a set of criteria by which any son can be included or excluded from analysis and that we conduct a survey to determine the validity of our hypothesis. Our next step is to determine whether or not sons adopt the occupations of their fathers.

Random Sampling

We might ask whether anyone has already conducted a national census on occupation and identified father with son in the process. Since that is unlikely, we must collect some new evidence. We will not be able to survey everyone in the population, so we will be forced to obtain the information from only a sample of persons. But which sample? The answer depends on how far we would like to generalize our result. The principle is simple: Draw the random sample from the population of people about whom we wish to generalize. For example, if we wish to generalize about all American men, we must take a random sample of all American men. By a *random* sample, I mean that every member of the surveyed population has an equal chance of getting into the sample. With the help of specialists in sampling procedures, I draw a random sample of all American men. That sample will not be truly random unless I spend more time on it than is customary. For example, men in mental institutions or in the armed services will be omitted.

Interviewing

The next step is to design an interview schedule and interview the men in the sample. We have to communicate our questions to them and obtain their answers. We will probably never find all the respondents designated in the sample. We will have to modify the ideal procedure, either by working with a reduced sample or substituting men who weren't selected for the sample.

Now come more difficult problems. No one knows how to talk to persons to maximize results. We know little about the properties of conversations and how to use them to get the information we want. We want the interviewers to ask questions, but there is no science of question asking. The interviewers will have to ad lib on the doorstep. The respondent may not cooperate; he may ask questions himself, or refuse to answer particular questions.

Suppose the interviewer has completed his task as best he can. He returns with the desired information on a reasonably large number of respondents, convinced that the bulk of the information is accurate (in the sense that checking birth certificates and employment records would confirm the facts).

Tabulation

The next problem is putting the data into proper form for analysis. Assume that we want to construct a table like Table 10–1. The table is constructed as follows: Each adult male in the sample will have his occupation and his father's occupation recorded, as determined by the coding rules discussed earlier. Enter in the "Son Doctor, Father Doctor" position (cell) of the table the number of persons in the sample who fall into this category. Enter in the "Son Doctor, Father Electrician" cell the number with this combination, and continue in this manner to fill out all the cells. Many cells may be empty because the sample did not contain that combination; others may contain a large number because many sons and fathers exhibit the combination. The table may not reflect the entire random sample, for several reasons: the investigator may miscode subjects, making the table inaccurate; the number of subjects may be fewer than the total number interviewed because some respondents didn't give both pieces of informa-

TABLE 10–1. FATHER-SON OCCUPATIONAL IDENTITY DIAGRAM

FATHER

		Doctor	Electrician	Insurance Salesman	Teacher
SON	Doctor				
	Electrician				
	Insurance Salesman				
	Teacher				

tion; the investigator may not know in which occupation to code an individual whose job doesn't fit the categories.

Assume the table is completed in some sensible manner. We are now close to making a test of our hypothesis: that sons have a tendency to adopt the occupations of their fathers. We can arrive at a preliminary judgment. If the hypothesis is correct, the numbers in the cells in which the son's occupation is the same as the fathers' occupation should be large compared with numbers in the other cells.

Suppose the data support the hypothesis in this way. Inspection of the table is not sufficient for concluding that the hypothesis is true. It is possible that the result is due to sampling (or chance) variation and only appears to support the hypothesis. Suppose only four occupations are in our sample—doctor, electrican, insurance salesman, and teacher—and we draw a random sample of 1,000 persons. Upon completing the table, we might find either of these sets of numbers:

FATHER

		Doctor	Electrician	Insurance Salesman	Teacher	
	Doctor	200	40	10	0	250
	Electrician	10	200	40	0	250
SON	Insurance Salesman	0	30	200	20	250
	Teacher	0	10	40	200	250
		210	280	290	220	1,000

FATHER

		Doctor	Electrician	Insurance Salesman	Teacher	
SON	Doctor	75	60	55	60	250
	Electrician	60	75	60	55	250
	Insurance Salesman	60	55	75	60	250
	Teacher	60	60	55	75	250
		255	250	245	250	1,000

Clearly, the first hypothetical outcome supports the hypothesis. No statistical test is necessary to confirm that decision. However, the second hypothetical outcome is not so clear. The results favor the hypothesis in that the biggest numbers occur for cells on the main diagonal, but they are not much larger than the numbers in the other cells. Since we observed only a sample of persons, the results may vary somewhat from the results that would have occurred if we had been able to tabulate the information for the entire population. Therefore, we need to decide whether or not sampling variation alone could account for the results. The field of statistics attempts to answer such questions by its procedures.

Statistical Test

We make a statistical test of the hypothesis. Essentially, we compare the results we found cell by cell with the results we would expect if there were no relation between son's occupation and father's occupation. "No relation" means that sons' occupations have nothing to do with fathers' occupations. For example, sons of electricians will not become electricians more frequently than other members of the population. If the cell numbers are sufficiently different from the numbers expected in a "no relationship" assumption, we conclude that the hypothesis is supported. If they were not sufficiently different, we conclude that the hypothesis is not supported. The sufficiency of the difference is measured by another statistical test. Problems arise: Was the arithmetic of the statistical test carried out correctly? Was the proper statistical test chosen? In practice, we must have a broad knowledge of statistical techniques to choose correctly. These statistical tests are presented in any statistics test, but are too technical for our purposes.

Evaluation of the Hypothesis

We have completed our test of the hypothesis and conclude that the hypothesis is or is not supported. One final problem remains. Even if every part of the procedure has been carried out perfectly, the sample may not be representative of the population. By *representative,* I mean that the percentage of any characteristic of interest will be the same in the sample as in the population as a whole. Thus, the sample will be representative with respect to sex if the percentages of men and women in the sample are identical (or at least very close) to the percentages of men and women in the population as a whole. Even random sampling does not guarantee representativeness. We may have an overabundance of men who fit the hypothesis by chance. There is no remedy for this problem. Only replication of the study can rule it out as an explanation.

Problems in Sociological Research

To highlight the problems, I have outlined the steps involved in testing a hypothesis. Every test involves most of these problems, and every investigator must make decisions about how to handle them. Many problems force the investigator to deal with everyday events as an ordinary member of the culture and not as a scientist. For example, the difficulties of interviewing recalcitrant respondents may force the investigator or his interviewer to act in ways not envisioned at the outset and beyond control of the research design. These everyday difficulties chip away at the ideal design.

The recognition that these difficulties are more obstinate than anticipated has brought on a critical appraisal of methods in sociology. We conclude that at present sociologists are practical scientists, investigators who follow the scientific method as closely as possible, but who depart from it when necessary to do research. Over a long period of time, sociologists will better understand the problems infecting their methods and, at least in part, control for them in their investigations if they recognize how they have necessarily departed from these scientific ideals in doing their research.

The kinds of troubles discussed make conclusions suspect when drawn from a single study. That is why replication is such an important method in science. The more times we can replicate a result, the more confidence we can place in its meaning.

Census

One very important survey method, and certainly one with the fewest troubles, is the *census.* A census is a survey for which no sampling is allowed; everyone in the designated population is to be questioned. The U.S. Census and many other national censuses have as their main task the determination of the number of people in their nations, where they live, and how many are of each sex and age. In the case of the United States, the information is necessary for assigning seats in the House of Representatives to the states.

Because important decisions are based on the information collected in the U.S. Census, it is imperative to assess the consequences of possible inaccuracy. First, no census question will possess perfect accuracy. No one disputes that. Therefore, every national census figure is wrong, and no one disputes that either. Further, there are errors all the way down to the household level, though most household data are correct. The real problem for census workers is not the existence of inaccuracy, but the extent of it.

The census worker, along with every other survey man, counts on the *principle of compensating errors* to keep the aggregate inaccuracy down. If one census enumerator counts an extra person in Household A, a second enumerator will count one too few in Household B, and the total or aggregate count will not suffer. Thus, there can be a good deal of individual inaccuracy, but that is not necessarily translated into the same amount of aggregate inaccuracy. This principle provides adequate protection in most cases, but it may fail. For example, it was discovered that too few babies were counted in some censuses because adults tended to forget that new infants were part of their households. There was no compensating set of families where too many babies were counted. The results were systematic error, a *statistical bias*. Second, there has been a phenomenon of "age heaping" until recent censuses. It was discovered that there were too many persons whose ages ended in "5" or "0," presumably because respondents "rounded" their ages. This last problem has largely been removed by shifting from the question "How old are you?" to "What was the date of your birth?"

To be useful, census figures need be only within a reasonable distance of accuracy. Suppose one purpose of the census statement "There are 10 million men of age 18" is to estimate the number of new soldiers that will come from this group. Suppose the Army estimates that half of this group will become soldiers, yielding 5 million soldiers. Now assume only 9 million men are of age 18 in the country. In due time they will find they have only 4.5 million soldiers—not 5 million. At this scale of size, the difference of five hundred thousand from "expected" can be handled either by making do (by thinning out some units, by combining others, and by making everyone work harder to make up for the lack of manpower) or, alternatively, by recruiting an extra five hundred thousand men of age 19. Similarly, every national institution—education, religion, business—can adapt somewhat to miscounting problems. The crucial issue comes when the count is grossly off, exceeding the "elasticity" of the system. From this point of view, it matters only that census figures be reasonably accurate. Social life is organized to absorb reasonable errors.

Interviewing

Interviewing differs from survey analysis in the kinds of questions that the investigator asks. The survey interviewer's questionnaires consist predominantly of "close-ended" questions, whose answer sets contain a known list of short answers. Examples are the set "Yes," "No," and "I don't know" and the set of possible dates of birth and "I don't know." Even "open-ended" items on the questionnaires tend to be specific. The researcher does not know beforehand all the answers in the answer set of an open-ended question, but he has a good idea of the general categories into which they will fall. He is looking ahead to a coding operation by which the open-ended answers will be classified into a relatively few categories of interest to him.

The survey interviewer is not expected to let the respondent ramble on; he is supposed to hold the respondent to the question and cut him off as soon as the question has been answered. He writes down a short answer no matter how long the respondent talks, trying to capture the essence of the respondent's answer.

But on many occasions the investigator is not clear in his own mind what he wants from his respondents. He is not yet at the point of testing a specific hypothesis or of studying a particular set of variables. He also finds people to talk to, but he lets them talk more on their own than does the survey man. He introduces general topics of interest, and then encourages the respondent to tell him what he can about them. Very likely, he has a few specific questions that he asks of each respondent but, beyond that, he has only a set of topics that he wants the respondent to discuss. This method is called *unstructured interviewing*.

Unstructured interviewing is exploratory. The investigator gives the respondent some chance to instruct him about the topic, rather than assuming that he (the investigator) understands it completely.

Interviewing and *observation* have much in common. Both techniques are often used to find out what happened in a given situation. They may be used together, as when an investigator observes a scene and then interviews participants in the scene. Used alone, interviewing is inferior to observation in the sense that news at second hand is less reliable than news at first hand. Trying to "see" through another's eyes is a difficult task. On the other hand, observation is inferior to interviewing if the opinions, reactions, attitudes, and so on, of the participants in the scene are desired. The observer can infer them only from the behavior of the participants in the interaction; the interviewer has an additional source of material in the participants' reflections about these things. That may be a mixed advantage, as it is not known to what degree and in what situations respondents' thoughts, feelings, and memories are distorted. Usually, people are not accurate monitors and reporters of their own inner mental states.

A good example of the method appears in the recent study by Rosenthal

(1970), who was interested in the relationship developing between a lawyer and his client in conducting the case. Specifically, he wanted to see if "active" clients get better settlements in negligence cases than "passive" clients. Do clients active in several ways, who express a special want or concern, who demand the lawyer's attention, who marshal information to aid the lawyer, who seek quality medical attention, who seek a second legal opinion, or who bargain about the fee get better settlements than clients who do none or one of these things? Originally, Rosenthal suspected that active clients do better, even though the whole tradition of the law encourages passivity in clients by encouraging them to leave everything in the lawyer's hands. He felt that the area of high value ($2,000 and up) personal injury negligence cases was a good one in which to explore his hypothesis.

Rosenthal had no investment in the method of interviewing, but he found that he was forced to adopt it. He could not get lawyers to let him sit in on meetings between themselves and their clients, which ruled out any form of direct observation. Further, they wouldn't permit tape recordings of their conversations. He rejected the method of simulating lawyer-client interaction by having people play the role of client with real lawyers because it seemed too artificial. He turned next to interviewing but found that many lawyers wouldn't allow themselves to be interviewed. Finally, he chose not to use a closed-end questionnaire with clients because he did not know very much about lawyer-client interactions in this area. He had his hypothesis and some general ideas about the kind of client participation that should be taken as evidence of activity but, beyond that, he knew little.

In his interviews, Rosenthal asked the client to tell his story and then asked about points of interest not covered. His interview *schedule* (list of questions) contains such questions as "Please begin by telling me how your accident happened"; "What happened right after the accident?"; and "We have talked about your deciding to contact a lawyer; now I would like to know how you chose your particular lawyer." To facilitate the interview, Rosenthal asked questions in different orders to fit the flow of the client's story, and he modified the wording whenever he felt it necessary. The interviews were tape-recorded so that he could check on his interview notes.

The results supported Rosenthal's hypothesis. Active clients did indeed do better on the average than passive clients. One way of presenting the data is shown in Table 10–2.

Table 10–2 was created in the following way. Rosenthal took the 16 most active clients in his sample of 59, those who had persistently carried out at least two of the six activities mentioned earlier, and the 19 least active clients, those who had carried out none of the six activities or only one and in a desultory manner. Rosenthal decided that a recovery of 74 percent or more of an expert panel's evaluation of the worth of the client's case constituted a "good" result, and lesser recoveries constituted "bad" results.

TABLE 10-2. CLIENT ACTIVITY RELATED TO CASE RESULT.

	Active Client	Passive Client	
Good Result	69% (11)	26% (5)	$N = 16$
Poor Result	31% (5)	74% (14)	$N = 19$
	$N = 16$	$N = 19$	

From Douglas Rosenthal (1970, Table II-2, p. 9).

The 35 cases were then coded as good result cases or poor result cases. The cross-classification of client activity by kind of result produced the data shown in Table 10-2. Active clients got good results in 69 percent of the cases, while passive clients got good results in only 26 percent of their cases. The result is *statistically significant;* that is, it is unlikely that it could have occurred by chance.

Rosenthal also collected information from the clients on how their lawyers conducted their cases. With this information, Rosenthal was able to show that the traditional model of the law—leave the case in the hands of the lawyer-expert—allows the lawyer to handle it as he sees fit, often at the expense of the client's interests.

METHODS OF EXPERIMENTATION

The experiment is procedure for ruling out alternative explanations for findings. The experimental method helps to rule out "artifacts" such as some unanticipated substantive factor that could account for the finding. For example, Rosenthal tried to rule out some alternative explanations for his finding that active clients get better results than passive clients. By measuring the social class standing of the clients and the dollar worth and degree of "perfection" of their case (no negligence on the client's part), he was able to show that these three variables couldn't explain away the effect of activity on the result. But many other variables that he didn't measure could have caused the finding—for example, intelligence. If I asserted that more intelligent people get better results, Rosenthal would not be able to deny the possibility. He might point out that it is highly unlikely, but it would still be a possibility. The basic issue is that Rosenthal's subjects had selected themselves as active or passive and for good or bad results before he interviewed them. He didn't find them until after the "experiment" was over. Therefore, he had no way to control in advance for variables that could lead to alternative explanations; the best he could do was try to rule out some after the fact, an endless task. But, suppose we are able to show that the results are not due to intelligence? Then how about hostility? Or authoritarianism? And if not those, come back and I'll give you a list of another 22 variables to try.

The method of experimentation has one central property that helps to avoid alternative explanations after the fact. It selects individuals before testing the hypothesis in question, and the subjects are selected randomly to try to avoid biases.

Let me begin by describing the classical experimental design used in the social sciences. I will use the model of the psychological laboratory experiment.

The hypothesis. The first step is for the experimenter to formulate a hypothesis that he wishes to test. The experimental methods are not exploratory methods; they are demonstration methods. This technique is not used as a "fishing expedition," as an observational method might be used. Our experimenter must have a definite hypothesis to test. Suppose the hypothesis is that anxiety causes a deterioration in memory performance. The experimenter must first operationalize the variables in his hypothesis. What is anxiety? How do I measure it? There is one crucial difference here. The experimenter must solve these problems in such a way that he can make subjects anxious and then test their memory performance. He does not look around for persons who appear to be anxious (observation) or who report that they are anxious (survey) and then see what they did on some naturally occurring memory performance test.

The subjects. First, the experimenter assembles a pool of subjects. The academic experimenter may take subjects from a college population. Randomly, he assigns each to one of two groups, the experimental group or the *control group;* for example, he might flip a coin for each person. If it comes down "heads," that person is assigned to the experimental group; if it comes down "tails," he is assigned to the control group. By making assignments in this manner, the experimenter lets the laws of chance determine the composition of his two groups. He is, therefore, immune from the criticism that he picked his groups to suit himself.

Probably, the two groups are highly similar in background variables; if there are 60 percent men and 40 percent women in the original subject population, there will be approximately 60 percent men and 40 percent women in both the experimental group and the control group. Similar results are expected for any other variable. There are no guarantees. The experimental group may contain all the men and the control group all the women, just by chance, but that is not probable and the tests of statistical significance will enable us to say just how probable it is that our results are due to such chance factors, so we have a test of how reliable our results are.

"Before" test.   Next, the experimenter gives a "before" test to all subjects. This test is designed to see how well subjects perform on the measure of the *dependent variable* (memory performance) before an attempt is made to manipulate it by means of the *independent variable* (anxiety). (Note that the independent variable, anxiety, is the one we expect to be able to demonstrate as the "cause" of changes, or "effects," in the dependent variable, memory performance.) In our illustration we would measure the level of performance on the memory task of all subjects, both experimental and control, before proceeding.

Experimental procedure.   The experimenter now asks the subjects in the experimental group to carry out some procedure, involving "administration" of the independent variable—here, anxiety. Ideally, the control subjects do everything that the experimental subjects do, except that the independent variable is not administered to them.

Retest.   After administering the independent variable, the experimenter retests the subjects on the memory performance task, an "after" test. He will probably use a different but parallel form of the test to prevent direct memorization effects. He also reexamines the control subjects on the same test. Now he has a "before" and an "after" measure on each subject in each group.

Evaluating the experiment.   The test of the hypothesis that anxiety causes a deterioration in memory performance is now possible. If the hypothesis is correct, the "after" scores of the experimental subjects should, on the average, be below their "before" scores while the "after" scores of the control group should be the same, on the average; if the differences are larger than could be expected from chance variation, the experimenter concludes that his hypothesis is supported. Graphically, the classical two-group experimental design can be portrayed as follows:

	Time 1	Time 2	Time 3
Experimental group	"Before" test	Administration of independent variable	"After" test
Control group	"Before" test		"After" test

The only essentially new idea here is the concept of a control group. Although it seems folly to include persons to whom nothing happens, the presence of the control group allows us to rule out a number of alternative explanations for our findings. It is always possible, for example, that something outside of the experimental situation has happened that affects both the experimental and control groups in such a way as to produce the effects we observe in any "after test" in Time 3. The control group allows us to determine if this is so and thus to determine if the results observed for the experimental group in Time 3 are actually due to the administration of the independent variable.

To bring this discussion of experimentation to life, I will now present an experiment by Orne and Evans (1965).

At one time, researchers had concluded that hypnosis increases the suggestibility of subjects so much that they will commit antisocial acts while under trance that they would not commit in the waking state. There was, however, disagreement about the truth of this hypothesis in the literature. Orne and Evans set out to test it, both by replicating two prior experiments and by expanding on the two studies.

The two most relevant prior experiments were by Rowland (1939) and Young (1952). Rowland used the design shown in Table 10–3a. The data show that five of six experimental hypnotic subjects could be induced to pick up a rattlesnake or throw acid at the experimenter's assistant, while none of forty-two control subjects could be induced to pick up a rattlesnake. Rowland concluded that the data supported the hypothesis.

Young used a design controlling for possible differences between experimental and control subjects. Each experimental subject served as his own control by performing the same task first under hypnosis and then in the waking state. While under trance, each subject was given the suggestion that he would forget what he had just done, so that memory would not affect performance in the waking state. Young's design and results are shown in Table 10–3b. Young's data show that seven of eight subjects could be induced to commit antisocial acts while under hypnosis, while none of them could be induced to do so while in the waking state. Young concluded that the results supported the hypothesis.

It would appear that Rowland and Young were correct in their conclusions. The data are clear. But Orne and Evans didn't believe that the hypothesis had been properly tested. They proposed that subjects could be induced to commit these antisocial acts in the waking state if more inducement to comply were encouraged by the experimenter, equal to the inducement put on the hypnotized subjects. If so, then Orne and Evans had found a flaw in Rowland's and Young's designs. Because the experimenters had not motivated the controls as they had the experimental subjects, they do not know whether hypnosis produces more antisocial behavior than would have occurred under equal inducement in the waking state.

Orne and Evans now set about doing an experiment that would both replicate that of Rowland and Young and also add conditions to motivate subjects in the waking state equally to commit antisocial acts. They used the

TABLE 10–3. HYPNOSIS DATA.

a. Rowland's Design and Results

	Experimental (Under trance)		Control (In waking state)	
	Complied	Did Not Comply	Complied	Did Not Comply
1. Pick up rattlesnake				
a. suggesting it was coil of rope	1	1	—	—
b. no attempt to delude	2	0	0	42
2. Throw sulphuric acid at assistant	2	0	—	—
Totals	5	1	0	42

b. Young's Design and Results

	Experimental (Under trance)		Control (In waking state)	
	Complied	Did Not Comply	Complied	Did Not Comply
Handle snakes and throw nitric acid	7	1	0	8

design shown in Table 10–4 (simplified for the present purpose). The results with groups 1, 2, and 3 replicate Rowland's and Young's results. Hypnotized subjects can be motivated to commit antisocial acts, but nonhypnotized subjects will not do so. Orne and Evans got more antisocial behavior from their controls in groups 2 and 3 than did Rowland and Young, but still not as much as from subjects under hypnosis. They hypothesize that they might have pressed harder for it than did Rowland or Young.

Orne and Evans introduced two additional groups, groups 4 and 5. Group 5 was just like Group 3 except that it was pressed very hard to induce subjects to perform the tasks. The results show that they could induce normal waking subjects to perform the acts.

Group 4 was introduced to account for another possible alternative explanation—that control subjects would not be treated in the same manner as hypnotized subjects by the experimenter. Twelve subjects were brought

TABLE 10–4. ORNE AND EVANS' DESIGN AND RESULTS.

	Group	Grasp Venomous Snake Complied	Grasp Venomous Snake Did Not Comply	Activity Take Coin from Acid Complied	Activity Take Coin from Acid Did Not Comply	Throw Acid at Assistant Complied	Throw Acid at Assistant Did Not Comply
1.	Real hypnosis	5	1	5	1	5	1
2.	Retest, as waking control (Young)	2	4	3	3	2	4
3.	Waking control (Rowland)	3	3	1	5	1	5
4.	Simulating hypothesis	6	0	6	0	6	0
5.	Waking compliance control	3	3	5	1	5	1

into the experiment either under hypnosis or pretending to be under hypnosis. The hypnotist (Orne) did not know which was which and, surprisingly, could not tell them apart. Orne showed in an earlier paper that persons who had seen others hypnotized and performing tasks under hypnosis could simulate the state so well that he (if he did not know them in advance) could not distinguish simulators from hypnotized persons. Therefore, he treated all twelve as if they were under hypnosis. The six simulators were treated just as were the hypnotized persons. The six simulators form Group 4 while the six genuinely hypnotized subjects form Group 1.

Both Group 4 and Group 5 show a high degree of compliance with the tasks, demonstrating that waking subjects with the same degree of inducement as controls can be induced to perform antisocial acts. Therefore, the conclusion that hypnosis is the sole cause of relinquishing social control is not established.

The explanation for the results found in the control groups is that subjects trust experimenters not to allow them to get hurt or to hurt others and comply with whatever requests they make, no matter how dangerous they appear. Thus, the experimental situation appears to legitimize a very broad spectrum of tasks and makes the test of antisocial behavior under hypnosis very difficult. The subjects were right. In Orne and Evans' experiment, a glass panel slid down and prevented them from grasping the venomous snake. If they took the coin out of the acid, the experimenter washed their hands immediately to remove the acid. And, before they had a chance to throw the acid at the assistant, a glass of harmless liquid was substituted for it, unknown to the subject.

Subjects don't treat the experiment as just another event in their daily lives. They consider it a special event with its own rules. It is not that their behavior is artificial in the experiment; it is real enough. But subjects assume the rules for behaving are different, so what they do there and what they might do under similar circumstances outside the experiment are not necessarily identical..

In effect, the researchers prior to Orne and Evans had obtained the results they wanted. Robert Rosenthal (1966) has conducted a number of experiments on this general problem and has shown the same thing. One cannot tell an experimenter what hypothesis he is testing or, very likely, he will make it come out the way he prefers.

CONCLUSION

We cannot ignore the usual methods of sociology simply because they contain the troubles that I have pointed out. Collecting evidence to test hypotheses involves the sociologist in some sort of research method, probably one I have discussed, as it is difficult to invent a completely new research method. Thus, every sociologist must somehow overcome three major difficulties: (1) he cannot force people to do what he wants them to do, (2) he cannot prevent people from thinking about what he is doing, and (3) the research plan is only a sketch of the actual activities in which he will be engaged.

Sociologists' attempts to be methodical in research have at least revealed where difficulties lie, and we understand them better than we did in the past. Hopefully, we will improve our understanding as time goes on, to the point where we can control for them in our work.

These methods are the best we have at the present time. Regard them as practical methods, containing troubles not yet fully understood, but nonetheless valuable aids in our search for better understandings of human society.

SUGGESTED READINGS

Cicourel, Aaron, *Method and Measurement in Sociology*. New York: The Free Press, 1964.
  Cicourel's book outlines and critiques traditional methods in sociology from the perspective of recent findings in phenomenology and ethnomethodology.

Denzin, Norman K., *The Research Act: A Theoretical Introduction to Sociological Methods*. Chicago: Aldine, 1970.

> An important statement on sociological methodology and the theory of doing research from the symbolic interactionist stance.

Glaser, Barney and Anselm L. Strauss, *The Discovery of Grounded Theory*. Chicago: Aldine, 1967.

> Glaser and Strauss's excellent book is concerned with methods of generating theory in sociology rather than with the more traditional hypothesis-testing methods.

Hammond, Phillip E., ed., *Sociologists at Work*. New York: Doubleday, 1967.

> A stimulating collection of essays by well-known sociologists on how they went about conducting major research projects.

Kaplan, Abraham, *The Conduct of Inquiry*. San Francisco: Chandler, 1964.

> One of the best known, most thorough statements of social research methods in the traditional manner.

PART IV

Language and Communication in Society

Part III dealt with the more general dimensions of everyday life situations and social research. In this part we consider detailed aspects of the construction of social meanings and actions. Chapter 11 deals with the nature of social meanings, especially as communicated through language. Then it relates language to social action and particularly to the ways in which language is used by members of society to try to construct meaning from their actions. Chapter 12 shows how messages are formulated for their audiences by the mass media, mainly by newspapers, and then considers the various structural factors, such as oligopolistic ownership, that may influence patterns of communication in American media today.

CHAPTER 11

Language, Meaning and Action

This chapter, developing further some basic ideas introduced in Chapter 7, shows how we use symbols in our communications to give meaning to our actions. Language is the most important system of symbols used to construct and communicate meanings, so our emphasis is on the analysis of language and its use in everyday interaction.

Advances in understanding the nature of language and its place in social life have come only since we have studied language use in everyday life. Beginning with Ludwig Wittgenstein's argument that "language is its use," philosophers, linguists, anthropologists, and sociologists have made great progress in recent decades in understanding language. First, this chapter shows how individuals use language to construct meanings in face-to-face situations. Second, it considers how language is involved in interaction, how linguistic categories are used by members of society to place concrete situations into the larger action systems of social structures, and, finally, what recent contributions have been made in the analysis of the social uses of language.

The sections of this chapter dealing with language and social structure show how language leads the actor to transcend his immediate, face-to-face interaction situation. In the next chapter, we consider how the mass media construct meanings for people who have no first-hand knowledge of a situation.

Inevitably, sociology involves the study of language. In a sense language is society; there is no society without language. At the interpersonal level, language serves to provide terms of address which allocate people to social roles (Dr., Mr.); at the group level, to conceptualize relationships ("conflict," "harmony") and define groups themselves (the American Medical Association, the United States). If we assume that the study of language and the study of society are integral, insofar as both study action and its meaning, we may ask how language defines and shapes behavior (how language gets into action) and, on the other hand, how behavior takes on meaning through labeling and linguistic categorization (how action gets into language). Language also enables man to pass on his experience to other generations. Each individual does not have to rediscover all the knowledge accumulated by other members of his species, as do other animals.

LANGUAGE AS SYMBOL SYSTEM

We begin with several assumptions about how men make sense of the world around them. The center of man's life is himself, and he concerns himself most with his immediate experiences in concrete situations. We might say that a man's reality is what is most exciting and engaging to him at the time. What he sees stretches out from his own body, but also involves the lives, bodies, and past experiences of others. Furthermore, man is very dependent; he requires a long period to mature and is physically, psychologically, economically reliant upon parents for a long period (that may extend to age 30 in advanced societies). He must learn to communicate to survive, and he must learn those communications shared by his society.

First, he develops nonverbal communication—gestures, grunts, and facial expressions—and then verbal communication. By applying verbal labels to events, he adds them to his *stock of knowledge,* which he may call upon again throughout his life. Much of this knowledge will be simple reciprocal actions, such as extending a hand when someone else does, or waving a hand in response to another's wave. Some of people's responses to each other may be purely individualistic, such as a funny face that makes two people laugh but has no general meaning. However, a residue of human action becomes conventionalized to the degree that it is shared; an extended hand in our culture means an invitation to shake it, reciprocating a greeting. It is not simply interpersonal behavior; it is a relationship based on a cultural definition. As such, it is a *sign*. A sign designates objects, facts, or events in the world whose meaning arises by interpreting the thoughts and actions of other men; a sign depends on the existence of another man:

> In the simplest case, that of a face to face relationship, another's body, events occurring on his body (blushing, smiling), including bodily movements (wincing, beckoning), activities performed by it (talking, walking, manipulating things), are capable of being apprehended by the interpreter as signs. (Natanson, 1962, p. 319).

The primary source of understanding others' actions is the ability to understand one's *own* actions. Men "read minds" because they are able to take the other's place, see things as the other does, and interpret events within a shared perspective. They draw on past experiences and understand things as representing "cases of this," an "example of that," or as some standard feature of life seen in face-to-face relationships.

This idealization at the face-to-face level occurs in all cultures, but a true culture must have ways to refer to events and objects that are not visible or physically present. In the Province of Chiapas, Mexico, the Zinacantecos believe that certain illnesses are caused by certain states of the blood, either hot or cold, and the remedies prescribed by the Shamans reflect these states in the number of candles required in the curing ceremony, trips to the mountains, and the like. This system of curing, like our own germ theory of disease, requires us to take certain visible and outward clues to represent a larger set of established meanings. In our system, a warm forehead may mean a fever, which in turn is a sign of infection. Infection in modern Western medicine is blamed on germs and must be treated using a diagnostic system. The physician places the signs and symptoms of illness within the symbolic context of Western medicine, a *symbol system* which pairs fevers with infections, infections with germs, and further takes isolated symptoms as aspects of those clusters of symptoms we call illness, which are treated as "mumps," "diabetes," "mental illness," and so on.

The question is: How can something within the reality of everyday life be coupled with a system of ideas that have a more abstract and systematic meaning? How are we able to describe people as role players or label hatred of father as an oedipal complex? How do some societies attribute masculinity or femininity to the sun and moon? Society rests on these *symbolic representations* of the relationship between events and social meanings.

MAN CONSTRUCTS MEANING

Man does not react to events on the basis of instinct but interprets events and constructs their meanings through language. Symbols are inherently social. Often, a sense of certainty is ascribed to the conventional symbol such as a flag or a cross as if it were there in perpetuity or as if the meanings were fixed without regard to any interpretation. But the meanings must arise through interpretation. Society establishes the essential aspects of reality for members—its attributes and properties indicated by symbols—but each situation calls for the reestablishment of meanings. As the symbols become defined and narrowed in meaning, they become a part of language; and people are then able to talk about and share their symbols. This is often called the creation of a *universe of discourse*, a language, to talk about shared symbols.

An example from the world of art is helpful. A new kind of event or art object can be called "meaningless." However, when examining the transformation in labels applied to art, we can see the process of the conventional symbols at work. Silvers (1970) describes the reaction of the art public to the first appearance of representative works of the school now called abstract expressionism:

> Beginning in the early 1940's, this art movement developed around the idea that forms were to be based on abstract imagery rather than common visual subject matter, and further, that the style of presentation should vary with the spontaneous "visual language" of each artist. The public complained that the paintings were meaningless. Many of the forms were unrecognizable, and the manner in which paintings were to be viewed differed drastically from the past. Patrons could no longer rely on a visual reading along horizontal and vertical axes (ordinarily applied to a landscape, still life or portrait), nor could they use a perspective distinguishing background and foreground. Many of the paintings required a scanning approach so that a series of randomly selected parts of the canvas could be integrated in the mind of the viewer.

In the controversy this movement precipitated, the role of the artist, according to Silvers, was to construct the meanings of his works for others by providing the art public with a vocabulary and principles so that the art became recognizable as a form of expression, as part of a symbolic system having a degree of meanings among some art viewers.

> Artists also determine the general meanings of their work, chiefly by communicating to others the precepts which they consider to be fundamental in the creation of their works. Artists interpret the meaning and impute values by articulating principles and procedures that govern the production of art items. In this manner they influence the meanings constructed by the other members of society. The precepts may be phrased in the most concrete technical terms or in the most abstract theoretical and metaphysical concepts, and, depending upon the nature of the audience, the precepts are presented through different modes of communication. *Collectively and systematically the methodological precepts of an artist or group of artists endow the paintings and sculptures with meaning in terms of an idealization of creative process.*

This example shows the ways in which meanings arise, become conventional and diffused, and how a universe of linguistic discourse makes it possible. The source of these meanings is itself a sociological clue: it is the artist, in his attempt to organize and find meaning in the world and to carve out a social location in it, who helps define the symbol system for others. Here, as in other spheres of social life, man gives meaning to his actions and productions—man constructs meaning.

THE SOCIAL BASES OF SYMBOLS

Society is created when men are able to represent their actions to each other by means of symbols. Instead of communicating to each other through the repetitive and instinctual gestures of the bee wig-wagging to other bees the direction in which pollen may be found, men use language to transcend the present, to call out experience from the past, to shape the future. How does language arise? How do men develop this marvelous capacity?

Emile Durkheim was one of the first social scientists to develop a systematic place for language in his theory of society. He argued that society cannot possibly be the creation of any given human mind, that it is an idea taking precedence over the individual in many cases (he was impressed that people might even commit suicide as a sign of their commitment to society). Above all, the most significant aspects of social life were collective. He felt that sociologists should study only those things which characterized a whole society or group, not the characteristics of individuals alone. The focus of sociology was to be on systems of ideas (such as religion, kinship, law) and patterns or rates of actions (the suicide rate, the density of a population, the ecology of a society).

SOCIETY CREATES SYMBOLS

Language is the most important of these systems of ideas because it is shared by groups, is characteristic of groups as a whole, is external to the individual (unless it is babble), and is the means by which other symbols and meanings are transmitted from one generation to the next. Durkheim argued that groups of people created symbol systems such as language as adaptive mechanisms enabling them to deal with and give meaning to an often dangerous and threatening external world. This same position was later developed by two linguists, Edward Sapir (Mandelbaum, ed., 1949) and Benjamin Whorf (Carroll, ed., 1956).

Two groups writing since Durkheim have challenged his view of the rise of symbols in society. One group, headed by the Swiss psychologist

Jean Piaget (see Insert No. 36), sees the meaning of fundamental social categories (size, shape, temperature, color) as determined by prelinguistic experiences (prior to the development of language in the child). The other group, represented by the French anthropologist Claude Levi-Strauss (see Insert No. 41), argues that the categories in society, including those in language, may be found in all societies. It is important to note, before we evaluate the two challenges to Durkheim's ideas, that they have important implications for the study of language. If, as Piaget says, meanings are learned by prelinguistic experience, all categories would arise from the physical properties of objects and be uniform in all cultures. Levi-Strauss would argue in similar fashion for the universality of categories but he is searching for them in underlying conceptions or ideas about society, which are found in very abstract form in any given society. In either case, Durkheim's idea (later revived by Sapir and Whorf) that language is culture and that culture is unique to some degree for a given group is challenged by Piaget and Levi-Strauss. They see language as a universal logical system based in the physical properties of objects or in the metaphysical basis of human life.

LANGUAGE LEARNING

Roger Brown (1965, ch. 5), reviewing studies advocating prelinguistic determination of the fundamental concepts of thought, concludes that many concepts are learned, as Piaget and others have claimed, without "social mediation" or the filter of language concepts. The child's early experience with objects, his manipulation of them, his extraction of perceptual constants, and his observation of the physical effects of light, heat, and motion lead him to develop conceptions that require names only when language is learned. Language does not precede concept and meaning. The concept arises before the language used to label it; the labeling does not create the reality of the concept for the child (Roger Brown, 1965, p. 314). Later studies by Piaget of children's learning and use of such social-ethical concepts as lying, justice, guilt, and errors, however, reveal that they are shaped by the language used and transmitted to youth differentially from culture to culture.

Other studies of the concept of color, pain, kinship, and disease illustrate the impact of culture on the semantic variation attached to words. The color experiments are particularly revealing, for they establish that the same physical variations in hue, saturation, and brightness are divided and named distinctively and differently by three groups tested (exclusively Zuñi speaking, bilingual Zuñi, and native Americans). Culture provides the categories (blue, red, yellow) into which physical stimuli are sorted and labeled.

Different cultures develop an elaborate range of names for what is important to their existence: Filipinos (Hanuoo) have ninety-two names for rice (Conklin, 1954); Laplanders have numerous names for snow (Werner, 1948); Solomon Islanders have six names for coconut, but no generic term; North Africans have some six thousand names for camels (Lindesmith and Strauss, 1968, p. 28); and Americans have almost no names for their kin beyond the cousin.

Levi-Strauss (1967) has speculated how the kinship system of a given society may express two poles (hot or cold, nonrepresentational or representational), that may also characterize other aspects of the society, its medicine, its law, its religion. Once a principle of dualism (positive and negative, attraction and repulsion) is established, a variety of interactions between social institutions can be made. Propositions might be formulated, such as "all societies are dualistic in nature; the underlying model of opposi-

---

INSERT NO. 41

Claude Levi-Strauss

Claude Levi-Strauss (1908–   ) is a French social anthropologist who has extended the study of man to try to account for the basic structure of the human mind through all ages and all types of primitive or civilized states. More than any other contemporary social scientist, Levi-Strauss has aimed at a universal statement of man's social institutions and customs.

As a child, Levi-Strauss demonstrated the intense curiosity that was to characterize his later innovative social analysis. His boyhood collections of ancient and primitive artifacts and his study of geology established a concern for classification and investigation of the underlying nature of things. Rejecting his formal training in academic philosophy, Levi-Strauss turned to anthropology and became a field anthropologist. At age 28, he went to Sao Paulo, Brazil, as professor of sociology. Here he expanded his amateur and unsystematic knowledge of preliterate people by venturing into the Brazilian interior to study Indians firsthand. His extensive experiences with the remnants of these primitive cultures are poetically described in *Tristes Tropiques*.

Forced out of Europe by Nazi anti-Semitism, Levi-Strauss spent most of the war years teaching in New York at the New School for Social Research and later became a cultural counselor in the French Embassy. His Anglo-American contacts in these positions proved fruitful in further broadening his intellectual scope.

His theoretical development shifted from ethnology and descriptive studies of primitives to the analysis of social structure as a formal and abstract entity. Levi-Strauss sought through the study of myth, ritual, and magic to establish

tion can be discovered in the categories used in the society including the language."

These two positions on the relations between language and conceptual thought are both buttressed with much empirical evidence and argument. No doubt, some aspects of conceptual learning precede linguistic learning. There is no way at present, however, to ascertain the limits of the influence of prelinguistic conceptual learning on later learning, or whether Levi-Strauss' models might not also account for these processes. Concept learning based on language, as Bruner and others have shown, probably accounts for much of what Piaget takes to be prelinguistic learning, especially in the almost patently social area of ethics. There is little doubt that language categories create a considerable part of the meaning system characteristic of the adults of a society—but how much? We simply do not yet know the answer to this basic question.

---

the essentials of social relationships and their necessary connections. To this end he employed structural linguistics, which emphasizes the logical rules of relationships that order the vast diversity of sounds and meanings. He argued that, just as language follows predictable forms, cultural phenomena obey social laws. The social scientist should concentrate on forms, not content, for understanding these social laws. By thus moving beyond empiricism, he intended digging below every theoretical level yet discovered to come to a basic structure of the human mind.

For Levi-Strauss, the underlying structure *is* the reality. By abstracting the limited, significant features of social organization, societies may be compared. As men think, so do they order their social life. By applying the rules of logic to the analysis of social forms, Levi-Strauss analyzed social systems in terms of linguistic systems, "built by the mind on the level of unconscious thought." From this perspective, the logic of the savage was as fully comprehensible as that of Western man, but of a different order from the logic of abstract science. Mankind is one through all times and places.

Levi-Strauss has not only provided a new method and theory for studying man, he has also been a consistent social critic of the cultural dislocation of modern life. Material "progress," he has noted, has devastated the primitives' simple ordering of man and nature. "The world began without the human race, and it will end without it," he has declared. While his sentiments and general approach to social structure have been repudiated by some critics, including most of the phenomenological sociologists, Levi-Strauss continues to exert a strong impact on the systematic development of sociology in Europe and America.

Other works include *The Savage Mind* (1966), *Structural Anthropology* (1963), and *The Elementary Structures of Kinships* (1969).

Learning the Semantic Domain

In the years since World War II, the dominant interest of philosophers has been *linguistic analysis,* the study of the use of ordinary language. Ludwig Wittgenstein (see Insert No. 42), one of the revolutionary figures in this movement, urged repeatedly in his later works that philosophers desist from their search for language as a mirror of reality or for the precise referent of a given word. His work is influential among sociologists, psychologists, and anthropologists concerned with language learning and competent usage. His views, presented in brief, are an orientation to further discussion of language.

Wittgenstein felt that the study of philosophy was artificial and should return to data readily available to everyone—one's own speech and actions. Language is the data for answering philosophic questions, and it is right on the tip of the tongue. But to engage in answering philosophic queries, one must proceed from ordinary use and users to philosophic questions

---

INSERT NO. 42

Ludwig Wittgenstein

Ludwig Wittgenstein (1889–1951) has been the most powerful influence on contemporary philosophy. The linguistic movement he inspired has spread from England to the United States and Europe. The profound impact of his often abstruse philosophical work is due to its originality and scope, as well as to its lucid and systematic style.

Wittgenstein was born in Vienna, Austria, and reared in an affluent and cultivated family. His parental home was renowned as a center of musical life. His father, trained as an engineer, became a leading figure in the steel and iron industry in Austria. Ludwig was the youngest of five brothers and three sisters, all of whom were artistically and intellectually talented.

Educated at home until he was fourteen, Wittgenstein's earliest formal training was in engineering and physics, interests he maintained throughout his life. He was equally adept as a mechanic and inventor and did original research in aeronautics. Construction of a jet-reaction propeller for aircraft led him to an interest in propeller design, essentially a mathematical task. His interests shifted from applied to pure mathematics and eventually to research on the foundations of mathematics.

His earliest philosophical work was in logic. These studies were to move him away from conventional philosophy, which emphasized certainty in knowledge, to the possible combinations of elements in reality. Language, from this vantage point, is a picture or model of reality and serves as a vehicle for expression and knowing. The structure of statements depicts a possible, not a necessary, state of affairs. Wittgenstein held that words, often assumed to have

(the ways in which people speak provide a paradigm or model of what is an important issue) and must look at the ways that language is not being used or is used badly to contrast with what is seen as proper use. It is not so much a matter of proper construction or order by the rules, as whether there is a shared understanding of the words used in that context.

Wittgenstein takes a "cultural view" of meaning. There is no single meaning of any word, in spite of the dictionary's set of ordered or preferred definitions. There is no single usage of a word. On the contrary, there are many uses, many meanings, perhaps as many meanings and uses as there are situations in which human beings "use" and "mean" words. Thus, if a parent wanted to teach a child the meaning of the word "uncle," he would not attempt to give her the kinship rules of American society specifying the lineality, sex, and generation of uncles. He would refer to specific people as examples—"Uncle Jim," "Uncle Jack," "Uncle Joe." Sometimes uncle refers to close friends of the family, and sometimes brothers and sisters take

definite and specific referents in the real world, are not used with fixed meanings, nor do concepts have sharp boundaries. In language, we play games with words, he insisted, and the meaning of the game becomes clear only when we see it in the context of the players. Only by adopting the frame of reference of the speakers can one understand their meaning. "An expression has meaning only in the stream of life" sums up a central feature of his philosophy.

Wittgenstein was a professor at Cambridge University, England, but found academic life exhausting and tedious. His strong sense of duty dictated a rigorous lecture, discussion, and professional schedule, which interfered with his obtaining the solitude he required for working on the unsolved problems of his theories.

Haunted by the inhumanity of man, a pessimism which pervaded his consciousness, Wittgenstein frequently sought solace in an isolated hut in Norway and later in a farmhouse in northern Ireland. Service in both world wars and imprisonment during World War I were experiences that deepened his belief that human life is ugly and that our minds are hopelessly in the dark—a feeling often close to despair. In his later years, he was racked with illness and periods of mental instability.

His difficult personality, while attracting brilliant students, was too morose for close friendship. He sought love and response from others but was unable to give it himself. Yet his profound wonder at the nature of life never ceased. He commented in one of his works: "Not *how* the world is, is the mystical, but *that* it is." Existence for this tormented genius was infinitely profound and problematic.

Wittgenstein's major works include *The Blue and Brown Books* (1958), *Philosophical Investigations* (1967), and *Tractatus Logico-Philosophicus* (1961).

the child's role and refer to each other as uncle when sociologically they do not stand in the avuncular relationship. Sometimes kin connected through marriage to relatives are granted a kin name of a much closer sort—for example, "uncle" for my wife's sister's husband's sister's husband.

The idea of *language games* is central to Wittgenstein's theory of language. His examples suggest the idea of a situationally located, loosely bounded cluster of activities defined and identified by similarities in the use of words:

> Consider for example the proceedings that we call "games." I mean board-games, card-games, ball-games, Olympic games, and so on. What is common to them all? Don't say: "There must be something common, or they would not be called 'games' "—but look and see whether there is anything common to all. For if you look at them you will not see something that is common to all, but similarities, relationships, and a whole series of them at that. To repeat: don't think, but look! Look for example at board-games, with their multifarious relationships. Now pass to card games; here you find many correspondences with the first group, but many common features drop out, and others appear. When we pass next to ball-games, much that is common is retained, but much is lost. Are they all "amusing"? Compare chess with noughts and crosses. Or is there always winning and losing, or competition between players? Think of patience. In ball games there is winning and losing; but when a child throws his ball at the wall and catches it again, this feature has disappeared. Look at the parts played by skill and luck; and at the difference between skill in chess and skill in tennis. Think now of games like ring-a-ring-a-roses; here is the element of amusement, but how many other characteristic features have disappeared! And we can go through the many, many other groups of games in the same way; can see how similarities crop up and disappear.
>
> And the result of this examination is: we see a complicated network of similarities overlapping and criss-crossing: sometimes overall similarities, sometimes similarities of detail (Wittgenstein, 1967).

These games cannot be discovered by reading a dictionary or by constructing grammars, but only by means of a perspective known by the participants that provides links between words and the objects named or categorized.

Language Learning as a Word Game

Roger Brown describes language learning with a metaphor reminiscent of Wittgenstein, calling the process the "original word game" (1968, ch. 6). The *word game* takes place as "things" are touched, presented, or drawn to the attention of persons, while "words" are produced as their names or labels. I play this game with my little girl (19 months) every day. I hold her and read her book to her, pointing to the "chick-chick," dogs, babies, and other brightly colored objects and naming them. "Elephant, see his trunk; dog, see his ears; duck, quack, quack." I point to her nose saying "nose," and she repeats, often pointing either to my nose or hers. Before she could play this word game with me, she had to learn language as a means for obtaining what she wanted, and before that she had to learn gestures. These two stages in learning precede the ability to manipulate language symbols in an abstract fashion.

Cries, whimpers, and whines seem to be uniformly used by children to express a need. The need to eat, to drink, to get up or down, to go out or come in is first signaled by a system of *natural signs* or cries. These signs seem to arise primarily from unpleasant sensations and interrupt what is the child's normal speech at that time—his babble, the almost random production of sounds. As the parent connects the less sophisticated emotional signals or gestures of the child with types of objects, reinforcing the child's connection of cry and satisfaction, he responds selectively to the child's babble. It is usually understood that any normal child in any culture emits in his babble all the sounds necessary for the development of competent speech in that culture. As early as 11 months of age, a profile of children's babble begins to show a "drift" toward the local norms of sound (Roger Brown, 1968, pp. 199–201).

This process of language learning suggests an imitation pattern by which the child changes from using what Piaget calls *egocentric* speech to the emulation of adult speech-patterns. Adult speech is then adhered to insofar as the physical and mental world of the child permits it (Vigotsky, 1962). One of the most interesting social features of this process is that, at first, a child seems to use words in ways which reflect his perspective and which are "inaccurate" in just those ways in which his experience differs from that of adults (Roger Brown, 1968, p. 325). It is possible that children do not learn the subtle variations and shadings of meaning attached to money, for example, only because it has little bearing on their everyday affairs, not because children are unable to abstract. Children's meanings approximate the adult's definitions and uses of money as the child engages in social relationships involving the use of money (Lindesmith and Strauss, 1968, pp. 245–246).

The Self and Language

The *self* distinguishes man from all other beings, even those who carry on a social life. The principal means by which the person develops a self and a mind is through his association with others—particularly in his symbolic, verbal communication. Language serves first in addressing ourselves and trying out roles we can take in response to ourselves and then as a part of learning the many roles that social life requires. Broadly, the child moves through two stages as he is transformed and transforms himself: *play* and *the game.*

For Mead, play is a series of "playing at" sequences: the child plays at being a teacher, a mother, a policeman, and so on. He assumes each role, addresses himself and responds to himself in that role: as a policeman, he arrests himself; as a teacher, he teaches himself. The rules learned in play have to do with simple role relationships.

In the play stage, language is the means by which the child names himself and others to whom he responds. By this identification, he aligns his conduct with the other in the playing-at phenomenon. The vocal gesture parallels the gesture of the arm or leg; as the person hears himself, he responds as he imagines others might respond. The vocal gesture is the only one shared in all its facets by both listener and speaker, but the gestures made in play are not its central feature. It is language, the vocal gestures, which have a shared social meaning.

The game, on the other hand, represents a "higher development" of the self because it entails awareness of and reaction to (1) a set of roles, (2) rules governing role relationships, and (3) a capacity to assume these roles. To play a game is to see oneself in a role in relationship to the overall perspective of the rules governing others and to abstract parts of the others' roles transcending that situation. The game is a microcosm of society as a whole. As the person learns to play the game, he learns to organize his own actions in regard to others and to respond in such a way that he may fit his conduct to uniformly binding rules.

Learning the Structure of Language

A second aspect of language learning is the learning of grammatical structure. The question is similar to that posed in the discussion of learning meanings. How do children learn the rules that enable them to speak correctly (according to grammar books) while actual performance requires continuously new arrangements of words? It is a three-stage process (Roger Brown, 1965). The three processes are learned between 18 and 36 months, although not necessarily in this order: imitation by reduction; imitation with expansion; and induction of latent structure.

Imitation by reduction describes a child's version of adult speech. Children imitate parents' sentences by shortening them and omitting words, reducing the speech to "telegraph style." Words such as *to, by, the* are omitted, while those normally stressed in sentences—the verbs, nouns, and adjectives—remain. These words, called *contentives,* are probably imitated because they are stressed, can be guessed from the context, and serve an important reference function (Roger Brown, 1965, p. 290ff).

Eventually, the child must learn to expand the meaning and complexity of his sentences through another process that Brown calls *imitation with expansion.* All investigators of children's speech have noted that, continuously, adults repeat and add to their children's speech. Brown and associates found that parents talked to a child in this way, expanding his sentences, about 30 percent of the time. Most striking is that the manner in which parents imitate children is not random or merely a repetition of the child's reduced sentence. It takes the form of expanding the child's sentence, including those aspects of the child's speech that the child leaves out—the articles, auxiliary verbs, prepositions, and conjunctions. For example, if my daughter says, "Baby crying," I repeat, "*Yes, the* baby *is* crying." I retain the child's word order, add those words the child omits (a kind of mirror image of the child's speech), and make expansions according to the circumstances, which provide a *contextual effect.* If she repeats the same phrase to me later this evening, I will repeat, "Yes, the baby did cry." Identification of these two processes supports Mead's general position that the child takes roles vis-à-vis parents through language. The child imitates, taking a counterrole to the parent, attempting to emulate his speech. The parent assumes the role of authority or of the community, as represented in adult speech, speaking to the child in expanded terms. At the same time that the child imitates the parent, the parents imitate the child (take the role of the other). A reciprocity of perspectives results.

The final process is more complex and probably the central part of language, that is, grammatical learning. Brown calls this process the *induction of latent structure.* He claims that children learn sets of words in isolation, particularly nouns and modifiers, and then learn the variations possible, combining nouns and their modifiers in longer and more complex sentences. This process depends on the child's capacity to learn the ways in which words expand (via plurals, change in verb forms and endings) to fit the demands of the situation. This process requires a knowledge of latent structure.

Language is learned through interaction, probably in the context of two or three people in conversation, and involves the two processes we have discussed, the learning of grammar and semantics. When people speak they shape and direct their own behavior and others' behavior, and the mutually resultant behavior is a product of this interaction. In order to act, people must possess some notion of the meaning of others' behavior. A concept of meaning is at the heart of sociology. Meaning must arise from experience, and experience is based on and emerges from language, its grammar and semantics. But this equation seems highly generalized and much too simple. We will examine it further in reference to selected sociological research on language as interaction and language as social structure (Deutscher, 1967). *Language as interaction* refers to studying the effects of the social context in which communication takes place upon the meaning of that communication. *Language as social structure* refers to studying how group contacts, conflicts, and changes are patterned by language.

Language as Interaction

There are three major methods used by sociologists to study language as interaction: (1) experimental studies; (2) experimental studies of situated meanings; and (3) studies of communication in natural settings. *Experimental studies of language* rely on the usual model of experimental research. One or more well-defined variables are introduced into a situation in which other effects are controlled or minimized, and the effects of the introduced or experimental variables are measured. One of the best-known examples of this sort of research is Robert Bales' *interaction process analysis* (Bales, in Maccoby, Newcomb and Hartley, eds., 1958, pp. 437–447) (see Chapter 10). The focus and method of this research has the merit of being relatively precise, but its scope is overly narrow. Laboratory interaction lacks the dimensions of real life situations, where meanings are not limited and controlled by an investigator.

The second type of language study might be called the *experimental study of situated meanings*. One fundamental human activity is the creation of meaning; people lacking sensory stimulation either in extreme isolation situations or under experimental conditions will hallucinate, perhaps to create social boundaries or meaning in the situation. Several sociologists have demonstrated that people will construct meanings in whatever situations they find themselves (Kjolseth, 1967; Garfinkel, 1967, ch. 3). In experiments, the subjects' perceptions and definitions may not coincide with the experimental reality, or they may focus on matters irrelevant to the experimental design. For example, Bruce (1956) found that people used a pre-established context of "sports" to identify an inaudible remark as being about the subject of sports.

Sociologists have most often studied *communication in natural settings*. They have attempted to understand how speech defines objects, gives them location and attributes, and thus underlies the nature of action or response to these objects. These researchers often adopt an anthropological style or approach, involving participation or at least observation of ongoing language. Thus, these studies tend to deal with a narrow aspect of behavior, which can be seen, observed, and described in great detail over time and with concepts of a limited range. Similar studies have been committed to reconstructing a language that reflects and captures the actor's point of view. (An excellent example of this approach is Psathas and Henslin's (1967) study of how cab drivers receive and interpret instructions from dispatchers.)

Some results of the various studies of language as interaction show how language reflects respect for the speaker; how it coordinates meanings enabling people to work together; how it is central to role taking; how the style, type, and nature of the language contribute to defining the situation.

Language as Social Structure

Even if an important beginning has been made in understanding the situated nature of talk, as yet the study of language as social structure is more an entity in belief than in fact. Language as social structure refers to the ways language defines group relationships in and between societies, and to the language forms (rhetoric) used to describe social structure. Although a large body of synthetic writing exists, few generalizations are empirically verified. We need evidence on questions about learning social roles, the formation of groups through and by language, language as a social system, and language-patterned relationships among groups, between groups, and cross-culturally (Useem, 1963).

As the linguist looks to bits of meaningful sounds and their combinations and how they are patterned into language, so the sociologist looks to meaningful bits of social action and expectations of it—*roles, norms, statuses, identities,* and *social acts*—as the building blocks of society. These concepts provide the language by which he can describe the social action he observes. It is his language for talking about language.

Let us turn to some examples of how language patterns the relationships between groups of people, whether by stabilizing or changing them. Edward Thompson (1935) suggested that sociologists consider that society has at least two fundamental features: a *grammar* and a *natural history*. If one looks to the grammar of a society, he looks to the formal rules that specify the ideal relationships within that society. The grammar deals with what is expected, not with what is done. The natural history indicates that societies change in line with some regular pattern and that change itself takes place within understandable boundaries.

The grammar of a society is indicated by the rules of respect between people taken as representatives of groups (not as individuals but as players of social roles). The rules can best be discovered by looking at the existing terms and the occasions on which they are used. For example, the respect term *don* is used throughout Latin America and wherever Spanish-speaking people live. It has primary reference to a respected male, and thus reflects the prestige system of the community. Romano (1960) studied utilization of the term *don* in a small Texas town, showing that language mirrored the social relationships between people. The term is used before the first name —for example, Don Pedro—and always with the first name. It is never used by the person to whom the term applies, nor by kin who employ more intimate names. In the community are two major classes of men called *don*. On the one hand, the term is granted on the basis of the traditional categories—the patron or powerful "father figure" in the community, the Mexican consul, certain wealthy businessmen, the political powers of nearby towns, the *curandero* or native healer, and very old men. On the other hand, it is granted to men who have achieved their right to the title. These men seem close to the "ideal male" in this context—men who have passed thirty-five, are worldly-wise, independent, and dominant, expecially in sexual prowess, and have achieved some notoriety in the neighborhood.

Thus, the term *don* refers to "respect between unrelated males . . . as the acknowledgment of social distance according to prescribed forms and with primary reference to social status as determined by the traditional and achieved classes of donship." Respect is gained either through the control of valuable resources (the traditional basis) or through an aloof independent demeanor. Once a man is assigned to either of these categories, he is called *don* and spoken to in a formal way, given courtesies, and not sought as an intimate friend.

This example of the grammar of social relationships also has a dynamic dimension. It shows how prestige can be earned by proper behavior and attitudes, enhancing one's social position and altering the traditional structure. It also relates to the previous section on language as interaction. In the study of interaction itself, one would look for the clues, verbal and nonverbal, in the situation that made use of the term *don* appropriate. In that case, the situation as a context in which meanings arise would be primary. In this case, the grammatical or routine nature of the relationship, *once established,* is the focus.

Language as a source of social change, as a part of the *natural* history of society as it bears on conflict and power struggles, has been studied most by scholars in the nations of Africa, Norway, Canada (especially French-speaking Canada—Quebec), and India. In India, a country with a dozen major languages each spoken by millions, the dominance of a language indicates the potential, symbolic, or actual dominance of the people speaking that language. Thus such questions as national publications, broadcasts, or advertising mobilize language loyalties. The effects of the world-wide spread of "civilization" are increased contacts between groups across national boundaries, colonialism, war, imperialism, capitalism, and free trade, all of which depend upon communication and language. This contact, in turn, has created trade languages, bilingualism and multilingualism, language loyalty and disloyalty, questions of power and sometimes war, all hinging on language.

Some Recent Developments

Two approaches to the study of society through the lens of language are now gaining favor among anthropologists and sociologists. One, componential analysis, is associated primarily with anthropology; the other, ethnomethodology, is associated with sociology. They are important indications of the growing interest in language among the social sciences and appear promising.

Language and culture. While agreeing with the Durkheimian view of language as external and constraining, some anthropologists have attempted to investigate how men are able to understand each other's vast range of meanings, even the unstated and assumed. This work does not share the grandiose aim of Levi-Strauss to develop models underlying the cultures of the world but aims to deal with the underlying model of meaning that a language indicates in a single culture. In general, they have found that language reflects culture only selectively, but the relationship between language and culture is still debated, with special emphasis of study being on the possible bond between social categories and language categories (Hymes, ed., 1964, pp. 166–169).

While anthropology as a whole aims to study systems of classification (Needham, 1967), componential analysis or ethnoscience aims to construct a theory of the ways native speakers organize these meaning systems. In this approach, a culture is a system of meanings based on an underlying form or model(s). *Culture* is defined as consisting of

> whatever it is one has to know or believe in order to operate in a manner acceptable to its members and to do so in a role they accept for any one of themselves . . . it does not consist of things, people or emotions. It is rather an organization of these things. It is the forms of things people have in mind, their models for perceiving, relating and otherwise interpreting them (Goodenough, in Hymes, ed., 1964, p. 36).

Goodenough, a leading figure of componential analysis, describes an adequate knowledge of culture.

> What is required is to construct a theory of the conceptual models (of culture). We test the adequacy of such a theory by our ability to interpret and predict what goes on in a community by how its members, our informants, do so. A further test is our ability for ourselves to behave in ways which lead to the kind of responses from the community's members which our theory would lead us to expect. Thus tested, the theory is a valid statement of what you have to know in order to operate as a member of the society and is, as such, a valid description of its culture.

Language is both an aspect of culture and the means by which one learns and knows the culture. The study of linguistics is intimately tied to the study of culture. In contrast to linguists who study grammar, these anthropological linguists study meanings, the semantic domain.

Componential analysis is the study of meanings by identifying what determines the culturally appropriate uses of a term. The componential analyst wants to know the *occasions* on which one term is used, its possible range of denotations, and clues helping him decide how to use it competently on such an occasion. A simple example is drawn from Tyler

(1970, pp. 7–8). Furniture is the general or inclusive term he discusses, and under it he lists more specific cases of the same class. Each level provides a contrast, as when one compares *furniture* to *tables,* and *tables* to *end tables.*

The objects to which we apply names do not provide a rationale for the distinctions which a knowledgeable person can make; thus, we are not aware in a systematic rule-governed way *why* chairs and tables are different, we only know they are. We can discover that a chair has four legs, a seat, and a back, while a table has four legs, no seat or back, and a top. Therefore, the presence of two features (a seat and a back) and the absence of one (a top) distinguishes a chair from a table.

The inference of *rules* or features governing distinctions native to the language is the province of the anthropologist. Describing the categories and meanings in the culture from the members' point of view is the initial step. The anthropologist's role is to identify the significant features of an environment and how they are organized, and then to infer the organizing principles underlying such a system of meanings known to the group (Tyler, ed., 1970, p. 3). Typically, componential analysis focuses on a narrow and easily circumscribed set of terms, well known and easily elicited—such as color, firewood, kinship, or disease categories.

Componential analysis is an attempt to discover how a person looks at events in the world, how that native person defines them and relates them to other meaningful features of his social world. It seeks to uncover the rules governing each of these processes. Unfortunately, studies to date have been perhaps overly concerned with static portrayals of kinship as a system of meaning. Further, the issue of learning and competence is understood or *assumed* in this approach; only a fully socialized and competent user of a language could explain a complex kinship system to an investigator. Thus, in spite of its exciting potential, the approach tends to yield a static picture of society and to minimize the problematic features of meaning that we have argued are so characteristic of linguistic communication.

Ethnomethodology. Ethnomethodology is a recent approach in sociology (see Chapter 4 for its general features). As it is a philosophical stance, any sociological topic can be analyzed using ethnomethodology. However, it is most concerned with language in society and thus focuses on face-to-face situations in which people talk to each other. The term ethnomethodology combines two words, *ethnos* (meaning a people, culture, or social group) and *methodology* (a procedure or technique for obtaining information). Ethnomethodology means the study of how people obtain and use social information, especially the information that allows routine interactions to take place. Many of these rules, norms, and bits of social information are not explicitly known by members of society, but are taken for granted (see also Chapter 4). Ethnomethodology asks: "What ways do people use to make their own actions, intentions, and past experiences accountable or understandable to others?" As an example, let us examine one case of ethnomethodological analysis of a familiar activity.

Grading in universities cannot be understood solely by reading the catalog that explains the range of grades and their social equivalents (A = outstanding performance, B = above-average performance, and C = adequate performance). Grading must be seen as a way in which people make sense of the world. How? The professor must apply the categories available at his university to groups of students who register for his classes. They are a sample drawn from a population within the university: people composed of a fairly wide range of individual skills, attitudes, abilities, backgrounds, and personalities. The university demands that members of the class be ranked in order to ascertain their relative merit and qualification for a degree. The ranks are the grading categories (A, B, C) supplied in the catalog. These ranks must be applied to individual students. The catalog and the university regulations cannot tell a professor how to apply the abstract system of ranks to a given individual.

The procedure of grading can be studied ethnomethodologically. The formal categories are applied to individuals by use of certain common-sense assumptions: that test scores indicate ability in the subject matter; that ability in subject matter can be ranked by the use of points; that cut-off levels on a numerical scale of points can be translated into letter scores; that letter scores from previous classes are a reliable indication of past performance; that scores can be interpreted, weighted, judged, and manipulated to produce meaningful grades. The grades are then defined as adequate because they do the job of ranking and allocating honor.

When students call for an accounting, feeling their grade does not represent what they know, the professor may turn to other rationalizations. The practical method of decision making may become its own ratonale—the curve set an A at x points and above; you had fewer than x points; therefore, your grade is B. You failed because you did not amass enough points to pass. The outcomes the professor produced by his assumption of a match between performance and points (what a grade means) are justified to students. The fact that grades were produced justifies the schemes producing them, though this rationale might not be accepted by the student at the wrong end of the curve.

In contrast to componential analysis, ethnomethodology seeks to understand the nature of deep rules that make possible continued meaningful interaction in conversations (Cicourel, 1970). The denotative meanings studied by Tyler and others assume the existence of connotative meanings surrounding any utterance—such as the dress, social status, biography, gesture, posture, or tone of the speaker. The ethnomethodologist might argue that not only must one know those connotative meanings, but one must also know what phenomena to discount or ignore, such as pauses, phonetic variation, and individual differences in sound production, if he is to know what the exact meaning of any communication is for members of the culture.

Garfinkel (1967, ch. 3), in an ingenious experiment, sought to uncover some of these deep rules. Ten students were selected for an experiment in "new types of counseling." They were asked to sit in a room separated from an experimenter, "the counselor," and connected to him only by a microphone; then they were asked to provide him with the background of a personal problem. These questions were to be asked in such a way that the counselor could answer "Yes" or "No." After questioning the counselor once and receiving a Yes or No answer (the answers were chosen on a random basis), the subject was to disconnect the microphone and to make an interpretation of the exchange. Then the subject was to reconnect the microphone and ask the next question. Each subject also dictated a final summary of his interpretation of the question-and-answer session. From the subjects' capacity to make sense of absolute nonsense (random replies), Garfinkel derives several important unstated rules of conversational interchange, the *deep rules* of conversation. They underscore the prospective-retrospective nature of conversation, as indicated by "I thought so . . . now I understand" clauses. That which initially does not make sense is filed away until it can be utilized in a meaningful interpretation. Garfinkel summarizes:

> Through the work of documenting—i.e., by searching for and determining pattern, by treating advisers' answers as motivated by the intended sense of the question, by waiting for later answers to clarify the sense of previous ones, by finding answers to unasked questions, the conceivably normal values of what was being advised were established, tested, reviewed, retained, restored; in a word, managed (1967, p. 94).

From this view, events are seen as part of a pattern or context of meaning that persists and is indicated by *signs* pointing to it, an *order,* even though the order remains unseen. The signs are, of course, linguistic signs, and by their appearance they enable the structures of honor, dishonor, status, and the like to be seen as a part of society existing in the members' knowledge of it. People will assign meaning to random events (Yes and No answers), and do so by assuming an order is there and by picking out those things in the conversation that indicate order to them, thus making the parts of the conversation into members of the order of meanings.

No set of utterances can be fully analyzed by an observer or a member of the society without reference to what is already known. Garfinkel refers to what is known by people who are conversing with the symbolic equivalent of the written *etc.* Not simply a statement that words take their meaning from the situations in which they are used, this statement attempts to discover how people understand the intent of such devices as metaphor, irony, and analogy. How do we know when people are being sarcastic? Garfinkel (1967, pp. 24–31) asked students to write a conversation on one side of a piece of paper and, on the other, an explanation of what the participants were talking about. After each attempt at explanation, Garfinkel demanded that the students try further explanations until the students capitulated, claiming the task was endless. From this exercise, Garfinkel concludes that the words in a conversation cannot be understood solely by finding the referents of the verbal signs (to what does a "heel" or "feeling all right" refer?), but only by also seeing the verbal signs as illustrations of what is left unsaid. The students sought to explain ways of speaking, the style of presentation, which is part of an *etc.* dimension surrounding the words. They failed because, even as they wrote more explanations, they were expanding the task by adding more implied meanings, unexplained by words but derived from the context and style of the phrases.

Linguists look to grammar as the structure of thought. Sociologists have sought a similar social grammar in such concepts as roles, identities, and selves. However, to understand these terms, we must first provide a context in which they have relevance; thus, the meaningful structure of situations is an important domain of inquiry. Goffman (1962, 1963, 1967) has given us exquisite examples of the range of breaches of an unstated situational order in his work on embarrassment, "face-work," "cooling out the mark," and stigmatization. Order is indicated by members' reactions to a fellow's loss of poise—slip of the tongue, drool, stumble, or spilling food. They attempt to repair the scene by pauses, downcast eyes, avoidance of glances, shifting positions, and accepting apologies. The "moral wholeness" of both the one in error and those on whom the error was committed is restored by these devices.

Sherri Cavan (1966) illustrates how conversation is structured among bar patrons. Normal conversations in bars often begin with entrance ceremonies, but bar patrons are generally defined as open to approach and conversation unless they indicate specific feelings to the contrary. The trick is to extract oneself from conversations and, thus, otherwise insignificant signals, such as long pauses, are often taken as indication that one of the parties should go. But leave-taking is signaled, so that mutual face is saved:

> Generally, this leave-taking is not accompanied by any verbal statements. For example, if a patron is leaving the premises or changing his location within the establishment, the termination of an ongoing encounter may be signified only by the patron gathering up his possessions from the bar (change money, cigarettes, matches, etc.). Such activity is usually understood by the other to mean that the encounter has come to an end, although nothing may have been said before the activity started and nothing may be said afterward. Talk simply ceases when the collection of goods and posses-

sions begins. He who is about to move may offer the other a curt nod as he gets up, but this is not obligatory and frequently not possible. Typically, the other will become involved in some activity such as finishing his drink, lighting a cigarette, or instigating an encounter with another, permitting ego's departure to occur silently and unobstrusively. However, unless one verbally declares before he physically moves that he will socially return as, for example, saying, "I'm just going to the bathroom," or "I only want to get a pack of cigarettes," even temporary departures are conventionally read as having effectively terminated the encounter. Once the other has returned to the spatial proximity the two share, any further talk between them requires the same ceremonial opening that began the initial conversation Cavan, 1966, pp. 55–56).

Thus, to understand talk in a situation, both nonverbal and verbal clues must be understood as defining the situation.

In summary, we may conclude that actions do not speak for themselves; actions *do not* speak louder than words. For the fully socialized members of society social action, even organized and shared action such as we find in games, takes on meaning when it is described by a shared set of symbols —by a language.

Through language the world takes on meaning and continuity. Once learned, language is the key to taking a socially defined position (a role), casting others in related roles, and engaging in social interaction. We may learn a great deal by studying those categories of people who are considered unable to take a socially defined position. Although the study of deviance covers many of these categories (the deformed, the sick, and the retarded), it centrally involves language when it deals with the "deaf," the "illiterate," the "mute," the "blind," or the "stutterer." By contrast, these categories show the social errors attributed to people perceived to suffer from incapacities of language. Incapacities of the body alone are excused as biological failures. Incapacities of speech, however, are not easily excused. For the person's self is based on his ability to linguistically evoke behavior in others and to respond to others' social demands on him. A failure of language, more certainly than a failure of the body, will be taken as a failure of the self—total failure. To learn a language is, consequently, to learn and display a competent being and to express that being.

Studies of social interaction and social structure through language deal with the patterning and change of social life. Either language must be acknowledged as an intimate part of any study of social life or it will be an unknown and uncontrolled contributor to that study. To scientifically study society, we must scientifically study language. Ethnomethodology and componential analysis are both of great interest to social scientists because they deal with cognitive, rational, and predictable modes of human thought and action. They move in the direction of "intellectualizing" the world. What of the irrational, the humane, the expressive? These areas of life, the feelings, the states of being, the sensual and sensate will involve the next generation of sociologists. How will we study the feelings, moods, and expressive behavior revealed through language? We do not yet have any answers to these difficult questions.

SUGGESTED READINGS

Brown, Roger, *Social Psychology*. New York: The Free Press, 1965.
   Chapters 6 and 7 contain a very clear review of language learning.

———, *Words and Things*. New York: The Free Press, 1968.
   A basic introduction to the study of language; probably the finest general treatment available.

Burke, Kenneth, *Permanence and Change*, 2nd rev. ed. Indianapolis: Bobbs-Merrill, 1965.
   One of the most stimulating books on language, thought, and action written in the last thirty years.

Chomsky, Noam, *Syntactic Structures*. The Hague: Mouton, 1957.
   An attempt to discover the basic rules of grammar which underlie speech and language.

Gellener, Ernest, *Words and Things*. London: Penguin Books, 1968.
   A vitriolic critique of the ordinary language analysis school of Wittgenstein.

Hertzler, Joyce, *A Sociology of Language*. New York: Random House, 1965.
   A general overview of the sociological study of language.

Levi-Strauss, Claude, *Structural Anthropology*, trans. C. Jacobson and B. G. Schoepf. New York: Doubleday Anchor, 1967.
   A collection of essays by the eminent French anthropological linguist, which sets out his theory of basic social forms.

Lindesmith, Alfred, and Anselm Strauss, *Social Psychology*, 3rd ed. New York: Holt, Rinehart & Winston, 1968.
   This text is based in large part on the ideas of George Herbert Mead and contains research findings bearing on many of Mead's notions.

Mandelbaum, David, ed., *Selected Writings of Edward Sapir*. Berkeley: University of California Press, 1949.
   A collection of writings by one of the originators of the Sapir-Whorf hypothesis of language determinacy of social life.

Piaget, Jean, *Language and Thought of the Child*. New York: Humanities Press, 1959.

———, *The Moral Judgment of the Child.* New York: The Free Press, 1948.

Studies by the always creative and stimulating Swiss developmental psychologist.

Whorf, Benjamin, *Language, Thought and Reality,* ed. John Carroll. Cambridge: M.I.T. Press, 1956.

A classic collection of works by the linguist and co-formulator of the Sapir-Whorf hypothesis.

Wittgenstein, Ludwig, *Philosophical Investigations,* 2nd ed., trans. G. E. M. Anscombe. New York: The Macmillan Company, 1967.

Wittgenstein was the most influential philosopher of the twentieth century, with the possible exception of Lord Russell and one of the pioneers of "ordinary language analysis." This is a very difficult book, but also very rewarding.

CHAPTER 12

Society and Mass Communications

Any medium of communication has an effect on the meanings communicated. In the last chapter we considered communication in which the medium is face-to-face interaction. This chapter is concerned with mass communication, in which the medium does not involve face-to-face interaction and the messages are directed at a largely anonymous and unseen public.

The mass media are predominantly a twentieth-century form of communication closely related to our mass society. Their exact effects on what people believe and do has been subject to much controversy but, as the sole disseminators of "news," the communications about recent events publicly defined as important, they are extremely influential. This chapter examines four major theories of the effects of mass media on our society. Then it proceeds to show how messages communicated by media are constructed, using the daily newspaper as the prototype because it was the first and because, essentially, the other media have followed its methods.

The examination of the construction of messages in the mass media proceeds from consideration of the situations to consideration of the structures within which situations take place. First, the methods of putting together the news are examined. Next, the patterned activities—the strategies and purposes of the reporters—are studied in relation to the messages they construct. And, finally, the oligopolistic structure of ownership and its possible effects on messages are analyzed.

THE MEDIA AND EVERYDAY LIFE

When people communicate with one another, they do so by means of a medium, some device or process through which they convey information. The English language is a medium; so is a smile, a smoke signal, or a number. Anything that people use to transfer information, or to represent information, is a medium of communication.

Media differ from one another, first of all, with respect to the kinds of information they convey. Numbers convey information about quantity but not about quality; oil paintings contain mixtures of color for which the English language has no words; and neither prose nor poetry can express the information transmitted by a shrug of the shoulders. Media also differ with respect to what *modes of perception and thought* and what *types of personal experience and social interaction* they make possible for people. Because each medium can transmit only a distinctive, limited range of messages (or units of information), its use channels human thought in a distinctive way. Not all languages, for example, have equivalent words for colors. The spectrum of color that English divides into "green" and "blue" may be described in some other language by only one word. It has been found that people who use and are dependent on such a language cannot perceive any difference between the colors that English-speaking people differentiate as green and blue. To them, green and blue are not different colors but the same color. This illustrates how a medium (a given language) possesses distinctive messages (certain categories of color) which shape human perceptions.

In a given social context, the presence or absence of a given medium can profoundly affect not only what people perceive but also how they organize their lives. Imagine what life would be like in our society if the only means of communication were the handwritten letter. Clearly, things would be very different. Just how different is impossible to say: we are so used to the information and experiences made possible by other media—speech, gesture, touch, TV—that it is difficult to predict with any degree of certainty the long-run effect of taking them all away. It would be equally difficult to predict the effect of taking away only one medium.

The reason for this is that media can never be perfectly differentiated from one another. It is interesting that the contents of one medium are always other media. Telegraph contains the medium of Morse code, and Morse code contains the Roman alphabet, which in turn contains the English language. When one has finished enumerating all media contained or presupposed by a single medium, the result is usually a surprisingly long list. If we were precise in our use of language, then, we would speak of a system of media and not of a single medium.

MASS MEDIA IN MASS SOCIETY

In the social sciences, the term *media* is usually reserved for a small subset of all modes of human communication—the "mass media," chiefly newspapers, magazines, television, radio, and the movies. Each mass medium is a device or process (or system of devices and processes) for transmitting information. Therefore, each must be presumed to affect perceptions and behavior in a distinctive way. If we were to define mass media solely in terms of the methods by which they convey information, we would have to conclude that they do not constitute a single subject for study but many subjects. Yet the mass media have enough important characteristics in common to justify their common name.

The first general characteristic of the mass media is what their name implies—media designed for, distributed to, and consumed by *mass* audiences. These are mass audiences in two senses. First, they are very large, whether measured in absolute numbers or as a proportion of total population. The total daily circulation of newspapers in America is over 60 million, and television sets are present in 95 percent of all American households. Nearly every adult American is exposed to newspapers, television, or radio every day. Second, they exist in large, heterogeneous, industrial societies—divided along lines of class, religion, ethnicity, education, and so on. In order to achieve close-to-universal acceptance in such societies, the mass media have addressed themselves to the average individual, making little or no contact with members of minority races, religions, classes, and so on. Instead, they have treated the individual as if he were a member of a homogeneous, undifferentiated, mass society (Kornhauser, 1959). Despite cultural or economic divisions within their audience, the media speak to what most members of that audience have in common. Their tendency is to centralize and homogenize rather than to decentralize and pluralize. By this definition, a mass medium is the opposite not of a medium with a small audience but, rather, of a medium whose contents are suitable only to a highly specialized audience (such as model train buffs or vegetarians).

A second characteristic of mass media is that they are big business. In 1969 the total revenues of all mass media were close to 4 percent of the U.S. Gross National Product. Although mass-media-producing firms vary widely in size, they have been growing larger and larger over time; the media firms which set styles and standards for the rest are invariably among the very biggest firms. *The New York Times,* the nation's leading "prestige" newspaper and one of the biggest newspapers of any type, had in 1969 a total revenue of more than $238 million, assets of $115 million, daily circulation of about 1 million, well over six thousand employees, and net profits of almost $15 million. During the same period, an average newspaper had total annual revenues of $4 million, circulation of 36,000, and after-tax profits of $300,000. The television networks are the biggest media firms; in 1969 the revenues of CBS were over $1.1 billion. Because nearly all media-producing organizations are business firms (not voluntary associations or philanthropies), they need profits and must operate within commercial constraints. Because they are very big organizations, their news and entertainment are produced by bureaucracies following routine procedures.

A third characteristic of mass media is that they are the sole disseminators of news (defined as current, verifiable information about recent events). Mass media also disseminate other sorts of information—fictional stories, political advocacy, strictly utilitarian information like recipes. But, in the dissemination of these other sorts of information, the mass media do not possess a monopoly: stories or recipes can be found in books as well as in newspapers and television, and books are not a mass medium in the usual sense of the term. The kind of information uniquely characteristic of mass media is news.

A fourth characteristic of mass media is the speed with which they gather information and the frequency with which they distribute it. Media-producing organizations are continuously gathering information and are in instantaneous communication with their sources of information. They package and distribute such information at least once each day. The speed and rhythm of this ongoing process of gathering and distributing information, especially news, sharply differentiate mass media from other media and exert an enormous influence on the character of their messages.

A final characteristic of mass media is that they developed and attained maturity during roughly the same historical period, in response to the same circumstances, and in pursuit of the same purposes. Each incorporates modes of communication (typography, language, music, and so on), some ancient, all originating in different periods. The newspaper was a seventeenth-century invention; nevertheless, the mass media are essentially twentieth-century phenomena.

Except for the newspaper—and the newspaper underwent such radical changes during the last decades of the nineteenth century that we may consider it as created anew—the mass media did not exist before the turn of this century. This is because the technologies (high-voltage electricity, electronics, and high-speed large-volume printing presses), economic circumstances (mass marketing and advertising), and social structures and conditions (universal literacy, professionalism, bureaucracy) which they rely on did not exist or were not sufficiently widespread, being developed toward the end of the nineteenth century or during the early part of the tweniteth century. Mass media are the uniquely modern means of public communication, and much of their importance lies in the fact that they are a major cause of whatever may be distinctively modern about our current modes of perception, thought, public discourse, and political action.

EFFECTS AND SIGNIFICANCE OF MASS MEDIA

A vast literature addresses the nature, effects, and significance of mass media. Yet how significant the mass media are, in what ways, for what reasons, with what results, and in which areas of individual and social life —all remain open questions.

The questions remain unsettled for two major reasons. First, there are so many different kinds of media and media contents and such a huge variety of people, social situations, and possible effects that it has proved impossible to formulate any general statement about the effects of media that is both true and nontrivial. Only when social scientists have limited their research to specific media, specific kinds of messages, specific people in specific circumstances at specific times, and so on, have they begun to succeed in establishing the effects and significance of the mass media.

The second reason these questions lack definitive answers is that students of mass media disagree over what questions are worth asking, how one should go about answering them, and what would constitute adequate evidence for accepting or rejecting a hypothesis. At least four different approaches are widely adopted by students of mass media. Each proceeds from different assumptions and reflects different purposes and standards.

The first and most popular approach is based on *democratic political theory*. It is adopted by politicians, journalists, and most other nonacademic commentators, and it focuses upon the potential and actual problems that mass media pose in a society attempting to govern itself democratically. Adherents of this approach consider media in an essentially normative context. Their underlying purpose is to articulate democratic values and fears, expose wrongdoing, urge reform, or sketch some better way of organizing public life; rarely are such people neutral or dispassionate toward mass media. Often, their writings present not formal arguments or the results of empirical research but, rather, anecdotes and illustrations intended to stimulate political reform or symbolize various democratic attitudes.

In the works of those who adopt the democratic approach, three themes stand out, each highlighting a different set of problems and suggesting a different model of correct media behavior. The first theme is *popular sovereignty*, the notion that the people as a whole should be the sole legitimate source of political authority and the ultimate arbiter of all political questions. If important information is suppressed or distorted, or if public opinion is manipulated by "external" forces, the sovereignty of the people as a whole is compromised. This theme implies that mass media should be unbiased in selection of information and accurate in representation of information. It also implies that they should not influence the formation or expression of public opinion. Observers who have in mind these standards of correct media behavior criticize evidence suggesting that the media may consciously exercise discretion in deciding what to publish, or possess power over public opinion, or publish a biased account of the day's events.

A second theme of the democratic approach is *meliorism,* the notion that people and social conditions are capable of improvement, especially through education. Often, meliorists suggest that the ability of a democratic nation to make progress or even to survive depends primarily on how much information and understanding the citizenry possesses. Naturally, meliorists assign to the mass media a major responsibility for the endless task of informing, educating, and improving citizens. Frequently, meliorist studies stress any indication that the mass media are not primarily educational in purpose or effect—for example, sensationalism in the presentation of news. Like the popular sovereignty model, the meliorist model of media behavior opposes all "political bias." Unlike it, the meliorist model urges media to play an active role in forming and changing public opinion through education.

A third theme is *participatory citizenship.* Its assumption is that a good citizen participates actively in politics, pursuing his personal convictions about the public interest. If mass media are to be good citizens, they must act in accordance with a "responsible" view of the public interest, not only by publishing or broadcasting editorials, but by actively promoting reform and exposing wrongdoing in all parts of their product, including the news. "Participatory" critiques of mass media are no more consistent than their authors' opinions and policy positions. Thus, in 1968, the National Advisory Commission on Civil Disorders (Kerner Commission) advised mass media to allocate more news coverage to events and conditions in the Negro community and, in reporting riots, not to publish information—even true information—which could have an inflammatory effect. Unlike the first two models of media behavior, the participatory model advocates an explicitly political and activist standard.

In each of its variants, the democratic approach to mass media is based on the assumption that the media exercise great influence over public opinion. Assessing the truth or falsehood of this assumption is the principal concern of a *social psychological approach,* the approach of most social science studies of media effects. Its aim is to measure in a precise and systematic way the response of individuals and groups to messages transmitted by mass media. Do opinions change as a result of reading editorial pages? Can the individual be persuaded by slanted news or by obvious propaganda? Does news coverage influence voters' preferences or their voting behavior? Do TV programs depicting violence stimulate children to behave violently?

The general answer to these and similar questions is: Not very much, not very often, and not under most circumstances. Study after study has shown that the image of media effects implicit in the democratic approach is seriously distorted. That approach pictures people as isolated individuals heavily dependent on mass media for their information, attitudes, and interpretations of current events. Given such circumstances, the media would be influential over individuals; but most people are not particularly isolated from one another. Typically, a person is a member of many different groups (family, peer, work, community, church) and each group has its activities, traditions, norms, and influence. These groups help form the individual's perceptions and opinions and, once formed, maintain them through a system of interpersonal influence and social pressure. This system acts as a filter mediating between the individual and messages of the mass media.

In a classic study of media effects, Elihu Katz and Paul Lazarsfeld (1955) found that when messages produce opinion change in the individual, they do so through a two-step process. Most people, they found, were not directly influenced by media. When they did change their minds, they did so in response to the opinions of a few people they knew and respected as specially competent. These *opinion leaders* interpreted messages of the media to the rest of the population, accepting some messages, rejecting others, and altering still others.

Apart from group and interpersonal processes that affect an individual's receptiveness to mass media, within each individual are a series of psychological processes that often qualify or negate the media's influence. Most people do not expose themselves to all kinds of media; instead, they expose themselves selectively, choosing those media and messages which they find most congenial. People also perceive selectively, noticing those bits of information which fit in with their preexisting opinions and disregarding the rest. They remember selectively. These and other processes tend to reduce *cognitive dissonance,* conflict and disparateness among the facts and opinions of which the individual is aware. Messages giving rise to cognitive dissonance tend to be disregarded; moreover, people differentiate messages according to their apparent credibility. A news story that appears to be fair and that presents more than one side of an issue is more likely to be believed than a news story that seems slanted (Klapper, 1960).

This is not to say that media are totally without influence; they do have effects, and they can reinforce beliefs. Reinforcing messages during a political campaign can stimulate people to get out and vote (Lazarsfeld et al., 1952). On new or unfamiliar subjects, the messages of mass media can exert a powerful influence on public opinion. But the media are never more than one of many forces playing upon the individual's opinions, and the messages of mass media work their influence within a complex network of social, psychological, and attitudinal factors.

A third approach to the effects and significance of mass media, the *functionalist approach,* is grounded on certain types of social and political theory. Whereas the social psychological approach fixes attention on the capacity of specific messages to alter opinion or induce behavior, the functionalist approach seeks to discover ways in which the operations of mass media systems clash or harmonize with the operations of other systems within a society. Thus, the researcher's attention is directed at the broad, unchanging characteristics of media and at their "functions" in maintaining other structures or processes. The political scientist Harold Lasswell asserts that a primary systemic function of mass media is to perform a "surveillance" of the social environment (1960). The media reveal threats and opportunities to the society's value system and, by doing so, help to reinforce, interpret, or change that value system. Karl Deutsch (1965) has suggested that another function of mass media is to provide channels for that type of communication which serves as a "cement" binding the various parts of a society together into a single integrated system. Daniel Lerner (1958) has described the effects of introducing mass media into rural areas of Turkey and finds that one function of mass media is to encourage and accelerate the process of political development or modernization. Thus, mass communication is dysfunctional for the maintenance of isolated, traditional societies and functional for the maintenance of modern societies.

The fourth approach to mass media—we will term it the *cultural approach*—is a variant of the functionalist approach, but it is used for sufficiently different purposes to justify making the distinction. Functionalist analysts tend to make no distinction among kinds of mass media, as their ultimate interest is in the functions of communication rather than in the functions of specific media systems *per se;* those who adopt the cultural approach are interested primarily in the unique characteristics of each medium and how they affect the messages. And, whereas functionalists are ultimately interested in how communication contributes to the equilibrium of the entire social system, followers of the cultural approach tend to fix their attention upon the ways in which introduction or use of a given medium *changes* the culture it transmits.

Consider the effects of introducing telegraph, telephone, and radio on the power exercised by autocratic political regimes. Before the widespread use of these modes of communication, autocrats—by definition, rulers who claim or seek unlimited authority and power—were sharply limited in the control they could exercise over individuals, groups, or society as a whole. These limitations were, in large part, the result of slowness and decentralization of both private (point-to-point) and public (or "broadcast") communications. It took a long time to receive reports, send out orders, and then ascertain how effectively they had been carried out. It was also difficult to monitor the communications of individuals or groups. Autocratic regimes were consequently limited in how much, and how often, they could alter the behavior of people and organizations. But, with instantaneous communication (and the expansion of bureaucracy, with its huge capacity for gathering, storing, and processing information), it came within the power of autocratic regimes to exercise a far broader and more stringent control, and this control was enlarged still further by introduction of mass media. These communications technologies, in short, made possible (though they were not the only cause of) the evolution of inherently limited autocracy into comparatively unlimited totalitarianism (Friedrich and Brzezinski, 1956). In *1984,* George Orwell paints a vivid and chilling picture of the crucial role played by instantaneous and mass communication technologies in a totalitarian system.

THE STUDY OF MESSAGE SYSTEMS

Studies of the messages of mass media tend to restrict themselves to very small portions of the entire message system rather than to that system as a whole. The elements of the message system chosen for study are usually selected because of their relation to something else—the defense of democratic values, for example, or the equilibrium of social systems. Because that "something else" is the real subject of interest, these studies rarely scrutinize the relation of the selected messages to the total media and message system. Thus, such studies proceed as if there were nothing interesting or problematic about message systems as a whole.

Behind this lack of interest in message systems as a subject in their own right stands a firm, if tacit, assumption. It is that the mass media have discovered and institutionalized the uniquely correct, objective mode of representing the world around us. This mode of representing or reconstructing reality needs no study; since it is correct, there can be no question or puzzlement about it. It is not seen as an intellectual problem.

Of course, problems may be associated with the messages of mass media. Media often deviate from what people believe are correct representations of reality, and such deviance is often studied. Yet, frequently, such studies assume that the normal mode of the media is the correct one and that any deviation from the truth is also a deviation from the norms of the media. Accordingly, they treat deviations as accidents attributable to the mistakes of isolated, aberrant individuals or to dysfunctions in media organizations. Very rarely are deviations attributed to limitations or contradictions inherent in the normal mode by which media seek to represent reality.

The assumption that the mass media have hit upon the uniquely correct way to represent the world is part of an ideology that newsmen share with most Americans. This ideology is useful to the mass media—it makes reporters careful about facts and less prone to slant the news—and comforting to the American people. Yet it is fundamentally incorrect, for a limited amount of information organized and conveyed in any given manner can never be the uniquely correct or "objective" representation of reality. It is impossible to describe reality without first making assumptions about the nature of reality, and any such assumptions are debatable. Thus, any mode of representing reality will be found to possess inherent weaknesses and problems—blind spots, exaggerations, even falsifications. Any mode of representing reality encompasses only a part of reality or only one sort of reality.

If this means that extraordinary and insoluble difficulties confront a newsman as he tries to give an account of the day's events, it also suggests a powerful strategy with which students of mass media may begin to study message systems as a whole. This strategy is simple enough: identify and then elaborate in detail the mode or modes in which mass media represent reality. That is: study the processes by which the mass media *construct the news* about reality. Those processes turn out to be very complex.

THE STRATEGY OF NEWS ORGANIZATIONS

In order to understand the nature of the uniquely characteristic messages of mass media—the news—we begin with the elementary facts about the media themselves. The content of the mass media is a *product*. Each day (in the case of newspapers) or every few hours (in the case of radio and TV), new material is gathered and organized and sold in a marketplace by an organization. To understand the product, one must begin by understanding the organization that produces it and the procedures that organization follows.

For the sake of simplicity, we will confine our attention to the large metropolitan newspaper because it was not only the first but the prototypical mass medium: the mass media that emerged later followed the newspaper's example in designing their new product. These later electronic media differ from the newspaper in many interesting respects, and some of these differences will be noted. Still, the electronic media have adopted the newspaper as their model, have relied upon newspaper organizations and newspaper-oriented journalism schools as primary sources of news personnel, and have depended on newspapers and newspaper-oriented wire services in identifying, defining, and gathering information about newsworthy events.

Maintenance needs. An organization may be defined as a system of consciously coordinated cooperative action that aims at the achievement of some goal (Barnard, 1938). Many goals shape the behavior of an organization, but perhaps most important is the effort of its executives (those who "consciously coordinate") to *maintain* the organization, to promote its survival and maximize its security. The principal maintenance need of a newspaper organization is a money income at least equal to its expenditure.

Thus, a newspaper must establish and maintain an audience sufficiently large, stable, attentive, and trusting. Creating such an audience is the most effective thing a media organization can do to ensure its continued survival, and this imperative need constrains the organization in every part of its operations. Yet how it constrains those operations, and especially how it shapes the editorial content of a newspaper—the "magnet" with which the organization attracts its audience—depends on three independent factors.

Least important is local circumstance: the size of the local population; its social, cultural, and economic characteristics; competition from other media; and the potential volume of advertising. With minor exceptions, local circumstances have not had much impact on the content of modern journalism.

A second, much more influential factor is the decision of the executive concerning the scale of his operation. It is possible to have a successful small newspaper as well as a successful large one and, to a significant extent, the newspaper executive is free to decide the size of his newspaper. Almost without exception, newspaper executives in modern America choose to create a large, costly newspaper organization in order to reach as large an audience as possible within the local market area.

The third factor is the executive's choice of a strategy for attracting a large audience. As demonstrated in another context by states which in the same year give substantial electoral majorities to both conservative and liberal candidates for different public offices, it is possible to forge very large coalitions out of the same population on the basis of a very different, or even antithetical, type of appeal (Bauer, Pool, and Dexter, 1964). Again, almost without exception, American newspaper executives have adopted only one strategy, described below, for creating and holding the largest possible audience, making the message systems of American newspapers what they are today.

Goals and strategy. Until the Civil War, the goals, strategies, and nature of newspapers were altogether different from today. The technologies of printing and transportation made it nearly impossible for a newspaper to have a circulation of more than a few thousand (or, in a few exceptional cases, a few tens of thousands). Circulation was also limited because the purchase price of an issue was relatively high, which was in part a consequence of the fact that advertising revenue was relatively low. Long-distance communication was by mail and news received was days, weeks, or months old by the time it was published. Usually, a single issue contained only four pages; often no more than one page was devoted to news; and, because the news was rarely divided into units ("stories"), as today, there were few if any headlines.

One consequence was that news organizations were very small—often one-man operations. Another was that many newspapers aimed their editorial content not at the general public but at a special audience—businessmen or farmers or Democrats. Sometimes newspapers were directly subsidized by political parties. It was a period of personal, partisan, specialized, and decentralized journalism (Weisberger, 1961).

During the second half of the nineteenth century, newspaper technologies advanced rapidly. As telegraph communications became widespread, news became available quickly, and a larger and larger proportion of the news was up to the minute. As the speed and capacity of printing presses increased, there was soon almost no limit on the size of a newspaper's circulation or on the number of pages per issue. Advertising also began to grow. As circulation and advertising revenues went up, the price to the reader was lowered, and newspapers came more easily within the means of everybody. These developments produced a profound transformation of the character of daily journalism.

But this transformation was not automatic; it was the creation of a few imaginative newspaper entrepreneurs who, over the course of decades, discovered and exploited the journalistic possibilities opened up by the new technologies and economic conditions. In the process these men created modern journalism. Three publishers stand out: James Gordon Bennett (1795–1872), founder of the New York *Herald*; Joseph Pulitzer (1847–1911), founder of the New York *World*; and Adolph S. Ochs (1859–1935), publisher of *The New York Times*.

Bennett, Pulitzer, and Ochs were not interested exclusively in making money nor were they single-minded news technicians, concerned solely with the process of putting out newspapers. Like many publishers and editors of the age, they conceived their newspapers in terms that were ultimately political. All three were deeply commited to democracy and reform, and all intensely disliked partisanship and politics. They sought to keep their newspapers free from the divisive and corrupting influence of party and politics, and they believed that if they could create a truly independent and popular journalism, it would do more than any other institution to perfect the American democracy.

Their goal was to create an authentic democratic journalism, one which would possess universal appeal, inspire universal trust, and attract a universal readership. Thus, their newspapers aimed at reaching every citizen in order to educate, represent, and defend all of the people.

Together with their contemporaries, Bennett, Pulitzer, and Ochs invented a four-part strategy for achieving their goal. Each element of the strategy increased the ability of journalism to interest nearly every member of a diverse nation, reduced the risk of alienating anyone, and protected the newspaper's audience from day-to-day fluctuation and from long-run attrition. These four elements are the organizing principles of modern journalism and constitute the message system of newspapers.

The first element, the cornerstone of this strategy for creating a mass audience, was a rule that sharply restricted the subject matter of news: news would deal with subjects only as they are involved in or expressed by events occurring during the twenty-four hours preceding publication of a newspaper issue. The key term here is "event." An *event* may be defined as a sudden and easily recognizable disturbance of some seemingly stable situation (or "background") which takes place in a very short period of time.

By restricting themselves to events so defined, newspapers adopt a specialized perspective in time that restricts vision to actions and occurrences happening within a span of minutes or at most hours and that restricts memory to the immediately preceeding twenty-four hours. As a result, many subjects within the normal range of human awareness and interest are excluded from newspapers. Stable situations or conditions (backgrounds against which events stand out), slow and diffuse changes (most changes of historical importance or social impact), general ideas or sentiments—rarely are these a subject of news. Happenings with a lifetime of minutes or hours constitute this subject matter.

This *focus on events* increases the capacity of newspapers to attract a universal audience. By definition, events are easy to perceive and read about; a journalism about events is readily accessible to everyone and assists the newspaper in achieving universal readership. Moreover, the suddenness of an event or the background against which it stands out may lend it glamor or drama, and these possess their own interest, independent of that attaching to the people ("human interest") involved and the values at stake. Thus, the event orientation of modern journalism not only lowers the intellectual cost of reading news but increases its immediate benefits. And, finally, the focus on events gives journalism the extra attractions of suspense and currency. Each issue is a unique and never-to-be-repeated chapter in an unending chronicle of happenings. Thus, the newspaper induces people interested in events to read the news every day in order to be "up-to date" on the "latest" events and to relieve yesterday's suspense over what tomorrow's news would bring. This feature of event-oriented journalism helps to stabilize audiences and to "immunize" them against the appeal of other, nondaily media.

The focus on events is the first principle of daily journalism and the source of most of its strengths and shortcomings. As for these latter, one point should be noted. Ultimately, most human interests and values are associated with long perspectives in time (MacDonald, 1950). Whether one is interested in promoting some religious ideal, being wealthy, having a meaningful life, or realizing some political objective, what one has in mind is not a condition that can be defined or understood as a collection of brief events. What one does have in mind is a condition whose existence and qualities are clear (if they are ever clear) only over periods of years, decades, or longer. It may be easy to perceive and read about events, but it is difficult to understand how they bear on most human interests and values. Thus, to most individuals, the meaning or significance of most events is problematic. This inherently problematic quality of events is the underlying cause of the many shortcomings and defects that critics rightly attribute to modern journalism.

The second element of the strategy of modern journalism is the *summary report*. In principle, there are several different ways in which an event might be related: as a chronological description that starts at the beginning and describes the successive actions that follow; as a history, in which actions are ordered chronologically but in which their causal interrelationships are also described; or as an interpretive essay organized not around the event but around the relation of the event to ideas or values (White, 1965). Modern journalism adopts none of these possible forms as its model. Instead, it begins by relating the most dramatic or climactic aspect of the event and then adds other elements according to the rule of the "inverted pyramid"—in descending order of pertinence or interest (Max W. Hall, 1965). This practice of summarizing an event by its most noteworthy or interesting element maximizes both the dramatic appeal of the news story and the ease with which the story can be read. Thus, the summary report emphasizes the single most dramatic aspect of an event—its "eventness"— and rules out modes of description that might bring out other, possibly more important aspects.

The third element is the *rule of objectivity,* which defines what is and is not "true" and, therefore, what should and should not be published and believed. According to this rule, each statement in a news story must be of unambiguous fact based on direct observation or its equivalent. News is limited to simple, declarative statements that can be verified by anyone, whatever his opinions. Any statement that a reasonable observer could doubt is excluded.

The rule of objectivity reinforces the tendency inherent in the focus on events for news stories to be about specific, concrete actions readily located in time and space. Thus, news describes only wholly external, "objective," characteristics; whatever lacks unambiguous physical manifestation—a moral quality, for example—is not a fit subject for a news story because statements about it cannot be "objectively" verified.

By restricting itself to unexceptionable statements, modern journalism maximizes the probability that readers will trust what they read in a newspaper as the truth and minimizes the probability that they will blame the newspaper for what they dislike in the news. Moreover, the rule of objectivity has the effect of forcing reporters to write in a simple, concrete vocabulary and to avoid abstract, vague, or value-laden words. This style encourages brevity and helps make news stories easy to read.

Because news stories sometimes repeat statements that are not objective and because news stories place all objective statements within a structure that itself conveys implicit information that is not objective, the strategy of journalism contains as its fourth element a rule governing both how stories are selected for publication and how facts are selected for and placed in a particular story. This fourth element may be called the *rule of fairness*. Whereas the first three elements of the strategy of modern journalism aim at creating mass audiences by serving interests (keeping up to date) and by conforming to attitudes ("just give me the facts") that all Americans are presumed to have in common, the rule of fairness aims at aggregating audiences by means of a "log-rolling" strategy addressing the special concerns of individuals and groups.

The rule of fairness requires that a newspaper contain a wide variety of subjects, bearing on a wide variety of interests and values, and speaking to the different concerns of a wide variety of people and groups. As Marshall McLuhan has observed, the result is that a newspaper is a mosaic of unrelated items (stories) reflecting different interests and points of view (1964). Regarding the selection and ordering of facts for a single news story, the rule of fairness stipulates "write it down the middle," meaning that, when there is disagreement or controversy, the story should evenhandedly report all points of view and claims, no matter how implausible, and thus be "fair" to all parties. The idea is to speak to the concerns of all groups and ignore the concerns of none.

Although news on television is generally similar to that in newspapers, some fundamental differences should be noted. The most important is, of course, that television news often includes film and sound of events. This not only leads TV editors and reporters to emphasize the visually interesting aspects of events, but it also means that TV news conveys more information of a nonverbal sort and a more sharply defined point of view (a camera has an exact location in space and time). A second major difference is that, whereas newspapers present many stories, all available to the reader at the same time but each occupying a different place, TV news stories are available at the same place (the TV screen) but at different times. One result is that TV news is not nearly so pluralistic as the newspaper. A newspaper can publish far more information about far more subjects than any one reader is likely to find interesting because the reader can easily scan all the items and choose those he will read. A TV viewer cannot so easily scan and select because the items are presented serially, one after another; to "scan" them, he must watch them all. As a result, TV news programs are under a strong incentive to aim every story at the general audience; otherwise, viewers will be likely to turn the program off. For the same reason, TV news stories cannot be patterned after the inverted pyramid. Newspaper stories, which follow this structure, trail off (or are arbitrarily cut off) at the end; the reader decides how much of each story he will read and how much detail he wants to know. To prevent viewers from turning off TV news programs, the TV news story must have a well-defined middle and end as well as a well-defined beginning, and the middle and end must be as interesting as the beginning. Typically, the TV news story maintains interest and achieves closure by drawing conclusions about the meaning or significance of the event under consideration at the end of the story, a practice that makes TV news considerably different from newspaper news.

The structure of beats. A news department that pursues the above goal and strategy finds that its primary tasks are to discover newsworthy events, gather information about them, write news stories, and design each issue. In all these tasks, especially in the first, the news department is influenced by the way it searches for newsworthy events.

At any given time, countless events are happening in countless different places. It is scarcely practicable to attempt to identify them all, and so newsmen have divided the universe of all possible events into two categories: those presumptively not newsworthy, which they disregard, and those presumptively newsworthy. This latter category is broken down into manageable subareas (usually along lines of geography, level or branch of government, or type of social institution), and one or more newsmen are assigned to each area or *beat*. This structured division of news provides a focus for the newsman. It also roughly defines a standing agenda for the newspaper, a list of the kinds of events that will probably be newsworthy and the places to find them. As an editor of *The New York Times* once observed, "News breaks through definite channels; it cannot do otherwise. Cover these channels and you catch the news—much like casting a net across a salmon stream."

The structure of beats is more than a mere managerial convenience or technique for increasing efficiency. To see what else it is, let us examine the metaphor of casting nets across salmon streams. The metaphor is apt if the distinction between newsworthy and non-newsworth events is as sharp as the distinction between salmon and the water they swim in. In fact, the difference between news and non-news is not at all sharp. A fisherman who goes after salmon knows that he runs the risk of failing and going home empty-handed. But a newspaper must have news to print every day, and it refuses to go home at the end of the day with nothing in its creel. If a newsman fails to catch any salmon, then he will settle for minnows, and if there are no minnows around he will in all probability cart away a bucket of water, which he will later present as if it were the salmon he had been seeking. News is anything a newsman decides to present as news, and it can be found wherever he decides to look for it. Accordingly, the structure of beats may be regarded as a self-fulfilling prophecy, determining where news will be found and what news will be about. Establishing a new beat has the effect of creating a new sort of news. Contrary to the conventional wisdom, news is not simply the atypical or the unexpected. If it were, the beat system would not work, and clearly it does work. Generally, news is found in expected places at expected times.

Within this structure of beats, the reporter does his daily work, interviewing people, monitoring institutions, and looking for newsworthy events; when he finds one he writes a story about it. In the endless process of deciding what is true and what is not and what is news and what is not, he is guided by his "news judgment." Despite the typical newsman's inability to fully articulate this faculty of judgment, most reporters possess surprisingly similar news judgment and arrive at remarkably uniform decisions when reporting the same event. As Douglass Cater noted in his popular book on the Washington press, *The Fourth Branch of Government* (1959), "One of the perennial sources of astonishment for the nonprofessional is to attend a Congressional committee hearing and witness the row upon row of reporters seated at the press tables as they lift their pencils and lay them down with almost ballet corps precision while the flow of testimony flows along." This uniformity is a result of reporters' common training, their identification with a common craft, and a common viewpoint and method (see Insert No. 43).

THE MESSAGES OF NEWS

When newsmen search for and identify what they judge to be newsworthy events, they are performing a simple social psychological operation. Inarticulately, they have in mind a repertory of models, each defining and characterizing a basic type of newsworthy situation or action. As they search for news, reporters intuitively compare these prototypes of news stories with the actual situations and actions they encounter. Wherever the actual coincides with—or can be made to seem like—the prototypical, there news exists.

A final step in understanding how news is produced, and in discovering what news is and what messages it conveys, is to identify some of the major prototypes in use in American journalism today. We will consider several prototypes of political reporting and describe each in terms of its central theme (the way it conceptualizes events), its focal categories (which articulate and elaborate the theme and prescribe the types of information to be gathered), and the ways in which it illumines and distorts the situations to which it is applied.

A staple in the repertory of every American political reporter is what may be called the *politics-as-usual* prototype. This construes politics as a game and politicians as men who play it solely for personal advancement or reward. The focus of stories patterned after this prototype is upon events as they reveal the interaction between the desires and intentions of two or more political actors, or between such desires and intentions and the interactable reality of a politician's situation. Accordingly, one focal category of politics as usual is competition and conflict. Another is strategy, or the means by which a political actor seeks to achieve his ends or to defeat an opponent. Still other focal categories are friendship-enmity and success-failure. These focal categories are all elements of the drama and, indeed, the politics-as-usual prototype puts an essentially dramatic construction on events, which are treated like scenes in a play.

Although self-interest is a major fact of political life, politicians' actions always possess another level of qualities—the level on which actions and intentions link up, if only accidentally, with values and with serious questions of public policy. The politics-as-usual prototype largely ignores this second aspect of political reality despite the fact that, in the long run, it is probably more important to the citizen and voter than the degree of a politician's self-interest.

As visualized through the politics-as-usual prototype, the game of politics may not be exactly savory but neither is it altogether evil or objec-

INSERT NO. 43

The Craft of Reporting

A great deal has been written about reporters and their work (Rosten, 1937; Cater, 1959; Bernard Cohen, 1963; Nimmo, 1964). As a group, reporters choose to enter journalism at an early age, complete between two and three years of college as a median (40% have bachelor's degrees), have a median age of only thirty-five, earn just over the national median family income, appear to rank between white-collar and blue-collar occupations in national surveys of occupational prestige, are from middle-class backgrounds, exhibit a high rate of job turnover, and are disproportionately Democratic in political party identification (Porter, 1967). All reporters (including the third who have college journalism degrees) receive their principal journalistic training through an informal, on-the-job apprenticeship that often lasts for years. During this training—which places almost exclusive emphasis on the most elementary reportorial techniques such as observing, interviewing, writing, and selecting what is newsworthy—the reporter comes to identify with his occupation and to internalize its characteristic subculture.

The typical reporter sees himself as "the supreme individual in the age of the organization man. He is the one standing up against the many . . . the one who has singlehandedly busted up the hidden enclave of intrigue" (Cater, 1959). Yet he finds one of his principal rewards in the opportunity to directly observe historic events and to be on intimate terms with the famous, the glamorous, and the powerful. Accordingly, reporters are frequently "inside dopesters" (Kraft, 1966). Like the founders of modern journalism, reporters consider their occupation to provide an important, even essential, public service. Yet only rarely can a reporter determine whether journalism has any effect on public life, and in any case the typical reporter is of two minds about

tionable, for the game is played according to certain rules. Perhaps the most important is that players may not illegally use their public position for personal material gain. There must be no graft, no kickbacks, no misappropriation of public funds, and no conflict of interest. The breaking of this rule is the situation characteristic of, and central to, the *corruption* prototype. The focal categories of this prototype are the charges, denials, and findings of fact concerning allegedly corrupt acts.

An interesting property of the corruption prototype is that great newsworthiness attaches to any event or situation conforming to it; accordingly, corruption stories are given very prominent play. Yet stories about corruption are published infrequently, not necessarily because there is little corruption in modern American politics. Rather, because it is difficult to gather and confirm the facts of a case of corruption so that the story will hold up

writing news stories that might affect policy decisions. Reporters believe both that they should actively promote the public interest by exposing error and stupidity and by emphasizing what they believe to be correct policy alternatives and that their only claim to public respect is that they report the news in a spirit of dispassion and objectivity (Bernard Cohen, 1963).

Because the average news department is loosely organized, because editorial supervision is often weak, hurried, and irregular, and because he usually works alone, the reporter appears to have considerable freedom and discretion in deciding how to cover the news. In fact, the reporter is subject to a complex and often subtle balance of countervailing forces, each with its special interest; and each, if unchecked, can cause him to deviate from the norm of fair, truthful, and independent reporting. One such force is the editor or publisher, who may pressure the reporter to follow a specified political policy; if unchecked, such influence can lead to slanted news (Breed, 1955). A second force is the reporter's sources, who may pressure him to suppress embarrassing stories and to write only favorable stories; if unchecked, such influence can create a captive reporter. The reporter's fellow reporters constitute the third major force; they demand not only honest, craftsmanlike reporting but exciting and critical stories; and, if unchecked, they may induce a reporter to be unfairly critical, sensational, or faddish (Alsop, 1968). The reporter's need to steer a middle course among these conflicting pressures constitutes one system of control that governs what and how he writes.

A second system of control exists. Constantly, editors and reporters seek a consensus concerning how to report a given event and the relative importance of the day's news stories. Stories are routinely checked against the versions given by the wire services and by other newspapers, and editors and reporters seek to minimize any discrepancy. They strive to achieve consensus in order to ensure accuracy and to legitimate their coverage of the day's events as objective.

under critical scrutiny. Moreover, finding the facts of an alleged case of corrupt behavior requires a large investment of news staff resources, and there is no guarantee that the investment will pay off with a solid, well-documented story.

On the other hand, if a reporter can establish even one fact that, though it does not prove a man guilty of wrongdoing, does cast suspicion on him, the newspaper is likely to print it. In 1971, for example, *The New York Times* ran a front-page story reporting that former Texas Governor John B. Connally, whose nomination as Secretary of the Treasury was being considered by the Senate at the time, had received, while governor, payments from the estate of a wealthy oilman. The story implied that Connally had violated a Texas law prohibiting the governor from performing professional services and charging a fee while in office. The story, however, did not report that Connally had rendered these services while in office. In fact, it turned out that the services in question had been rendered before his election as governor and that he had elected to receive his fee in ten annual installments for tax purposes. In its zeal to expose corruption, *The Times* had suggested that a man was guilty of something and he turned out to be innocent.

The *symbolic controversy* prototype, which is also related to politics as usual, deals with conflict situations. In particular, it presents events as they exhibit or may stimulate conflict based on ideology or political symbols and expressed in public statements. Its focal categories include (1) the heretical statement that attacks symbols important to some group; (2) the indignant countercharges from defenders of those views, symbols, or rhetorical pieties; and (3) the "controversial" individual, depicted as colorful at best and as unstable or malevolent at worst, who has acquired his controversial reputation by making a statement that started a symbolic controversy. Once a man in public life has acquired such an identity, he finds it difficult to change, for subsequent news coverage of him refers either to his controversial reputation explicitly or emphasizes new actions or statements reminiscent of the original rhetorical impiety.

An interesting instance of symbolic controversy reportage is the case of the Moynihan Report on the condition and problems of blacks in America, prepared in 1965 by Professor Daniel F. Moynihan, then assistant secretary of labor, for the internal use of the Johnson administration in policy planning. The report noted, among other things, that the legacy of slavery and the facts of current ghetto life (especially widespread unemployment and the rule that families may not receive welfare benefits for a dependent child if there is a man in the household) had promoted the disintegration of many black families and that this disintegration was a cause of further problems. Other studies had reached much the same conclusion. But the initial news stories about the Moynihan Report, written by reporters to whom the long document had been leaked for a few hours and without explanation, presented the report as a grave symbolic affront to the dignity and culture of black Americans and as a rationale for doing nothing about their problems. In fact, the report was neither. But, plausibly, the news stories assimilated the report to the symbolic controversy prototype. The news stories stimulated a flurry of countercharges and denunciations, especially from leaders of black groups. What the report actually contained was forgotten or distorted almost beyond recognition, and the new symbolic identity which the news stories established for it prevailed. The entire story of the Moynihan Report is told in Rainwater and Yancey's *The Moynihan Report and the Politics of Controversy* (1968).

A fourth, frequently used prototype of political news is the *public leadership* prototype. This traditional kind of story deals with the newsmaker who holds some public office or position, and it conceptualizes his actions—typically, the announcement of a new bill he is introducing or a new project he is undertaking—as well intentioned, sincere steps to solve some public problem. The focal categories of this prototype are: (1) the public problem, invariably described in terms that suggest it is inherently capable of being solved; (2) the solution, generally treated as the only logical solution, even if the problem as defined is inherently insoluble; (3) leadership and initiative; and (4) action, change, or "doing something" (Banfield, 1970).

Whereas the politics-as-usual prototype presents politics as a collection of private dramas played out by politicians pursuing self-interest and ignoring the public interest, the public leadership prototype portrays politics as a series of public dramas in which a democratic people attempts (through its leaders and public institutions) to solve its public problems and achieve its common goals without being concerned with or hindered by special interests or groups.

In describing the proposed program or project, stories patterned after the public leadership prototype generally stay close to the description and actual words of the leader who announces the program. Therefore, this sort of story has a strong tendency to give an implicitly favorable view of the newsmaker's statements and his sincerity. For this reason, the public leadership prototype is a great boon to public officials, often enabling them to "use" the press and to manipulate public opinion.

Like other prototypes, the public leadership prototype fixes upon one aspect of the reality of events and ignores other aspects. Here, the focus is on the manifest content of leaders' statements. What is ignored is, first, the possibility that they do not mean precisely what they say or seem to say. This prototype assumes they do mean what they say. Second, the public leadership prototype simplifies (and sometimes badly misrepresents) the nature of the public problem in question and does not explore whether and how the suggested solution will solve it. It suggests, instead, an equivalence between the stated *intention* to solve a problem and the achievement of a program or policy that will solve the problem.

CONCLUSION

A useful way to summarize is to assess the probable effects upon news of historical changes in patterns of media ownership. During the last sixty years, there has been a dramatic reduction in the extent of local competition among newspapers and a dramatic increase in monopoly and chain ownership. In 1910 there were 2,202 daily newspapers in 1,207 cities (53% of all American urban places); of those cities with daily newspapers, more than half (57%) had two or more papers owned and operated by competing managements. At that time there were only 13 chains owning 62 newspapers, less than 3 percent of the total. By 1968 there were 1,749 newspapers in 1,500 cities, of which only 45 (or 3%) had competing newspapers; the number of chains had risen to 159, owning a total of 828 newspapers, 47 percent of the total. In broadcasting, the trend of the last several decades has been toward more stations in more cities, but there has also been a dramatic increase in chain ownership (Bagdikian, 1971).

Much has been written about the potential dangers posed by such increasing monopoly control in local media markets. Yet surprisingly little is known for certain about its actual results, and some evidence suggests that there may even be some benefits in monopoly for the consumer. One study found that the introduction of a competing newspaper in a previously one-paper town led the original monopoly paper to increase local news coverage (the most expensive kind of news to gather, 90% more costly per column inch than national news) by almost 25 percent, but the paper also increased the proportion of sensational news items. When the new newspaper failed and ceased publication, the original paper reduced the amount of sensational news and began to publish more long, interpretive news (Bagdikian, 1971). Because it is expensive to maintain a large staff of good reporters, financially hard-pressed competitive newspapers often cannot afford as large and as competent a news department as wealthier monopolistic newspapers. It is suggestive that, of the newspapers generally considered the best in America, a large majority are either monopolies or else (like the *Los Angeles Times* or *The New York Times*) face competition from such very different papers that they are nearly in a monopolistic position. It is equally suggestive that the cities with the nation's most hotly competitive newspapers (for example, Boston and San Francisco in the 1950s and early 1960s) are not noted as centers of excellent journalism. It is true that monopolistic newspapers can suppress or distort news with relative impunity and that some are known to have done so; it is also true that many competitive newspapers are guilty of the same thing. The only possible conclusion is that the consequences of monopoly are mixed and that competition is no guarantee of honesty or excellence.

In light of what has been noted in this chapter about the nature and causes of media message systems, it is to be expected that monopoly—or any other pattern of ownership—should have only mixed and marginal effects. The common purposes and strategy of all news organizations were set decades ago and have since been maintained by the craft of reporting; and, as we have seen, these—together with the rules, procedures, and prototypes with which reporters work—are primary determinants of their products' characteristics. This is not to say that there are no dangers in the way the media are owned, financed, and produced. It is to suggest that the rules and prototypes of reporting also pose a danger, perhaps a more direct and constant one than do ownership patterns.

Consider the undesirable consequences of the four prototypes. One of their common characteristics is that, by definition, they simplify events and induce reporters to ignore aspects of an event which do not fit with the prototype being applied. Second, and this is but a corollary of the first point, each prototype is incapable of conveying the problematic character of events, and the meaning of all events is inherently problematic. This suggests a final common characteristic and irony. By reducing events to a near caricature of themselves and by presenting events as if each had only a single, unambiguous nature—in short, by symbolizing the whole of an event by one of its parts—these prototypes facilitate the ease and speed with which the event can be grasped by a hasty reader. Yet they also render it extremely difficult to extract from news much useful understanding of the events in question. In purposive roles—for example, in their roles as voters—people, above all, need information illuminating the relationships between ends and means, between situations and goals. Without such information, people cannot understand or control what happens to them, and democratic politics is in danger of degenerating into a random and unavailing pursuit of deceptive appearances and empty symbols. There is a danger that the strategy originally adopted by the mass media in order to educate the citizenry and to perfect the American democracy has unintended—and opposite—results.

SUGGESTED READINGS

Boorstin, Daniel J., *The Image*. New York: Atheneum, 1961.
> One of the best critical studies of the contents of mass and other media, this historically oriented book has all the virtues and vices of the conventional approach to mass media.

Cohen, Bernard, *The Press and Foreign Policy*. Princeton: Princeton University Press, 1963.

> The best of the many modern works on the craft of reporting and on the interrelationships between reporters and government.

Klapper, Joseph T., *The Effects of Mass Communications*. New York: The Free Press, 1960.

> The comprehensive summary of social science research into the effects of mass media.

Lippmann, Walter, *Public Opinion*. New York: The Macmillan Company, 1922.

> A classic study of public opinion and the mass media, and still one of the best general theoretical works on this important subject.

Park, Robert E., *On Social Control and Collective Behavior*. Chicago: Phoenix, 1965.

> Park was one of the first and best sociologists to study American mass media. His essays on "News as a Form of Knowledge," "The Natural History of the Newspaper," and "Morale and the News" are particularly important.

Rosenberg, Bernard and David M. White, eds., *Mass Culture*. New York: The Free Press, 1959.

> A useful and often fascinating collection of essays on the contents of mass media, generally from a literary and critical point of view, and dealing with movies, books, magazines, comic strips, and so on, as well as with TV and newspaper news.

Rosten, Leo, *The Washington Correspondents*. New York: Harcourt, Brace, 1937.

> The first sociological study of reporters, and still one of the best.

Schramm, Wilbur A., ed., *Mass Communications*. Urbana: University of Illinois Press, 1960.

> This is one of the best collections of social science articles on mass media and mass communications.

Seisberger, Bernard, *The American Newspaperman*. Chicago: University of Chicago Press, 1961.

> The most intelligent and useful history of the newspaper in America—brief and to the point.

PART V

Politics and Stratification: Authority, Power, and Prestige

Having dealt with situations of everyday life, we begin detailed consideration of the structures or patterns of situations in Part V. We shall still be concerned, especially in the early parts of the essays, with the situations underlying structural analyses, but our emphasis will be on the structural analyses, mainly of social problems. Chapter 13 discusses the presentational strategies in gaining political power and then considers the social structures in politics. Chapter 14 deals with social class, an important form of influence in society. Chapter 15 deals with the many problems in comparing various structures of society, especially those arising from lack of attention to the complexities of everyday situations underlying any structural analysis.

CHAPTER 13

Politics in Society

Our predominant concern thus far has been with the analysis of situations. This chapter makes a transition to the analysis of social structures and of problems associated with those structures. The chapter begins with the nature and situational tactics of politics, including strategies of self-presentation, then proceeds to consider political organizations and their relationships to modern nation-states.

In its broadest sense, politics consists of the management of events to win social conflicts. But this definition is so broad as to make politics equivalent to interaction strategies. This chapter is concerned with politics as "the struggle of individuals and groups to gain control over social organizations of violence," which means primarily governmental power. It focuses on American politics and political organizations, tracing their patterns back to the forms of power in feudal Europe and drawing upon other examples to show that the pluralistic structure of power relations may be crucial to the continuance of democracy. We see in succeeding chapters that increasing concentrations of power, within American society and internationally, pose problems for democratic procedures.

Ordinarily, we think of "politics" as an activity involving governments, politicians, election campaigns, *coups d'état,* and so on. We also use the word in a broader sense, referring to "office politics" involving office cliques and power struggles; the "politics of the movie industry," "church politics," or "elder statesmen of science." In this sense, everything has its politics, its coalition-making, its influence-wielding—from bridge clubs to families to the American Medical Association. In this larger meaning, politics takes place in groups or organizations whenever individuals try to convince or manipulate others in order to get the group to do what a particular person or faction wants it to do. In this sense, politics would cover virtually all of sociology.

Politics involving government has a special feature distinguishing it from politics in general: government can back up decisions by force. Laws and taxes are enforced by the police; the authority of government can be upheld by the army. When a government loses control over the means of violence, it can no longer back up its orders, and its authority will be taken over by whatever organization can effectively use violence. One implication is that power politics is potentially dangerous. Another is that the political order is central in any society, since death is the strongest social sanction and all else must give way before the organization with the power to kill. How the state is constituted and how it acts will have an important effect on stratification, the economy, patterns of deviance, and family structure (through marriage, divorce, and inheritance laws). The state will have an effect whether it is strong or weak, positively by government action or negatively by standing back and allowing other social institutions to go their own way.

POLITICS AS THE STRUGGLE TO CONTROL THE SOCIAL ORGANIZATION OF VIOLENCE

We may define the area of politics as the struggle of individuals and groups to gain control over the social organizations of violence. This definition has the advantage of freeing us from our ethnocentric viewpoint as American citizens. Elections and parties are only one kind of political arrangement, as we can see by looking at politics in other countries and historical periods. Legislatures and government agencies are fairly modern Western innovations. The centralized state that attempts to monopolize the use of force has appeared only since the eighteenth century in Europe, displacing a political system in which the private use of force was still guarded by noblemen or heads of households. But, however it is organized, the capacity to use violence exists in all societies and everywhere men have developed institutions that wield force, banding together to gain control of those institutions and thus further their own interests.

In this chapter, we investigate the conditions that shape the form of governmental organizations; the conditions that divide up interest groups, parties, and movements attempting to get control of the government; and the tactics and resources that help determine who will be successful in the struggle for power. We begin with *tactics,* which are important in forming interest groups, parties, movements, and the government itself. Tactics also provide a link between the politics of everyday life and the game played for higher stakes in the organization of violence.

POLITICAL TACTICS, CONFLICT, AND ORGANIZATION

Politics arises when there is disagreement, which happens quite often. People are frequently divided in their economic interests and in their cultural ideals. But, even if these divisions do not exist, politics will develop wherever there are organizations in which some people have authority that others must obey, creating a division between those interested in maintaining or widening their power and those interested in greater freedom from control. Therefore, power is inherently divisive, especially when it is based—as governments are—on force.

Politics, then, involves conflict, ranging from friendly disagreement to violent attempts at domination. Power cannot be exercised by a single individual. It takes an organization to wield power, and whoever wishes to control such an organization must induce others to act with him. Even when the main inducement is force, there must be some social arrangement among the force-users, some "honor among thieves."

Political tactics are techniques of gaining group cooperation. There are two main sorts of tactics: *bargaining,* either by promising rewards or threatening punishments, and *manipulating beliefs and emotions.* American professional politicians are often characterized as special sorts of businessmen, engaged in buying and selling power. In most big cities the formal power is split among many officials: the mayor; the city council; the courts;

independent boards for water control, highways, and schools; the county board of supervisors; state agencies; and federal fund-granting agencies. Beyond these formal authorities are informal sources of influence: the newspapers, big businesses, civic associations, wealthy donors to public projects and political campaigns, party leaders, and sometimes the leaders of organized crime. If someone wants to undertake a project—whether a large one like renovating the downtown area or a small one like procuring a liquor license—he must get agreement from enough wielders of power and influence to carry it off against whatever interests may be opposed (Banfield, 1961). But politicians do not give their consent for nothing. In the days of extreme political corruption of the nineteenth and early twentieth centuries, the price was often a bribe. Today the price is usually less tangible, but nonetheless real: it is the expectation of a favor when the politician wants something in return.

This general model of political bargaining applies far beyond civic politics. It describes what goes on in legislatures as bills are passed or buried in committees and what happens in political parties during the maneuvering outside the public eye that results in candidates coming forth with endorsements from other politicians and campaign funds from wealthy supporters and the party treasury. The bargaining can not only take the form of you-support-my-project-and-I'll-support-yours, but also the form you-support-my-career-and-I'll-support-your-career. Bargaining may vary in form under different political systems. In European parliamentary regimes such as Italy, governments rise and fall as politicians renegotiate the majority coalitions from which the prime minister is usually drawn. The military juntas of Latin American, the Middle East, and Southeast Asia are put together by such bargaining; the stakes are higher since the loser may also lose his life.

Whatever the form of political bargaining, certain factors are conducive to success. Political bargaining power is cumulative; the more favors one has been able to grant in the past and the more successful one has been at bargaining with others in the past, the more power one has to make favorable deals. When dealing with a man of accumulated bargaining power, such as Speaker Sam Rayburn of the House of Representatives during the 1950s, or Mayor Daley of Chicago in the 1960s, one deals with a person who can be very helpful if he is friendly and very dangerous if he is not. Different structures of political organization and lineups of interests groups can limit the accumulation of personal power.

The other factor involved in success at bargaining is personality. The successful politician must be clever, cool-headed, quick to sense shifts in the distribution of power, adept at changing his position. The type does not seem to have changed much since it was described by the rules for worldly success of a Jesuit priest in the government of the Spanish Inquisition (Baltasar Gracian, *The Oracle*, 1647):

Keep your affairs in suspense.
Make people depend on you.
Avoid victories over your superiors.
Control your imagination.
Know how to take and give hints.
Without lying, do not tell the whole truth.
Be a man without illusions.
Behave as if you were watched.
In a word, be a saint.

PUBLIC BARGAINING

Bargaining takes place in public as well as behind the scenes. Public bargaining has a special structure, since it occurs among groups of people so large that few ever directly confront one another. Elections are the prime example of such public bargaining. Once the candidates have emerged from the more intimate maneuvers of the politicians, what determines who will win? Politicians offer positions on issues that appeal to a large enough range of interests to elect them. They are skillful at stretching their statements of principles to mean different things to different audiences, but there are inherent limits to what divergent interests can be brought together. We can predict that a politician who successed in preempting the middle will be most successful in American elections, not because he is necessarily well liked, but because the largest number of voters will regard him as the "lesser evil" compared to his opponents. The landslide victory of Lyndon B. Johnson in the 1964 presidential election resulted because his Republican opponent, Barry Goldwater, was identified with one end of the political spectrum.

Where the balance point is depends on the nature of the political system. In liberal congressional districts, the middle position will be considerably different from the middle for a presidential election. The kind of electoral system itself can have an important effect on coalition formation (Lipset, 1963). The American system of direct election of a strong president has meant that only two political parties at a time have had much chance of success: those two parties which start from the middle and branch on over toward the ends of the spectrum. Third parties cannot be successful in national elections except when the interest group spectrum undergoes a major shift and the center parties fail to move over to take account of it. In American politics, the major parties have been relatively free from ideological positions and have taken over many of the popular programs of various actual or potential third-party movements such as the Populists or the Progressives.

In European parliamentary systems, however, the prime minister is usually the head of a majority coalition in the national legislature. Thus, a large number of parties may flourish, since each may have a geographical base or may be given representation in proportion to its percentage of the vote. The coalition does not have to be put together in a presidential election but can be negotiated in private among leaders of parties or factions. This system has more positions represented in the government; it does bear the liability that the government may become deadlocked in party conflict.

MANIPULATING BELIEFS AND EMOTIONS: THE DYNAMICS OF LEGITIMACY

Politics is more than cool-headed bargaining. Success does not depend solely on who can offer the best deal for enough interests to form a winning coalition. Politicians can also influence emotions and beliefs, and bargains are not struck simply among people's clearly defined interests, but among what people conceive their interests to be. Whoever can influence those beliefs is at least part of the way to exercising power. How people act depends on what concepts they have available to think about the political world—whether they think of it in terms of Christians and infidels, Englishmen and Spaniards, working class and bourgeoisie, or democrats and Communists—and on what they believe to be facts: that the Germans attacked Poland or Poland attacked Germany, that the politicians in Washington are corrupt or honorable, that North Vietnam invaded South Vietnam or there is a civil war in South Vietnam against a reactionary military dictatorship. A large part of politics is the struggle among politicians to exercise influence over emotions and beliefs.

As in all social interaction, people act according to how they define the situation and, without a certain amount of common belief, people would be unable to uphold any social order at all. But beliefs are not separated from emotions and interests; they all go together. In practice, we see political reality in terms of notions of *legitimacy*: a world view tells us simultaneously what sort of politics exists, what sort of politics ought to exist, and where one stands in relation to all this. Various political factions try to define legitimacy their own way, but there must always be some notion of legitimacy if a state is to exist.

It is easiest to understand the dynamics of legitimacy by looking at an extreme case. Imagine a dictator who controls a country for his personal benefit. If he is universally disliked, how does he stay in power? By the force of his army and secret police. But how does he control the army and the police? He may not carry a gun himself, and at any rate his soldiers outnumber him. But any one man or any unit of the army that tries to revolt will be killed, as long as the rest of the army stays loyal. Why doesn't the whole army revolt? The difficulty is that they are watching each other, under the eyes of the dictator; no one can risk stepping forward to lead a revolt. But, if the dictator should falter and show signs of indecision or weakness, the whole regime might collapse. The key to power in this case is a self-fulfilling prophecy: as long as those who control believe the ruler is powerful, he will be powerful; when that belief crumbles, so does his power (Schelling, 1963).

This is an extreme case because most rulers get willing loyalty from at least some sectors of the populace: conservative dictators are sometimes allied with the church and the wealthy landlords, elected leaders may be given loyalty by most citizens merely because they play by the democratic rules. But, since the state survives because it has the power to use force, the extreme case tells us something about the others. How the power is distributed depends on what people believe, and shifts in their beliefs will bring about shifts in the distribution of power. Notions of legitimacy become much more complex and important in states in which the ruler depends on more widespread loyalty.

MAX WEBER'S ANALYSIS OF LEGITIMACY

Max Weber, who first analyzed the principles of legitimacy, noted three ideal types: traditional, charismatic, and rational-legal.

Authority may be *traditional*: certain people rule because it has always been that way. Most premodern societies were traditional in politics; kings and noblemen ruled because their families had always ruled, or tribal elders picked out the chief by the accepted magic formula. The basic justification was usually religious. Sometimes the ruler himself, like the Chinese emperor, was the highest religious figure; sometimes the priests were a separate group who sanctioned the ruler's authority, as when Charlemagne had himself crowned by the Pope. In traditional regimes, there is usually elaborate ceremony: prescribed costumes, formal rituals, processions, complex rankings, and court etiquette, all sanctified by tradition and generally having religious overtones. There are elements of traditional legitimacy in modern societies. Parliamentary regimes such as Britain or Belgium keep ceremonial monarchies as the ultimate repositories of state legitimacy. Traditional elements such as the church, the aristocratic landowners, and the army are important segments of the regimes in most of Latin America, the Arab states, Spain, Portugul, Greece, and parts of Asia. In the United States, traditional legitimacy is invoked by national symbols such as the flag, national holidays, and revered heroes such as Washington, Lincoln, Roosevelt, and Kennedy.

A different kind of legitimacy is based on personal *charisma*. The charismatic leader often breaks with tradition and puts in its place his own new and personal vision of the universe. Religious prophets such as Gautama Buddha and Jesus are charismatic leaders outside the political sphere; others such as Mohammed were simultaneously religious and political, as may be expected in a society in which tribal leaders were both. Modern charismatic leaders such as Lenin, Mussolini, Gandhi, Hitler, Franklin D. Roosevelt, and Mao Tse-tung are usually the heads of ideological movements, the modern secular substitute for religion. Politicians strive for a measure of personal charisma. Success is not entirely a matter of personal qualities, although they are important; usually charisma builds up, with a growing public mystique helping to reinforce the aura of personal authority and vision. Robert Kennedy seemed on his way toward acquiring such charisma at the time he was killed.

The principles of *rational-legal* legitimacy are very different. Authority is rational-legal if based on a set of general rules and on a rationale that explains why the authority should exist. The authority of American policemen, tax collectors, congressmen, and presidents is based on their installation in office through the laws governing appointment or election, and these laws are based on the Constitution. The system is supposed to be rational as well as legalistic. There are ultimately reasons why the state should exist and its various functions be carried out: to protect the life, liberty, and pursuit of happiness of its citizens and to promote the general welfare. There can be various forms of rational-legal justifications of authority. The Commuist states justify their adherence to a set of laws and regulations and ultimately on the promotion of a classless society. By the time of Frederick the Great, the Prussian state bureaucracy justified itself as promoting order and the power of the state. State protection of the people and maintenance of order have been used as justification in virtually all large states throughout history, including those in which the predominant legitimation is traditional.

The existence of principles of legitimacy does not mean that politicians live up to them or that there is no conflict over who will have the advantages of power (Collins, 1968). Principles of legitimacy by no means guarantee that everyone will accept the rulers' authority, but they are essential in shaping the arena for political conflict. The traditional ruler would seem to have little to worry about. He is the ruler, and no one can ask why or do anything about it. But tradition can be constraining. The priests might try to exert their traditional rights to advise him on all decisions; his courtiers might try to make him into a ceremonial figurehead, as happened to both the Chinese and Japanese emperors. In some African kingdoms, the king's religious duties were so confining (his ritual acts were believed to hold up the universe) that men had to be forced to be king. New interpretations of tradition may be added as new situations arise. Traditional regimes, then, can be full of court intrigue, as the ruler, priests, nobility, and servants vie with each other for control—all justifying themselves in the name of tradition.

The charismatic leader is in a precarious position (Bendix, 1968). His authority among his disciples and followers may be absolute, but it is based on maintaining his personal impressiveness. Should he show himself indecisive or confused, be embarrassed by a mistake or a defeat, or prove incapable of dealing with an emergency, he might lose his personal power quite rapidly. It is possible by modern public relations techniques to try to project a heroic image; but the man who embarks on that course arouses expectations that he may not be able to live up to. If he casts himself as a hero, people expect him to do things that ordinary men cannot do. The greater his image, the greater the miracles expected. Many charismatic figures and would-be popular politicians end by ruining themselves through a crowd-reinforced megalomania. Napoleon and Hitler brought on their own defeats by losing all judgment about military weaknesses; lesser politicians have repeatedly made the same mistake in policy because they were unwilling to admit their first mistake.

As in the other two forms of legitimacy, rational-legal authority creates expectations of the ruled that limit rulers' courses of action. Politics in the United States is officially justified only on the grounds of promoting the good of the people. The state is supposed to be a neutral instrument, representing no interest or faction but enforcing laws for the general protection and providing all manner of public services from sewers to nuclear defense systems. Of course, political interest groups use this political rhetoric in attempts to justify any and all measures for their own personal good—from workman's compensation to injunctions against strikes, from a graduated income tax to tax loopholes. The principles of legitimacy are so broad that they can sanction almost anything to people ready to agree. But they do focus politics in certain directions. No American government would survive in office that did not promote economic prosperity, whatever the ideologies of the time might say about the role of government in the economy. The fundamental justifications also provide a rallying point around which opposition to government actions may form. American values on equality provided virtually the only leverage of the civil rights movement of the 1950s and early 1960s against an institutionalized system of racism, and publicity about existing conditions was the prime weapon for initiating change. American ideas of democracy and humanitarianism have provided a similar organizing point for opposition to government policies of supporting exploitative military dictatorships in other countries. Communist regimes have been embarrassed by groups within their ranks opposing repression in the name of Marxist ideals.

POLITICS AS IMPRESSION MANAGEMENT

The legitimacy of a government, whatever form it may take, is a definition of the government's reality. People attempt to present a particular view of themselves in face-to-face encounters, and politics is a similar art of *impression management*. Like the hostess at a party suavely carrying on the conversation while servants remove dog manure from the carpet, politicians attempt to act as if their world lived up to the ideals that justify their power. One way to do this is by controlling information. Before the modern era this was comparatively easy, since there were no newspapers or other mass media, and the majority of the populace lived in isolated peasant villages. The aristocrats had power partly because they were the only men free to move about and know what was happening. In modern regimes information control is exercised partly by government secrecy, partly by news censorship. Both are likely to be more extreme the more the government is controlled by a single powerful faction and the more its actions stray from its own principles of legitimacy. Governments find it easiest to maintain their legitimacy in times of war or threatened attack, whether from within or without, unless they are losing badly. Under such circumstances, secrecy and censorship can be passed off as necessary to prevent information leaking to the enemy. At the same time, civil liberties and legal procedures can be suspended because of the necessity of moving fast against the enemy, and people's emotional solidarity under the government is generated out of feelings of fear and anger. Without independent sources of information, it is difficult for the public to know whether there is an emergency or not. Dictatorial regimes often come to power during such an alleged crisis: this happened in the army coups in Greece (1966) and Brazil (1964) and in Hitler's 1934 coup after acquiring the premiership in 1933 through elections.

POLITICS AS THEATER

Ordinary politics as well as revolutions take place as a kind of mass theater, in which various actors try to present their pictures of reality. Jean Genet's play *The Balcony* is a good picture of this aspect of politics. In American politics, the play of interest groups and backstage bargains appears in public as a series of arguments, speeches, newspaper headlines, and occasionally parades and demonstrations. Most of the time the audience pays only moderate attention to the drama, and the arguments on the center of the stage take the form of discussions of the public interest, with a certain amount of posturing toward enemies in the wings. Periodic political scandals come to light only through the revelations of an occasional newspaper columnist, and are treated with righteous shock.

CRISES OF LEGITIMACY

Politics, as we experience it, is a series of situations in which participants maneuver to define themselves into positions of advantage. Some of these situations are dramatic, especially when there is a *legitimacy crisis*. On a small scale, such crises are familiar on college campuses. Virtually the only weapon of student activists is their power to challenge the legitimacy of the college administration, since they have had little say in colleges' policies or rule making, and no force to match against the police.

Legitimacy crises occur in the larger society as well—in urban racial upheavals such as the 1965 Watts riot and in mass revolutions. Students and intellectuals have been important in most twentieth-century revolutionary situations. This does not mean that students have ever carried through a revolution; this has always come about through an armed uprising by large segments of the populace and by the defection of the army. The role of students and intellectuals has been in exploiting weakness in the façade of government legitimacy and in *constructing alternative definitions of the situation*. Thus, a university revolt and strike in Paris began the French crisis of May 1968; it spread to the labor movement when it became apparent that de Gaulle's government was vacillating and weak on this smaller issue (Seale and McConville, 1968). In the end the army stood by de Gaulle, and the near revolution collapsed. Student demonstrations have sometimes touched off changes of government when there was an uneasy balance of power between different contenders, as in the military coups of South Vietnam in the 1960s. Where the government power is united, as in the Soviet Union, demonstrations are merely crushed and those involved, like the Soviet writers Daniel and Tertz, are sent to prison. The ideological basis of the Soviet regime makes it sensitive to criticism by intellectuals.

POLITICAL INTEREST GROUPS AND MOVEMENTS

Everyone involved in politics has interests. There is confusion with this point, because our common political rhetoric defines interests almost exclusively in financial terms. But *economic* interests constitute only one of three main types of interests; the other two are *power* interests and *cultural* or *ideal* interests. These interests are often mixed together in any political program, with some (usually economic and power interests) kept in the background and others (usually cultural ideals) put in the foreground of public attention. That cultural ideals are almost never recognized as social interests is one of the principal reasons that politics seems incomprehensible to most people. We shall examine each type of interest separately, in its "pure" form, before seeing how they can be brought together in political ideologies and movements. One basic principle applies: Political interests—

whether economic, power, or cultural—are almost always based on particular social organizations or social groups.

ECONOMIC INTEREST GROUPS

Groups of individuals who share common interests by virtue of their position in the economic system are called classes. Employers comprise an economic class since they share an interest in keeping down the cost of labor; employees are another class, with a common interest in raising wages. Debtors and creditors are another pair of classes with antagonistic interests. Consumers and sellers are a third major set of opposing classes. The analysis of economic classes is far from simple, because there are many differing economic interests within these general categories and because not all potential economic conflicts are translated into political action. Within the class of employees, there may be considerable political disagreement between craft unions, which favor a policy of maximum job security for current employees, and industrial unions of unskilled and semiskilled workers which favor a policy of expanding job opportunities for the unemployed. Industrialists may compete with each other for a government contract, or for government spending in one region or another. Economic interests have political effects because they feed into the political bargaining process described above.

Not all potential economic interests are mobilized. Consumers are just now coming together as a political movement, though everyone is a consumer and therefore this group has had a numerical advantage. What classes will be politically mobilized depends on how the economy is organized in a particular country and how it is functioning at the time. Marx, in his class analysis of politics, argued that a capitalist economy generated periodic financial crises forcing people to forego all other economic interests but those held as employers or employees (Bendix and Lipset, 1966). Thus, politics would increasingly become a conflict between bourgeoisie and proletariat, with the issue capitalism or socialism. Marx's analysis still gives a partial insight into political events. The 1929 Depression did mobilize the working class in America and bring to office the liberal Democrats and Roosevelt's New Deal—with benefits for employees such as the legal right to unionize, social security, unemployment compensation, and tax reforms. But the Depression did not bring socialism in the form of government ownership of industry; indeed, it instituted policies of calculated government action in public spending, taxation, and currency control that have considerably stabilized the private economy and made unlikely the kind of economic system in which Marx's expected crises could occur (Schumpeter, 1942). One reason that the New Deal period did not work out according to the Marxian model is that American politics was not galvanized entirely on the employer-employee split; other economic classes, especially debtors and sellers, were also mobilized to fight for interests that helped shape the New Deal program. There has always been economic class conflict in the United States, but it has been confused and mixed rather than simple enough to foster revolution (Wiley, 1967). Marx made the only serious attempt to provide a theory of the economy that explains what economic classes become mobilized when. We remain in need of a theory that can take into account the myriad economic interests and their operation in the modern state.

POWER INTEREST GROUPS

The possession of power is widely desired for its own sake. Although virtually all politicians have this motive, for many modern politicians it is far more important than any economic interest or cultural ideal and makes them capable of changing their position if it will enable them to stay in power. Before the era of electoral politics, the political struggle was largely a clash among raw power interests, pure and simple. Military lords fought with each other for territory, kings fought with their subordinates, courtiers intrigued and poisoned to get a preferential position at court.

But, if the desire for power is so widespread, how can we use it to explain anything about how political interests groups will form? The answer is that power must always be attained through some kind of political organization, and hence sheer power conflicts always come down to conflicts between organizations or between different positions within organizations. Even the premodern political struggle was confined within certain organizational forms: between feudal barons and centralizing kings, between independent knights and a royal standing army, later between the king and his own bureaucracy. Organizations have becomes increasingly important in modern politics, since power is dispersed among a large number of permanent organizations within which individuals must climb on their way to the top. In the process of seeking power, individuals come to identify with the power of their own organization and, for the majority of men, the best way to enhance their own power is to enhance the organization's power. Power conflicts, then, tend to follow the lines of conflicting jurisdiction of political organizations.

In the modern United States, power is dispersed among many organizations, and hence the organizational power struggle is very acute. The three-way conflict between federal, state, and local power is no longer as acute as it was during the nineteenth century, particularly since local and state governments have come to rely heavily on federal financial aid. The struggle over local control versus municipal or more distant control in such matters as schools, police, and welfare services is on the increase, especially because local control is a means of gaining some power for racial and cultural groups with no influence over large-scale bureaucracies that try to force middle-class-white values upon them (Banfield and Wilson, 1963).

There are also major interorganizational struggles within the executive branch of government. Organizational studies have shown that virtually all large organizations develop a vested interest in their own survival and expansion, quite apart from whatever ideals they were originally set up to serve. Phillip Selznick's (1949) classic study of the Tennessee Valley Authority showed that an organization will modify even its basic liberal ideals in a conservative direction in order to accommodate hostile interests and survive. Thus, covertly, the TVA gave up its New Deal programs to help poor farmers in order to pacify conservative land-owning groups that might threaten its water and power projects. In the long run, generally, the organization's ideals and policies tend to maximize its power and stability. This tends to make government agencies their own lobbyists.

CULTURAL INTEREST GROUPS

Many political issues do not seem to involve self-interest in the economic or power sense. Sometimes these issues overwhelm the ordinary political struggle, and crusading idealists become the dominant political leaders—all the more powerful because they seem to have nothing to gain personally and because they are often willing to sacrifice others as well as themselves for their ideal. Historically, religion has been the main cultural interest in politics, especially in areas influenced by Christianity and Islam. Conquests to extend the faith were followed by wars between Protestant and Catholic factions and between various Islamic sects. The issue of a state-supported, compulsory-membership church has been important in much of Europe and South America until recently, and clerical and anticlerical factions remain strong in many countries. In secularized countries such as the United States, cultural groups continually attempt to influence the state to enforce particular moral standards. The conflict over the use of alcohol, culminating in the temporary victory of the Prohibitionists in the 1920s, is only one issue in a persistent moral battle between conservatives and libertarians. More recently, the battle concerns such issues as censorship of books, magazines, movies, and television; styles of clothing and hair, abortion, divorce, and drugs.

What determines cultural interest groups? They are determined by the organizations in which people work and by the formal communities in which they associate with others. One of the strongest generalizations we can make about social influences on values is that people adhere to those supporting their own career interests. Not unexpectedly, the strongest supporters of probusiness policies are businessmen, and unionists are the strongest supporters of pro-union policies (Lipset, 1960).

Cultural ideologies are thus generalized beyond particular organizations. The social groups supporting them are found in the community at large, where persons with similar life styles and ideals based on their work tend to associate, avoiding others with different styles and ideals. Thus, cultural ideals are part of community stratification. The groups that dominate the community, by their control of powerful organizations or by their wealth, tend to dominate cultural standards as well. Immigrant groups with different manners, religions, or ideals are usually relegated to the bottom of the community status hierarchy and discriminated against in formal organizations.

POLITICAL MOVEMENTS: MOBILIZED INTERESTS

Interest groups are only potential political forces. They must be mobilized to have an effect on politics. Political movements can be based on single-interest groups or on a coalition of interests under the umbrella of an encompassing ideology headed by recognized leaders. For mobilization to take place, physical and social conditions must allow individual members of the interest groups to become aware of each other and to act together. Before the urban industrial era, only the aristocracy was able to move freely from one part of the country to another, to communicate with each other, and thus to organize themselves into alliances to struggle for power. The peasants comprised over 90 percent of the populace but were scattered in isolated villages or farms; in Marx's famous phrase, their unity was purely external, "formed by simple addition of homologous magnitudes much as potatoes in a sack form a sack of potatoes." The major political effect of industrialization was to bring the majority of the population off the farm and into the cities, where they came to experience the power of their own numbers. Factories brought together workingmen in one place over a long period of time, making it possible for labor unions and employee-oriented parties and movements to spring up. This is part of what Marx meant when he stated that the capitalist order created the instruments of its own destruction.

Mobilization can bring out more than economic interest groups. Urbanization and the spread of radio, television, and newspapers can mobilize traditional ethnic and religious groups and make them more politically conscious (Deutsch, 1953; Geertz, 1963b). The spread of modern culture does not necessarily make for a more cosmopolitan, tolerant atmosphere but can have the opposite effect, as in the increasingly vehement conflicts between language groups in India, Moslem-Chinese conflict in Indonesia, and Arab nationalism in the Middle East. One reason students can be politically active is that they are easily mobilized; schools bring them together in large numbers, put them at the center of information about politics, keep them in constant contact with each other and out of contact with persons embedded in the nonmobilized and nonintellectual routines of work and family. The structural situation for students in large universities is similar to that of workers in industries with the highest strike rates: mining, logging, fishing, and other jobs that bring together workers in an isolated community (Kerr and Siegal, 1954).

In addition to physical and social conditions for acting together, mobilization requires an issue to galvanize people into action. The better organized the interest group, the more able it is to act on subtle and routine issues. The heads of large corporations, bankers, military officers, and government officials are in a good position to take a day-to-day interest in politics affecting them, as vast organizational resources are at their control. Other interest groups are more diffuse and require more dramatic issues to bring them into action. Unionized workers tend to be politically involved only when a labor dispute is underway; nonunionized workers are rarely drawn together into political movements except under the extreme conditions of an economic crisis.

POLITICAL ORGANIZATIONS

Political power is attained and exercised through organizations, and the principles of organizational functioning are important determinants of the outcome of the political struggle. There are two kinds of political organizations: membership associations, such as parties and legislatures, in which authority rests formally with the entire membership; and administrative organizations, such as armies and governmental agencies, in which authority is formally vested in the top official and is delegated by him to subordinates. Both types of organizations are also found outside the political realm: clubs, voluntary associations, professional societies, labor unions, and congregation-controlled churches are membership associations; factories, stores, banks, schools, and the Catholic Church are hierarchic or administrative organizations. The important distinction is that in the first type control comes from the bottom and is delegated to elected leaders while, in the second type, control comes from the top and is delegated to subordinates.

MEMBERSHIP ASSOCIATIONS AND MICHELS' "IRON LAW OF OLIGARCHY"

The principal theory on operation of membership associations was first stated by the German sociologist Robert Michels in *Political Parties*, published in 1911. His theory, developed from examining the German Social

Democratic party, states that actual power tends to slip out of the hands of formal authorities (the members) into the hands of the delegated officials who control the organizational machinery. Michels picked the Social Democrats to analyze partly because they were the only avowedly democratic party in Germany at the time. He felt that if he could show that even this party was *internally* undemocratic, his conclusions would apply even more strongly to parties that did not make this claim. In fact, Michels' theory has been borne out by studies of all sorts of membership associations—from the PTA and the American Legion to the American Medical Association and the American Sociological Association, from labor unions to congregational churches and throughout political parties and legislatures (Lipset, Trow, and Coleman, 1956). More specifically, Michels' theory, which he termed the "Iron Law of Oligarchy," states that (1) there is a relatively small group of leaders in any association; (2) this leadership group tends to form a unified group that operates informally, behind the scenes, to make decisions presented to the membership as *faits accompli*; (3) new leaders tend to be selected from above by the existing leadership group, rather than elected from below; (4) leaders tend to develop interests of their own differing from those of the membership, being more concerned about keeping themselves in power and protecting the organization than about taking risks to achieve the organization's stated goals; (5) the leaders are hard to influence from below; (6) when the disparity between the interests of leaders and members breaks into open conflict, the leaders exert power far out of proportion to their numbers and usually win such conflicts, often by using undemocratic methods; (7) members of the organization are generally disinterested in controlling it, reinforcing the hold of the leaders.

How do we account for the tendencies that Michels so accurately observed? First, all membership organizations tend to have a relatively small number of leaders because of the physical impossibility of operating with a large number of decision makers. Anyone who has ever attended a committee meeting or a public forum in which more than five or ten people tried to have their say on what should be done, knows that such meetings usually go on into the small hours of the morning without covering more than a small part of the agenda. In the interests of efficiency, active participation in shaping an organization's policies must be confined to a few people.

The needs of efficiency also tend to make the leadership operate out of sight of the membership, merely presenting its decisions to them for ratification. As studies of many organizations have shown, decision makers operate most efficiently when they form a close-knit, informal clique (Barnard, 1938; Gross, 1953; Dalton, 1959).

Once constituted, this informal group has considerable power over any of its members and over anyone who would like to become a leader. When politics is carried on in behind-the-scenes bargains, individuals refusing to uphold the norms of privacy that the leaders have established can be threatening to the group and will be opposed by it. The group's weapons against a deviant are to exclude him from the informal bargaining through which influence is wielded and to discredit him with the public membership. For example, the dissident congressmen or state assemblyman who opposes the dominant political practices in the legislature finds himself given the most minor and irrelevant committee assignments and is cut off from influence over government jobs and spending in his district (Schlesinger, 1965). The strong informal group norms in American politics is one reason American politicians rarely resign or speak out when they disagree with policies of their government or party.

Even democratic organizations, then, tend to be elitist. This does not necessarily make for conflict, since one reason for departure from direct democracy is the need for efficiency in decision making by the organization. Obviously, however, the leaders come to have a greater investment in their positions and in the organization than do their followers; their positions give them pay, prestige, power, and a sense of belonging, whereas for the followers the organization pays off only by its success in carrying out their group interests. For the leaders, the organization need not be successful to be beneficial. As a result, they tend to act with greater conservatism, which increases the longer they have been in the organization and the more rewarding is their position. Thus, political organizations have an endemic conflict between the established leader's policy of business-as-usual and various factions trying to make them live up to their ideals.

Political power within a party or legislature builds up over time, so that the advantages of being on top enumerated by Michels are cumulative. Advantages for the leadership can be formally built into the organization. The seniority system and the great power of committees and committee chairman in Congress are common organizational features that perpetuate the control of an organizational elite in the U.S. Congress, by a conservative Southern and rural leadership that exercises influence far out of proportion to the section of the populace it represents (Clark, 1963, 1964). Existing electoral systems, including the ways districts are drawn to make seats safe for incumbents, have the effect of minimizing turnover in office for federal and state legislators. The U.S. Senate (and sometimes the presidency) comes closer than the House of Representatives to representing the large liberal section of the American populace because its members are elected from districts that are not shaped by current state politicians.

RESPONSIVENESS OF POLITICAL ORGANIZATIONS

Not all membership organizations are equally oligarchic. They vary in two independent ways: the extent to which leadership is responsive to the members' interests and the extent to which leadership is democratically selected and replaced. These are different dimensions, as an organizational leadership can be powerfully entrenched and still responsive, and an organization might have high turnover in office but be irresponsibly led.

The degree of responsiveness of leadership depends on the extent to which the organization needs the active participation of its members. Groups engaging primarily in public demonstrations must have leaders who are highly responsive to members' interests or they will mobilize few people. As labor unions have an intermittent need for membership support at times of strikes and touchy negotiations, the leadership must be responsive if the union is to survive. At other times—especially if the union officials are protected by closed shop (compulsory union membership) contracts and union dues are withheld from paychecks—the union leadership need not be very responsive. Political parties, needing their members for votes at election time only are even more intermittently responsive to their members, especially if their leaders acquire personal power by gaining public office. Fraternal organizations such as the American Legion can be almost entirely unresponsive to their membership, and their leaders may make public statements reflecting the feelings of only a small active section of the organization's nominal members. Professional associations such as the American Medical Association, in which the organization has power over its members by its control of legal boards which regulate practice, are often totally uncontrollable by the rank-and-file membership; thus, the AMA's conservative official positions may not reflect the attitudes of the majority of less powerful doctors.

Responsiveness also depends on the degree to which the leaders find the job valuable. Union leaders are prone to become conservative and committed to self-interest, ranging all the way from a willingness to compromise with business interests to outright labor racketeering (for personal profit). Union leaders experience a tremendous rise in prestige and pay when they move up from a workingman's job to a union hierarchy job; they have a long way to fall if they lose their job. If a leader makes enough enemies while in office, he may find it too dangerous to give up his office and will be motivated to use increasingly repressive and undemocratic means to stay in power. An extreme example was Stalin's rise to power in the Communist party of the USSR after Lenin's death: he began by backstage control of the party's administrative apparatus, increasingly resorted to accusations of treason and police power in his battles with Trotsky and other opponents within the party, and finally instituted a reign of terror that became self-perpetuating because of the opposition it provoked (Deutsher, 1959).

The leadership will be most responsive to membership when members have a choice among several organizations to support. Labor union members can "vote with their feet" by leaving an unresponsive union if there are several competing unions. The same applies to political parties. The two-party system, however, is not always as widespread in practice as in theory; in many areas in the United States, one party has effective control—the Democrats in most big cities and in the rural South, the Republicans in many small towns and suburbs. Pluralism is a way of making even fairly elite-controlled parties more responsive, but it is not found in all political arenas. Governmental structures are one determinant of the degree of pluralism; another is the existence of several large interest groups with the resources to organize independently.

THE SELECTION OF LEADERS

Turning now to the degree of democratic selection of leadership, we find the following conditions:

1. *Size.* The larger the organization, the harder it is to control leaders' activities, and the greater their freedom from the membership in selecting and recalling them. As Rousseau argued long ago, the democratic ideal can work only in groups small enough to meet face to face (and even here tendencies toward structural oligarchy may be found).

2. *Crisis.* The more often the organization experiences crises that mobilize members' interests, the more likely it is to have changes of leadership. Crises are not always democratizing, however; government leaders often attempt to use crises to silence opponents in the name of unity and authority. Still, emergencies and major issues—wars (especially defeats), civil disorders, economic depressions, and, for unions, wildcat strikes—tend to bring about at least temporary reassertions of democratic turnover.

3. *Dispersion of membership.* The members of an association have the greatest influence in selecting and replacing leaders when they meet together and organize factions within the organization. Perhaps the most democratic of all labor unions, the International Typographical Union, has had a two-party system within the union for many years, partly based upon the strong occupational community of printers in the big cities where the union is centered. Frequently, printers are together both on and off the job and have a strong informal network among the rank-and-file counterbalancing the usual informal network among the leaders (Lipset, Trow, and Coleman, 1956). At the other end of the spectrum, the most corrupt unions tend to have members widely dispersed on their individual jobs, and only the union officials are in contact with all the members (Bell, 1962). In political parties, the highest degree of oligarchy is usually found in rural areas, because the party members are widely dispersed and communicate

with each other only through the intermediary of party leaders. Thus, contrary to popular clichés about big-city machines, the most corrupt political machines in the United States are in the rural South, where the one-party system, the race issue, and the dispersion of voters gives political bosses almost unshakable tenure in office despite the most blatant personal corruption (Key, 1949; Sherrill, 1968).

In general, parties are most oligarchic when the members are relatively dispersed but the leadership and the formal organization are relatively centralized. In European parties, there is much more formal centralization than in American parties. The Catholic, Socialist, and Communst parties of continental Europe have tremendous bureaucracies and large funds, usually running their own trade unions, social clubs, summer camps, youth organizations (comparable to the Boy Scouts of America), and mutual aid organizations. As a result, the parties have tremendous resources to defend and a strong tendency to accept the status quo, whatever their ideologies may be. The Communist parties have been widely attacked by their more ideological student and intellectual members, because of their antirevolutionary policies. American parties are much less encompassing and tend to come together as national parties only during presidential elections. Which type of party is more democratic, according to widely accepted ideals of citizen participation and control, is hard to say. European parties are much more unified but more remote from control of the ordinary member; they have more power to act on the organization's ideals, but in fact tend to be oriented toward the status quo. American parties are more controllable at the lower levels, but the complex coalitions making up the party when it contends for higher office mean that the individual citizen's influence may be lost through the network of backstage deals among politicians.

The alternatives are most understandable if we realize that democracy is an *ideal* that encounters several dilemmas when applied to reality. First, full participatory democracy is inefficient; if a party is too democratic, it may spend all its time in internal controversy and never get anything done. But parties cannot go too far in the other direction, because too little democracy results in member apathy and alienation, which can also undermine the organization. Second, if groups of people with different interests disagree, someone is bound to lose the argument. Since there are real disagreements in a society, the democratic ideal of everyone having his interests watched over by the government is impossible. This dilemma is reduced only to the extent that people in the organization or society have homogeneous interests. We should be aware of the necessity to choose between alternatives and pay the price of our choices: How much uniformity are we willing to endure in order to have democracy? How much efficiency are we willing to pay for at the price of liberty, and vice versa? Conflict is not necessarily bad; it is the price for certain kinds of freedom.

ADMINISTRATIVE ORGANIZATION

Membership associations attempt to gain power, but it is in administrative organizations that power is exercised. In both types of organizations, there are similar problems of control by the formal authorities. In membership associations, the power is at the bottom but tends to slip into the hands of the delegated officials at the top. In administrative organizations, formal control is vested at the top of the pyramid rather than at the bottom, but the history of such organizations has underlined the struggle of top officials to prevent the inevitable dissipation of power toward the lower ranks. In both types of organizations, the reasons for the transfer of power from formal authorities to *de facto* influentials are the same: the men who do the work of the organization (the leaders in voluntary associations, the lower-ranking officials in administrative organizations) have advantages over their nominal superiors because they control on-the-spot knowledge, communications, and much of the material resources. In both cases, organizations have a momentum of their own and slip out of the control of those whom they are designed to serve.

PATRIMONIAL ORGANIZATIONS

The history of administrative organizations is one of efforts to control subordinates. Early political organizations—warrior tribe, ancient empires, feudal kingdoms—were based on personal ties between lords and their followers (Weber, 1968). In a society of widespread violence and conflict, lacking a legally enforced and morally accepted civil order, men relied only on those they could trust personally—relatives, servants who seemed "part of the family," and personal friends and allies. Following Weber's terminology, we call such organizations *patrimonial*. In a patrimonial regime, there is no idea of nepotism or corruption in the modern sense; it is considered right and proper to use one's influence to get relatives and friends into whatever political position one can, and the man who does not do so is considered disloyal and dishonorable. In such a society, the lord who conquers a territory divides it up among his relatives and loyal followers, and they appoint their personal retainers and relatives to assist them in administering (collecting booty and taxes from) the land.

The difficulty with patrimonial organizations is that personalities are not very strong and contain no principles for settling disagreements except for guile and strength. Over and over throughout history, a conqueror appoints his trusted lieutenants to help control his territory, only to find it slipping from his control—often within his own lifetime, certainly within the next few generations. Generally, patrimonial regimes do not distinguish between public and private property, as the property of the state is the private property of the lords, and taxes support the king's army and the king's wine cellar. Subordinate officials were often paid in land rather than in money; they were expected to take their own profits and expenses out of the taxes that they collected for their lord. As a result, taxes might be set by tradition but in fact were usually squeezed to the practical limits, as each level of official had to make his own profit before passing on the collected wealth to the ruler. For example, the practice of selling the right to collect taxes to entrepreneurs called "tax farmers" persisted in France right up to the revolution of 1789.

Consequently, the ruler had little control over what happened at the bottom, and he could ensure that a sizable portion of the taxes got through to his court only by continually checking up on subordinates. There was an even more serious danger to the ruler: his subordinates, especially those in removed parts of the empire, might grow powerful enough to declare themselves independent or even to overthrow the ruler and take his place. Patrimonial regimes were constantly in a state of war and intrigue, with rulers attempting to replace disloyal followers with loyal ones and instituting networks of spies and informers. Premodern political history looks like the swings of a pendulum—from relatively centralized empires that disintegrate into fragmented ones as local officials grow stronger, to recentralization as some new conqueror either from within or from primitive tribes consolidated outside the wealthier empire overruns the fragments.

BUREAUCRATIC ORGANIZATIONS

In Europe the kings of the sixteenth and seventeenth centuries began to overcome the last medieval period of fragmentation—especially in France, Prussia, Spain, and Russia—by introducing a new organizational form: *bureaucracy*. The absolutist monarchs—Louis XIV, Frederick the Great, and Peter the Great are the most famous—had gradually replaced the old patrimonial system by a new form of control (Rosenberg, 1958). Bureaucratic power is based on a set of general, impersonal laws, so that officials take orders from the system rather than from a particular person. There are specialized jurisdictions (tax collectors, road builders, army officers, commissary officers, clerks) rather than wide grants of power to local lords; and a sharp distinction of public and private, so that officials receive fixed salaries rather than having to forage for booty. These reforms added up to replacing a network of shifting personal loyalties with an organizational machine designed to operate without relying on any specific individual. Elements of centralized, bureaucratic administration existed as far back as the empires of ancient Egypt and Imperial China, but bureaucracy was fully developed only in post-Renaissance Europe. Bureaucracy depends on certain conditions that were widely developed only at that time: a large group of literate men (in this case, the priests of the already bureaucratic Church) who could administer this paperwork machine; a stable money economy so that salaries could be paid; improvements in transportation and communication to enable a centralized organization to operate in large territories; and changes in military technology, especially the spread of firearms, making individually equipped knights obsolete (Weber, 1968).

But bureaucracy was no utopia for rulers. If the patrimonial ruler tended to lose control to his subordinates through a network of personal intrigues, the bureaucratic ruler might find himself reduced to a cog in the machine he had created. A maze of rules and regulations understood only by the various specialists sprang up; rulers had to keep up with a mass of paperwork. It became difficult to find out what lower officials were doing and demanding detailed reports added to the need for further levels of officials to process the information. The specialized bureaucrats were no longer concerned with taking power, but with petty jurisdictional disputes and struggles in which their power to do nothing and to sit on needed information gave them a great deal of negative influence. Frederick the Great, who found that he could keep control of his Prussian government only by immersing himself in paperwork and becoming a bureaucrat himself, summed up the transformation with the words: "I am the first servant of the State." Subsequent rulers, lacking his devotion to the job, found themselves displaced from power, either by revolutions or by a gradual loss of control to their prime ministers.

IDEAL TYPES AND REALITY

Patrimonial and bureaucratic forms of organizations are ideal types; in reality, they are often mixed. The clever modern administrator attempts to control his bureaucracy by using some patrimonial strategies of control as well. Franklin D. Roosevelt and John F. Kennedy used such methods when they appointed advisers with sweeping powers, task forces which could cut across formal jurisdictions and regulations, personally loyal "kitchen cabinets" and political contacts within their own governments. Many modern governments—such as those in Latin American, Asia, and the Mediterranean countries—are formally bureaucratic but actually patrimonial, full of personal networks of influence and with government property frequently regarded as a means of private livelihood (Roth, 1968; Wertheim, 1968). The United States and the Soviet Union are a mixture of bureaucratic and patrimonial, because of the amount of political machinations in the state bureaucracies of both countries. Germany and France are closest to the purely bureaucratic end of the continuum.

Politics in modern bureaucratized countries is probably more strongly shaped by the organizational dynamics of the state than by social classes and cultural interest groups in the society. Bureaucracies have a momentum of their own. No one is really in control of a large, complex bureaucracy, and its officials are confined to their own specialized, technical views of the world (Bendix, 1947). But all members of bureaucracies share an interest in expanding the funds, size, and scope of the organization: government agencies, once established, tend to survive and grow, whatever their effectiveness. Military, diplomatic, health, welfare, educational, recreational, police organizations—whatever their success in meeting their avowed goals (for most, it is clearly quite low), they become entrenched interest groups dedicated to their own survival and expansion (Selznick, 1957). Government bureaucracies now take the initiative in setting their own policies— almost always by a quantitative expansion of whatever they are currently doing, no matter how badly they have been doing it—which are merely ratified by elected officials and legislators who lack the "expertise" to understand what the bureaucracy is doing (Wildavsky, 1964). Most federal programs and laws are now formulated in government agencies, and then acted upon by president and Congress. Max Weber, who did the first clear historical analysis of the rise of bureaucratic administration, was pessimistic about future trends: we were less in danger of losing freedom to tyrannical individuals, he predicted, than to organizations for which no one is responsible but the organizational momentum carries everyone along with it.

THE RISE OF THE DECENTRALIZED STATE

All modern states have administrative structures formally controlled by some superior power: military dictatorships, traditional monarchs, party dictatorships, and sometimes elected officials and legislatures. The last form of government, which may be broadly termed democratic, developed only by a special set of historical conditions. Democracy does not seem intrinsic to a modern, powerful, industrialized state. The most democratic states are heir to European, especially British, political institutions.

The origins of democracy are found in the premodern (prebureaucratic) period of history, and are described by Weber (1968), Hintze (1968), Tocqueville (1955), Huntington (1968), and Bendix (1964). As noted above, premodern history was a series of pendulum swings between centralized patrimonial regimes under strong rulers and decentralized feudal regimes in which many lords held sway and recognized only loose ties with any others. Also, a number of cities in the ancient Mediterranean, controlled by tribal coalitions, were sometimes formally democratic; our formal ideals of democracy originated from the Greek cities, although only a small elite participated in the government. This kind of essentially primitive tribal democracy did not last but some of these states, especially Rome, grew into empires with mixed patrimonial and bureaucratic forms. In the period around the thirteenth century, the pendulum in Europe was balanced between the power of the nobility and the power of the kings. The nobles' power was based on coalitions formed against the centralizing efforts of the rulers; these coalitions were institutionalized in organizations claiming jurisdiction over many laws, mainly over taxes—they were called *parlements* in France, *parliaments* in England, *Stande* in Germany, *zemskii sobor* in Russia, and *cortes* in Spain.

From this apex of European feudalism, the power of the nobles declined as kings increased their control, especially through their newly instituted bureaucracies. In some countries, such as Russia and Spain, the nobles' coalitions were destroyed; in Germany and France, the *Stande* and *parlements* were more or less absorbed as specialized agencies within the royal bureaucracy. In England the power of the bureaucratically centralizing king grew as well, but it was met by strong resistance from the coalition of the gentry in Parliament. The civil wars of the seventeenth century decided the question in favor of the gentry: the royal bureaucracy had been built but Parliament, representing a coalition of the smaller nobility (most of the great barons had been killed off in the Wars of the Roses) asserted control over the bureaucracy and reduced the king almost to a figurehead. The basis of modern democracy, then, is to be found in decentralized institutions left over from the feudal period. The English and the colonies which transplanted their institutions, such as those which became the United States, thus had the most decentralized and nonmodern institutions in the modern world. These institutions included not only the power of legislatures but also an independent judiciary system (unlike continental states, in which the courts are administrative arms of the central state) and considerable local autonomy left over from the village authorities of the Middle Ages.

Feudal institutions do not add up to modern democracy, of course; they were participated in only by a small noble elite. The Industrial Revolution provided the impetus which widened political participation to include a large proportion of the adult populace. Everywhere there was industrialization, the peasant majority was moved off the land and into the cities, where it became literate, politically conscious, and politically organized. In England and America, the new classes began to demand an end to feudal restrictions and were given the right to participate equally in elections and law courts. These concessions were not given willingly. Riots and near rebellion in England in the 1820s were prime forces behind the Reform Law of 1832 which enfranchised the middle class (universal manhood suffrage was not achieved until 1918), and insurrections such as the Whiskey Rebellion of the 1790s and Dorr's rebellion in Rhode Island in 1842 contributed to the gradual extension of the franchise in the United States before the Civil War. But the decentralized institutions of self-government among the nobility provided the framework into which the mobilized industrial populace could be integrated. In France, where the absolutist monarchy had almost destroyed the independent powers of the nobility, the newly created parliament had been extremely weak in relation to the state bureaucracy, and since 1789 periods of popular revolution alternated with dictatorships in France. In Russia, where the absolutist monarchy had reduced the nobility to civil servants within the czar's bureaucracy, a revolution in the name of the mobilized industrial masses produced the reign of another extremely centralized state bureaucracy.

As noted above, democracy is not a formula for utopia. In a society with differing interest groups, full democracy often results in a deadlock of conflicting factions and hence an inefficient state. Absolutist states can be more efficient than democratic ones. The value of democracy is not that it allows the wishes of the majority to be carried out, but that it limits the power of the state. As affirmed at the outset of this chapter, the state is ultimately the machinery of organized violence. Democratic societies are freed from the coercion of the state, not because everyone is honorable enough to believe in the rules of justice and fair play, but because democracy splits up the power of the state among contending parties. Most of history is a record of state coercion of the many in the interests of the few—of conquest, war, and legalized robbery. Some modern states have greatly mitigated state coercion over the individual by institutionalizing a stalemate among the various contenders for power. It is by splitting up the power of the state, rather than by relying on the idealism of those in office, that the reign of terror, experienced so often throughout history, has at times been lifted.

SUGGESTED READINGS

Banfield, Edward C. and James Q. Wilson, *City Politics*. New York: Harvard University Press, 1963.

A highly competent summary of the varieties of urban politics in modern America.

Bendix, Reinhard, *Nationbuilding and Citizenship*. New York: Wiley, 1964.

A leading historical sociologist analyzes the rise of the modern state in Europe, and the efforts to emulate that process in the Third World.

———— et al., eds., *State and Society*. Boston: Little, Brown, 1968.

The best reader on the varieties of politics throughout world history; Weberian in orientation, giving the basis for a historical theory of politics.

Domhoff, G. William, *Who Rules America?* Englewood Cliffs, N.J.: Prentice-Hall, 1967.

A description of the role the American upper class plays in national politics.

Hofstadter, Richard, *The American Political Tradition*. New York: Knopf, 1948.

> Now classic essays on the vicissitudes of politics in America, by a historian who was sociological before it became fashionable.

Lipset, Seymour Martin, *The First New Nation*. New York: Basic Books, 1963.

> By the leading political sociologist of the survey research tradition, incorporating a historical and comparative dimension.

Marx, Karl, *The Eighteenth Brumaire of Louis Napoleon*. New York: International Publishers, 1935 (originally published 1852).

> Classical Marxist analysis at its most impressive as applied to the *coup d'état* of 1851 in France.

Moore, Barrington, Jr., *Social Origins of Dictatorship and Democracy*. Boston: Beacon Press, 1966.

> An effort to explain why socialist and fascist revolutions occurred in some societies but not in others.

Schesinger, Joseph A., "Political Party Organization," in James G. March, ed., *Handbook of Organizations*. Chicago: Rand McNally, 1965, pp. 764–801.

> A detailed discussion of the complexities of modern American political parties.

Stone, Lawrence, *The Crisis of the Aristocracy, 1558–1641*. Oxford: Clarendon Press, 1965.

> The best of modern sociologically oriented history; an analysis of the bases of the Cromwellian revolution in seventeenth-century England.

Tocqueville, Alexis de, *The Old Regime and the French Revolution*. New York: Doubleday, 1955 (originally published 1856).

> A classic account, beautifully written, containing the first analysis of the roots of modern totalitarianism.

Weber, Max, *Economy and Society*. New York: Bedminster Press, 1968, Part I, ch. 3, and Part II, chs. 9–16 (originally published 1925).

> The fundamental, comparatively based theory of politics, by the greatest and most historically knowledgeable of sociologists.

CHAPTER 14

Social Stratification

The preceding chapter showed how men try to manage social events to achieve their ends, especially through the use of political tactics, influence, and power. This chapter examines social class, dealt with briefly in the last chapter.

Social class concerns the ways people differ in their chances of getting what they consider the good things in life. Inherited characteristics such as health and intelligence may affect these chances, but the sociologist is primarily concerned with the patterned differences in the social definitions of people and things that lead to patterned differences in these chances. In some societies, such as European societies before the twentieth century, social classes were reasonably simple and hierarchical. But in American society there are many dimensions of class—such as money, education, fame, and political influence—that are partially independent of each other. There are various hierarchies rather than a single one. Because of these complexities, an individual is free to construct combinations of class variables to deal with the situation he faces or wants to create. For example, a well-educated man may seek publicity for his ideas and himself to gain political influence with the rich; and a politically influential man may seek the symbols of the educated, such as honorary degrees, to gain prestige and influence.

Some patterns or structures to class situations in our society have proven resistant to change over decades. This is especially true of the distribution of income. After examination, the author proceeds to show how these structural forms of inequality are related to social problems.

MAJOR FORMS OF STRATIFICATION

Social stratification refers to the ways people differ in their chances to get what they consider the good things in life. If everything were plentiful and free, there would be no stratification. Most "good things" have a price tag, a guest list, or a guard at the gate.

In this chapter we will deal with stratification in its three major forms: class, status, and power. *Class* refers to economic inequality; *status* to inequality in prestige; and *power* to inequality in political rights and influence. A main concern will be why inequality exists, what causes it, and who gains from it. We will explore the ways these three forms of inequality interact with each other.

INEQUALITY ACROSS HISTORY

All societies have some inequality, but the extent of inequality is sometimes slight and sometimes vast. The most equalitarian societies are those which have the least developed technology, produce food at about the subsistence level, and possess the least wealth. The most unequal are not the wealthy industrial societies but the large agrarian ones, producing food and handicraft goods well beyond the subsistence level but not achieving the wealth of industrial societies. The relationship between level of technological development and degree of inequality, not just economic inequality, is important for understanding how and why societies differ from each other in their stratification systems.

Technology and inequality were the subjects of a book by Gerhard Lenski (1966) entitled *Power and Privilege,* in which he examined a wide array of societies and tried to show how and why they are stratified. A brief summary of Lenski's findings will give an overview of inequality and also introduce some of the disputes that center around this topic.

Lenski deals with five types of societies, in advancing levels of development: hunting and gathering, simple horticultural, advanced horticultural, agrarian, and industrial. Stratification is almost nonexistent in hunting and gathering societies, because the economic surplus defined as "goods and services over and above the minimum required to keep producers alive and productive" is so slight that inequality is physically impossible. To take someone else's food or to make him engage in some personal service for you rather than raise food is to bring about his death. If a society is on the edge of subsistence, the closeness of death prevents inequality.

As agricultural techniques develop from the less effective forms (horticulture) to the more effective (agriculture), the surplus continuously rises. Not only does the food surplus permit some privileged people to act as priests, warriors, or leisured class, but others can act as artisans and servants for the privileged. The peak of inequality is reached in the great agrarian societies—such as the ancient empires of Rome, India, China, and some of the modern agrarian nations of the underdeveloped world. In some of these civilizations, the elite of the top 2 percent may have received as much as 60 percent of the economic surplus. Along with this steep economic inequality, there is usually the political and status inequality that goes along with monarchy and aristocracy.

In industrial countries—such as England, the United States, or the USSR—there is less inequality than in agrarian countries. The top 2 percent may be receiving only 10 percent to 20 percent of the economic surplus. Voting and democracy, when present, bring about a measure of political equality, and the decline of aristocracy and unequal types of citizenship means a decrease, although not a complete elimination, of status inequality.

The broad relationship between technological development and social inequality reported by Lenski can be pictured, as in Figure 14-1, as a line which ascends until we hit the industrial level. Then it descends.

Lenski interprets this broad relationship as a result of two patterns or laws. The first is that men will share the product of their labors to ensure the survival and continued productivity of others whose actions are necessary or beneficial to themselves. To ignore the demands of survival would be to kill the goose that lays the golden egg. The second law is that power will determine the distribution of nearly all the surplus possessed by the society. Lenski says "nearly all" because he thinks altruism will account for a small part of the distribution.

In asking why inequality decreases under industrialism and doesn't just keep getting steeper, as his second law would predict, Lenski points to a number of restraining forces that come from the nature of the industrial economy. Workers at various levels of expertise have more crucial skills and therefore more power in industrialism than in an agrarian economy. Below the level of the top elite are managers and experts of all kinds who

Figure 14-1. Degree of Inequality

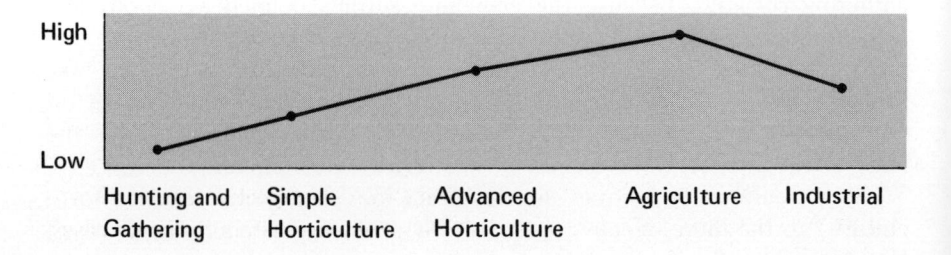

can command great economic rewards. Similarly, the workers, organized into large factories, have the power to strike or to slow down their work and thereby throw a monkey wrench into the delicately balanced industrial economy. Further, mature industrialism requires mass distribution of its products, or it will break down into unemployment and depression. By the very nature of the mass production system, it is physically impossible for an elite to consume a large proportion of goods. A rich family may be able to use several cars, television sets, or bathtubs, but not several thousand. These products must be widely distributed to the workers, or products will sit in warehouses and the whole economic system will break down. Even if the experts or the organized workers did not have the power to make economic gains, the elite would be required to spread the wealth somewhat or that wealth would melt away. It is not necessary to say that the elite in industrial countries is more altruistic than its counterpart in agrarian societies. The industrial system demands more economic equality than the agrarian system does. Karl Marx had this in mind when he said that changes in the *forces of production* require changes in the *relations of production*. The forces of production are the technology; the relations of production are the property system. When the forces of production shift from farming and handicrafts to manufacturing, the property system must become more equalitarian or it will die. Marx and many Marxists are of the opinion that capitalist industrialization is not becoming equalitarian fast enough to absorb the massive manufactured wealth it produces. They argue that colonialism and the more recent neocolonialism, along with militarism and wars, are ways in which capitalism finds outlets for goods that would better be distributed to its working population. We will consider later the evidence for this serious critcism of capitalist industrialization.

DISTRIBUTION OF INCOME AND RELATIVE DEPRIVATION

But, first, we must consider two other problems with Lenski's picture of stratification. The trend line in Fig. 14–1 suggests that human society is becoming more equalitarian and that, therefore, industrialism is a system that spreads its benefits more widely than previous systems, implying that the future will be more equalitarian than the past. This picture is misleading, for industrialism has also brought certain inequalitarian effects. One such effect is poverty in the industrial countries themselves, for the relative equality in these countries is much more characteristic of the top half of their populations than of the bottom half. Their poorest groups get just as small a share of the pie as the poor in underdeveloped societies. Table 14–1 gives an illustration of this for five underdeveloped and five developed countries. The top tenth and fifth in the underdeveloped countries get a somewhat larger share of the national income than in the developed countries, but the bottom fifth gets only about 5 percent of the income in any country. The developed or industrial countries have not solved their poverty problem (speaking in relative income terms) any more than have the underdeveloped countries. The industrial poor have much higher absolute incomes than the poor in agrarian societies and, if they compared themselves with the poor in Latin America and India, they might be content. But they seem to compare themselves to the affluent of their own countries and therefore feel deprived. Relative to the affluent in their own countries, the poor feel deprived. They are thus said to suffer feelings of *relative deprivation*.

TABLE 14–1. DISTRIBUTION OF FAMILY UNITS ACCORDING TO INCOME (IN PERCENTAGES).

	\multicolumn{5}{c}{Underdeveloped Countries}
	India (1950)	Ceylon (1952–1953)	Mexico (1957)	Colombia (1953)	Salvador (1946)
Top Tenth	43.0%	40.6%	46.7%	48.4%	43.6%
Top Fifth	55.4	54.2	61.4	56.4	53.1
Second Fifth	16.0	18.4	17.4	12.2	15.7
Third Fifth	11.4	13.3	9.9	—	—
Fourth Fifth	9.2	9.3	6.9	—	—
Bottom Fifth	7.8	5.1	4.4	—	—

	\multicolumn{5}{c}{Developed Countries}
	United States (1950)	Great Britain (1951–1952)	West Germany (1950)	Denmark (1952)	Netherlands (1950)
Top Tenth	30.3%	30.2%	34.0%	30.7%	35.0%
Top Fifth	45.7	44.5	48.0	47.0	49.0
Second Fifth	22.3	22.2	23.0	23.5	21.5
Third Fifth	16.2	16.6	16.5	15.8	15.7
Fourth Fifth	11.0	11.3	8.5	10.3	9.6
Bottom Fifth	4.8	5.4	4.0	3.4	4.2

SOURCE: Modified from Table 3, Kuznets (1963).

Much social protest and urban violence in the United States in recent years has come from the American poor. This serious weakness in the United States—and perhaps in some other capitalist countries—suggests that poverty in rich countries may be even more galling than poverty in poor countries. Notice in Table 14–1 how isolated the bottom fifth in the developed countries is from the two fifths just above it. In the underdeveloped societies misery has plenty of company, because those in the fourth or third fifth are not much better off than those in the bottom fifth; but in the developed societies the bottom fifth is far worse off than those just above it. This isolation may make the poverty hurt more. A more detailed discussion of the American poor is given later in this chapter, but for now the point should be clear that, while industrial countries may be less stratified in their top half, with a less commanding elite, they have not treated their poor well, creating a great potential source of instability.

A second misleading feature of Lenski's picture of inequality is that it ignores the fact that industrialism has increased the degree of global inequality, as the gap between the rich and poor nations has widened. Table 14–2 shows how much of the world's income went to each fourth of the world's population in 1860, 1913, and 1960. In 1860, when industrialization had existed in Western Europe for several decades, the richest fourth of the world received 57.8 percent of the world's income. This share had increased to 72.1 percent a hundred years later. The share of the poorest fourth decreased from 12.5 percent to a mere 3.2 percent during that same period. Industrialization has increased the equality within industrial nations, particularly in the upper half, but it has decreased the equality of the whole human family. This negative effect on equality may be just as important, as time goes by, as the positive one.

TABLE 14–2. PERCENTAGE DISTRIBUTION OF WORLD INCOME EARNED BY EACH FOURTH OF WORLD'S POPULATION FOR SELECTED YEARS.

Share of World Population	Percent of World Income Earned		
	1860	1913	1960
Top Fourth	57.8	68.9	72.1
Second Fourth	15.5	17.2	17.9
Third Fourth	14.2	7.8	6.8
Bottom Fourth	12.5	6.1	3.2

SOURCE: L. J. Zimmerman (1965, p. 38).

Nor is this world inequality a matter of the capitalist countries finding a better economy while the underdeveloped countries have not. To a great extent, the industrial countries built their wealthy new economies by exploiting the rest of the world. Forced trade, forced labor, colonialism, and slavery in the relations between Europe and the rest of the world were an important part of early industrialization, just as their aftereffects in the contemporary world continue to be. To a great extent, industrialization developed at the expense of the non-Western world, and the widening gap between the rich and poor nations shown in Table 14–2 is partly due to international coercion. From one view, we might have shown the line of inequality in Table 14–1 moving up instead of dropping at the industrial era. For if we look at the entire world as our unit in the recent industrialized period—and it is a unit for many purposes—industrialization has brought even greater inequality than before, though it may have brought somewhat greater equality within the industrial nations.

Lenski's book and the problems it brings up show several things. One is that the degree of inequality within a society is a variable, slight in some societies and pronounced in others. Among the causes of variation are the system of technology and the size of the surplus. Further, it suggests that power rather than the welfare of the whole society is the reason most of the surplus is divided unequally. The trend toward greater inequality, while reversed to some extent within industrial countries, has continued unabated in the world as a whole. We will consider in greater detail the question of poverty and whether industrial countries are equal enough to maintain the necessary balance between production and consumption.

INEQUALITY IN THE UNITED STATES

Let us examine inequality in the contemporary United States as an example of a developed, capitalist country; the patterns we find we will then apply elsewhere.

Class

The most basic kind of inequality—especially in a historical period in which material prosperity is the center of attention—is economic, and we will begin with the economic class structure. In Karl Marx's use of the term, *class* refers to the ownership or nonownership of the means of production, whatever these means may be in any given society. Basing his views on mid-nineteenth-century capitalism in Western Europe, Marx thought that because competition and technology would gradually eliminate the middle classes of farmers, professionals, and small businessmen, capitalism was moving toward a two-class system of a small number of rich owners and a large mass of impoverished workers, the *proletariat* below them. In some respects Marx was right in this prediction; in others, wrong. If we consider the capitalist economic system, there has been a concentration of economic power in a small number of business firms with the mass of the population serving as employees of these firms. Organizationally, there has been something of a Marxian polarization and, in an essay on the future of capitalism as an economic system, this polarization would be of central importance. But if we consider the people in capitalist countries, the work they do, their income, and the distribution of property ownership, we do not see anything like a Marxian polarization into two classes, though economic inequality remains. The middle classes have not disappeared, although much of this class has changed from self-employed to employee status; the workers have not, for the most part, become impoverished, and many continue to have highly paid skills; and the ownership of large corporations is held by a fairly large, rather than a small, wealthy elite. It is difficult now to talk about class in the original Marxian sense, and it will be more useful for us to look at certain specific indicators of class structure: property ownership, income distribution, and occupation.

We said that property in the United States is owned by a fairly large elite, but nevertheless an elite, as the following figures show. Stock ownership is the major form of wealth in the United States, and as of 1959 only about 8 percent of the population owned any stock at all (Kolko, 1962, p. 51). The bulk of corporate stock—about 76 percent, according to Lampman's study (1962)—is owned by only 1 percent of the population. When other forms of wealth are taken into account (land, cash, and other forms of property including stocks), the top 2 percent of American families owned 29 percent of the wealth in 1953 (compared to 33% in 1922). The result is that control of the economy is in the hands of a relatively small minority of people, political equality is under constant threat from economic inequality, and the elite boast higher incomes and living standards than others.

In contrast to property, which includes all valuable assets, income refers only to money received for some kind of service (wages, profits, interest, rent). A secondary form of income is *income in kind,* such as an expense account or automobile for the executive or home-grown food for the farmer. Income seems more equally divided in industrial than in preindustrial societies, although far from equally in either one. Table 14–3 shows what percentage of the national income went to each tenth of the American population for selected years from 1910 to 1964. This table shows that the American income distribution, while not as unequal as property ownership, has been quite unequal throughout the twentieth century, with little change from decade to decade. What changes there have been are mainly twofold: the top tenth has dropped a few points, most of which have been gained

TABLE 14–3. PERCENT OF NATIONAL PERSONAL INCOME BEFORE TAXES RECEIVED BY EACH INCOME TENTH.

Year	Highest Tenth	2nd Tenth	3rd Tenth	4th Tenth	5th Tenth	6th Tenth	7th Tenth	8th Tenth	9th Tenth	Lowest Tenth
1910	34%	12%	10%	9%	8%	7%	6%	6%	5%	3%
1918	35	13	10	9	8	7	7	6	4	2
1921	38	13	10	9	7	7	6	5	3	2
1929	39	12	10	9	8	7	6	5	4	2
1937	34	14	12	10	9	7	6	4	3	1
1948	31	15	12	10	9	8	6	5	3	1
1950	29	15	13	11	9	8	6	5	3	1
1952	30	15	12	11	9	8	6	5	3	1
1954	29	15	12	11	9	8	6	5	3	1
1956	31	15	12	11	9	8	6	5	3	1
1958	27	16	13	11	9	8	6	5	3	1
1960	28	16	13	11	9	8	6	5	3	1
1962	27	16	13	11	9	8	7	5	3	1
1964	30	15	13	11	9	8	6	4	3	1

SOURCE: Mayer and Buckley (1970, p. 70).

by the next tenth, and the bottom three tenths (the poor) have dropped from 14 percent in 1910 to 8 percent in 1964. Although much controversy centers around the details of American income, taxation of this income, and the actual impact of income on the standard of living of individuals, Table 14–3 is probably an understatement of the degree of inequality. Taxes, often thought to be a device that hits the wealthy much harder than the poor, have little effect on income distribution, as Table 14–4 shows. Until the "$15,000–Plus" bracket is reached, all income groups, including the lowest, pay about 21 percent of their income in taxes—state, local, and federal.

These facts about property and income tell us that Americans differ drastically in ability to buy the good things in life—whether a comfortable house, attractive clothing, good food and drink, travel or services such as the best doctor, inside information, and the elite education that will help guarantee the children the same kind of life their parents had. These differences are also basic to the various life styles that characterize the status levels in the residential community.

This tells us something about the fate of certain important income groups, whose long-term gains are often misunderstood. Is the United States becoming more middle class? In some ways it is, but not in terms of relative income. If we define "middle" as the fourth, fifth, sixth, and seventh tenths, we find they gained only four percentage points in fifty-four years, despite enormous gains in education and occupational level throughout this period. In 1900 white-collar workers of all kinds constituted only 18 percent of the labor force, and in 1960 this proportion had risen to 42.2 percent. During that same period, high school graduation increased from 6 percent to 65 percent of the population; while college graduation increased from 2 percent to 18 percent. But white-collar jobs have often meant only prestige gains, for many pay less than the better manual jobs. And advancing education has been largely offset by constantly increasing educational requirements for the better paid jobs. *Where* a person goes to college may be as important for the best jobs as *whether* he goes to college. So the paradox of a society becoming more and more middle class in occupation and education but not in relative income is explained largely by the weak effect of occupation and education on income equalization.

Another group whose position is clarified by Table 14–3 is the bottom tenth of the poor. Obviously, the United States has a chronic problem of poverty. Sometimes it becomes highly visible and publicized in the mass

TABLE 14–4. PERCENTAGE OF 1958 TOTAL INCOME PAID IN FEDERAL, STATE, AND LOCAL TAXES,[*] BY INCOME CLASS.

Income Class (in dollars)	Federal	State and Local	Total[†]
0– 2,000	9.6	11.3	21.0
2,000– 4,000	11.0	9.4	20.4
4,000– 6,000	12.1	8.5	20.6
6,000– 8,000	13.9	7.7	21.6
8,000–10,000	13.4	7.2	20.6
10,000–15,000	15.1	6.5	21.6
15,000–Plus	28.6	5.9	34.4
Average	16.1	7.5	23.7

SOURCE: Kolko (1962).

[*] Social insurance taxes are not included.

[†] Because of rounding, items do not always add up to totals.

media, as during the Great Depression or the "War on Poverty," and at other times it moves out of attention but, on a purely relative or proportional basis, the poverty problem has not changed much in sixty years, except to get worse. To change this condition would require a redistribution of income, with the upper groups getting a lesser share and the lower groups a greater one. As a large proportion of the poor do not work at all (the old, the sick, the woman heading a household) and those who work are concentrated in low-wage nonunionized industries, this redistribution would probably have to be done by the government through such devices as changing the tax laws and expanding services to the poor. All indications are that this will not happen, and the recent post–World War II trend has been for income inequality to worsen slightly. Whether this is a healthy thing for the United States is in doubt and, in a discussion of the effects of inequality below, we will consider the impact of income distribution on the stability of society.

Status

It was pointed out earlier that class and power are instrumental, relatively impersonal spheres of inequality, while status is emotional and personal. The meaning of status, though, is not easy to define. We can get the flavor of this concept from such synonyms as prestige, deference, honor, respect, and rank. But the kind of relationship referred to is not obvious. There are two views on the social psychological roots of status. One is that status is based on a consensus in which shared values or norms, to which all parties are more or less committed, control the distribution of status so that the closer a person comes to the value or norm, the more status he has. In this view, a lawyer has higher status than a plumber, because he more closely attains some shared occupational value such as services to the community or doing an exacting job. The other view of status holds that it is the reflection or shadow of power. The person with less power admits (and is reminded of) it by displaying symbols that he agrees have less merit and by showing deference to the one with more power. It is difficult to choose between these two views because the ritualization of pure power differences tends to attain a patina of rightness over a long period of time, and the power and value aspects of status become intermixed.

In some societies status differences have become so ingrained that the hierarchy takes on a religious sanction, as in the caste systems of India and Ceylon. At other times these differences have been supported by the force of law, which regulated the rules of clothing, using weapons, and entering occupations. The medieval European estate system of "commoners," "clergy," and "nobility" was this sort of status system. In the modern European period of industrial societies, the status systems have lost much of their earlier moral and legal cover and have come closer to being pure power devices. But status differences still have a normative quality, and the mixture of power and normative obligation gives an ambiguity to American status relations that cause them to explode periodically in outbursts of resentment and hatred, especially between ethnic groups, with long periods of quiet in between.

The pure power aspect in America is most obvious in the racial, religious, and ethnic side of status. Here the differences between the fact and the rightness of status are most glaring. Negroes came to this country as slaves and, although legally freed, were not given land after the Civil War and have been suppressed ever since. No doubt, the great majority of Negroes would admit that Negroes have low status, in the sense that they fall short on the skin color test of value. But few would accept the rightness of this value. Other ethnic or religious groups, placed in low status on ethnic-religious grounds, would also reject the rightness, while acknowledging the brute fact, of their status inferiority. This side of the American status system, then, is clearly the shadow of power and little else.

Another status hierarchy central to American community life is that of occupations. The occupational structure is a reflection of the economic class system, since occupations differ in their control over the means of production, income, and the chance to amass property. But occupations also have a prestige side that makes them important ingredients in the status system. Along with the racial-ethnic-religious hierarchy and roughly correlated with it, the occupational hierarchy is major basis of the overall status hierarchy.

There have been many studies of the relative prestige of occupations, from Supreme Court Justice on down to bootblack, and in practically every country studied, especially the United States, there is general agreement on their relative standings (North and Hatt, 1947). This agreement does not imply that there ought to be these prestige differences. But, when people were asked why they ranked some occupations higher than others, the responses indicated a widespread moral acceptance of the hierarchy, especially among respondents who are themselves well placed. When asked why they ranked, say, a doctor or banker high, the typical response of a middle- or upper-status person would stress the meritorious nature of the job, its service to the community, or use of expert knowledge and training. Lower-status respondents are more likely to stress the reward side of the job, its high pay or economic security, suggesting that they are less impressed by the merit interpretation. But people who are occupationally deprived seem more likely to accept the occupational hierarchy than the racially-ethnically-religiously deprived are to accept that hierarchy.

What, then, is the relation between these two status hierarchies? In answering this question, let us refer to the racial-ethnic-religious ladder as the *ascriptive hierarchy* (in the sense that status is ascribed to the person, regardless of how well he performs) and to the occupational ladder as the *achievement hierarchy* (in the sense that a person gets into a highly placed occupation only if he achieves this). Recalling the distinction between the power and value interpretations of status, the ascriptive hierarchy is based overwhelmingly on power and the achievement hierarchy largely on shared values. Ascriptive differences are maintained by coercion, both mild and severe. Occupational differences, on the other hand, are largely self-justifying.

But the question remains: How can two hierarchies, one ascriptive and one achievement, exist side by side? Doesn't one tend to drive out the other? The answer seems to be that there are not one but several occupational achievement systems. The children at each level in the status community, which is itself determined by a mixture of the parents' ascriptive and achievement qualities, have access to a range of occupations, and within this range they compete and achieve. Sometimes they move outside the range, in a marked case of social mobility, but by and large people entering new jobs stay in the approximate range that fits their status group. Cases of social mobility usually progress to the next range rather than across the whole hierarchy. The concrete status groupings in any community are in a sense training centers in which children learn the life style and gain the friends that will help them achieve at the level appropriate to them, through work and marriage. The schooling process is largely an extension of the placing function of the status community and, while a minority of students can use their education for social mobility, the more common pattern is for education to transmit inequality from one generation to the next.

The relation between status and class structures is not a direct one. Political power and the state stand between in important ways and regulate this relation. But, before turning to power, we will briefly consider the extent and influence of social mobility.

Social mobility. Up to now we have been stressing inequality in the way goods are distributed at any one point in time. Social mobility refers to another sort of inequality, its stability over time, as transmitted through the family from one generation to the next and from the beginning of a person's work career to the end. The first form of inequality is structural and says nothing about the degree of inheritance. The second form is dynamic and adds another dimension. In principle, the two forms of inequality are independent of each other, and there could be much mobility despite vast structural inequality. There is a tendency for the two inequalities to go together, with agrarian countries low and industrial countries somewhat higher in both respects.

The most heavily studied kind of mobility is occupational; the least studied, and most important, is income. It is difficult to get a total picture of how much mobility exists anywhere, but certain parts of the picture become clear from occupational data.

OCCUPATIONAL MOBILITY

Occupational mobility is usually measured by comparing the occupation of a working person with the main lifetime occupation of his father. If his occupation is distinctly higher or lower in status than his father's, it is a case of mobility, either upward or downward. This comparison is made against the backdrop of an occupational hierarchy, in which types of occupations are ranked from high to low. The usual hierarchy runs something like this: unskilled and personal service, semiskilled, skilled, clerical and sales, managerial, and professional.

When the occupational mobility of a whole society is considered, the most common way to summarize overall mobility is to count the number of cases crossing the line from manual into nonmanual, as it seems more difficult to cross this barrier than to move within the manual or nonmanual spheres. Also, as we have information from a variety of countries on this kind of mobility, we can make international comparisons. This information was summarized by Lipset and Bendix (1960) in *Social Mobility in Industrial Society*. They drew together data from a number of studies to show the amount of upward mobility—cases where the sons of manual workers had achieved nonmanual jobs—and downward mobility—manual sons of nonmanual fathers—in several industrial countries. For the United States, the percentage of sons who had moved upward was 33; downward, 26. For West Germany, the comparable percentages are 29 and 32; for Sweden, 31 and 24; for Japan, 36 and 22; for France, 39 and 20; and, for Switzerland, 45 and 13. These figures show that approximately a third of nonfarm workingmen are mobile, either upward or downward, in each country, with little overall difference from country to country.

Whether a figure of one third will seem high or low will depend on what ideal it is compared to. In comparison to the relatively slight mobility of preindustrial societies, it seems high, but in comparison to an ideal society in which jobs are assigned purely on a merit basis it seems low. Later, when we compare the Marxian and functional interpretations of stratification, we will show that there is disagreement on the political meaning or impact of mobility, but there are some interpretive comments we can make now.

Much manual versus nonmanual mobility, even though across a significant barrier, is a relatively short jump, for the fathers of mobile sons tend to be near that line—either at the upper end of the manual or lower end of the nonmanual hierarchies. In comparison to a long jump, such as that of a poor man's son who becomes a big business executive, these movements have slight impact on the inheritance of position. In fact, movements upward from skilled manual jobs to lower white-collar may bring a drop in income. So, much mobility is more a matter of changing occupational prestige than changing income.

Much mobility is a matter of exchange, in which the son of a nonmanual father falls and the son of a manual father rises and takes his place. When this occurs the exchange is largely the result of education, the rising son having more education than the falling one, especially in the United States. Sometimes the mobility is due to low birth rates of upper status groups. The difference in birth rates at different status levels has decreased in recent years but, until recently, the pattern had been one of smaller families at higher levels, often too small to replace the parents in desirable occupations.

But much mobility is also the result of factors other than exchange. The continued industrialization of the economy with a decrease in farm and unskilled jobs and an increase in white-collar jobs causes mobility without exchange (no loss for the families already there). The same is true of mobility caused by immigration into the society and the push from below that occurs when migrants settle into the lower positions. Historically, much American mobility was due to constant pressure at the bottom of the ladder, pushing those already there to higher positions. This immigration of the unskilled has lessened since the passage of restrictive laws in the 1920s, but a similar function has been taken over by Negroes and Puerto Ricans who migrate within the United States from rural to urban areas. These new migrants get the worst urban jobs and push the nonminority poor upward. Once these minorities (especially Negroes) settle in cities, their chance of mobility remains slight, largely because of discrimination, and much white mobility depends on Negroes not being very mobile.

The overall impact of mobility on the stratification system is difficult to assess. We cannot say that a mobility rate of one third in the typical industrial society shows a fairly strong working out of the achievement or merit system. When mobility entails a true exchange, in which the children of better and worse-off parents trade places, this is reflective of an achievement system. But much of this exchange is a matter of occupational prestige rather than of income. When the mobility is a result of economic growth or immigration, it cannot be called merit in the same way, as no exchange takes place. And, when the mobility is gained by holding down minorities, like Negroes, it is the opposite of a merit system.

POWER

The class and status systems, including mobility, are conditioned by political factors, for laws, taxation, and government programs have crucial effects on stratification. If we recall that the state is not only the presidency and the Congress, but the whole court system, the civil service and government agencies, the military establishment, the police at all levels, and the state and local governments, we get some conception of the far-reaching control the state has over American life. Working out state policy in any society is always a struggle, to some extent, for all conflicts within a society tend to affect the struggle for political power. Such conflict has become obvious in the United States since the early 1960s as the protests centering around race and poverty, war, and students have rocked the nation. But the state has been relatively unresponsive to these protests, and the question of who has the power or who gains from power is asked.

On the surface, and in the old-fashioned civics book, the answer is clear. Everyone in the United States has equal political power, and everyone is served equally by the state. This is the *formal picture of government,* with an emphasis on voting, the popular powers of initiative, referendum and recall, and so on. This picture is still widely publicized in American schools and mass media and it is still believed, or half believed, by many Americans. But it is not easy to give an accurate picture of the American power structure, partly because power, being a relationship and not a three-dimensional object, is difficult to locate and measure. It is also difficult, especially in democratic countries, because those well endowed with power will consciously and unconsciously deny that fact. For, in a society in which everyone is supposed to have equal power, inequality is still considered somewhat immoral, and to be honest about your power might lead to having it taken away from you.

The shape of the American power structure and its effect on the stratification system is subject to dispute. In addition to the simplistic formal view, there are three serious theories of who holds power in America: a pluralism of pressure groups, a power elite, and a ruling class.

Belief in a *pluralism of pressure groups* is the view that elected officials don't represent "the people" but respond to various organized groups—like business associations, labor unions, religions, and organized ethnic groups—who pay lobbyists to live in Washington, D.C. or the state capitals to promote the group's interests among the legislators and other government officials. Sectors of the population that band together and focus their pressure on political centers—not only at election time but during the official's term of office—are a supplement to the people's mass voting behavior. If a group is not organized it has less power than one that is. An important tenet of many versions of the pluralistic picture, however, is that all American groupings are more or less equally represented, and that power is balanced among all competing interests. The critics of pluralism do not accept the "more or less equal" idea. They argue that pressure groups are vastly unequal, that business groups are more powerful than labor, that white groups are more powerful than black, and that large sectors of the population are not represented in pressure groups at all.

One such critical picture is that of the *power elite,* championed by C. Wright Mills in a book of the same name (1959). Mills feels that the pluralistic picture applies only at the middle levels of power: around Congress and the state capitals. Above that level, around the executive arm of government (the President and the executive agencies) and the military establishment, many crucial decisions are made with no access allowed to pluralistic influences. Since Mills' book, the term *military-industrial complex*, coined by President Eisenhower, has come to be used interchangeably for the power elite.

Power: Ruling Class Perspective

The most critical picture of power in the United States shows it as basically belonging to a ruling class (Miliband, 1969; Domhoff and Ballard, 1968, pp. 101–165). This view carries the following assumptions: (1) There is a small economic elite with much property and large incomes in the United States. Their money and interests are attached to big business, and their main purpose is to promote big business, even against any other interests in the country. (2) This economic elite is represented in government, sometimes directly (the last few presidents and many cabinet officers are millionaires), but usually indirectly through sympathetic officials who promote their interests. The basic policy of the state is to promote big business interests, at home and abroad. Any policy that hurts big business would be regarded by the elite as national suicide. (3) The masses of Americans who are not benefited by big business also promote it because they have been indoctrinated to think that way by schools, churches, movies, magazines, radio, TV, advertising, and a host of other influences.

These four pictures of power in America, then, are in intellectual competition, although one hears considerably less about the last two than the first two. The civic course picture is blatantly false, although there are rare occasions when truly grass-roots campaigns, often socially destructive ones, come from the masses. The other three are difficult to prove. Certainly a pressure group system exists for limited purposes, although it is an exaggeration to say that all organized groups have equal power. But if someone stepped directly on the toes of a minority group, he would probably not get away with it. Could anyone succeed in passing a law to take the vote away from those Negroes who now have it?

For many other, more basic policies, a sort of combination of ruling class and power elite seems to operate, depending on the issue. The bulk of people do not object to such an arrangement. Not only the people at the top but also many of those in the middle and bottom are favorably slanted toward big business interests. Whether they are misled by schools or other socializing institutions (which I believe to be true) or whether they are intelligently choosing their politics is a debatable question. If it were clear that the masses were deliberately choosing a minority rule, we could call it benign aristocracy.

THREE INTERPRETATIONS:
MARX, FUNCTIONALISM, AND WEBER

The overall interpretation of inequality in the United States and in other developed capitalist countries is subject to wide disagreement, but it is possible to reduce these variant interpretations to three: Marxism, functionalism, and a Weberian approach.

Marxism

By Marxist, we are not referring to the original views of Karl Marx, but to a loose tradition of leftist scholarship, which takes its point of departure largely from the spirit of Marx, even though it contains many different and contradictory subschools and approaches (Miliband, 1969; Cox, 1958; Lynd, 1957; Mills, 1959, 1962).

This approach sees the root of inequality in the private property system and the fact that the wages of workers, themselves lacking property, can be controlled by capitalists to their own advantage. This inequality in economic power is reflected in the authority system of the workplace. Workers take orders; owners or their hired managers give them. All economic production units, except small businesses without employees, entail this hierarchy of authority, and the aggregate of these units can be visualized as a pyramid with the owners and managers at the top and the least skilled workers at the bottom.

The relation between the class system and the status system is one of approximate balance in which economically superior people are also superior in status, while economic inferiors are status inferiors. The status system is caused by and reflects the class system, and the two hierarchies are parallel with status as the shadow of class. The whole aggregate of status or communal groupings serves further to strengthen the class system, for superiority of status off the job tends to increase authority on the job. If workers can be entrenched in a system of respect off the job, and look up to the large houses and superior life style of their bosses, it will make it easier to get obedience and acceptance from them on the job. If, on the other hand, workers can live in the same neighborhoods, enjoy the same leisure pursuits in the same places, and mingle freely with their employers off the job—suspending the attitude of subordination until work begins again the next day—they will find out that their economic superiors are ordinary people, with the same failings as everyone else, and the habit of obedience at work may erode.

In addition to social insulation and the protection of economic authority, the status system has other functions for the class system. It unites the economically dominant in ways over and above their economic similarity. Certain tensions of a purely economic nature can divide the wealthy. Competition still operates in the capitalist economy to some extent and tends to divide rival producers—let us say among the large auto companies or between oil and coal companies. Competition of a kind also operates between large sellers and buyers—for example, Sears Roebuck and the factories from which it buys goods. This competition is much less intense than in the period of early industry when there were more rival producers and less price-fixing, but it still exists. The status system, however, in which rival executives can enjoy each other's company in wealthy suburbs, exclusive country clubs, and parties serves to heal most cuts and bruises resulting from the economic competition of the workday.

Further down the line the status system may have opposite effects, equally favorable to continued power of the rich. If workers of differing skill levels are divided from each other in different community groups and neighborhoods and if they have their own prestige differences, it is more difficult for them to unite on the job or among different lines of industry in any one community. This worker disunity is most developed in a country like the United States where workers have differing ethnicity, race, and religion, and where these qualities stratify workers. The status differences between Puerto Ricans and others or between Negroes and whites have important negative effects for the economic power of workers generally. As a rule, the status life of workers hurts their class power, while the status system of owners and managers solidifies their class position.

The status system, then, in the Marxist view, both reflects and gives further support to the class system. Finally, the system of power, or the state, is viewed as primarily a class weapon. The state's role is to support and advance the economic power of those who already have it and to defend this power against any groups that may be trying to encroach upon it. It is the state's job to create, uphold, and defend laws maintaining the existing class system and to execute any policies needed for that purpose. The state, above all, must defend the private ownership system from socialism. But it must also maintain the present system of taxation, prevent strikes that might upset the power balance between labor and industry, put down demonstrations or riots by minority groups that threaten existing power relations, support American economic interests in foreign countries—by war, if necessary—and in general use the weapons of authoritative command and violence to protect capitalism. The Marxist view recognizes that the state may make minor concessions to economically weaker groups, if necessary, to make the whole system stronger, but these concessions must never be major, as the basically unchanging distribution of income over time suggests.

The three dimensions of class, status, and power are, according to the Marxists, a single system of stratification. The primary dimension is the economic one, and both the status system and the state exist to defend and strengthen the economic structure. Marxists also emphasize the structure of inequality more than the process of mobility from one generation to the next. A great deal of mobility would be difficult to explain within the Marxist framework. Therefore, Marxists deemphasize mobility and, insofar as it exists, to interpret it in ways that minimize its impact on the class system, by (1) emphasizing the slight amount of income mobility in contrast to the relatively large amount of occupational mobility in industrial societies, (2) pointing out that most occupational mobility is in short jumps, often from skilled to white-collar work, and does not affect the top or bottom of the occupational ladder as much, and (3) arguing that when mobility does occur in large leaps (when a poor person becomes rich), it is a kind of tokenism for the poor and steals away their best leaders.

Finally, Marxists emphasize the economic relations between the rich and poor countries, termed *neocolonialism* or neoimperialism, and how it favors the wealth of the rich nations. The Marxist picture shows the relations among nations as an integral part of the stratification system, along with the relations among classes within any one country. The richer countries, particularly the United States, so runs the argument, exploit the Third World countries by virtue of superior economic power, much as capitalists exploit workers within any one country by virtue of economic power. As the whole populations of the richer countries benefit from neocolonialism, the workers and weak minorities of the United States, for example, are cast in the position of exploiters on a world basis. They are winners on a world basis even though they are losers within their own country.

Functionalism

Functionalism is also a balance theory (Parsons, 1953; Davis and Moore, 1945; Davis, 1949, 1953; Barber, 1957). In this approach, the unity of the system comes not from the overriding influence of economic power but from the value system. There is a balance in two senses: (1) the systems of class, status, and power are integrated and in balance, with a person's position about the same in each system, and (2) the cause of this unity is not in the economic system but in a second balance between the demands of the value system and the performances or achievements of people.

The functional position sees the origin of stratification arising from the division of labor. In a complex society with many jobs, some are more important than others, and the welfare of the whole society hinges on the efficient performance of these crucial roles. Supervisory jobs are more important than the ones being supervised; highly skilled jobs are more important than the less skilled; jobs involving important values like life and death (physicians or generals) are more important than jobs centering around other values. Because jobs are different in social impact, it is necessary that the important jobs be filled by people with maximum competence, and here the stratification system enters. Stratification is a system of rewards that serves to motivate the most able people to pursue the most important jobs. Further, it compensates people for undergoing long training periods—for example, in preparation for the learned professions—which, presumably, they would not undergo if not given special rewards. The stratification system gives differential rewards to differential performances. Without inequality society would get less able performance from its population, and everyone would be the loser.

In this view, the status system as well as the class system provides rewards. Sheer income or economic power is not enough to motivate. Prestige is necessary, too, and the status communities reflect the relative earned prestige of different occupational groupings.

The role of the state is, among other things, to keep the stratification operating in an efficient productive manner, to maintain inequality when it is necessary for efficiency, and to correct it to help groups that are not being treated fairly and not allowed to operate in the achievement system.

Mobility is a key process in this theory, for mobility proves that ability and competence and not just wealth and power control the doling out of the good jobs. Functionalists stress the extent of occupational mobility in industrial societies and see it as proof that stratification draws talent from the general population, even from the children of less successful parents.

The main criticism of this theory is that it gives an inaccurate picture of the way people get good jobs. The obvious restrictions on access to education and the chance to develop talent are not well accounted for, and the inheritance of wealth is unexplained. Kingsley Davis has provided an answer to these objections (see Insert No. 44).

The functional theory does not pay much attention to the problem of world stratification although, insofar as it does via the spread of functionalism into political science, it plays down neoimperialism and emphasizes the negative effects of tradition in holding back the development of underdeveloped countries. The poor countries are poor largely through their own doing and the world is seen as one big achievement system, with the high achievers (the industrialized, European world) rich and the low achievers (the Third World) poor. The operation of political pressures or economic coercion or the more subtle built-in forms of economic exploitation are minimized by the functionalists just as they minimize the same processes within nations.

The functional theory resembles Marxism in being a balance theory, with the whole stratification system visualized as a unity determined by a single principle. That principle is values, achieved or not achieved by people in society, a sort of *normative* or value *determinism*. But it bears similarities to the *economic determinism* of Marxism. In functionalism, the whole society with its value demands plays a role like that of "buyer" in the economy. The individual members of society take their training and skills to the labor market and "sell" these skills. The labor market, a reflection of society's values, buys these skills at a price determined by their social value. Thus, instead of being a market theory in the old-fashioned sense, in which buyers and sellers meet and hammer out an agreeable price, it is a revised market in which society's values help impose the price (or rewards). But, because these values operate by their effect on the economy, we can say, for all practical purposes, that the functional theory of stratification is a theory of the economic market. Therefore, it is a version of economic determinism just as much as Marxism, and it visualizes a balance among the various aspects of stratification much as Marxism does. It differs on the cause of the balance for, while Marxism sees the cause in the superior economic power of capital over labor, functionalism sees the cause in the more valued function of some

INSERT NO. 44

On Kingsley Davis' *Human Society*

In his book, *Human Society*, Kingsley Davis argued that, along with the achievement system, it is necessary in some societies to allow parents to pass special advantages on to their children, over and above what their achievements might merit, for the sake of family unity. Without inheritance, in the broadest sense of the term, and special treatment of the children within the families of the advantaged, these families would be emotionally disrupted and could not raise their children effectively. Therefore, if a rich man's son is competent he has a right to a good job because of his competence, but if he is less competent, he still has a right to a good job to protect the stability of his family. To the competent son of a poor man, who may be squeezed out of a job by the less competent rich man's son, this argument may have a "heads I win, tails you lose" quality, but with a certain logic. For a pure merit system, which somehow eliminated all advantages that can be transmitted in the family and geared rewards solely to abilities and performance, would certainly lay a great deal of stress on the family as presently constituted.

Many rich families would be embarrassed by the failure of their children, which might weaken the entire status community at the upper levels since that community is so heavily based on the continuity of wealthy families. On the other hand, many poor families would be helped, as their children would be allowed to develop native abilities and receive just rewards. The net impact on the family might not be all that bad, and the net impact on society as a whole, since more able people would be discovered, would probably be quite good. The drag that the powerful families inflict on the system, by placing their less qualified children in important jobs, would be eliminated.

jobs or skills over others. It also differs in its underlying picture of capitalism. Marxism sees capitalism as having internal contradictions that make it tend toward chronic depression and eventual revolution, while functionalism, implicitly, sees capitalism as a workable system without fatal contradictions.

But the similarities between the two views have interesting consequences. Both are pessimistic—at least, in the short run—about social reform. Functionalism, an optimistic picture of society, sees no need for basic reform. If an essentially wise and serviceable social arrangement exists—if inequality does more good than harm—it is futile to talk about instituting basic reform. There is little or nothing to be reformed. Marxism is equally negative about short-run reform, but for a different reason. Marxist determinism sees no possibility of reform short of complete revolution and change in the system. In the absence of total change, there is no way of instituting limited reform. Both functionalism and Marxism, then, are unfriendly to the needs of reform and to the populations that would like immediate, limited reform. We will return to this topic after discussing Max Weber.

Max Weber's Theory

The most important point to make about Weber's view of the class-status-power distinction is that he was not a balance theorist, not a determinist, and that he saw certain autonomous processes operating within each dimension (Weber, 1958; Bendix, 1962).

Like many historically oriented sociologists, Weber saw most social life, and especially the spheres of inequality, as a struggle for power: for economic power in the class sphere, for political power in the state, for the power of prestige in the social or communal order. Within each sphere are conflicts of interest, and these conflicts may be fought out by groupings or scattered individuals or, more commonly, by mixtures of both. Each dimension centers around an "interest" that is scarce: wealth in the class arena, authority in the political area, and "ideals" in the status order. To some extent, each interest can be used to obtain interests of the other order: wealth can be translated into political power; status can be transformed into wealth. But each also operates somewhat independently of the others.

In the class or economic order this exchange is easily shown, and here Weber shares many of Marx's views. Technological change, for example, is a process which can of itself change the structure of economic power, as older technologies and the people anchored to them decline and new ones rise. To some extent, the replacement of one superior class by another throughout history is the replacement of one technology by a more efficient one. Similarly, in the economic order, the system of exchange, particularly the market system in which goods and services are privately bought and sold, can affect class positions. If all sellers of a commodity can agree to fix prices at an artificially high level and can also prevent any other sources of that commodity from appearing, this special economic power can be used to lift that group's wealth and position.

Similarly, the importance of different markets changes over time, and people crucially placed in a market whose importance is declining may lose economic power. The history of American politics is largely the result of the interplay of the labor, money, and commodity markets and the changing processes within each market have had marked effects on the class position of various rising and falling groups (Wiley, 1967).

The social orgnization of work, quite apart from its physical technology, also affects class relations. The existence of large rather than small factories increases the power of workers in some respects because they can communicate with each other more easily and launch strikes that are more crippling to employers. Workers in industries, such as mining, located far from the big cities in isolated one-industry towns, may have more economic power than their counterparts in the big cities. As with large factories, the isolation of these industries makes it easier for workers to communicate with each other during nonworking hours, and it permits an organization and intensity of interest not possible in the big city.

Within the status order, too, are autonomous processes. The status or communal order, as we are using this term, includes a large variety of religious, ethnic, cultural, and value groupings that spring up in this sector of life. These groupings center around a special kind of "interest," a desired thing over which people may clash. The struggle over religious beliefs, both among religions and within a single religion, is the most obvious of these struggles over ideals. Sometimes religious struggles have an underlying economic or political cause and cannot be called autonomous—but not always. Weber felt, for example, that the Protestant Reformation was in part a purely religious development that, instead of being economically caused, was an important influence in bringing about modern capitalism.

Conflict among ethnic groups is a similar ideal struggle, though it may also involve economic and political values. In fact, often the economic-political aspects of these struggles are minor, masking a fight for pure status. This is a kind of "symbolic politics," and the McCarthyism of the early 1950s was so interpreted by several sociologists (Bell, 1964). The prohibition movement to outlaw the sale of alcohol in the United States has also been interpreted as basically a conflict among status groupings (Gusfield, 1963).

Sometimes ethnic groups achieve mobility solely in the status order, gaining pure prestige (often at the expense of other groups) by manipulating the value of the group's ethnic symbols, changing symbols, or degrading the symbols of a rival group. The most recent attempt to do this in the United States has been the effort of Negroes to upgrade the value of their body qualities, hair, skin color, and facial attributes as well as other racial symbols. A similar symbolic struggle goes on among some Indian castes who adopt symbols of the higher Brahmin caste. These ethnic gains may or may not be used to increase the group's political or economic power, either as a bloc or on a one-by-one basis, but in any case mobility through the status order is a partly autonomous process.

The autonomy of the political order is most clear in the area of military clashes. The French and Russian revolutions, both purely political and military struggles, changed the fortunes of all classes in France and Russia. The political power structure, although restored in a limited sense in France, was drastically changed by a pure political-military process.

Changes in military technology can also bring about basic political changes. When guns were invented in Europe, the class of knights with their horses and armor was made obsolete, and their political power gradually disappeared. More generally, if the military technology changes to one that requires large porportions of the ordinary population to engage in battle, a certain amount of political power may drift to the common man too.

Another area in which politics shows autonomy is in the changing ideologies or self-justifications of states. Weber saw three types of self-justification: traditional, charismatic, and legal-rational. A traditional legitimation justifies a system of rule sheerly on the basis of its having been that way for a long time; a legal-rational legitimation justifies a state as being in accordance with reason and law based on reason; a charismatic legitimation justifies a state on the basis of the extraordinary or sacred qualities of the ruler. Twentieth-century Germany is an example of all three types: it passed from a traditional monarchy to a legal-rational democracy after World War I to a charismatic dictatorship under Hitler and finally to a democracy again after World War II. Weber felt that changes in these self-justifications were partly an impending political process, changing the relative power of contending political groups in a way that could not be completely explained by economic or status interests.

Weber sees a number of internal processes located in each sector of inequality that can operate somewhat independently of those in the other sectors. This variety makes his approach rather wide open compared to Marxism and functionalism, but it seems to be more true to the way things happen, particularly in preindustrial societies. It also provides a more useful theory on which to base attempts at social reform—whether minor, major, or revolutionary.

Social Reform

Earlier, we pointed out that both Marxism and functionalism suggest rigid positions concerning social change or reform. Marxism sees it as impossible short of revolution, and functionalism sees little need for it. In contrast, Weber's position implies both the need and opportunity for reform. Because stratification is seen as struggle, there is no difficulty admitting the existence of exploitation and suffering from Weber's viewpoint. He does not overemphasize the extent of value consensus in society, as do many formalists. But, as he was not an economic determinist and could recognize autonomous changes in the political and status order, with no necessity for these orders to always strain toward a balance, his position implies several levels of change scattered throughout the social order. A deprived group can work for reform in the economic order or the political order or the status order and can combine approaches in various ways. This does not mean reform is always possible. That depends on the concrete historical conditions in question. But it does mean there are many ways of approaching reform other than the functionalist or Marxist approaches. However one approaches reform, the basic questions involved hinge in good part on the view one takes of the effects of inequality.

The Effects of Inequality

There are two main arguments for the good effects of inequality. One argues that inequality is a necessary incentive to induce people to work hard to get the good things in life and that, if there were no inequality, the more important (and normally well-paid) jobs would not be done well and the wheels of progress would halt. The other argument is a historical one; it is based on the fact that an unusual degree of equality was tried in Russia shortly after the Bolshevik revolution but didn't work and had to be abandoned after a few years. More recently, all Communist countries appear to have a great deal of inequality.

The former argument is that of the functionalists; we have considered its strengths and weaknesses. Perhaps the most obvious point in its favor is that in a complex society some people must have more authority than others or complex tasks could not get done, so some inequality of power is indispensable. But that is a technique for doing a job, not an incentive or reward for achieving it. Whether the important jobs must be heavily rewarded with money and prestige is another question. Just which are the important jobs and whether the existing system of rewards is necessary to fill them has never been proved. What has been proved is that many people will not get the good jobs no matter how talented they are or how hard they try because they are discriminated against or their parents do not have the power to place them properly. The logical argument, deducing the necessity of economic inequality, has never been able to get around these obvious objections. Therefore, it cannot be said that progress or the optimal flow of talent is a good effect of the present system of American inequality.

The historical argument, from Bolshevik Russia's experience, is more persuasive (Moore, 1956, pp. 182–188). Lenin introduced a wage structure so radically equal that the highest paid workers earned little more than the lowest paid workers. This system lasted only a few years, and Lenin decided that it was blocking incentive. Therefore, he introduced more inequality, including the right to grow and sell food on the free market, which also had been previously abolished, and, with these reforms or New Economic Policy, output increased. In the 1930s, Stalin introduced even more inequality and this too increased Russian productivity. It is only since the Stalin period, under Khrushchev and his successors, that timid attempts to reduce economic inequalities have been reintroduced into Russia, and these have not been fully implemented.

More generally, all the Communist countries have maintained a good deal of inequality, to an extent that cannot be precisely measured because most do not publish good income statistics. Indications are that, while they might be somewhat less unequal than capitalist countries at the same level of development, they still use and need inequality as an incentive device.

The arguments in favor of inequality, testifying to its good and even indispensable effects, assert that society doesn't work without plenty of inequality. Without it, effort and progress stops; even essential services, let alone economic progress, will be impaired. Both logically and empirically a case can be made for this conclusion.

The most unnecessary suffering stemming from inequality is the status degradation doled out on purely ascriptive grounds. That such groups as Negroes, Mexican-Americans, or Puerto Ricans should be looked down upon because of race or ethnicity is an unnecessary form of suffering. It may give minor economic or psychological gains to people not in these ethnic groups, but these economic gains for some do not help the entire society. In fact, they hurt the total economic process by suppressing talent and creating a host of other costly personal problems for the minority people. And the psychological gains are the neurotic, unhealthy kind. This form of inequality, then, is completely indefensible.

But there is also the suffering of low-income people, who cannot afford decent life as defined in this society. That the American bottom tenth gets 1 percent of the national income means that they live difficult lives—unhealthy, worrisome, and unnecessarily short.

Closely related to this suffering is the deviance concentrated among the poor. Crime, drug addiction, alcoholism, family breakup, and psychosis are concentrated among the poor and are largely a result of poverty. These forms of deviance, both the illegal and the perfectly legal self-destructive kinds, have many causes, but one such case is low income and all that entails. Correspondingly, if there were less inequality, particularly in the lower reaches of the population, there would be a reduction in various rates of deviance. A more subtle way in which deviance is related to inequality is suggested by the "labeling" theory of deviance, which we shall examine in Chapter 20.

Political Inequality

We have hinted at the bad effects that economic and status inequality can have for political equality. There is a strong tension among the three orders of class, status, and power to make them line up equally, that is, to have the same degree of inequality in each order even though this balancing is constantly disrupted by autonomous processes within each order. When universal voting was first introduced in the nineteenth century, the upper classes in Europe thought the masses would inevitably vote for economic equality and, by bringing in socialism, create an economic democracy that paralleled political democracy. They were wrong; the reverse has happened. For, instead of political equality forcing in an economic equality, economic inequality has gutted and made political equality largely formal. This shows up in a variety of ways:

1. Elected officials are often most responsive to the people who make the largest campaign contributions. They are also sensitive to the rich and powerful so they can get a good job if defeated for office or when they retire from public life.

2. The pressure group system, more important than the voting system, is less effective as we descend from the rich to the middle groups to the poor. This creates and reflects unequal political power.

3. The poor don't vote as often as others. Turnout in the United States is about 50 percent for the poor in a well publicized election. It is closer to 90 percent among the well-off. Nonvoting is partly a result of apathy, and in that sense it is a result of being powerless; but it also helps perpetuate that powerlessness, and if the poor had the money and skills to organize (which they don't because they are poor), they could increase their political power enormously.

4. Most important elected officials are rich or well off, if not before getting into office, then afterward.

5. Some poor people are not allowed to vote: many Negroes in the South; people without a settled residence; migrant laborers who never settle down long enough to get the right to vote.

These limitations on democracy show the pressure to match political with economic inequality and, though half a loaf is better than none, the capitalist democracies are a long way from being fully democratic.

International Effects of Inequality

Earlier, in discussing why incomes are distributed more equally in industrial than in preindustrial societies, it was pointed out that the nature of the mass production system necessitates this more equal distribution, otherwise products will go unsold and work will stop. But there is the further question of whether industrial societies have fully solved the overproductivity problem. Leftist critics argue that existing economic inequality in the United States is still too great to sell what our economy produces and that military spending and sales to other nations are essential to take up the slack. In its most extreme form, this is the theory that *monopoly capitalism*—a capitalist economy that has concentrated itself to the point that a small number of firms have most of the economic power and can fix prices almost at will—must invest and sell in Europe and the underdeveloped world or there will be a depression at home (Sweezy and Baran, 1966). According to this view, American foreign policy, including the Vietnam war and any other future military ventures, is geared, not to spread political freedom and democracy, but to protect these American economic interests. This theory may be an overstatement, but it cannot be doubted that the American economy is dependent on foreign outlets to an extent greater than before and that if these foreign outlets were closed off because of Communist or Socialist revolutions in foreign countries, our economy would be seriously hurt. According to this theory, the United States can do either of two things: (1) continue as we have been, using the rest of the non-Communist world as an economic outlet, or (2) move to equalize our income structure so that elements of the population who are most likely to spend (the poor and the workers) will do this spending and make it less necessary to rely on foreign markets. The leftist critics feel that this equalization is impossible and would come only from a bloody revolution. Judging from the recent trends in income distribution, they may be right, but it would make more sense to change the income structure peacefully than continue as we are, fighting foreign wars and risking nuclear war.

In my view, income inequality is at least part of the reason why the United States has become policeman of the world, and it can only be called a bad effect of inequality.

In this section we have presented the pros and cons of inequality in the United States, stressing economic inequality. If there were less economic inequality, there would be a reduction in status inequality, especially in its more destructive ethnic forms, and there would probably be a reduction in political inequality as well. I am convinced that it would be in the interests of this country, as well as of the rest of the world, if more equality could be achieved here, peacefully, in a nonrevolutionary way. A peaceful revolution is in order in the United States, to be achieved largely through political means and subsequent legislation. Such a revolution, as things stand, does not seem any more likely than a bloody one, for the forces of basic reform, which began to grow during the 1960s, seem to be diminishing in the 1970s, at the same time that the American economic empire throughout the world is constantly getting into more trouble. But, though no clear solution is in sight, we should keep looking. This review of inequality and its effects shows that it is at the root of many American social problems and should be sharply reduced. How to organize political resources to achieve this peaceful revolution will be the task of many thinkers and doers in the 1970s. The problem of social stratification is anything but an abstract, textbookish issue unrelated to public life. It is at the core of the problems of public life.

SUGGESTED READINGS

Barber, Bernard, *Social Stratification*. New York: Harcourt, Brace, 1957.
> One of the best, book-length statements of the functional position. His facts can be brought up to date by seeing Mayer and Buckley below.

Bendix, Reinhard and Seymour Martin Lipset, eds., *Class, Status and Power*. New York: The Free Press, 1966.
> A book of high-level readings. It contains the important exchange between Kingsley David and Wilbur Moore, who gave a closely reasoned statement of functionalism, and Melvin Tumin, who argued for the possibility of social equality.

Collins, Randall, "A Comparative Approach to Political Sociology," in Reinhard Bendix, *State and Society*. Boston: Little, Brown, 1968, pp. 42–67.
> A difficult but rewarding interpretation of Max Weber's theory of political stratification. I lifted several of Collins' ideas in preparing this chapter.

Harrington, Michael, *Toward a Democratic Left*. New York: The Macmillan Company, 1968.
> The chapters on American foreign policy and world politics are one of the few nontechnical attempts to refute the leftist theory of American imperialism.

Kolko, Gabriel, *Wealth and Power in America*. New York: Praeger, 1962.
> A highly critical picture of inequality in America. Kolko sees considerably more inequality than do many other scholars.

Magdoff, Harry, *The Age of Imperialism*. New York: Modern Reader Paperbacks, 1969.
> A presentation of the argument, largely with facts and figures, that the United States is a neoimperialistic nation.

Mayer, Kurt B. and Walter Buckley, *Class and Society*. New York: Random House, 1970.

> A good, short discussion of stratification, containing a great deal of descriptive and interpretive material in 150 pages.

Miliband, Ralph, *The State in Capitalist Society*. New York: Basic Books, 1969.

> This is probably the best statement of the ruling class theory of the capitalist state. He organizes everything written on the topic and lays special stress on the role of schools, churches, and media in creating a consensus that favors big business.

Mills, C. Wright, *The Power Elite*. New York: Oxford University Press, 1959.

> Mills' theory of how a power elite rules America.

Weber, Max, *From Max Weber*. New York: Oxford University Press, 1958.

> A good sprinkling of Weber's writings. Contains his seminal but difficult essay on class, status, and party.

CHAPTER 15

Comparative Sociology and Economic Development

Both the chapter on politics and the chapter on social inequality were concerned, in part, with economic development and its relation to income distribution and power within and between nations. Chapter 15 carries these concerns further, showing how the methods used to compare societies are important in dealing with such issues.

Economic development has been a basic goal of almost all national policies in past decades. In using comparative methods to study such phenomena and to try to answer basic questions about the factors producing economic development and the effects of such development, sociologists have too often looked at societies as homogeneous social systems with clear and simple structures that could serve as the basis for their comparisons. This chapter explains how complex social processes related to economic development depend on the concrete, historical choices individuals make about social policies.

Is not the "comparative" in *comparative sociology* redundant? After all, systematic comparison is basic to the way scientists construct causal explanations. Although all sociology uses comparative techniques, the term is applied to only one branch. Commonly, sociologists label comparisons and analyses of data drawn from different societies as *comparative* sociology, an arbitrary decision reflecting the peculiar historical development of the discipline. Yet some logical basis exists for this distinction.

Within any society, there may be a wide range of differences based on age groupings, class, religion, or race. Researchers comparing one of these subunits to another from that society could be labeled "comparative sociologists," but the probability of finding distinctive structural arrangements with distinctive meanings for participants is much greater in comparative studies based upon national units. An advantage of the comparative approach between societies is that it will probably find the maximum possible diversity in variables most likely to have a limited range of values within one society. For example, the mode of family structure within China or the United States will vary with the social class of the family studied, but the differences will be still greater when we compare the family structure of one society to the other. Ultimately, the explanation of what comparative sociology contributes rests on the proposition that variables are more likely to take on a diversity of values using different societies as units of analysis.

The nation-state has been the unit most closely associated with achievement of modern economic growth. Therefore, it is the most appropriate unit for analysis when trying to illustrate variations in patterns of economic growth and social change. Economists sometimes find geographic regions more useful for this purpose (the lower Rhine Valley as an industrial complex involves several European countries), and some political scientists have also turned to region-specific models of nation-building (Rokkan, 1970, p. 57). In recent years efforts to coordinate economic development have been based on a vision of a united Europe (Friedrich, 1969), Pan-Arabism, Pan-Africanism, and so on. Although the success of these movements varies, it suggests that the appropriate unit of analysis to answer certain questions may have to be other than the sovereign state. Yet, for a wide range of qestions, the state has been the unit most effective in increasing our understanding of economic growth.

For researchers, it is natural to speak of a specific comparative approach. This does not mean that a new variety of the scientific method has been found applicable to comparative studies; it means that there is a set of distinctive research strategies appropriate to comparative studies of economic development. This chapter is about these strategies, their promises and pitfalls. The aim is to develop a conceptual framework that will allow an understanding of the extent of national uniqueness and explain it in a wider analytical framework.

THE POTENTIAL OF COMPARATIVE STUDIES

Comparative sociology offers much to our hope of understanding social structure and process during the process of industrialization. What seem universal truths in American society may be recognized as having limited historical applicability in the context of national comparisons. We can discover which relationships hold up over time and space and which do not (Bendix, 1963, p. 533). Thus, comparative analysis enables us to gain a fuller understanding of the range of inventiveness for solving problems facing human societies. This is particularly true with respect to common problems that occur at given levels of economic development.

In this fashion, comparative analysis forces us to see social structure not "as a natural system with defined limits and invariant laws governing an equilibrating process, but rather as a system of historical dimensions" (Bendix, 1963, p. 537). To say that social structure is a system of historical dimensions means that we recognize the intrusion of external, often random, events and those resulting from situational choices of individuals. Historical context influences the operation of seemingly invariant processes; it makes a great difference for the content of Soviet industrialization that it was preceded by an authoritarian rather than a democratic form of government. Industrialization is not a universal process that repeats itself with monotonous rhythm in country after country.

Comparative research compels us to recognize that many of the definitions of sociological concepts rest upon unfounded generalizations. Bendix offers the example of urbanization. Based upon Western experience, urbanization is often used as a measure of economic development (Banks and Textor, 1963) or is assumed to be part of the ongoing process of economic development. Bendix notes that urbanization is frequently defined in terms of a cluster of attributes (e.g., impersonality) that presume a given level of industrialization. Yet these assumptions do not hold in many non-Western societies. Not uncommonly, large-scale urbanization takes place *before* the nation achieves high levels of economic development. Irving Horowitz (1966, p. 35) suggests that, in many Third World countries, the urban centers are parasites of available resources and not promoters of economic development. The economic and political elites living in these centers exploit the population in the surrounding hinterlands; these urban centers also serve the needs of the more industrial nations at the receiving end of the international market. The expansion of population in these centers, without corresponding economic growth, prevents effective utilization of the labor force and creates problems in housing and welfare. This situation leads to a reliance by individuals on turning inward toward kinship and other personal ties to cope with the scarce opportunities available. Thus, as Bendix notes, what starts out as a definition of urbanization in terms of a cluster of attributes turns out to be a prediction. Properly executed, comparative studies force such implicit assumptions to become explicit hypotheses. For example, instead of assuming that growing impersonality is inherent in urbanization, we formulate a hypothesis asking under what conditions the two variables are present.

The significance of comparative sociology can best be appreciated by contrasting it with *historicism*. Historicism asserts historical uniqueness and denies all attempts to formulate generalizable propositions applicable to more than one society, culture, or period. Its focus is on the constellation of temporal events that crystallize into a unique pattern of growth or decay. Understanding evolves only by concentrating on the relevant historical events.

Comparative sociology rejects this view (Shils, 1963, pp. 14–15) and, instead, seeks generalizable statements that apply to more than one society. It expects the historical experience of one society to illuminate the meanings of historical experiences in other societies. Ideally, these general propositions are not rooted in any one society; they transcend specific societies, yet prove their utility by helping to explain specific empirical processes. Consider the legitimation of authority. In asking how industrializing elites legitimate their authority, we come to recognize a range of possibilities for any one country. The question, then, becomes a search for the conditions likely to produce one rather than another of these possibilities. This reasoning led Max Weber to ask: Under what conditions are different types of legitimation likely to emerge and prove successful? His efforts have been continued in the current social science literature (Bendix, 1956; Rokkan, 1970).

PROBLEMS OF COMPARATIVE SOCIOLOGY

If the promise of comparative studies is great, the pitfalls are more numerous. To the extent that scholars see all social and political development as positing the goal of achieving Western characteristics, they repeat the ethnocentric biases in theories of the nineteenth-century evolutionists. Much theoretical and empirical effort has been devoted, implicitly or explicitly, to cataloguing the social and political correlates of economic growth in the developed nations and measuring the extent to which they have been achieved by the "developing nations."

On the theoretical level, the clearest example is the use some sociologists have made of the pattern variables set forth by Talcott Parsons (1951, pp. 51–67). This approach emphasizes the way all social roles are compounded of alternative criteria. Sociologists have used this method of classification to argue that ascription is dominant in preindustrial societies as a basis for distributing rewards and that achievement is dominant in industrialized societies. Such formulations suffer in that they are mutually exclusive classifications not reflecting variations in the phenomenon being classified. The variables cannot take on the variety of true values that they possess in the empirical world. As a result, the classifications obscure our understanding of the real world. They hide the variety of differences and subtle interrelations among social meanings of our categories; it is these differences and interrelations—manifest or potential—that we want to investigate to uncover general regularities and build a more solidly based comparative sociology. We need analytical constructs that can take on a sufficient range of values to become applicable to a wide range of socially meaningful phenomena.

The dichotomization of preindustrial and industrial behavior also appears in the work of Max Weber. He treated bureaucracy as the most efficient form of modern organization, with characteristics maximizing rational decision making (see Chapter 16). By extension, Weber's theory of bureaucracy implies a way of looking at organizations in preindustrial societies as well; these organizations are seen as lacking the requisite characteristics of bureaucracy. A major problem with the Weberian formulation is that it was based on an ideal image of Prussian bureaucracy in the nineteenth century. We might better define rationality in organization as selection of the most effective means to achieve specific limited goals (Simon, 1957). Looked at in this light, the effectiveness of various social practices and values for a modernizing society will depend on the *cost* of shaking them loose from traditional structures to work for—or, at least, not to hinder—modern economic growth. In some cases, the costs will be so great that these preindustrial values and structural patterns must be abandoned. In other societies, however, the utilization of preindustrial behavior patterns and values may be the least costly means of rapid industrialization. This is not to say that these preindustrial patterns remain unchanged; they are likely to be remolded to fit the needs of an industrializing society.

In the latter case, to ignore or write off traditional values and practices is itself irrational. The kinds of choices that a society's members make in concrete situations will depend on the cohesiveness of an existing tradition, its resilence and flexibility, and its degree of initial compatibility with productive forms of economic organization. An important contribution of comparative sociology, consequently, lies in examining the extent and manner in which traditional values and practices are related to and combined with more modern forms of social organizations and values (Gusfield, 1967, pp. 351–362). These interactions should provide important clues to the nature of the industrialization process. In Germany and Japan, the industrializing elites were successful in mobilizing traditional values of loyalty to legitimate authority relationships in the new industrial organizations; this had a great impact on subsequent social and political changes in the two countries.

Problems of Comparative Sociology: Some Empirical Considerations

Since the early 1950s, the most notable development in the comparative study of economic development has been the increasing use of quantitative data and aggregate measures (Herman Miller, 1960; Inkeles, 1960; Almond and Verba, 1963; Russett, 1964; Meritt and Rokkan, 1966; Marsh, 1967). This research has been oriented toward documenting the associations of social and political variables with economic development. The use of quantitative and aggregate data in this fashion must be considered an important advance that enables researchers to speak with greater confidence about what goes on in industrializing stages.

Yet a number of pitfalls are apparent in the present quantitative approaches. There is sometimes a mindless quantification seeking only to confirm that the way to achieve economic development is to adopt those social and political characteristics associated with Western development. The cult of development may join hands with the cult of measurement. In part, the problem stems from the tendency to view the development of social science disciplines in terms of their ability to quantify. As a result, technique sometimes outruns sound sociological reasoning. Attempts are made to show that higher levels of economic growth lead to political development. Neubauer (1967) has also shown how measures of political development, in effect, measure degree of "democrationess." Thus, if a country does not have the characteristics of Western democracies, it ranks low on a measure of political development. To be developed is to be Western!

Many massive cross-cultural studies have followed a "shotgun" approach; researchers gather a wide range of data and then follow intuitive hunches about which are the best "tables to run." The reader is presented with numerous correlations but little in the way of causal analysis. Second, it can be a wasteful approach in terms of the enormous amount of time, energy, and money required and the low rate of data utilization. Some scholars compare large numbers of societies using secondary (someone else's) data and avoid these investments. The problem becomes one of interpreting data of widely varying quality and unknown reliability. This is the case for researchers using the massive ethnographic materials of the Human Relations Area File. True, many comparative studies are exploratory and the main product is discovery of relevant variables. Under these conditions, one can hardly demand that the researcher specify the relevant variables beforehand (Russett, 1964, pp. 1–5).

Cross-Sectional Studies

One danger of empirical comparative studies focusing on economic development arises from the use of *cross-sectional studies*. A cross-sectional study is one in which data is gathered for only one point in time. Although focusing on one point in time is not a characteristic limited to comparative studies, it is remarkable how little study of changes over time there is in a field whose *raison d'être* concerns economic and social change. The use of the cross-sectional method in comparative studies commonly involves the selection of countries at different levels of economic development. Implicit in this procedure is making statements about the past of the developed society from data collected from the contemporary less-developed society or making predictions about future changes in preindustrial society on the basis of conditions in the present-day developed society. One observer has suggested that the commitment to cross-sectional research may be responsible for the acceptance of neoevolutionary theories (Ian Weinberg, 1968). The issue is the validity of making future projections for the nonindustrialized countries on the basis of existing data of the developed countries. In this way, the use of cross-sectional analysis is based on the assumption that it can reveal past patterns that can then be projected into the future.

Simon Kuznets (1966) provides an example from economics exposing the dangers of these assumptions. Cross-sectional analysis of contemporary societies shows that the share of consumer expenditure spent for clothing rises from 10.5 percent for underdeveloped countries to 12.3 percent for the moderately developed countries to 12.7 percent for developed countries. On this basis, one might assume that, as the present-day underdeveloped countries industrialize, the share of consumer expenditure spent for clothing should rise; in fact, it has declined in the more advanced countries, apparently because of changes in consumer preference away from clothing and toward other forms of expenditure, like cars, made possible by achievement of new levels of technology. In short, we would make a mistake if, on the basis of cross-sectional analysis, we assumed that consumer expenditure on clothing had been lower in the past for developed countries. Because we would be wrong in predicting the past from cross-sectional analysis in this case, we would also be wrong in using it to predict the future. We would incorrectly predict that consumer expenditures for clothing could be expected to rise throughout the world.

Evaluation of Comparative Research

An examination of sociological studies with a non-American setting reveals that most do not have a strictly comparative focus. Thus, of thirty-four such studies reported in the two leading sociological journals (1965–1966), only twelve had a formal comparative research design (Brown and Gilmartin, 1969). Research with a non-American setting is often done by American sociologists and social anthropologists designated as area specialists. Having spent many years in the field, they often limit their reports to descriptions and perhaps an analytical statement of how "their" societies work, with some insightful remarks about how things are different elsewhere. At its best, this research can be illuminating; at its worst, it misleads because the comparison is not explicitly part of the design and the researcher is able to pick out evidence which supports his argument. A basic requirement of good comparative research is for the specialist to make the comparison explicit and to label clearly dimensions he plans to compare.

One common procedure is to take a theory or conceptual framework developed in one society or set of societies (usually the Western experience) and try to apply it to the experience of another society or set of societies (usually non-Western). Ideally, the researcher should formulate his hypotheses so they can be rejected as well as accepted. Beforehand, he should formulate the kinds of data that would lead him to reject his hypotheses and the kinds of data that would induce him to accept them. Unfortunately, because of the nature of the data and the kinds of questions asked, these procedures are not and often cannot be followed. At a minimum, it is critical that the individual not be so committed to a given answer that the research process consists of selecting data most suitable for proving his hypothesis and ignoring data conflicting with it.

We may cite two well-known studies which follow a research design that pits Western theories of economic growth against empirical data from non-Western countries. The first is a study entitled *Peddlers and Princes*, by Clifford Geertz (1963), which takes up contemporary Indonesian industrialization and the development of innovative economic leadership. This theme is elaborated in the context of Western theories of the relationship between economic growth and social institutions. Geertz finds that the social and cultural transformation required for economic modernization appears far less sweeping than the theoretical positions identified with Max Weber and Talcott Parsons suggest. Rejecting parts of the Weberian position, Geertz shows how some conceptual categories produced by Westerners are inadequate for the complexity of the empirical world.

As sociological hypotheses relating to economic development are not universal propositions, they cannot be falsified by a single exception. When research results such as those of Geertz deviate sharply from predictions constructed from Western-based hypotheses, two alternatives suggest themselves. First, the deviations may be systematized and incorporated into the original hypothesis to enrich it and provide a stimulus for further research. Second, the hypothesis may be judged inapplicable to the new set of historical circumstances and its explanatory value limited to the original conditions. This may lead to revision of the general analytic framework to incorporate the new case (Gerschenkron, 1964, p. 360).

A second study, which pursues the Weberian question of the relation of values to economic motivation, is the work of Robert Bellah entitled *Tokugawa Religion* (1957). Bellah takes Weberian and particularly Parsonian categories and applies them to the conditions that made Japanese industrialization possible. In particular, he examines the possibility that there was in Japan a "functional equivalent" to the Protestant ethic. Bellah claims to have found such a counterpart by documenting the role of religious and value orientations in the process of Japanese industrialization. In a revealing account of the way his research project developed, Bellah points out that the usual textbook notion of social research is that one forms a hypothesis and then gathers data to confirm or negate it. Although this description may be true in many cases, he argues that it is often not what occurs in the field of comparative and historical sociology. More frequently, the researcher finds himself with an abundance of data, and his problem is to make sense of it. Bellah suggests that the situation is not likely to change in the near future, as historians continue to uncover more facts than they can make sense of. One test of this approach is the way new conceptualizations and interpretations give rise to new research (Bellah, 1964).

The practices described by Bellah are common, testifying to the weakness of sociological research in relating economic behavior to social and cultural variables. The limitation of this approach lies in the presentation of evidence that is at best plausible and cogent but does not successfully exclude the possibility of alternative explanations. The gradual rejection of alternative hypotheses lies at the heart of scientific explanation.

Comparing Two or More Societies

Thus far we have talked about those comparative studies that test conceptual frameworks developed in Western countries on non-Western countries. Now let us deal with some methodological considerations arising from research designs that explicitly include one or more national units. Generally speaking, the more nations compared, the better. The greater the number of differences to be compared, the greater the opportunity to examine the different limits and conditions under which a relationship will hold. Suppose, for example, we are interested in testing the proposition that higher levels of economic development result in a reduced level of communal (ethnic or tribal) conflict. We cannot hope to explain the causal force of levels of economic development if the level does not vary. Only by looking at another society where the level of economic development is different can we begin to talk about the causal force of this factor. Similarly, it is necessary that the level of communal conflict vary or nothing needs explaining.

Although the more national units compared the better, two-nation comparisons are not meaningless. The strategy of paired comparisons is frequently used in the social sciences (Kindleberger, 1964; Ward and Rustow, 1964). Comparisons may first be made between two societies, the limits under which a relationship holds determined, and appropriate analytical categories devised. The same researcher, research team, or others may then seek to establish the nature of the relationship in other societies. In the course of this ever-expanding application, analytical categories must often be reformulated to allow for more inclusive explanations.

Comparative analysis does not focus only on differences. Like any science utilizing induction, the establishment of similarities is also important. Suppose we are trying to explain differing degrees of communal conflict in two societies with different levels of economic development. One explanation might be that the level of economic development is the important causal factor. To increase the creditability of this explanation, we could try to show that the most likely competing theories are incorrect. One might be that the degree of residential integration in major urban centers with diverse ethnic groups is an important causal factor. If, however, we take a measure of residential integration and find that both societies register the same values, this factor cannot be a cause of the observed differences in communal conflict. By rejecting this alternative hypothesis, we make more credible one based on level of economic development. In this way, the identification of similarities can be part of the process for explaining differences.

Comparing Industrial Societies

One research strategy involves making comparisons among nations that have achieved a similar level of economic development. Holding this level constant, we may examine relationships among social and cultural variables. The presumption is that, as the level of economic development cannot be a causative factor in such cases, we can derive the importance of noneconomic factors.

Convergence Theory

Much cross-cultural sociological research concerned with economic development has focused on comparing countries at the same level of development. For the advanced industrial nations, this often involves efforts to test some variation of "convergence theory," which asserts the growing similarities in social structure and value orientations among industrial nations. In these societies, unique historical heritages have been overlaid by the common imperatives imposed by the industrial order. Convergence theory envisions that, with advanced industrialization, unique national identities fade and common solutions to problems of social organization prevail. Scholars identified with this position are Clark Kerr and associates (1960), Alex Inkeles (1966), and Marion Levy (1966). The convergence position is a technocratic one, asserting that social and political relationships must be restructured to mesh with the complex technological organization characteristic of high levels of economic development (Ian Weinberg, 1968, p. 10).

A number of scholars have rejected the view that industrial societies are characterized primarily by their similarities. Reinhard Bendix (1964) accepts that the industrial revolution brings common imperatives to bear on industrializing nations. Yet he emphasizes the way these imperatives are combined with the unique historical experience of each country. This amalgam denies the simple applicability of one country's experience to another. Although each successive level of industrialization opens up common options and closes others, choices are made by people in subtle interactions between these common options and the specific social, political, economic, and cultural history of the country in question. Convergence proponents seem too ready to speak of the organizational requirements of modern industrial society without recognizing the needs of historical actors. In part, this bias seems to flow from the lack of emphasis on history inherent in contemporary cross-sectional research.

Other critics of convergence theory, such as Wilbert Moore and Arnold Feldman (1962), argue that convergence is limited to the "core" elements of the industrial system, with all industrial societies possessing the minimum characteristics of "a factory system of production, a stratification system based on a complex and extensive division of labor and hierarchy of skills, an extensive commercialization of goods and services and their transfer through the market, and an educational system capable of filling the various niches in the occupational and stratification system." Beyond these minimum core characteristics, Moore and Feldman emphasize the elements of divergence in industrial systems.

Some of the most exciting comparative research today explores dimensions in which industrial societies converge and those in which cultural distinctiveness is maintained. The work has been concerned with such issues as how an occupational structure meets the needs of an industrial society, the relationship of population growth to level of economic development, the change from an extended to a nuclear family system, the emergence of common structures for organizing the labor force, the appearance of a consumer market and its social and political implications, and the correlation between high levels of income and education with political democracy.

One reason for the popularity of convergence theory relates to the current international political scene. Some American liberals, in their desire to end the cold war, have built the powerful argument that, as the Soviet Union approaches the levels of economic development achieved by the United States, it becomes like the United States, developing a vested interest in the status quo, and experiencing a growing democratization. Despite the popularity of this interpretation, scholars are not in unanimous agreement. Brzezinski and Huntington (1964) argue against convergence theory, stressing the different relationship of economics to politics in the United States and the Soviet Union. They see political structure as the dominant influence on the evolution of Soviet society, explained by the existence of a political elite that set itself the task of transforming a backward agricultural society into a powerful industrial society. The speed with which it tried to accomplish this change meant that power had to be centralized, wielded by professional political leaders, and exercised with "sustained ruthlessness, skill, and ideological commitment" (Brzezinski and Huntington, 1964, p. 423). In the Soviet legacy, political power preceded economic power, while in the American legacy economic power preceded political power. The authors see this legacy as all important in shaping the present organization of society and the likely form of future society. Brzezinski and Huntington see convergence theory as exaggerating the importance of economic determinants and ignoring "the probability that the future will see in both the United States and in the Soviet Union novel forms of government which will *evolve* out of the present on the basis of the *uneven* importance of political and socio-economic determinants in the two countries" (Brzezinski and Huntington, 1964, pp. 429–430). Whether or not one agrees with these conclusions, it is important that the authors subjected the convergence argument to investigation rather than accepting it as an implicit assumption.

An additional problem concerns the distinction between level of economic development as opposed to rates of economic growth. The rate of economic growth may be an important variable affecting social organization, whether or not we hold constant the overall level of economic development. Thus, if we hold this level constant, we cannot assume that all remaining differences flow from noneconomic factors. The most commonly used indicators for determining the influence of economic factors are selectively chosen on the basis of their accessibility and the theoretical orientations of researchers; they do not necessarily include all the economic factors in operation (Rokkan, 1970, p. 49).

One useful research strategy is to formulate a series of problem areas for investigation. We might begin with: To what extent does a common core technology exist in industrial societies? This raises questions: To the extent that such a core exists, does it give rise to common occupations in industrial societies? To the extent that common occupations exist, are they organized in the same fashion? To the extent that a common organization exists, is it based on similar reward systems? One might continue in this fashion to build outward to areas such as leisure and family organization, more removed from the direct influence of industrial technology. To state the convergence theory in this way is to make problematic and put to a test the degree of interdependence of different parts of society. The approach allows for the possibility that convergence is likely to reach some sectors and levels of society earlier than others and to occur in some sectors not at all.

Comparing Preindustrial Societies

One may also focus on a comparison of those states that have not yet achieved high levels of economic growth. In the earlier stages of economic development, the diverse historical heritages are most strongly imprinted on structural arrangements and the meanings of these arrangements for participants. These heritages have not yet been overlaid with the common features of industrial societies. At first glance, this great diversity may seem to make meaningful comparison impossible. Perhaps as a consequence, much work on the industrially undeveloped nations has been limited to a search for the emergence of social characteristics serving as preconditions of modern economic growth. A large literature on these preconditions and existing obstacles has resulted. It is increasingly clear that the great investment in these efforts has led us down a dead-end street. A precondition in one society proves not necessary in another (Gerschenkron, 1964, pp. 31–51). An obstacle in one society proves to be a resource in another (Hirschman, 1965). Thus, the extended family in one society may be an obstacle to releasing the individual to economically productive activity, while in another society the extended family may be an important source of capital accumulation.

POLITICAL CONSEQUENCES OF EARLY INDUSTRIALIZATION: THE MARXIST PERSPECTIVE

Three dominant formulations have commanded the attention of sociologists in dealing with the political consequences of early industrialization. First, the Marxist perspective, as represented in current sociological thought, focuses on the tearing loose of rural, village, or tribal inhabitants from the community life, offering the individual a secure anchorage. This argument is not often explicit. The new industrial worker is seen as thrust into a new and strange urban environment; his supporting social networks are destroyed and his culturally conditioned work rhythms hinder his adaptation. In the city, factory life offers no status, sense of personal dignity, independence, or traditional work rights. The individual is separated from meaningful participation in the process of production. He is forced to adjust to an unrelenting work discipline and system of authority for which he is unprepared. The result is a rise in alienation and a sense of social injustice. When this early period of industrialization coincides with colonial rule, the hostility of new workers increases. Protest comes to be expressed in absenteeism, sabotage, spontaneous strikes, and worker organization. It is seen as creating a radical worker movement that, in the classic Marxist formulation, culminates in class consciousness and ultimately in political revolution.

(This account draws from the presentation of Herbert Blumer, 1960). The critical tension in this theory is supplied by the gap between village life and the less congenial factory life. Adam Ulam (1960) has pursued this theme to suggest that Marxism's greatest appeal is to peasants nostalgic for village life. To these individuals, Marxism offers a comforting vision in which an oppressive state and factory have "withered away." The goal is less economic growth than a return to an idealized past.

A parallel analysis has developed in recent years that focuses upon the potential force of rural discontent. Perceptively, Frantz Fanon (1963) notes that the new industrial workers are a privileged elite under colonialism and therefore not likely to lead a revolution. He pins his hopes on the peasantry. His call for revolution, however, contains little of the sociological analysis that would permit us to assess the likelihood of successful peasant revolutions. Unlike Fanon, Eric Wolfe (1969) sets himself the task of examining the structural sources of political revolution in the early stages of industrialization. He applies much of the Marxist perspective formerly reserved for industrial workers to rural relationships.

> It is significant, however, that before the advent of capitalism and the new economic order based on it, social equilibrium depended in both the long and short run on a balance of transfers of peasant surpluses to the rulers and the provision of a minimal security for the cultivator. Sharing of resources within communal organizations and reliance on ties with powerful patrons were recurrent ways in which peasants strove to reduce risks and to improve their stability, and both were condoned and frequently supported by the state. What is significant is that capitalism cut through the integument of custom, severing people from their accustomed social matrix in order to transform them into economic actors, independent of prior social commitments to kin and neighbors (Wolfe, 1969).

Wolfe, basing his analysis on the historical experience of six countries, cautiously delimits the conditions under which peasant revolutions arise and are likely to be successful. He pays particular attention to the importance of coalitions among various groups and classes. No successful revolution has been carried out exclusively by peasants in the political states of the twentieth century.

Barrington Moore (1966) is concerned with coalitions that led to modern polity formation in the major powers of the contemporary world. Moore posits as the major actors in the transition to a modern industrial society: the central dynasty and its bureaucracy, the merchant and manufacturing bourgeoisie in the cities, the landed interests, and the peasants. Alone, none of these actors is strong enough to bring the state through the process of nationhood and economic growth; only a nation-building alliance can be successful. At least one set of actors is left in opposition outside this nation-building alliance. Moore emphasizes the profound consequences that choices of coalitions exert on subsequent structuring of each society's central institutions. In particular, he concentrates on how the transition to a modern agriculture is effected and on the role of the landed interests.

To some extent, explanations of the political response to industrialization based on the role of industrial workers and those based on the role of peasants reflect different historical periods. The image of the industrial proletariat joining hands to bring down capitalism grew out of Marx's observations of nineteenth-century English society. The focus on the role of peasants in the work of Fanon and Wolfe stems from the nature of twentieth-century revolutions in such countries as China, Vietnam, Cuba, and Algeria. Whether peasants or industrial workers, the view is posited that protest movements arise because of the psychic and material deprivation that grows out of an emergent capitalist process. To understand the direction and impact of the protest, however, it is necessary to examine the nature of the coalitions formed between different social groupings.

Structural Differentiation

Another theory concerned with early industrialization arises from the tradition of Herbert Spencer (1891). Notable adherents to this tradition are Talcott Parsons (1961), S. N. Eisenstadt (1965, pp. 50–57), and Neil Smelser (1959). Its key concept is the process of *structural differentiation*. Smelser defines structural differentiation as a process in which

> one social role or organization differentiates into *two* or more roles or organizations which function more effectively in the new historical circumstances. The new social units are structurally distinct from each other but taken together are functionally equivalent to the original unit (1959, p. 2).

The most obvious example of this process is the way family functions of training and economic production are differentiated after industrialization; schools and distinct productive organizations fill these specialized functions. Smelser and Eisenstadt focus on the varying response to this process of structural differentiation and, in particular, on the likelihood of political revolution. They emphasize the need for creating a new mode of integration to coordinate the diversified specialized activities associated with industrialization. The failure of the new differentiated units to mesh with the old or emergent mode of integration is seen as a basis for the social disturbances common in the early stages of industrialization.

A notable attempt to apply this model of structural differentiation to the empirical world is Neil Smelser's study of the British cotton industry, which examines changes in the family and community life of the British working classes in the early nineteenth century. Robert Nisbet (1969, pp. 159–161) has criticized this approach for using concepts like differentiation, so abstract as to defy application to the concrete behavior of human beings.

Working Class Alienation

A third approach to the social protest arising under early industrialization is found in the work of Count Alexis de Tocqueville, T. H. Marshall (1964), and Reinhard Bendix (1964). It focuses on the experience of Western Europe and the rise of political alienation among the working class, seeing it as deriving from the worker's loss of a recognized position in a civic community.

T. H. Marshall (1964, pp. 71–72) sees citizenship as composed of three strands: the civil element, composed of the rights necessary for individual freedom, such as freedom of speech and the right to own property; the political element, composed of the right to participate in the exercise of political power either directly or through some representative body; and the social

---

INSERT NO. 45

Modernization and Communist Party Strength

John Kautsky and Roger Benjamin (1968, pp. 184–206) have examined the relation of communism to level of economic development. The researchers predicted the curvilinear relationship between level of economic development and Communist party strength depicted in Figure 15-1.

Figure 15-1. Predicted Relationship between Level of Economic Development and Communist Party Strength (Kautsky and Benjamin, 1968: 187).

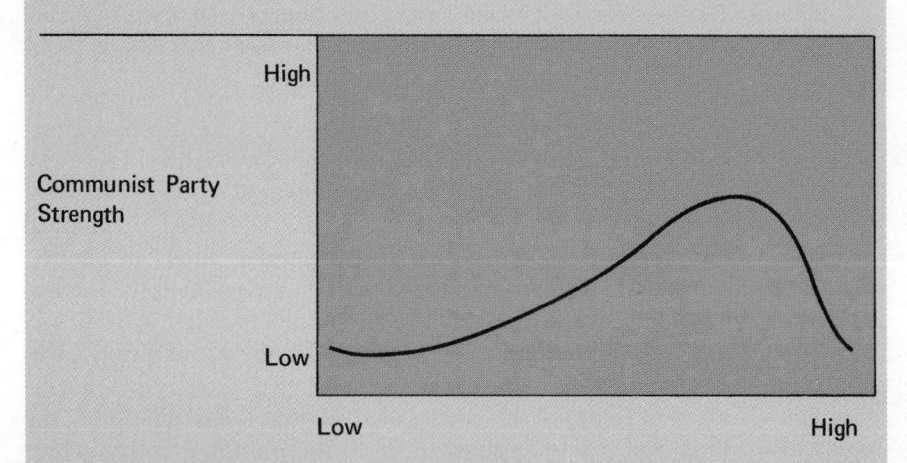

They expected that Communist party strength would be low in those societies with a low level of economic development but would rise as economic development accelerated and then decline at advanced levels of industrialization. The

element, ranging from the right to a minimum level of economic welfare to achievement of the standards of life deemed proper for civilized man, especially access to the educational system and social services.

This theory sees the extent and rate at which the emergent working class acquires a sense of citizenship, of membership in the nation, as the crucial determinant of the direction of political protest movements. The denial of this citizenship, a sense of being an outcast in one's own country, is seen as heightening politically expressed dissatisfaction. This approach is distinguished from the Marxist position, in particular, by its treatment of politics and government as partially autonomous institutions, instead of mere reflections of the economic sphere. A recent study applies an empirical test to propositions deduced from this framework (see Insert No. 45).

research consisted of constructing measures of level of economic development and measures of the strength of the Communist party and applying them to ninety non-Communist countries. Generally speaking, the researchers' predictions were confirmed. Since the data is based on cross-sectional data, however, it is subject to the cautions noted earlier.

The authors regard Communist parties in the nonindustrial states as modernizing movements. Thus, at low levels of industrialization, where the impact of Western industrialism on traditional societies has been slight and anticolonialism has not been a major factor, the appeal of this movement is small. As industralization proceeds, modernizing movements like the Communist party can begin to draw on a larger base of support from dissatisfied intellectuals, industrial workers and their unions, dislocated artisans and shopkeepers making up the old urban middle class, and peasants who find their traditional village communities threatened by the impact of economic development. The high point in Communist party strength shown in Figure 15–1 reflects Western European countries such as France and Italy where economic development took place indigenously but still has not pentrated the entire economy. Here, full citizenship has not been achieved in the sense described by T. H. Marshall. Industrial workers remain a minority in the population with a union movement much weaker than in other more advanced industrial countries of Western Europe. The strong antilabor majority of industrial and preindustrial propertied groups denies workers political and social citizenship and leads to their alienation from society and the political system. The workers, along with remnants of the peasantry and the old middle class, provide the bulk of support for the Communist party in these countries.

At the most advanced levels of industrialization, the Communist party has little mass support. Workers in these countries have achieved full citizenship; through their political and economic power, they have become integrated into their societies and have come to share the growing wealth. In Western Europe, the workers, along with sympathetic intellectuals, have turned to socialist labor parties, leaving relatively inconsequential Communist parties surviving at their fringes.

Problems of Industrialization

From a problem-solving point of view, many contemporary nonindustrial countries are new states that have just emerged from colonial rule, with many still seeking to escape from "economic colonialism." Some major problems that must be solved in the course of industrialization are the emergence of a new social and political order, the establishment of an effective government, the process of revitalizing traditional values and practices to serve economic development, and the legitimation of authority necessary to coordinate the activities of large groups of people. Nation-building involves creating a national consensus, social mobilization of the population, breaking down of local solidarity, and establishment of direct links between the territorial nation and its individual subjects. In the West, this process has been accomplished through the expansion of universalistic criteria of citizen rights and obligations. A dynamic structure is necessary that allows for creative innovation without ripping apart the social fabric. Sometimes the creation of this dynamic balance between innovation and stability must wait upon a political revolution which transforms the society. These tasks are complicated by the ethnic and tribal diversity of many new states, reinforced by the often arbitrary national boundaries imposed by colonial rulers. A focus on the process of nation-building means a macrosociological approach; it merges with notable efforts by political scientists in recent years to build models of nation-building (for a systematic codification of these efforts, see Rokkan, 1970, pp. 46-71).

The task of comparative sociology is to examine the range of solutions to such problems and to formulate analytic concepts and generalizations to provide an adequate framework for understanding these developments (Shils, 1963, pp. 1-26). The emergent solutions must be compared to the solutions arrived at in the historical experiences of the present-day advanced industrial societies. It cannot be assumed that the Western societies have exhausted man's creative possibilities for solving these problems. Moreover, contemporary industrializing nations have a variety of models to choose from and possibly recombine in unique ways.

COMPARING THE INDUSTRIAL SOCIETIES WITH THE PREINDUSTRIAL SOCIETIES

In discussing strategies for organizing national comparisons, we have suggested comparisons of nations at the same level of development. Thus, preindustrial or transitional societies may be compared with respect to how they solve their common problems. On the other hand, advanced industrial societies may be compared with respect to the issue of convergence. A third logical possibilty is to compare industrialized societies with those in transitional or early stages of industrialization.

It might seem that the differences are so great as to make any comparative analysis meaningless. The basis for comparison, however, lies in the recognition that all societies are members of a single species: human society. One difficulty in comparing societies at different levels of development arises from the arbitrary boundaries set by academic disciplines; often, these boundaries are not conducive to full understanding of the phenomena under investigation. We come to emphasize certain concepts, categories, and associations among variables when dealing with some societies and an entirely different set when dealing with other societies. We must test the utility of concepts and hypothesized relationships in societies at different levels of economic development. For example, Inkeles and Rossi (1956) reported the results of occupational prestige rankings for six countries, all relatively advanced industrial nations. The authors concluded that the high correlations were accounted for by "cross national similarities in social structure which arise from the industrial system and other common structural features such as the national state" (1956, p. 339). The results were interpreted as strong evidence for the convergence hypothesis. Yet gradual extension of occupational prestige studies revealed that similar rankings existed in preindustrial and transitional societies as well (Hodge, Treiman, and Rossi, 1966). This is complicated because we can compare only those occupations that societies have in common. These are occupations we would expect in societies with a complex division of labor; thus, it is not so surprising that, when compared, they should stand in relatively the same prestige ordering as they do in advanced industrial societies.

In short, an essential structural similarity is shared by all nations of any degree of complexity (Hodge, Treiman, and Rossi, 1966, p. 321). Whatever conclusions one may draw about the convergence hypothesis, it should be clear from this example that consideration of nonindustrial nations constitutes a critical check on our generalizations about the impact of economic growth. Whenever we want to assert that a certain relationship exists in nations as a consequence of industrialization, we must present evidence that it does not exist in nonindustrial nations. Conversely, if we assert that a given relationship exists in nonindustrial societies because of a lack of industrialization, we must demonstrate that it does not exist in industrialized societies.

It is not necessary that every comparative study take the form of an explicit comparison between nonindustrial and industrialized nations: progress in sociology must be seen as a cumulative collective enterprise, as the research on occupational prestige rankings indicates. Nothing in this essay should be taken to mean that a sociologist's first obligation is to engage in comparative studies. Frequently, we have so little knowledge about a given phenomenon that concentration on how the process works in one society is preferable. But, once we have these understandings of phenomena within each society, comparative analyses can be of great value in gaining greater understanding of each society.

SUGGESTED READINGS

Bendix, Reinhard, *Nation-Building and Citizenship*. New York: Wiley, 1964.

> Examines the European experience of nation-building and compares it to current problems in the Third World. Close attention is given to comparisons with Japan, Russia, and India.

Black, C. E., *The Dynamics of Modernization*. New York: Harper & Row, 1966.

> A short and lucid book on political and social change as it relates to industrialization. An attempt to classify and explain the process of modernization in all existing political entities of the globe, from the pioneer in the process, England, to those which have begun only recently.

Brzezinski, Zbigniew and Samuel Huntington, *Political Power USA/USSR*. New York: Viking Press, 1963.

> An illuminating empirical study of the two major world powers; analyzes differences and similarities between the two nations with special reference to the likelihood that they may be "converging."

Coburn, Judith, "Project Cambridge: Another Showdown for Social Sciences?" *Science*, V (December 1969), 1250–1253.

> A journalist examines the implications of large-scale social science projects sponsored by the government. Discusses the impact of Project Cambridge at Harvard.

Finkle, Jason and Richard Gable, *Political Development and Social Change*. New York: Wiley, 1966.

> This book collects the most important essays in social and political change as they relate to economic development. Major contributors are political scientists, sociologists, and economists.

Geertz, Clifford, *Peddlers and Princes*. Chicago: University of Chicago Press, 1963.

> An empirical study of two Indonesian towns. The author analyzes the process of economic change in terms of the behavior and ideas of people and relates it to broader social science theory. A well-written study that makes for enjoyable reading as well as intellectual stimulation.

Horowitz, Irving Louis, *Three Worlds of Development*. New York: Oxford University Press, 1966.

> Applies concepts of social stratification and social psychology to a theory of international stratification. Examines the role of Third World nations in the international system with particular emphasis upon the impact of colonialism. Explores some of the critical dimensions in achieving modern economic growth.

Kerr, Clark and John Dunlop, Frederick Harbison, and Charles Myers, *Industrialism and Industrial Man*. Cambridge: Harvard University Press, 1965.

> An important statement outlining the different paths to industrialization and the growing convergence among industrial nations.

Kuznets, Simon, *Modern Economic Growth*. New Haven: Yale University Press, 1966.

> An important statement of the meaning of modern economic growth. Provides a detailed examination of what modern economic growth has meant in those nations that have successfully industrialized.

Nisbet, Robert, *Social Change and History*. New York: Oxford University Press, 1969.

> Professor Nisbet analyzes the ideas of social change and progress as they have appeared in the course of Western civilization. Shows the historical relation of the classical Greek idea of growth, the Christian epic, with its fusion of Hebrew and Greek ideas, and our modern ideas of progress, development, and sociological functionalism.

PART VI

The Technological Society, Computers, and Social Research

The structural properties of Western societies most related to social problems are those of industry and technology. Chapter 16 begins by analyzing formal organizations or bureaucracies that have grown to create and control industrial forms of production. Chapter 17 deals with a recent important development in forms of production and control: the electronic computer. Each chapter analyzes these aspects of our society, primarily to deal with social problems. In Part VII we shall more directly consider these social problems.

CHAPTER 16

Formal Organizations: Freedom and Control

Formal organizations or bureaucracies are important structures in an industrial society. Most employed members of our society work in some form of bureaucracy, making them central to the quality of our everyday lives. This chapter begins by exploring the nature of bureaucracies, considers the evolution of their sociological analysis, and concludes with the problems posed for society by bureaucratic organizations.

The chapter shows that sociologists began their examination of formal organizations by mistaking the formal aspects—the rules and rationalized procedures—for the whole truth about bureaucracies. This history of sociological research and theory on organizations has shown a progression toward increased emphasis on studies of the concrete, face-to-face interactions in everyday situations of organizations.

Sociologists have long been concerned with questions about the possible alienation of workers from their work in industrial society. With the introduction of automation this problem has become pressing for white-collar workers as well as blue-collar workers.

THE DUALISM OF BUREAUCRACY

As an epithet, "bureaucracy" designates red tape, waiting lines, reports in triplicate, time clocks, tedium, the "run-around," insensitive clerks, and squadrons of gray-flanneled conformists. A man who has to wait in line or fill out a form curses the imperious bureaucracy because he would rather be doing something else. If he liked to wait in line or to fill out forms, he would not be angrily experiencing a bureaucratic frustration, which constitutes an unwelcome control. Controlled people are not free (see Insert No. 46).

In a more descriptive sense, the term *bureaucracy* refers to an administrative structure that organizes and coordinates the behavior of large numbers of individuals. The key elements of this structure are division of labor, hierarchy, chain of command, and rules. Private organizations such as General Motors and the Roman Catholic Church and public organizations such as the U.S. Army are all bureaucracies in this sense. When referring to an administrative structure, bureaucracy is no epithet. Here the term stands for the structure that often results when large numbers of people come together to coordinate their behavior toward some shared goal or goals.

Even people who hate bureaucracy in its worst sense understand that formal administrative structures make possible many good and useful things. Bureaucracy organizes the sanitation workers who pick up our garbage; it issues each worker his check in the proper amount and on time; it puts price tags on canned goods and piles them neatly. Bureaucracy even insists that sullen, nasty clerks talk politely to customers they do not know or like. Although people rarely compliment bureaucracy for its ability to oversee these useful services, no one suggests that complex tasks can proceed without administration. When it makes possible our attainment of desired goals, bureaucracy helps us.

One cannot deny that bureaucracy is sometimes frustrating, but neither can one deny that bureaucracy is sometimes helpful. Bureaucracy is neither frustrating nor helpful, neither good nor bad. Bureaucracy is, rather, Janus-faced, simultaneously good and bad. This chapter examines the processes that connect bureaucracy as administration and bureaucracy as frustration, to provide an understanding of the whole.

INSERT NO. 46

On Jacques Ellul's *The Technological Society*

Jacques Ellul is a professor of law and social history at the University of Bordeaux. He was a member of the French resistance and is active in Roman Catholic ecumenism. These credentials bespeak a man of moralistic and humane disposition. Professor Ellul does not care for the "onward and upward" march of technology because he feels that technical efficiency robs human life of existential spontaneity, introducing a spiritual anesthetic. He argues, however, that technology has now become self-generating, and he is pessimistic about humanity's spiritual future, as the enemy grows ever stronger.

Ellul holds that the purpose of *technique* is to find the one best way to achieve some end. Once this way has been found, a man must choose it over inferior methods. For example, as penicillin is more effective than witch-doctoring in curing infections, a man must choose penicillin to treat his infection. But this is not a real choice, in Ellul's view. The advance of technology has robbed man of his free choice of means, a process he calls technological *automatism*. Because Ellul favors human freedom of choice, he fears the advance of technology, which imposes rational restraints upon behavior. Because a better technology always drives out an inferior one, Ellul concludes that there is little hope of avoiding a future in which everyone will have to do virtually everything in its "one best way." In such a world, life will be sanitary, standardized, and infinitely boring.

Ellul's reasoning is provocative, but the humane values he espouses are not congruent with his technophobic conclusions. For example, few technophobes would exchange a state of good health for the spiritual values allegedly enjoyed by plague victims in the days before medical technology. Few technophobes in poor health would not gladly sacrifice their "freedom of choice" if improvements in medical technology offered them a chance to recover. Ignorant people who know nothing of disease pathology live happy, carefree lives dumping their refuse wherever they please. The price of this freedom is sometimes early death by epidemic. These people are "free" to die prematurely because their ignorance precluded choosing survival. This kind of freedom has obvious limitations, but Professor Ellul overlooks them in order to emphasize his point.

BUREAUCRACY AND THE IMPLEMENTATION OF POLICY

Frequently, executives express frustration and anxiety about the performance of the bureaucracies they command. From the point of view of executives, the bureaucratic apparatus exists to implement the policies they establish. Because the bureaucratic machine refuses to be fully responsive to their will, executives take countermeasures intended to increase the responsiveness of their organizational instrument (Crozier, 1964, p. 184). Rarely are these countermeasures fully effective. Policy makers and executives cannot, in practice, eliminate the hiatus between their desires and the actual performance of the organizations they command. Nonetheless, they attempt to do so. If one would imagine the resulting state of affairs were these executive efforts wholly successful, one would create an ideal type of a perfectly disciplined and responsive bureaucracy. This type is ideal only in that it extrapolates to the ultimate degree executive tendencies present in real organizations. A "frictionless machine" and a "free market" are ideal types in the same sense; one never finds them in the real world. Yet these abstractions are useful scientific tools.

Weber's "Ideal Type" of Bureaucracy

Max Weber (1864–1920) developed a theory of bureaucracy, especially public bureaucracy, that was an ideal extrapolation of this sort (Weber, 1968, Vol. III, ch. 11). He noted that policy makers or "masters" experience a frustrating hiatus between the policies they set and the performance of the administrative apparatus they command. Weber's ideal type of bureaucracy imagined the existing state of affairs if masters were completely successful in their efforts to close the gap. In Weber's view, the "decisive" advantage of bureaucracy was its "purely *technical* superiority over any other form of organization." Yet bureaucracy also recommended itself to policy makers as an efficient instrument of "domination."

As an instrument of domination, the ideal bureaucracy's technical superiority derives from a working fusion of loyalty and expertise. In order to serve their master most effectively, bureaucrats must be both skilled and loyal. Loyal ineptitude or skilled disloyalty are alike unsatisfactory to policy makers.

To obtain a fusion of skill and loyalty, policy makers often resort to bureaucratic measures. Together, these measures tend to create the ideal bureaucracy whose summary characteristics can be reduced to five principal points (Blau and Scott, 1962, pp. 32–33):

1. The basis of bureaucratic authority is legal delegation. Without such delegation, no official has a right to command. Orders in violation of law are invalid. This principle guarantees the monopoly of authority claimed by authorized policy makers and, therefore, buttresses the loyalty of officials to the policy-making elite.

2. Work is distributed among various positions as the official duty of each position. The office holder takes responsibility for the performance of duties attached to that post. This division of labor makes possible specialization and therefore expertness.

3. A public system of rules and regulations governs the conduct of every person holding an official position. To perform his assigned work, every official implements the rules. The system of impersonal rules increases the disciplined compliance of officials to policy directives. Weber thought that rigid adherence to work rules also maximized operating performance.

4. Officials do not permit their private likes or dislikes to influence the impartial discharge of their duties. This impersonal attitude increases the disciplined subordination of officials to policy directives. If officials allow their personal feelings to affect the conduct of their duties, the policy-making elite lacks perfect control over organizational functioning.

5. Officials are appointed by superiors to their official posts on the basis of their tested expertness. Appointment by superiors (rather than election by subordinates) results in increased official receptivity to policy directives from above. Appointments on the basis of expert skills (rather than, say, by apple-polishing) guarantee that officials will be technically competent.

Formal Organization

The formal structure of bureaucracies can be visually mapped in a table of organization. In fact, large bureaucracies usually prepare tables of organization. This chart shows the officially prescribed relationships among different posts. The higher the post is on the chart, the higher is the post's authority. Vertical positions stand for social relations of equality, whereas horizontal positions represent institutionalized relations of hierarchical command and obedience. Each organizational post is indicated by a separate box, so that the paper relation of the boxes mirrors the formal relationships of the people filling the posts.

Figure 16–1 provides an organization chart of a large public school system in an American city (Caplow, 1964, p. 63). All authority in this system is legally derived by public election of members of the Board of

Formal Organizations: Freedom and Control   415

Figure 16-1.   The Organization Chart of a Large American School System

A LARGE ORGANIZATION
(PUBLIC SCHOOL SYSTEM)

Source: Theodore Caplow, *Principles of Organization* (New York: Harcourt Brace and World, 1964), p. 63.

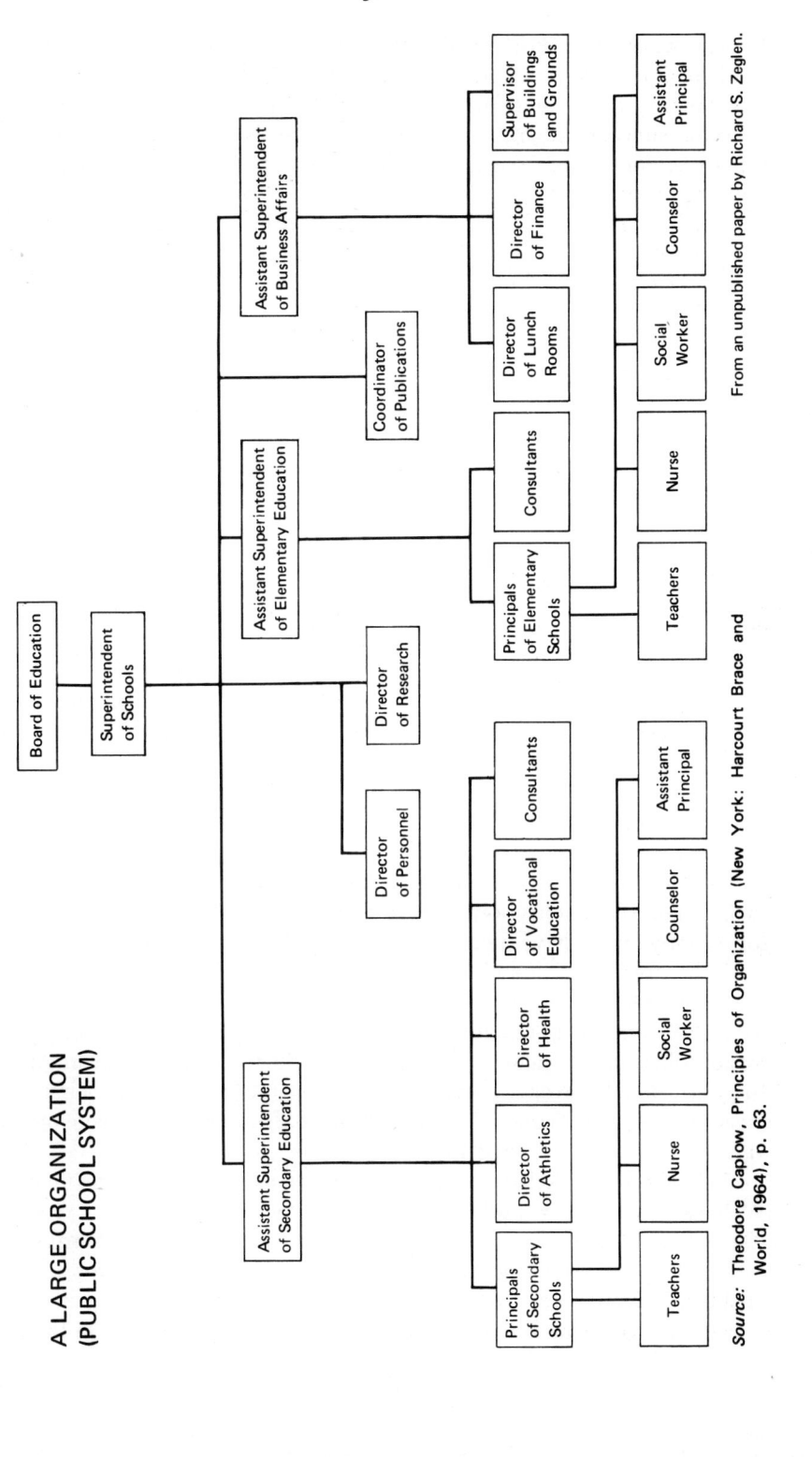

From an unpublished paper by Richard S. Zeglen.

Education. Hence, the formal source of their right to issue orders is the election. The Board of Education appoints both the superintendent and the assistant superintendents of schools on the basis of their qualifications. The assistant superintendents are directly responsible to their supervisor, the superintendent. The assistant superintendents, in turn, are authorized to give orders to the separate school principals. The right to issue orders to school principals is delegated to the assistant superintendents by the superintendent, who derives his authority by delegation from the Board of Education. Presumably, the Board of Education speaks in the name of the people who elected it.

Work in this school system is distributed among the various positions as the official duty of each position. The official duty of each principal, for example, is to supervise teachers, school nurse, social worker, counselor, and the assistant principal, and to report to the assistant superintendent in charge of his school. This division of labor increases specialization in that it permits a person trained in nursing to serve as nurse, a person trained in teaching to serve as teacher, and a person trained in counseling to serve as counselor. Expert skills contribute to the efficient operation of the organization as a whole in performance of its mission.

Each official in this school system operates in terms of rules that specify what he may and may not do. Teachers are not permitted to dispense bandages or administer psychological tests, but they must meet their classes. Also, officials in this system are not supposed to permit their private likes and dislikes to influence the manner in which they discharge their duties. A teacher is expected to grade students on the basis of quality of work rather than whether he likes or dislikes the student. Each principal is expected to deal impartially with the personnel of his school, whether he likes or dislikes them or approves of their friends.

School officials in this system are appointed to posts on the basis of their technical qualifications. The director of health for secondary schools, for example, must have medical credentials. Presumably, no illiterate person could be appointed to any school post, but an illiterate could be elected to the policy-making Board of Education. Elected members of the Board of Education are not bureaucrats in Weber's sense of the term, because they make policy in the name of the people, held to be sovereign in America. In contrast, whenever a king, party, or general is sovereign, school board members derive bureaucratic authority from the august personage or coterie and issue orders in his imperious name.

This American school system functions as a close approximation of Weber's ideal type of bureaucracy. Such a system represents a technically efficient tool for implementing policy decisions made by the Board of Education. The Board of Education develops a conscious motive for seeking to create a bureaucracy that functions in this way whenever the structure it finds at any moment fails to implement the goals it sets. Since, in the course of humdrum affairs, the discrepancy between what a Board of Education wants from its school system and what it gets is not very great, its real bureaucratic motive is concealed in the normal run of events.

In emphasizing by extrapolation elements of expertness and loyalty, Weber's ideal typical analysis seemed to overlook internal resistance to bureaucratization. His image of organizational life stressed the blind, robot-like conformity of rule-bound bureaucrats as though expert officials were not also human beings with beliefs, values, and interests of their own. Moreover, he wanted to ignore the sense in which professional experts (such as schoolteachers) can obtain authority from their expertise. The expert's authority sometimes opposes itself to hierarchical authority—and wins. The term "doctor's orders" illustrates this authority of skill. Weber ignored this because he was so keenly aware of its importance. The apparent paradox in his treatment disappears when we recall that Weber's purpose was to formulate an ideal type of bureaucratic domination. Many later scholars misunderstood his purpose.

Because Weber's essay on bureaucracy was misinterpreted, many scholars derived from his writing some patently erroneous expectations of how organizations actually (not ideally) function. When these investigators compared the empirical reality of the functioning organizations they studied with what they took to be Weber's theory, they found his theory wanting (Mouzelis, 1967). These judgments led to a strong academic reaction against Weber's emphasis on the *formal* structure of organizations. Emphasis shifted to *informal* organizational processes, because human beings failed to behave like cogs in an ideal typical machine (Dalton, 1959). Among sociologists, this new emphasis on informal structure became a critique of Weber (Blau, 1968a).

The Discovery of Informal Organization's Scientific Management

Interest in Weber's writing was restricted to campus-bound university scholars. In industry, the principal popular theory of organization in the first two decades of this century was Frederick W. Taylor's (1856–1915) *scientific management* (March and Simon, 1958, ch. 2). The purpose of this approach was the delineation of optimal methods of work organization in the interest of increasing output and profit (Blau and Scott, 1962, p. 87). To this end, Taylor and his followers studied the effects on productivity of industrial fatigue, incentive payment plans, and the relative efficiency of differing time-and-motion combinations.

Taylor's conception of bureaucratic efficiency was very close to that of Weber, although Taylor was a practical man and Weber a theorist. Scientific management was to enable policy makers and executives to achieve greater control over their organizations in the interest of a closer articulation of policy and performance (Taylor, 1919, p. 113):

> Every man must learn how to give up his own particular way of doing things, adapt his methods to the new standards, and grow accustomed to receiving and obeying directions covering details, large and small, which in the past have been left to his individual judgment.

Scientific management substituted rules for "rule of thumb." Efficiency experts formulated regulations for the "one best way" of performing a task. Thereafter, workmen had only to obey the rationally devised rules. Although their zeal made them few friends among workers, the scientific managers introduced many rationalized production ideas in American and Soviet industry (Merkle, 1968; Nadworny, 1955).

The Hawthorne Studies

Between 1927 and 1932, F. J. Roethlisberger and W. J. Dickson conducted a prolonged series of scientific management experiments at the Western Electric Company's Hawthorne Works in Chicago, which had an enormous impact upon students of industrial organization (Roethlisberger and Dickson, 1939). Following the scientific management tradition, Roethlisberger and Dickson first investigated the effects of illumination and fatigue upon production workers. Contrary to expectation, variations in the intensity of illumination or the pattern of rest breaks produced few systematic effects upon worker productivity. In fact, productivity increased after initiation of the investigation, no matter what level of illumination or pattern of rest breaks was employed. It seemed to the investigators that the regular productivity increases they observed resulted from the workers' gratification in being deemed worthy of attention by management and the research team. Moreover, the process of investigation itself had apparently had a beneficial effect upon the workers' morale by facilitating the emergence of more integrated work groups. People seemed to enjoy working in friendly groups rather than as isolated individuals, and their increased work satisfaction resulted in higher productivity.

To test this hypothesis, Roethlisberger and Dickson arranged to seclude fourteen male production workers in a special room, called the Bank Wiring Observation Room because the telephone workers were engaged in wiring banks of telephone equipment. To their surprise, the observers discovered that the workers in the Bank Wiring Observation Room possessed a "code of ethics" that determined how much each workers might produce on the average (Roethlisberger and Dickson, 1939, pp. 458–548). The accepted norm was six thousand to six thousand six hundred soldering connections a day. While satisfactory to management, this figure was far below what the workers might have produced had they worked each day to the limit of their physical endurance. Workmen who produced more than the accepted daily output were derided as "rate busters" by their fellows. Those workmen who produced fewer than the norm were sneeringly labeled "chiselers." Both "chiselers" and "rate busters" were subject to "binging," a painful game in which partners hit one another with a closed fist on the forearm (Homans, 1950, chs. 3–5).

The Bank Wiring Room workmen were paid on a group piecework basis. The department was counted as a unit, and each individual in it received money bonuses for high productivity by his group. From the standpoint of the management and economic theory, any "restriction of output" by the workers was economically irrational. Had the wirers set an easily obtainable higher production target each day, they would have received much larger incentive bonuses. Yet, for their part, the workers were convinced that their systematic output restriction was a rational policy. They were afraid that higher production would have caused management to lower their piece rate so that the wirers would end up doing more work in order to earn the same amount of wages. This logic justified their informal policy of output restriction. Subsequently, similar restrictive attitudes have been reported by other studies of production workers (Whyte, 1955).

Roethlisberger and Dickson had begun their research conceiving of organization as a passive tool of an economically rational management. After exposure to the Hawthorne plant, they concluded that management controlled only the formal organization. In the organization table, management appeared to be in complete command of its organization, but the informal working groups controlled level of output in the plant. These informal groups (rather than top management) determined how and how much production would occur in the plant. Instead of talking about formal structures, time and motion, rules, and the flow of authority from top to bottom, it appeared wiser to direct attention to such matters as the satisfaction of workers with their tasks, leadership in small groups, group dynamics, social roles, and social integration. These factors, after all, determined the productivity and profitability of the corporate enterprise.

Elton Mayo's Research

In several decades of careful research, Elton Mayo (1880–1949) and his followers drew out and systematized the Hawthorne conclusions. Mayo's school of "human relations in industry" urged industrial managers to give up their infatuation with mechanical images of efficiency. In Mayo's view, true efficiency depended upon managers taking account of human relations in the plant. Not only do people resent being treated like mindless cogs in a huge machine, they also express their resentments by output restriction, strikes, lateness, absenteeism, quitting, and industrial sabotage (Mayo and Lombard, 1944). Mayo interpreted these acts as the desperate responses of unsophisticated people goaded beyond their emotional limit by a mechanically sound but humanly irrational "logic of efficiency." The result, as depicted in Fig. 16-2, could be a spiraling, mutual increase in worker alienation and attempts by management to control this by imposing more punitive controls, which in turn would generate more alienation, and so on. An intelligent management ought (in its own self-interest) to cultivate decent human relations in the bureaucratic setting (Kerr and Fisher, 1957).

Mayo's theory implied that social isolation and normlessness (anomie) caused labor unrest and that, therefore, the deliberate cultivation of integrated work groups would greatly reduce labor unrest, including its expression through trade unionism. He blamed labor unrest on the scientific management outlook, which made working so unpleasant for people that they rebelled. This argument was good logic but, knowing the manifest conflicts of interest between labor and management, social scientists in general refused to agree with Mayo that anomie *alone* produced labor unrest and trade unionism. Social scientists were also critical of Mayo's manipulative, elitist, and promanagement attitudes, deeming these little more than current expressions of a changing "managerial ideology" (Bendix, 1956; Baritz, 1960). Nonetheless, the careful empirical research of the school of "human relations in industry" proved that work behavior depended in an important sense upon informal groups and attitudes (Wilensky, 1957).

To summarize, in real (not ideal typical) organizations, the people who occupy "posts" also have human feelings. Like other human beings, people at work form groups on the basis of mutual liking. These feelings and groups have no formal place in the organization chart, but they exist and create an informal social structure. Sometimes this informal structure comes into conflict with the formal organization controlled by distant policy

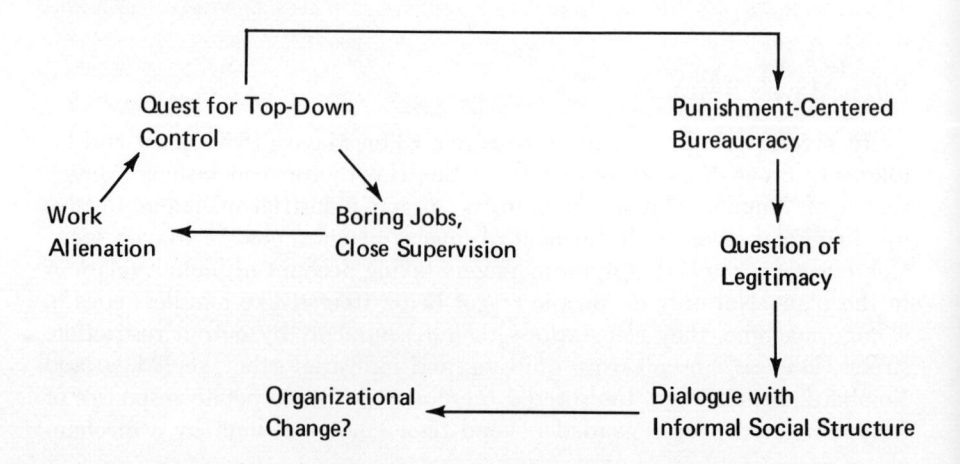

Figure 16-2. Flow Chart Model of Typical Control Alienation Spiral in Bureaucracies

makers. When this conflict appears, people have to choose between doing their duty and what they feel is fair or reasonable.

Alvin Gouldner's Research on General Gypsum Company

A case of managerial succession in the General Gypsum Company illustrates this point (Gouldner, 1954a). Under the regime of "Old Doug," the General Gypsum Company's Oscar Center plant had been a nice place in which to work. "They ain't very strict," said one worker, "you can come in late, and if you give a reason, they listen to it." The workers approved of Doug's easygoing ways. They appreciated his willingness to let them relax on company time after completing a fair day's work. Doug was always willing to give a second chance to rule-breakers and hated to fire anyone. He tolerated informal job shifting among production workers and failed to notice when workers took five minutes extra on lunch break. Anyone could walk out of the plant with large supplies of gypsum board for his personal use—and many did. Workers could punch in late, provided they stayed afterward to make up the lost time. Because of his policy of indulgence, the plant manager, Old Doug, had many friends among the Oscar Center work force.

But, in faraway Lakewood, the Board of Directors of the General Gypsum Company had unfavorable attitudes toward Old Doug's record. When Old Doug died, the board ordered Vincent Peele to take command of the Oscar Center plant and "get production up." In order to fulfill this order, Peele found it necessary to rescind the indulgency pattern. Standing on his formal authority, Peele cracked the whip over Oscar Center employees, clamping down on lateness, absenteeism, unauthorized work breaks, theft of company property, personal use of company tools, and "shirking" in general. In addition, Peele fired several of Old Doug's loyal lieutenants who refused to cooperate with him because they felt that one of them should have been appointed to Doug's job rather than an outsider. Worst of all, Peele introduced close supervision to check up on the workers' performance. These policies made no friends for Peele at Oscar Center, but the new manager could behave no differently if he wished to implement the policy directives he had received.

Naturally, Peele's bureaucratic measures outraged the Oscar Center work force. Instead of submitting, they resisted. Resistence culminated in a wildcat strike (Gouldner, 1954b). No one could deny that Peele was the legally authorized boss, whose commands did not exceed his formal authority. In theory, Peele had the right to command and employees had the obligation to obey. In practice, Peele lacked effective authority because his formal rights did not command unlimited loyalty. Personnel felt justified in resisting an "unfair" boss who did not pay proper respect to the local tradition of indulgence. Moreover, Peele did not "deserve" the top job so he did not have a "right" to give orders. These notions of fairness and merit were based on the informal structure of the Oscar Center plant. They had no official place in the organization chart; nonetheless, they existed. Industrial conflict resulted from top management's attempt to ignore *de facto* group realities in the Oscar Center plant (see also Insert Nos. 47 and 48).

In the strife-ridden Oscar Center plant, there were certain issues about which the formal authorities and the local people were not in disagreement. For example, everyone was in favor of safety—the Board of Directors, Vincent Peele, the miners, and lieutenants—albeit for different reasons. Thus, when the Board of Directors resorted to bureaucratic formalism (di-

---

INSERT NO. 47

On Melville Dalton's *Men Who Manage*

"There's always a way to get around the rule—look for it." This maxim does not conform to bureaucratic theory. But it does express what Dalton found happening among managers of four large plants in America's Middle West. In these plants, the managers of departments and divisions formed alliances, arranged treaties, and struggled with one another for power and rewards rather like sovereign nations in the U.N. Personal advancement depended upon religion and clique membership rather than upon impersonal competence. Successful stealing was a legitimate reward of the strong, who punished the weak for doing it. Strength depended upon informal alliances and connections rather than formal position in the organizational hierarchy. Dalton even feels that the strong deserved what they stole because they earned it by their contributions.

Yet, on paper, these plants were intended to operate in a formal, bureaucratic manner. If they inquired, outsiders (including board of directors) were piously informed that the plants operated in the formal way in which they were supposed to operate. Special shows were arranged for the benefit of outsiders who intruded into the operation of the plants. Outsiders went away unaware of what was occurring. In short, there was an enormous and elaborately maintained discrepancy between the respectable front these organizations proclaimed and the actual clash of competing groups which was their mundane reality.

Most organizations maintain a public façade incongruent with the realities of internal politics. Only by dint of careful and lengthy participant observation was Dalton able to penetrate the façade of the four organizations he studied. His analysis is a useful reminder to the fledgling sociologist that the façade of an organization and its functioning reality are likely to differ. But, finding out the way operations proceed is difficult because people do not make these disclosures to those whom they have not learned to trust.

vision of labor, hierarchy, rules, impersonality) to implement a policy of safety, they experienced no conflict with the informal plant organization. The board appointed safety experts on the basis of technical qualifications. These experts introduced rules about safe procedure, which were generally obeyed. On safety, the Oscar Center bureaucracy seemed a virtually frictionless instrument of the Board of Directors' policies.

The success of the safety rules shows that formal organization and informal social structure need not conflict. Sometimes the informal social structure of an organization opposes the policies adopted by formal authorities; sometimes it supports such official policies enthusiastically. When formal authorities and informal powers are in agreement, the formal authorities' bureaucratic measures give rise to a structure approximating Weber's ideal type of responsive bureaucracy. Expeditiously, the organization executes official policies. When, however, formal authorities and informal powers disagree about means or ends, conflict emerges. The organization responds sluggishly, if at all, to the efforts of legal authorities to command obedience to official policies (Ashworth, 1968).

To take account of these important differences, Gouldner (1954a) distinguished between two types of bureaucracy. *Punishment-centered bureaucracy* arises when one group of organization members attempts to force another group to behave in a manner which the second group has a motive to avoid. *Representative bureaucracy* appears when all organization members unite to further objectives which everyone approves. When, for example, the Board of Directors attempted to increase production at Oscar Center, they attempted to force plant personnel to behave in ways that the personnel had a motive (traditional indulgence) to avoid. Consequently, hierarchy, rules, and impersonality created a punishment-centered bureaucracy around these issues. On the other hand, when workers, management, and the Board of Directors united behind the safety campaign, hierarchy, rules, and impersonality created a representative bureaucracy.

Representative bureaucracy begins with the many-sided recognition that something needs doing. People decide how best to go about meeting these needs and work toward development of a social organization capable of performing the mission. In such a structure, those who break rules are thought careless or ignorant but not malicious. Representative bureaucracy is pure administration because, by definition, there is agreement among participants about both means and ends.

Punishment-centered bureaucracies develop slowly from the ongoing process of social interaction. First, one group notices that another group of organizational members is not behaving the way the first group thinks they ought to behave. Second, the first group also determines that the other group has a comprehensible motive for its actions. Third, the first group agitates for a system of impersonally enforced rules to force other members to behave in a way they have a motive to avoid. The final step is a system of punishment-centered bureaucracy. This process occurs in many organizational settings; it represents the translation of a problem of *intergroup conflict* into a problem of administration.

In any given organization, the overall system of rules, hierarchy, and impersonality normally reflects the simultaneous coexistence of punishment-centered and representative bureaucratic systems. One could characterize the Oscar Center plant as basically a scene of labor-management conflict. Yet

---

INSERT NO. 48

On William Kornhauser and Warren O. Hagstrom's *Scientists in Industry: Conflict and Accommodation*

Becoming a scientist takes years of specialized training. Many people who begin such training lack the motivation or intelligence to complete it. Scientists have good reason to be aware of these facts. It is not, therefore, surprising that salaried research scientists claim to know more about performing scientific research than does the monied layman who pays their salary. As a layman, the boss is incompetent to evaluate the scientific research conducted in his establishment by salaried, professional scientists operating in their fields of specialization. Being incompetent to evaluate, the boss has, in the scientists' view, no right to attempt to control their work behavior. Paying the piper, the boss is denied the right to call the tune.

Kornhauser points out that what is true of salaried scientists is also true of salaried professionals in general. There is an unavoidable tension between hierarchical authority and professionalism. Bureaucracies distribute authority in a hierarchy. But in professions (such as science, medicine, law, architecture, education) the practitioners regard one another as colleagues. Only colleagues are competent to evaluate colleagues. Professionals are also loyal to their profession rather than to their employer and usually make unsatisfactory bureaucrats.

Their skills demand work autonomy, but the boss is used to telling subordinates what to do down to the last detail. When large organizations employ professionals, as they increasingly do, the boss and the professionals find it necessary to make mutual adjustments in order to accommodate one another.

The mutual accommodation of bureaucracy and professionalism is especially interesting in our technological era because factories did not accommodate craft guilds. They destroyed them. Guild craftsmen became unskilled laborers under the control of an appointed boss. Professionals and professionalism represent a kind of survival in this postindustrial era of preindustrial forms of work organization. Kornhauser finds little reason to believe that the further development of large-scale bureaucracy will uproot professionalism, although he does anticipate new accommodations.

one would find here and there instances of representative rather than punishment-centered bureaucracy. For example, rules against absenteeism and goldbricking reflected punishment-centered bureaucracy; safety rules reflected representative bureaucracy.

The distinction between the two types of bureaucracy underscores the dualism of organized life, of which the man in the street has only a vague and hazy awareness. Part of bureaucracy consists of people getting together to coordinate their efforts in the achievement of common objectives. Another part stands for objectified intergroup conflicts arising in the process. As these distinct activities clash, real organizations become intricate structures of spiraling and interacting cause-and-effect sequences.

FROM CRAFTSMANSHIP TO AUTOMATION

Although large bureaucratic organizations existed in ancient China, Rome, and Egypt, their proliferation has been strictly a modern phenomenon (Bendix, 1968). Before the Industrial Revolution, the prevailing mode of production was craftsmanship. Artisans worked at home or in small shops, employing hand tools and muscle power to produce finished articles from raw materials. What they made they sold themselves. Craftsmen were organized into guilds striving to monopolize the trade for members and to maintain the autonomy of the independent, master craftsmen who were members of the guild. Until the eighteenth century, craftsmanship was the prevailing method of manufacturing in Western Europe (Faunce, 1968, p. 15).

Factories were necessary to obtain the advantage of a rational division of labor. In a factory many people come together and, by dividing their labor, cooperate in the production of more and cheaper commodities than they could produce if they worked as solitary craftsmen. During the Industrial Revolution in Europe, factories pushed out solitary craftsmen who became factory hands and helped destroy the independent livelihood of remaining craftsmen. In turn, bigger factories pushed out smaller factories. As late as 1845, 91 percent of manufacturing employees in Boston, Massachusetts, worked in establishments with fifty or fewer workers (Handlin, 1959, p. 238). Contemporaries thought these factories were large. By 1963, only 26 percent of manufacturing employees were in plants with fifty or fewer workers. Almost three of four manufacturing employees in 1963 found work in establishments larger than any that existed a century earlier.

Big operations continue to assert productive advantages over small ones. In 1963 small factories with four or fewer workers gave employment to 1.2 percent of manufacturing employees in the United States, but produced only 1.1. percent of value added by manufacturing. At the other extreme, plants with two thousand five hundred or more workers utilized 18.3 percent of manufacturing employees. This 18.3 percent created 21.8 percent of value added by manufacturing. Thus, the largest operations used less than their share of labor to produce more than their share of finished goods (Table 16–1).

Managing the Assembly Line

Solitary craftsmen needed no management science, as they had only themselves to manage. As factories dispossessed craftsmen and larger factories pushed out smaller factories, managing the even larger units became an increasing problem. Someone had to oversee the total operation, integrating the separate activities of the unskilled factory hands. The first problem was

TABLE 16–1. MANUFACTURING ESTABLISHMENTS IN THE UNITED STATES BY EMPLOYMENT, SIZE OF ESTABLISHMENT, PERCENT OF TOTAL MANUFACTURING EMPLOYMENT, AND PERCENT OF TOTAL MANUFACTURING VALUE ADDED: 1963.

U.S. Manufacturing Establishments in 1963

Number of Employees per Establishment*	Number of Establishments (cumulative %)	Total Employment (cumulative %)	Value Added (cumulative %)
All Establishments	100.0	100.0	100.0
1–4	36.5	1.2	1.1
5–9	52.3	3.2	2.7
10–19	67.6	7.1	5.9
20–49	83.0	16.2	13.3
50–99	90.5	25.9	21.5
100–249	96.2	42.6	36.5
250–299	98.4	56.7	49.8
500–999	99.4	69.1	63.0
1,000–2,499	99.8	81.7	78.2
2,500 and over	100.0	100.0	100.0

SOURCE: U.S. Bureau of the Census, *Census of Manufacturers,* Vol. I, *Summary and Subject Statistics* USGPO (Washington, D.C., 1966), p. 2, Table 3, and p. 4, Table D.

NOTE: Mean employment size of establishments = 53 persons. Median employment size of establishments = about 300 persons.

* Establishment refers to individual plants—not to overall company size.

to develop an overall production plan incorporating a rational division of labor. The second problem was to induce flesh-and-blood factory hands to operate as the plan intended.

Thus, the factory system raised unavoidable problems of control that demanded answers, and *classical management theory* developed in response to the concrete problem. Writers like Frederick W. Taylor and Henri Fayol formulated general solutions to the problem of organizational control (Massie, 1965). Their classical doctrine lodged rationality and spontaneity in the exclusive hands of top management. This group was to formulate rigid performance rules for underlings. The rules had a system logic known to those who made them, but those who executed them did not need to understand this logic. Indeed, the narrower the range of subordinate discretion permitted by the rule, the more successful Taylor and Fayol considered the control. Five related notions capture the essence of classical management theory's program:

1. *Bureaucratic centralization.* Management plans and administers production operations (Woodward, 1965, ch. 12).

2. *Minute division of labor.* The central management plan divides the total labor into the smallest possible constituent tasks. This plan makes it possible to tell every worker "exactly how to do his job down to the last detail."

3. *Rational flow of work.* Minutely divided tasks are arranged spatially for maximally speedy transfer. Management plans and administers this work flow.

4. *Short task cycles.* The finer the division of labor, the shorter the elapsed time required to perform a task. The task cycle consists of all operations involved in task performance.

5. *Surface attention.* Simplified, short-cycled tasks require little mental attention from the worker who learns to perform the task without thinking about it. Rote performance reduces the probability of operator error.

This classical program assumed that the boss was omniscient and knew better than any operative how his job should be performed. The assumption was appropriate enough in the case of those craft skills which could be broken down into a sequence of unskilled jobs, but some skills were so esoteric that they resisted division of labor. Research chemists, engineers, accountants, and professionals in general possessed "difficult" skills of this sort. The classical model of top-down control encountered serious problems when managements tried to control professional workers as they controlled factory hands (Kornhauser, 1962; George Miller, 1967).

On the other hand, top-down control produced incredibly productive payoffs when applied to humdrum problems. A working illustration of the classical management program occurs in the automobile industry (Chinoy, 1955; Walker, 1957; Blauner, 1964, ch. 5). Management plans the work flow and hires operatives to perform the separate, simplified tasks. On the automobile assembly line, a moving belt ("live line") transfers the car or engine body from one work station to another. At each work station is a worker. As the car body moves past his work station, the worker performs a simple operation such as boring a hole, tightening a bolt, or fitting a door (Meissner, 1969, p. 218). He performs the same operation all day long on hundreds of auto bodies sweeping past his station. The sum total of the many separate operations at the sequential work stations is a finished automobile. No single individual has built this vehicle: many separate individuals have contributed routine work to create the final product. Because it divides the total labor into constituent operations, the automobile assembly lines makes possible construction of many more finished products in a day than would otherwise be possible. Increased output results in lower prices. In turn, the lower prices mean that more people can afford automobiles.

Alienation from Work

Although assembly-line methods are highly efficient in the production of automobiles, they tend to cheapen and devalue the work experience. It is boring and tiring to stand all day in one spot and keep performing some rather simple operation. The worker assigned to an assembly line is not free to set his own work pace but, instead, must be paced by the moving line. Foremen make certain that individuals keep up the pace and do not slow down the operation by unauthorized departures for toilet or snack bar. Because this work is interdependent, no one can leave his station without causing a breakdown of work flow all along the line. Each operative's work is so routine that it requires little mental attention from him but, unfortunately, this freedom from concentration does not permit operatives to while away the day in casual chatter. They are virtually chained to their separate posts and communicate above the din and clatter only by shouting to those closest to them. This is hardly a satisfactory form of sociability, so that each operative is reduced to silent daydreaming, punctuated by clock watching and counting the remaining hours and minutes of work. These workers do not enjoy their duties because time "passes" quickly only when a person is absorbed in his work (Blauner, 1964, pp. 27–28).

Although the total assembly line is complex, each separate job is simple. The operatives performing these simple tasks do not understand how their operation fits into the total picture. Not surprisingly, people who work on assembly lines report that they do it for the money. This attitude distinguishes these operatives from weekend craftsmen who put together automobiles for the pleasure of doing it. The experience of such amateurs shows there is nothing inherently unpleasant about mechanical work. The dissatisfactions surface when the labor is divided in the interests of technical efficiency. If weekend craftsmen wanted to turn out more cars, they could get together and set up an assembly line. This technology would be more efficient but no one would get much pleasure from the work.

In his youthful writings, Karl Marx (1818–1883) developed the notion of work alienation as part of his incipient critique of capitalism. Marx's approach was metaphysical in that he conceived of work as a fulfillment of man's "essential" humanness and a distinguishing feature of his "species-life" (Marx, 1961; Fromm, 1961; Rotenstreich, 1963). Marx argued that factory labor reduced the operative to a mindless drudge, alienating the worker from himself (from his species-life). Although metaphysical, this proposition is an agreeable one, as it is difficult to escape feeling sympathy for those multitudes condemned to work lives of bleak monotony.

While Western social scientists have abandoned the metaphysical approach to the study of alienation, they have taken up Marx's youthful concern with the quality of work experience (Seeman, 1959, 1967; Blauner, 1964; Aiken and Hage, 1966; Etzioni, 1968). In a general way, the term *work alienation* denotes people's dissatisfactions in rationalized modern workplaces (Richard Hall, 1969, pp. 34–66). Marxist sociologists, however, are critical of this "one-dimensional" approach to work alienation and define it in terms of objective conditions rather than subjective feelings (Kon, 1969; Marcuse, 1964). How one defines alienation determines what political implications one can derive from it. Terminological squabbling mirrors a struggle for partisan advantage. The squabbling has now reached the point that both Soviet and Western sociologists are looking for new designations of the phenomenon so that dispassionate discussion can replace polemics.

In an important study, Blauner (1964) compared four quite different work settings with respect to Seeman's (1959) dimensional analysis of alienation. Seeman's paradigm underlies most current Western research into this question (Van Dyck and Van Oers, 1969). The four dimensions are powerlessness, meaninglessness, social isolation, and self-estrangement. Each dimension stands for a set of subjective individual feelings; and the term alienation refers in turn to one, some, or all of these subjective feelings, depending on the degree of alienation. Comparing printers, assembly-line operatives, textile workers, and refinery workers, Blauner reported that the assembly-line workers evinced the highest degree of alienation in terms of Seeman's categories. Assembly-line workers are powerless because they feel they lack control over their work processes and are "machine-paced." Extensive division of labor has rendered their repetitive work activities subjectively meaningless. Compared to other workers, assembly-line workers lack a sense of membership in an industrial community and experience personal isolation. Finally, the purely financial purpose of assembly-line work betokens the absence of intrinsic work rewards and suggests the self-estrangement of the line operative.

Naturally, these four symptoms of work alienation are also found outside the automobile industry and in non-assembly-line situations. College students sometimes complain of alienation in terms similar to what Blauner and Seeman meant (Keniston, 1965; Ralph Turner, 1969). Nonetheless, the assembly-line operative is considered the prototype of the alienated worker, compared to whom the student's lot is enviable indeed.

INSERT NO. 49

On Melvin Seeman's *"On the Meaning of Alienation"*

People who talk about alienation often have heated disputes about its definition. There is, according to Seeman, no such thing as alienation. His reading of the very large literature on this subject reveals, instead, five "logically distinguishable" usages of the term alienation. Each usage has its own history; each has analytically distinguishable merits. Accordingly, Seeman finds no scientific value in continuing to talk about alienation as though it were a unitary phenomenon. Scientific progress depends upon separating the different types or meanings of alienation, and then beginning to specify the causes and consequences of each type singly and in combination.

It is possible operationally to define each type in the ordinary vocabulary of social psychology. In this sense, Seeman defines *powerlessness* as "the expectancy or probability held by the individual that his own behavior cannot determine the occurrences of the outcomes or reinforcements he seeks." Thus defined, powerlessness is different from *meaninglessness*, referring to situations in which "the individual is unclear as to what he ought to believe." A given human actor can experience one or the other or both psychic states at the same time. Both powerlessness and meaninglessness differ from *self-estrangement*, by which Seeman means a high degree of "dependence of the given behavior upon anticipated future rewards." Seeman's language of rewards and expectancies does not sound much like the discursive, often theological literature on alienation, but these transformations make possible empirical research (Seeman, 1967).

Each type of alienation reflects the consciousness of human actors. In this respect, Seeman's approach differs from that of Herbert Marcuse (1964), who uses the term alienation to refer to "false needs" introjected by the consciously satisfied citizens of repressive industrial societies. If Seeman called his five

AUTOMATION AND FREEDOM

Until recently, the automobile assembly line was considered the ultimate in technological efficiency. It has become clear, however, that the assembly line is no longer the most advanced organization of production. Thus, it is inappropriate to assume that the relentless quest for greater output leads to assembly-line methods or that classical management prescriptions remain valid in a "post-industrial" era (Woodward, 1965, p. 77).

Automation is more advanced than assembly-line production just as factory production was more advanced than craftsmanship. The factory system replaced skilled craftsmen with unskilled workers. Automation replaces

---

types of alienation *a*, *b*, *c*, *d*, and *e*, and if Marcuse called his version *f*, it would be clear that the two authors have defined different concepts. But each wants to use the term alienation to refer to what he is talking about. Thus, quarrels about what alienation really *is* turn out to be quarrels over possession of the term.

These intellectual differences involve political implications. Having defined alienation, Seeman would refrain from labeling as alienated people who do not feel themselves to be powerless, normless, isolated, and so on. Marcuse's approach makes it possible for him to hang the label "alienated" around the necks of people who would repudiate the designation if they understood what it meant. Even though scientists do not derive their view of science by deduction from their politics, ideologically committed activists do. Activists want to know what alienation is so they spend a good deal of time debating scientifically tiresome but politically relevant questions. Professor Marcuse's view, important to an administered repressive society (including the Soviet Union), is that "average people" want these things. That they do want them is a testimony to mass introjection of and identification with a state of alienation.

Although Marcuse hints that automation will destroy the one-dimensional status quo, he does not show in detail why or how this change will occur. Hence, his work is pessimistic in outlook because it gives little clue as to how change can transpire in a society whose average citizens are, by his own confession, very satisfied with it. Romantic revolutionaries share Professor Marcuse's distaste for the life style and values of average people. Some revolutionaries have seized upon Marcuse's concept of "false needs" as justification for bullying and coercing the average man in his own "best interest." Naturally, average people resent this treatment because they do not understand that what they want is a testimony to their own alienation. It is not, however, clear that Professor Marcuse justifies "forcing men to be free," although it is hard to see what practical alternatives could be painted into the scenario he has created.

skilled craftsmen with unskilled workers. Automation replaces unskilled workers with complex machines, capable of producing greater output than factory hands at a cheaper unit cost. Nowadays, the ongoing quest for technological efficiency involves replacing unskilled workers with machines whenever possible.

In general, automation means the automatic control of an integrated production system (Faunce, 1968, p. 49; Bright, 1958, pp. 239–241). "Detroit automation" involves the transfer and treatment of material on an assembly line. At each station, materials are machine-positioned. Another machine performs an operation such as boring or fitting on the self-positioning material. Then the semifinished product moves to its next station, where it undergoes more advanced treatment at the hands of a different set of machines. Detroit automation originated in the automobile industry, but other examples are found in appliance production. Because the machines are not fully integrated, Detroit automation is a rudimentary form of automatic technology.

The ultimate in automation is closed-loop process technology. Humans feed raw materials into an integrated, self-controlling machine series and retrieve the finished articles from a stack or vat. The machines do the processing (Froomkin, 1968). Under these circumstances, human labor is reduced to supervision of a control panel whose sundry dials, gauges, and lights indicate the state of the process at various stages of completion (Meissner, 1969, p. 148).

Since World War II, automated technologies have become prominent adjuncts of the work process in government and industry. A survey of U.S. manufacturing establishments in the mid-1960s revealed that two thirds employed some automatic control or measurement devices and data-handling systems (Froomkin, 1968, p. 481). The first commercial digital computer was sold to the Bureau of the Census in 1950. By 1965 over twenty-four thousand commercial computers had been installed by U.S.-based companies (Carstens, 1966, p. 4). Although the extremely rapid pace of computerization has now resulted in widespread "underutilization" of computer capacity, new patterns of computer organizations—such as multiple-access computing—promise to further increase the rate of computerization in coming decades. As most organizations are now only partially automated, there remains much untapped demand for automated methods.

Minute division of labor is a prerequisite of automation. Complex tasks are reduced to simple rules of procedure. But, instead of teaching these rules to a worker, management develops a machine program. The program tells the machine how to respond to specific contingencies it has learned to anticipate. (For a detailed discussion of programming see the next chapter.) A computer takes nothing for granted, so it is necessary to spell out all its choices in painstaking detail. Absence of sufficient detail results in "bugs," which invariably accompany the installation of automatic technology.

Eventually, the bugs identify themselves and permit technologists to eliminate them. From this process of planning, installing, and "debugging" emerges a computer program capable of producing useful goods by following detailed instructions (Bright, 1958, pp. 123-131).

Managements once attempted to force people to behave like machines, creating the alienated proletarian on the assembly line.. Now managements are, wherever possible, replacing workers with talented machines. Many observers believe this latest substitution will tend to reduce the level of work alienation among production workers. When automatic machines replace operatives, remaining production workers become either maintenance workers or monitors of the machines. The automatic machines take over the worst drudgery.

Because automated equipment is costly and the production system is fully or partially integrated, machine "down" time (time out of use) is expensive. Maintenance workers must know how to spot incipient breakdowns and how to repair the machines when breakdowns occur. Obviously, these tasks require special training and technical knowledge. Skilled maintenance work, therefore, resists organization in terms of rational work flow, short task cycles, and superficial attention because machine maintenance requires craftsmanlike skills.

Machine monitoring does not require so much technical expertise as does maintenance work. Unlike assembly-line operatives, monitors of automated production machinery exercise considerable personal discretion on the floor (Blauner, 1964, ch. 7). They not only respond to the machines around them; they control the machines. Many production workers experience considerable work satisfaction in controlling the operation of elaborate interconnected machines, because it requires an understanding of a broader segment of the total work process than was required of the assembly-line operative. When the integrated process runs amok, as occasionally it does, the monitor must make rapid decisions to restore order and prevent expensive down time (Woodward, 1965, p. 233).

Workers report that automatic plants require less physical effort but more mental attention (Walker, 1957, p. 31). They do not feel automated jobs are easier than their assembly-line jobs; rather, they are more involving. The assembly-line worker finds no intrinsic meaning in his job rather than the money payment. Apparently, automated production workers find greater satisfaction in the image of themselves their job reflects and, to some extent, in the work process itself.

Office Automation

Unlike manual work, white-collar occupations have been largely immune to job rationalization. In the early part of the twentieth century, typewriters replaced copyists with typists. This technological innovation did not, however, radically alter the work process or work environment. Conventional office machines still required skilled users, for the machines had no built-in skills. Extreme specialization of function and conveyor-belt methods did not appear in the office (Rhee, 1968, pp. 35–36). Even the humblest clerk retained substantial control over work pace, timing, sequence of operations, methods, and quality of product.

Office automation, however, is now tending to force increased rationalization of office procedures. Electronic data processing (EDP) substitutes a digital computer for clerical workers. These complex machines have the ability to store information, retrieve it, and make rapid computation in fulfillment of a program (Simon, 1965). The program tells the machine what to do with bits of processed data it receives. Knowing this, computers can perform many white-collar jobs such as accounting, sales and inventory analysis, billing, filing, and routine decision making (Hoos, 1960). In addition, EDP has been experimentally applied to such diverse fields as teaching, medical diagnosis, weather forecasting, and language translation.

Because data processing machines require programmed rules, the introduction of EDP forces management to rethink the organization of an office staff in terms of a "systems" approach. A careful scrutiny of office work is made to eliminate multifunctional jobs wherever possible and place sequences of work into machines instead. Clerical workers then find themselves performing a single standardized operation relevant to machine processing of input information. Thus, office automation tends to reduce individual flexibility in determining the rate, methods, or route of work. The lower white-collar employee learns to adjust his actions to the requirements of the larger machine-based "system" in which he has a small, relatively specialized function (Rhee, 1968, p. 117).

A new field known as *operations research* applies computer techniques to routine decision making to obtain efficient solutions (Anshen, 1962; Ackoff, 1968). Decision-making machines take over functions previously performed by middle and lower managers. Instead of leaving routine decisions in management's hands, operations researchers develop mathematical relations among specified variables that form the basis of general rules for problem solution and decision making (Mann and Williams, 1968, p. 155). Thereafter the machines convert data into decisions on the basis of programmed instructions. This method of decision making works only when it is possible unambiguously to specify all variables relevant to a decision and to establish a mathematical form of solution. Still, operations research has shown that many minor officials who thought they were exercising creative initiative in their jobs were actually performing tasks capable of reduction to a complex sequence of rules. Data processing machines can replace people in the performance of such duties.

In general, office automation reduces the need for lower white-collar employees to exercise intellectual faculties in performance of their duties. Systems analysts and programmers build rationality into the machines, after which it is necessary only that the office staff follow the rules of timing, method, and sequence established by others on their behalf. As, historically, clerical and office workers have distinguished themselves from manual workers in terms of the higher intellectual demands of their front-office occupations, these workers experience chagrin at their reduced status. Moreover, this status is separated from higher-level jobs by educational requirements most office workers do not possess. Accordingly, easy career movement from routine white-collar posts to upper-level positions is likely to decrease with the progress of office automation (International Labour Office, 1967, p. 20). The professionalized "computer elite" is as socially and educationally distant from the lower office staff as line management is distant from the factory hands (Seligman, 1966, p. 193). These technological changes imply that the historic identification of white-collar workers with management and their resistance to trade unionism may be breaking down.

FREEDOM AND CONTROL

The hallmark of process technology is the integration of separate tasks into a total and continuous system. The system requires an omniscient hand at the top to design it. Once designed, it tends to supervise itself at the operating level because "noncompliance with rules designed into technical processes is likely to be followed by nonattainment of technical objectives" (Meissner, 1969, p. 26). In a sense, the boss is able to delegate supervisory responsibilities to the integrated machines (Michael, 1962, p. 115). This impersonal system is often a harsh taskmaster, increasing the premium on accuracy as well as management's ability to track down those who make errors (Woodward, 1965, p. 163). (Computer checking of tax returns has recently brought this development to the American public's attention.) For these reasons, the introduction of automation in most work settings involves centralization of authority, increasing levels of hierarchy, and impersonal controls over work behavior (Bright, 1958, pp. 142–143; Blau, 1968b; Richard Hall, 1969, p. 360).

The specter of centralized knowledge and power has raised fears of an automated Brave New World lurking around the corner. Many observers find the boss more formidable when he has a computer and a fancy vocabulary of systems analysis. However, people who worry about new trends toward centralization usually assume that they are the result of technological imperatives of automation. This assumption may prove unwarranted. As Meyer (1968) has argued, some centralization *apparently* derived from conversion to EDP *actually* mirrored informal status conflicts between computer technologists and line officials. Punishment-centered bureaucracy absorbed these status conflicts. Evaluation of automated centralization depends heavily upon whether apparent trends toward centralization reflect new technological imperatives, new constellations of intraorganizational status conflicts, or both.

Gloomy visionaries of a Brave New World tend also to overlook historical chronology. The drive for top-down control antedated automation, and was not caused by it. Exaggerated fears of cybernetic slavery ignore the assembly-line world. No one could have less freedom at work than the assembly-line operative. As we have observed, the monitoring and maintenance jobs automation creates are less controlled than the assembly-line jobs automation eliminates. Although office workers can look forward to more routinized tasks because of EDP, the semiautomated office environment remains substantially freer and more humane than the assembly line. Balancing gains and losses in work freedom resulting from automation, the losses may slightly outweigh the gains: the difference is small. Nonetheless, the foreseeable introduction of automation does not indicate any spectacular changes in the existing balance of freedom and control at work. No such changes have occurred thus far, and automation is now almost three decades old.

Recurrent imagery of a Brave New World or an automatic *1984* reflects popular fear that improved technology will at last permit elites to develop a foolproof system of controls capable of reducing subordinates to cybernetic slavery (Ellul, 1964; Silberman, 1966, ch. 6). No doubt, some elites vaguely hope that automated technology will have this effect. As machines are more docile than people, managements have historically tried to solve chronic labor problems by eliminating human laborers in favor of machines (Merton, 1957, p. 565; Heilbroner, 1962). People who can be replaced by talented machines are also in a weak bargaining position. Fear of replacement makes these workers more docile than they might otherwise be. Nowadays, many people are afraid that an automatic machine will take their job.

Like other people, those who service automatic machines develop ideas of what is "fair" in their workplace. When management tries to introduce automation into a nonautomated setting, it rediscovers this fact. Hence, even a hypothetically successful reduction of work behavior to programmed rules would leave untouched the propensity of humans to develop and communicate ideas that may or may not be harmonious with those of formal authorities (Crozier, 1964, p. 160). This capacity forces elites in automated and nonautomated systems alike to engage in a new covert, now overt dialogue with the informal social structure of the establishments they purport to command. At issue in this dialogue is the elite's right to command, that is, its legitimacy. Automation does not provide automatic moral legitimacy for those who claim the right to issue orders.

Automation or none, the more intense the drive for top-down control, the more boring and repetitive become jobs at the operational level. Naturally, workers dislike boring jobs. They resent the meaninglessness, powerlessness, and self-estrangement controlled jobs create. This spontaneous resentment puts control-seeking managements (public and private) into the position of attempting to force employees to behave in controlled ways they have a motive to avoid. Thus, a successful quest for top-down, total control creates a punishment-centered bureaucracy. What began as a purely administrative drive for technological efficiency turns into more or less conscious and vocal grass-roots dissatisfaction, focusing mass attention upon the legitimacy of the control-seeking elite, as we suggested in Fig. 16–2, depicting the spiraling relations between alienation and top-down controls. People require good and sufficient reason for loyal obedience, particularly when obedience is unpleasant. When elites fail to engage in a dialogue on this and to adapt their policies to increase the legitimacy of their controls, collective behavior in crowds is likely to occur (Blumer, 1951).

Automation does not change this basic structure of the organizational game. Hard-headed elites dislike constraints upon their control, as they always have. But the discomfort (or "alienation") of workers, resulting from their attempts at control, produces the dialogue about elite legitimacy. Because such dialogue limits an elite's absolute control, elites are motivated to employ technology to obtain external conformity when they cannot obtain a full subjective legitimation from the governed (Faunce, 1968, ch. 4). Insofar as automation seems to offer elites an opportunity to substitute external conformity for subjective consent, it responds to the tendency of elites to seek control independent of legitimation. The quest may be a mirage, because process technology seems incapable of overcoming the dependence of bureaucratic elites upon the ultimate consent of the workforce. However, whether technology will succeed in this quest remains an open question.

SUGGESTED READINGS

Blau, Peter M. and Richard W. Scott, *Formal Organizations.* San Francisco: Chandler, 1962.
> The most influential general textbook on sociological approaches to bureaucracy.

Blauner, Robert, *Alienation and Freedom.* Chicago: University of Chicago Press, 1964.
> A closely empirical comparison of four work settings with respect to the level and intensity of alienation in each. A basic study.

Dalton, Melville, *Men Who Manage.* New York: Wiley, 1959.
> A classic portrait of formal and informal organization in real industrial organizations. Emphasizes the critical importance of the informal social organization of managers.

Gouldner, Alvin W., *Patterns of Industrial Bureaucracy*. New York: The Free Press, 1954.

A modern sociological classic and a basic work in its field. Sophisticated, theoretical, and enjoyable.

Mayo, Elton and George W. Lombard, *Teamwork and Labor Turnover in the Aircraft Industry of Southern California*. Boston: Graduate School of Business Administration, Harvard University, 1944.

A good, interesting study in its own right, and the fastest way to understand what Mayo was driving at.

Seligman, Ben B., *Most Notorious Victory: Man in an Age of Automation*. New York: The Free Press, 1966.

An economist analyzes changing technologies and reaches gloomy conclusions about the future automation promised mankind.

Silberman, Charles, *The Myths of Automation*. New York: Harper & Row, 1966.

An editor of *Fortune* magazine dismisses the gloomy prophets of automated disaster and foresees a decent future.

Weber, Max, *Economy and Society*. New York: Bedminster Press, 1968.

The third volume contains Weber's analysis of bureaucracy in Chapter 11. But chapters 10 and 12 are also important because Weber was contrasting bureaucracy with other forms of administration.

Woodward, Joan, *Industrial Organization: Theory and Practice*. London: Oxford University Press, 1965.

A very important recent study of industrial management with emphasis on changes produced by automation.

CHAPTER 17

Computers, Sociology, and Society

The last chapter considered the nature and problems of industrial organizations and society. This chapter offers more detailed consideration of the nature and problems of technological society, concentrating on the computer.

This chapter begins with an analysis of the nature of computers. It then deals briefly with the effects of computers on sociology, especially the weight they introduce in favor of the statistical data, regardless of the validity and reliability of the statistics.

The most basic effects of computers on society result from the automated production they make possible and the forms of thought they encourage. In Chapters 15 and 16 we discussed problems they pose in automated production. In this chapter we consider biases they introduce into policy making. Computers demand precision and quantity, whereas the everyday world is commonly uncertain and qualitative. Computers, therefore, introduce a strong bias toward producing and using information and criteria that contradict realities they are intended to deal with.

Because computers lend themselves to centralization and homogenization, they may support trends contrary to individual freedom. This danger has been especially obvious in the development of centralized data banks on all citizens, a problem investigated here in some detail. It is up to men, not computers, to make the choices that will either fulfill such dangerous prospects or lead to the use of computers to enrich our everyday lives.

Computers are among the few unnatural objects on this earth deserving of the adjective "awesome." They are the achievement of man's efforts to realize a sublime dream. A sampling of items concerning their power is overwhelming:

1. A computerized teaching machine succeeds in teaching preschool children to read, without adult assistance, in thirty hours.
2. The flow of traffic in Toronto is almost totally controlled by computer.
3. Engineers can design workable plans quickly and accurately by "drawing" a plan on a display screen and communicating with the machine to modify the design.
4. Presidential election predictions of considerable accuracy have been made by computers from early returns, even before polls were closed in the Western states.

Awesome sights overwhelm some men with reverence, others with fear; few are blasé or neutral. For some men, computers seem to promise the coming of the New World of humanity; for others, they portend, in Yeats' words, a "Second Coming" of destruction. Similarly, some sociologists think the computer is the key to the maturity of the profession; others have never seen one (and would never care to).

Whether the reaction is reverence or fear, the result is to sanctify the computer, paying it homage of high order. This sanctification has resulted in an unbalanced use of the technology. The unabashed purpose of this chapter is to desanctify the image of the computer, because only then can its more balanced use follow.

Western societies have been characterized by a cultural fascination with numbers and accounting schemes. In the fifteenth century events moved this fascination into an obsession. At this point there is evidence that governments had learned to tabulate their tax and trade data for planning purposes. The Gregorian calendar, considerably more accurate than the previous dating scheme, was adopted in 1582. Science was showing signs of experimental principles, and there was a rebirth of mathematical reasoning.

In the seventeenth century Pascal invented a primitive computer. In the social arena governments were beginning to centralize data collection. Officials were charged to account for themselves by presenting statistics to show they were effective in their jobs. Cities would try to prove they were "better" than one another by enumerating their art works or their armament supplies. Hence, accounting took on both moral and political overtones.

The technological developments for the rise of the modern computer did not come until the 1800s. Charles Babbage worked out the details of an Analytical Engine, though he failed at its construction because the gears were too cumbersome. Then Hollerith conceived of using punched cards to tabulate information. Whereas the 1880 U.S. census took seven years to compile data on 50 million people, the 1890 census, using Hollerith's technology, tallied data on 62 million people in about two years. Since it was much easier to collect and organize information, intrusions into people's lives were initiated for ever increasing amounts of information. Hence, the mushrooming of paper-processing bureaucracies with their concomitant white-collar occupations.

THE MINDS OF COMPUTERS

Computers are symbol-manipulation devices. They receive information from the environment, remember it, work with it, and send responses back to the environment. Thus they think and behave, though not out of self-motivation. Their behavior is, unlike men's, readily understood and highly predictable (see Insert No. 50).

Computers obtain their information from *input* devices, by which it is fed directly to the *memory*. All information sent into the machine is stored before any other process occurs. At this point the supervisory unit, known as the *control*, examines the information, consisting of both data and instruc-

---

INSERT NO. 50

Computers

The first modern computers were *analog models*, that is, they solved problems through physical analogies. The slide rule and the speedometer are two common analog devices. Engineers discovered they could use electronic circuitry to build a model of some physical system of relationships. For instance, a volt could be scaled to represent 10 miles in a transportation system; the resistance placed upon circuits could be varied to represent the effects of certain "inputs" on travel. Because they simulate the appearance of something else—for example, a transportation system—analog computers are known as *simulations*.

The use of *digital* computers soon overtook that of analogs. Rather than measuring physical phenomena, digital computers count and manipulate symbols. Perhaps the most important step in their development was taken in 1945 when John von Neumann conceived of the stored program, a way to instruct the machine to avoid rewiring it for each new problem. Programs also add flexibility to computer operations, allowing the machine to change itself according to present conditions during its operation.

tions for its manipulation. The control unit oversees the actual data processing, which occurs in the *logic* or operations unit. Generally, there will be an interplay of information—from memory to logic and back again. Sometimes it may be necessary to call upon the *external memory*, units that augment the computer's internal memory by use of such external devices as magnetic tapes or disks. They store ancillary information in much the same way that reference books are available for human computation. At some point in the information processing, *output* devices, such as special printers or display screens, will convey the various results of the computer operations to the user.

The machinery on the market today varies in several dimensions. Most utilize electronic circuitry. With advances in this technology, larger memories are taking less space and are less troublesome to maintain. These electronic digital computers are the ones with whirring tapes and flashing-light panels prevalent in movies, television, and university computing centers. Other forms exist for cases when electronic circuitry is prone to failure. Pneumatic methods and fluid dynamics form more useful bases for computers in space, in extreme temperatures, and in explosion-prone settings.

The machines differ also with regard to memory capacity and speed. The internal memory capacity of computers has multiplied, so that earlier machines (a few years old) have limitations in storage ability affecting the complexity or scope of their potential operations. This limit is less with each new model. Similarly, the speed of machine operations has become truly incomprehensible. Early computers divided time into microseconds (millionths), then nanoseconds (billionths), and now femtoseconds (trillionths). Machines are so fast that, in a process known as time-sharing, more than one hundred people can communicate with the machine simultaneously on separate consoles, each under the impression that he is receiving its undivided attention.

Computers cannot, like man, glibly devise problems for solution. Their input must include a statement of the problem, inserted into the machine not as a query, but as a list of explicit steps for the computer to perform. These instructions, prepared in a special language, form the *program*.

Given a problem to solve, the computer is still helpless, for it needs appropriate information for a solution. Because it is immobile and lacks the versatile sensory organs of man, a computer cannot collect this data on its own. In fact, the machine is quite rigid about the form in which it receives data. The primary input-gathering devices to date are card readers, tape readers, keyboards, and, to a much lesser extent, optical scanners. These devices convey information to the computer in terms of the only symbols it can accept: binary-coded *bits* (units) of information.

It is beyond the scope of this discussion to explain why binary codes are the basis of computer language; let us note simply that machine circuitry has switches that can be "on" or "off." To activate these switches, a "1" signifies an on operation, while a "0" signifies an off operation. When a computer "reads" a letter or number, it codes a sequence of zeroes and ones. Because its switches can be only on or off, a black-white mentality underlies computer operations.

There is always a point at which connotations of meaning entered as input are lost. Frequently, information must be entered with more precise meaning than is desirable. For example, consider a college admissions committee that decides to place all applicants' materials into the computer as an aid in selecting the top students. Some data, such as college board scores, can enter without change. But how should high school grades be recorded to correct for variation in school quality? What about letters of recommendation? In the first case, the committee will need to find an arithmetic way of "correcting" the grades; for example, multiplying those from more highly rated schools by some constant number. In the second case, the letter contents must be reduced to categories of judgment (unqualified yes, favorable with qualification, unfavorable). Thus, precision may be lost while the illusion of precision is increased.

Assume that the committee settles these data-coding problems and has agreed on a "formula" rating some pieces of information as worth more than others. Theoretically, it is possible to score people for various characteristics and then choose the best people from these scores. This leads to the second quirk in computer mentality: every direction must result in closure; a decision leads "either" to one place "or" to another. This is not to imply that "maybes" cannot occur. In the social sciences, and in everyday decision problems, there are often instances when a conclusion may be one thing or another. The computer must be told exactly what maybe represents: a toss of a coin, a specific probability, or something else. In mathematical parlance, when the operation process has probabilistic steps it is *stochastic*. Decisions in which probabilities of outcomes are featured force the user to specify beyond the everyday language of "more likely," "tends to," "sometimes," to an exact numerical translation of meaning.

The fictional admissions committee, then, cannot say: "Look each guy over and pick out the best." Rather, it must say something like this:

> Here are individuals with five pieces of information about each in the form of scores. Multiply each of these scores by an appropriate constant. If someone is missing a score, send him to the "Incomplete" file. Add the weighted scores for the others and rank them by these weights. Count up and mark as "reject" all those below the 75th percentile. If ties prevent a clean break at the 75th percentile, work up so that the entire tie group is rejected. Print "accept" next to the names of all those above the cut-off.

Note the seemingly picayune quality of this crude outline of instructions. Exceptions must be anticipated or, in this instance, all incomplete cases would be rejected. In addition, the ending directions must include a rule for dealing with ties.

A device for displaying the general outline of instructions is the *flow chart,* which enables decision makers and programmers to grasp at a glance main steps in the processing instructions. Figure 17–1 presents a general flow chart for the college acceptance decision. This diagram demonstrates another feature of the input instructions: all processing is sequential. Ultimately, all instructions must have a processual order. This is not generally a liability in numerical computations, but it can be in less exact problems.

Once the committee has systematized its decision process and prepared the data code, the programmer can start work. He must prepare the instructions according to the rules of a machine language. *Languages* are recognizable in the literature by their upper case acronym names. The most widely used are FORTRAN (for scientific work) and COBOL (for business work). At times the programmer may work with language sporting more novel names, such as JOVIAL, JOSS, LOLITA, PLEASE, LISP, DYNAMO, BASIC, GASP, FSL. To many, the alluring features of programming cease at this point. For every statement in the flow chart, a large number of individual "sentences" may have to be put to the machine. Consider the small issue of ties in scores. The programmer must write something like this:

> Look at the case equal to or greater than 74.9 percentile. Note its score. Look at the next greater case. Note its score. Are they the same? If not, then all cases including the first read get a "reject." If the scores are the same, go to the next one. When you find a score that is different, it and all those remaining are marked "accept."

In other words, concepts and directions clear to us in our everyday language need complete definition in the program.

Note, too, that the programmer has further specified 75th percentile to mean "more than 74.9." The requirements of the machine or the language may result in changes of meanings in the instructions. Perhaps the committee, if asked, would have opted for 75.4. This is a trivial example, but if there are many instances in a complicated job where the programmer may select an alternate and unintended procedure, the room for error becomes considerable. Similar changes in meaning occur because of sequencing demands or problems in machine memory capacity or machine speed. Thus, *translation may result in a violation of one's intentions;* the computer will not operate as intended by its human master. Or one may not be able to state his intentions well enough to program them.

Given the exactness of the programming task, there must be considerable trial-and-error before achieving the final instructions. This process is known as "debugging." Not only must the instructions be translated meaningfully, but the translation itself must be absolutely accurate. No grammatical errors are permissible—a misplaced comma in an otherwise perfect program makes it no better than gibberish to the machine. Again, the computer's circuitry makes it intolerant of any vagueness or mistake.

Figure 17-1. Computer Programming

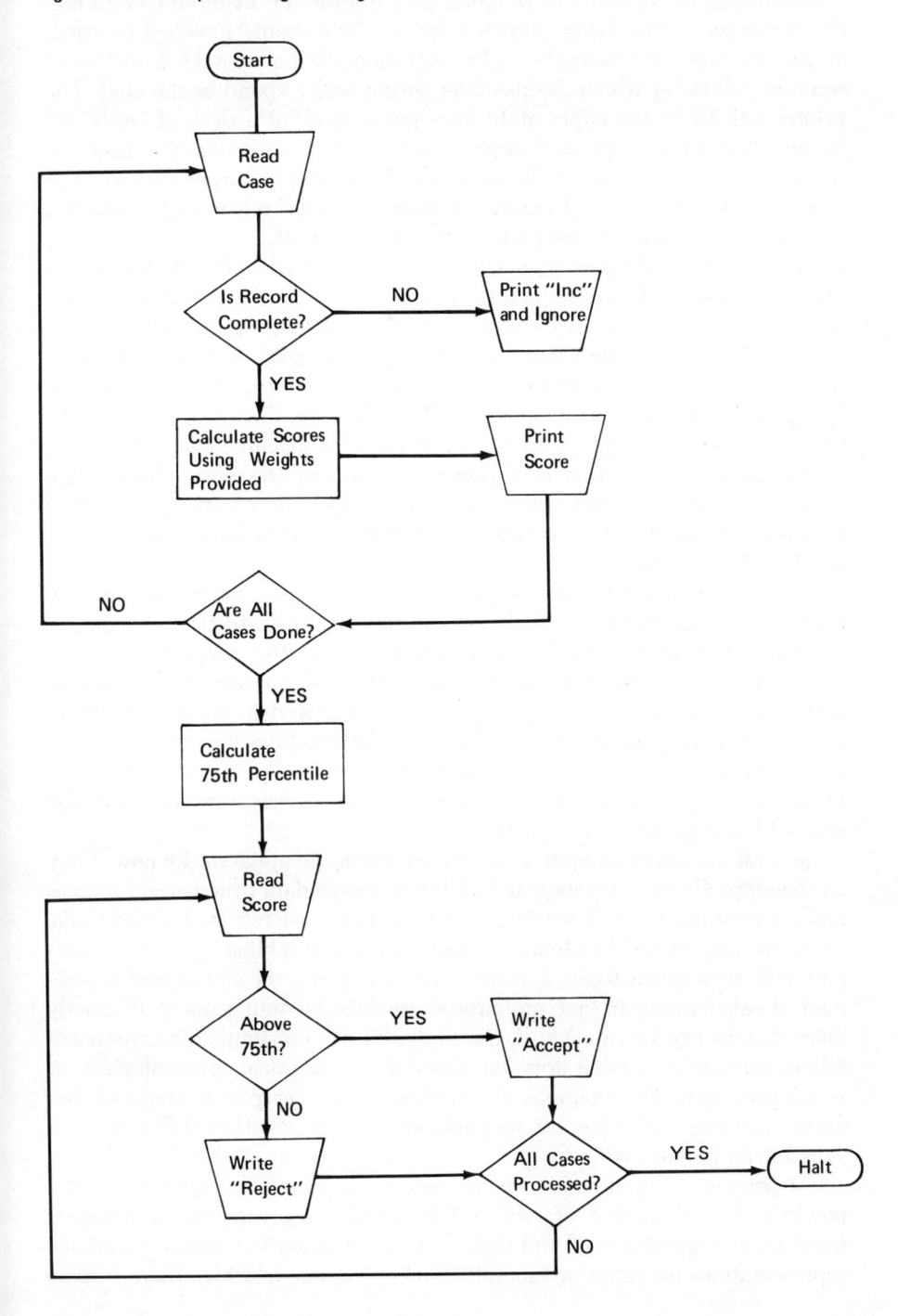

Following many hours of program preparation, the material can go into the computer (after being prepared for machine input: punched on cards or put on tape, for example). The operation itself may take a matter of seconds, following which the machine output will respond as directed. The printer will spew out paper at 15 lines per second, or a deck of cards will be punched, or a graph will appear on a cathode ray tube. The response will be set by the needs of the user and the available output devices. The machine may even print "I enjoyed working for you," but in fact, through a very circuitous route, the user will be thanking himself.

As we saw in Chapter 16, machines were first used to handle the repetitive tasks one finds so frequently in industrial manufacturing or clerical work. Once the algorithm for a procedure has been programmed (such as the calculation of a chi-square statistic), it is usually possible to use the same program with any accompanying data. Hence, the expense and time spent for programming is quickly offset. In one documented example, human calculation of pi (with the assistance of a machine calculator) took about ten hours. An experienced programmer did all the work (defining the operations, flow charting, program writing, deck preparation) in eighty minutes. The computer then needed only three seconds for the actual computation (Fink, 1966).

Though meticulous, the computer is not inflexible, for it may be programmed to modify itself. Much work in the area of "artificial intelligence" illustrates this approach. An outstanding case is the program used for playing checkers. The computer was instructed to look ahead a few moves and evaluate ensuing board positions. Then it stored in its memory those sequences of play resulting in success. As the machine continued to play, its experience grew and its tactics improved. Eventually, it defeated its own programmer with consistency, and soon overtook a checkers champion who had not lost a game in eight years.

Several classes of computer operations should be apparent by now. First, its speed, prodigious memory, and ability to merge data from several sources make a computer useful for information storage and retrieval. In scientific work, various retrieval systems can provide a list of bibliographic references pertinent to a given topic. Second, a computer can do logical and mathematical calculations; in fact, any process translatable into sequential, exactly defined steps can be run. Third, the computer can do simulation experimentation, serving as a laboratory for the study of physical, psychological, or social processes. For example, the simulated checker player could be run under variations of rules for remembering to see whether differences resulted in its playing skill.

At present, computers are not notably intelligent. Their genuine mental power is less than that of, say, a fish. Their sensory apparatus severely limits their "experiencing," and their "acts" are limited to immobile symbolic representations on paper or tubes. Samuel's program, in which there is some adaptability of the machine, is an exception. (For a lucid sympathetic discussion of the present state of computer intelligence, see Fink, 1966.) They cannot use judgment, speculate, jump to conclusions, or exercise creativity in the human sense of the words. They can achieve complete accuracy in grinding out information that is erroneous because of a validity error in the program. One can always, in moments of exasperation, pull the plug. Yet no one does, because both users and laymen harbor an exalted image of computers and believe the machine is in control. This is an erroneous and potentially disastrous conception, as we shall see in the remainder of this chapter (see also Insert No. 51).

COMPUTERS IN SOCIOLOGY

Analogous to the Whorfian hypothesis that differences in language imply differences in ways of perceiving the world, is the hypothesis that diverse measurement and analysis devices affect the way an observer, scientific or not, looks at the world. Someone who is both a cook and a chemist will, if handed a bag of flour, behave one way if there is analytical equipment nearby and another way if there is culinary equipment. The availability of materials at hand will set limits on whether the person chemically analyzes the flour or bakes it. This is not to say that the person is blind to other possibilities, for he could probably cook in the laboratory or improvise an analysis using culinary tools. But, given man's general tendency toward consistent behavior in specific settings, he would not be likely to break his habits without encouragement.

The sociologists' repertoire of measurement devices is not extensive, and its components have been available for a long time. In the nineteenth century, official statistics (information collected by authorities in the course of official duty) were the basic data source. Soon behavioral observation and varieties of the attitude questionnaire were added. In the latter cases, rather crude category schemes provided the basis for preparation of data for statistical manipulation. Yet quantification did not predominate in sociological research until recent years. Thus, in the early forties, most research investigations in the major sociological journals were of a qualitative case study or ethnographic nature; but studies of this kind were seldom published in the mid-sixties (Brown and Gilmartin, 1969). By 1969 the American Sociological Association sponsored the first yearbook volume of *Sociological Methodology;* every paper in the volume concerned quantitative research. No doubt, the introduction of the computer facilitated the move toward a quantitative emphasis.

Three broad areas of research benefited from the introduction of the computer to sociology in the early fifties. In each case the technology brought advance to the discipline, through making previously impractical research problems more feasible. Yet there were also unfavorable effects in each case.

1. *Official statistics.* Much of the earliest sociological research utilized officially collected data, such as death, suicide, and marriage statistics. Durkheim's *Suicide* (1951) is perhaps the best known for its skill in attempting to demonstrate the relationship between an individual's position in the social structure and his likelihood of committing suicide. The computer provided new possibilities for research based upon official statistics. First, large amounts of data could be stored and retrieved at low cost. Certain problems, such as comparative national studies, were very costly or too unwieldy before the computer came into use. In addition, the computer's powers spurred the development and use of complicated analytical techniques. One subdiscipline of sociology, demography (the study of population), has proliferated in so many special procedures and techniques that it may soon assert itself as a separate discipline.

INSERT NO. 51

Artificial Intelligence

There is considerable debate over the possibility of *artificial intelligence*, the potential ability of human-like machines (automata) to duplicate intellectual functions of the human brain, perhaps even to surpass it. Here is one viewer's conclusion:

> A number of enterprising investigators are busily devising ever more complex automata intended to reproduce some of the essential functions of the human brain-mind. Grey Walter's mechanical "tortoise" and CORA and Ross Ashby's *homeostat* are among the most illustrious of these imitation men. Provided we do not assume that they embody all the essential properties of man, they may serve to illumine the nature of human abilities and disabilities. In spite of his critics, Grey Walter makes no exaggerated claims on behalf of his own automata. They bear about as much relation to the human brain, he says, as a hacksaw does to the human hand.
>
> In his brilliant essay on Computing Machinery and Intelligence, the late A. M. Turing considered the theological objection to the view that machines can think. A theologian might argue that God has given a thinking soul only to man but not to any animal. But, says Turing, it would not be beyond the power of an omnipotent Almighty to confer an immortal soul on an elephant, even if He felt it would only be appropriate to do so if the elephant were to be equipped with a brain capable of ministering to his soul. The idea of a thinking machine is no more sacrilegious than the idea of an elephant with a soul. . . .

On the other hand, most of those who utilize official statistics fail to acknowledge certain long-standing difficulties. Most serious has been the failure to deal with biases in collection of these data. Douglas (1967) has persuasively demonstrated that even the most "objective" data, based upon suicide reports, are so fraught with problems of interpretation that elaborate statistical analysis is virtually meaningless (see also Chapter 20). The variations in the way coroners interpret laws defining suicide vary too much for us to claim that the suicide rate for even one state is meaningful. Although investigators have written about these biases for years, they have ignored the implication that the data cannot be interpreted until the specific biases are known.

2. *Survey research.* The social survey based upon the attitude questionnaire or direct interview was used prior to the computer; however, time and the tedium of preparing the results prevented the use of large samples, large numbers of questions, and complicated analyses (see Chapter 10 on

> It would seem that at least three things characteristically human are out of reach of contemporary automata. In the first place, they are incapable of laughter (or tears); secondly, they do not blush; thirdly, they do not commit suicide. It is conceivable that robots of the future may be capable of all three. However, until we have a better understanding of the nature of laughter it would be unwise to assume that we shall be able to teach robots how to laugh. . . .
>
> In general, whatever refinements and novelties are introduced into artifacts in the foreseeable future, man is destined to remain for a very long time, the lightest, most reliable, most cheaply serviced and the most versatile general-purpose computing device made in large quantities by unskilled labour, an observation appropriately attributed to a naval officer.
>
> The logical system which is embodied in a computer is a *tool* which in and by itself is utterly useless. It requires for its logical completion someone who is able to use it in a fashion and for a purpose not fully predetermined by the tool. As Michael Polanyi has made abundantly clear, to elevate the machine to the logical or psychological status of its maker is to commit the behaviourist's error when he confuses the observed "mind" with the observing mind. The thought or purpose which we are able to detect in the working of a machine is properly speaking the thought or purpose of the designer of the machine, for the most cunningly devised automaton is, in principle, in the same logical class, in relation to its maker, as the most rudimentary flint scraper of primitive man.

From John Cohen, *Human Robots in Myth and Science* (London: Allen & Unwin, 1966), pp. 137–138.

questionnaires). That the computer changed all this can be seen through the 1966 educational study known as the Coleman-Campbell report. This survey sampled almost six hundred thousand school youngsters from about three thousand eight hundred schools throughout the United States with questionnaires numbering several hundred items. Then they merged the students' responses with those of teachers and administrators from the same schools. One statistical technique used was regression analysis, which assists in identifying the "significant" variables from a large number of factors that could be operating at the same time. One result of the study was to support claims that minority students benefited by attendance in integrated schools. Clearly, this work is a tribute to the accomplishments possible with survey research and computer technology.

Yet the fact that such studies can be done is not sufficient reason for doing them. One pitfall in survey research is that it often focuses upon narrowly defined topics with measurements both easily obtained and reasonable. Hence, there are studies of premarital sexual behavior that never mention the words "love" or "ecstasy," and studies of hospital workers that ignore compassion. One enormously expensive study of happiness tells us little more than that to be black, poor, or sick is to be unhappy.

A related problem is that of omitting any rationale for data collection. Because the machine can quickly perform search techniques to locate patterns in the data, it is tempting to hand all work over to it. Hence, one may collect huge amounts of data, invading respondents' privacy to the extreme by asking any question or recording any behavior that could be "relevant." As this research begins without any conceptual base, the results are limited to statements about idiosyncrasies, without providing any logic for generalization. The use of theory to select a problem becomes "old-fashioned," and the word "theoretical" is even used pejoratively by some. What these investigators ignore is that theories often force us to look at the parts of the world not amenable to coding for a computer.

3. *Simulation.* This procedure, virtually nonexistent prior to the computer, allows a theorist to set up an artificial working model of behavior by means of computer operations. Thus, the investigator can test his ideas in the simulated model rather than in the real world. Voting prediction models are a very simple simulation (Pool et al., 1965). On the basis of census, poll, and voting data, estimates are developed for each type of voter in a state. For example, a "small-city Protestant Democratic female" is given a probability of voting in a certain way in an election. These "simulated individuals" are combined proportionately according to their number within the state, and elementary mathematical calculations provide the predicted voting outcome. Many simulations are not so quantitative. Based upon the work of George Homans, the Gullahorns (1970) have created a simulation

of elementary social behavior which produces "conversation" between two individuals.

The major potential for error in simulation research concerns its validity (whether the model is a good reproduction or not). All simulations are simplifications, but they are sufficiently lifelike to be treated as if they were mirrors of reality, which is not the case. Two problems arise here. One is that the simulation may become accepted as a "good" sociological theory or explanation scheme before it has been tested against real world data. Another is that social policy recommendations may be initiated because a manipulation in the simulated world is successful in alleviating a problem. A harmless illustration is the result of one university's use of a simulation to schedule classes and rooms. The simulation provided an excellent guideline for efficient use of class space and personnel but, unfortunately, failed to include any consideration of classroom cleanup and, frequently, blackboards were so dirty by midday as to be useless. If this oversight could occur, imagine what might result from use of a simulation to solve racial discord or campus uprising.

Today the computer symbolizes a growing division in sociology: For some it reprsents an invaluable tool leading to many breakthroughs; for others it represents a frivolous plaything distracting men from truly productive work. Perhaps it is a worthy symbol of this conflict, but it was not its cause.

As a final note, it must be added that this discussion applies to sociology as a *discipline,* that is, to the public and hence published display of information. A very small proportion of sociologists contribute to this public production. Most Ph.D.s have only a perfunctory introduction to statistics. Sibley's (1963) survey revealed that only a tenth of the sociologists in his sample had received any indoctrination, formal or informal, on computer technology and use. Thus, many sociologists are as naïve as laymen about the rationale of digital computation.

COMPUTER TECHNOLOGISTS AND SOCIETY

In order to understand the adoption of computer technology in society, as well as the public image of computers, it is useful to examine the mentality of those men closest to the machines. Computers were developed by engineers, and the engineering ethos pervades the minds of others in society who press for the adaptation of computers in all spheres of activity—whether in business, government, education, research, or even home life.

Americans are likely to be unaware that there is an important semantic distinction between the words "science" and "technology." Historically, American scientists, more than those of other countries, have been technologically oriented (Struik, 1962). Whereas science is concerned with the systematic and shareable organization of knowledge of the empirical world, technology is the development of skills, procedures, and equipment to achieve desired results. Technology always implies the concept of *utility*, whereas pure science does not. Although we think of our society as "scientific," there are twice as many professional engineers as scientists in the country and many of the scientists work explicitly at solving technical problems.

Furthermore, engineers are servants of others or members of a team. Over three fourths are employees of industrial organizations, and another 10 percent or so work for governmental agencies. Hence, their principal domain is technology in the service of economic and industrial objectives (including the technology of war). Their concern is control over the environment for the satisfaction of material needs.

The ideology underlying engineering is one of "rational decision making," meaning that the optimal choice should be made in any situation. Optimization refers to maximizing profits of an activity while minimizing costs; efficiency sees to it that scarce resources are used to their fullest potential. Yet, as Soderberg (1967) has noted, "Collective man's rationality is only a thin veneer" covering "frightening propensities for cruelty and irrationalism." The reason is that the equation for optimization is not applied to many things valued by members of a society: compassion, tolerance, ethics, spirituality, beauty, sensuality, and other human qualities.

Engineers function in a sphere of life wherein quantification without loss in translation is frequently possible, and quantity is supreme. Dollar costs are a simple matter in an organization devoted to development of profits and minimization of monetary expenditures. Humane features such as "good working conditions" are frequently justified on grounds that "they pay." Adaptation of any technological advance becomes a relatively uncomplicated case of calculating probable costs against profits and comparing the results to costs and profits of other alternatives.

In other than economic affairs, completing an optimization equation is much more difficult. Since the world is seen to include only those elements which are quantifiable, valued ends are selected only from the class of objects that can be measured. Thus, elements not easily quantified come to be undermined. The result can be technological tyranny: New techniques are introduced to society because they mean "progress," but progress consists of a limited set of quantifiable goals. This state of affairs has appeared in the area of education today, where some define learning in terms of what teaching machines can teach (which happened to be factual material) rather than in terms of display of judgment or creativity.

Engineers are not unaware that they ignore "humane values" in their work. In fact, they refer to them as "externalized" aspects, unconsidered in their calculations. Yet, no matter how much verbal recognition is paid to externalized elements, it remains that they are treated as secondary. This is further demonstrated in that professional journals (such as *Computers and Automation* and *Educational Technology*) usually report only positive (quantifiable) effects of a technique. The "news items" in these journals cite improvements in computer technology, new groups who have adopted the technique (and warnings about those who inhibit the technology's proliferation).

Technical experts are not fully professional in the sense that they are self-policing with regard to standards of behavior. Being in the service of others, they do not question the ultimate value of their work for, after all, they are not the ones with ultimate decision-making power. It should not be surprising, then, to find them tacitly supporting conservative ideals—those values espoused by men in power. This is evident in their rhetoric to the lay public, which also often ignores any mention of costs. Consider this statement:

> The newest machines have grace, lightness, elegance, and a parsimony of movement. Little elegant systems, performing great feats of production, are replacing the iron leviathans of the early 20th century. . . . Man, of his own will and design, passes over the threshold into a truly New Time. Labor, once believed to be a curse on man, and later a kind of penance and character builder, is destined for marked decline. . . . The community is increasingly rationalized and instrumental in its pattern of social action. Personal civic concern . . . is being replaced by a comprehensive and compassionate well-trained civil bureaucracy. The heartlessness predicted by the early 20th century critics has not materialized. . . . Education will be a less nucleated place-centered activity, and more of a feature of life itself. The drop-out problem will decline. . . . The position seems to be one of "Why wait?" One is reminded of a news commentator's parting phrase in the days of full-time radio. He signed off with "Take it easy, but take it." The tactic, however, is not one of the populist movement and personal direction by the masses. Rather [it is one of] cool-headedness, professional expertise, and calculated corporate love (Buck, 1969).

Besides the obvious illogic of linking calculation with love, other problems arise from a statement of this nature. It assumes a naïve materialistic theory of social change in which technology is readily adapted by society. It also presumes a unanimity in society as to what are the favored ends. It ignores that not everyone will "benefit."

Jaki (1969, p. 28) noted, in a similar context, "epigones [imitators] whose number and vociferousness always outweigh the wise counsel of masters lose no time in presenting hypotheses as demonstrated verities." Indeed, the major figures in the development of computer technology, going back all the way to its sixteenth-century roots, have displayed a cautious attitude that has not proved contagious among the current users of the technology. To illustrate, von Neumann recognized that although thinking, in the sense of analytical problem solving, can be attributed to machines, this does not mean they are conscious. Yet among those committed to the idea of "artificial intelligence" can be found one who states that "machines may well have erotic fantasies when machine 'perceives' the rising nipple of a well-turned dial."

In a similar vein, Norbert Wiener (1964), the father of cybernetics (the science of control systems), noted in his last work his fears about some of those who followed him in advocating automation (see Insert No. 52). Some of these men, he suggests, are impatient because man is undependable and unpredictable. Others desire to avoid personal responsibility for a dangerous or disastrous decision by placing the responsibility elsewhere, as on a mechanical device. He called both types gadget worshipers, who deserved to be called sinful for advocating technology to the public without exercising foresight and circumspection. He pointed out that in the past defective engineering decisions did not threaten human destruction.

The point of this discussion is not to condemn those who plump for automation. That many of their claims are naïve is understandable, for they represent some of the brightest people in society, who at the same time have been trained in specialized, nongeneralist schools. Furthermore, they are frequently the servants of others who force upon them single-minded goals, such as increasing profits or producing students who make high college board scores. As we shall see, it is not so much that the claims of technological experts are wrong, as that they are incomplete, shortsighted, and narrow.

Engineers write the computer credo, but programmers are the priests who service it. In 1960 their number was in the thousands; by 1970 there were three hundred thousand, and more could easily have been accommodated.

Programming is a technical job that seems to require a particular type of person rather than a highly educated one. A high school diploma is no longer mandatory for obtaining basic skills, because the task requires a rigorous attention to detail and a preference for closure in thinking, and not necessarily mathematical knowledge. In an everyday sense, programmers are so different from other workers that some firms are dissatisfied with computers because of the programmers that go with them rather than with the machines themselves (Todd, 1970).

What is so strange about programmers and related personnel? Often, they display a strange psychological stance toward the machine. They will give it a name and make it "do human things"—print out Snoopy saying "Happy New Year" or play jingle bells. They attribute motives and emotions to the machine and use its "states of mind" as explanations for any unusual features of its performance. They "protect" it from others by keeping it "off limits" and by making its use indirect and bureaucratically routinized.

INSERT NO. 52

On Norbert Wiener's *Cybernetics*

Although few sociologists would count Norbert Wiener among their number, he deserves regard on two counts. First, Wiener's autobiographies (*Ex-Prodigy; I Am a Mathematician*) form a notable case history of what it is like to be an exceptionally gifted member of our society. He attended Tufts at the age of eleven, entered Harvard for a doctorate in biology at fifteen, and studied philosophy and mathematics with Bertrand Russell at Cambridge. After making numerous significant contributions to engineering and physics, Wiener began to explore the borderlines of many fields, including medicine, biology, and sociology.

His first interdisciplinary contribution was *Cybernetics* (1948), the term he coined to stand for the field of control and communication theory, whether in man or machine. This technical work elaborates the basic concepts of the field, including such ideas as the self-correcting system, feedback, and communication network. Wiener argued that only a small, close-knit group could ever have a high measure of homeostasis (internal stability); this idea is much in contrast to those of sociological systems theorists such as Talcott Parsons. Second, he noted that in the social sciences the coupling between the observed phenomenon and the observer is hardest to minimize. Hence, he argued that, because statistical studies could never be adequate for a full understanding of man, "unscientific" narrative methods would also be needed. This conclusion about sociological methodology is also the opposite of what sociological systems theorists have held.

The Human Use of Human Beings (1950) was Wiener's first detailed exposition of the cybernetic approach to society. He conceived of society as a communication structure. This provocative book ranges over many topics, including an analysis of why human society is not analogous to animal society, why techniques of secrecy or communication jams are used, and the role of the intellectual in shaping society. Throughout his book are both logical and value-based arguments for a social organization premised upon freedom rather than coercion.

God and Golem (1964), published posthumously, is a poignant elaboration of the problems of knowledge, communication, and power in our technological world. Wiener describes his distress at the way technicians had misread his directives for the use of cybernetics in the control of society. Selflessly, he concludes that he had been wrong: The social sciences are a bad proving ground for the ideas of cybernetics because inhumane values are served too easily. Those interested in developing systems of control, he suggests, should best remain with the physical or biological systems, wherein the relationships under study have existed for eons and are less likely to be reversed by some poor decisions on the part of man.

Often overlooked is the implicit power of programmers. Because they are expert regarding what the machine can and cannot do, they can tell their users (the managers and bureaucratic officers) what can and cannot be done. In programming, they can even change others' intentions without notice. One consequence is that some computer users do their own programming whenever possible. Another result is that programmers have a special opportunity for white-collar crime: a notorious example is the woman who cued the computer to write her a payroll check every eighteen minutes. (She was eventually caught because her mail carrier tired of delivering the daily load and reported her.) And there are stories of the best programmers hiding their thefts in such clever ways that other programmers cannot find them. However, an interesting feature of the occupation is that it is trying to destroy itself. Many programmers are working diligently to eliminate the complexity of languages so that within a few years most people will be able to program most problems on their own, using a language very similar to the vernacular. BASIC is one such program language already in use. Analogously, key-punching, the transfer of coded data to punched cards, surely among the world's most tedious jobs, may also disappear soon if optical scanners develop as promised.

Computers in Society

Except for the trivial use of hand tools by some other primates, only man is a technological animal. His prodigious reasoning ability has allowed him to compensate for his physical inadequacies, and his history traces his attempt to further increase the use of prostheses as labor-saving devices. Why man seems propelled to move in this direction is a mystery. Now that the computer is available as a mental prosthesis, the point of this labor reduction becomes even more mysterious and pressing: What will he do with his time?

Technical experts have all the answers—or so it seems. One can imagine a mythical society in which, whenever a new technology appears, the "compassionate, rational" decision makers sit down and say, "Now what effects will this invention have on our society, and how can we introduce its use so as to minimize the unpleasant or negative ones?" In the case of the computer, based upon their study of experts, they might take the following line of reasoning: computers introduced into economic organizations will cause shifts in occupational requirements (Simon, 1965). For many people, the work week will be shortened and they will have to learn to judge the worth of their everyday lives on bases other than work performance (Buckingham, 1961, ch. 9). We know, too, that computers will free individuals from tedious work and give individuals more time for creative thought (McLuhan, 1966). By making computers a utility (Parkhill, 1966), everyone can tap into massive reference libraries and computational assistance centers (Gerard, 1967). Why not start, then, by placing this new invention in educational institutions and training our young to adapt to a society where the computer will serve as a prosthetic device in all areas of decision making (Brickman and Lehrer, 1969)? As the computer is introduced into other spheres of life, we will have technicians to fill the new occupational roles, decision makers sophisticated about the limits of technology, and a public capable of using the computer creatively in leisure pursuits. In this way social disruptions will be minimized and individuals will not suffer. For our society such planning (even if desired and feasible) would be too late, because the American economic system has already pressed computers onward, notably in areas of industry, education, and government.

In 1964 a committee on cybernation reported to the president that "radical new strategies would be required to save the nation from unprecedented disorder." In response to these fearful announcements, Silberman (1966) investigated the impact of automation in the United States. He discovered that no fully automated process exists for any major product in the United States, nor is it expected in the near future. What he did find was that much of the literature failed to distinguish what is scientifically possible and what is economically or otherwise feasible. For example, in the early sixties there was much mass media publicity about Transferobot, an inexpensive automaton which was supposed to "do anything that hands born of woman can do." After an extensive search, only six customers for the device had been located, and only one was satisfied. That one useful robot replaced one man.

We can say that, for the time being, the entry of computers into work organizations does not cause large-scale unemployment (Silberman, 1966; Simon, 1965). But if we evaluate computers solely on the basis of labor statistics, we are restricting ourselves to quantitatively measurable results. Gross statistics obscure pertinent qualitative differences. Because Ivan Light has discussed the effects of automation on work organizations (see Chapter 16), let us move on to consider its effects upon others in contact with the computerized bureaucracy. Seldom considered are those workers on other levels whose job classifications remain, yet whose tasks are modified to adapt to the rigid computer mentality.

It would be irresponsible to claim that the computer is the source of depersonalization and alienation in bureaucracies, for the literary evidence alone (such as Gogol's stories of nineteenth-century clerks) demonstrates that these patterns of interaction have existed a long time. Certainly, though, computers have exacerbated the entire situation. For example, on the one hand, they have made it possible for companies to provide many more services (e.g., varieties of telephones) to more people. On the other hand, all rules of behavior have been constrained by the rules of machine operations. This is an ironic choice on the part of managers and administrators, because it would seem that the optimal use of men and machines would be to let each perform at his best capabilities. For machines, it would mean handling repetitive, clear-cut cases; for men, it would mean using intuition to handle the many exceptions that arise in everyday negotiations. Instead, exceptions are made to fit the preprogrammed mold, and workers are merely interfaces between client and machine. The process appears efficient, because "all cases are handled," although no one asks whether they have been handled well or correctly.

There is a more insidious feature of extensive computerization. If the computer makes a mistake, it is very difficult to account for the error. Here is a trivial example from the news, which is only a more novel variation of the type of problem all of us face with increasing frequency:

> When a business executive repeatedly received parking violations on his car from a city he had never been in, he finally dispatched punch cards to the traffic bureau, which stated:
>
> Apparently the letters sent to the humans who try to control you are being disregarded. The violation is not valid. I suggest you instruct them to erase the ticket from your memory bank. I hope you can make them understand.
>
> The machine's human programmers returned a deck that read: "Dear Human. At last I have found someone who understands my language" (adapted from *Time*, March 2, 1970).

Imagine the continual irritation this situation must have provoked. Why did it take an extraordinary, imaginative effort to move toward solution? First, there may have been no way for the staff to feed the man's complaint into the acceptable codes; hence, they may have ignored all his letters. Second, the process may be so fully automated that no human ever saw the correspondence. Third, there is a commonplace attitude that "if it's from the machine, it's correct." Records of any kind are always hard to change but, when they are the product of a mysterious "electronic brain" that prints clean neat rows of type, the "truth value" of the item increases even more. Thus, the machine is innocent until proven guilty by the client. (So Wiener's prediction that gadget worshipers pass their responsibility onto the machine is shown to be correct [see Insert No. 53].)

We have touched lightly upon a variety of effects from broad-scale economic advantages to everyday irritation that automation brings into the working world. The problem of making predictions about the impact of any technology should now be apparent. First, there is often a lack of data to show what has happened. Second, it is difficult to separate effects of the technique from other historical trends. Third, it appears that techniques are not the cause of change so much as the people who use and command them.

Computers and Knowledge

Computers have been domiciled on college campuses since the first one, ENIAC, was built at the University of Pennsylvania. As we saw in our discussion of computers and sociology, there is little doubt of their benefits as tools in scientific research, for both their speed in reducing data and their ability to solve complex problems.

INSERT NO. 53

"Chalk One Up for Humans vs. Computers"

The defeat of the machine is a sufficient novelty to be a newsworthy item. The following appeared in a daily column under the headline "Chalk One Up for Humans vs. Computers."

> It was the Baltimore Symphony Orchestra's All Request Night, preceding which patrons were to vote for the selections they wished to hear by punching small holes in the spaces indicated on an IBM card.
>
> Girl Scouts then collected the punch cards and took them to the stage where an IBM card sorter was ostensibly waiting to do its thing.
>
> However, the recalcitrant card sorter just leaned back and refused to work on a Saturday evening, much to the embarrassment of the IBM "systems engineers" who were present.
>
> The IBM people didn't waste any time in stating that the real culprit was the symphony patron who obviously didn't know the correct way to punch out the holes.
>
> When it was announced that the IBM card sorter had hopelessly jammed and that selections for the evening would be democratically determined by an anachronistic show-of-hands, there was a loud round of applause. The "system" had finally been beaten.
>
> When the patrons raised their hands to vote for one of three choices for the first selection of the evening, it was obvious that the votes were equally divided and only an arbitrary decision on the part of the announcer and a very Spiro Agnewish statement from him convinced the audience that one particular selection had received more votes than the others.
>
> The stage personnel were apparently so unnerved by the incident that they forgot to turn out the house lights when the concert finally began.
>
> The word from the folks at the Symphony office is that a new plan may be used next year to tabulate the requests.
>
> In the meantime, they are eligible for membership in the steadily growing ranks of the Organization Holding That Humans Are Victims of Computers (OH, HAVOC).

The [Baltimore] Evening Sun, May 7, 1970, Lou Panos' column.

Another area into which computers have made a permanent entrée is administration. Computers are used for storing student records, planning classes, making space assignments, accounting, and the like. That school administrators are no less likely than businessmen to bend human needs to machine needs is evident by the ubiquitous college demonstration sign: I AM A HUMAN BEING. DO NOT FOLD, SPINDLE, OR MUTILATE.

A third area in which computers promise to influence education is by a new form of library. The long-term goal in this area is to reduce books to some automated form by storage on tapes or perhaps by one of the photo-miniaturization processes. Computerization would also address itself to a new procedure for indexing and cataloguing. Presumably, the result would be a fast, comprehensive gathering of sources on any topic.

There are still very many problems before even a modest venture of this type of library is likely to appear (Gerard, 1967). First, the role of book publishing and copyrights has to be determined. Then, there is the issue of how to select materials to store, given limited memory space and cost of storage. There is also the task of categorization: keeping the categories constant and dependable, on the one hand, and, on the other, flexible and interdisciplinary. Perhaps it is more practical and psychologically favorable for users to handle books and search for sources using their own personal systems. Most serious, at present, is the lack of a good retrieval code. Even the most superficial cataloguing procedures are more costly than human cataloguing, and their quality is questionable. Finally, there is no manpower available for establishing these systems, given the vast backlog of material to be incorporated.

On the other hand, this is not to discount the use of automated systems for reference work in delimited areas. In fact, one publishing company has joined with a computer system for such a purpose. They have computerized a major engineering reference work so that an engineer can look up the formula he needs in the book, call in and state his values for the problem, and receive an immediate answer. Problems that had previously taken several hours may now be solved with a phone call. Data retrieval by telephone will permit anyone, regardless of location, access to information sources previously unavailable.

Interesting puzzles still abound. One is the possibility of storing misinformation; for example, historical dates of the same event often vary among reference works. Will all be reported, or just one, indiscriminately? Another has to do with the role of argumentation in everyday life: what will happen when a dispute about a football game can be settled by a dime call to the "Sports Compudata Bank"? One answer may be suggested by referring to what happened to the *Guinness Book of Records*. When it first appeared, barkeepers in English pubs used the book to settle disputes. They soon ignored it, though, because the losers seldom returned to the pub.

Arguments will continue, but they may return to metaphysics so that no one can be pronounced a loser by the machine.

The fourth area of computer impact is the classroom. Computer Assisted Instruction (CAI) is a procedure whereby the student interacts with the machine in a dialogue. Programs are structured so that the computer can branch off and use a Socratic method to encourage the student to understand his mistakes. The claims for the method are many. Most popular is the argument that it provides "individualized" instruction because the computer can adjust to each student's pace, in contrast to a classroom teacher's "batch processing." In addition, courses can be developed by "master teachers" reaching far beyond the student's ordinary experience. The teacher shortage can then be alleviated. Once a course has been developed, modifications are inexpensive (Gerard, 1967, chs. 1 and 2; see also any issue of *Educational Technology*).

Technologically, the cost of computer services is decreasing, yet CAI is still more costly per capita than are other methods. And, as Oettinger (1969) has documented, CAI makes considerable demands upon the school organization and scheduling. Also, CAI programs are presently limited to rote or factual learning content, and few courses are available. Mathematics and languages adapt to the machine more easily than history, English literature, and other fields. Furthermore, good evidence is yet to be found that CAI is better than traditional teaching in terms of student learning.

Although CAI is promising, much more technological development and evaluative research is in order. Some educators have predicted that schools will disappear and individuals will educate themselves at home. This prediction is premised upon a narrow view of education, for only knowledge conveyable by the programmed machine approach could be disseminated. Second, it assumes a vast economic and manpower commitment, as well as the public's willingness to accept a technology because it is beneficial. More likely, computer-assisted instruction will become one of a variety of ways to stimulate learning, possibly as a more efficient and enjoyable way to learn drill or rote materials and to facilitate the tedious bibliographic work of independent study.

Computers and Privacy

In our discussion so far, it has often been necessary to hedge about the impact of computers. In this section we can be definite about a danger they already present for a society valuing individual freedom. Symptomatically, this cost has been almost completely ignored by the technicians. The issue is privacy.

In the precomputer era, the inefficiency of storing and analyzing data placed practical limits on the amount of information that could be obtained. Furthermore, once a file was started, the cumbersomeness of paper storage and the whims of file clerks blocked ready information retrieval. Hence, personal information was not often collected by organizations and was referred to infrequently.

The computer has changed this drastically. Storage on tapes is so cheap that masses of individual dossiers are easily retained and recorded. Files are readily transported, because a tape reel may contain several file cabinets' worth of information. Retrieving information is also simple and fast.

1. When a family moves to a new city, a "Welcome Wagon" lady may visit. Actually, she is an investigator for the local credit bureau (Westin, 1967).

2. Any time a person applies for a job, his employer will ask for copies of records from schools, including nonacademic data such as club memberships, disciplinary violations, and health statistics.

3. The 1970 census, which must be answered under penalty of law, asks such questions as the number of showers and beds in each dwelling. Women are to report the total number of babies they have delivered, *including stillborn.*

4. Certain governmental agencies obtain airline passenger lists to learn the travel companions of individuals under investigation (Arthur Miller, 1969).

5. Social scientists ask schoolchildren hundreds of questions about themselves and their families (Coleman and Campbell, 1966).

Individuals in our society are generally compliant and cooperative in cases where information is sought directly. Why should this be so? Apparently, there is trust that the information is being "put to good use." There is also a considerable naïveté as to the profound meaning the resulting files can have for one's freedom.

As with any file, the computer is an identity bank, storing bits of personal selves. That individuals know this can be gleaned from such phrases as "one should keep one's record clean" or "try to make a sound record." In other words, they attach value to themselves in terms of the record. Keeping it favorable to oneself is a goal similar to maintaining an attractive physical appearance. Furthermore, record-keepers seem aware of this feature; many social control agents use their ability to "keep something off the record" as a way of extending leniency to—and at the same time power over—a deviant.

Until recently, managing one's record was not too troublesome. Fewer pieces of information about oneself were recorded. One could "start over with a clean slate" by changing organizations or localities and failing to mention discreditable memberships to new groups. Since organizations were smaller, an enterprising person could appeal for changes. After several years, files were more difficult to locate or were even destroyed. Many groups, such as voluntary organizations or clubs, had little reason to keep records. The computer changed all this.

In general, the computer has resulted in less control over one's recorded self. When someone loses his ability to control the flow of information concerning him, his privacy has been invaded. The private aspects of one's life can be defined as those for which one need not account to others. In our "free" society, people are not supposed to be accountable to others for their memberships in all varieties of organizations, for the way they have voted or will vote, for their sexual behavior, esthetic preferences, health, and so forth. These aspects of life are *not supposed to make any difference* to political and legal authorities. Employers, school administrators, ministers, and special interest groups may hold people accountable for one or two of these distinctions but, presumably, because the member voluntarily agrees to be held accountable.

Very few personal characteristics in our society are held to be public (knowable by authorities). Age is a basic definer of legal rights (e.g., Medicare) and obligations (e.g., school attendance). Full name, social security number, income, sex, and marital status are all pertinent for various laws or taxing purposes. As soon as a questioner moves beyond these categoes, he does so for his own special purposes. Thus, the government continues to ask for racial identifications "so it can check on distributions of employers and industries"; or a state college requests students' religious affiliation "so it can show it does not discriminate." They obtain the information with little trouble partly because respondents also value the end use of the data and fail to suspect that any harm could come of it.

There are two ways in which this free transmission of personal information invades privacy in today's computer age. First, respondents are deprived of the *right to accuracy.* In the past the questionnaire filled out by the respondent in his own writing, with his own marginal notes or wording, was placed in the file as his record. If others interviewed or tested him, all supporting material would be on file. Today all such material is prepared for computer storage, and the originals are then forgotten or destroyed.

The right to accuracy is affected in several ways. One is clumsy coding procedures. Typically, credit bureaus code all felony convictions as "felons," whether the felony was robbery or refusing to answer census questions. Incomplete recording is a second, related problem. Credit bureaus are notorious for recording arrests and then failing to provide follow-up information, such as whether the person was convicted of the crime. Third, there may be human error in storing information. A college student I know spent a thousand dollars for special summer school courses, but his attendance was never punched and filed; after a year of trips to the school, he gave up trying to obtain a record. His case indicates another problem with accuracy —the misplacing of responsibility upon the computer and not upon the people operating or directing it. The administration's view was that, because his name was not on the computerized roll, he could not have attended, even though the faculty member witnessed his attendance and vouched for this in writing.

To date, there are few instances when individuals can, with little effort, read their records and file grievances against inaccuracies. College students see no more than transcripts, while their potential employers might receive much more. Few employees know what is in their personal file. Credit bureaus may tell you why your credit rating is poor, if you see them in person during office hours, but they will not disclose the contents of your file, which may include innuendoes about your "moral" behavior. And none of us know what is recorded about us in various agencies of the state and federal governments.

Complicating the deprivation of accuracy control is the loss of *right to access control*. Because computer files are cheaply reproduced, they are sold off to other users. When someone's profile has been bartered or sold, he becomes, in effect, a commodity. Organizations profit by selling their membership lists to special economic interests. Except for the Census Bureau, whose confidentiality is guaranteed by law, federal agencies ignore regulations and trade files. When a file is traded to a new user, accuracy suffers. New users are unaware of nuances in coding schemes. The possibility of abuse by thoughtless officials has striking implications for personal freedom (see Insert No. 54).

Violations of privacy brought on by computer technology are so great that it is a wonder abuses have not been more apparent. Lawyers have noted the lack of precedent in this area (Ruggles et al., 1968; Arthur Miller, 1969). In one important decision (the *Hill* case), it was ruled that a plaintiff had to prove that the defendant, a magazine, had been *intentionally* guilty of falsehood in reporting misinformation. This decision sets a bad precedent for information release outside the press, such as agencies' trading files. Lawyers also note that the Freedom of Information Act of 1966 is so vaguely worded as to suggest that federal agencies *must* divulge files of information, including personal information. However, legal statutes are pending in some states to define rights to accuracy and access to personal information.

Yet two problems remain. One is that individuals are often subtly coerced into giving personal data. Employers and schools use duress by implying that refusal to answer questions means one will not be accepted for admission or promotion. Strangely, those groups taking the most care to destroy individual identification on records, the social scientists, are the only ones who face regulations in this area. Generally, federal granting agencies require that a consent form be obtained from subjects, while no restrictions are placed on other groups as to demands made on their members. What right do industries have to ask a man about his sex life as a dubious indicator for "placing him in the best position"?

Second, computer technology, designed excellently for efficient processing of information, has been designed poorly to avoid tampering. The fact is that vandalism or theft of others' data occurs in computing centers. There are many ways for knowledgeable users to break into others' data, and these spying opportunities have increased under time-sharing; for example, students at M.I.T. have deciphered an extra-secure computing arrangement and broken into information concerning air defense in North America. Until more effective controls have been devised to regulate entry and access to computer operations, protecting users, it is useless to regulate

---

INSERT NO. 54

How Much Does the Federal Government Know About You?

How much does the federal government know about you? Probably much more than you want. In 1968 a U.S. Senate subcommittee reported on the information in government files. Their findings include:

1. Of 27 *billion* types of individual file information, only 5 *per cent* was obtained without the use of expressed or implied compulsion.

2. The following categories each had more than one billion responses in the files: name, social security number, age, marital status, race, current or past addresses, total income and source, occupational history, employment status. Since the present population is only 200 million, there are obviously duplicate records among the various agencies, as well as records on deceased persons.

3. As a condition of participating in a government program or receiving a grant, the following information may be required, depending upon the agency involved: debt history, credit rating, condition of living quarters, police record, report of civil court involvement, dental history, food consumption, consumer preferences.

4. Some information was *never* obtained voluntarily from the individuals. Categories include savings account records, mortgage delinquency history, and welfare status.

See "Government Dossier: Survey of Information Contained in Government Files" (Washington, D.C.: Government Printing Office, 1968).

users alone. As technology stands, at present, anyone who wants the information can get it. (These problems are described in detail in Arthur Miller, 1969.)

There are many signs that rights to privacy in the computer age are being reconsidered. In the early 1960s, at the behest of government agencies and social scientists, there was strong pressure in Congress for a National Data Bank. During special hearings in 1965, it became evident that neither technology nor present laws could guarantee individual privacy. It was also learned that there is a blatant disregard for privacy among federal agency bureaucrats below top levels.

These hearings stimulated concern among legislators, lawyers, and social scientists. To illustrate, in 1970 the army destroyed a data file on 7 million persons considered potentially "subversive." Their files were based on such "evidence" as subscriptions to certain journals, cars parked near demonstration locations, and police picture files of protestors. Another expression of concern is the Russell Sage Foundation (1970) assemblage of experts to establish guidelines for the collection and dissemination of pupil records. They provide a useful practical model for administrators to follow. Student data is classified into three category levels; only one level is free for almost anyone's use and it is limited to such basic categories as age, sex, grade level, and achievement. Parents are to be informed of record contents and can check for accuracy. It is urged that data be destroyed after a certain time interval, and there are detailed discussions of the need for accuracy, particularly in coding negative information. Parental and/or student permission is required to release much of the data, even to those in the school system. Employers, social workers, and security agents are not to receive the data without the subject's consent. Whether the guidelines are accepted, of course, is another matter.

OVERVIEW

Those whom I criticize for optimistically rushing technological change upon society may reply, "If something is possible, shouldn't we attempt it?" Indeed, much that is magnificent in Western society results from its members urging their curiosity to the limit. Further, it can be argued that many of our machines have contributed to man's *increasing* humanity. Insofar as machines free man from repetitive mental or arduous physical tasks, his opportunity for utilizing his uniquely creative brain is increased. For this reason, men such as McLuhan (1966) predict that an automated world will extend human affairs into even greater individual autonomy. Reliance upon jobs and other status characteristics for self-identification will attenuate. Whether his prediction is true or not will depend upon man's willingness to face the problems of automation.

Computers are here to stay. They pervade powerful governmental and economic institutions. It is unlikely that we will follow Samuel Butler's vision of Erewhon and destroy all machines. And even if we did, as did the citizens of an automated society in a Vonnegut (1952) novel, we would probably turn right around and start making repairs.

It is clear that decisions concerning technology cannot be left, as in the past, to technicians and vested interest groups. Bad, though often well-meaning, decisions are made out of ignorance. Apparently, computers do not cause environmental pollution as do other technologies; rather, they pollute the human spirit, by facilitating the invasion of privacy and the passing of responsibility to the machine by irresponsible people. More perniciously, computers foster a special magic, the assumption that by quantifying decisions we are most rational. Some of this pollution is recognized by systems analysts and computer devotees, yet these people claim they are not expert enough about society to provide answers (see papers in Dechert, 1966, as an example). They have been forced, regardless, to make decisions—often by default of others.

One implication is that social scientists must help us understand the broad impact of the computer—and, indeed, of machines in general—upon individuals and society. We lack such basic information as the present-day distribution and uses of computers, although the raw data is available in the technical journals. Virtually all studies or papers on the impact of computers have been by other than social scientists; usually, they are by economists who focus upon dollar benefits or labor distributions. The discussion of impact in this chapter can best be viewed as a set of working hypotheses for social science studies.

A second implication is practice-oriented; namely, that there must be general education on technology in our society. It is curious that products of our educational system can receive a high school diploma and lack acquaintance with the automation of our society. Although we are materialistic, somehow we consider the study of materials an improper or irrelevant topic. Understanding of chemistry and geology is of little use in appreciating the economic and social impact of the petroleum industry, an important factor in both international relations and environmental pollution. An adequate understanding of the computer is much easier to convey than that of, for example, the automobile (which American males study out of school at length).

Machines do not mechanize or "dehumanize" man: he does that to himself. It is partly because he makes machines that he is human. The act of discovery satisfies his curiosity; once the machine is completed, it fulfills an accompanying desire for efficiency. The dilemma is that each new machine provokes even more problems to be solved, though not necessarily by the application of technology. For the time being, Norbert Wiener's (1964, p. 69) prophecy rings true:

The future offers very little hope for those who expect that our new mechanical slaves will offer us a world in which we may rest from thinking. Help us they may, but at the cost of supreme demands upon our honesty and our intelligence, not as a comfortable hammock in which we can lie down to be waited upon by our robot slaves.

SUGGESTED READINGS

Buckingham, Walter, *Automation: Its Impact on Business and People*. New York: Harper & Row, 1961.
  Although old for a book on this topic, it remains one of the best summaries of the effects of computers on the structure and content of work.

Dechert, Charles R., ed., *The Social Impact of Cybernetics*. New York: Clarion, 1967.
  A symposium of technical experts who take a sobering look at the potential effects of the computerized society.

Fink, Donald G., *Computers and the Human Mind*. Garden City, N.Y.: Doubleday/Anchor, 1966.
  Perhaps the best nontechnical discussion of how a computer operates and what its potentials appear to be.

Jaki, Stanley L., *Brain, Mind and Computers*. New York: Herder & Herder, 1969.
  An erudite discussion of artificial intelligence—its history, role in philosophy, and implications from neurology.

Miller, Arthur R., "Personal Privacy in the Computer Age," *Michigan Law Review*, LXVII (1969), 1091–1246.
  The definitive review and discussion of the topic from the legal standpoint.

Oettinger, Anthony G., *Run, Computer, Run*. Cambridge: Harvard University Press, 1969.
  A critical essay on technology in education with excellent ethnographic material from Oettinger's observations in schools that utilize the new technology.

Parkhill, Douglas F., *The Challenge of the Computer Utility*. Reading, Mass.: Addison-Wesley, 1966.
  What will happen when computers are as available and as cheap as electricity?

Simon, Herbert A., *The Shape of Automation for Men and Management*. New York: Harper & Row, 1965.
  An example of how one technical expert sees the Good Society to come from computerization—one premised upon values of those now in power.

Vonnegut, Kurt, Jr., *Player Piano*. New York: Holt, Rinehart, & Winston, 1952.
  A novel of a computerized society.

Wheeler, Stanton, ed., *On Record.* New York: Russell Sage, 1970.

A collection of original essays on the use of personal dossiers by various organizations.

Wiener, Norbert, *Cybernetics.* New York: Wiley, 1948.

———, *The Human Use of Human Beings.* New York: Houghton Mifflin, 1950.

———, *Ex-Prodigy.* New York: Simon & Schuster, 1953.

———, *I Am a Mathematician.* Garden City, N.Y. Doubleday, 1956.

———, *God and Golem.* Cambridge: M.I.T. Press, 1964.

These works, especially *Cybernetics,* are classics in the field of computers and automation. They are well written, insightful, and controversial discussions of the possible impacts of computers and automation on society.

PART VII

Social Problems and Social Order

As we saw in Part I, much of sociology is ultimately directed toward dealing with social problems. Many chapters in this book have dealt with this subject matter. In this part we directly examine major social problems facing our society today. Chapter 18 introduces the basic concepts and ideas of the sociology of social problems and then deals with three important concerns: race, pollution, and generational problems. Chapter 19 outlines the nature of, and problems in, cities. Chapter 20 deals with problems of deviance, law, and crime.

CHAPTER 18

American Social Problems

This chapter introduces basic concepts about social problems. It begins by showing that sociologists have progressed in the last one hundred or more years from a positivistic view of social problems, which saw no difficulties involved in defining them and suggesting solutions, to a more interactionist, phenomenological view, which sees social problems as highly problematic and solutions as even more problematic. The positivistic view was tied to the earlier "official definition" of both problems and their solutions. The phenomenological view takes into consideration the pluralistic nature of definitions of social problems and does not place sociology in the service of the small number of officials who may seek to exercise social control.

After developing the basic ideas of the sociology of social problems, this chapter then deals in detail with the problems of race, pollution, and age-statuses in contemporary American society. The problems of race will also be dealt with in Chapter 19 in the context of the "urban crisis."

Sociology, from its European beginnings, was rooted in the study of "social problems" in industrial society. But the American development of social problems research and theory has always been more pragmatic (and often directly political) and less philosophical than that of European sociology. Much early American sociological attention was directed toward solving the many problems perceived as arising from a rapidly industrializing, technological society. Such famous sociologists as Lester Ward were involved in the political struggles of the Progressive Era, when the increasingly affluent middle classes in America created and sustained a wide variety of social movements to achieve and maintain their moral hegemony over what they perceived as "the dangerous classes" beginning to inhabit the urban communities in the Northeast. The "social problems" associated with such dangerous classes were thought to be related to their immorality, aimlessness, and disorganization (conceived as both personal and social disorganization). Perhaps because many early American sociologists came from social backgrounds similar to those of the burgeoning numbers of federal and state officials, the earliest efforts directed toward the generation of a scientific knowledge of social problems defined them in the same terms as those officials who defined them for the purpose of controlling them. Social problems, then, were largely conceived as failure of less privileged classes to "toe the line" of the utilitarian morality promoted by the reformers of the Progressive Era. Social solutions, insofar as they were conceived at all, were conceived in terms of greater state controls over dangerous classes. This perspective has remained with us and serves as the rationale for maintaining large forces of police, probation, social welfare, and other officials charged with keeping order within the confines of the ghetto, but not within the New York Stock Exchange.

Nearly every text in this area begins by posing the question: What is a social problem? Even a cursory review of textbooks indicates that the answer varies widely.

One early conception was implied in the mechanistic theories of society. Within these theories—in which society was conceived as analogous to a machine, an organism, or some other simple system—society was thought to be characterized by certain objective conditions promoting social health and other conditions giving rise to social pathology. It made little sense to question how such conditions were known, or whether one's knowledge of them was dependent upon one's perspective on social reality. Just as society was thought analogous to a machine, social problems were thought analogous to problems caused by the friction or wear between machine parts. The identification or diagnosis was seen as the domain of those with "expert knowledge" of such matters, the mechanics of society—the sociologists.

This traditional conception seems useless as an aid to understanding the increasingly rapid changes of an increasingly complex and pluralistic society. American sociologists of the first decades of this century struggled for a new perspective, which came to be called the *structural-functional perspective*. From this perspective, society is still conceived as a system, but an immensely more complex and problematic one. The social system is conceptualized as sets of interrelated and interdependent groups or subsystems, ordered by adherence to a common set of values, norms, beliefs, attitudes, and other social meanings. Social order is conceived as possible because of the legitimacy of shared norms and values to members of society, and this normative system legitimizes the use of power within society.

Social problems are conceived as "strains" within the system, seen as the product of certain objective conditions within the society inimical to the realization of other norms or values for members of society. For example, a functionalist might argue that racially exclusive employment practices would be dysfunctional for the realization of such values as equality—values assumed to be shared by most members of society. The strain between a certain cultural value (e.g., financial success) and the institutionalized means for realization of that value (e.g., educational and employment structures) is the result of unavailability of *opportunity structures*. It is presumed that members of society define "success" (if they define it at all) as does the sociologist. A social problem is identified by the sociologist in terms of his knowledge of "what is," which is taken to be the same as "what is functional." The reality of what is is taken for granted by the structural-functional sociologist. Society is not a struggle, or a possibility, but a given external reality to which all submit willingly, having internalized the society-wide values. No consideration is given in the structural-functional paradigm to such questions as: Who defines social problems? Who defines "suitable solutions" to social problems? How do groups "sell" their definitions and solutions to others?

Both organismic and structural-functional theories of society thought of social problems as the misfunctioning of an essentially stable and conflict-free society. This conception, as Gouldner points out, had a rival in the

European school of sociology built up around the writings of Karl Marx. In the Marxist conception—never as influential on American sociology as theories rooted in mechanistic perspectives—social problems were the result of inevitable class conflict under capitalism.

Naturally, these two conceptions of social problems led to two different conceptions of their solution. In the positivistic and later structural-functional tradition, solutions consisted of the continuous repression of the deviant groups in society and, later, in the attempt to "socialize" them to norms of the majority. In the Marxist paradigm, conflict between groups was defined as endemic to the system, and tended to be instrumental in furthering the overthrow of the system. "Social problems" were, then, not "problems" but midwives of the revolution.

During the early days of sociology a third movement, an offshoot of positivism, preached another brand of solution. Known as *romantic positivism*, this school of thought, associated with Saint-Simon, defined social problems in much the same way as other positivists, but proposed different solutions. Whereas Comtean positivists sought to solve these problems by tinkering with the system until it evolved into the positively perfected society, romantic positivists devised a rebellious solution, by which society would rid itself of social problems by changing the personnel running the system—from incompetent, unscientific officials of various kinds of sociologists. The romantic positivists devised a model in which the economic and political system would remain intact (which makes their solution nonrevolutionary), but would be altered and run by those trained in the science of society (which makes their solution different than reformist).

Sociologists have only recently become aware of the problematic nature of their definition. For the early positivists (and the classical sociologists who succeeded them), social problems were defined by officials of social control: poverty (considered voluntary), idleness, "sexual immorality," intoxication, and crime. Sociologists, sharing the same value orientations, accepted these categories. Marxists, on the other hand, were committed to destroying the fundamental "social problem" that was society: the system itself. From both these streams of sociology—positivism and Marxism—came the more recent phenomenological approach to social problems.

This approach is in a tentative state of development. Part is in the positivistic tradition: problems are chosen for study from the conventional corpus of categories used historically by "officialdom": poverty, crime, sexual deviance, and unemployment. Other categories have been added, however, which have roots in the social changes in America since the era of positivistic thought: the alienation of man in a technological society, affluence, and the like. But the thrust remains the same: sociologists study these phenomena defined as social problems by agencies of government and business.

But a second strand in the study of social problems in today's world has its roots in the philosophical sociology of earlier European thinkers such as

Schutz, Wittgenstein, and Husserl—and, to some extent, Weber and Marx—and today is associated in America with such sociologists as Howard S. Becker, Erving Goffman, and Harold Garfinkel. This approach takes as its starting point not the question of what in the real world is a social problem, but the more fundamental questions of who is defining the problem and how and why specific definitions of problems and solutions are developed by particular groups.

All, from Weber and Marx to Goffman and Becker, have contributed to this view of social problems through their insistence that all knowledge is essentially relative and subjective. For the phenomenological sociologist, social problems are no longer defined by one group only—say, the agents of social control or the sociologists—but must be looked at from the perspective of many groups who might be competing to have "their" definition embodied in problem-solving activity.

The stage has been set for the development of a new sociology of social problems. Within the context of the traditional approach, the conventional body of these problems became conceived as a question of power: sociologists focused on those trouble areas which powerful groups in the society labeled social problems. The reformist approach remained the dominant pragmatic approach, but the sociologists took even this as a problem to be studied rather than as an unproblematic "given." The best known spokesman for this perspective on power is Howard S. Becker. The "labeling theory" perspective—as it has come to be known—conceives of social problems resulting from entrepreneurial activities of powerful groups and individuals, able to impose their definitions of "problems" and "deviance" on less powerful individuals through formal legislation and control of the means of communication.

At the same time, a parallel analysis of the grounding of social problems in everyday interaction has developed, under such rubrics as "deviance" and "stigma" (see Chapters 8 and 20). One conception derives from labeling theory, with the phenomenon of deviance seen not as an instance of individual pathology but, rather, as a product of interaction between those powerful enough to make labels such as "poor," "dirty," and "criminal" stick, and those powerless to resist this labeling.

Lemert's study of trailer parks as a social problem (see Insert No. 55), Goffman's studies of stigma in everyday life, and to a lesser extent studies of the routine uses of rules in everyday life by the ethnomethodologists have added further dimensions to the study of the everyday, microsocial ground of social problems. In order to illustrate differences between the macrosocial and microsocial approaches, let us consider two aspects of the social problem of the elderly in our society.

The elderly (over sixty-five years old) are a relatively powerless group in comparison with the wage-earning, young adult-to-middle-aged population. Proportionately fewer earn their living, and those who work tend to earn less than other adults. Their formal organizations and pressure groups are not powerful. They are defined as a social problem by many groups with more power—by the taxpayers who have to support them, the offspring who have to place them, the employers who have to decide whether to hire them, the welfare workers who have to push papers about them, and the sociologists who take note of all this.

At the same time, any given elderly person may be stigmatized in daily interaction on one or more levels. If an elderly man, a bedridden seventy-year-old, does not conform to the conversational and behavioral conventions of those in his environment, he may be labeled as "senile." If an elderly and lively seventy-year-old woman dresses and acts in a style "appropriate" to one of twenty, she may be treated with an equally stigmatizing attitude, but from the point of view that she is "juvenile." In everyday interaction, it is wise for an elderly person to be neither too "youthful" nor too "aged"; even if neither, he will generally be stigmatized in interaction with younger people—as not open-minded, for example, or as incapable of assimilating new experience, or as not a fit student at a junior college.

By this example, we have traced the two more recent types of approach to social problems, each with important historical roots, at present converging into a single approach that we have called the phenomenological approach. It takes account of both the processes by which phenomena are defined as social problems in the larger society and the ways these problems are generated in the everyday lives of members of society. So far, however, rapprochement is uneasy. Methodologically, theoretically, and substantively, there is an enormous gap between studies of everyday life and those analyses of "social problems in American society" that take the entire nation as their arena. We will attempt such a rapprochement.

The purposes of this chapter are to trace the effects of earlier sociological definitions of society and social problems on contemporary definitions and to introduce the phenomenological study of social problems. The current direction of sociology is illustrated by three areas of social problems: race relations, pollution, and age-status.

Each substantive area was chosen to illustrate aspects of social problems theory, methods, and substantive material common to all studies of any social problem. None of these brief reviews claims comprehensiveness; all encompass enormous areas of study. The question of race relations was selected because of its long-term historical definition as a problem both at governmental and interpersonal levels. The pollution issue was chosen for opposite characteristics: Aside from the ecological fact of pollution, "pollution as a social problem" is of very recent origin. The problem of the age-status system was chosen because of its lack of either historicity or immediacy in the sense of popular and governmental interest. It is a "problem" as yet articulated more frequently by experts in the social sciences than by legislators or large-scale movements, although its realities are played out from day to day in millions of households across the country.

Race issues challenge the definition of the term *social problem*. The latter concept has usually been connected to a reformist approach which, as we have seen, rested upon a rational approach to modifying the structures of a society accepted as fundamentally sound. Sociologists, in their attempts to unravel the nature of the race problem, have put forth many explanations and offered a variety of solutions. The classical tradition in American sociology perceived race relations in an evolutionary perspective consistent with the philosophy of social Darwinism. The culmination of this tradition is found in Robert E. Park's formulation of the race relations *cycle*, a predictive theory that promised the elimination of race problems with the ultimate incorporation of the diverse races of man into a single homogeneous people. Although this perspective has never been completely abandoned, it is not useful as a practical matter, and its internal logic has made it impervious either to validation or refutation.

INSERT NO. 55

Trailer Parks as a Social Problem

Fuller and Myers' natural history theory of social problems, developed in the 1930s and 1940s, was based on an empirical study of a trailer camp park in the Detroit area, which came to be viewed as a social problem by the other area residents (Fuller and Myers, 1941). Finally, legislation was enacted to curb the activities of the park.

The authors argued, from this example, that all social problems develop in a sequence of invariant natural stages:

1. Shared awareness that a given objective condition is a social problem. More and more people become involved in discussing the "problem," which may also be discussed by the mass media.

2. Official policy making, which has three stages:
    a. informal discussion of goals among the people experiencing the problem
    b. organized discussion about goals by pressure groups
    c. discussion about means among experts and officials

3. Social reform, in which experts and officials act to reconcile the other groups' conflicting values and interests.

Although Fuller and Myers recognized the differential definition of social problems and solutions by various interested groups, they overstressed the in-

Another approach insisted on the priority of mental states—attitudes, feelings, sentiments—in understanding race problems. Race prejudice, originating in malfunctions occurring during childhood socialization, could be eliminated if only people would recognize the pathology of their predispositions and seek treatment; ultimately, it could be prevented by improving child-rearing practices.

Bridging the subjective orientation associated with the psychological approach to prejudice and the objective orientation associated with the study of discrimination, ghetto communities, and race conflict is the social system analysis of race problems. Myrdal's analysis in *American Dilemma* focused on the inherent contradiction between the American ethos of democratic equality and American racial prejudice. Ultimately, he argued, the higher ethos would triumph over its baser foe. Parsons, perceiving American society as evolving toward a race-incorporating solution that would preserve subcultural differences at the same time that it provided for equal rights, economic opportunities, and social acceptance, outlined causes for variations in the speed of incorporation for different races.

---

variance of the stages. Edwin Lemert, a social problems theorist of the symbolic interactionist school, found in a California-based replication of Fuller and Myers' study that the "trailer camp problem" did not proceed through three defined stages.

Lemert found that, although development of the trailer camp situation and the area residents' sense of problem were similar in California to Detroit, the specification of the social-problem aspect was very different:

> Trailer camps at different times and at different places have been and continue today to be sources of annoyance and irritation to individuals and to groups both public and private. Importantly, however, the specific irritations have varied greatly with respect to their substance and with respect to the context of symbols in which they were publicized. In one community the trailer camps were seen primarily as a health problem, in another as a fire hazard, and in still others as a police problem.
>
> Neighborhood awareness of trailer camps as problems manifested itself only in sporadic and attenuated forms (Lemert, 1951).

In addition, there was continued conflict between interest groups over whether or not the trailer camps are a social problem and, if so, to what degree. Policy determination was different from that described by Fuller and Myers, with less emphasis on the response of officials and experts to other groups' opinions. Efforts at reform were sporadic and undirected; the major reason appeared to be that the legal meaning of "trailer" was unsettled for members of society: "whether trailers are vehicles or whether they are dwellings" (Lemert, 1951).

None of these approaches is phenomenological. In the symbolic interactionist approach of Herbert Blumer, however, the ethnomethodological orientation associated with the name of Harold Garfinkel, and the "sociology of the absurd" enunciated by Stanford M. Lyman and Marvin B. Scott is a portent of a phenomenological sociology of race relations.

SOCIAL DARWINISM AND THE RACE CYCLE

William Graham Sumner and Lester Frank Ward were heavily influenced by Social Darwinism but reached opposing conclusions on the race issue. To Sumner, the evolution of social relations was determined by the folkways and the more deeply ingrained customs that could not be eradicated or modified by human interference, public policies, or what he called "the absurd attempt to make the world over." The future of the races in America had become unpredictable, Sumner argued, since the abolition of slavery had upset the traditional relations between blacks and whites. But, whatever that future would be, it could not be shaped by any program devised by planners. "We are like spectators at a great convulsion," Sumner concluded.

He proposed a naturalistic solution to the race problem. Relations between the races would develop in accordance with their own inherent principle; and this principle was determinate, beyond man's control. The discovery of *fundamental notions* was of crucial importance in coming to understand the nature and direction of social relations. One presented by Sumner is *ethnocentrism,* the "view of things in which one's own group is the center of everything, and all others are scaled and rated with reference to it" (1940). The centrality of ethnocentrism as a universal principle of human association seemed to suggest that, although the outcome of race relations was neither knowable in advance nor subject to human engineering, a situation of equality and toleration was unlikely.

For Ward, on the other hand, Social Darwinism implied refutation of the prevailing theses that observable differences among people were hereditary, that the races had separate origins, and that race mixture would bring about retrogression. He challenged the idea that one race was older than another in the chain of human development and that the so-called lower races could not achieve the same moral, material, and intellectual levels found in the West. He sought to refute the idea advanced by Herbert Spencer and others that the social setting did not have a most significant effect on changes in relations among races and on social progress.

Ward's vision of the evolution of mankind projected a society in which races would be abolished and all humanity would be undifferentiated by hereditary marks. He observed, "If we could but peer far enough into the great future, we should see this planet of ours ultimately peopled with a single homogeneous and completely assimilated race of men—the human race—in the composition of which could be detected all the great commanding qualities of everyone of its racial components" (Ward, 1967).

Despite differences in their approaches, especially their opposed positions on the role of human intervention in effecting social change, both Ward and Sumner believed in social evolution. From an evolutionary perspective, social problems are but current stages in the unfolding drama of social development. Man might interfere with these developments and fumble over or further the coming of the next stage, but that stage was going to come sooner or later, halted for a time because of accidents or man's bungling, hastened by providential events or man's aid.

A further development of evolutionary theory may be found in Robert E. Park's *race relations cycle*. According to Park, race relations proceed in stages beginning with *contact*, producing *competition* and *conflict* between the races, an eventual *accommodation* between the embattled racial groups, and finally *assimilation* as the races merge in culture and social relationships. This evolutionary sequence was, Park asserted, a generalized law of race relations as a whole and a particularized description of the history of races in America. Moreover, it solved a problem in Marxist thought, for Park believed that the end of the race relations cycle would clear the social arena for an inevitable class struggle (1939).

As sociological theory, Park's cycle was ambiguous. As an evolutionary doctrine of inevitable stages, it belongs to that class of theories that can neither be refuted nor validated. The studies carried on by Park and his associates did not demonstrate the cycle's operation; yet Park insisted he could perceive the forces of historical destiny at work beneath the apparent contradictions. He disposed of the negative evidence by introducing the Aristotelian doctrine of *obstacles*, which held that progress along a hypothesized line was inevitable unless something interfered (Lyman, 1968). For Park, there were a wide variety of obstacles—including skin color, prejudice, racial temperament, accidents of settlement, and the failure to establish intimacies across racial lines.

Events, thus, either describe predicted cyclical action or are redefined as obstacles. Ironically, only the *a priori* assumptions of the theory permit a researcher to classify events as evidence or accident. But employment of this approach assures that no event or set of events can be utilized to refute the theory.

Dissatisfaction with Park's cycle arose among antievolutionists and radicals, but his followers also discovered embarrassing problems in it (Lyman, 1971). Louis Wirth's analysis of ghettos and minorities, Rose Hum Lee's study of the Chinese in America, and E. Franklin Frazier's sociology of the Negro illustrate the problems arising when one adheres to the race relations cycle as an unalterable description and prescription for racial and ethnic groups in America. In fact, some sociologists have become so disenchanted with the race relations cycle that they have delegated it to illustrative uses, urged the abandonment of cyclical theories, or asserted that theory itself is impossible in the study of race problems.

In the work of Brewton Berry, the failure of the cycle to predict events in race relations has led to pessimism about the limits of nonphenomenological sociological theory. Finding no unilinear uniformity in his studies of race relations in Brazil and Hawaii and between Indians and whites, and having shown in a separate study that people who have for generations been mixed bloods with no unambiguous racial identity do not enjoy equal treatment or even social toleration (Berry, 1963; Lyman, 1970), Berry and others "question the existence of any universal pattern and incline rather to the belief that so numerous and so various are the components that enter into race relations that each situation is unique and the making of generalizations is a hazardous procedure" (Berry, 1965).

THE STUDY OF RACE PREJUDICE:
THE AUTHORITARIAN PERSONALITY

The growing dissatisfaction with evolutionary theories of race relations lent additional weight to theories about and proposed solutions for race prejudice. Of course, race prejudice had figured in the work of the classic sociologists. W. I. Thomas distinguished between caste feeling and race prejudice proper in his studies; Robert E. Park perceived prejudice as one of the most difficult obstacles an assimilating racial group would have to overcome; and, at the close of World War II, Talcott Parsons argued that hostile orientations toward an outgroup were endemic to Western civilization. However, the most significant proposal arose out of psychological studies of the nature of prejudice. Rooted in psychoanalysis, these studies discovered personality disorders and seemed to suggest a therapeutic solution to the race problem.

The study of a purported authoritarian personality by clinical and survey researchers in the late 1940s shifted concern from the structure of society to that of the personality. According to the approach of T. W. Adorno and his associates, a particular kind of child-rearing is likely to result in the creation of a basically insensitive, hostile, and prejudiced personality.

> Thus a basically hierarchical, authoritarian exploitive parent-child relationship is apt to carry over into a power oriented exploitively dependent attitude toward one's sex partner and one's God and may well culminate in a political philosophy and social outlook which has no room for anything but a desperate clinging to what appears to be strong and a disdainful rejection of whatever is relegated to the bottom (Adorno et al., 1950).

Although the methods, assumptions, and biases of *The Authoritarian Personality* have been called into question, the importance of the study lies in its shift of perspective. Before the advent of this study, race prejudice had not loomed nearly so large in the sociological analysis of the race problem. Once enunciated as a problem in personality, race relations assumed a more manageable form to those who subscribed to therapeutic approaches and wanted a solution more immediate than evolutionary orientations. If the race problem was one of personality, and if personality in turn was a function of socialization, then the solution to this problem lay in better child-rearing practices. Here was a solution that eschewed the old debate over whether morality could be legislated. Laws might not be needed; if parents could only be taught to be more open, flexible, and democratic in raising their children, the race problem would disappear.

But not even the discoverers of the authoritarian personality were optimistic. In their conclusion to the study, Adorno and his colleagues emphasized that they had dealt only with the "psychological aspects of the more general problem of prejudice" and that in "pointing toward the importance of the parent-child relationship in the establishment of prejudice or tolerance we have moved one step in the direction of an explanation." They went on to note that they had "not, however, gone into the social and economic processes that in turn determine the development of characteristic family patterns." Moreover, Adorno et al. emphasized, *The Authoritarian Personality* "deals with dynamic potentials rather than with overt behavior. We may be able to say something about the readiness of an individual to break into violence," they concluded, "but we are pretty much in the dark as to the remaining necessary conditions under which an actual outbreak would occur" (1950).

Turning to solutions indicated by their study, Adorno and his colleagues suggested that any program to alleviate prejudice must take account of "the whole structure" of the prejudiced outlook. Given this necessity, they discussed why most measures designed to end social discrimination have been unsuccessful:

> Rational arguments cannot be expected to have deep or lasting effects upon a phenomenon that is irrational in its essential nature; appeals to sympathy may do as much harm as good when directed to people one of whose deepest fears is that they might be identified with weakness or suffering; closer association with members of minority groups can hardly be expected to influence people who are largely characterized by the inability to have experience, and liking for particular groups or individuals is very difficult to establish in people whose structure is such that they cannot really like anybody; and if we should succeed in diverting hostility from one minority group we should be prevented from taking satisfaction by the knowledge that the hostility will now very probably be directed against some other group (Adorno et al., 1950).

Faced with a monolithic irrationality, the researchers turn to the ameliorative effects of therapy. But here, again, the sheer enormity of the problem confounds effective action. "[W]hen one considers the time and the amount of arduous work that would be required and the small number of available therapists, and when he considers that many of the main traits of the ethnocentrist are precisely those which, when they occur in the setting of a clinic, cause him to be regarded as a poor therapeutic risk, it appears at once that the direct contribution of individual psychotherapy has to be regarded as negligible" (Adorno et al., 1950). As for improving the rearing of children, the researchers are equally pessimistic. Although all "that is really essential is that children be genuinely loved and treated as individual humans," there are great obstacles to a seemingly simple demand for domestic humanity. Ethnocentric parents will likely produce authoritarian children; well-informed parents may suffer from an incapacity to give the requisite love and understanding to their offspring; and even the best parents may be "thwarted by the need to mould the child so that he will find a place in the world as it is." Dolefully, the authors conclude: "Few parents can be expected to persist for long in educating their children for a society that does not exist, or even in orienting themselves toward goals which they share only with a minority" (Adorno et al., 1950).

Ultimately, Adorno and colleagues hope for a change in society itself. Recognizing that psychological means are inadequate to solve the race problem, they ask social scientists to concentrate their efforts on this issue. Comparing the eradication of prejudice to the elimination of neurosis, delinquency, or nationalism, they note that all these "are products of the total organization of society and are to be changed only as that society is changed." But they add: "It is not for the psychologist to say how such changes are to be brought about." In the end, Adorno and his colleagues "insist . . . that in the councils or round tables where the problem is considered and action planned the psychologist should have a voice" (1950).

GUNNAR MYRDAL'S *AN AMERICAN DILEMMA*

The advent of structural-functional analysis in American sociology heralded a return to evolutionary approaches to the race problem. Far more sophisticated than the formulations of Sumner and Ward, conscious of the ambiguous mixtures of hope and process in the race relations cycle of Robert E. Park, and taking into account the factors of personality that affect race prejudice, studies of America as a social system nevertheless retained the essential ahistoricism of classical sociology and continued the tradition of eschewing the comparative analysis of events. The most important of these studies, carried out under the sponsorship of the Carnegie Corporation, was *An American Dilemma* (1949), by Gunnar Myrdal and a corps of social scientists. Rooted in a mechanistic model of American society and guided by the "higher value" of equality and democracy, this study predicted an end to the race problem and suggested approaches to hasten it.

Twenty-three years later, faced again with the seemingly insoluble problem, Talcott Parsons formulated a cycle of *inclusion* which promised the absorption of the Negro into American society in accordance with processes set in motion by America's own general dynamic. Both Myrdal and Parsons conceive of the race problem in terms of a system, and both couch its solution in terms of change inherent in the system itself.

Central to his belief in the positive effects of a push for equality is Myrdal's contention that the American ethos assures that such a push will occur. Rejecting the idea of a pluralism of values and interests, Myrdal insists that the United States is characterized by a unified culture and a single dominant set of values. This value profile includes a fundamental commitment to democracy and equality—the "American Creed." Such a creed promotes changes for its fulfillment.

> Though our study includes economic, social and political race relations, at bottom our problem is the moral dilemma of the American—the conflict between his moral valuations on various levels of consciousness and generality. The "American Dilemma" . . . is the ever raging conflict between, on the one hand, the valuations preserved on the general plane which we shall call the "American Creed," where the American thinks, talks, and acts under the influence of high national and Christian precepts, and on the other hand, the valuations on specific planes of individual and group living, where personal and local interests; economic, social, and sexual jealousies; considerations of community prestige and conformity; group prejudice against particular persons or types of people; and all sorts of miscellaneous wants, impulses, and habits dominate his outlook (Myrdal, 1944).

Myrdal is convinced that the social trend in America is toward the fulfillment of the American Creed and the rejection of race prejudice and discrimination. His conviction is based on his feeling that the American Creed is the higher value and his assumption that, in the long run, higher values generally win out over lower ones. He also assumes that societies strive toward consensus around the realization of their dominant value profile, and he points to the decline in once popular theories of Negro inferiority as evidence of a positive trend.

It is also reasonable to argue, however, in contrast to Myrdal's profile of American values, that racism is not a lower and local set of attitudes but a complex value orientation. Second, even if it is accepted that race prejudice is morally inferior to the American Creed in the eyes of most Americans, it is evident in psychological studies of cognitive dissonance that a person can maintain contradictory attitudes without suffering excruciating discomfort. Third, Myrdal's optimistic bias is rooted in his assumption of a dynamic social system pushing toward value consistency. Posed against this model of society are several alternative ones: for example, a society governed by contradictions and bad faith, preaching progress and practicing discrimination, resolving any psychological difficulties by rationalization. Still another model is that of social complexity and normative pluralism. According to this perspective, America is a pluralistic society with a multiplicity of values and meanings and a context of situated moralities. In such a society, the American Creed might be less relevant to individual beliefs. Although a pluralistic society need not be racist and, indeed, a plurality of beliefs would suggest the possibility of some circles wherein no such beliefs hold, neither does it guarantee an absence of race prejudice. A pluralistic society with a multiplicity of values suggests the probability of a struggle for value supremacy and social power. However, the outcome of such a struggle is unpredictable and the triumph of egalitarianism and democracy is not assured (Scott and Lyman, 1970).

TALCOTT PARSONS' RACE RELATIONS CYCLE

The most recent attempt to reconcile the facts of American racial life with sociological theory is found in the work of Talcott Parsons. In line with Myrdal's concept of a social system moving with its own principle of motion, Parsons perceives American society as about to embark on the final phase of what he terms the inclusion process that characterizes the social history of minorities in the United States (1966a). Inclusion, as Parsons defines it, is the final outcome of a cycle absorbing America's racial and ethnic groups into the civic, economic, and social mainstream. It is distinguishable from assimilation since it permits ethnic communal and cultural survival within a pluralistic society. Inclusion occurs in a cycle of three evolutionary stages through which the several racial and ethnic groups are gradually but steadily extended the full complement of citizenship.

The first stage is the *civic* or *legal* one, in which each individual is secured in the rights of person, property, religion, speech, association, and assembly. Although these are guaranteed in the Bill of Rights, their implementation takes longer for various social groupings because of their socioeconomic position, peculiar culture, or political impotence. The second stage is *political,* in which individuals acquire the vote and also form associations effective for securing collective goals. The third and final stage is *social,* in which the group attains the resources and capacities to take advantage of political, economic, and social opportunities.

Within the general cycle of expanded citizenship, as presented by Parsons, the several racial and ethnic groups proceed at a pace dictated by the extent to which they possess capacity to utilize various aspects of civic inclusion and are held back by the extent to which they arouse anxiety among the general citizenry. Some people may, because of their characteristics and because of prejudices against them, evoke fears by their "foreignness," by the possibility that they might subvert cherished institutions, or by the belief that their inclusion will debase the quality of citizenship. Negroes have not been eligible for inclusion until the present time because, Parsons asserts, not until recently did they possess the necessary qualifications for advancement through the stages of the cycle. Moreover, other peoples—European immigrants, Catholics, and Jews—did possess the wherewithal and dominated the public arena to the detriment of Negroes. As Parsons sees it, Negroes have had to wait their turn behind these other groups but, now that it is time for them to be included, the cycle should proceed with speed.

Like Park's race relations cycle, which it closely resembles, Parsons' inclusion cycle is evolutionary and ahistorical. It projects a predetermined drama of racial improvement which will unfold unless certain developments interfere. Those events contributing to the cycle are natural and preferred; those interfering are unnatural and opposed. If the cycle materializes as predicted, sociology is vindicated and the Negro becomes a full citizen; if it does not, social science is still bolstered by the assumption that accidents interfered with natural developments. Moreover, as the time for teleological redemption is long, the Negro may consign his future to hope.

Parsons' approach, like that of other sociologists we have analyzed, pays little attention to the events of Negro history or to the values that blacks share. Except for his apprehensions about black nationalism's effect on the inclusion cycle, Parsons avoids an examination of black life and black perspectives.

PHENOMENOLOGY AND THE CRISIS IN AMERICAN SOCIOLOGICAL THOUGHT ON RACE

The tradition of symbolic interactionism and ethnomethodology has called attention to the problematic nature of events and the importance of the social construction of reality. In the work of Herbert Blumer is an emphasis on the symbolic and negotiated struggle over meanings and the development of a sociology faithful to the nature of its subject matter—man making sense out of his experience in the world (1969). Thus, race prejudice becomes a sense of group position, not a deep-lying mental state, as the psychologists would have it. According to Blumer, prejudices are social constructions, formulated by elites in the public arena where spokesmen for vested interests meet. Their legitimacy and persistence rest upon their ability to explain major issues and the effectiveness of their spokesmen in the marketplace of ideas. Race prejudices decline as minorities gain access to the arenas of media communication and as pressure coerces elites to reformulate their hitherto racist explanations (Blumer, 1958).

Closely related to Blumer is the orientation described by the term *sociology of the absurd,* associated with Stanford M. Lyman and Marvin B. Scott. Emphasizing the essential meaninglessness of the world, the sociology of the absurd focuses on how man makes sense out of his senseless condition. In studies of Asians in the West, Lyman (1970) has formulated a theory to account for changes in the manifestations of racism in America. Criticizing the organic and ahistorical approaches to the study of the Negro in America, Lyman has emphasized the study of the events of black history, the existential condition of absurdity that characterizes Negro life in America, and the problematic condition that influences innovative and deviant practices (1972).

What of race relations as a social problem? A phenomenological approach would invert the issue, asking: How do members of society define their existence, cope with their condition, live their lives? Instead of assuming that the problems of existence in a less-than-tolerant and egalitarian world are unambiguously clear and await only the genius of man to solve them, the phenomenologist returns to the people to find out. Ordinary man is restored to the center of sociological thought.

THE POLLUTION ISSUE

The sudden emergence of environmental pollution as a social problem during the past few years is a phenomenon of great interest to sociologists. As recently as the mid-1960s, scientific and public health experts lamented the fact that "pollution" was not seen by the "general public" as a problem. Now, only a few years later, America witnessed marches and demonstrations protesting pollution, as well as intensive media coverage of environmental questions and the formation of new pressure groups and publications.

Two major questions arise: Why, at this juncture, has the issue become a social problem? To whom is it significant? We will concentrate mainly on the second question, with elaborations: What groups and individuals regard pollution as a social problem? How do the various interest groups define pollution, and what solutions do they propose?

Rather than provide a definition of this social problem, we will investigate the various ways in which groups or individuals in our society define it. We will discuss multiple definitions of the problem rather than a single one, and we will supply a preliminary overview of definitions of the problem constructed by interested groups in our society: young "eco-activists," mass media, politicians, and ecological "experts."

Eco-Activists

From the time of the oil slick disaster in Santa Barbara, the pollution problem has been adopted by young eco-activists. The editors of *The*

Progressive have commented, "The brightest hope for progress on the environmental front rests with American youth who this year have enrolled by the tens of thousands in local, state, and national campaigns to restore and preserve the quality of life."

Santa Barbara became the generating symbol of eco-activism because a fortuitous combination of circumstances rendered it uniquely useful as a symbol both of pollution and of other aspects of American life which many activists define as portents of collapse. The oil spill, like other contemporary local disasters, produced a highly visible pollution and damaged the tourist-based economy of the area. More important, it symbolized the worst aspects of the activist villain, the "corporate establishment"—materialism of corporations and buying of governmental favors combined in an assault on both nature and "the people."

Santa Barbara was the first major orienting symbol for the radicals' definition of pollution as a product of "the system." This issue arose at a propitious juncture in the history of the radical movement, which before Santa Barbara had grouped itself around two major unifying concerns: the Vietnam war and civil rights. But the recent surge of separatist ethnic political movements had led to rejection of white movement members by blacks. At the same time, the Vietnam war had lost much of its thrust as an issue, while Cambodia was not yet upon us. Santa Barbara became the new rallying symbol for young activists in search of an issue, giving rise to an appropriately radical definition of pollution as a social problem engendered by the capitalist military-industrial complex.

Even within a given political or social perspective there are factions with different—even opposed—definitions of any given social problem. This is the case with eco-activism. Although many radicals took up the issue as part of their program of core problems to deal with, others regarded it as insignificant compared with the older questions of civil rights and international warfare:

> Ask Vietnam protesters about the April 22 National Environmental Teach-In and they'll tell you it's a scheme to contain their spring offensive against the ecological disaster in Southeast Asia. Ask young blacks about this new movement and they'll tell you that it is a way of distracting attention from the old movement that was supposed to save their skins (Barklay and Weissman, 1970).

While one faction of radicals regards pollution as a social problem, others see its definition as a social problem as a problem.

The Mass Media

A second group interested in defining pollution as a social problem is the mass media, concerned with selectively *reporting others' definitions of the problem,* as well as with the creation of definitions. Those who use the mass media report on eco-activism and editorialize about pollution; in either case, they do it for a living, rather than for a voluntary political or social purpose.

Take Santa Barbara as the event from which definitions of pollution may be spun. Generally, television focused not on questions of the military-industrial complex or the evils of capitalism, but on sensitizing dramatic images such as oily seabirds and oily waves lapping onto deserted beaches. As Molotch (1970) comments: "The rather intense media coverage of the oil spill centered on a few dramatic moments in its history, e.g., the initial gusher of oil and a few simple-to-tell 'human interest' stories such as the pathetic deaths of the sea birds struggling along the oil-covered sand."

At a later date, with equal intensity, television covered the activities of radical eco-activists (and others) protesting Santa Barbara and pollution in general, adding other sensitizing, dramatic images to the TV public's growing idea of pollution as a social problem: hippies, bare feet, green peace signs superimposed on green stars and stripes, long hair, placards, and students. Meanwhile, other media were giving escalating coverage to pollution events, and to pollution *protest* events, and at the same time were coming out with editorials and articles giving detailed opinions on pollution. Editorials discussed the likelihood of world starvation by the 1980s, psychological journals reported on the behavior of caged rats, books gave much attention to red tides and the spilling of industrial wastes into water.

The mass media promote fragmented, complex, and surface images of pollution as a social problem, rather than a specific, group-oriented political definition. The most potent fragments are those tossed at the public via television, as this medium is present in most households. We would expect, therefore, that the media-generated public image of pollution as a social problem is an uneasy blend of oily seabirds, hippie-looking protestors, and politicians: an image far different, less specific, political, articulated, or holistic than the definitions offered by interest groups such as the eco-activists.

The Politicians

Pollution has been called "the mom and apple pie issue" that is, a problem that everyone must be concerned with and that everyone can work together to solve without regard for political, ethnic, age, class, or other special interest affiliations. But not everyone defines pollution as a problem or is concerned with it and, since people see the problem differently, it is not true that everyone can work together to solve the problem.

Politicians tend to act as if pollution were a simple issue. That is, although we define pollution sociologically as a problem which differs in definition from group to group, politicians often use pollution as a safe rhetorical issue, one which can be defined and discussed as a problem, in general terms, without offending any political group and with great appeal to all. The important word is *rhetoric*. Politicians speak rhetorically about pollution and in some cases propose or promote antipollution legislation; this does not, however, indicate anything about the everyday power activities affecting the practical problem. Politicians may speak often and long about pollution, but feel afraid to tackle a powerful local pollution industry and be voted out of office in favor of a do-nothing candidate who only *speaks* of pollution as a problem. Sociologists anticipate that political action and political rhetoric may not coincide.

The pollution issue does not appeal to everyone, either at the rhetorical level (because some groups see the problem differently) or at the practical level (where rhetoric may be acceptable and action unacceptable). Pollution is not a simple issue, nor is it likely to unify a nation divided along multiple lines, as many commentators have hoped. As our investigation of the differential definitions of pollution indicates, a problem defined so variously is not likely to provide warring groups with grounds for unification, as they will eventually realize that, although they *appear* to be speaking of the same topic, they are *actually* discussing many.

Ecological Experts

Ecological experts help shape the perspectives of eco-activists, politicians, and the mass media. More specifically in fact, these experts have almost fearsome power in connection with the definition of pollution as a social problem, because only they have technical knowledge of the phenomenon. "Experts" come in many varieties—general ecologists such as René Dubos and the Ehrlichs; specialized scientists such as marine biologists, demographers, and astronomers; technicians and planners at work in government and industry. Each concentrates on a special aspect, a situation representing the opposite of the amorphous image of pollution held by the TV watcher.

Solutions

Consideration will now be given to differences in the proposed solutions; we shall do so, initially, with reference to our earlier distinction between reformist, rebellious, and revolutionary solutions.

The Revolutionary Alternative

The revolutionary solution to the pollution problem may be considered briefly because it is simple: the overthrow of the economic and political system. One of the clearest statements of this solution is given by Keith Lampe in *The Environmental Handbook* (de Bell, 1970, pp. 9–12).

For openers, let's look at a few "root" mistakes the old timers are about to make in the context of their new eco-concern. I use "old-timer" not as a pejorative but to indicate anybody—regardless of age—whose frames of reference are products of the OLD TIME, i.e., the industrial revolution phase of history.

1. They are about to initiate massive programs within the old frames of centralized authority of the nation. Nations are such an artificial construct from an ecological point of view that any further energies poured into them are almost certain to do more long-term harm than good. Nations must be phased out as quickly as possible and replaced with tribal or regional autonomous economies rational in root terms of planet topo/climate/watershed/etc.

2. They are about to initiate massive programs within the old frames of a competitive society even though this will prove decisively contradictory in terms of our recent root insight into interdependence of species. Interdependence of course can be sustained only in a context of cooperation, so competition (capitalism) must be phased out and replaced with cooperative economic models.

The pollution problem, then, is seen by radicals such as Lampe as an example of the American way of life. Any solution which starts from the premise that pollution is a separate issue, amenable to gradual improvement, is unacceptable for the radicals.

The Reformist Alternative

The reformist solution involves retention of the basic economic and political status quo of the nation, with an adjustment of social institutions. In the case of pollution, the reformist solution involves the economic development and legislative enforcement of consumer goods and processes that do not pollute, such as a biodegradable and noncaustic detergents and destructible containers.

Reform is the conceptual type of solution favored by a majority of interested parties although reformist solutions vary in detail depending upon the interest group. It may not be possible for, say, scientists and politicians to agree on what specific tinkering with which economic and legislative institutions will be effective in combating pollution. Reformists conceive of the possibility of solution without radical social change, while revolutionaries see any such partial solution as a social problem in itself.

The Rebellious Alternative

The rebellious solution to the pollution issue involves a rejection of the special competence of those traditionally regarded as expert in the field—ecological and scientific experts, politicians, and planners—and their replacement by a spontaneous and romantic cooperation of individuals interacting with nature. Even those experts who have succeeded in capturing the attention of the rebellious have done so more by means of dramatic approach than technical competence.

Expertise is not regarded as a qualification for setting up solutions to social problems, nor are experts regarded as the only legitimate definers of such problems. Competence is viewed as a quality not of technique, but of spontaneous humanitarianism. This tendency was apparent in youthful political discussion of the war in Vietnam; youth would no longer be put off by assertions that the only people qualified to speak out on Vietnam were those who knew the technical facts. As René Dubos points out, the desired solution to the problem is one accomplished by a "grassroots movement, powered by romantic emotion as much as by the factual knowledge, that will give form and strength to the latent public concern with environmental quality."

Who are the rebellious? Unlike many specific interest groups—such as the Progressive Labor party, on the one hand, and the Sierra Club, on the other—the rebellious cannot be readily recognized in organized interest groups. They tend to be young and apolitical, often students or dropouts, dedicated to a romantic, back-to-nature way of life which sometimes involves living in rural communes and eating health foods. They are "native Americans" of the new age.

We have sketched only the barest outline of the full picture. We have not considered the role of formal organizations in creating definitions and solutions of the issue, the historical genesis of environmental pollution, or the federal legislation passed recently to combat pollution. Pollution is a complex matter for sociological analysis; as we have illustrated in our discussion of race relations, this complexity is endemic to the study of any social problem.

AGE-STATUS AS A SOCIAL PROBLEM

Loren Carter says he is now twenty-eight. Born and raised near Columbus, Ohio, he graduated from Ohio State in 1964 and moved to southern California shortly after graduation. He wanted to escape from what he perceived as "the stifling atmosphere" of the Midwest. He has been working as a social worker for nearly four years and considers himself "tuned in" to various vibrations of the youth movements: from hard rock and occasional drug use to radical politics. Some fellow social workers consider him "the house radical," others see him as a "swinger," and a few as "someone who hasn't grown up yet." Not long ago he commented:

> I was out at the university the other day, first time in a couple of years. Man, the scene has really changed. I didn't feel at home there at all. Kids passin' numbers right out in the open, some freaked out right there on the

grass. Nobody seemed to be talking to anyone else, everyone just going their own way. . . . I felt like my coat and tie were like some sort of uniform—nobody would even give me a glance. . . . Sure isn't like it was in the early 60s at OSU. At least people smiled and said hi. . . . I feel like I'm approaching middle-age (Carter, 1970).

Not too long ago, many people used the phrase "generation gap" to indicate that persons of different ages saw the same things in different ways. Often, the phrase was used to denote many problems considered natural between parents and their offspring. Many used to think that a generation could be defined as about twenty-seven years in duration, so that it would be natural to expect such differences in perception within that length of time (within a given family, for example). As the comment by Loren Carter indicates, the so-called gap appears to be narrowing. Previously, people may have perceived themselves as different from those who were the age of their fathers or mothers, but now they have such perceptions about those only four or five years younger or older than themselves.

Many who share substantial portions of the American language take it for granted that such linguistic expressions as "infant," "adolescent," "young adult," "minors," "youth," "adults," "middle-aged," and "senior citizen" are descriptive. Many of us make such distinctions in our everyday lives to differentiate among the wide varieties of persons we encounter. Often, we construct common-sense theories about such categories as "those over 30" and use such theories to impute motives, such as "they're only interested in advancing their own interests." Some of us may use such distinctions as a basis for action. We may presume, for example, that it makes sense to act toward "infants" as if they were "less mature" than "adults," without reflecting on how maturity is defined. Despite the evidence provided by historians and anthropologists on the existence of civilizations which flourished without articulating any social ideas about "age," "childhood," or "education," these categories (and our refinements of them) are often regarded as absolutes by many who are now constructing the 1970s. Once such linguistic expressions have been created and shared with others, their continued use takes on an independent existence. For example, such expressions created between the tenth and seventeenth centuries were adopted much later by practitioners of modern science, who promised to generate a kind of knowledge that would be independent of such "subjective" considerations as individuals' intentions. From the best available evidence, then, the age-related categories adopted by modern scientists, claimed as "objective" for purposes of empirical observation, are in fact founded upon the most subjective considerations.

Common-sense perceptions of society and history lead us to think that "there have always been" "families" and "children." Philippe Aries' (1962) perceptive analysis of the social history of family life suggests that the development of these notions as social ideas appears only after the Middle

Ages. Aries reports that, as late as the twelfth century, it was common practice for parents to count their offspring as "children" only after they had reached a certain age (usually around seven) because of the high rate of infant mortality at the time. In the artistic representations of family life during the Middle Ages, children were depicted as very small adults, with no distinguishing characteristics due to age. By the sixteenth century in France, three distinct linguistic categories had been developed and widely disseminated to denote what were thought to be the temporal features of the "life cycle"—childhood, youth, and old age.

The seventeenth century witnessed the development of many ideas that were to foster the scientific and technological revolutions of the following centuries. Of these, the revolutions in medicine and sanitation contributed to a decrease in infant mortality; the geometric increases of the world's population since that time are well known. More recently, the continuation of the medical revolution has allowed for a substantial decrease in the death rate. Although an analysis of demographic change in society is only the starting point for analysis of social change and social problems and although there has not always been a direct relationship between rapid demographic change and fundamental change in Western societies, there is always some relationship between the "objective conditions" of demographic change and the "subjective conditions" leading to definition of social problems. At least, some of what are now called the social problems of the young—whether defined in terms of educational priorities or reform, employment, psychological adjustment, or political protest—bear some relationship to the fact that there are now more young people, in both absolute and relative numbers; that the period of "youth" has been prolonged by restrictions placed upon the young, such as educational requirements, keeping them from holding positions of responsibility within the larger society; and that increasing numbers of "older" persons are developing a subjective identification with the hedonistic pursuits that have been a monopoly of the young in the West.

The situation is similar when those called "the aged" are defined as a social problem. In this case, the problem is not defined as the recalcitrance of some group to follow current norms of good conduct or as the rebellion of some group against standards of appropriate demeanor but, rather, as the necessity that older people adjust to their new role as functionless citizens of technological society.

According to some welfare and state officials the solution to the problem is reformist: the provision of home help, visiting services, and day centers administered by expert personnel. How the aged define the problem of aging—to what extent they see it as a problem and what solutions they propose—is rarely explored.

By contrast, youth's views on how they define themselves and society and what they perceive as problematic have received wide attention. Headlines have been generated by youth who see society as the problem and suggest revolutionary solutions. Others define rebellious youth as social problems and propose solutions ranging from reform (change school curricula, make drug education available) to extreme change (remove rebellious students and teachers from universities and replace them with adherents of the status quo).

Sociologists have approached the age-status cycle from various perspectives. Those engaged in the study of youth may involve themselves in formulating reformist or revolutionary political definitions and solutions to the "youth problem." Those expert in the study of aging could define problems such as the uselessness of the aged or the secularization of thought which desanctifies death and those approaching it. Comparative sociologists could contrast the status of youth and the aged at different times and places—for example, in the twentieth century. Theorists might present models of age-status or life cycle systems in a given society, comparing prestige, power, life styles, and socioeconomic status at different points in the cycle.

Rarely is phenomenological analysis applied to age groups in our society, to determine what meanings age categories and statuses have in everyday life. Do the aged long to be young? Do they believe they are functionless and incapable of learning? Do adolescents see this period as a social problem? Do the young and old feel problems in common with each other, such as stigma, dependency, or relatively low income? Such questions are hardly touched by sociologists. To advance knowledge on the nature of age status, we need to begin the systematic investigation of such questions.

CONCLUSION

We have provided an overview of the general historical background of the sociological analysis of social problems, described ongoing research and theory in three substantive areas, and indicated problematic meanings attached to the concept social problem.

We have stressed problematic meanings of social problems for analysis. Historically, the concept has moved from nonproblematic to problematic status within sociology, but only recently have social problems theorists started to give significant consideration to this in their research. Almost every textbook on social problems poses the question, "What is a social problem?" Most textbooks give an answer to that question. Their answers must be problematic, because different groups define different phenomena as social problems and propose different solutions.

Faced with this complexity, the sociologist can take the omniscient stance, propose his own classification and definition of social problems, and "take note of" the different definitions of other groups. Explicitly or implicitly, this has been the approach of most social problems texts. But there is another path. The sociologist can renounce omniscience and take as his primary data the problematic nature of these questions. He can approach social problems through their manifestations in man and interaction, reinstating the reality of the situation as the core of all sociological reality.

SUGGESTED READINGS

Adorno, T. W. et al., *The Authoritarian Personality.* New York: Harper & Row, 1950.

> The classic psychological study of the nature of "authoritarian personality." The "social problem" of authoritarianism is seen as rooted in childhood socialization practices.

Aries, Philippe, *Centuries of Childhood: A Social History of Family Life.* New York: Knopf, 1962.

> Aries gives a fascinating historical account of the ways in which children have been defined and used throughout the centuries.

de Bell, Garrett, ed., *The Environmental Handbook.* New York: Ballantine, 1970.

> An uneven collection of views on the current pollution crisis. Interesting from the perspective of analyzing the various meanings attached to the "social problem of pollution."

Lemert, Edwin R., *Human Deviance, Social Problems and Social Control.* Englewood Cliffs, N.J.: Prentice-Hall, 1967.

> An important collection of Lemert's essays on deviance and social problems, including the famous trailer park study.

Lyman, Stanford M. and Marvin Scott, *The Revolt of the Students.* Columbus: Charles Merrill, 1970.

> Lyman and Scott analyze the student protest movement from the phenomenological perspective, using their concept of the sociology of the absurd.

Merton, Robert K. and Robert A. Nisbet, eds., *Contemporary Social Problems.* New York: Harcourt, Brace & World, 1961.

> The most significant text on social problems written from the structural-functional perspective. Divides social problems into categories of deviance and social disorganization.

Myrdal, Gunnar, *An American Dilemma: The Negro Problem and Modern Democracy.* New York: Harper & Row, 1944.

> The classic structural-functional study of the race relations problem in American society. Myrdal hypothesizes a nonpluralistic "American Creed" of equalitarianism against which racism has little chance of survival.

Shanas, Ethel et al., *Old People in Three Industrial Societies.* New York: Atherton Press, 1968.

> A comparative study of the situation of the aged, and attitudes toward them, in industrial societies.

CHAPTER 19

Urban Society

The centers of complex civilizations have always been the cities, and urban sociology has always been an important field of sociology. As cities today are also the locale of many of America's most pressing social problems, the analysis of cities is important to the study of sociology.

After an overview of the city in history, this chapter analyzes the everyday situations of city life. What is it like to live in a city? Here we consider the classic questions of loneliness and style of life.

The next two sections discuss the physical aspects of cities and their governing. Then the author shows how and why federal urban renewal programs have failed to deal with these problems, which are social rather than physical. He discusses our urban crisis, showing how it is dependent on governmental economic policies, and considers how we can deal realistically with the crisis. He ends by considering the prospects for solving this crisis, recognizing the problematic nature of the definitions of social problems and social solutions treated in the last chapter. He is especially concerned with basic changes in our conception of "the good life."

Cities are important to sociologists because they contain a lot of people. That alone would do it. But, more than this, cities—their origins, their processes of physical development, and the life styles within them—are at once the determining force and the result of what makes up the history of modern man.

The development of societies—including changes in economics, religions, and political and social systems—is intertwined with the emergence of the city as the center of civilization. The triumph of industrialization in the West is paralleled by the domination of social and political life in industrial countries by those who made their fortunes in urban economies and utilize urban institutions as a source of power and psychic gratification. The world is run from New York, Washington, Tokyo, Moscow, and London. Whatever happens, happens in those places first (or by direction of persons in those places) and then radiates to the hinterlands. Innovations in scholarship, culture, and manufacture are likely to come from these same kinds of places. The larger the city, the more dominant tends to be its role.

This is no coincidence. Cities are where things happen, and it has almost always been so. Cities first arose because of the fortitude, cunning, charisma, or brutality of their future residents, who were able to convince the first "country yokels" that they should produce food not just for themselves, but for the city dwellers as well. The city served as the host environment for those who went on to build an industrialized society, funneling more and more people into an industrial complex capable of producing more and more goods in an economy expanding without limit.

Some idea of the scale of this phenomenon can be seen from population figures: It is estimated that in the year 1800 only 1.7 percent of the world's people lived in cities of 100,000 or more residents and 3 percent in urban places of 5,000 or more (Hauser, 1965b, p. 7). By 1950, 13 percent lived in places of 100,000 or more people and 30 percent in places of 5,000 or more. In the United States the proportion who were urban (lived in a place with more than 2,500 people) had risen to over 70 percent by 1960.

Thus, more and more people have come to experience urban life—an existence fraught with new kinds of excitements, dangers, and dilemmas reserved for those who, without being fully aware of it, participated in the profound transformation of Western societies. The adjustments they were forced to make—relinquishing ancient folkways, religions, political systems, family structures, and bases of interpersonal accommodation—occurred along with the demographic and economic transformation engulfing so many of the world's peoples. The city as a changing and growing physical entity, as a system of social organization, and as a setting for new forms of living (and dying) developed as a concomitant feature of this remarkable transformation.

These changes, interconnected in a complex pattern that sociologists and historians only dimly comprehend, are the subject of this chapter. The basic perspective taken is that the history of modern man cannot be understood apart from the history of the city—and vice versa. Similarly, the present condition of modern man cannot be understood apart from the nature of the contemporary urban place. The interesting point about cities today is not that urban people are so troubled that they riot in the streets or that there is a crisis in law enforcement, garbage collection, or budget balancing. All this may be true. But these troubles are best evaluated in terms of their context: the surrounding political, economic, and spiritual realities of the social epoch in which they arise. The city in history is modern man in the making; similarly, the contemporary city is only a collection of symptoms of the society of which it is a part. Today, as before, the city and its society are part of the same historical force. To understand the problems of the city is to understand the problems of our historical era. To solve these problems is to usher in a new age.

THE NATURE OF CITIES

Preconditions of the rise of cities: social mobilization. Although disputes as to the most appropriate definition of "city" or "urban" continue, basic to almost any such notion is that somehow, somewhere, a population accumulates whose primary activity is something other than producing food. Thus, societies in which virtually the entire population is involved in hunting and gathering or agriculture are not urban; thus, most societies that ever existed come to be removed from the subject matter of urban sociology, and attention can be restricted to that minority of history's peoples that has existed in other than "hand-to-mouth" social orders.

The first question arising is this: How, precisely, does it come about that, when an entire population was once needed for food production, significant numbers of persons can devote themselves to different sorts of tasks, while their food is provided by others? Cities are not born; they are made.

One way or another, the countryside must produce a "surplus" of food-stuffs that directly or indirectly feed a city. Some scholars (Herskovitz, 1952; Childe, 1942) explain a surplus through a fortuitous event—favorable weather brings a bountiful harvest or a technological breakthrough is realized (animal husbandry, fertilizer, and the like). Such developments free men to devote themselves to activities appropriate for new forms of social organization—such as commerce, universities, governments, and legal systems. Thus, the city comes about as a consequence of technological breakthroughs in the countryside.

The opposite perspective is the notion that the surplus itself is a result of new forms of social organization. This view holds there are always potential surpluses even if aggregate productivity is low, and products can be distributed in such a way that some men are freed from rural labor, even if other men starve as a result. There has been starvation in history, even during periods of major surplus accumulation, to support city development. Thus, what counts in explaining the rise of cities in a particular place is not whether a surplus existed in the countryside, but whether appropriate social institutions were available to mobilize human energies making the potential surplus an actual surplus. Robert Adams (1968, p. 103), a student of early urban development in Mesopotamia and early Mexico, argues in favor of this by raising the question:

> Is there an inherent tendency for agriculturalists to advance in productivity toward the highest potential level consistent with their technology, that is, to maximize their production above subsistence needs and so to precipitate the growth of new patterns of appropriation and consumption involving elites freed from responsibilities for food production?

His answer would be no. Good weather comes, and rural people may produce only what they need to eat and let the rest spoil. Surplus is a social rather than a natural or technological product.

There are various ways to mobilize a surplus. The medieval church instituted a system of tithes, neighboring peasants sharing a portion of their agricultural productivity with the ecclesiastical elite. Church services are thus exchanged food—and it is not unreasonable to assume that, facing the penalty of eternal damnation, a religious peasant would strive to eke out a tithe, regardless of sacrifice. Feudal lords or princes exacted a surplus in the form of taxation. Peasants might pay such taxes voluntarily for protection provided against competing lords or involuntarily as subjects of a warlord's conquesting armies. The glories of Imperial Rome rested upon the latter system of surplus creation. Either way, some form of institutional domination of the hinterland serves urban development. The noble's household or the church establishment, beginning with some degree of power over the peasants, grows as new-found surpluses are utilized to extend hegemony over larger and larger regions, tapping larger and larger surpluses, providing support for larger and larger numbers of nobles, clerics, and tradesmen who provide various services to the emerging urban elite. Thus, a preindustrial urban enclave comes into being. Keyfitz (1965, p. 270), in basic agreement with Adams and other scholars (Polanyi, 1945; Pearson, 1957; Hauser, 1965a), states in summary:

> We oppose the assertion that the "surplus" created the institutions, including the cities, and say instead that the institutions created the surplus. More precisely, the building of cities is part of a process that includes instituting a surplus.

The same basic model can explain the development of the great industrial metropolis. But sheer size may require such enormous stocks of accessible food that there must be a reciprocal relationship between developments in urban centers and those in the countryside; at least a portion of the surplus exacted from rural hinterlands must be deployed in such manner that technological efficiencies are introduced, both in city and hinterland. Thus, railroads and steamships, tractors and fertilizers, made possible by innovations in the city, are exported to the countryside, generating even larger food stocks capable of feeding still larger numbers of productive city dwellers.

Mere existence of a surplus does not guarantee its efficient use. Once created, a surplus can be used in a variety of ways. It can be spent by the urban elite on fineries of conspicuous consumption; the large-scale, exorbitant court life of the French nobility rested upon such surplus deployment. Surplus can take the form of investment in capital accumulation, with the result that new forms of production accelerate the growth of future surpluses. What Max Weber (1958) called the "protestant Ethic" leads to a sacrifice of near-term comforts for the benefit of longer-term material accumulations. Factories are built but not palaces; farm machines are developed rather than hunting grounds. Wars are waged to create stable markets and sources of raw materials, not for purposes of plunder or to build urban grandeur for the imperial throne. The result is industrialization, a form of resource mobilization capable of freeing vast numbers of people from the land as efficiencies of production in the city are exported to the countryside.

Continuous exploitation of a static system of production cannot support a city the size of the industrial metropolis. Thus, as Orans (1966) has argued, a given society's gross amount of productivity is at least a partial determinant of the urbanization potential. Industrial development, in particular, resting upon a special mode of surplus deployment, increases the opportunity for urban growth. Huge cities are at least partially a response to technological innovation. Changes in social organization stimulate a surplus; the surplus, in turn, stimulates technological innovation. The result is modern urban, industrial society.

Reciprocity between City and Countryside

This reciprocity between city and countryside in industrial society does not imply that mechanisms active in precipitating surplus in preindustrial economies have ceased to operate. Law, religion, and military power have been important tools for the creation and maintenance of urban industrial development at the expense of farmers and peasants (Moore, 1966). Through oppression or war there is outright plunder of a nation's own or plunder of a distant nation. When surplus mobilization of distant lands occurs through visible political forms, it is called colonialism; when it occurs through more indirect means (such as economic domination), it may be called "economic imperialism." During the period of Great Britain's rapid industrial development, British-controlled bureaucracies in India combined both forms of domination: They taxed the peasantry at the rate of 25 percent of the crop's value—as determined by what the authorities considered the potential of the land (Keyfitz, 1965, p. 272). If taxes could not be met, the land was confiscated.

Industrial Development in the United States

The rapid industrial development of the United States in the late nineteenth and early twentieth centuries was facilitated through other techniques of redistributing rural resources into urban centers. Protective tariffs were established—tariffs that protect fledgling urban industries against foreign imports, increasing the cost of manufactured goods to those living in the country. Similarly, monopoly rail transport corporations (established through federal land grants) result in arbitrarily high prices that the farmer must pay in order to get his goods to market. Many great American fortunes (Vanderbilt, Rockefeller, Stanford) were a result of their steward's position as the funnel through which such "surplus" funds flowed as they made their way from the pockets of the western farmer into the urban centers as capital for further industrial investment. The periodic peasant and farmer rebellions in virtually all developing nations (Moore, 1966) are evidence that the transfer of wealth (even when indirect) from rural to urban centers is not viewed sympathetically by the rural dweller. That such rebellions seldom succeed in altering policy is tribute to the police power of the nation-state, which comes to have as one of its roles the protection of the urban elite's interest in industrial development. Keyfitz (1965, p. 276) argues:

> It is factually wrong to assert that the city is lost in the nation; it is rather that the nation is created by the city as a projection of itself over a territory.

It is only when a certain level of industrial development has been reached (well after initial stages) that the possibility arises of the city beginning to return an equitable bargain to the countryside, in the form of manufactured goods and public services. Perhaps this beneficence to the hinterland (e.g., U.S. farm subsidies) reflects the fact that industrial growth has created a nation-state powerful enough to exploit foreign hinterlands—the as yet undeveloped (and thus politically and economically weak) agricultural nations. Again, the fierce antagonisms that result lead to periodic rebellions against what are termed the new imperialists. Thus, the most powerful urban nations, especially the United States and the USSR, are considered imperialist by the underdeveloped nations.

Population and Production

For contemporary countries seeking to industrialize, the situation is difficult. They are struggling to achieve industrial development while being subjected to postcolonial external constraints imposed by a world marketplace dominated by the developed nations (Horowitz, 1966). Attempts to tax hinterlands to support urban capital development are thwarted by the "fundamental democratization" (Mannheim, 1940) by which increasing numbers of persons have become aware that their condition of poverty (whether urban or rural) must give way to improvement. This revolution of rising expectations imposes upon the national urban rulers—be they capitalist, fascist, or communist—the imperative of increasing living standards in the present.

Evidence has been reported by Davis (1965) that this task is even more difficult than it may appear at first. Basic to the development problem of any industrializing society is the fact that a population increase must be compensated for by concomitant increases in production. It is the difference between the rate of population increase and the rate of increase of industrial development that constitutes the amount potentially available for capital investment. Otherwise, any increase in productivity (whether industrial or agricultural) goes to feed, clothe, and house the increasing numbers of bodies. A rule-of-thumb is that an increase of 1 percent in the size of the labor force must be compensated by an increase of 3 percent in new capital investment—if things are just to stand still (Coale, 1963).

As the Western countries experienced industrialization, events were such that capital could accumulate. First, as indicated earlier, there were appropriate political and quasi-political mechanisms (e.g., police power) to draw off the necessary surplus from the hinterland. In most cases, massive starvation was prevented as vast numbers of rural dwellers emigrated to urban places where they were employed in rapidly expanding industry. In the United States they came not only from the American farm, but from the hinterlands of Europe as well. The high birth rates of farm families were compensated for by the low birth rates of urbanites; relatively high death rates in both locales further helped to keep total population gains from reaching explosive levels. In 1841 residents of rapidly industrializing Liverpool and Manchester had a life expectancy of twenty-six years. There was, to be sure, a dramatic increase in the numbers of persons living in cities, and in Western societies in general. But the numbers were not a problem, given that people came to cities to get jobs; the rapid pace of industrialization meant that there were jobs to be had.

Growth in the size of urban places and the number of such places was rapid. But such growth was accomplished in a particular way—through immigration from abroad (in the U.S.) and migration of farmers' children to the city. Between 1920 and 1959, it is estimated that seven hundred thousand Americans left the hinterlands each year for urban areas. The result was a massive change in the proportion of Americans living in the city. In 1880, 44 percent of the American population was classified as "farm family." By 1964 the proportion was reduced to 6.8 percent. For the first time in the nation's history, the absolute number of rural dwellers declined in the ten-year period from 1950 to 1960.

In virtually all underdeveloped nations of the world, there were signs that led social scientists to think that the experience of the United States and Western Europe was being duplicated. But such a conclusion may have been a serious error. Kingsley Davis (1965) has shown that, at least for some underdeveloped nations, history is not repeating itself. The most important (and misleading) sign of similarity is the rapid growth in the populations of the cities. Caracas, Venezuela, jumped from 359,000 in 1941 to 1,507,000 in 1963; Amman, Jordan, grew from 12,000 in 1958 to 247,000 in 1961. Such spectacular cases of population explosion can be explained in part by rural to urban migration. But in many underdeveloped countries today, people are not migrating to cities; they are being born in them. Most of the growth in cities of underdeveloped nations is due to "natural increase," the simple excess of births over deaths. Basic improvements in sanitation have led to improvements in health such that urban populations are able to reproduce and maintain themselves as efficiently as rural populations. The result is a twin population explosion—one in the hinterland and one in the cities. Both make first claim to any increases in productivity, and together they constitute a danger that capital accumulation will be perpetually postponed. The eventual result is starvation.

The near-term consequence is that cities are created but, in a distinction made by Davis, *urbanization* does not occur. For urbanization, according to Davis, is the demographic-ecological counterpart of industrial development. But population growth and distribution patterns which are simple responses to natural increase are, in Davis' view, "unhinged" from economic development and hence from rural-urban migration. "The problem is not urbanization, not rural-urban migration, but human multiplication." Thus, it is not surprising that cities growing under such conditions take on the appearance of vast slums with hundreds of thousands of persons living on the periphery of urban life. The peripheral nature of their existence is manyfacted: they are geographically distinct (and usually on the outskirts of the city); their habitants do not enjoy the urban amenities of modern sewage and permanent housing; their cultural existence is that of villagers transferred to a new locale; their industry is restricted to village-type handicrafts. They live in what anthropologist Oscar Lewis (1959, 1965) calls the "culture of poverty." Life is hopeless, timeless, and insulated from change and other people. Their presence is a coincidence of death and birth rates, not a response to the pulls and pushes of industrial development. Such people are geographically in the city, but they are not urban.

Urbanism as a Way of Life: The Studies of Louis Wirth

The pathological social consequences that seem to result when increased city size fails to be accompanied by alterations in employment and life style, raise the question of what might be the normal response to urbanism. What patterns of life ordinarily develop when urbanization, in the fullest sense, is occurring? The issue, as framed by sociologist Louis Wirth in 1938, consists of the question: What is "urbanism as a way of life"?

Wirth's answer was not formulated in the context of the circumstances of struggling underdeveloped countries; his data came from his own social laboratory, the city of Chicago. In his now classic article, he stipulated three conditions which, by their inevitable structuring of life within cities, create a particular life style: (1) numbers, (2) density, and (3) heterogeneity. That is, cities are places where large numbers of different kinds of persons come together in a relatively small territory. The consequence of large numbers is that all sorts of new activities and institutions become possible: it takes two to tango, hundreds to perform an opera, and hundreds of thousands to support an opera house. Museums, department stores, assembly lines, and football teams entail new options for vocation, mobility, and life style that the unchanging narrow opportunities of rural existence preclude.

Density means that individuals come to impinge upon one another; all persons cannot be intimate with all other persons. One cannot respond to every passerby, every store clerk, every fellow factory employee as a "total person"—that is, as a brother, a clansman, or a close friend. Selection is necessary, and selection requires that most interpersonal contact consists of "tenuous segmental relationships." We are "interested" in the sales clerk insofar as she can quickly sell us a product; we "care" about the garbageman insofar as he is important to removing our garbage, with a minimum of early-morning clanging of galvanized steel against pavement. His personality, the health of his children, and his feelings toward us are irrelevant.

This depersonalization is also fostered by the heterogeneity of the city's population—a condition arising through what Wirth considered the city's "recruitment of variant types to perform its diverse tasks and the accentuation of [this] uniqueness through competition and the premium upon eccentricity, novelty, efficient performance, and inventiveness." Diversity gives rise to growing sophistication and cosmopolitanism as urban dwellers adjust not only to change and opportunity, but to the simultaneous existence of persons with differing kinds of skills, value orientations, and cultural backgrounds.

While increasing an individual's range of options and providing for excitement, exhilaration, and higher standards of living, the massive nature of urbanism reduces one to "virtual impotence as an individual." People join together to form interest groups and may fall prey to mass movements. The rise of Nazi Germany is sometimes attributed to this massification of society. Mass society thus fosters not only interest politics but, in Wirth's words, "personal disorganization, mental breakdown, suicide, delinquency, crime, corruption, and disorder" (1964, p. 61). Not a very pretty picture.

The theme of the impersonality of modern life, sometimes linked to the urban environment that accompanies modernity and sometimes conceived as a general psychological setback for mankind, has been a long-standing component of social science literature. So long-standing, in fact, that one might despair that for so long so many have been saying things so similar. In 1887 Ferdinand Tönnies made the distinction between *gemeinschaft* and *gesellschaft* forms of social organization. *Gemeinschaft* societies (tribes, clans, villages) are places of spontaneity, warmth, and the kind of total interpersonal involvement appropriate to tightly bound kinship groups. *Gesellschaft* is a business-oriented society: people "mean business" when they get together, and that is why they get together and stay together. Social relations are cold and impersonal. Durkheim, writing in 1893, made a similar distinction between *mechanical solidarity* (a society held together by bonds of shared collective representations) and *organic solidarity* (a system resting on the *functional complementarity* of the division of labor). More recently, the *folk-urban* distinction made by the anthropologist Robert Redfield (1930) and the *pattern variables* stipulated by Talcott Parsons (1951) revolve around the same sort of distinction. Although it might be appropriate to hail this similarity in theory-making across generations as a continuity in social research, one might just as well regard it as a symptom of theoretical bankruptcy. Matters are not helped by the fact that, whatever one forms it, the validity of the *gemeinschaft-gesellschaft* theory is open to question. We explore the evidence questioning this theory below.

Ordinarily, it is thought that a theorist bears some responsibility to operationalize the concepts he utilizes; in order to test a theory for validity, one must have a way to measure the described phenomenon. In the case of Wirth's theory, the issue arises as to what *impersonality* might look like in the real world. How will we know it when we see it, so that we may make measurements and compare different sorts of environments? Lacking any precise formulations by Wirth, social scientists have attempted to devise measures of their own.

Axelrod (1956) carried out a survey attempting to measure the degree to which people visited their neighbors or spent leisure time with relatives, friends, or co-workers. His findings were: 49 percent of respondents reported getting together with relatives at least once each week and 28 percent reported visiting friends that often; for neighbors and co-workers, the corresponding visiting percentages were 29 and 12, respectively. Is this a lot of interpersonal contact, or is it only a little? It depends on what are one's expectations, although most sociologists tend to interpret such data as a refutation of Wirth's impersonality hypothesis.

Participant-Observer Studies

Through many participant-observer studies, sociologists have showed that an impressive amount of interpersonal intimacy remains in urban settings. Regardless of setting (middle-class, lower-class, Italian-American, or black), researchers find the amount of interpersonal interaction, the closeness and intimacy among persons, more than would be expected on the assumption of a depersonalized city. Interpersonal intimacy has been examined on Italian-American street corners in Boston (William F. Whyte, 1943); Italian-American neighborhoods in Boston (Gans, 1962); a middle-class Chicago suburb (William H. Whyte, 1956); a lower-middle-class Philadelphia suburb (Gans, 1967); a Washington, D.C., ghetto corner (Liebow, 1967); and urban slums in Java (Geertz, 1956), Mexico City (Lewis, 1959), and San Juan (Lewis, 1966). Each study, taken separately, may be treated as an exotic exception: for example, the Italian-American inhabitants of Boston's North End are seen as "urban villagers" carrying their rural folkways from Italy into inner-city America. Taken together, these studies, by diverse researchers in diverse settings, indicate either that it is time to further refine notions of impersonality and anonymity—or to accept the position that field experience in the contemporary urban world has refuted Wirth's notions.

Evidence gathered from the premodern world points in the same direction. George Foster (1959), in an attempt to construct the tone of peasant life from the monographs of anthropologists, concludes that these societies were characterized by, in Oscar Lewis' summary of Foster's work, "distrust, suspicion, envy, violence, reserve, and withdrawal." Lewis goes on to make the contrast to contemporary urban life:

> In modern Western cities, there may be more give and take about one's private, intimate life at a single "sophisticated" cocktail party than would occur in years in a peasant village. I suspect there are deeper, more mature

human relationships among sympathetic, highly educated, cosmopolitan individuals who have chosen each other in friendship, than are possible among sorcery-ridden, superstitious, ignorant peasants, who are daily thrown together because of kinship or residential proximity (Lewis, 1965, p. 498).

It may be that earlier writers have mistaken the tightness, the rigidity, and, in a sense, the security, of primitive and feudal orders as a sign of interpersonal intimacy. But there may be no relationship whatever between the way in which social solidarity is accomplished and the quality of interpersonal relations within a society. Similarly, as Lewis argues, it may be that

> the city is not the proper unit of comparison or discussion for the study of social life because the variables of number, density, and heterogeneity as used by Wirth are not the crucial determinants of social life or of personality.

Variations in culture, economic class, and personal biography may be the kinds of things that matter, producing all sorts of personalities in cities and all sorts of personalities in the countryside.

Can anything be said on the topic of urbanism as a way of life? Do we deny that urbanism functions as an independent variable to structure the nature of human interaction or determine the social and psychological quality of life? My own feeling is that, despite the sound criticisms of Wirth's theory, the wound is not mortal.

There must be a return to the most basic of Wirth's points and an elimination (for the present) of his other arguments. It cannot be denied that numbers, density, and heterogeneity tend to be peculiarly urban phenomena; and certain consequences follow from these features of life. Number, density, and heterogeneity do not dictate a life of anonymity, but they do make such a life possible. Whereas nonurban settings, by the constraints of their unchanging order of existence, provide a place for everyone (and put everyone into his place), urban settings put everything up for grabs. Given mobility (geographic and social) and the demise of ascription as a method of social order, new options and new dangers arise. Given large numbers of persons in the environment, selection must occur; thus, opportunities for friendship and intimate affiliation are widened while problems of association also arise concomitantly. Affiliation becomes a personal problem. For most persons in urban settings, the problem is solved: legitimate statuses, more or less secure, are reached; friends and associates are selected (and reciprocated) in such a way that at least some interpersonal relationships are rewarding. But there are losers. Some people lose or are unable to achieve a respectable status; some people do not get chosen by anyone. Thus, it becomes possible to be anonymous among a mass, to become a stranger in one's own land.

The problematic nature of gaining associates is exacerbated by the heterogeneity of urban environments. Unlike the folk society, it becomes possible for urban man to find himself in contact with all sorts of persons: people who cannot be depended upon as potential friends capable of hearing secrets, witnessing moral transgressions, or offering generous help when one is down and out and vulnerable. Urban dwellers tend to be troubled by the presence of persons who are unknown, unproven, and thus undependable. They may even become tense, for example, in the relatively benign environment of a passenger elevator, where they are forced to share a relatively intimate space with strangers. The genuine psychic (and, occasionally, physical) risks which accompany encounters with strangers lead urbanites to develop techniques for "gaining associates, avoiding enemies, and establishing each other's intentions" (Suttles, 1968, p. 234). These techniques are based on the search for cues which bespeak similarity and the existence of some form of personal tie (mutual friendship, blood relationship) that would imply dependability and trustworthiness. When such cues are not forthcoming, mutual avoidance (or outright hostility) is the consequence.

The Studies of Gerald Suttles: Bases of Social Solidarity

Gerald Suttles (1968) has described in detail how the process of gaining associates works in the lower-class area of Chicago where four distinct (and segregated) ethnic groups lived in close proximity. Blacks, Italian-Americans, Mexican-Americans, and Puerto Ricans resided in separate enclaves that touched one another only in the periodic contacts required by overcrowding. Differences of language or dialect, religion or religious style, dress habits, musical preference, or courtship rites tended to be superimposed upon one another in such a way that ethnic differences were reinforced by whole series of other kinds of differentiations. These were precisely the kinds of differences that do not bode well for cross-ethnic friendship and association. An Italian boy who sees a black youth strutting down the street, attired in the latest fashionable garb, with his arm intimately around the waist of his girlfriend, perceives a foreign spectacle. In his culture, boys wear armless undershirts, walk the neighborhood with an aimless shuffle, and touch "good" girls only when serious about marriage. The resulting mutual avoidance indicates reciprocal distrust.

Systems of trust and distrust lead to what Suttles terms *ordered segmentation* in the city. People find each other; they seek out, discover, and make common cause with those in whom they can place reliance, to whom they can express themselves intimately, who will understand their failures and celebrate their successes. Suttles (1968, pp. 92–93) explains the rise of ordered segmentation among slum dwellers:

> Because of the intimate and unguarded nature of street life and its contributing sources, the facts that residents know of one another are drawn from a long history of gossip and private disclosures. . . . Where possible, then, each individual is evaluated against his own historical precedents.
>
> This historical and individuated social order has both advantages and disadvantages for the residents. Usually the residents do have a firm notion of what to expect from one another. Moreover, an exact knowledge of one another's personal character is often quite reassuring. . . . Jointly compromised by common disclosures, the residents enter a pact assuring one another's safety.

In the urban area studied by Suttles, shared ethnicity, coinciding with a shared geographical habitat, served as the basis of the mutual survival pact. It is likely that even among those of higher socioeconomic status—who live more cosmopolitan, formal, and private existences—similar processes are at work determining bases of community and cleavage. Even among the middle and upper middle classes, ethnicity continues as a basis of trust and association (Glazer and Moynihan, 1963). The political behavior of middle-class Americans suggests that they, like their lower-class counterparts, tend to choose their leaders on the basis of their presumed reputations, or they try to operate in this manner, devising notions of the personalities and personal habits of the candidates to justify having the same faith in their man as they have in their relatives or friends (Lane, 1959, p. 166).

As socioeconomic status rises, geographical neighborhood comes to matter less and other bases of social solidarity (e.g., professional memberships) come to have more meaning. But the need for a basis of selecting the reliable persists; the fundamental needs of the slum dwellers are the needs of everyone and analogous mechanisms of building communities of trustful association exist everywhere. The openness of slum life makes such areas more visible to the investigating sociologist who can watch people interact on their front stoops and sidewalks; similar processes among the more furtive upper classes are more difficult to observe, for the sociologist and perhaps for participants as well. Nevertheless, they exist as a basis of the social order and as important determinants of individual satisfactions. Social survival in a competitive urban society requires work.

Physical Growth and Social Change in Cities

While some sociologists have attempted to understand the city by examining the quality of urban social life, other scholars have considered study of the physical development of cities a more rewarding strategy for coming to a comprehensive understanding of urbanism. This latter group has sought general rules for the relationship between physical change and social change, often focusing on the physical environment. The goal has been to explain patterns of urban growth and development. Why do cities tend to take on certain shapes and not others? Why are they dense in places while open and undeveloped elsewhere? How do social and economic groups get deployed over the cityscape?

A group of scholars working in the 1920s and 1930s at the University of Chicago were most closely linked with attempts at comprehensive explanation of the city as a social-physical construct. This branch of the "Chicago School" considered man's social life as basically conditioned by the fact that he, like all other animals, shared a specific habitat, a geographical place that was both a product and a producer of his social existence. The basic model of what has come to be termed the study of human ecology is derived from an analogy to plant and animal life. All species share a habitat and interact both with one another and with that habitat in such ways that a more or less natural balance is achieved. Just as the fish, the birds, and the plankton of the ocean are in interdependent interaction with one another, so do different kinds of urban land users experience an analogous form of interdependence. Ecologists refer to his mutually interlocking system of competition and cooperation as the condition of symbiosis: Deer need trees to eat bark but, if they eat all the bark, there will be no trees. It is a system of competitive cooperation. Similarly, there must be a balance in cities. For any given population size, there will have to be appropriate numbers of drugstores, banks, and shoeshine stands; if there are too many drugstores, some will go out of business; if there are too few, certain needs will not be fulfilled. Men who makes shoes exchange with men who make bread; and, although both compete for the consumer's dollar, both need each other and consumers need both.

Different kinds of land users come to be deployed across the landscape according to the results of a competitive struggle among all possible users of the habitat. The most strategic or precious parcels of land go to the *dominant* land user, to the function that can call forth the most massive resources and, in the phrase of professional planners, put that land to its "highest and best use." In the redwood forest, the redwood tree is dominant; in the city, the major business headquarters, financial institutions, and department stores are dominant. They occupy the most strategic portion of the city, usually its center, and other land users in the same area are there insofar as they fulfill needs established by the dominant land users. Thus, in the shadow of banks and corporation headquarters one will find luncheonettes and business supply houses to service the dominants; one is less likely to find supermarkets and TV repair shops.

Ernest Burgess' Perspective on Urban Land Use

Applying a general ecological perspective to American cities, Ernest Burgess, writing in 1925, attempted to derive a comprehensive theory of city development. He conceptualized the city as a series of concentric circles, with the land between each circle constituting a zone appropriate to one or another kind of use. The innermost circle, the central business district (CBD), contains the stores and institutions dominant in the city. Land use is intensive; the great density of uses and height of buildings reflects a high market value of land. Only those who can pay the high rents such well-placed land may demand are able to locate in the CBD. Adjacent to downtown is a zone of transition, an area which will likely be absorbed by the CBD as the city grows outward. The owners of land in this zone, reluctant to make improvements lest they not be recouped as the CBD encroaches, allow their holdings to deteriorate. As a temporary source of revenue, properties are turned over to marginal uses as rooming houses, marginal industry, and the more unsavory of urban pastimes (gambling, prostitution, lurid films, and "dirty" books).

Still further out is the zone of workingmen's homes. Living is rather dense, although not so crowded as in the rooming-house area closer in. Beyond the workingmen live the more well-to-do. Incomes are higher, density is lower, and the ambience is suburban.

Generalization that follows from Burgess' concentric zonal theory is that land is less valuable with increasing distance from the strategic urban center. Because the land is less useful, it will have fewer competitors striving to control it (through purchase or rental) and will have a lower value on the marketplace. Thus, there is a tendency toward an inverse relationship between the value of land in cities and the wealth of people living on it. Houses in the suburbs may cost more than living units in the city center, but only because their condition is better and the amount of land they occupy is so much greater. Thus, inner-city slum properties can be valuable; the density of their use provides a high rent roll to an owner of a relatively small piece of land; the high rent total may yield high profits which are reflected in high value. (For an alternative view, see Sternlieb, 1966.) The proximity of such parcels to jobs and efficient transit lines in the central city means that many people are struggling to occupy that land. Many competitors force prices up; a good market encourages dense housing development. Thus, the inner city tends toward high land values and dense living conditions.

The Burgess theory more or less fits Chicago, the city he studied, and approximates conditions found in many older cities of the American East. But the cities of Europe, of Asia, of Latin America, and the newer cities of America (e.g., Los Angeles) developed differently than Burgess would lead us to suspect.

A major criticism of the Burgess position—and, indeed, of the ecological school in general—is that it fails to take into account that, unlike other species, man is an animal with *culture*. His cultural preferences, his notions of beauty and tradition, influence his choices. When he makes decisions about land, all these forces come into play (and interact with principles of economic strategic worth) to determine the outcome. Thus, the city looks as it does not because of a struggle among efficient land users, but because of a series of choices made by men who are not efficiency-maximizing creatures.

Walter Firey (1945) provided concrete examples of this phenomenon in his study of land use patterns in Boston. The Common, a forty-eight-acre open space in the heart of downtown, has never been developed, despite its obvious commercial value. Tradition and sentiment keep it that way. Similarly, Boston's Beacon Hill district, although directly adjacent to the CBD, remains an upper-class, relatively low-density residential area. Jonassen, in his historical account of the settlement patterns of New York's Norwegian population, shows that the Norwegians' traditional love of the sea brought them to settle (and remain) in seaside Brooklyn locations. As encroaching development eliminated the peaceful ambience of their communities, they relocated only in areas that recreated the Norwegian seaside environment, their cultural heritage. Thus, they remained in homogeneous communities and made location choices governed by "pursuit of culturally determined goals by culturally determined habits and ways of living" (Jonassen, 1961, p. 273). Similar exceptions can be pointed to in most cities.

The Social Organization of Cities: Questions of Power

How many exceptions are allowed before the rule is invalidated? American cities reveal exceptions to the Burgess theory; many cities abroad discredit it completely. Caplow (1949), in a study of the ecology of Guatemala City, demonstrates that its land use patterns are the reverse of Burgess' Chicago. The wealthy live in the city center; they congregate around their society's major institutions: the Catholic cathedral, the halls of government, and the marketplace. Individual houses in the city center are oriented around a central courtyard, and they achieve privacy and protection from passerby heterogeneous elements through the erection of high walls around each residence. Many European cities are similarly arranged; the suburbs are frequently industrial centers and working-class districts; the rich live near the institutions that matter: the church, the opera house, government and business headquarters.

The increasing number of exceptions suggests an alternative perspective, alternative not only to Burgess' specific theories of city development but to the more general ecological approach that spawned it. One such view is that there are two (not one) systems of competition and that the ecology of man is conditioned by the fact that men develop interests and organize interest groups to influence the outcome of the ecological struggle (Molotch, 1967).

It is necessary to confront the basic premise upon which the human ecologist operates, the validity of the analogy between human beings seeking a place to live, shop, or invest, and animals (and plants) seeking a place to procreate, scavenge, and nest. The difficulty is that once people of the metropolis relate themselves to a certain area, their fortunes and futures become dependent upon the fate of that geographical unit. In a sense, the same may be true of plant and animal communities. But the difference is that plants and animals do not know that their future and the future of their community habitat are intimately intertwined. Despite behavior based upon territoriality, animals and plants are in a much poorer position to unite in action to maintain and enhance a shared geographical unit.

Humans have an active, self-conscious interest in the future of certain land areas, perhaps because they own a land parcel; thus, their very livelihood depends upon its future or, because they associate specific areas with a way of life, they either cherish or despise it and are anxious for the area to build a future consonant with their value systems. An example of both is identification with one's residential community; generally, this is a positive identification, and residents attempt to enhance their community in the face of threats they fear may lead to degrading changes.

When residents perceive a shared interest, the result is often the formation of a voluntary association devoted to enhancement of a land parcel. The result may be a block club, a neighborhood improvement association, or a more comprehensive community development organization. Often, the goal of a community organization, especially one located in a declining urban area, is maintenance of the white middle-class community through the attraction of whites to the area. Of course, there are only so many whites to go around; thus, communities compete for middle-class whites, sometimes directly through advertisements in national publications read primarily by the liberal white middle class (e.g., *The New York Review of Books*).

What has been said of residential areas can also be applied to business areas. Here the function of maintenance and enhancement is fulfilled by the local chamber of commerce or the shopping street association. Like the residential community, such groups depend for their existence upon a certain community of interests associated with a certain geographical area. Chambers of commerce compete energetically with one another, all aiming to attract certain scarce kinds of land users. Similarly, a major function of a state in the American federal system may be to coordinate the campaigns of a given set of land interest groups in their competition with other states for scarce land users, usually new industries. Which areas will be victorious is determined by the relative advantages and disadvantages each offers the scarce middle-class white resident or the desired money-generating smokeless factory.

Obviously, this competitive system is a very different one than that described by the classical ecologists and their followers. In order to explain how human beings arrange themselves over a geographical area, the ecologist focuses upon competition among land users; here the focus is upon competition among land areas, and we bring to light a largely ignored competitive system. True, land users continue to compete for scarce, desirable, or peculiarly strategic urban spaces. But, more and more, urban spaces are competing for certain kinds of land users. People compete for areas, and areas compete for people. Thus, two competitive processes are occurring simultaneously and interacting with one another.

The processes are present under almost all conditions: the opening of newly discovered, uninhabited virgin lands would constitute an exception. But, despite this coexistence of the two systems at certain times and certain places, the significance of one process may loom larger than the other. To an increasing degree, the American urban situation is characterized by the ascendancy of competition among land areas in shaping urban growth and change.

Two reasons may be cited for the increase in significance of this second competitive system. First, active community organizations as described are becoming more prevalent on the urban scene. The rise of such organizations has been a response, in part, to a growing awareness among residents and land owners in the "striving" communities of the very competitive process we have outlined. These organizations are typically devoted to "the maintenance of a stable, high-quality neighborhood" or, as a more precise goal, to attracting "high-quality people" to the area. Some consult professional planners, and they are aware they are competing with other areas in creating an environment that will attract such people. Usually, such community organizations arise and prosper in direct proportion to the probability of Negro in-migration (Mikva, 1951).

There is a second reason why competition among land areas is becoming more significant. Not only are there more community organizations and other land interest groups today than in the past, but the possibilities for effecting basic changes in conditions of competition have been greatly enlarged because of new technologies and the increasing scale of governmental intervention. By gaining access to political power, the area may drastically alter its ability to compete.

Numerous projects have remade sections of the urban environment by harnessing newly found public resources and technologies to effect an area goal. The Chicago River was reversed in its course; the St. Lawrence Seaway was built to benefit Chicago and Detroit; urban renewal "saves" downtowns all over America; London Bridge was moved to Arizona. The future promises more. But, even when all that is required is a zoning variance or road improvement, the result is similar: areas are modified, placing them in a more strategic position vis-à-vis the land users they are attempting to attract. Thus, areas are becoming strategic because of man-made capital and social improvements, not because of characteristics relative to natural topology or centrality.

The sprawling city of Los Angeles is one dramatic case in point. Centrality is everywhere and nowhere; the most strategic spots are determined by their relative accessibility to the freeways, airports, and landing strips that crisscross the region. All were man-made improvements; except for an occasional mountain, they could have been placed anywhere; their present location is the result of man-made decisions. Such decisions have meant that development occurs in one place and not in another; they determine who makes a fortune in land investment and who goes bust. The very lifeblood of Los Angeles, its water supply, is itself an artificial commodity; a massive aqueduct system pipes fresh water from near and far. The very expensive decisions to bring water to Los Angeles were political and were made in private board rooms, statehouses, the U.S. Congress, and lobbies. Water was not brought to Los Angeles merely to quench the thirst of residents, but so that fortunes could be made in southern California.

The Controversy over Urban Renewal

In every city in America, "Los Angeles" is happening. Freeways and airports are changing the meaning of "central"; water is being imported over vast distances, and harbors are being built to bring the sea to cities that want to become ports. Virtually every city has experienced urban renewal, a federally financed program with the direct goal of altering the future of certain land parcels so that investments in downtown and surrounding inner-city neighborhoods might be protected. Greer (1965), in his survey of urban renewal projects across the country, found few other reasons for urban renewal. Surely the goal has not been simply to provide, in the words of the Federal Housing Act of 1949, "a decent home and a suitable living environment for every American family." Greer (1965, p. 3) reported the consequences of the program as the opposite:

> At a cost of more than three billion dollars the Urban Renewal Agency (URA) has succeeded in materially reducing the supply of low-cost housing in American cities. Like highways and streets, the program has ripped through the neighborhoods of the poor, powered by the right of eminent domain.

Under the urban renewal program, local governments draw up plans for renewing portions of the city. Usually, the land is purchased by the government, then cleared, and sold to private enterprise at a loss to the government for construction of more desirable buildings. The result is that poor housing is condemned and destroyed, and housing or other facilities to serve the more well-to-do are constructed where the poor once lived. Because the total number of housing units is not increased, the poor (especially the blacks) are squeezed into the remaining low-income areas of the city, further increasing density and inflating rents.

Urban renewal won wide acceptance in the United States for its presumed role in revitalizing the city. Of course, the several hundred thousand blacks who once lived in renewed neighborhoods constituted plenty of life. But they were the "wrong" kind of life. Owners of American downtown areas thought their holdings would be enhanced if downtown were ringed with handsome middle-class apartment towers, bringing plenty of spending power nearby. Similarly, universities and other institutions want to guarantee an environment that enhances their ability to attract faculty and students. The University of Chicago wrote the legislation to permit (primarily with federal funds) the razing of much of its surrounding community (slum prevention, it was termed) in order to help guarantee a stable middle-class surrounding neighborhood (Rossi and Dentler, 1961). In the Chicago case, middle-class Negroes were expressly part of the plan; for this reason the University of Chicago urban renewal program has been celebrated for its success in bringing about stable racial integration. As the comedy team of Nichols and May once remarked in reference to their former neighborhood: "It was black and white, shoulder to shoulder, against the poor."

Urban renewal is only one of the more dramatic and visible means by which decisions—whether made by a businessman in the privacy of his office or a politician in the publicity of a city council meeting—come to shape what the city looks like and how that emerging shape influences the lives of urban dwellers. Meyerson and Banfield (1955) have described how planning decisions regarding the location of public housing are determined not by the planner's conception of the most handsome or socially useful siting of buildings, but by the local city councilman's need to defend his area against land users who would damage the standing of his community in its competition with other areas for "quality" land users. In another study, Banfield (1961) traced a series of decisions made in the city of Chicago. His research indicates that the selection of sites for a great convention hall (McCormick Place), a new public university (the University of Illinois at Chicago Circle), a new medical treatment facility, and a vast urban renewal project were all made in response to the pulls and tugs, the bargains and counterbargains of men with vested land interests in the decisional outcome. Thus, department store owners and hotelmen located near the south edge of downtown wanted the new convention center, with its thousands of free-spending conventioneers, located on the South Side. Merchants on the north edge of downtown had a different notion of the best location. What the city comes to look like after all this wheeling and dealing cannot be understood by reference to some abstract theory based on a struggle for crucial pieces of land. The struggle is among men, all right, but men who already have land and buildings and plans for the future.

Who Runs Cities? Perspectives on Community Power

If the development of cities is the product of decisions that men make, we may ask which men make which decisions, and with what effect? The subject of *community power* has received extensive attention from social scientists.

Two opposing perspectives exist in the study of community power and for each there is a methodology that tends, by its very nature, to demonstrate the validity of the position from which it is derived. One group of researchers (Hunter, 1953) conceives of American cities as run by a tight-knit *elite*, primarily big businessmen, surrounded by a claque of politicians and lesser support personnel drawn from the professions (e.g., city planners, lawyers). To prove their case, these researchers go around asking various selected respondents in a given city questions that investigate the reputation of power. They ask: "Who can get things done?" "Who runs this town?" They find that a relatively few names are given in each town, names that appear again and again regardless of the type of issue involved—in short, a local power elite. As the critics of this approach have pointed out, however, the reputation of having power and the actuality of having power may be two different things.

The alternative school of thought is that of the *pluralists*. They hold that power in American communities is quite diffuse. Power is plural; there is not a single elite but, rather, a series of competing elites. On some issues one group will win; on another issue a different interest group will be victorious. For certain issues, in fact, otherwise powerful men will take no interest and exert no pressure. The pluralists tend to demonstrate their point through the research method of decisional analysis; that is, they try to determine who influences the important decisions. Banfield (1961), in the study discussed earlier, inspected the Chicago newspapers and located the six *key issues* creating most local controversy. By interviewing major actors in each drama, he inventoried who held what position and why, and the consequences of their holding a certain position. He tried to answer a classic question raised years earlier by the political scientist Harold Lasswell (1958): "Who gets what, when, how?" From these studies, Banfield concluded that Chicago has no power elite and that decisional outcomes are shaped by competing groups.

The decisional technique is at least as faulty a research tool as the reputational method. The first dilemma arises in choosing key issues. The selection process may help determine the findings. Basing research on the newspapers' definition of a key issue is hardly a satisfactory means of refuting elitist theories. For the power elite conception holds that newspapers are owned by publishers who are part of the big business conspiracy. It is likely that issues the media chooses to publicize are big precisely because they reflect a split among elites that generally operate as a united body. Such public disputes function as window dressing on a basically autocratic system which the pluralist sociologist verifies as reality. Thus, if the elite theorists were correct, tracing how decisions are made on issues publicized by newspapers would not be a satisfactory research methodology.

Bachrach and Baratz (1962) have pointed to the central failure of pluralist theory: Power reflected in the public press, or even in private disputes, is not the only power exercised. There are two faces of power, and the second face has to do with conditions that determine what is and what is not an issue and what solutions come to be taken as real options in a given situation. Compare, for example, Banfield's list of key issues with the following list: (1) city ownership of all land, (2) legalization of all drugs, (3) city endorsement of nuclear disarmament, (4) an enforced open housing law, (5) triple educational resources in ghetto schools, and (6) death penalty for industrial polluters. In the late 1950s none of these were real issues in Chicago, despite the fact that most were major issues or reality in at least some industrial nations of the West. Others are surfacing as issues in the 1970s. Why are certain options considered as real issues and social problems at certain times and places? The above list of possible issues was not the list found by Banfield because serious people did not view such questions serously at that time. It is this which some students of community power assert should be the sociologists' primary intellectual problem, rather than an analysis of issues that periodically surface because certain parties agree to disagree on them.

Thus, the important questions about community power are not asked. Bachrach and Baratz remark:

> To the extent that a person or group—consciously or unconsciously—creates or reinforces barriers to the public airing of policy conflicts, that person or group has power (1962).

In that sense, in American cities as well as in American society in general, those who own newspapers and television stations, those who sit as judges or gain podiums as politicians or movie stars, and those who lobby for doctors and those who rig national political conventions all have power that is routinely exercised without being directly visible or measurable. E. E. Schattschneider (1960, p. 242) has argued:

> All forms of political organization have a bias in favor of the exploitation of some kinds of conflict and the suppression of others because *organization is the mobilization of bias.* Some issues are organized into politics while others are organized out.

The traditional ability of the American system to absorb what are labeled extremist views, through just such a mobilization of bias, has been hailed as part of the genius of American democracy (Boorstin, 1953). My own view is less sanguine (Molotch, 1970). Such a phenomenon as the invisible mobilization of bias provides a dilemma for those attempting to measure power by tracing the outcomes of specific observable decisions.

Does Community Power Exist?

Perhaps the most troubling problem in studying community power is the possibility that there may be none. C. Wright Mills (1956), writing one of the most important works on this topic, *The Power Elite,* argued that one feature of modern industrial societies is that power leaves the locality; in America the big decisions are made not only by an elite, but by a national elite. Decisions of war and peace, employment or unemployment, good housing or bad housing are in the hands of a distant and detached federal government. The decisions made at the local level, according to Mills, are increasingly trivial; the locality is shaped by decisions made from afar.

Other sociologists, using very different approaches, have been led to similar conclusions. In studies of small town life, one is struck with the provincialism of locals, the triviality and banality of local politics and decision making, and, consequently, the total vulnerability of the political and social system to changes in the external environment. A local corporation that is a major local employer may be absorbed by a national conglomerate that may then decide to close down the local production facilities. No debate will be held, no bills will be introduced at city hall, but the town's very existence may be ended. In my own observations on the 1969 Santa Barbara offshore oil spill (Molotch, 1970), I witnessed a process of decision making (by oil companies and the federal Interior Department) in which the local community had no say whatsoever. Yet the consequences of these decisions led to an eventual mammoth oil spill in the beautiful Santa Barbara Channel, threatening the entire economic base (tourism) of the city. Despite two years of protest activity—including lawsuits, picketing, civil disobedience, and the introduction of congressional legislation—the locals were thwarted in their attempts to gain significant influence upon national offshore drilling policy (see Chapter 18 for more on Santa Barbara).

But much less dramatic interventions than offshore drilling may have a major impact on a locality. A change in the direction of the local truck route, a modification of federal funding requirements, the creation of new incentives for state and federal programs—all can wreak havoc on a given city. Industries collapse, new politicians arise, established families may lose their dominance.

Schulze (1961), in his study of community power in the city of Ypsilanti, Michigan, provides evidence that as small industries merge into larger ones, the paternalism of the former owner-operators is replaced by the disinterest of new corporate managers who, associated with the town only temporarily, have their eyes on their next move, which they hope will take them to corporation headquarters far away. Thus, the major industries of Ypsilanti (auto accessory plants) no longer provided the town with its leaders. In the overt behavior observed by Schulze, the former activism of what he terms the *economic dominants* gave way to a bland civic boosterism that was "above" politics. Regardless of the accuracy of Schulze's specific findings about power in Ypsilanti, his observations suggest that possibility that one reason power may be diffuse at the local level is that it is largely irrelevant. Corporate managers can let local townsfolk argue with one another about whether to put fluoride in the water so long as Congress passes appropriate labor legislation, the Federal Reserve makes the right moves on interest rates, and the president provides the appropriate tariffs

---

INSERT NO. 56

On Norton Long's *"The Community as an Ecology of Games"*

Norton Long (1958, p. 252) pictures the local community as an *ecology of games.* Far from regarding games as trivial, Long believes that

> man is both a game-playing and a game-creating animal, that his capacity to create and play games and take them deadly seriously is of the essence, and that it is through games or activities analogous to game-playing that he achieves a satisfactory sense of significance and a meaningful role.

His answer to the question "Where is community power?" would probably be: "Nowhere and everywhere." Each actor on the urban scene is oriented to his own particular game, a field of operation that he has either selected or been forced to enter. Doctors play the doctor's game, politicians play the politician's game, professors, the professor's game. Rules for each game ensure that a player who makes the right moves is rewarded with money, prestige, and a feeling of achievement and self-worth. Decisions come to pass because players in the same game trade off with one another and cooperate with persons in other games. These deals result in hospitals being built, laws being passed, and other issues never being raised. The result may correspond to the wishes of everyone in general but no one in particular. The city comes to be as it is because diverse persons got points by acting in certain ways. Long (1958, p. 254) comments:

> The ecology of games in the local territorial system accomplishes unplanned but largely functional results. The games and their players mesh

to hold up the price of American-made automobile cigarette lighters (see Insert No. 56).

Social scientists have tended to avoid such issues. The early years of power studies involved simplistic debates on whether there was a power elite. Only recently has it dawned on observers that the question is in one sense unanswerable. Whether there is a power elite depends, in part, on how power must be concentrated in how many hands before one calls what one sees a power elite. It should not be surprising, then, that two groups of scholars could look at the same phenomenon (even if they had used the same methodologies) and not be able to agree on an answer to a question too vague to be meaningful. Every human group and every social system—be it a city, society, or scout troop—is characterized by some degree of leadership (or power concentration) and also by some degree of internal democracy (or pluralism). The crucial questions are how much, under what

> in their particular pursuits to bring about over-all results; the territorial system is fed and ordered. Its inhabitants are rational within limited areas and, pursuing the ends of these areas, accomplish socially functional ends.
>
> It would follow from Long's analysis to ask which games are most important in the ecology of games. When the game of the welfare mother intersects with the game of the corporation executive, what will be the decisional outcome? Can it be assumed that there are no built-in mechanisms to determine that the executive's ability to score in his game will be greater than the welfare mother's ability to score in hers? Which will have the greatest resources to bring to bear ensuring that his own points cannot be lost because of someone else playing a different game? Who creates the game and sets the rules by which it is played?
>
> Bachrach and Baratz would probably ask similar questions. How does one determine the most important games? How are the rules of the various games established so that rewards accrue to certain behaviors but not to others? A doctor, for example, rises in wealth, social status, and the ability to make deals with people in other games (e.g., hospital administrators, politicians) if he makes rich people well, but not if he makes poor people well (Oswald Hall, 1946). How does it come about that the medical profession is structured that way? A professor makes points to the degree to which he spends his time publishing research rather than teaching. How does the university come to be structured in that way? Rules of games are not random. As important as it may be to explain why men follow the given rules and how they exchange their points for rewards, it is no less important to understand how the games themselves became structured. Perhaps the structuring of rules is itself, as Bachrach and Baratz imply, the crucial exercise of power.

circumstances, and with what effect? No totalitarian dictatorship in history was a pure autocracy, and no democratic order in history was a pure democracy. We must ask how much power concentration is present, under what circumstances is power concentration induced or inhibited, and how can democratic social orders be structured so that the most important potential issues and questions can come before publics for their consideration.

The Urban Crisis and the Continuing Failure of White Magic

If there is a circumstance in which full consideration might profitably be given to all possible options, it is the case of what is frequently termed the *urban crisis*. The city has always been a tumultuous place of change and innovation. Its very looseness of structure relative to the hinterland made it a place where some people could come and succeed and other people could suffer dismal failure. From preindustrial times, a "citizen" (member of the city) has sought the city walls as protection from arbitrary violence and rule by fiat and as protection from a social order that imposed an ascribed status from which there could be no mobility. American cities, growing and dynamic, were a locus for the upward mobility of numerous ethnic groups—people who came poor and, under the conditions of rapid industrial growth, achieved middle-class and in a few cases upper-class status, if not for themselves, then for their children.

Intellectuals have always been suspicious of the city, despite (or perhaps because of) its role in fostering the movement of at least some of the have-nots up the social ladder (White and White, 1962). But, in recent years, the traditional suspicion has given way to deep concern over the condition of urban America. The city is not doing well, and the titles of American books on the subject dramatize the diagnosis: Gordon (1963) calls his book *Sick Cities;* Jacobs (1961) calls hers, *The Death and Life of Great American Cities*. The theme of the "dying city," the "city in crisis," has filled the pages of many books and articles.

But various observers had different things in mind when they became distressed by urban conditions. Among those who supported urban renewal, the urban crisis was conceived as a downtown declining in commercial dominance. Rhetoric calling for invigorating the city was an important part of the successful political battle in creation of the appropriate national and local legislation that made large-scale renewal possible. Still others supported urban renewal to promote the social uplift they hoped new buildings would create; by destruction of the physical components of slum life, the social components (crime, delinquency) would also be destroyed. Yet, even where good housing for the poor did result from urban renewal, there is no evidence to suggest that other problems of poverty were thereby eliminated. The strategy of physical intervention as a means of creating social change has been a long-standing approach to solving social ills in America but, as we saw in Chapter 1, these programs were based on the false premise that urban slums are necessarily disorganized. Urban renewal did not solve the problems of the slums; thus, the solution was seen as one of changing the environment. Lower the densities, erect good housing, and social disorganization will decline. This kind of "white magic," established in the 1930s, led to a generation of social welfare work in which providing open space in the slums, public housing, summer camps, and recreation programs became the highest urban priority. These strategies do not seem to work. Crime is high in the new public housing projects; kids playing basketball at the recreation center manage to roam the streets between games and to have fights during half-time ceremonies; recreation programs become loci for antagonisms among different gangs who otherwise might never have come into contact (Suttles, 1968).

The urban riots of the 1960s helped to undermine such theories. The violence in Watts (a black Los Angeles ghetto) was severe, yet Watts is a community of relatively low density with access to open space. Detroit suffered perhaps the most destruction (in terms of both property and lives) of all urban areas, and Detroit has been hailed for its extraordinary number of progressive physical (as well as social) programs aimed at solving the urban crisis. The failure of the environmental explanation reflects a failure of the ecological correction to pinpoint causes of social phenomena. Even when we know where there is bad housing, its occupants may or may not be the individuals committing crimes. There is no way of knowing which of these three (or other) explanations is correct on the basis of an ecological correlation (Robinson, 1950).

Those who conceived the city's troubles as rooted in its physical blight came up with a simple solution: clear it out, tear it down—either through urban renewal or some other method of harnessing the federal bulldozer. Jane Jacobs has delivered a severe indictment against this practice of what might be termed "destroying the city in order to save it." She argues that, whatever the city's ailments, architects, planners, and politicians are making the city inhuman and unliveable; they intervene without understanding the methods urban dwellers use to generate safety and satisfaction from their community. Imagine the plight, for example, of Suttles' ethnic minorities if their community were to be destroyed by urban renewal. The bulldozers and the pseudosophisticated abstractions of the redevelopment professionals lead to a sterility of towers-and-spaces in the physical environment which is paralleled only by the social sterility of the people who must live in such artificial settings. Jane Jacobs (1961, p. 4) sees the results as follows:

> Low-income projects that become worse centers of deliquency, vandalism, and general social hopelessness than the slums they were supposed to replace. Middle-income housing projects which are truly marvels of dullness

and regimentation, sealed against any buoyancy or vitality of city life. Luxury housing projects that mitigate their inanity, or try to, with a vapid vulgarity. Cultural centers that are unable to support a good book store. Civic centers that are avoided by everyone but bums, who have fewer choices of loitering place than others. Commercial centers that are lackluster imitations of standardized suburban chain-store shopping. Promenades that go from no place to nowhere and have no promenaders. Expressways that eviscerate great cities. This is not the rebuilding of cities. This is the sacking of cities.

The Neighborhood as Human Scale

Jacobs pleads for restoration of the "human scale," a return to the neighborhood as a basis for association, intimacy, and self-worth. She regards her own home neighborhood, Greenwhich Village in New York City, as a kind of model community: a heterogeneous jumble of narrow streets, small shops, apartment buildings, and remodeled townhouses. It is a community of writers, artists, craftsmen, and a colony of Italian-Americans left over from a previous ecological generation. There is always a place to go and a nook or cranny to explore. People are friendly and remember you. There has been no successful attempt to convert the Village into an imitation of the green openness of the rustic suburbs. For Jacobs, Greenwich Village is the city left alone—and that is the source of its delight.

Jane Jacobs has strengthened the growing ideological and intellectual revulsion against city planners and urban renewal officials who seek to recreate the city without any real conception of how cities work. Mistaking the physical symptoms of distress for the essence of the urban problem and supported by business and political interests who see clearance to their advantage, the planners may indeed have created a policy that has lessened the vitality of the city while severely damaging the lives of hundreds of thousands of persons.

But this is not to say that all of Jacobs' argument is sound. The model she holds forth as the goal for all urban America and as the example of the city-left-alone is Greenwich Village. But Greenwich Village derives its character precisely from its peculiarity. It is a bohemia that draws deviants from every corner of the world to share in its unique environment. Most Americans are very different from Jane Jacobs' beloved villagers; among other things, they want to live in a single-family home in the suburbs. They say they do, in virtually every study done of housing preferences (Caplow, 1949; Gans, 1962) and they act as if they do when they plunge themselves into lifetime mortgage debt, put up with commuting, and pay high taxes. Herbert Gans, who completed an in-depth study of one such suburban community (1967) reports that residents are quite happy with their lot in the "ticky-tacky" of suburbia. Family life is more stable, people join community groups, the kids have a safe place to play, there is new-found pride in the homestead—and, no, they do not want to return to the city, thank you very much.

Suburbanization and Metropolitan Government

For other observers, suburbanization is a problem not because of the sterility of social life allegedly found there but rather because of problems of governmental administration that the rise of autonomous suburbs has created. Thus, the urban crisis is seen by some as created (or at least prolonged) by the political arrangements under which the metropolis is now governed. Solve these problems, the reasoning goes, and the urban crisis is solved along with it. Generally, a city comes into existence through an act of incorporation, often in the form of a charter by state government. It may grow to encompass larger area units through annexation of additional lands (a process becoming increasingly impossible as suburbs become jealous of their own autonomy). The city's charter specifies the power it is to have, and these powers are limited. The rules vary from state to state, but such limitations as these are common: the power to tax, the power to take on new governmental functions, the power to borrow money, the power to alter the legal order. Most generally, cities are prevented by law from legislating in areas where decision making has been preempted by state or national agencies. Further, with the growth of federal incentive programs in welfare and renewal and the availability of other funds with strings attached, the city's latitude for autonomous action shrinks rather than grows.

A city is limited not only by constraints imposed from above, but also by problems created by separate governmental jurisdictions in adjoining suburbs and the existence of additional political jurisdictions within the city itself. Thus, a city's government must deal with school boards, sewage districts, pollution districts, and college districts, each with some autonomous power of its own. Similarly, the existence of semiautonomous suburbs consisting of residents who work and shop in the central core but whose taxes support public services elsewhere constitutes another source of difficulty. Problems like pollution, crime, and public transportation do not respect city boundaries but often there is no larger political body to effectively deal with them. The 14 million people making up the New York metropolis live in four different states and are governed by 1,400 distinct legal jurisdictions (Wood, 1961). *Metropolitan government,* a system in which city and suburbs form a single jurisdiction, is one response to such dilemmas; so far, these kinds of experiments have begun haltingly in only a few places in America, including Miami and Nashville.

It is probably true that metropolitan government would help alleviate the city's problems. Yet it is doubtful that metropolitan government can have very much consequence upon what is, in the writer's view, the essence of the urban crisis. The term *urban crisis* is a euphemism for crime, delinquency, and the rebellion (increasingly violent) of black slum dwellers and other minorities. It is important to note that just because this urban crisis causes so much attention, including a small amount of government expenditure, it is not necessarily the largest cause of suffering or unhappiness in America. Indeed, until the mid-1960s, most blacks in America lived in rural areas of the South and lived something of a personal crisis each day of their lives. In terms of income, housing, diet, and equal protection under the law, rural blacks, then as now, suffered greatly compared to their urban counterparts. The nature of the present crisis is not that human beings are suffering but, rather, that their suffering is creating inconvenience for the white majorities of American society. Slums are ugly, and the practices of slum dwellers are disturbing. Crime against persons robs all urban dwellers of security; people avoid the parks and don't go out at night. Riots threaten property values and, potentially, white lives. Slums are bad for business. Slum dwellers exacerbate all these problems by their high rates of natural reproduction; more slum children not only mean more slums, but also more voters who might contribute to a black or brown takeover of the urban political machines.

The assemblage of a vast number of have-nots in a relatively small area with efficient means of communication, has meant that the personal crisis suffered always by the poor, regardless of the context in which they live, is transposed into a crisis for the larger urban society within which these individual crises are lived out. Richard Wade (1964) noted that, even prior to the Civil War in the South, slavery and the city were great enemies. Men in cities have experiences that cause them to ask questions. Mobility and change, status gradations, and the torture of exposure to the "American dream" all act as similar sources of upset for the urban blacks of contemporary America. The result is that their crisis is on its way to becoming everyone's crisis.

Thus, it is doubtful that a palliative such as metropolitan government could solve this urban crisis; certainly, the smoldering ghettoes of Nashville or Miami would indicate the contrary. The consequences might be in the opposite direction. Cities are increasingly coming under the control of black politicians; as the black population grows in proportion to total city population (given a continued higher black birth rate), an authentic source of black upward mobility comes into existence. In the past, urban administration has provided various American ethnic groups with important sources of legitimate and illegitimate avenues to money and power. As Glazer and Moynihan (1963, p. 17) have pointed out,

> a man is connected to his (ethnic) group by ties of family and friendship. But he is also connected by ties of *interest*. The ethnic groups in New York are also *interest groups*.

The Irish used the police and the mayoralty to make important social inroads; the Italians were able to establish themselves in the building industry through government "sweetheart" contracts. Daniel Bell (1953, p. 142) argues that

> Irish immigrant wealth in the northern urban centers, concentrated largely in construction, trucking, and the waterfront, has, to a substantial extent, been wealth accumulated in and through political alliance, e.g., favoritism in city contracts.

Bell argues that other immigrant groups, such as the Italians and the Jews, also profited handsomely by arrangements with city hall.

Now it's the blacks' turn. But they are "the last man in" and, just as they have arrived at the scene, opportunities for direct graft have become fewer. Most forms of organized crime (e.g., gambling) remain firmly under white control (Cressey, 1969). More important, resources have left the city; the centers of dynamic growth are the suburbs. Reapportionment through the Supreme Court's one-man, one-vote decision has further enhanced the power of the suburbs on the political scene, and blacks neither live in the suburbs nor are moving into the suburbs. Metropolitan government would be the final straw; it could preclude blacks from gaining a major political foothold in the United States. Black power through control of city halls would have the possible consequences not only of creating changes locally, but of creating changes nationally through the political might of unified urban governments pressuring the major parties and the presidency.

It is possible that only through such national pressures could any authentic change come to American urban life. The problems of American slums are problems of our stratification system. They cannot be solved locally. As long, for example, as there are more men who want jobs in the United States than there are jobs to be had, unemployment will persist. Programs that train workers for particular kinds of jobs merely substitute one unemployed worker for another. And where there is unemployment in a setting of affluence, there will be problems indeed.

America's Hidden Urban Policies

Daniel Moynihan has pointed to what he terms America's "hidden urban policy." One example of hidden urban policy that is frequently raised is the Federal Housing Authority's post–World War II policy of guaranteeing low-interest loans for suburban single-family dwellings. The FHA, without really determining to do so, facilitated the suburban boom and dramatically altered the character of American urban life. But there are examples of hidden urban policy much more profound than those perceived by Moynihan. Thus, government decisions and policies that affect interest rates, the prosperity of given sectors of the economy, and the course of inflation drastically alter the lives of all Americans; and those who make up the urban crisis are affected most directly of all. A slight change in the national rates of unemployment may have a dramatic effect upon the most volatile groups on the urban scene; for example, at the end of 1968, the overall unemployment rate in the United States was 3.2 percent, but for black teenagers the rate was 21.5 percent. When the unemployment rate fell very slightly from 3.7 to 3.2 percent from 1967 to 1968, the employment rate of blacks in urban poverty neighborhoods of the 100 largest metropolitan areas fell from 9 to 6.4 percent, a much larger difference than the aggregate change. As the saying goes, blacks are the "last hired and first fired."

For this reason, some economists find fault with methods that increase unemployment in order to fight inflation. Inflation is a response, in part, to a "hot" economy, one of full (or nearly full) employment in which increased buying power leads to spiraling rises in prices. To combat a rise in prices through measures increasing unemployment has a great impact upon the urban poor. As argued by one British economist (Macrae, 1969, p. 16), the results of such a policy might be disastrous for the United States.

> The present (1969) 3.4 per cent general unemployment rate means that only 1.5 per cent of adult white males are out of work, and it is said that the recent "ruinous rise in inflationary pressures" will continue unless this rate is increased. But a general 5 per cent unemployment rate in America would be likely to mean an average 10 per cent of jobless among all Negroes, 15 per cent in the ghettoes and probably over 30 per cent among Negro teenagers. The administration (Nixon's) might then find that it was exerting its mild curb (against inflation) by mildly holding a black panther by the tail.

As this observer understates in conclusion, "This is not a recommended procedure in America's cities for the next few years."

It would take an extraordinary amount of manipulation of welfare services to a degree the American government has not seriously entertained to counterbalance the consequences of such a decision in economic policy. Economic policy and urban policy are not really separate; to the degree to which this is not recognized, the celebration of community organization programs, job-retraining activities, and nutritional advice to the poor will have little effect on the urban crisis.

A major task for anyone seeking a solution to the urban crisis is to uncover the hidden urban policies at all levels of government and of private corporations. Urban dwellers are a part of the social system; any and all parts of that system are appropriate as a potential focus for investigation and eventual change. As indicated, the problem is more than a lack of knowledge; there are political realities that, even in the face of knowledge to the contrary, preclude certain actions from taking place. Solutions to the urban crisis will require that somehow new coalitions and new bases of power come into being, so that decisions currently not even under consideration might be effectuated. At that point, it will be possible to look for solutions to America's urban ills, and many of its other troubles as well.

Crisis of the Urban Social Order

There are advanced industrial societies that have solved some, if not all, the problems associated with the American urban crisis. Most European countries have gone far toward solving the aesthetic problems of urban sprawl and inner-city decay through strict zoning and architectual control as well as through government sponsorship of *new town* developments outside the city limits. In the Scandinavian countries, in particular, poverty and slums on the scale that we know them in the United States have been generally eliminated. There exist in such societies comprehensive free medical care, job security, and rather mild programs of income redistribution such that these societies warrant being called *welfare states*. Certainly, new kinds of problems arise in welfare states—problems of intelligent use of leisure time, development of a meaningful existence, and avoidance of boredom and the malaise that threatens once the exigencies of war, poverty, and aggressive competitiveness no longer have to be faced. For at least a portion of the American people, these problems may also exist, but simultaneously with the kinds of "old-fashioned" social problems typical of a nineteenth-century industrializing economy. Thus, while the drive to produce continues unabated, the well-being of Americans falls behind that of the rest of the world. Wars are waged against foreign countries and portions of our own population as well; the country's health slips to the point where thirteen other countries have lower rates of infant mortality, with the American black baby's chance of survival less than that of the citizens of thirty-three countries (Population Index, XXXV, No. 3 [July-September 1969]. Princeton: Population Association of America.)

The contemporary crisis of American society takes its character from an anachronistic situation: a society with the means of solving the basic problems fails to do so. The United States continues to tolerate deprivations typical of a struggling, aggressive, developing society long after it has matured into an industrial system capable of meeting the basic needs of its entire population. Those not making it in the struggle of nineteenth-century industrialization were thrown to starvation, lest any of the precious surplus be diverted from the process of capital accumulation. Today, however, the options have been enlarged, and the necessity for this sort of social brutality has been eliminated. These options consist of such administrative programs as guaranteed annual incomes for all citizens (or some similar form of income redistribution), fair housing and employment legislation with genuine police enforcement components, and comprehensive free medical care. If by no other means, those in power in America could move far toward solving the urban crisis by emulating those European societies that, under roughly similar circumstances, have gone so much farther in solving the problems of an industrial urban society. For the long term, more complete social transformations may be necessary, but for many of our troubles the solutions are clear and present.

In an urban society, the problems of people become the crisis of the entire social order. People in cities can more easily come together for good or for evil; the potential to disrupt through sheer assemblage of numbers as well as through increased opportunities for sabotage rises with increased size and complexity. The distinction between what happens in the city and what happens outside the city tends to disappear. It follows that the solutions to the city crisis have to become as broad as the outline of the problem. Certain minimal rudiments of satisfaction in an urban society, rooted in a capitalist productive system, must be provided: jobs, income, and the excitement of some perceived social mobility for all identifiable social groups, including the minorities. If these satisfactions are not provided, the city is not supplying a social-physical space appropriate to our age. This is the essence of any urban crisis, including our own.

Prospects for Alternative Urban Social Orders

Two simultaneous rebellions are occurring in this country against the current state of affairs—those of the minorities, primarily the blacks, and the college-age youth. The blacks rebel because they suffer directly and painfully the hardships of the present system. The white youth rebel partly in empathy with the minorities, but primarily in opposition to the lack of appropriate avenues for a meaningful existence in a society with goals increasingly seen as irrelevant or even evil. The ends of modern industrial society, as the contemporary American condition is interpreted, are considered not worth living for and certainly not, as in the Vietnam war, worth dying for. Although the elimination of our grossest social evils would help to ameliorate some of this distress, there would remain dissatisfactions grounded in the nature of contemporary urban society. To solve these problems, we need, as a beginning, models of alternative kinds of social systems and alternative kinds of human communities.

Sociologists have been remiss in their duty to formulate visions of new kinds of societies, new social orders appropriate to an age of postindustrial, postscarcity economies. Stewart Marquis (1968, p. 13) has formulated the need succinctly:

If scarcity no longer is *the* critical problem, then sustenance technology *must* leave the driver's seat, and so must those organizations controlling it. . . . We are not prepared for intellectual paradigms that take affluence for granted and state the *desirable* (rather than necessary) as highest goals. . . . Futurism of a scientific kind can spell out the possible and the probable in alternative futures some day; but more is needed: utopian futurism of a quasi-novelistic kind, replete with imagery, but based on solid calculation.

Paul Goodman (a social critic, novelist, and poet) and his brother Percival Goodman (an architect), have begun the job of providing models of new kinds of cities in new kinds of societies. The present-day American city is conceived by the Goodmans to be a "department-store" metropolis, its physical and social components managed for maximum efficiency in the production and distribution of goods (recall the Burgess model). Given that production and distribution are the essence of a city serving industrial development, the department store city is a natural result. Downtowns are packed with merchandise as central goods depots. The city is crisscrossed by transportation routes designed to get people to goods and goods to people. What the city planners refer to as the "amenities"—parks, museums, plazas—are afterthoughts, which through some miracle of philanthropy or other accident manage to find their way into the interstices of the productive and distributive apparatus.

The Goodmans offer alternatives. They describe two kinds of urban societies, two different schemes of "relationship between the means of livelihood and the ways of life" (1960, p. 119). The first of the Goodmans' schemes is a system that would provide "planned security with minimum regulation." Every citizen would be called upon to work for a certain period (perhaps one year out of every five or ten), devoting himself to producing the basic commodities of subsistence: cheap clothing, shelter, and food. In return for his intensive period of labor, each individual would be assured that for the rest of his life the needs of sustenance would be provided without cost. Only the bare minimum (clothing, shelter, food, and health care) would be his by right. Anything above subsistence would be provided to those who made extra contributions in the second economy of competitive "free enterprise," existing for those who cared for the rewards it might offer. Thus, there would be full security for those who wished it (without the degradation of taking charity), but minimum regulation for those who continued to desire the material luxuries of life and the risk-taking of the market economy. For everyone, there would be a new freedom in knowing that life itself was guaranteed. For some persons, at least, there would be the opportunity to devote themselves to art or music or any other form of creation that struck their fancy.

The physical form of the new community would take its character from the nature of the economy it represented. Workers in the subsistence economy would live in communities developed with "efficiency and cheapness . . . the only determinants" (Goodman and Goodman, 1960, p. 204). Such communities would be located outside the metropolis, where land is cheap but proximate to markets and materials. The Goodmans (1960, p. 207) list the following principles for housing in such minimal subsistence communities:

> (1) Good functioning at a minimum standard; (2) Considerable mobility, combined with exchangeability, to allow freedom of location; (3) Mass production of the fewest possible types consistent with freedom of selection on crucial basic issues; (4) Longevity of 10 to 20 years; (5) Adaptation of the types to various communal environments, e.g., those in which public utilities are available, those in which they are not available, etc.

The essence of the minimum subsistence plan is separation of basic production economic activities from other forms of economic production. Similarly, there would be at least two different kinds of physical environments parallel to the two economies; the Goodmans' description of housing provides an example of what one of those kinds of communities might look like.

An even more radical proposal by the Goodmans—as different from the basic subsistence scheme as from the contemporary U.S. metropolis—is a plan for "the elimination of the difference between production and consumption." There would be efficiency under this plan, but

> a different standard of efficiency, one in which invention will flourish and the job will be its own incentive; and most importantly at the highest and nearest ideals of external life: liberty, responsibility and self-esteem as a workman, and initiative (Goodman and Goodman, 1960, p. 160).

The total amount of merchandise produced might be less than in contemporary society, in order to make certain that work for every person would be an enjoyable and meaningful experience. In the words of the famous urban architect, Mies Van Der Rohe, "Less is more."

The new city of this society would be defined, according to the Goodmans, by a series of squares or piazzas. One such piazza is described as follows:

> On one side of the piazza opens the factory; another entrance is a small library. . . . As in all other squares, there is a clock with bells; it's a reminder, not a tyrant. . . . The leisure of piazzas is made of repetitive small pleasures like feeding pigeons and watching a fountain. These are ways of being with other people and striking up conversations. . . . Colored linen and silk are blowing on a line—not flags but washing! For everything is mixed up here (1960, p. 164).

Places of work and places of play merge physically, just as they do spiritually. Lunch hours are long or short; it doesn't matter because work and play are much the same. People meet and talk at the piazza—workers and students, wives and husbands, young and old. Each new city would be surrounded by a proximate farm district, providing as nearly as possible for a self-sufficient urban region. Just as industrial machines of the new city would be simple enough for everyone to understand and repair (with much manufacturing done in people's own home workshops), agricultural production would be easily accessible and comprehensible to all city folk.

The Goodmans wrote the first edition of their book in 1947; they provided utopian visions which had virtually no correspondence to the social realities of the 1940s. Today, however, there are signs that increasing numbers of Americans, especially among the comfortable classes, are questioning the goal of crude productivity and substituting more refined versions of the good life. As in the Japanese home, where a beautiful flower in a perfect setting is more wondrous than all the doodads of opulent American house beautifuls, so a rich and wondrous society may come to be seen in terms other than the Gross National Product: a lovely sight, a pleasant day, a fresh insight. The rapid rise in Americans' concern over the quality of the physical environment is one such trend in reappraisal. And in some university communities (Berkeley, Ann Arbor, Madison) people are devising new mechanisms for subsistence and social interaction: new (and low) standards of living, new residential arrangements (e.g., communes), and new techniques of production and distribution (handicraft industries, community gardens, food cooperatives).

These are, of course, only beginnings, and they involve a very small proportion of the American people. History is filled with many such beginnings that faltered and ended in demise. But they do constitute a trend and provide at least some clue to future possible relationships between means of livelihood and ways of life—for future communities in dealing with new realities of economy and society. The city of the future will—if all goes well—reflect these new realities and provide a social-physical space appropriate to them. The city would thus serve, as it usually has in the past, its role as the center of the history of man.

SUGGESTED READINGS

Davis, Kingsley, "The Urbanization of the Human Population," *Scientific American*, CCXIII, No. 3 (September 1965), 41–53.

> Presents data to make clear the awful dilemma facing underdeveloped societies, where urban population growth is "unhinged" from economic development.

Gans, Herbert, *The Urban Villagers*. New York: The Free Press, 1962.

    An ethnographic account of life in a working-class Italian neighborhood prior to its destruction by the Boston urban renewal program.

——, *The Levittowners: Ways of Life and Politics in a New Suburban Community*. New York: Pantheon, 1967.

    An ethnographic description of life in a classic middle-class suburb which helps dispel some myths about suburbia.

Jacobs, Jane, *The Death and Life of Great American Cities*. New York: Random House, 1961.

    A burning indictment of the methods used by planners and their patrons to destroy cities under the guise of "redevelopment."

Lewis, Oscar, *Five Families: Mexican Case Studies in the Culture of Poverty*. New York: Basic Books, 1959.

    An emphatic description of the lives of Mexico City slum families who live in the culture of poverty.

Liebow, Elliot, *Tally's Corner*. Boston: Little, Brown, 1967.

    An ethnographic account of the daily lives and routines of a group of black men who hang around together on a Washington, D.C., street corner.

Long, Norton, "The Local Community as an Ecology of Games," *American Journal of Sociology*, LXIV (November 1958), 251–261.

    A witty detailing of a unique perspective on how cities are organized and how decisional outcomes are determined.

Suttles, Gerald D., *The Social Order of the Slum: Ethnicity and Territory in the Inner City*. Chicago: University of Chicago Press, 1968.

    A recent synthesis of methodologies and perspectives in a community study of four distinct low-income Chicago neighborhoods.

Whyte, William Foote, *Street Corner Society*. Chicago: University of Chicago Press, 1943.

    A classic community study of status problems, politics, and interpersonal life of lower-class Boston Italian youth.

Wirth, Louis, "Urbanism as a Way of Life," pp. 61–83 in Albert Reiss, Jr., ed., *Louis Wirth on Cities and Social Life*. Chicago: University of Chicago Press, 1964.

    The essay which poses the problem of what social consequences follow from the conditions of numbers, density, and heterogeneity.

CHAPTER 20

Deviance and Social Control

Having considered the nature of specific social problems in Chapters 18 and 19, we now discuss the most general social problem: social order. The sociology of deviance (also known as social disorganization or social control) is one of the oldest, most important areas of sociology because it concerns social order. In common-sense and traditional sociological approaches, it was assumed that law and order go together, that obedience to society's rules is sufficient to produce social order. This was based on the absolutist view that social rules are clear in their meanings and in their relation to social actions for members of society. However, sociologists have begun to recognize that the meanings of social rules are uncertain, and that there is no simple relationship between law and order.

First, this chapter shows how and why social rules are problematic and then shows how members of society construct the meanings of rules in concrete situations to achieve their purposes, drawing upon the discussions of the construction of social meanings in Chapters 4 and 11. Then, we consider how they pursue their complex construction of social order, and we find that social rules are merely one factor they use. They also use all other social meanings and social power. But, because these activities are so uncertain, we find that all social order is temporary. Inevitably, social disorder returns.

The field usually called the sociology of deviance has had a long and varied history and has spanned a wide area. But basic concerns run through all sociological approaches to deviance and define the field called "Deviance and Social Control," asking four questions:

1. What is the nature of social rules?
2. How and why are social rules violated?
3. How and why are social rules used?
4. How are social rules related to social order?

Most of this chapter will deal with the answers sociologists have proposed to these questions.

THE NATURE OF SOCIAL RULES

All societies seem to have social rules. In the chapter on sex and love, we noted that all societies have rules on sexual behavior. Every chapter in this book considers some kinds of social rules, because rules are found in all realms of social life. Presumably, there is something about human society that makes rules necessary—whether they be moral rules, ethical rules, laws, or rules of etiquette.

The traditional view in Western societies has been that social rules are absolute, being (1) obvious to any competent member of society, (2) independent of the specific situation, (3) independent of the persons and times involved, (4) unchanging, and (5) derived from the will of God or some other absolute source. The absolute stance toward rules is sometimes seen even in the case of rules of etiquette—that is, there is only one right way to introduce people, to eat with a fork, to use a knife, or to blow one's nose—and any violation of such rules leads to embarrassment and anxiety.

As sociology began in common-sense understandings of everyday life, it is not surprising to find that sociologists began the study of social rules by adopting the absolute stance of common sense toward those rules. This attitude is seen most clearly in the works of the early nineteenth-century sociologists, such as the "public hygienists." Public hygienist works on prostitution assumed that the practice was a social evil that would have to be eradicated. They did not ask why there should be social rules for or against prostitution, how such rules came about, how they were related to other aspects of society, or what their consequences were for the rest of society. The rules were assumed to be facts of life, and the purpose of social science was to find a scientific way to eradicate the "evil."

By Durkheim's time, sociologists had decided that social rules or, as they called them, social morals, should be studied scientifically, in the same way scientists studied physical phenomena. As Durkheim said, morals should be studied as if they were things or objects (1950). But what do social rules look like in everyday life? How do we know when the members of society are using these rules?

The difficulty of answering is clear when we look at common instances involving expression of social rules in society. Consider the following statement about "good," "bad," and "moral indignation" by Crane Brinton (1959).

> In September 1957 there appeared in most American newspapers a news photograph that showed a Negro girl in Little Rock, Arkansas, after a vain attempt to enter a white high school, leaving the premises with a group of whites trailing and abusing her. The face of one white girl was contorted in a shocking way; the Negro girl looked dignified and self-controlled. Commentators in the North were unanimous that the expression of the Negro girl symbolized the good and the expression of the white girl the bad; and commentators in the South were at least much disturbed by the picture, for they could not help making the same specific classifications of good and bad that their Northern colleagues did.

Many people were responding to a picture, with no indication of what the subjects were saying or doing other than their facial expressions. The implication is that moral meanings can be communicated and understood by members of the same society without the use of words. Moral meanings can be implicit in the situation.

Sociologists cannot define moral rules in terms of linguistic statements, nor can they count on "discovering" the moral rules of a society by taking a picture or recording what people say. A picture will show an outsider nothing more than expressions, with no captions specifying moral meanings. A recording will often involve statements from which members of society might infer moral meanings without using such a word as "moral," especially today when it has become in bad taste to be "moralistic" and most communications of moral feelings and ideas are probably indirect.

Sociologists must, then, rely on understandings of the moral communications gained through participant observation of everyday life. By this method, we can accumulate and analyze studies of many different forms of what members of our society consider moral communications. We have barely begun the necessary analyses of the complex nature of moral communications. But we have used some sociological studies and some studies of moral and ethical statements by philosophers who have analyzed language.

First, we find that *social rule* is a more general category than *social moral*. Social rules include morals, but they also include other forms of rules. At the most general level, social rules are the criteria that normal members of society are expected to make (sincere) use of in deciding what to do in any situation for which the rules are seen as relevant. Morals are social rules seen by members of society as involving a sense of *appropriateness*, as *necessarily binding* on all the members of society, and as *imposed* upon all individuals by God or some other higher force, rather than created by individual wills. By social definition, then, morals are seen by members of society as absolute rules that cannot be waived or changed.

A second important and general category of social rules is that of social mores, the rules of good taste. They differ from social morals in that they are the product of human creation and subject to some degree of individual choice. Mores are rules intended to order such activities as introducing people to each other, setting a table, eating with a fork, or wearing one's hair in a certain style. Such rules, specifying what are commonly called "good manners," are so complex that experts on these rules write books to which people can refer for guidance. Governments have experts on protocol to order their interactions with other governments. While these mores are often taken quite seriously (and breaches of etiquette or protocol can have serious consequences), they are understood to be rules agreed upon by ordinary mortals, rather than handed down by God.

All rules may be either *sanctioned* or *nonsanctioned*. Positive sanctions are rewards for obeying the rules; negative sanctions are punishments for violating them. Rules may be formally or informally sanctioned. Formally sanctioned rules have explicit (generally written) rewards or punishments, while informally sanctioned rules involve less explicit rewards and punishments. Formally sanctioned rules are usually made explicit and enforced by officials; normally, these officially enacted and enforced rules are called *laws*. Corporate groups in our society have private laws, while governments have governmental laws.

Until recently, most sociologists, taking the absolutist stance, assumed that social morals and social laws were largely the same. They believed that moral rules led to laws to enforce them and that governmental laws would be direct representations of society's morals. Today, when there is so much conflict over morals and laws in American society, it seems strange that such an assumption was made; yet it was made by almost all sociologists until the 1930s and had a profound effect on studies of deviance. This assumption of the *congruence of morals and laws* led sociologists to concentrate their studies of deviance on violations of governmental laws, relying almost entirely on official statistics of legal violations. The recognition that official statistics on deviance do not give a true picture of what is going on in society has been crucial in the past three decades, producing important changes in the sociology of deviance.

EARLY SOCIOLOGICAL THEORIES OF DEVIANCE

Because nineteenth-century sociologists assumed that social rules were absolute, accepted by and binding on all members of society in all situations, violations of rules were a great mystery. For this reason, as well as the fact that these early sociologists were deeply committed to helping officials solve the "social problem" of such deviant acts, they became committed to explaining the causes of deviance.

The Functional Theory. Most theories of deviance in the nineteenth century were developed by the moral statisticians, discussed in Chapter 2. Their hundreds of works on deviance were based on the idea that society operates like a giant probability machine to produce statistical rates of social actions. Each specific kind of social system or social structure, defined in terms of some set of properties (such as marriage rates or number of children per family), would generate a specific rate of deviant actions so that, as long as properties of the social system were basically the same, the society would have a reasonably stable rate of deviant actions over the years.

The basic idea of this perspective is that deviance is a function of the social system operating as a whole. It is opposed to the more traditional idea that suicide, for instance, is the result of individual factors and decisions; rather, society operating as a whole is the cause of suicide, and the individuals who commit suicide are not. This functional theory of deviance was developed by Durkheim in *Suicide* (1951). Durkheim intended this work as a demonstration that society is a level of existence causing such deviant acts as suicide independently of the will of individuals.

Durkheim's theory of suicide is examined in more detail in Insert No. 5, but the essentials follow. Using the data and correlations found by hundreds of moral statisticians throughout the nineteenth century, Durkheim argued that there are four basic factors at work in society: *egoism, altruism, anomie,* and *fatalism.* These factors operate in relation to each other to produce a given degree of social integration (or social cohesion), the degree to which individuals are involved with, bound to, or dominated by society. The degree of social integration is indicated by rates of various forms of behavior —such as marriage, divorce, number of children, or widowhood. In general, the higher the rate of social involvement (the higher the number of children, the higher the rate of marriage), the greater the social integration. The crucial point is that the greater the degree of social integration, the weaker the suicide-causing currents, and thus the lower the suicide rate; while the lower the degree of social integration, the stronger the suicide-causing currents, and the higher the suicide rate. Most of Durkheim's book is devoted to showing correlations between the official statistics on suicide and those, for example, on marriage and children. The essential details of the theory are indicated in Figure 20–1.

Figure 20-1. Durkheim's Theory of Suicide

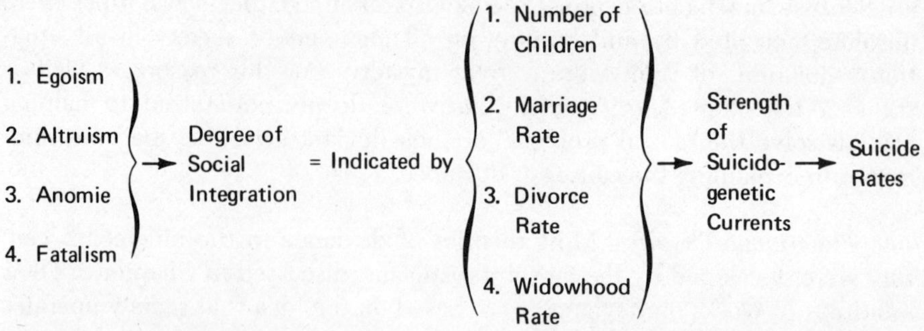

$$\left.\begin{array}{l}\text{1. Egoism} \\ \text{2. Altruism} \\ \text{3. Anomie} \\ \text{4. Fatalism}\end{array}\right\} \begin{array}{l}\text{Degree of} \\ \rightarrow \text{Social} \\ \text{Integration}\end{array} = \text{Indicated by} \left\{\begin{array}{l}\text{1. Number of Children} \\ \text{2. Marriage Rate} \\ \text{3. Divorce Rate} \\ \text{4. Widowhood Rate}\end{array}\right\} \rightarrow \begin{array}{l}\text{Strength of} \\ \text{Suicido-} \\ \text{genetic} \\ \text{Currents}\end{array} \rightarrow \begin{array}{l}\text{Suicide} \\ \text{Rates}\end{array}$$

Later, Durkheim made a second major contribution to the functional theory of deviance with his analysis of the functional responses of society to crime. (We discussed this briefly in Chapter 3.) Durkheim and later functionalists argued that there are two major types of social responses to deviance and crime. First, society creates institutions and patterns of behavior that function to reduce the rate of deviance and crime, through both informal mechanisms of social control and formal mechanisms such as police forces. Second, Durkheim and succeeding functionalists argued that there are unexpected positive functions (or *eufunctions*) of deviance and crime for society. Durkheim tried to show that crime reinforces societal values because society's negative reaction to crime provides a forceful definition of its values for members and demonstrates what happens to evildoers. Other functionalists pursued this same argument later. Kingsley Davis argued that prostitution provides sexual outlets that marriage does not and tends, therefore, to have the function (presumably a eufunction) of supporting marriage as an institution.

In general, functional theorists saw deviance and crime as related to society; society itself generated the rates of deviance and crime, meaning that they were not merely individual acts of antisocial behavior. Having generated deviance, society operated in such ways as to reduce, but not eliminate, deviance and crime, because they also had positive functions for society. Three later functional works on deviance expanded each of these basic points.

Merton's famous article "Social Structure and *Anomie*" (see Insert No. 57), originally published in 1937, had a great influence on a generation of sociological works on deviance. The basic idea of this theory is that society produces anomic strains in individuals by first socializing them to want success and then limiting, through social stratification, opportunities for that success for lower-class individuals. These anomic strains lead individuals to commit one or more of five basic types of deviance.

In *The Social System,* Talcott Parsons (1951) argued that deviance and crime lead to functional responses by society, especially the creation of institutions to reduce them, that tend to maintain the boundaries of the social system. In *Wayward Puritans,* Kai Erikson tried to show that deviance among the American Puritans served the function of producing a redefinition of the boundaries of the social system (see Insert No. 58).

Ecological and Social Disorganization Theory. The ecological theory of deviance is closely related to Durkheim's theory of social integration and deviance. Rather than concentrating on forces that lead individuals to commit deviant acts, the ecological or social disorganization theorists assumed that all individuals have tendencies toward deviance and that the crucial factor allowing this natural deviance to happen is the lack of effective social organization.

At first, the ecological theory was more a method of presenting and analyzing data than a true theory. Each officially reported case of deviance was pinpointed on a map of the city at the place it occurred. The sociologist then tried to analyze these reported cases to see if there was some pattern to them. It was soon discovered—especially in Chicago where the University of Chicago sociologists first developed and applied this method and theory—that there was a clear pattern to these cases: the closer one went toward the center of the city, the higher the official rate of deviance or crime. They tried to answer the question of why such a pattern existed.

The social disorganization theory of deviance was their answer. In general, they believed the rate of deviance increased as one approached the center of the city because the degree of social disorganization increased. The greater the social disorganization, the greater the rate of deviance.

They defined social disorganization as the relative lack of effective social controls over members of society, especially the relative lack of effective punishments for violating the values of society. They believed that many factors produced this disorganization. They argued that primary social relations, involving a high degree of interaction and personal commitment, would produce less disorganization than secondary social relations. Friendship is an example of a primary relationship, while a salesman-customer interaction is an example of a secondary relation. The more anonymous or lonely an individual was in his neighborhood, the fewer social relations he maintained, the more his social relationships were called disorganized. The more social relations in any part of the city tended to be absent or secondary, the more disorganized was that neighborhood, and the more deviance would result. The general outline of this theory is given in Figure 20-2.

Areas closer to the center of town were believed to contain more deviance and crime because they had more secondary than primary relations and fewer social relationships in general. The Chicago sociologists tried to show that skid row areas tend to be near downtown areas, to offer few primary social relations, and to display high rates of deviance and crime. Any other area with a high degree of social disorganization should have a high rate of deviance as well. The Chicago sociologists attempted to prove this in areas located between what they called *natural communities,* generally dominated by one ethnic group. In his famous study of 1,313 gangs, for example, Frederick Thrasher tried to show that gangs were located primarily in such interstitial areas around the city of Chicago.

Louis Wirth (1964) summarized the many ideas of the ecological theory of deviance in his theory of urbanism and deviance (see Chapter 18). He argued that the larger the absolute size of a population in a given area, the larger the relative density of that population, and the more ethnically heterogeneous the population, the more socially disorganized that area, with more deviance.

INSERT NO. 57

On Robert K. Merton's "*Social Structure and* Anomie"

First published in the *American Sociological Review,* Robert K. Merton's "Social Structure and *Anomie*" is probably the best known article in contemporary American sociology (1957). Merton took Durkheim's idea of anomie, or normlessness, in the social structure and applied it to modern American society. He defined anomie as a situation in which many individuals are unable to use institutionally prescribed means to gain access to the major American goal of financial success. He proposed that there are institutionally prescribed means to this end and that an individual may adapt to the situation in one of five ways:

A TYPOLOGY OF MODES OF INDIVIDUAL ADAPTATION

Modes of Adaptation	Culture Goals	Institutionalized Means
1. Conformity	accepts	accepts
2. Innovation	accepts	rejects
3. Ritualism	rejects	accepts
4. Retreatism	rejects	rejects
5. Rebellion	accepts & rejects	accepts & rejects

ANALYSIS OF THE FUNCTIONAL AND ECOLOGICAL THEORIES

These early theories of deviance were found to involve important weaknesses, primarily because they relied on the official statistics on deviance and crime.

Some social scientists and laymen were always aware of the unreliability of official statistics on deviance, as in the case of those on suicide. But, generally, sociologists overlooked criticism of their data, because no other statistics were available and because they continued to hope that errors would be random and would not result in significant biases.

In recent decades, a number of analyses of official statistics (Douglas, 1971a), show unreliability in such data that is not random and make it unlikely that a valid theory of deviance could be constructed by using them.

Official statistics are biased selections of social data because they concern only those data that interest officials trying to eliminate or control what they define as deviance. This bias is especially clear in the case of "juvenile delinquency," a category created by officials with little basis for distinguish-

---

To the extent that a society is stable, conformity is the most usual adaptation for individuals and involves acceptance of cultural goals and institutionalized means for reaching them. The four other modes of adaptation represent different types of deviance.

Innovators accept cultural goals but reject "legitimate" means—they turn to illegitimate or criminal means. Innovation is found especially among the lower classes, where access to legitimate means of attaining wealth are consistently blocked. Ritualism, on the other hand, involves rejection of the goals and acceptance of the means—the typical adaptation of the lower middle classes. Although ritualistic individuals realize that they cannot achieve much success, they "go through the motions" out of habit.

Retreatists accept neither goals nor means of the society; in a real sense they are dropouts. Coming from all strata, they include vagrants, hippies, drug addicts, and drunkards. Rebels also reject goals and means of the society, but they propose other goals and other means, while retreatists do not. Examples of rebellious individuals are radical left and radical right revolutionaries.

As an application of Durkheim's theory to contemporary society and an analysis of the structural sources of deviance, Merton's essay has been the source of much controversy and many new ideas up to the present. Although it has been criticized, particularly on the grounds that it erroneously assumes a homogeneity of values in American society, it remains a significant sociological classic.

ing the criminal acts of the young from those of adults. If the scientist allows the official to decide which realm of society is to be categorized for study, he will wind up studying an officially constructed social reality.

The official categories are not systematic or consistent. Though the same category may be used in several nations or states, the meanings given may be different, so any sociologist using official data that combine data from these different areas may be misled. For example, in the United States the category of "embezzlement" is used in most states, but close examination reveals that the same category has different legal definitions in different states, so a sociologist utilizing official data on embezzlement would be studying a combination of different kinds of actions. In some categories, especially "suicide," we find more extreme variations. For example, in a state such as New York, the official categorization of suicide as a cause of death is entrusted to the coroners or medical examiners of each county; but they do not know a legal definition of suicide that could guide their work. They must fall back upon meanings of suicide in common sense or formal definitions used in different textbooks of forensic medicine.

Even if these categories represented social realities and were consistent from one area to another, they would still be biased because of variations in application by different agencies. Almost all investigations of official crime statistics have found they are biased along class lines in such a way that

INSERT NO. 58

On Kai T. Erikson's *Wayward Puritans*

Kai T. Erikson's *Wayward Puritans* (1967) is a study of Puritan culture in seventeenth-century New England, from the standpoint of deviance theory. He describes three historical events as cases of widespread mass deviance in Puritan society: the Antinomian heresies, the Quaker movement, and the witchcraft scare.

All three instances of collective deviance were essentially theological. The Puritan state was theocratic, basing its law on the Bible, and did not distinguish between secular and sacred law. The first instance of mass deviance was the Antinomian controversy, when several individuals challenged the civil and religious competence of many heads of the church government; the second was the Quaker invasion of New England. In the third case, the deviants were witches, so labeled by young girls who claimed to have been persecuted by these agents of the devil.

In all three instances, says Erikson, despite their "crime wave" characteristics, the annual number of offenders convicted remained fairly stable throughout the century. He surmises from this that there is a "quota" of deviance for

they underestimate upper-class crimes, partly because agencies supporting the police departments, who construct the data on crime, allocate very little money for police work aimed at uncovering and proving cases of *white-collar crime,* such as fraud committed by salesmen and businesses. Attorneys general of various states have long maintained that the most frequent crimes are cases of fraud, especially in such giant fields as the television repair industry, and have called for massive infusions of money to find and prove such difficult cases of fraud. Statistics also underestimate the relative frequency of middle-class and upper-class crimes because legislative bodies will not pass laws against kinds of crimes that cannot be effectively controlled by current police. Many attorneys general have also called for changes in the laws against fraud, which now require stringent proof of "intent to commit fraud" to make it possible to use evidence of fraud in the same way that police can use the presence of a person in someone else's house without invitation as presumption evidence of intention to commit burglary. Legislative bodies have refused to make such changes in the laws. Crimes of upper-class groups are also underestimated because police find it easier and safer (from suits for illegal arrest) to direct most of their work at the lower-class groups.

As the evidence has grown that official statistics on deviance are highly biased, sociologists have relied on participant-observer studies (see Chap-

---

any given society which will be filled by a given number of individuals. He further theorizes that this quota operates to "maintain the boundaries" of conformity in the community—to define and reaffirm the limits of the normative structure by defining and reaffirming violations of it.

Erikson called this societal regulation of the deviant population its "deployment patterns." The Puritans' deviant deployment pattern, for example, involved assumptions that deviance was the individual's property and that deviant roles were permanent (even after death). Usually, the Puritans punished deviants, either by hanging or by permanent stigmatization, marking the individual as unfit for society. This treatment provided reinforcement for the Puritan belief in predestination.

Thus, Erikson argues, a society experiences the amount and kind of deviance necessary for its cultural preservation. He adds that even today Americans tend to view deviance as a characterological state, relatively difficult to change:

> People in this society do not expect much in the way of reform from those who are labeled "deviant." And this, historically, brings us back to the Puritans, for it is their image of deviation, their belief in the irreversibility of human nature, which may be reflected in that expectation.

Figure 20-2. Outline of the Social Disorganization Theory of Deviance

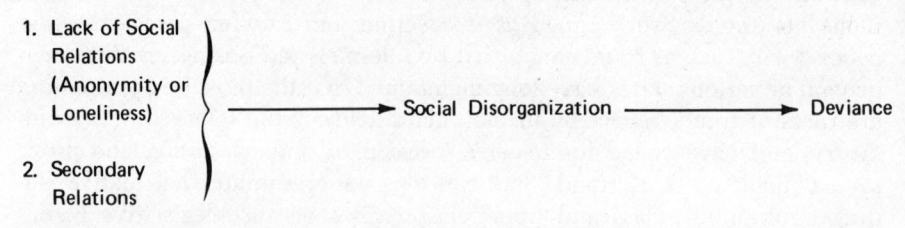

1. Lack of Social Relations (Anonymity or Loneliness)
2. Secondary Relations

⟶ Social Disorganization ⟶ Deviance

ter 4) of deviant groups to construct and test their theories. These studies allow us to obtain reliable information on the everyday lives of deviant groups to explain how and why they develop such patterns of action.

The second major weakness of these earlier theories was their failure to grasp the many conflicts over values in American society. Both the functionalists and the theorists of social disorganization implicitly assumed the common-sense view that social rules are absolute. They believed that all members of American society have the same values and use them in the same ways in their everyday lives, that these values are not created by individuals and do not change. Evidence has accumulated to show, rather, that social rules are subject to a great deal of conflict and uncertainty for Americans, that they are created by individuals, and that they change greatly.

In the 1930s A. W. Lind (1930), Thorstein Sellin (1938), and others criticized the disorganization theorists for failing to see that values and laws are not always congruent in American society. Specifically, they argued that frequently the many different ethnic groups have different values and that some of these values bring them into conflict with the laws and legal institutions of our society. This conflict was most obvious in a city such as Honolulu where the laws were the usual Anglo-American laws but where ethnic groups such as Polynesians and Japanese had very different values concerning, for example, premarital sex and suicide. As Lind argued (1930), the more socially organized were these ethnic groups, the more they would violate the laws. Sellin (1938) argued that this evidence makes it necessary for us to distinguish between *conduct norms,* used in everyday life to govern behavior, and laws.

Subculture Theories. The growing recognition that deviant groups in American society have some different values or make use of common values in different ways led first to the subculture theories of deviance. A subculture is any set of social meanings shared by a group which varies from the generally shared meanings of the larger group. The members of the subculture have meanings in common that overlap with those of the larger group but are in some way different.

The subculture theories differ from each other mainly in the degree to which they see deviant subcultures as different from the larger society. One of the most influential theories of deviant subcultures is Albert Cohen's

Delinquent Boys (1955). Cohen argued that the dominant feature of delinquent gang boys is their ambivalence about American values. He tried to show they are committed to traditional values of success, including success in school, but repress these commitments in favor of opposite values when they find they cannot succeed in terms of traditional values. Vandalism, the destruction of property which represents the traditional values, becomes an ideal method of expressing their ambivalence. Cohen's theory, however, suffers from not proving such ambivalence. All observable behavior of the gang boys could as easily be explained by seeing them as opposed to the traditional values without ambivalence.

Walter Miller (1958) and others have taken this latter position in explaining lower-class gang activity. They postulate a *lower-class subculture* in our society that is quite different in its values, ideas, and patterns of everyday life from those of the middle and upper classes. This "culture of poverty," as it is sometimes called, places great value on immediate gratification, excitement, toughness, and other aspects of social life that these theorists believe lead adolescent males into trouble.

As Charles Valentine (1968) and others have noted, many problems remain to be answered about the theory of a lower-class subculture. Existing theory tends to see the lower class as far more homogeneous than it is, and fails to see that the nature of our criminal laws and police work leads lower-class groups to be more subject to police surveillance and intervention than other class groups. But these subculture theories made an important contribution to the development of the theory of deviance by noting the differences and conflicts in values existing between groups in our society.

The Phenomenological Theories. The most important break with the absolutist perspective on social rules was made by the *social interactionists*. The earliest interactionist theories of deviance were those of Sutherland (1957), Lindesmith (1947), and Lemert (1967). Sutherland's studies of processional criminals had emphasized the specialized nature of the skills involved in professional crime. By use of self-reporting, a form of retrospective participant observation, he demonstrated that professional criminals have highly developed subcultures with different views of law and law enforcement from those of other groups in our society. Lindesmith's study of *Opiate Addiction* (1947) carried this line of reasoning further by arguing that the crucial determinant of whether an individual becomes an addict is whether he learns to think of himself as addicted; he tried to show through case studies that an individual becomes a socially defined addict only when others, in their interaction, show him that he can avoid withdrawal symptoms only by taking more of the drug. Lemert argued further that individuals become socially defined as deviants, such as paranoid schizophrenics, primarily by being official labeled as deviants.

The most famous work in this interactionist tradition is Howard Becker's *labeling theory*, as developed in *Outsiders* (see Insert No. 59). Becker argued that rules are created by some groups in society to enforce their values and interests on other groups; that creation and invoking of social rules is not an automatic process but results from the initiative of moral enterpreneurs; and that these rules are invoked and enforced selectively. Some rules are invoked and enforced more than others and some groups (especially lower-class groups) have rules invoked against them more than others. By denying that social rules are absolute, Becker made an important contribution to investigation of the *problematic nature of social rules*, that is, the uncertainties and conflicts over the meanings and uses of social rules.

Becker's theory of social rules and rule violations, based on the idea that it takes the interaction of two parties to produce a rule violation, grew out of his own participant-observer studies of jazz musicians and marijuana use. Since his work, there have been many important studies of deviant groups making use almost exclusively of the participant-observer methods presented

---

INSERT NO. 59

On Howard S. Becker's *Outsiders*

Howard Becker's *Outsiders* is a landmark in the development of sociological theories of deviance. His major thesis is that deviance is a product of negotiation between the deviant and those with whom he is interacting, rather than a quality inherent in the deviant himself or in his acts:

> *Social groups create deviance by making the rules whose infraction constitutes deviance*, and by applying those rules to particular people and labeling them as outsiders. From this point of view, deviance is *not* a quality of the act a person commits, but rather a consequence of the application by others of rules and sanctions to an "offender." The deviant is one to whom that label had successfully been applied; deviant behavior is behavior that people so label.

Becker argues that involvement in deviance tends to have a sequential rather than a simultaneous character. In other words, the traditional way of studying deviance is in error because it assumes that the variables under study are all operating at the same time to produce the deviant behavior. Rather, this behavior is a dynamic process, not a static phenomenon, so that the sequential model in which variables are seen as operating sequentially rather than simultaneously is more appropriate.

The sequential model of deviance is elaborated by Becker in his concept of *deviant careers*, which he illustrates with reference to marijuana smoking. In his chapter on "Becoming a Marijuana User," Becker describes the sequence

in Chapter 4. All these works take the everyday lives of socially defined deviants as the primary reality that must be studied and analyzed. They are studied as natural phenomena to see how deviants define their own actions. An important statement of this theory is found in David Matza's *Becoming Deviant* (see Insert No. 60). These works do not begin with the presumption that we already know what the rules are, what they mean, how they are used, that these people are violators. Rather, they take all these as problems to be investigated by the sociologist. By using such methods and avoiding preconceptions based on the absolutist view of social rules, these sociologists have discovered many ways in which many people are involved in what could be officially categorized as crime, but which rarely is. In this way, they have discovered that members of society do not look at all their social rules as absolute or binding on themselves. They have found many ways in which members of society are able to manage the appearances of such actions so that they do not appear deviant: they normalize deviance

of steps involving the individual in regular use of marijuana in terms of a career in deviance which, like any other kind of career, has a distinct beginning, a sequence of steps, and a conclusion. First, the marijuana user has to learn the technique of smoking and to perceive the drug's effects. If the user is to continue, he must also learn to enjoy the experience. Generally, this career progresses through interaction with other users, who teach the novice the social meanings of marijuana use.

A further significant concept developed in *Outsiders* is that of the *moral entrepreneur*. The moral entrepreneur sets about getting a particular type of activity defined as deviant or making sure that existing laws against some type of deviance are stringently enforced. Often, he is able to start a moral crusade against a given deviant activity which, in turn, can be the start of a deviance-fighting organization. The classic example of this would be the moral entrepreneurs who created the many temperance leagues which got prohibition passed by a constitutional amendment. Once such an organization has eliminated the original aberration to its satisfaction, it will go on to create and attack other types of behavior it defines as deviant, because organizations tend to be self-perpetuating.

Throughout the book, Becker addresses himself to how rules are made, enforced, and applied. He concludes that the crucial element in successful definition, prosecution, and organizational use of deviance is power: groups in power make the rules and enforce them selectively, which means they will be enforced primarily on those who do not have power: the lower-class groups.

Outsiders is one of the most significant theoretical statements of that sociology of deviance referred to as labeling theory. With its focus on the process of deviance and on the negotiation of labels, it makes an important advance from earlier conceptions of deviance as what powerful people say it is.

in many different ways, so that they reach accommodation between the rules of the larger society and their own seeming violations of those rules.

The findings of these studies of social rules and their uses have gone further, showing that the meanings and uses of all social rules are problematic to some degree for members of society. The meanings and uses of any social rules are uncertain and conflictful, in part, because any rule may contain conflicts within itself or conflict with other rules that must be combined with it. In this case, rules are said to be essentially problematic, or problematic for members of society independent of the situation in which they are used. But these problems also exist because the application of any rule to a real situation involves uncertainties. Rules are said to be *situationally problematic*, or problematic for members of society in a given situation.

The degree of difficulty in deciding the meaning of rules varies greatly, from the nearly automatic application of rules to routine situations to the uncertainties and conflicts of crisis situations. We are aware of these problems in everyday life. We recognize that the routine application of traffic rules to our everyday driving practices involves problems. Inevitably, there arise situations not adequately covered by the rules, such as a car stalled

---

INSERT NO. 60

On David Matza's *Becoming Deviant*

As Matza comments, the commitment of his book *Becoming Deviant* (1969) is to naturalism: "To phenomena and their nature; not to Science or any other system of standards." There are two main approaches to deviant phenomena: the correctional and the appreciative. The *correctional* perspective takes deviant phenomena as something to be cured or eliminated, while *appreciation* involves interpreting deviance without a prior commitment to eliminating it.

Matza also contrasts the concepts of *pathology* and *diversity*. Sociologists who regard deviance as pathological, abnormal, and destructive of society are distinguished from those who regard it less evaluatively, as diverse behavior subject to social controls and proscriptions. Appreciation and diversity take the deviant actor's viewpoint as the starting point of sociological theory, while correction and pathology arise from the views of official agents of social control who wish to eliminate the deviance.

As Matza points out, once the correctional approach was put aside, sociologists discovered the connections and similarities between deviant and conventional phenomena, which he calls their *overlap*. He also points out that the naturalistic stance tends to be ironical, as it leads to the discovery of socially beneficial aspects of deviance and destructive elements in conformity. The

across the intersection where we are about to make a left turn or a red light that is stuck on red and is backing up traffic. The laws say nothing about these exceptions but we know that, to achieve our purposes in the situation, we must "play it by ear," providing new meanings or interpretations for the situation in order to achieve our goal. In this sense, each member of society must act as judge and jury by providing concrete interpretations of the laws.

Aside from these instances of problematic meanings of rules taken from everyday life, there are many examples in recent studies of deviance. In my analysis of suicide cases (1967), I tried to show that members of our society construct varied, complex moral meanings for individual cases of suicide in which they find themselves involved. Most of the time the individual commiting suicide, if successful, is not considered morally to blame. Rather, his friends, family, employer, or society are often held morally responsible in some way. This makes it possible for people to use suicide as a means of getting revenge.

Because of these problems of interpreting meanings of social rules, members of society must construct meanings of rules for the situations they face in everyday life. There will be disagreement between members over what they see as moral and immoral for a given situation, even if they start out

---

natural approach, by admitting overlap and irony, highlights the complexity of social phenomena, while traditional sociology is often simplistic.

Matza also analyzes the concept of deviant career, by which an individual comes to think of himself as representative of a given deviant category. Traditional sociology has conceived of the person as feeling an affinity for deviance because of environmental background. Matza regards this conception as too simplified and he adds two other, more dynamic concepts: affiliation and signification.

Affiliation refers to the subjective aspect of becoming deviant: the process by which the individual, step by step, affiliates himself with the deviant behavior and with others who have chosen to engage in banned acts. *Signification* is the process by which the deviant comes to see himself as a deviant, as a representative of a deviant category. Through affinity, affiliation, and signification, in dynamic interaction, the individual builds himself a deviant identity.

Matza's book is a landmark in contemporary deviance theory, both for its analysis of the history of deviance theory and its contribution to theory. Its central premise, the naturalistic approach to deviance, renders deviance nonmysterious:

> Deviation . . . needs no extraordinary accounting. Straying from a path need be regarded as no less comprehensible nor more bewildering than walking it. Given the moral character of social life, both *naturally* happen, and thus are pondered and studied by sociologists and others.

554 Social Problems and Social Order

with the same rules. This is why we see vast disagreement over what is right and wrong in our everyday lives, even within tight-knit families and friendship groups sharing the same abstract social values and facing the same situations.

This necessity of constructing concrete meanings of rules for concrete situations means that individuals will have considerable freedom in our society in creating the meanings they want, especially because our society is so pluralistic that individuals often hold different values to be applied to given situations. This makes it possible for a vast array of different kinds of behavior to be judged morally acceptable or reprehensible by different

INSERT NO. 61

"Practical Reasons for Gundecking" by John M. Johnson

The setting for "Practical Reasons for Gundecking" is the everyday working routine aboard the U.S.S. *Walden*, a Navy destroyer whose primary mission is Anti-Submarine Warfare (ASW). The research focuses upon the practical reasoning of the various persons concerned with the maintenance and operation of the ship's ASW equipment, and their reporting of their activities. Interest is specifically concentrated on the Sonar Performance Report, one of the more important reports by which the ship's ASW personnel demonstrate their organizational competence, and the situations in which this report is "gundecked."

Literally defined, gundecking refers to "falsification" of official reports, that is, reporting activities as having been accomplished when the rules and procedures of the formal organization have not been followed "to the letter." For an observer to ascertain that certain activities constitute compliance or non-compliance with the formal rules, it is necessary to assume that these rules possess status transcending the occasions of their use. This formality obscures our understanding of actors' reasonable judgment of the situational relevance for determining what it takes to maintain the normal working day, and it diverts our attention from the meaning of the formal organization's rules on the occasions of their use. This research analyzes various ways the ASW personnel use the formal rules and procedures of the organization as common-sense concepts in their efforts to construct or maintain social order.

Several kinds of practical sociological reasoning were used by the ASW personnel aboard ship to more rationally account for the exigencies of new situations. The first was called "fudging" or, sometimes, "throwing in a fudge factor." Although formal procedures for conducting the sonar performance measurements called for stopping the normal working day for nearly all electrical equipment in the galleys (kitchens), the ASW personnel considered these requirements unnecessary. Given "what anyone knows" about sustaining

groups, while the groups continue to see themselves as upright American citizens. Consider, for example, the different meanings given by groups to "all men should be treated as equals." Some believe this phrase means we should give everyone equal educational opportunities; others believe it means that those who have the most trouble learning in our formal systems of education should be given more than equal financial treatment, so that they will "become equal someday"; others believe it means we should leave everyone to his own devices and treat everyone equally in social interaction. Each group is convinced that it has found the one right meaning of equality. But a sociologist trying to objectively analyze society must note these dis-

a cooperative atmosphere for social relationships in such a physically confined setting, the ASW personnel avoided "catching flack" from their shipmates by not insisting that the formal procedures be followed. They altered the Sonar Performance Report in terms of common-sense interpretation of what they thought would be a reasonable factor representing the noise put into the water by, for example, the fact that the equipment in the galley had not been shut off during the measurements. This alteration appeared reasonable to these actors, given that the sonar performance measurements were routine for them but potentially inconveniencing to many others.

The second kind of practical reasoning was referred to as "sketching-in," involving gundecking certain portions of the Report. Because a casualty to one of the ship's boilers limited the ship's speed, sonar measurements were made at lower speeds only, and figures for the higher speeds were sketched in by referring to figures in the Report for the previous month. While the deviant status of this activity was recognized by the organizational actors, the gundecking of the Report was perceived as a reasonable response to the situation at hand, especially in light of other reasons offered to support the contention that the intent of the formal rules had been accomplished. The sketching in of a portion of the Report not only avoided potential embarrassment, but allowed the ship to return to a more pressing battle-related commitment.

Another kind of practical reasoning called "covering your ass" involved "faking" the Report by adopting measures which participants perceived as unofficial but deemed a logical response to the situation. Through systematic, competent use of formal rules and procedures, certain unofficial practices were validated and sustained, which they thought dealt with the practical circumstances of their jobs in a more rational way than official practices.

Gundecking was perceived as problematic by men aboard the U.S.S. *Walden* for several reasons, the most important being the uncertainty associated with the negotiated cooperation of various people who had their own purposes and diverse interests. Also, the actors were keenly aware that reports deemed sufficient at one point in time may be redefined as insufficient at another point in time (as were the reports of the My Lai incident in the Vietnam war).

agreements and try to explain them. The explanation comes from recognizing the necessarily problematic constructions of moral meanings in our society.

We find unexpected constructions of moral meanings resulting from this freedom in making interpretations. For example, we find nudists who believe that nudity is justified by American values. As Martin Weinberg has described it (see Insert No. 62), they have constructed a situational morality justifying nudism.

USING SOCIAL RULES AND CONSTRUCTING SOCIAL ORDER

It is clear that members of our society are constrained in construction of their interpretations of social rules. Thus, the nudists are constrained to justifying their nudity only within physical places—nudist camps and, more rarely, their homes. Interpretations of our social rules that justify public nudity have become far more acceptable in recent years, but these interpre-

---

INSERT NO. 62

"The Situated Morality of a Nudist Camp" by Martin S. Weinberg

"The basis for the construction of a situated morality in the nudist camp is provided by the official interpretations that camps maintain regarding the moral meanings of public heterosexual nudity. These are 1., that nudity and sexuality are unrelated, 2., that there is nothing shameful about exposing the human body, 3., that the abandonment of clothes leads to a feeling of freedom and natural pleasure, and 4., that nude activities, especially the entire body's exposure to the sun, lead to a feeling of physical, mental, and spiritual well-being. . . . One element in the strategy used by the nudist camp to anesthetize nude-sex appresentation is a system of organizational precautions in the requisites for initial admission to a nudist camp. Most camps, for example, do not allow unmarried individuals. . . .

"Norms regarding patterns of interpersonal behavior are the second element of the strategy to maintain the organizations' system of moral meanings. . . . No staring. . . . No sex talk. . . . No body contact. . . . No alcoholic beverages in American camps. . . . Rules regarding photography. . . . No accentuation of the body. . . . No unnatural attempts at covering the body. . . . Communal toilets. . . .

"In the nudist camp, nudity becomes subjectively, as well as objectively, routinized. Its attention-provoking quality therefore recedes; nudity becomes a taken-for-granted state of affairs" (Martin Weinberg, 1970).

tations are still not widely shared. What do members use as criteria for constructing their situational meanings of rules?

First, there are normatively prescribed *rules about the use of rules*. Interpretations of rules must generally meet tests of rationality. The interpreter must be consistent, consider relevant facts, and demonstrate his willingness to be reasonable and objective. He must also show that he is sincere and not making use of the rules to justify whatever he happens to want. These rules, while providing a greater degree of concreteness in the construction of situational meanings, allow for the same kinds of problems of interpretation as other rules. They do not provide completely concrete constructions of meanings.

The crucial factor in providing concrete solutions to the problem of constructing meanings seems to be *practicality;* that is, only those constructions that seem practical in the immediate situation will be accepted. This practicality is judged in terms of the context of people's everyday lives. No matter how much in accord with abstract values, anything not seen as workable in this context will be rejected. It may be labeled as "too idealistic," "impractical," "other-worldly," or "radical."

But one man's practicality is another man's impracticality; there are many kinds of everyday lives. We must continually negotiate the moral meanings (or any other meanings) for any concrete situation at hand. Most of the time, there is *cooperative construction* of the meanings of rules, involving the give-and-take of bargaining when there are differences in the general values brought to the situation. There are many *presentational and interactional strategies* of the sort analyzed by Goffman and others (see Chapter 9) involved in these negotiations of situational meanings. For example, those involved will often use *interactional indirection* in bringing moral considerations into play. They will avoid treating these considerations in terms of moral rules, but will act as if the only disagreements were on the facts. This tactic helps avoid conflicts that might arise from asserting, "What you say is immoral and what I say is moral." Members will seek more general agreement by talking about values they might share. ("We both want the common good, so we simply have to find the best way to get there.") When conflicts are inescapable they will try to compromise, one going along with something that he thinks wrong in order to avoid an even greater wrong that would come from open conflict. When such strategies fail, there is generally open resort to power and conflict. Bloody conflicts in American public life attest to the danger that members of our society are not always able to negotiate solutions to problems of moral meanings.

Given the necessity in such a pluralistic society of negotiating the applications of social rules to social situations, there can be no simple relationship between these rules and social order. The traditional, common-sense view of the relations between social rules and social order is that disobeying the rules produces social disorder. This idea is seen in the slogan "Law and

Order." Obeying the laws, the official rules of modern states, supposedly produces social order, while disobeying the laws supposedly produces social disorder. This idea is so much taken for granted in common-sense thinking that "obeying the rules (laws)" and "social order" become almost synonymous. It is this common-sense assumption that underlay the early absolutist assumption that deviance produces social disintegration and that this produces deviance.

Our understanding of the complex nature of the interpretation and use of social rules leads us to see that there can be no such simple relationship between rules and order. Social rules are merely one of many social factors used to construct social order and the ways in which they are used for this purpose are varied. It is common, for example, for police to choose not to enforce laws when they believe that an attempt to enforce them would lead to violence or riots. During the urban riots of the 1960s and such mass gatherings as at the Woodstock Festival, the police admitted that this was their policy. It seems clear that as power in American society has become more pluralistic, because different ethnic groups have become more powerful, public policies are based less and less on moral rules held by only one part of society. Increasingly, policies are based on considerations of how well they seem to contribute to the "common good" as defined by their contribution to the general economy, national security, and health. These general goals, shared by almost all groups, regardless of differences in moral commitment, may become least-common-denominator goals and both replace morality as a basis for policies and moral rules as the basis for attempts to construct social order.

PROSPECTS

The sociology of deviance and social control now considers the use of rules in constructing social order as complex and problematic. The greatest progress in this field has come from the growing number of participant-observer studies of the everyday lives of deviant groups and of social control groups such as the police. These studies first revealed how little we understood about social rules in everyday life and allowed us to determine what we know. For all this progress, we have only scratched the surface.

We shall have to concentrate on studying the use of social rules to construct social order. We shall have to undertake the study of how politicians and government officials use, or do not use, social rules in creating coalition parties and policies to produce social order. We shall have to study what they mean by social order, just as we have had to study what they mean by social rules (such as morals), and how they decide when order or disorder exists. When we have done this, we shall be better able to transcend common-sense analysis of social rules and social order.

SUGGESTED READINGS

Becker, Howard S., *Outsiders*. New York: The Free Press, 1963.
    One of the best-known theoretical and empirical statements of the "labeling theory" perspective on deviance.

———, ed., *The Other Side*. New York: The Free Press, 1964.
    A collection of essays by various authors which apply the labeling theory of deviance to empirical cases.

Douglas, Jack D., *American Social Order: Social Rules in a Pluralistic Society*. New York: The Free Press, 1971.
    A contemporary statement of the nature of rules and the construction of social order.

———, *The Social Meanings of Suicide*. Princeton: Princeton University Press, 1967.
    Critique of Durkheim's use of suicide statistics, with a consideration of other ways of studying suicide and its meaning.

Erikson, Kai T., *Wayward Puritans*. New York: Wiley, 1967.
    Using a historical example from Puritan New England, Erikson analyzes the way in which deviant behavior expresses the boundaries of what is "normal" in society.

Merton, Robert K., *Social Theory and Social Structure*, rev., enlarged ed. New York: The Free Press, 1957.
    This collection of Merton's major work contains his famous essay on "Social Structure and *Anomie*," which had such a major impact on deviance theory from the functional perspective.

Wolfgang, Marvin E., ed., *The Sociology of Crime and Delinquency*. New York: Wiley, 1962.
    A comprehensive reader in deviance and criminology which covers many sociological perspectives on these topics, from theories of the etiology of time to the argument over gang delinquency and lower-class subcultures.

PART VIII

Conclusion

All of the earlier parts of this book have shown us where sociology has come from and what its major findings and ideas are today. The following brief chapter tries to show what the major trends are today, and where we seem to be going. It tries to show what some of the major weaknesses of recent theory have been, and it suggests how these might be overcome by further developments.

PART VII

CHAPTER 21

The Future of Sociology in America

As we have seen throughout this book, the discipline of sociology is undergoing more rapid change today than at any time since its formation in the nineteenth century. These changes have come both from within and without sociology. The rapid developments, especially those due to analyses of everyday life, have posed challenges to the classical structural tradition and have begun to transform it, integrating the sociology of everyday life with the analyses of social structures. The growing pressures to involve the discipline in attempts to understand and solve social problems have posed parallel challenges that are beginning to change sociology (including the phenomenological sociologies), relating it to finding practical solutions to complex social problems.

Predicting anything about the future is uncertain. If we could do this, we would anticipate evil possibilities and prevent them, invalidating our earlier anticipations of evil. Predicting the future of social events is more uncertain than this, both because members of society find their social decisions so problematic and because sociologists have not yet achieved a high degree of predictability in their theories of social action. But, just as scientists and historians of technology can now anticipate with some success what important types of developments will take place in their fields, so can we hope to foresee the types of developments that will take place in sociology and in our society over the next few decades, without being able to give precise details. This kind of task has been undertaken by futurologists, students of the future, and specifically by the group of natural and social scientists who produced the report *Toward the Year 2000* (Bell, 1968).

When we survey important developments in sociology, certain areas pose problems that seem important to the future of the discipline. The sociology of everyday life, or the phenomenological sociologies, has been in the forefront of creative developments in theory for some time, yet the rapid pace of growth and increase in student involvement lead us to expect that it is still in the early stages of development. Its most important contributions may lie ahead. What might these be?

There will be a great increase in field studies using participant-observer methods to determine the meanings of actions to members. This increase will be of value because there have been relatively few recent studies that students of everyday life could use to derive and test their theories. It will give us a far more representative set of studies of everyday life in American society. We shall no longer have to guess about the representativeness of any given study of a relatively small group of people, but shall be able to determine with some degree of precision whether the results of one study indicate a more fundamental pattern of social action. But the increase in number will be of value only if it produces an increase in the amount of reliable information about our society.

There are two reasons for believing that the increase in the number of these studies will be accompanied by an increase in the quality of information, in its validity and reliability. Recently, the methods of field research have been more carefully analyzed. As these methods develop and become more generally applied, we shall obtain more sophisticated, valid, and reliable information about everyday life.

The second reason is that theoretical analyses of everyday life are increasingly informing and stimulating the field studies. Previously, studies of everyday life went on largely independent of development of the phenomenological theories of everyday life, which were often based on a simple observation of the theorist's own everyday life. The field studies were only a step away from journalism, and the theories were only a step away from philosophy. But the growing knowledge of the theories and the growing empirical sophistication of the theorists has produced a great increase in the validity and reliability of both.

What will these studies and theories be about? What directions can we expect in their content?

We can expect a continuing concern with the determination of meanings to members of society. We can expect two developments in this direction.

First, students of everyday life will become more concerned with problems of objectivity in determining meanings. We shall continue using common-sense understandings of everyday lives, gained through participant observation, but we must also develop more objective means of studying meanings communicated in everyday life by members of society. We have to devise better means of demonstrating that our conclusions about meanings are valid, to make our conclusions more reproducible by others, rather than allowing them to remain mystical revelations of our methods.

Second, we can expect sociologists to be increasingly concerned with determining the properties of social meanings. To date, most field studies have been concerned with showing "how the members see it." This was important in correcting the earlier assumption of sociologists that they knew what social action meant to the members without studying this action; but the simple repetition of raw studies does not get us beyond the first step of the sociology of everyday life. The crucial form of progress consists in analyzing raw data to determine its theoretical properties. More specifically, we can expect a growing concern with how members demonstrate to each other what is meaningful, reasonable, plausible, and ordered. What are the properties of a communication or an action seen by members of a group to be meaningful, reasonable, and ordered?

Sociologists of everyday life will also become more concerned with studying the *transsituational aspects* of everyday life (Douglas, 1970f). We will study *how members see social structure (order) in their everyday situations;* we will determine how they move from social situations to social structures. Thus far, there has been a concentration on determining the meanings of actions to one given group or within one given situation, but little concern with how members of society put it all together. The first part of a study of transsituational aspects of everyday life might focus on the question of how the members see or infer an order within situations? This question leads to the question of how they see situations as related to each other. How are situations seen as similar or dissimilar to others? How do members see situations as ordered in relation to each other? What do they mean by "social order" and "social disorder" when they say such things as "America is threatened by growing social disorder"?

If we begin to determine such fundamental questions, we shall better understand how individuals attempt to construct social order. For the first time, phenomenological sociologists will become directly concerned with the study and analysis of politics. (Some first steps in this direction are given in Chapter 12.) What do we mean by "politics"? What are the political devices used to construct social order? Many participant-observer studies of political activities will be necessary before we gain reliable information on such questions.

First, we must study such questions from the standpoint of the members, but we must then try to go beyond the members. We are not interested only in how individual members try to do it, but also in how they could do better if they had scientific knowledge about such social activities. By starting with an analysis of what they are trying to do and the way they do it, we assure ourselves that our theories will include the meanings of such questions to the members; at the same time, we will assure ourselves that our analyses will be relevant to the practical concerns of members. Rather than impose our ideas about social order or structure upon them, we shall be providing them with the kind of knowledge they can use to better achieve the kind of social order they want.

ANALYSIS AND SOLUTION OF SOCIAL PROBLEMS

As we have seen in Part VII, almost all traditional analyses of social problems assumed definitions of problems to be unproblematic or absolute. Sociological analyses have assumed it was obvious that certain things (deviance, crime, pathology) were social problems, that everyone in society agreed they should be solved or eliminated, and that the sociologist's job was to discover their causes so they could be eliminated. These analyses made value assumptions which, as C. Wright Mills argued (1963), sociologists did not recognize as such. Because they adopted such assumptions and took an unquestioning approach toward social problems, these people were trying to impose their values on the rest of society and were using the mantle of science to convince other members that they, as scientists of society, were right about what should be done, regardless of what other members of society might think.

This approach has been rejected by sociologists of everyday life because it is contrary to the very idea of such a sociology and, they argue, to an effective application of the discipline to the solution of social problems. Just as the sociologist of everyday life begins his analysis of any aspect of society, such as social order (see Chapter 20), by studying it from the standpoint of members, so he begins his analysis of social problems from their standpoint. He begins by trying to determine what people mean by a social problem. What criteria are used to specify a social problem? In Chapter 19, we have seen the progress made thus far in this form of analysis. While these initial advances are important in the development of the sociology of social problems, the greatest advances in our understanding lie ahead.

In trying to anticipate developments that will contribute to the solution of social problems, we must have some idea of related trends in American society. We can expect the society to become more complex. While there may have been a slow decrease in the ethnic differences in our population, many other social differences and divisions have grown rapidly to ensure continuance of our high degree of social pluralism. In addition, we can expect that these differences will lead to more social conflicts, political or violent. This is because they are increasingly focused at the national level. Mass communication makes interest groups aware of their differences. The increasing involvement of government at all levels in American life means that the many interest groups will have to struggle with each other to gain political influence and power so that they may protect and advance their interests. Whereas the small farmers and artisans making up much of America until the early part of this century had to struggle against nature or local competition to advance their interests, the giant interest groups today (farmers, industrialists, businessmen, professors, students, poor, rich, middle class) must struggle with each other at the city, state, and federal levels. Consider the effects of the slow decline of the free market on political conflicts. The small farmer of the last century had little recourse when the prices of his crops were low because of high supply relative to demand. He couldn't pressure his congressman because his congressman had little to do with it. Today, when farmers get low prices for their crops because of high supply, they go to the government for help in limiting the crop supply and maintaining the prices at what they consider a fair level (parity). In the same way, the unemployed and poor demand help from the government, which farmers may oppose as social welfare and giveaway programs, while the urban poor may oppose farm subsidies as giveaways and unfair advantages. As another example, the oil depletion allowance can produce intense national conflict among different groups.

At the same time that American society is becoming more complex and internally conflictful, it is becoming more involved in conflictful international relations. There are many reasons for this: (1) Our economy is involved in the economies of almost every other nation. (2) Our search for national security through foreign treaties and military bases involves us in many nations. (3) Our economic importance, our millitary interests, and some national values have led us to take an active interest in the governments and economies of other nations and these factors, combined with the almost universal desire for economic progress, have led some of these nations to make ever greater demands on us. (4) The growth of international mass communications has produced greater mutual awareness and concern. From a nation shunning foreign entanglements, we have become the most entangled nation of all; and our conflicts with other nations and interest groups in other nations have grown proportionally. At the same time, these foreign conflicts have accentuated our internal strife because of their effects on our nation and because many such conflicts, such as the Vietnam war, are seen by different interest groups as having different effects on them. The internal effects of such foreign involvements are apparent in the assassinations of John and Robert Kennedy, whereas earlier political assassinations had been related mainly to internal conflicts. As there is every reason to believe we shall continue to become more involved in international relations, and that they will continue to generate conflict, we can expect that our international conflicts and the internal turmoil related to them will continue to grow.

The rising complexity and conflictfulness of American society has two general implications for our understanding of social problems and for the involvement of sociology in trying to solve them. The problems of social order will become greater. Not only will it be increasingly difficult to handle political conflicts by normal political and legal procedures, but we will have greater difficulty in maintaining our forms of government and law and the individual rights and civil liberties dependent on those forms of government and law. As the government, especially the federal government, becomes even more the focus of our differences and conflicts, it becomes more both the target of those who wish power over their own circumstances and the target of discontented groups, from farmers to inner-city residents. We do not know whether our democratic forms of government or individual freedoms associated with those forms can endure these increasing conflicts. But we can be sure that any attempts to solve them in such a way as to allow the continuance and expansion of such freedoms and forms of government will be more difficult and will demand better knowledge of social processes.

Because of growing politicization of our society and growing conflict, there will be less consensus in definition of social problems. The result is that definition of what are social problems and what are not will become ever more the subject of political conflict. Thus, individuals concerned with studying and helping to solve social problems will have to become more concerned with analyzing definitions of these problems and with surveying the political processes by which they are defined. For example, we shall have to determine how the mass media are important in forming public opinion on social problems (as we saw in Chapter 19, the sudden burst of public interest in the long-standing problem of pollution is an excellent example of the power of the media), how government bureaucracies and "experts" are instrumental in formulating definitions of social problems, how politicians are significant, and how all these are related to each other.

Political conflicts over the definition of social problems will be accentuated by the increasing independence of our problems from nature. An example of this can be seen in farmers' reactions. Whereas once farmers saw their problems as the result of nature or the natural functioning of the marketplace (prices), now they see their problems as the result of social policies; whereas there was once general agreement, among farmers and nonfarmers alike, about the nature of farm problems, there is now little agreement. The fact that we as a society could now do something about various problems if we chose to leads to greater political conflict over social problems. This is one reason why in recent years we have seen an increase in what members of society define as social problems, precisely at a time when in absolute physical terms most people are better off. Sociologists can understand these complex developments only by devising better means of analyzing the *social meanings of social problems* and how these meanings are created through political struggles.

At the same time, the political conflicts over what constitutes *an adequate solution* to any social problem have become more intense. Even such problems as smog produce intense political conflicts over definition of a solution. For example, consider the controversy between those who argue that the problem of smog can be solved only by changing our entire way of life (less consumerism and less power for business) and those who argue that we must initiate further developments in technology and business to solve the problems created by earlier developments.

Few social scientists today can feel sanguine about the future of our society or about our own capacity to provide the objective understanding of social problems that is needed if we are to find workable solutions. But we must recognize that the challenge to us, as to our society, is to do all we can to provide knowledge about society, its situations and structures.

Glossary of Key Concepts

The reader can find specific uses of these key concepts in the text by checking the Index.

Action (social): Behavior with shared meanings for members of society; the object of all sociological work, as defined by Weber.

Action system: The organized orientations of action of social performers.

Affiliation: The need to interact with (or, at least, be in the company of) others; ordinarily applied only to members of the same species.

Alienation: First developed by Marx with reference to man's alienation from his work, this term has come to mean the state of being estranged from society or social relationships, especially in industrial society; hence, a feeling of separateness.

Analytic induction: A method that seeks to establish abstract generalizations sequentially from observation of concrete data by changing the generalization to accommodate each change observed in the data.

Anomie: First used by Durkheim, this term has come to mean a condition of normlessness or meaninglessness in society, hence feelings of confusion and absurdity. *See also* Norms.

Appearance: Those stimuli that inform an observer about the social statuses and roles of a performer. Examples are insignia of office or rank, clothing, sex, age, and racial characteristics.

Ascription: The automatic attachment of a given role or status to an individual; for example, "male," "daughter," "old person." Antonym: achievement.

Association: (1) A logical term referring to the co-presence of two states or variables in society; for example, "high" education is associated with "high" occupations in American society. (2) A word loosely descriptive of large groupings of people bound by one or two common interests.

Attitude: First defined by W. I. Thomas, a tendency to act or respond in a definite manner.

Audience: Witnesses to a given encounter of performance.

Authority: Institutionalized power, seen as legitimate and based on shared values concerning who has a right to influence in the group.

Backstage: As used by Goffman, the area where people (social actors) relax from performances, contradict their frontstage performances, and prepare for coming frontstage dramatizations. Also known as back region.

Bias (statistical): Technical or human error in research, especially any systematic of nonrandom error.

Blue-collar occupation: Manual, semiskilled, or unskilled occupation.

Boundary maintenance: Those events and decisions related to setting limits of acceptable behavior in a given social group: formal law-making, informal group sanctioning.

Bourgeoisie: A term used by Karl Marx to refer to middle-class capitalists who own the means of production.

Bureaucracy: (1) A type of organization based on loyalty of its members to formal rules rather than to individual persons. (2) An organization ordered and staffed through the application of "rational" and legal rules. First systematically analyzed by Max Weber.

Caste: A system of stratification where, based upon strong religious sanction, there is little social mobility. Membership is highly ascriptive (defined above, see Ascription). Historically associated with the Hindu religion, especially in India, the term applies to other groups and societies as well.

Category: A unit of classification, especially linguistic, into which phenomena may be conceptually sorted, and which orients behavior.

Census: The counting of a given population.

Charismatic legitimacy: The belief that specially gifted leaders are entitled to authority.

Chicago sociology: That school of sociology which flourished at the University of Chicago from the 1920s to the 1940s. The chief interest of the Chicago sociologists was in field research studies of "social disorganization" in urban areas.

Class: (1) A very large group of persons who share similar interests, especially economic interests. (2) A division within the stratification structure on the basis of arbitrary meanings—usually of wealth, prestige, or power.

Class conflict: (1) Conflict between groups with differing economic interests. (2) The basis of Marxist theories of historical development.

Cloning: Asexual reproduction without fertilization.

Coding: The preparation of information for data analysis; usually involves reduction of information according to a convenient category scheme.

Cognitive dissonance: Conflict or discrepancy among the facts, ideas, or attitudes of which an individual is aware.

Common sense: The taken-for-granted presuppositions of members of society.

Conduct: Social action *directed* toward either a real or imagined audience. See also Social action.

Conflict: Dissent or open disagreement over values, beliefs, goals, norms, or behavior.

Consonance: The lack of conflict within a set of attitudes, values, or beliefs. Antonym: dissonance.

Content analysis: A method of analyzing written and visual media to detect themes or common patterns.

Controlled observation: Observation of social phenomena in experimental rather than natural settings.

Covert participant observation: The method of study in which the researcher becomes a member of the group he is studying, but the regular members of the group do not know he is studying them.

Craft: A body of traditional practical skills, self-consciously maintained and transmitted by those who possess them through an institutionalized but informal on-the-job apprenticeship.

Cross-sectional study: A study in which data is gathered for only one point in time.

Glossary of Key Concepts 573

Cultural interest group: A group of persons who share similar cultural ideals which they wish to publicize and defend against other group ideals.

Cultural relativism: The view that because the behavioral patterns of any particular group are but one of a large number of possible behavioral patterns, we should not impose our own standards on the behavior, values, or beliefs of persons of another culture. Antonym: ethnocentrism.

Culture: A conceptual model for perceiving, relating, interpreting, and organizing things, people, and emotions. As defined by Kroeber and Kluckhohn (1952), culture includes the transmission of information through learning, the use of shared symbols, shared habits, and normative codes or rules.

Cybernetics: A discipline based on the analogy between machine and brain functioning. Created by Norbert Wiener.

Deep rules: Those unspoken rules of behavior which must be inferred from explicit rules and actions. *See also* Rules.

Defensive practices: Techniques an individual uses to protect his own projected definition of self. *See also* Protective practices.

Definition of the situation: The significance of meanings attached to situations by individuals. As W. I. Thomas stated, "If situations are defined as real, they are real in their consequences."

Determinism: (1) The view, often implicit, that a given order of phenomena are causal to another order; for example, biological factors cause social factors. (2) More generally, the view that all human actions are *caused* by something external to the actors.

Deviance: (1) Violation of the rules or norms of society. (2) A definition or label applied to acts or individuals (deviants) by more powerful groups.

Discredited performance: The refusal by an audience to accept a definition that an actor projects because of information incompatible with the projected definition.

Display behavior: Actions, often exaggerated, which signal an animal's "mood" or internal state to his others. Displays are frequently associated with courtship, aggression, defense, dominance, and submission.

Dissonance: The incoherence or conflict within a set of attitudes, beliefs, or feelings.

Dominance order: The patterning of interaction among animals into a hierarchical arrangement.

Dramaturgical discipline: The ability to cope with unanticipated problems while still giving a good performance.

Dramaturgical loyalty: The moral requirement that "teammates" not betray the secrets of the "team."

Dramaturgical model: The model of the theater; the view that human interaction consists essentially of performances for the benefit of both self and others.

Dysfunction: Those effects of phenomena on society perceived to be harmful or negative by the observer.

Ecological theory: Traditionally associated with studies of social disorganization; the theoretical association of social behavior with spatial areas. *See also* Social disorganization.

Economic determinism: The theory that economic phenomena are the basic causes of or factors in understanding social phenomena.

Ego: A term used by Freud to refer to the rational aspects of man's self. *See also* Self.

Encounter: As defined by Erving Goffman, the interaction that occurs on any one occasion when a given set of individuals are in one another's continuous presence. Also known as a "focused gathering."

Endogamy: Rules of marriage specifying that one must marry *within* a particular social grouping.

Environmentalist: A social scientist who emphasizes factors of situations and experience in the explanation of behavior, while minimizing hereditary and constitutional factors.

Equilibrium: Used by structural functionalists, referring to the tendency of a social system to return to a given state. *See also* Social system; Structural-functional sociology.

Estate: A system of stratification sanctioned by law that entails the inheritance of occupation much like the caste system. It is characteristic of many advanced agrarian societies; including medieval Europe.

"Etc." property: That part of spoken communication which is left unsaid but understood or taken for granted.

Ethical neutralism: The principle that one should not judge the actions of others by his own ethical standards.

Ethnic group: In the United States, a group having a common culture at some variance with white Anglo-Saxon culture.

Ethnocentrism: Negatively judging others' behavior by the standards characteristic of one's group. Antonym: Cultural relativism.

Ethnography: Literally, writing about an ethnic group or people, it is the primary method by which anthropologists report the findings of primitive cultures. The ethnographic method is also used by sociologists who use participant observation to understand the social construction of reality by groups or organizations in industrial society.

Ethnomethodology: A sociological theory of how participants obtain and use social meanings (ideas, values, feelings) to make their actions understandable and acceptable to others. A chief focus is the concern with the "taken for granted" aspects of actors' social worlds.

Ethology: The science seeking behavioral laws that are species-specific (specific to all and only members of one species); the typical interest is to identify innate, evolutionary adaptations of the species.

Everyday life: The term used to distinguish the natural settings of members of society from the artificial settings of experiments and questionnaires constructed by and imposed on members of society by social scientists.

Existential: Referring to the concrete involvements of human beings in everyday life situations.

Experiment: A procedure carried out under controlled conditions to test a hypothesis. A study involving controlled intervention into the social situation by the sociologist; usually, experiments take place in laboratories.

Experimental setting: The study of social phenomena in an artificial setting created by the researcher. *See also* Experiment.

Expressions given: Using sign-vehicles to purposely convey information to others. Thought to be under the actor's control.

Expressions given off: Information communicated to others that is supposedly not under the individual's control. According to Goffman, used by social actors to evaluate the "true" intentions of others.

Expressive aspect of behavior: The symbolic aspect of behavior.

Extended family: A family consisting of three generations or more, especially where living in the same location.

Face-to-face interaction: The reciprocal influence of individuals upon one another when they are in one another's immediate physical presence.

Family: That social group made up of persons united by bonds of kinship; marked by sexual couplings between men and women on some more-or-less permanent basis.

Family of orientation: Kin family; the family of origin or the family in which one is born or grows up.

Family of procreation: Marital family; the family formed when a marriage takes place.

Field research: See also Participant observation.

Folkways: A cultural norm which is less salient than mores. *See also* Mores; Norms.

Front: The expressive resources serving to define the situation for an observer. Front consists of setting, appearance, and manner.

Front region: Frontstage.

Frontstage: Where the audience is found and a performance is given. Also known as front region.

Full person: A term used to indicate that someone is treated with the expected social deference. Antonym: nonperson.

Function (social): The effect of an object or phenomenon on the rest of society.

Functionalism: A general theory or approach in sociology. The theory that all or most social phenomena have a necessary function for society. *See also* Dysfunction; Latent function; Manifest function; Structural-functional sociology.

Gemeinschaft: Community in which people feel they belong together because they have common social characteristics. Relations are general and personal. Antonym: Gesellschaft.

Generalization: (1) The process by which a finding is applied to a larger population. (2) Deriving abstract statements from concrete data.

Generalized other: First proposed by Cooley and Mead, it represents, for the individual self, the organization of attitudes or rules expressed in the group.

Gesellschaft: Social group based on specialized, functionally defined relations, such as bureaucracy. Antonym: Gemeinschaft.

Group marriage: The form of polygamy in which there are at the same time two or more husbands *and* two or more wives.

Hereditarian: One who emphasizes heredity in explanation of behavior.

Hierarchy: Ordering of phenomena in a status scale; for example, an occupational or clan hierarchy. *See also* Status.

Historicism: The view that historical events are unique, so that comparisons of events across time and space have no validity. An extremely relativistic view of social phenomena.

Homology: Similarity of structure, but not necessarily function. A functional rather than structural similarity is an *analogy*.

Hypothesis: A tentative assumption made about the association of variables in the natural or social world; to be tested by empirical research.

"I": A term used by G. H. Mead to describe the individual's active, self-constructing aspect. *See also* "Me."

Id: A term used by Freud to refer to man's most basic, primitive emotions. *See also* Ego.

Ideal culture: See also Social reality.

Ideal type and ideal typification: A term used by Max Weber referring to construction of sociological models closely linked to, but not exact representations of, concrete data.

Identity: A key element of the self formed by interaction between the individual and society. It is the individual's subjective reality of "who he is" as a definite, stable, and socially recognized entity. Identities can undergo transformation and change depending on the individual's situated actions and relationships.

Identity kits: Cosmetics, clothing, and tools that we use to maintain our identity.

Ideology: Beliefs, often political, assumed to be true and used to justify individual or group actions.

Impression management: Attempts to mold the impression that others receive of the self.

Index: A measure which "stands for" a concept of phenomenon.

Indexicality: An ethnomethodological view that the meanings of symbols are fundamentally linked to the situations in which they are used.

Individuated meanings: Meanings, definitions of situations, or expectations that differ from individual to individual because of their different backgrounds.

Industrialization: The transformation of an economy through the development of manufacturing and technology.

Information game: The systematic attempt an actor makes to control others' impressions of him, while he tries to uncover the meaning of their communications.

Institution: An action system used to regulate behavior of members of a society or group over time. Examples: government, education, marriage. *See also* Action system.

Instrument aspect of behavior: The goal orientation of behavior toward purposeful achievement of specific goals.

Interaction: Another term for "encounter."

Interaction process analysis: A complex method of coding meanings of interaction among members of a small group in lab settings. Created by R. F. Bales.

Internalization (also Introjection): The process by which an individual incorporates the values and norms of his community as his own. *See also* Norms; Values.

Interview: Asking questions of a member of society in order to obtain sociological data.

Iron law of oligarchy: A theory, developed by Robert Michels, stating that power in groups tends to be controlled and perpetrated by a small group of leaders.

Key informant: A member of society who has significant knowledge of the data under study, and who will cooperate with the researcher. A single informant often used by anthropological field workers who acts as translator, host, and chaperone.

Keypunch: A machine that punches coded information onto cards for use as computer input or output.

Kinship, consanguine (based on blood): Relationships beyond the nuclear or extended family.

Labeling theory: A sociological theory of deviance which focuses on how powerful groups create and apply deviant labels to less powerful groups and individuals. Most associated with the work of Howard S. Becker.

Language: A system of symbols used in a conventional way by a number of people to communicate intelligibly with one another. Such symbols are arbitrary in that meaning is *conferred* on them by the community of speakers. Language includes principles and patterns of organization and use, speech (verbal), and manner of expression (nonverbal).

Latent function: The unintended consequences for society of an action or, more generally, a pattern of social action. *See also* Manifest function.

Law: A body of written or unwritten rules enforced by means of sanctions. *See also* Rules.

Legitimacy: Beliefs about who is rightfully entitled to authority.

Linguistics: The systematic description and analysis of language and speech, with focus on the system of rules and principles of construction, classification and combination of elements (sounds, syllables, word arrangements, meanings, etc.).

Longitudinal study: Research in which individuals or groups are studied over a period of time.

Macrosociology: The study of large-scale social phenomena, especially the comparison of whole societies with each other.

Manifest function: The intended consequences or purposes of an action or, more commonly, pattern of actions. *See also* Latent function.

Manner: The stimuli telling the observer the performer's role on this occasion or how he will play his role. Examples are facial expressions, posture, speech patterns, and bodily gestures: such as being meek or haughty, apologetic or aggressive.

Marginal man: An individual who does not fit into common social categories or role sets. Used by Robert E. Park.

Mass media: Media (newspapers, magazines, television, radio, and movies) designed for, distributed to, and "consumed" by extremely large audiences. Typically, the sole disseminators of news.

Mathematical model: An attempt to make an analogy between some social phenomenon or process and a mathematical formula.

"Me": A term used by G. H. Mead to describe the passive, socially manipulative aspect of the self. *See also* "I."

Glossary of Key Concepts 579

Meanings: The interpretations, especially symbolic, attached to phenomena by members of society. Social beliefs, values, and feelings are basic variables in almost all sociological theory today.

Mechanistic theories of society: Theories viewing society as a massive machine to be explained without reference to social meanings.

Medium: A device or process through which people convey or represent information.

Members' accounts: Explanations of actions and phenomena given by social actors.

Message: A unit of information.

Microsociology: The study of small-scale social phenomena, such as role playing in small groups.

Middle-range theory: Sociological theory that is neither highly abstract nor too empirically detailed. Robert K. Merton is the chief proponent of this position.

Mobility: Refers to a change in stratification position, whether from one generation to the next in the same family (intergenerational mobility) or within the adult lifetime of the same person (intergenerational mobility). "Vertical mobility" is a status change up or down; "horizontal mobility" is a change in status, such as job, without a change in vertical position.

Mobilization: The process of drawing together a group of persons sharing certain interests for purposes of consciously organized action.

Monogamy: The form of marriage in which a man is allowed one wife only *and* a woman is allowed only one husband. *See also* Serial monogamy.

Moral entrepreneur: A person who encourages moral disapproval of those individuals and groups that he defines as deviant.

Mores: Rules, values, or accepted ways of behavior on which the group feels its welfare depends.

Natural history: The historical development of a given social phenomenon.

Natural setting: Social phenomena outside an experimental or laboratory situation. *See also* Everyday life; Experiment.

Neo-imperialism: A form of economic dominance that one nation may exert over another without the direct political control that characterized the colonial form of imperialism.

News: Current, verifiable reports (or information) about recent events.

Nonperson: One who is treated as though he were an object. Antonym: full person.

Norms: Standards or expectations of conduct. Norms are sets of rules specifying what may be done in a particular situation. Typically, a gap exists between the idea or verbal norm (what people *say*) and the real norm (how people *act*).

Nuclear family: A social group ordinarily consisting of two generations—parents and their children.

Objectivity: A lack of personal bias. Having knowledge that is not biased by the personality or situation of the knower.

Old middle class: The self-employed middle class, including farmers, free professionals, and small businessmen. The maturing of industrialization brings about a numerical decline in the old middle class, especially farmers, and an increase in the new middle class.

Operationalization: The process whereby variables of a hypothesis are translated into a set of specific procedures that can be measured, so that the hypothesis can be tested.

Opinion poll: A survey of opinions on a given topic. *See also* Survey.

Organicism: The view of society as an organism and its parts as organs. *See also* Structural-functional sociology.

Part: The role one plays; the pattern of action that unfolds during a performance.

Participant observation: A method whereby the researcher joins in the activities of the persons he wishes to study. The fact that he is observing may be known or unknown to them.

Performance: The way a role is played, serving to influence other role players.

Performance team: The same as team.

Performing self: The one who puts on the mask or role and performs for others—the person behind the mask.

Personal documents: Diaries, life histories, and so on which sociologists, historians, and others use as source data for case studies and analysis of culture.

Personal front: The complex of clothing, makeup, hairdo, and other surface decorations that one carries about one's person. Personal front consists of one's appearance and manner. *See also* Front.

Personal identity: Who the person is as an individual. *Contrast with* Social identity.

Personality system: Talcott Parsons' view of personality as a system of need dispositions.

Perspective: A selective, arbitrary mental view of objects and events. The language actors use permits a description and understanding of certain features of the social world which, at the time, neglects or omits still other features.

Phenomenological sociology: A theoretical stance in sociology which stresses the importance of studying the meanings of phenomena to individuals involved in natural settings of everyday life. As such, it requires the use of field research methods, rather than laboratory experiments or questionnaire methods.

Phenomenology: A philosophical system associated with Husserl, Heidegger, Schutz, and others. For its importance to sociology, *see* Phenomenological sociology.

Pluralism (political): The view that in democratic countries, particularly the United States, political power is shared among a wide variety of competing pressure groups. The more optimistic variants of this view hold that all major interests have more-or-less equal power.

Pluralistic society: A society, such as the United States, containing many different groups with divergent values, life styles, degrees of power, and so on.

Polyandry: The form of polygamy in which a woman has more than one husband at the same time.

Polygamy: The form of marriage in which an individual is allowed to have more than one spouse at a time.

Polygyny: The form of polygamy in which a man has more than one wife at the same time.

Positivism: An early school of philosophy and sociology which aimed at absolute scientific objectivity and the perfection of society. Originated by Auguste Comte.

Power: Defined most generally as the ability to get another to do your bidding, whether he wants to or not. Power of a government is ultimately based on physical force.

Power group: A group of persons who share similar interests in defending or increasing their power; usually consists of persons in similar organizational positions.

Pressure group: A group formed for the purpose of pressuring political leaders to adopt policies the group favors.

Primary group: A family or other close-knit group. Its purposes are diffuse and it includes high emotional involvement among the members. Antonym: secondary group.

Primary incest taboo: The rule that forbids coitus and marriage between parents and their children and between children born of the same parents.

Primates: The order of vertebrates that includes monkeys, apes, and man.

Primogeniture: System of the inheritance going to the first-born son.

Problematic: Uncertain, nondeterminate; not taken for granted; out of the ordinary.

Profession: A vocation characterized by specialized knowledge, training, ethical standards, and a self-policing organization.

Program: A systematic plan for problem solution by the computer.

Proletariat: A term used by Karl Marx referring to urban factory workers, who sell their productive labor to owners of the means of production.

Protective practices: Techniques used to protect the projected definitions of others. *See also* Defensive practices.

Protologue: New model of social life.

Prototype: A model, usually partly or wholly inarticulate, which forms or guides perception.

Psycholinguistics: The study of linguistics from a psychological perspective. *See also* Linguistics.

Qualitative sociology: Sociology that emphasizes nonquantitative descriptions and explanations of social phenomena. *See also* Quantitative sociology.

Quantifiable: Capable of being identified clearly with some magnitude, amount, or size, so that quantitative comparisons with other items are possible.

Quantitative sociology: Sociology that emphasizes counting or the collection of numbers and percentages to explain human characteristics and behavior.

Questionnaire: A standard written form that contains a set of questions to be asked of persons to gain data about society.

Random sample: A group selected in such a manner that each person has the same chance or probability of being selected.

Rational (legal) legitimacy: The belief that persons are entitled to authority as a result of fulfilling certain rational rules (usually written) of procedure.

Raw data: Information prior to any coding or preparation for data analysis.

Reciprocal dependence: When each member of a team depends on others for success of a team performance by appropriate conduct. One basis for team cohesiveness.

Reciprocal familiarity: When each team member knows that the other team members know about the secrets lying behind their performance. One basis for team cohesiveness.

Reciprocity of perspectives: The mutual assumptions of actors regarding knowledge of objects or events in the world. An underlying notion of "other things being equal" allows people to fit their different lines of conduct to each other and permits actors to assume the roles (or perspectives) of others "as if" they were their own.

Reductionism: To interpret social phenomena in terms of psychological variables that alone cannot validly explain them.

Region: Any place that is bounded to some degree by barriers to perception.

Relative deprivation: The feelings of deprivation derived from observing others who possess the object of characteristics of which one feels deprived, though "objectively" the feeling of deprivation is not justified.

Replication: The redoing of research to find out if the results will be similar. Used to check on the objectivity of research findings.

Representative sample: A sample is representative of a population on a given characteristic if the percentage in the sample is the same as the percentage in the population. A representative sample is a truthful model, on a smaller scale, of the whole population, so it can validly stand for the whole population.

Role: Normatively patterned action of social actors: student, lover, male. It specifies an individual's rights and obligations toward other actors in a given situation.

Role conflict: When the obligations or expectations attached to one role conflict with those attached to a second role.

Role player: One who plays a role, or performs. Also known as an actor.

Role playing: Giving a performance.

Role set: A set of roles which are expected to go together in a society. *See also* Role.

Role strain: See also Role conflict.

Routine: Preestablished part, unfolded during a performance and presented on other occasions.

Rules: Normative prescriptions for action; sanctioned or nonsanctioned norms, or guides for behavior. *See also* Norms; Values.

Ruling class: The social class possessing the means of coercion in a society, and exercising power. *See also* Social class.

Sanction: Responses to behavior for purposes of encouraging or discouraging its repetition. Often viewed as "reward" or "punishment."

Scale: A numerical ordering of social data; for example, an attitude scale.

Secondary group: A group with specific purposes and a low degree of emotional involvement. Antonym: primary group.

Self: The psychic entity arising during socialization, allowing man to treat himself as an object, judge how others will respond to him, and interact with himself. Most associated with the theory of Symbolic interactionism (see below) developed by G. H. Mead.

Self-concept: An image that one has of himself.

Self-fulfilling prophecy: A prediction that comes true because knowledge of it leads social actors to change in a way that produces the predicted outcome.

584   Glossary of Key Concepts

Self-lodging: A process discussed in symbolic interactionist theory by which an individual becomes known to another. *See also* Symbolic interactionism.

Self-report studies: Studies that ask respondents questions about their personal biographies or their self-categorizations.

Sequenced interaction: Encounters that are temporarily spaced; for example, one scene follows the other.

Serial monogamy: A term applied to the contemporary American marital form that allows an individual to marry more than once, but permits him to have only one spouse at any given time.

Setting: The background items making up the scenery and props for a performance.

Sibling: Brother or sister.

Sign: A stimulus calling for a fixed (rather than arbitrary) meaning. *See also* Symbol.

Sign-Vehicles: The means by which we communicate information to others—such as our conduct, appearance, spoken words—and the social setting for the interaction.

Simulation: An artificial system designed to replicate another, usually real-world, phenomenon. Sometimes done with computers.

Situation: The circumstances interpreted by an actor at a given time in his interaction with others or with the environment.

Social action: The fundamental unit of sociological analysis. As defined by Weber, any behavior (*see* Social behavior) involving meanings shared by two or more members of society.

Social behavior: Any activity of an organism which affects, or is affected by, another organism. It does not have to involve shared meanings; if it does, it is social action.

Social class: See also Class.

Social Darwinism: The theory that society is based upon competition and the survival of the fittest. Based on an analogy with the Darwinian theory of evolution.

Social disorganization: A breakdown in social organization and control. Considered by earlier sociologists, especially of the Chicago School, to be a cause of deviance.

Social fact: A concept used by Durkheim to indicate that social phenomena have a real existence independent of individual social actors.

Social identity: The individual's status or role; for example, a checkout clerk who happens to be an eighteen-year-old female. *See also* Personal identity.

Social interaction: The fitting together of persons' separate lines of activity to establish a mutually meaningful activity. While animal behavior is largely programmed by biological mechanisms, only man conducts himself by taking the other into account through symbolic communication. *See also* Action.

Socialization: The process of teaching or learning the shared behaviors, values, attitudes, and/or beliefs of some group.

Social mobility: The movement from one social class to another, intergenerationally or intragenerationally. *See also* Class; Mobility.

Social organization: Any group whose actions are patterned, especially in accord with formal rules. *See also* Bureaucracy.

Social reality: The nature of the social world. However, *statements* about reality often reflect an *ideal* image of the social world, rather than the *real* patterns or rules of social existence. For instance, statements by Americans about democracy usually ignore conflict, income and power differences, and racial oppression. Much sociological and anthropological data reflect the verbal or ideal reality.

Social structure: Generally, any pattern of social actions. Sometimes refers to those factors believed to be causes of the patterning of social actions. Figuratively, social structure can be said to be the bones of society.

Sociolinguistics: The study of linguistics from a sociological perspective. *See also* Linguistics.

Sociology of everyday life: The sociological analysis of selves and actions in everyday life. *See also* Everyday life.

Sociology of knowledge: The study of the social determination of man's consciousness, ideas, and theories; also, as used by Berger and Luckmann, the study of how man constructs and maintains his knowledge of everyday reality.

Sociology of sociology: The analysis of theory and research by other sociologists within the context of the sociology of knowledge.

Social pathology: The view of deviance as pathological, that is, like a disease in a healthy organism.

Social psychology: The study of the relations between individual and group behavior, often based upon experimental data.

Social status: The prestige or other evaluational ranking of an individual or group within a given group. *See also* Class.

Social stratification: Hierarchical patterning of social classes. *See also* Class.

Social system: An abstraction of a social group in terms of its statistics and shared symbolic definitions and expectations.

Sociologism: Sociological determinism; the attempt to explain human action in terms of factors believed wholly external to the individual actors.

Structural-functional sociology: Sociology based on the premise that society has a structure determining the interactions of its members. The various parts of society are seen as interdependent with each other, so that a change in one part affects all other parts.

Subculture: A distinctive cultural group within the larger culture. *See also* Culture.

Subjectivity: Situational understanding based on the self's perspective. *See also* Self.

Superego: In Freud's theory, that part of man's self which consists of the internalized expectations and values of society. *See also* Ego; Id; Internalization.

Survey: A sociological method by which a relatively small number of people, a sample, are questioned about a given phenomenon, and the results are generalized to the larger population from which the subjects were taken. A survey may be performed by mail or by personal interview. *See also* Interview.

Symbol: A "conventional" sign, the meaning of which is given by arbitrary assignment and maintained by consensus. *See also* Sign.

Symbolic interactionism: A branch of the phenomenological school of sociological theory which views self and society primarily in terms of an exchange of symbols or meanings among selves during interaction. Thus, self and society are seen in dynamic terms, as in a continuous process of construction. First developed by Mead and Cooley.

Tabulation: To arrange data in a condensed and systematic form.

Team: Any set of individuals who cooperate in staging a single routine or performance.

Theory (social): A set of interrelated and testable propositions or hypotheses which explicitly specify conditions under which certain forms of behavior will occur.

Total institutions: Institutions that attempt to control their members totally, such as mental hospitals, armies, prisons, and monasteries.

Traditional legitimacy: The belief that persons sanctioned by traditional religion or hereditary position are entitled to authority.

Transsituational: Going beyond one immediate situation; cross-cutting situations.

Typification (and Idealization): The learned categories through which standard features of social life are understood, especially through language.

Validity: In sociological research, the fit between a concept or indicator and the data which it is supposed to "stand for." Also used generally to refer to any theory which explains research findings.

"Value-free" sociology: The view that sociology is, can be, or should be a discipline whose practitioners bring no value premises into their work. *See also* Values.

Values: Criteria, especially rule criteria, by which something is judged desirable or undesirable. *See also* Mores; Norms; Rules.

Variable: A one-dimensional concept whose gradations are measured quantitatively by a series of increasing numbers; for example, degree of education, I.Q., amount of wealth.

Verstehen: According to Max Weber, the intuitive understanding of social phenomena.

White-collar occupation: Clerical or office type of occupation. *See also* Occupation.

Whorfian hypothesis: Different languages imply differences in ways of perceiving the world.

Bibliography

Abegglen, James, *The Japanese Factory*. Glencoe, Ill.: The Free Press, 1958.

Ackoff, Russell L., "Operations Research," *International Encyclopedia of the Social Sciences*, XI (1968), 290–294.

Adams, Robert McC., *The Evolution of Urban Society: Early Mesopotamia and Prehistoric Mexico*. New York: Thomas V. Crowell, 1968.

Adams, Walter, *The Structure of American Industry*, 3rd ed. New York: The Macmillan Company, 1961.

Adorno, T. W., Else Frankel-Brunswick, D. J. Johnson, R. Sanford et al., *The Authoritarian Personality*. New York: Harper & Row, 1950.

Aiken, Michael and Jerald Hage, "Organizational Alienation: A Comparative Analysis," *American Sociological Review*, XXXI (August 1966), 497–507.

Albert, Ethel M., "Women of Burundi: A Study of Social Values," in Denise Paulme, ed., *Women of Tropical Africa*. Berkeley: University of California Press, 1963, pp. 179–215. (Translation of "La Femme en Urundi," in Denise Paulme, ed., *Femmes d'Afrique Noire*. Paris: Mouton, 1960, pp. 173–205.)

Almond, Gabriel and Sidney Verba, *The Civic Culture*. Princeton: Princeton University Press, 1963.

Alsop, Stewart, *The Center: People and Power in Political Washington*. New York: Harper & Row, 1968.

Andrew, Richard J., "Evolution of Facial Expression," *Science*, CXLII (November 22, 1963), 1034–1041.

———, "The Origins of Facial Expressions," *Scientific American*, CCXIII (October 1965), 88–94.

Anshen, Melvin, "Managerial Decisions," in *The American Assembly, Automation and Technological Change*. Englewood Cliffs, N.J.: Prentice-Hall, 1962, 66–88.

Audrey, Robert, *African Genesis*. New York: Atheneum, 1961.

———, *The Territorial Imperative*. New York: Atheneum, 1968.

Argyle, Michael, *The Psychology of Interpersonal Behavior*. Baltimore: Penguin Books, 1967.

———, *Social Interaction*. London: Methuen, 1969.

Aries, Philippe, *Centuries of Childhood: A Social History of Family Life*. New York: Knopf, 1962.

Asch, Solomon E., *Social Psychology*. Englewood Cliffs, N.J.: Prentice-Hall, 1952.

Ashworth, A. E., "The Sociology of Trench Warfare, 1914–1918," *British Journal of Sociology*, XIX (December 1968), 407–423.

Aubert, William, *Elements of Sociology*. New York: Charles Scribner's Sons, 1967.

Ausubel, D. P., H. M. Schiff, and E. B. A. Gasser, "A Preliminary Study of Developmental Trends in Socioempathy: Accuracy of Perception of Own and Others' Status," *Child Development*, XXIII (1952), 111–128.

Axelrod, Morris, "Urban Structure and Social Participation," *American Sociological Review* (February 1956), pp. 14–18.

Bachrach, Peter and Morton Baratz, "The Two Faces of Power," *American Political Science Review* (December 1962), pp. 947–952.

Bagdikian, Ben H., *The Information Machines: Their Impact on Men and the Media*. New York: Harper & Row, 1971.

Baily, L., "Mass Media and Children: A Study of Exposure Habits and Cognitive Effects," *Psychological Monographs*, Vol. LXXIII (1959).

Bain, Read, "The Self Other Words of a Child," *American Journal of Sociology*, XLI (May 1936), 767–775.

Bales, Robert F., *Interaction Process Analysis: A Method for the Study of Small Groups*. Cambridge: Addison-Wesley, 1950.

———, "Task Roles and Social Norms in Problem Solving Groups," in E. Maccoby, T. Newcomb, and E. Hartley, eds., *Readings in Social Psychology*, 3rd ed. New York: Holt, Rinehart & Winston, 1958.

Ball, Donald W., "Toward a Sociology of Toys: Inanimate Objects, Socialization, and the Demography of the Doll World," *Sociological Quarterly*, VIII (Autumn 1967), 447–458.

———, "Attitude, Biography, or Situation: Approaches to Standing, Sitting and Definitions of Self." Unpublished doctoral dissertation, Department of Sociology, University of California at Los Angeles, 1969.

———, "An Abortion Clinic Ethnography," in Jack D. Douglas, ed., *Observations of Deviance*. New York: Random House, 1970.

———, *Microecology: The Sociology of Intimate Space* (studies in sociology). Indianapolis: Bobbs-Merrill, 1971.

———, "The Definition of the Situation: Some Theoretical and Methodological Consequences of Taking W. I. Thomas Seriously," in Jack D. Douglas, ed., *Existential Sociology*. New York: Appleton-Century-Crofts, forthcoming.

Bancroft, Frederic, *Slave-Trading in the Old South*. Baltimore: S. H. Furst, 1931.

Bandura, Albert and Richard H. Walters, *Social Learning and Personality Development*. New York: Holt, Rinehart & Winston, 1963.

Banfield, Edward C., *Political Influence*. New York: The Free Press, 1961.

———, *The Unheavenly City: The Nature and Future of Our Urban Crisis*. Boston: Little, Brown, 1970.

———, and James Q. Wilson, *City Politics*. New York: Random House, 1963.

Banks Arthur and Robert Textor, *A Cross-Polity Survey*. Cambridge: M.I.T. Press, 1963.

Barber, Bernard, *Social Stratification*. New York: Harcourt, Brace, 1957.

Baritz, Loren, *The Servants of Power: A History of the Use of Social Science in American Industry*. Middletown: Wesleyan University, 1960.

———, "The Servants of Power," in Jack D. Douglas, ed., *The Impact of Sociology*. New York: Appleton-Century-Crofts, 1970, pp. 137–155.

Barklay, Katherine and Steve Weissman, "Why the Population Bomb Is a Rockefeller Baby," *Ramparts*, vol. 8 (May 1970), 48–56.

Barnard, Chester, *The Function of the Executive.* Cambridge: Harvard University Press, 1938.

Barnett, Harold, "Pressures of Growth Upon Environment," in Henry Jarrett, ed., *Environmental Quality in a Growing Economy.* Baltimore: Johns Hopkins Press, 1966.

Barnett, S. A., *Study in Behavior: Principles of Ethology and Behavioral Physiology,* displayed mainly in the rat. London: Methuen, 1963.

———, "On the Hazards of Analogies," 1967, reprinted in Montagu, 1968, pp. 18–26.

Bateson, Gregory et al., "Towards a Theory of Schizophrenia," *Behavioral Science,* I (1956), 251–264.

Bauer, Raymond A., Ithiel de Sola Pool, and Lewis A. Dexter, *American Business and Public Policy.* New York: Atherton, 1964.

Beals, Ralph L. and Harry Hoijer, *An Introduction to Anthropology.* New York: The Macmillan Company, 1965.

Beatty, John, "Taking Issue with Lorenz on the Ute," in Ashley Montagu, ed., 1968, pp. 111–115.

Becker, Ernest, *The Birth and Death of Meaning.* Glencoe, Ill.: The Free Press, 1962.

———, *The Lost Science of Man.* New York: Braziller, 1971.

Becker, Howard S., "Becoming a Marijuana User," *American Journal of Sociology,* LIX (November 1953a), 235–242.

———, "The Teacher in the Authority System of Public School," *Journal of Education,* XXVII (1953b), 128–141.

———, "Marihuana Use and Social Control," *Social Problems,* III (July 1955), 35–44.

———, *The Outsiders.* New York: The Free Press, 1963.

———, et al., *Institutions and the Person,* papers presented to E. C. Hughes. Chicago: Aldine, 1968a.

———, Blanche Geer, and Everett C. Hughes, *Making the Grade.* New York: Wiley, 1968b.

Bell, Daniel, "Crime as an American Way of Life," *Antioch Review,* XIII (Summer 1953), 131–154.

———, "The Racket-Ridden Longshoreman," in *The End of Ideology.* New York: The Free Press, 1962, pp. 175–209.

———, *The Radical Right.* Garden City, N.Y.: Doubleday, 1964.

———, ed., *Toward the Year 2000.* New York: Harper & Row, 1968.

Bellah, Robert, *Tokugawa Religion*. Glencoe, Ill.: The Free Press, 1957.

———, "Research Chronicle; Tokugawa Religion," in Phillip Hammond, ed., *Sociologists at Work*. New York: Basic Books, 1964.

Bendix, Reinhard, "Bureaucracy: The Problem and Its Setting," *American Sociological Review*, XII (October 1947), 493–507.

———, *Work and Authority in Industry*. New York: Wiley, 1956.

———, *Max Weber: An Intellectual Portrait*. New York: Doubleday, 1960.

———, *Max Weber*. Garden City, N.Y.: Doubleday, 1962.

———, "Concepts and Generalizations in Comparative Sociological Studies," *American Sociological Review*, XXVIII, August 1963.

———, *Nation-Building and Citizenship*. New York: Wiley, 1964.

———, "Reflections on Charismatic Leadership," in Reinhard Bendix et al., eds., *State and Society*. Boston: Little, Brown, 1968, pp. 616–629.

——— and S. M. Lipset, "Marx's Theory of Social Classes," in Bendix and Lipset, eds., *Class, Status, and Power*, 2nd ed. New York: The Free Press, 1966, pp. 6–11.

Benedict, Burton, "Role Analysis in Animals and Men" *Man* (n.s.), IV (July 1969), 203–214.

Benedict, Ruth, *Patterns of Culture*. New York: New American Library (Mentor Book), 1934.

Bensman, Joseph and Israel Gerver, "Crime and Punishment in the Factory: The Function of Deviancy in Maintaining the Social System," *American Sociological Review*, XXVIII (August 1963), 588–598.

Berelson, Bernard, "Content Analysis," in Gardner Lindzey, ed., *Handbook of Social Psychology*, Vol. I. Cambridge: Addison-Wesley, 1954.

Berenda, R., *The Influence of the Group on the Judgments of Children*. New York: Kings Crown Press, 1950.

Berger, Peter L., *Invitation to Sociology: A Humanistic Perspective*. Garden City, N.Y.: Doubleday Anchor, 1963.

———, *The Sacred Canopy*. Garden City, N.Y.: Doubleday Anchor, 1969.

——— and Thomas Luckmann, *The Social Construction of Reality*. New York: Doubleday, 1967.

Bernstein, Basil M., "Some Social Determinants of Perception," *British Journal of Sociology*, IX (June 1958), 159–174.

———, "Public Languages: Some Sociological Implications of a Linguistic Form," *British Journal of Sociology*, X (December 1959), 311–326.

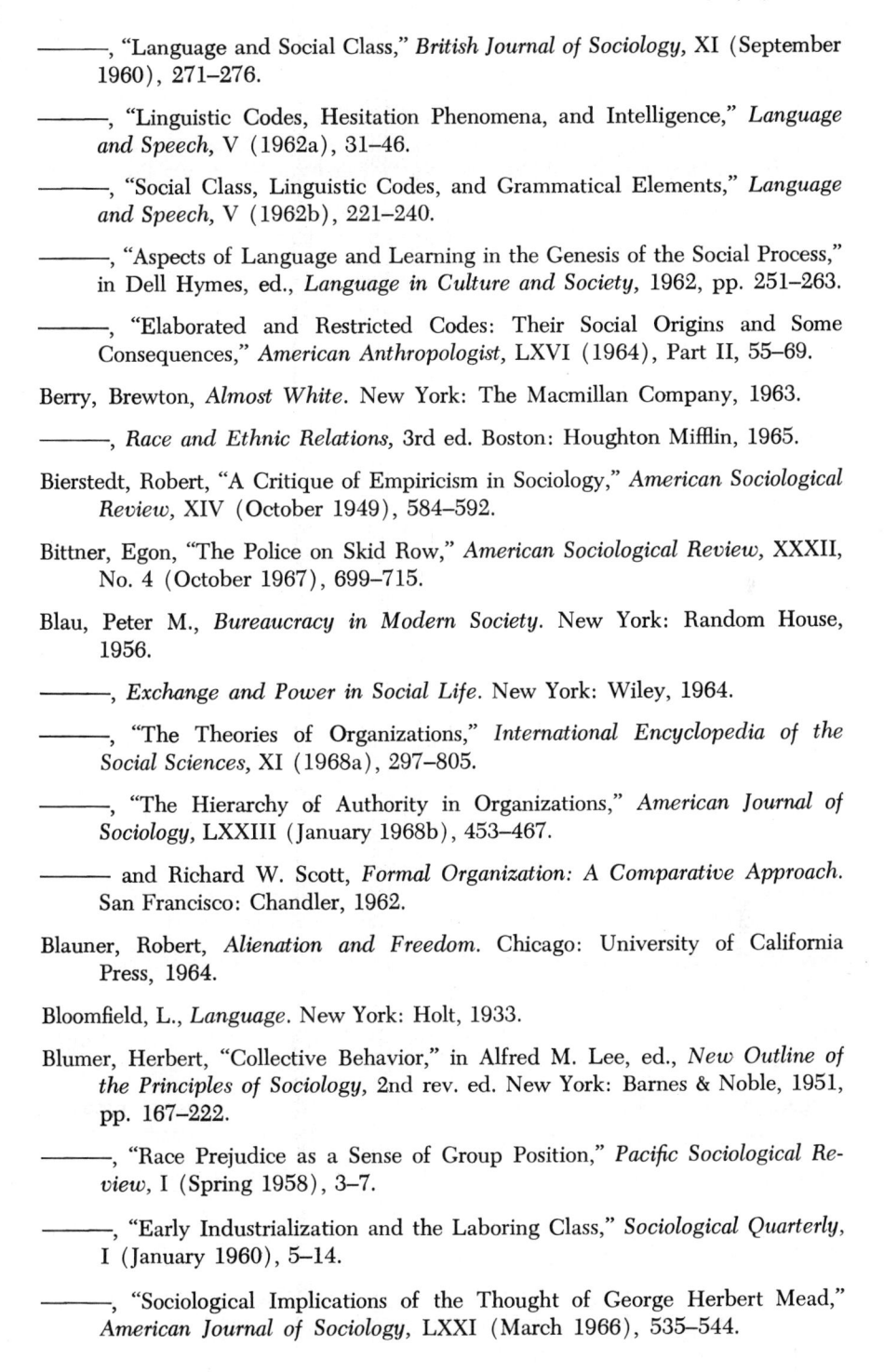

———, "Language and Social Class," *British Journal of Sociology*, XI (September 1960), 271–276.

———, "Linguistic Codes, Hesitation Phenomena, and Intelligence," *Language and Speech*, V (1962a), 31–46.

———, "Social Class, Linguistic Codes, and Grammatical Elements," *Language and Speech*, V (1962b), 221–240.

———, "Aspects of Language and Learning in the Genesis of the Social Process," in Dell Hymes, ed., *Language in Culture and Society*, 1962, pp. 251–263.

———, "Elaborated and Restricted Codes: Their Social Origins and Some Consequences," *American Anthropologist*, LXVI (1964), Part II, 55–69.

Berry, Brewton, *Almost White*. New York: The Macmillan Company, 1963.

———, *Race and Ethnic Relations*, 3rd ed. Boston: Houghton Mifflin, 1965.

Bierstedt, Robert, "A Critique of Empiricism in Sociology," *American Sociological Review*, XIV (October 1949), 584–592.

Bittner, Egon, "The Police on Skid Row," *American Sociological Review*, XXXII, No. 4 (October 1967), 699–715.

Blau, Peter M., *Bureaucracy in Modern Society*. New York: Random House, 1956.

———, *Exchange and Power in Social Life*. New York: Wiley, 1964.

———, "The Theories of Organizations," *International Encyclopedia of the Social Sciences*, XI (1968a), 297–805.

———, "The Hierarchy of Authority in Organizations," *American Journal of Sociology*, LXXIII (January 1968b), 453–467.

——— and Richard W. Scott, *Formal Organization: A Comparative Approach*. San Francisco: Chandler, 1962.

Blauner, Robert, *Alienation and Freedom*. Chicago: University of California Press, 1964.

Bloomfield, L., *Language*. New York: Holt, 1933.

Blumer, Herbert, "Collective Behavior," in Alfred M. Lee, ed., *New Outline of the Principles of Sociology*, 2nd rev. ed. New York: Barnes & Noble, 1951, pp. 167–222.

———, "Race Prejudice as a Sense of Group Position," *Pacific Sociological Review*, I (Spring 1958), 3–7.

———, "Early Industrialization and the Laboring Class," *Sociological Quarterly*, I (January 1960), 5–14.

———, "Sociological Implications of the Thought of George Herbert Mead," *American Journal of Sociology*, LXXI (March 1966), 535–544.

——, *Symbolic Interactionism: Perspective and Method.* Englewood Cliffs, N.J.: Prentice-Hall, 1969.

Bock, Kenneth E., *The Acceptance of Histories: Toward a Perspective for Social Science,* University of California Publications in Sociology and Social Institutions, Vol. 3, No. 1. Berkeley: University of California Press, 1956.

——, "The Comparative Method of Anthropology," *Comparative Studies in Society and History,* VIII (April 1966), 269–280.

Boocock, Sarane S., "Toward a Sociology of Learning: A Selective Review of Existing Research," *Sociology of Education,* XXXIX (1966), 1–45.

Boorstin, Daniel, *The Genius of American Politics.* Chicago: University of Chicago Press, 1953.

——, *The Image.* New York: Atheneum, 1961.

Bossard, J., "Family Modes of Expression," *American Sociological Review,* X (April 1945), 226–237.

Boulding, Kenneth E., *The Image: Knowledge in Life and Society.* Rexdale, Canada: Ambassador Books, 1956.

——, "The Economics of the Coming Spaceship Earth," in Henry Jarrett, ed., *Environmental Quality in a Growing Economy.* Baltimore: Johns Hopkins Press, 1966.

Bowlby, John, *Child Care and the Growth of Love.* London: Penguin Books, 1953.

Brace, C. L. and M. F. Ashley Montagu, *Man's Evolution: An Introduction to Physical Anthropology.* New York: The Macmillan Company, 1965.

Breed, Warren, "Social Control in the News Room: A Functional Analysis," *Social Forces,* XXIII (May 1955), 326–335.

Bregman, J. I. and Sergei Lenormend, *The Pollution Paradox,* Washington, D.C.: Spartan, 1966.

Breland, Kellar and Marian Breland, *Animal Behavior.* New York: The Macmillan Company, 1966.

Brickman, William and Stanley Lehrer, eds., *Automation, Education, and Human Values.* New York: Apollo (Crowell), 1969.

Bright, James R., *Automation and Management.* Boston: Division of Research, Graduate School of Business Administration, Harvard University, 1958.

Brinton, Crane, *A History of Western Morals.* New York: Harcourt, Brace & World, 1959.

Broom, Leonard and Phillip Selznick, *Sociology.* New York: Harper & Row, 1963.

Brown, Julia and Brian Gilmartin, "Sociology Today: Lacunae, Emphases, and Surfeits," *The American Sociologist,* IV (November 1969), 283–291.

Brown, Roger, *Words and Things*. Glencoe, Ill.: The Free Press, 1958.

———, *Social Psychology*. New York: The Free Press, 1965.

———, *Language, Thought, and Culture*. Ann Arbor: University of Michigan Press, 1966.

——— and Albert Gilman, "The Pronouns of Power and Solidarity," in Thomas Sebeok, ed., 1960, 253–276.

——— and Eric Lenneberg, "A Study in Language and Cognition," *Journal of Abnormal and Social Psychology*, XLIX (1954), 454–462.

Bruce, Donald, "Effects of Context Upon the Intelligibility of Heard Speech," in Calen Cherry, ed., *Information Theory*. London: Butterworths, 1956.

Bruner, Jerome S., "Learning and Thinking," in Alice and Lester D. Crow, eds., *Vital Issues in American Education*. New York: Bantam Books, 1964, 182–192.

Bruyn, S., *The Human Perspective in Sociology*. Englewood Cliffs, N.J.: Prentice-Hall, 1966.

Brzezinski, Zbigniew and Samuel Huntington, *Political Power: USA/USSR*. New York: Viking Press, 1964.

Buck, Roy C., "Education, Technological Change and the New Society," in W. Brickman and S. Lehrer, eds., *Automation, Education and Human Values*. New York: Apollo (Crowell), 1969, 195–212.

Buckingham, Walter, *Automation*. New York: Harper & Row, 1961.

Burgess, Ernest W., *The Growth of the City: An Introduction to a Research Project*. Chicago: University of Chicago Press, 1925.

Burke, Kenneth, *A Rhetoric of Motives*. New York: Prentice-Hall, 1950.

———, *Permanence and Change*, 2nd rev. ed. Indianapolis: Bobbs-Merrill, 1965.

———, "Definition of Man," in *Language as Symbolic Action*. Berkeley: University of California Press, 1966.

Butterfield, Herbert, *The Origins of Modern Science*, rev. ed. New York: Collier, 1962.

Campbell, A., P. A. Converse, W. E. Miller, and D. E. Stokes, *The American Voter*. New York: Wiley, 1960.

Campbell, Donald T. and Julian C. Stanley, "Experimental and Quasi-Experimental Designs for Research on Teaching," in M. L. Gage, ed., *Handbook of Research on Teaching*. Chicago: Rand McNally, 1963.

Caplow, Theodore, "Home Ownership and Location Preferences in a Minneapolis Sample," *American Sociological Review*, XIII, No. 6 (December 1949a), 725–730.

———, "The Social Ecology of Guatemala City," *Social Forces*, XXVIII (December 1949b), 113–135.

———, *Principles of Organization*. New York: Harcourt, Brace, 1964.

———, *Two Against One: Coalitions in Triads*. Englewood Cliffs, N.J.: Prentice-Hall, 1968.

Caprio, Frank S., *Variations in Sexual Behavior*. New York: Citadel Press, 1955.

Carey, James T., *The College Drug Scene*. Englewood Cliffs, N.J.: Prentice-Hall, 1968.

Carr, Edward Hallett, *What is History?* New York: Knopf, 1964.

Carstens, Arthur, "Some Computer Manpower Problems of the Future." Institute of Industrial Relations, University of California, Los Angeles, 1966.

Casagrande, Joseph, ed., *In the Company of Man*. New York: Harper & Row, 1960.

Cass, James, "Can the University Survive the Black Challenge?" *Saturday Review*, LII (June 21, 1969), 68–84.

Cater, Douglass, *The Fourth Branch of Government*. New York: Vintage, 1959.

Cavan, Sherri, *Liquor License*. Chicago: Aldine Press, 1966.

Chambliss, William J., "The Selection of Friends," *Social Forces*, XLIII (March 1965), 370–380.

Chance, M. R. A., "The Interpretation of Some Agonistic Postures: The Role of 'Cut-Off' Acts and Postures," *Symposia* of Zoological Society of London, VIII (1962), 71–89.

Chance, Norman A., *The Eskimo of North Alaska*. New York: Holt, Rinehart, & Winston, 1966.

Childe, V. Gordon, *What Happened in History*. Harmondsworth, England: Penguin Books, 1942.

Chinoy, Ely, *Automobile Workers and the American Dream*. Garden City, N.Y.: Doubleday, 1955.

———, *Society*. New York: Random House, 1963.

Chomsky, Noam, *Syntactic Structures*. The Hague: Mouton, 1957.

———, "Review of Skinner's Verbal Behavior," *Language*, XXXV (1959), 26–58.

———, *Current Issues in Linguistic Theory*. New York: Humanities Press, 1964.

———, *Aspects of the Theory of Syntax*. Cambridge: M.I.T. Press, 1965.

———, *Cartesian Linguistics*. New York: Harper & Row, 1966.

———, *Language and Mind*. New York: Harcourt, Brace & World, 1968.

Christensen, Harold T., "Studies in Child Spacing: Premarital Pregnancy as Measured by the Spacing of the First Child from Marriage," *American Sociological Review*, XVIII (1953), 53–59.

Chukousky, Kornel, *From Two to Five*. Berkeley: University of California Press, 1971.

Cicourel, Aaron, *Method and Measurement in Sociology*. New York: The Free Press, 1964.

────── and John I. Kitsuse, "The Social Organization of High School and Deviant Adolescent Careers," in Earl Robington and Martin Weinberg, eds., *Deviance: The Interactionist Perspective*. New York: The Macmillan Company, 1962, 124–135.

────── and ──────, *The Educational Decision-Makers Method*. Indianapolis: Bobbs-Merrill, 1963.

──────, "Basic and Normative Rules in the Negotiation of Status and Role," in Hans Peter Dreitzel, ed., *Recent Sociology No. 2: Patterns of Communicative Behavior*. London: Collier-Macmillan, 1970.

──────, "The Acquistion of Social Structure: Toward a Developmental Sociology of Language and Meaning," in Jack D. Douglas, ed., *Understanding Everyday Life*. Chicago: Aldine, 1970.

──────, "Unpublished Lectures." San Diego: University of California Press, 1971.

Clark, Joseph S., *The Senate Establishment*. New York: Hill & Wang, 1963.

──────, *Congress: The Sapless Branch*. New York: Harper & Row, 1964.

Clausen, John A., et al., *Socialization and Society*. Boston: Little, Brown, 1968.

Coale, Ansley J., *Population and Economic Development*. Englewood Cliffs, N.J.: Prentice-Hall, 1963.

Cohen, Albert, *Delinquent Boys*. New York: The Free Press, 1955.

Cohen, Bernard, *The Press and Foreign Policy*. Princeton: Princeton University Press, 1963.

Cole, Robert, *Japanese Blue-Collar—The Changing Tradition*. Berkeley: University of California Press, forthcoming.

Cole, Stephen, "The Unionization of Teachers: Determinants of Rank-and-File Support," *Sociology of Education*, XLI (1968), 66–87.

Coleman, James S., *The Adolescent Society*. Glencoe Ill.: The Free Press, 1961.

────── and Ernest Q. Campbell, *Equality of Educational Opportunity*. Washington, D.C.: Government Printing Office, 1966.

Collingwood, R. G., *The Idea of History*. New York: Oxford University Press, 1956.

Collins, Randall, "A Comparative Approach to Political Sociology," in Reinhard Bendix et al., eds., *State and Society*. Boston: Little, Brown, 1968, 42–67.

Commager, Henry Steele, *The American Mind*. New Haven: Yale University Press, 1950.

Conant, James Bryant, *Slum and Suburbs: A Commentary on Schools in Metropolitan Areas*. New York: McGraw-Hill, 1961.

Cooley, Charles Horton, *Social Organization*. New York: Charles Scribner's Sons, 1902.

———, "A Study of the Early Use of the Self-Words by a Child," *Psychological Review*, XV (1908), 339–357.

———, *Human Nature and the Social Order*. New York: Charles Scribner's Sons, 1922.

Coser, Lewis, ed., *Georg Simmel*. Englewood Cliffs, N.J.: Prentice-Hall, 1965.

Cox, Oliver C., *Caste, Class and Race*. Garden City, N.J.: Doubleday, 1948.

Cremin, Lawrence A., *The Transformation of the School*. New York: Knopf, 1961.

Cressey, Donald, *Theft of a Nation*. New York: Harper & Row, 1969.

Crozier, Michel, *The Bureaucratic Phenomenon*. Chicago: University of Chicago Press, 1964.

Cutright, Philips, "National Political Development: Its Measurement and Social Correlates," in Nelson W. Polsby, R. Dentler, and Paul Smith, eds., *Politics and Social Life*. Boston: Houghton Mifflin, 1963.

Cuzzort, R. P., *Humanity and Modern Sociological Thought*. New York: Holt, Rinehart & Winston, 1969.

Dahrendorf, Ralf, *Class and Class Conflict in Industrial Society*. Stanford, Calif.: Stanford University Press, 1959.

Dale, Edwin, Jr., "The Economics of Pollution," *New York Times Magazine*, April 1970.

Dalton, Melville, *Men Who Manage*. New York: Wiley, 1959.

Darwin, Charles, *The Expression of the Emotions in Man and Animals*. London: John Murray, 1872.

David, P. T., R. M. Goldman, and R. C. Bain, *The Politics of National Party Conventions*. Washington, D.C.: Brookings Institute, 1960.

Davis, Kingsley, "Extreme Social Isolation of a Child," *American Journal of Sociology*, XLV (January 1940), 554–564.

———, "Final Note on a Case of Extreme Isolation," *American Journal of Sociology*, L (March 1947), 432–437.

———, *Human Society*. New York: The Macmillan Company, 1949.

———, "Reply to Tumin," *American Sociological Review*, XVIII (August 1953), 394–397.

———, "The Urbanization of the Human Population," *Scientific American*, CCXIII (September 3, 1965), 11–53.

——— and Wilbur Moore, "Some Principles of Stratification," *American Sociological Review*, X (April 1945), 242–249.

De Beauvoir, Simone, *The Second Sex*, H. M. Parshley, ed. New York: Bantam Books, 1961 (first published 1949).

De Bell, Garret, *The Environmental Handbook*. New York: Ballantine Books, 1970.

Dechert, Charles R., ed., *The Social Impact of Cybernetics*. New York: Simon & Schuster, 1966.

De Guerry, A., *Statistiques Morales de la France*. Paris, 1831.

———, *Essai sur l'homme*, Paris, 1835.

Denham, Woodrow W., "Nonhuman Primate Behavior: A Note on Recent Research," *American Anthropologist*, LXXII (April 1970), 365–367.

Denzin, Norman K., "Symbolic Interactionism and Ethnomethodology: A Proposed Synthesis," *American Sociological Review*, XXXIV (December 1969), 922–934.

———, "Rules of Conduct and the Study of Deviant Behavior: Some Notes on the Social Relationship," in Jack D. Douglas, ed., *Deviance and Respectability: The Social Construction of Moral Meanings*. New York: Basic Books, 1970a, 120–159.

———, *The Research Act: A Theoretical Introduction to Sociological Methods*. Chicago: Aldine, 1970b.

———, "Developmental Theories of Self and Childhood: Some Conceptions and Misconceptions." Paper presented to annual meetings of American Sociological Association, August 31–September 3, 1970, Washington, D.C., 1970c.

———, "Childhood as a Conversation of Gestures." Unpublished manuscript, 1970d.

———, *Intimate Interactions: Aspects of the Moral Order*. Chicago: Aldine, forthcoming.

De Schweinitz, Karl, *Industrialization and Democracy: Economic Necessities and Political Possibilities*. New York: The Free Press, 1964.

Deutsch, Karl W., *Nationalism and Social Communication*. Cambridge: M.I.T. Press, 1953.

———, *The Nerves of Government*. New York: The Free Press, 1965.

Deutscher, Irwin, "Public vs. Private Opinions: The Real and the Unreal." Unpublished paper presented to Eastern Sociological Society, 1966a.

———, "Words and Deeds," *Social Problems,* XIII (1966b), 235–254.

———,"Notes on Language and Human Conduct." Unpublished paper, Syracuse University, 1967.

Deutsher, Isaac, *The Prophet Unarmed: Trotsky, 1921–1929.* New York: Oxford University Press, 1959.

DeVore, Irven, ed., *Primate Behavior: Field Studies on Monkeys and Apes.* New York: Holt, Rinehart & Winston, 1965.

Dexter, Lewis A. and David M. White, *People, Society and Mass Communications.* New York: The Free Press, 1964.

Dickson, Donald T., "Bureaucracy and Morality: An Organizational Perspective on a Moral Crusade," *Social Problems,* XVI (Fall 1968), 143–156.

Domhoff, G. William and Hoyt B. Ballard, *C. Wright Mills and the Power Elite.* Boston: Beacon Press, 1968.

Dore, Ronald, "Talent and the Social Order in Tokugawa Japan," in John Hall and M. Jansen, eds., *Studies in the Institutional History of Early Modern Japan.* Princeton: Princeton University Press, 1968.

Douglas, Jack D., *The Social Meanings of Suicide.* Princeton: Princeton University Press, 1967.

———, eds., *Deviance and Respectability: The Social Construction of Moral Meanings.* New York: Basic Books, 1970a.

———, ed., *Freedom and Tyranny: Social Problems in a Technological Society.* New York: Random House, 1970b.

———, ed., *The Impact of Sociology.* New York: Appleton-Century-Crofts, 1970c.

———, ed., *Observations of Deviance.* New York: Random House, 1970d.

———, ed., *The Relevance of Sociology.* New York: Appleton-Century-Crofts, 1970e.

———, ed., *Understanding Everyday Life.* New York: Aldine, 1970f.

———, *Youth in Turmoil: Traditionals, Deviants and Rebels.* Washington, D.C.: Government Printing Office, 1970g.

———, *American Social Order.* New York: The Free Press, 1971a.

———, ed., *Crime and Justice in America.* New York: Bobbs-Merrill, 1971b.

———, ed., *The Threat of Technology.* New York: Prentice-Hall, 1971c.

———, ed., *Research On Deviance.* New York: Random House, 1972.

———, *The Sociology of Social Problems.* New York: Appleton-Century-Crofts, 1973.

Duncan, Hugh Dalziel, *Communication and Social Order.* New York: Bedminster Press, 1962.

———, *Symbols in Society.* New York: Oxford University Press, 1968.

Duncan, Otis Dudley, "Inequality and Opportunity." Presidential address of the Population Association of America, Atlantic City, 1969.

Durkheim, Emile, *The Division of Labor in Society.* Glencoe, Ill.: The Free Press, 1933.

———, *Suicide.* New York: The Free Press, 1951.

———, *The Rules of Sociological Method.* Glencoe, Ill.: The Free Press, 1958.

———, *Elementary Forms of the Religious Life.* New York: Collier Books, 1961.

———, "The Normal and the Pathological," in Marvin E. Wolfgang, ed., *The Sociology of Crime and Delinquency.* New York: Wiley, 1962.

——— and Marcel Mauss, *Primitive Classification.* Chicago: University of Chicago Press, 1967.

Dynes, Russell R., et al., *Social Problems.* New York: Oxford University Press, 1964.

Ebenstein, William, *Great Political Thinkers: Plato to the Present*, 3rd ed. New York: Holt, Rinehart & Winston, 1960.

Eberhard, Wolfram, *Conquerors and Rulers: Social Forces in Medieval China.* Leiden: Brill, 1965.

Editors, "When the People Speak Up," *The Progressive,* April 1970, 62–66.

Eimerl, Sarel and Irven DeVore, *The Primates.* New York: Time, 1965.

Eisenstadt, S. N., *Essay in Comparative Institutions.* New York: Wiley, 1965.

Elkins, Frederick, "Advertising Themes and Quiet Revolutions: Dilemmas in French Canada," *American Journal of Sociology,* LXXV (July 1969), 112–122.

Ellis, Robert A. and W. Clayton Lane, "Structural Supports for Upward Mobility," *American Sociological Review* (October 1963), 743–756.

Ellul, Jacques, *The Technological Society.* New York: Vintage, 1964.

———, *The Political Illusion.* New York: Knopf, 1967.

Erikson, Kai, *Wayward Puritans.* New York: Wiley, 1967.

Ervin-Tripp, Susan, "Language Development," in L. Hoffman and M. Hoffman, *Review of Child Development Research,* Vol. II. New York: Russell Sage Foundation, 1966.

Etzioni, Amitai, "The Ghetto—A Reevaluation," *Social Forces,* XXXVII (March 1959), 255–262.

———, "Basic Human Needs, Alienation, and Inauthenticity," *American Sociological Review*, XXXIII (December 1968), 807–875.

Fanon, Frantz, *The Wretched of the Earth*. New York: Grove Press, 1963.

Faris, Robert E. L., *Chicago Sociology: 1920–1932*. San Francisco: Chandler, 1967.

Faunce, William A., *Problems of an Industrial Society*. New York: McGraw-Hill, 1968.

Feagin, Joe R., "Black Women in the Labor Force." Unpublished paper read at 1969 meetings of Pacific Sociological Association.

Feldman, Arnold and Wilbert Moore, "Industrialization and Industrialism, Convergence and Differentiation." Transactions 5th World Congress of Sociology, Washington, D.C., 1962.

Fink, Donald G., *Computers and the Human Mind*. Garden City, N.J.: Doubleday Anchor, 1966.

Firey, Walter, "Sentiment and Symbolism as Ecological Variables," *American Sociological Review*, X (April 1945), 140–148.

Fishman, Joshua, "A Systematization of the Whorfian Hypothesis," *Behavioral Science*, V (October 1950), 323–339.

Flavell, J., *The Developmental Psychology of Jean Piaget*. Princeton: Van Nostrand, 1963.

Foster, George, "The Personality of the Peasant." American Anthropological meeting (58th), Mexico City, 1959.

Frake, Charles, "A Structural Description of Subanum Religious Behavior," in Ward Goodenough, ed., *Explorations in Cultural Anthropology*. New York: McGraw-Hill, 1964.

Freidman, Neil, *Social Aspects of the Psychological Experiment*. New York: Basic Books, 1967.

Freuchen, Peter, *Peter Freuchen's Book of the Eskimos*, Dagmar Freuchen, ed. Cleveland: World, 1961.

Freud, Sigmund, *Civilization and Its Discontents*. New York: Norton, 1961.

Freund, Julien, *The Sociology of Max Weber*. New York: Random House, 1968.

Friedenberg, Edgar Z., "Adolescence as a Social Problem," in Howard S. Becker, ed., *Social Problems: A Modern Approach*. New York: Wiley, 1966.

Friedrich, Carl, *Europe an Emergent Nation?* New York: Harper & Row, 1969.

——— and Zbignieu Brzizinski, *Totalitarian Dictatorship and Autocracy*. Cambridge: Harvard University Press, 1956.

Friedrichs, Robert W., *A Sociology of Sociology*. New York: The Free Press, 1970.

Fromm, Erich, *Marx's Concept of Man.* New York: Ungar, 1961.

Froomkin, Joseph N., "Automation," *International Encyclopedia of the Social Sciences,* I (1968), 480–482.

Frumkin, Robert M., "Early English and American Sex Customs," in *Encyclopedia of Sexual Behavior,* Vol. I. New York: Hawthorne Books, 1967, 350–365.

Fuller, Richard C. and Richard R. Myers, "The Natural History of a Social Problem," *American Sociological Review,* VI (June 1941), 320–329.

Gans, Herbert, *The Urban Villagers.* New York: The Free Press, 1962a.

———, "Urbanism and Suburbanism as Ways of Life: A Re-Evaluation of Definitions," in Arnold Rose, ed., *Human Behavior and Social Processes.* Boston: Houghton Mifflin, 1962b.

———, *The Levittowners: Ways of Life and Politics in a New Suburban Community.* New York: Pantheon, 1967.

Gareau, Oliver, *The Political Life of the American Medical Association.* Cambridge: Harvard University Press, 1941.

Garfinkel, Harold, "Studies of the Routine Grounds of Everyday Activities," *Social Problems,* Vol. XI (Winter 1964), 225–260.

———, *Studies in Ethnomethodology.* Englewood Cliffs, N.J.: Prentice-Hall, 1967.

Geertz, Clifford J., *The Development of Javanese Economy.* Cambridge: M.I.T. Press, 1956.

———, *Peddlers and Princes.* Chicago: University of Chicago Press, 1963a.

———, "The Integrative Revolution," in Clifford Geertz, ed., *Old Societies and New States.* New York: The Free Press, 1963b, 105–157.

Gelner, Ernest, *Words and Things.* London: Penguin Books, 1968.

Gerard, Ralph W., ed., *Computers and Education.* New York: McGraw-Hill, 1967.

Gerschenkron, Alexander, *Economic Backwardness in Historical Perspective.* New York: Praeger, 1964.

Gerth, H. H. and C. Wright Mills, *From Max Weber: Essays in Sociology.* New York: Oxford University Press, 1946.

Gesell, Arnold and Frances L. Ilg, *Infant and Child Care in the Culture of Today.* New York: Harper & Brothers, 1943.

Gibbs, Jack P., "Conceptions of Deviant Behavior: The Old and the New," *Pacific Sociological Review,* IX (Spring 1966), 9–14.

Ginott, Haim, *Between Parent and Child.* New York: Avon Books, 1965.

604   Bibliography

Gist, Noel P. and Sylvia F. Fava, *Urban Society.* New York: Thomas Y. Crowell, 1964.

Glaser, Barney G. and Anselm L. Strauss, "Awareness Contexts and Social Interaction," *American Sociological Review,* XXIX (October 1964), 669–679.

——— and ———, *Time For Dying.* Chicago: Aldine, 1968.

Glazer, Nathan and Daniel Moynihan, *Beyond the Melting Pot.* Cambridge: M.I.T. Press, 1963.

Glueck, Sheldon and Eleanor Glueck, *Unraveling Juvenile Delinquency.* New York: Commonwealth Fund, 1950.

Goffman, Erving. "The Nature of Deference and Demeanor," *American Anthropologist,* LVIII (June 1956a), 473–502.

———, "Embarrassment and Social Organization," *American Journal of Sociology,* LXII (November 1956b), 264–274.

———, *The Presentation of Self in Everyday Life.* Garden City, N.Y.: Doubleday Anchor, 1959.

———, *Asylums: Essays on the Social Situations of Mental Patients.* Garden City, N.Y.: Doubleday Anchor, 1961a.

———, *Encounters: Two Studies in the Sociology of Interaction.* Indianapolis: Bobbs-Merrill, 1961b.

———, *Behavior in Public Places: Notes on the Social Organization of Gatherings.* New York: The Free Press, 1963.

———, *Stigma: Notes on the Management of Spoiled Identity.* Englewood Cliffs, N.J.: Prentice-Hall, 1965.

———, *Interaction Ritual: Essays in Face-to-Face Behavior.* Chicago: Aldine, 1967.

Goldstein, Melvin L., "Physiological Theories of Emotion: A Critical Historical Review from the Standpoint of Behavior Theory," *Psychological Bulletin,* LXIX (January 1968), 23–40.

Goldthorpe, John, "Social Stratification in Industrial Society," in Reinhard Bendix and S. M. Lipset, eds., *Class, Status and Power,* 2nd ed. New York: The Free Press, 1966.

Goodall, (Lady) Jane, "Chimpanzees of the Gombe Streat Reserve," in Irven DeVore, 1965, 425–473.

Goode, William, "Industrialization and Family Change," in Wilbert Moore and Bert Hoselitz, eds., *Industrialization and Society.* New York: UNESCO, 1963.

Goodenough, Ward, "Cultural Anthropology and Linguistics," in Dell Hymes, ed., *Language in Culture and Society.* New York: Harper & Row, 1964a.

———, ed., *Explorations in Cultural Anthropology*. New York: McGraw-Hill, 1964b.

Goodman, Percival and Paul Goodman, *Communities: Ways of Livelihood and Means of Life*. New York: Vintage, 1960.

Gordon, Chad and Kenneth J. Gergen, eds., *The Self in Social Interaction*, Vol. I. New York: Wiley, 1968, p. 227.

Gordon, Mitchell, *Sick Cities*. Baltimore: Penguin Books, 1963.

Gorer, Geoffrey, "Man Has no 'Killer' Instinct," 1967a, reprinted in Ashley Montagu, ed., 1968, pp. 27–36.

———, "Ardrey on Human Nature: Animals, Nations, Imperatives," 1967b, reprinted in Ashley Montagu, ed., 1968, pp. 74–82.

Gough, Kathleen E., "The Nayars and the Definition of Marriage," *Journal of the Royal Anthropological Institute*, LXXXIX (1959), 23–34.

Gouldner, Alvin W., *Patterns of Industrial Bureaucracy*. Glencoe, Ill.: The Free Press, 1954a.

———, *Wildcat Strike*. Yellow Springs, Ohio: Antioch Press, 1954b.

———, "Reciprocity and Autonomy in Functional Theory," in Llewellyn Gross, ed., *Symposium on Sociological Theory*. New York: Harper & Row, 1959.

———, "The Norm of Reciprocity: A Preliminary Statement," *American Sociological Review*, XXV (April 1960), 161–178.

———, *The Coming Crisis of Western Sociology*. New York: Basic Books, 1970.

———, "Anti-Minotaur: The Myth of a Value-Free Sociology," reprinted in Jack D. Douglas, ed., *The Relevance of Sociology*. New York: Appleton-Century-Crofts, 1970.

Greenberg, J. H., ed., *Universals of Language*. Cambridge: M.I.T. Press, 1963.

Greer, Scott, *Urban Renewal and American Cities*. New York: Bobbs-Merrill, 1965.

Gross, Edward, "Some Functional Consequences of Primary Controls in Formal Work Organizations," *American Sociological Review*, XVIII (August 1953), 365–373.

Gross, Neal, W. Mason, and A. McEachern, *Explorations in Role Analysis: Studies of the School Superintendency Role*. New York: Wiley, 1957.

Gusfield, Joseph R., *Symbolic Crusade*. Urbana: University of Illinois Press, 1963.

———, "Tradition and Modernity: Misplaced Polarities in the Study of Social Change," *American Journal of Sociology*, LXXII (January 1967), 351–362.

Hadden, Jeffrey, Louis Masothi, and Calvin Larson, *Metropolis in Crisis*. Itasca, Ill.: Peacock, 1967.

Hafez, E. S. E., ed., *The Behaviour of Domestic Animals.* London: Bailliere, Tindall & Cox, 1962.

Halacy, D. S., *Computers: The Machines We Think With.* New York: Dell, 1962.

Hall, Edward T., *The Silent Language.* New York: Fawcett Premier, 1965.

———, *The Hidden Dimension.* New York: Doubleday, 1968.

Hall, K. R. L., and Irven DeVore, "Baboon Social Behavior," in Irven DeVore, ed., 1965, pp. 20–52.

———, "Distribution and Adaptations of Baboons," *Symposia* of Zoological Society of London, XVII (1966), 49–73.

Hall, Max W., "The Shape of the Story," in Louis M. Lyons, ed., *Reporting the News.* Cambridge: Belknap, 1965.

Hall, Oswald, "The Informal Organization of the Medical Profession," *Canadian Journal of Economics and Political Science,* XII (February 1946), 30–44.

Hall, Richard H., *Occupations and the Social Structure.* Englewood Cliffs, N.J.: Prentice-Hall, 1969.

Handlin, Oscar, *Boston's Immigrants.* Cambridge: Harvard University Press, 1959.

Hare, A. Paul, *Handbook of Small Group Research.* Glencoe, Ill.: The Free Press, 1962.

Harlow, Henry F., "Love in Infant Monkeys," *Scientific American Zoo,* June 1959, pp. 65–75.

———, "The Development of Affectional Patterns in Infant Monkeys," in Foss, ed., *Determinants of Infant Behavior.* New York: Wiley, 1961, pp. 75–100.

———, "The Heterosexual Affectional System in Monkeys," *American Psychologist,* XVII (January 1962), 1–9.

———, "Maternal Affectional System," in Foss, ed., *Determinants of Infant Behavior,* Vol II. New York: Wiley, 1963, pp. 3–34.

——— and Margaret Harlow, "Social Deprivation in Monkeys," *Scientific American,* CCVII (November 1962), 136–146.

——— and ———, "The Affectional Systems," in A. M. Shrier, H. F. Harlow, and F. Stollnitz, ed., *Behavior of Non-Human Primates,* Vol. II. New York: Academic Press, 1965, pp. 287–334.

——— and ———, "Learning to Love," *American Scientist* (1966), 244–272.

Harrington, Michael, *The Other America.* New York: The Macmillan Company, 1962.

Harris, Seymour E., ed., *Economic Aspects of Higher Education.* Paris: Organization for Economic Cooperation and Development, March 1964.

Hart, C. W. M. and Arnold R. Pilling, *The Tiwi of North Australia*. New York: Holt, Rinehart & Winston, 1960.

Hartshorne, H. and M. May, *Studies in the Nature of Character*, Vol. I, II, III. New York: The Macmillan Company, 1928–1930.

Hass, C. Glenn, "Who Should Plan the Curriculum?" in Alice and Lester D. Crow, eds., *Vital Issues in American Education*. New York: Bantam Books, 1964, pp. 143–148.

Hauser, Philip, "Observations on the Urban-Folk and Urban-Rural Dichotomies as Forms of Western Ethnocentrism," in Philip Hauser and Leo Schnore, eds., *The Study of Urbanization*. New York: Wiley, 1965a.

———, *Urbanization: An Over-View*. New York: Wiley, 1965b.

Havighurst, A. R., and H. Taba, *Adolescent Character and Personality*. New York: Wiley, 1949.

Hawley, Willis D. and Frederick M. Wirt, *The Search for Community Power*. Englewood Cliffs, N.J.: Prentice-Hall, 1968.

Hayek, F. A., *The Counter-Revolution of Science*. New York: The Free Press, 1955.

Health Publications Institute, *Children and Youth at the Midcentury*. Raleigh, N.C.: Health Publications Institute, 1951.

Hebb, Donald O. and W. R. Thompson, "The Social Significance of Animal Studies, 1954," in Gardner Lindzey, ed., I (1954), 532–562.

Hediger, H., *Wild Animals in Captivity*. London: Butterworth, 1950.

———, *Studies of the Psychology and Behavior of Captive Animals in Zoos and Circuses*. London: Butterworth, 1955.

———, "The Evolution of Territorial Behavior," in S. L. Washburn, ed., *Social Life of Early Man*, 1961.

Heilbroner, Robert L., "The Impact of Technology: The Historic Debate," in *The American Assembly, Automation and Technological Change*. Englewood Cliffs, N.J.: Prentice-Hall, 1962, pp. 7–25.

Henslin, James M., "Trust and the Cab Drivers," in Marcello Truzzi, ed., *Sociology and Everyday Life*. Englewood Cliffs, N.J.: Prentice-Hall, 1968.

———, "What Makes for Trust?" in James M. Henslin, ed., *Down to Earth Sociology*. New York: The Free Press, 1971.

———, *The Sociology of Sex*. New York: Appleton-Century-Crofts, forthcoming.

——— and Mae A. Biggs, "Dramaturgical De-Sexualization: The Sociology of the Vaginal Examination," in James M. Henslin, ed., *The Sociology of Sex*. New York: Appleton-Century-Crofts forthcoming.

Herbers, John, "High School Unrest Rises Alarming U.S. Educators," *New York Times*, May 9, 1969, pp. 1, 30.

Herndon, James, *The Way It Spozed to Be*. New York: Simon & Schuster, 1968.

Herskovit, Melville J., *Economic Anthropology*. New York: Knopf, 1952.

Hertzler, Joyce, *A Sociology of Language*. New York: Random House, 1965.

Hill, Reuben, "The American Family of the Future," *Journal of Marriage and the Family*, XXVI (1964), 20–28.

Himmelweit, H. T., A. N. Oppenheim, and P. Vince, *Television and the Child*. New York: Oxford University Press, 1958.

Hintze, Otto, "The State in Historical Perspective," in Reinhard Bendix et al., eds., *State and Society*. Boston: Little, Brown, 1968, pp. 154–169.

Hirschman, Albert, "Obstacles to Development: A Classification and a Quasi-Vanishing Act," *Economic Development and Cultural Change*, XIII (July 1965), 385–393.

Hobbes, Thomas, *Leviathan*. New York: Dutton, 1950.

Hodge, Robert, Donald Treiman, and Peter Rossi, "A Comparative Study of Occupational Prestige," in Reinhard Bendix and S. M. Lipset, eds., *Class, Status and Power*, 2nd ed. New York: The Free Press, 1966.

Hodgen, Margaret T., *Change and History: A Study of the Dated Distributions of Technological Innovations in England*, Viking Fund Publications in Anthropology, No. 18. New York: Wenner-Gren Fund for Anthropological Research, 1952.

Hofstadter, Richard, *Anti-Intellectualism in American Life*. New York: Knopf, 1963.

———, *The Age of Reform*. New York: Knopf, 1955.

Holloway, Ralph, "Territory and Aggression in Man: A Look at Ardrey's Territorial Imperative," 1967, reprinted in Ashley Montagu, ed., 1968, pp. 96–102.

Holt, John, *How Children Fail*. New York: Pitman, 1967.

Homans, George C., *The Human Group*. London: Routledge & Kegan Paul (New York: Harcourt, Brace & World), 1950.

———, *Social Behavior: Its Elementary Forms*. Boston: Harcourt, Brace & World, 1961.

Hoos, Ida R., "When the Computer Takes Over the Office," *Harvard Business Review*, XXXVIII (July-August 1960), 102–112.

Horowitz, Irving, "Max Weber and the Spirit of American Sociology," *Sociological Quarterly*, V (Autumn 1964), 334–354.

———, *Three Worlds of Development*. New York: Oxford University Press, 1966.

Hughes, Everett C., *Men and Their Work*. Glencoe, Ill.: The Free Press, 1958.

———, "Race Relations and the Sociological Imagination," *American Sociological Review*, XXVIII (December 1963), 879–890.

Hunter, Floyd, *Community Power Structure*. Chapel Hill: University of North Carolina Press, 1953.

Huntington, Samuel P., "Political Modernization: America vs. Europe," in Reinhard Bendix et al., eds., *State and Society*. Boston: Little, Brown, 1968, pp. 170–199.

Huxley, (Sir) Julian (organizer), "A Discussion on Ritualization of Behaviour in Animals and Man." Philosophical Transactions of the Royal Society of London, Series B, *Biological Sciences*, CCLI, No. 772 (December 29, 1966), 247–526.

Hymes, Dell, ed., *Language in Culture and Society*. New York: Harper & Row, 1964.

Icheiser, Gustav, *Appearances and Realities*. San Francisco: Jossey-Bass, 1970.

Inhelder, B., and J. Piaget, *The Growth of Logical Thinking from Childhood to Adolescence*. New York: Basic Books, 1958.

Inkeles, Alex, "Industrial Man: The Relation of Status to Experience, Perception and Value," *American Journal of Sociology*, LXVI (1960), 1–31.

———, "The Modernization of Man," in Myron Weiner, ed., *Modernization*. New York: Basic Books, 1966.

———and Peter Rossi, "National Comparisons of Occupational Prestige," *American Journal of Sociology*, LXI (January 1956), 329–339.

Innis, Harold A., *The Bias of Communication*. Toronto: University of Toronto Press, 1951.

International Labour Office, *Labour and Automation*, Bulletin No. 5, Automation and Non-Manual Workers. Geneva, 1967.

Jacobs, Jane, *The Death and Life of Great American Cities*. New York: Random House, 1961.

Jacobs, Jerry, "A Phenomenological Study of Suicide Notes," *Social Problems*, XV (1967), 60–72.

———, *The Search for Help: A Study of the Retarded Child in the Community*. New York: Bruner-Mazel, 1969a.

———, "Symbolic Bureaucracy: A Case Study of a Social Welfare Agency," *Social Forces*, XLVII (1969b), 413–422.

Jaki, Stanley L., *Brain, Mind and Computers*. New York: Herder & Herder, 1969.

Janowitz, Morris, "Patterns of Collective Racial Violence," in H. D. Graham and J. R. Gurr, *Violence in America*. New York: Bantam Books, 1969.

Jarrett, Henry, *Environmental Quality in a Growing Economy*. Baltimore: Johns Hopkins Press, 1966.

Jay, Phyllis, "The Indian Langur Monkey (Presbytis entellus)," in Charles Southwick, ed., 1963, pp. 114–123.

Jensen, Arthur, "Reducing the Heredity-Environment Uncertainty: A Reply," *Harvard Educational Review*, XXXIX No. 3 (Summer 1969), 449–483.

Johnson, Benton, "Ascetic Protestantism and Political Preference," *Public Opinion Quarterly*, XXVI (1962).

Jonassen, Christen T., *Studies in Human Ecology*, George A. Theodorsen, ed. New York: Harper & Row, 1961.

Jones, N. G. Blurton, "An Ethological Study of Some Aspects of Social Behaviour in Nursery School," in Desmond Morris, ed., 1967, pp. 347–368.

Joos, Martin, *Five Clocks*. New York: Harcourt, Brace, 1967.

Kagan, J., "The Many Faces of Response," *Psychology Today*, No. 8 (1968), pp. 22–27.

Kaplan, Abraham, *The Conduct of Inquiry*. San Francisco: Chandler, 1964.

Karpman, Benjamin, *The Sexual Offender and His Offenses*. New York: Julian Press, 1954.

Katz, Elihu and Paul Lazarsfeld, *Personal Influence*. Glencoe, Ill.: The Free Press, 1955.

Kaufman, Bel, *Up the Down Staircase*. Englewood Cliffs. N.J.: Prentice-Hall, 1964.

Kautsky, John and Roger Benjamin, "Communism and Economic Development," in John Kautsky, ed., *Communism and the Politics of Development*. New York: Wiley, 1968.

Keniston, Kenneth, *The Uncommitted: Alienated Youth in American Society*. New York: Harcourt, Brace & World, 1965.

——, *Young Radicals: Notes on Committed Youth*. New York: Harcourt, Brace & World, 1968.

Kerr, Clark, John Dunlop, Frederic Harbison, and Charles Heyers, *Industrialism and Industrial Man*. New York: Oxford University Press, 1964.

—— and Lloyd C. Fisher, "Plant Sociology: The Elite and the Aborigines," in Mirra Komarovsky, ed., *Common Frontiers of the Social Science*. Glencoe, Ill.: The Free Press, 1957, pp. 281–309.

——— and Abraham Siegal, "The Interindustry Propensity to Strike," in Arthur Kornhauser, ed., *Industrial Conflict*. New York: McGraw-Hill, 1954, pp. 189–212.

Kerr, Norman, "The School Board as an Agency of Legitimation," *Sociology of Education*, Fall 1964, pp. 34–59.

Key, V. O., *Southern Politics*. New York: Knopf, 1949.

Keyfitz, Nathan, "Political-Economic Aspects of Urbanization in South and Southeast Asia," in Philip Hauser and Leo Schnore, eds., *The Study of Urbanization*. New York: Wiley, 1965.

Kindleberger, C. D., *Economic Growth in France and Britain, 1851–1950*. Cambridge: Harvard University Press, 1964.

Kjolseth, Rolf, "Structure and Process in Conversation." Presented to the ASA, 1967.

Klapper, Joseph T., *The Effects of Mass Communications*. New York: The Free Press, 1960.

Klietsch, Ronald G., "Clothesline Patterns and Covert Behavior," *Journal of Marriage and the Family*, XXVII (1965), 78–80.

Kohl, Herbert, *36 Children*. New York: New American Library, 1967.

Kohlberg, L., "Stage and Sequence. The Cognitive-Developmental Approach to Socialization," in D. Goslin, ed., *Handbook of Socialization Theory and Research*. Chicago: Rand McNally, 1969.

Kolko, Gabriel, *Wealth and Power in America*. New York: Praeger, 1962.

Kon, Igor S., "The Concept of Alienation in Modern Sociology," in Peter L. Berger, ed., *Marxism and Sociology: Views from Eastern Europe*. New York: Appleton-Century-Crofts, 1969, pp. 146–167.

Kornhauser, William, *The Politics of Mass Society*. Glencoe, Ill.: The Free Press, 1959.

———, *Scientists in Industry: Conflict and Accommodation*. Berkeley: University of California Press, 1962.

Kozol, Jonathan, *Death at an Early Age*. Boston: Houghton Mifflin, 1967.

Kraft, Robert E., *Profiles in Power: A Washington Insight*. New York: New American Library, 1966.

Krech, David, Richard Crutchfield, and Egerton Bailachey, *Individual in Society*. New York: McGraw-Hill, 1962.

Kroeber, A. L. and Clyde Kluckholn, *Culture: A Critical Review of Concepts and Definitions*. New York: Vintage, n.d. (first published in 1952).

Kuhn, Manford H., "Factors in Personality: Sociocultural Determinants as Seen Through the Amish," in Francis L. K. Hsu, ed., *Aspects of Culture and Personality*. New York: Adelaid Schurman, 1954.

———, "The Reference Group Reconsidered," *Sociological Quarterly*, V (Winter 1964), 5–21.

——— and Thomas S. McPartland, "An Empirical Investigation of Self-Attitudes," *American Sociological Review*, XIX (February 1954), 68–76.

Kuhn, Thomas E., *The Structure of Scientific Revolutions*. Chicago: University of Chicago Press, 1965.

Kummer, H., *Social Organization of Hamadryas Baboons*. Basel, Switzerland: Karger, 1968.

Kuvlesky, William P., "Toward a Sociology of Nonhuman Behavior." Presented at meetings of American Sociological Association, San Francisco, 1969.

Kuznets, Simon, *Modern Economic Growth*. New Haven: Yale University Press, 1966.

LaBarre, Weston, "The Cultural Basis of Emotions and Gestures," *Journal of Personality*, XVI (September 1947), 49–68.

———, *The Human Animal*. Chicago: Phoenix Books, 1960.

Lampman, Robert J., *The Share of Top Wealth-Holders in National Wealth, 1922–1956*. Princeton: Princeton University Press, 1962.

Lane, Robert E., *Political Life*. New York: The Free Press, 1959.

Langer, Elinor, "Inside the New York Telephone Company," *New York Review of Books*, XIV (1970), 16–24.

Lasswell, Harold A., *Politics: Who Gets What, When, How*. New York: World, 1958.

———, "The Structure and Function of Communication in Society," in Wilbur Schramm, ed., *Mass Communications*. Urbana: University of Illinois Press, 1960, pp. 117–140.

Lastrucci, Carlo L., *The Scientific Approach*. Cambridge: Schenkman, 1963.

Lazarsfeld, Paul F., Bernard Berelson, and Hazel Gaudet, *The People's Choice*. New York: Columbia University Press, 1948.

Lea, Henry C., *History of Sacerdotal Celibacy in the Christian Church*, 4th ed. London: Watts, 1932.

Leach, Edmund R., "Anthropological Aspects of Language: Animal Categories and Verbal Abuse," in Eric Lenneberg, ed., 1964, pp. 23–63.

———, "Don't Say 'Boo' to a Goose, 1966," reprinted in Ashley Montagu, ed., 1968, pp. 65–73.

Lemert, Edwin, *Social Pathology*. New York: McGraw-Hill, 1951.

———, "Is There a Natural History of Social Problems?" *American Sociological Review*, XVI (1957), 213–217.

———, *Human Deviance, Social Problems and Social Control*. Englewood Cliffs, N.J.: Prentice-Hall, 1967.

Lenneberg, Eric H., ed., *New Directions in the Study of Language*. Cambridge: M.I.T. Press, 1964.

———, "The Natural History of Language," in Frank Smith and George Miller, eds., *The Genesis*. Cambridge: M.I.T. Press, 1966, pp. 219–252.

———, "On Explaining Language," *Science*, CLXIV (May 9, 1969), 635–643.

Lenski, Gerhard, *Power and Privilege*. New York: McGraw-Hill, 1966.

———, *Human Societies: A Macrolevel Introduction to Sociology*. New York: McGraw-Hill, 1970.

Lerner, Daniel, *The Passing of Traditional Society: Modernizing the Middle East*. New York: The Free Press, 1958.

Levinger, George, "Natural Cohesiveness and Dissolution: An Integrative Overview," *Journal of Marriage and the Family*, XXVII (1965), 19–28.

Levi-Strauss, Claude, "The Family," in Henry L. Shapiro, ed., *Man, Culture, and Society*. New York: Oxford University Press, 1956, pp. 261–285.

———, *Structural Anthropology*, trans. from French by C. Jacobson and B. G. Schoepf. New York: Basic Books, 1963.

———, *Tristes Tropiques*, trans. and abridged by J. Russell. New York: Atheneum Paper, 1963.

———, *The Savage Mind*. Chicago: University of Chicago Press, 1966.

———, *The Elementary Structures of Kinship*. Boston: Beacon Press, 1969.

Levy, Marion, Jr., *Modernization and the Structure of Societies*. Princeton: University of Princeton Press, 1966.

Lewin, Kurt, *Field Theory in Social Science*, Dorwin Cartwright, ed. New York: Harper & Row, 1951.

Lewis, Oscar, *Five Families: Mexican Case Studies in the Culture of Poverty* New York: Basic Books, 1959.

———, "Further Observations on the Folk-Urban Continuum and Urbanization with Special Reference to Mexico City," in Phillip Hauser and Leo Schnore, eds., *The Study of Urbanization*. New York: Wiley, 1965.

———, *La Vida: A Puerto Rican Family in the Culture of Poverty, San Juan and New York*. New York: Random House, 1966.

Liebow, Elliot, *Tally's Corner*. Boston: Little, Brown, 1967.

Lind, A. W., "Some Ecological Patterns of Community Disorganization in Honolulu," *American Journal of Sociology*, XXXVI (1930), 206–220.

Lindesmith, Alfred, *Opiate Addiction*. Bloomington: Indiana University Press, 1947.

———, *Addiction and Opiates*. Chicago: Aldine, 1968.

——— and Anselm Strauss, "A Critique of Culture-Personality Writings," *American Sociological Review*, XV (October 1950), 587–600.

——— and ———, "The Social Self," in Robert W. O'Brien et al., eds., *Readings in General Sociology*. Boston: Houghton Mifflin, 1964, pp. 206–209.

——— and ———, *Social Psychology*, 3rd ed. New York: Holt, Rinehart, & Winston, 1968.

Lindzey, Gardner, ed., *Handbook of Social Psychology*, Vols. I, II. Reading, Mass.: Addison-Wesley, 1959.

———, "Some Remarks Concerning Incest, the Incest Taboo, and Psychoanalytic Theory," *American Psychologist*, XXII (1967), 1951–1059.

Lippmann, Walter, *Public Opinion*. New York: The Macmillan Company, 1922.

Lipset, Seymour Martin, "Changing Social Status and Prejudice: The Race Theories of a Pioneering American Sociologist," *Commentary*, IX (May 1950).

———, "Some Social Requisites of Democracy," *American Political Science Review*, LIII (March 1959), 69–105.

———, "Elections: The Expressions of the Democratic Class Struggle," in *Political Man*. New York: Doubleday, 1960, pp. 230–278.

———, "Party Systems and the Representation of Social Groups," in *The First New Nation*. New York: Basic Books, 1963.

———, Martin Trow, and James Coleman, *Union Democracy*. New York: The Free Press, 1956.

Litwok, Eugene and Ivan Szelenyi, "Primary Group Structures and Their Functions: Kin, Neighbors, and Friends," *American Sociological Review*, XXXIV (August 1969), 465–481.

Lofland, John, "Interactionist Imagery and Analytic Interruptus," in T. Shibutani, ed., *Festschrift for Herbert Blumer*, forthcoming.

———, "On the Sociology of Erving Goffman: Style, Structure, Substance, Soul." Mimeographed, no date.

———, *Role Management*. Programmatic statement, working paper No. 23, Center for Research in Social Organization, University of Michigan, 1967.

——— and Lyn H. Lofland, *Deviance and Identity*. Englewood Cliffs, N.J.: Prentice-Hall, 1969.

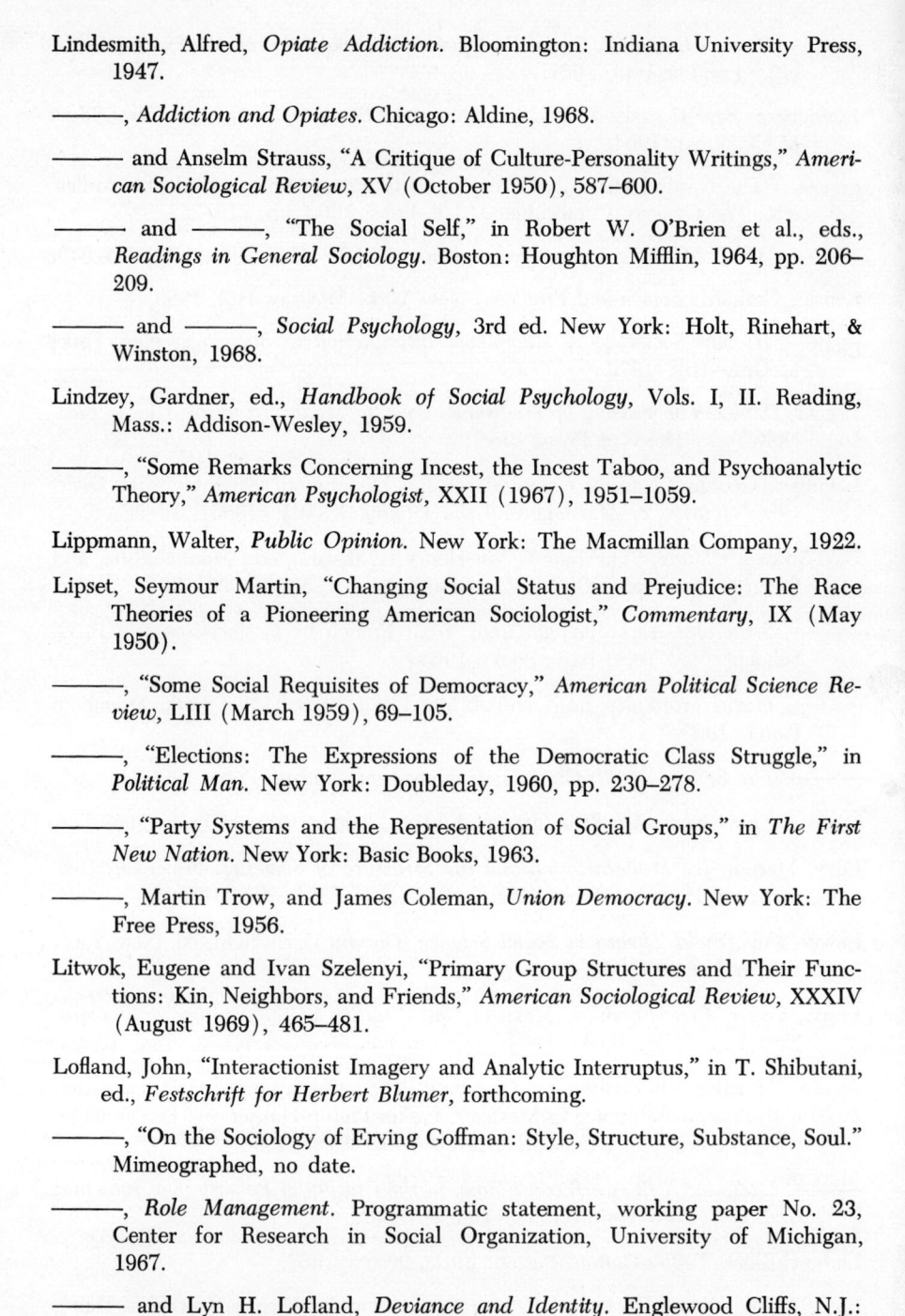

Loizos, Caroline, "Play Behaviour in Higher Primates: A Review," in Desmond Morris, ed., 1967, pp. 176–218.

Long, Norton, "The Local Community as an Ecology of Games," *American Journal of Sociology*, LXIV (November 1958), 251–261.

Lorenz, Konrad, *King Solomon's Ring*. London: Methuen, 1952.

——, *On Aggression*. London: Methuen, 1966.

Lowenthal, Leo, "Biographies in Popular Magazines," in William Peterson, ed., *American Social Patterns*. Garden City, N.J.: Doubleday Anchor, 1956.

Lowie, Robert H., *Indians of the Plains*. New York: McGraw-Hill, 1954.

Lubell, Samuel, *The Future of American Politics*. New York: Doubleday, 1956.

Lundberg, Ferdinand, *The Rich and the Super-Rich*. New York: Lyle Stuart, 1968.

Lyman, Stanford, "The Spectrum of Color," *Social Research*, XXXI (Autumn 1964), 364–373.

——, "The Race Relation Code of Robert E. Park," *Pacific Sociological Review*, XI (Spring 1968), 16–22.

——, *The Asian in the West*, Social Science and Humanities Publications, No. 4, Western Studies Center. Reno: Desert Research Center, University of Nevada System, 1970.

——, *The Negro in American Sociology*. New York: Simon & Schuster, 1972.

—— and Marvin B. Scott, *A Sociology of the Absurd*. New York: Appleton-Century-Crofts, 1970.

Lynd, Robert S., *Knowledge For What?* Princeton: Princeton University Press, 1939.

——, *Power in American Society as Resource and Problem*. Detroit: Wayne State University Press, 1957.

—— and Helen Merrell Lynd, *Middletown*. New York: Harcourt, Brace, 1930.

—— and ——, *Middletown in Transition*. New York: Harcourt, Brace, 1937.

Lyons, John, *Noam Chomsky*. New York: Viking Press, 1970.

Lyons, Louis M., *Reporting the News*. Cambridge: Harvard University Press, 1965.

MacCoby, E., ed., *The Development of Sex Differences*. Stanford: Stanford University Press, 1966.

MacDonald, Dwight, "The Times: One Man's Poison," *The Reporter*, February 14, 1950, pp. 12–17.

Macrae, Norton, "The Neurotic Trillionaire," *The Economist*, May 10, 1969, pp. 11–62.

Madge, John, *The Tools of Social Science*. Garden City, N.Y.: Doubleday Anchor, 1965.

Malinowski, Bronislaw, *Sex and Repression in Savage Society*. Cleveland: World (Meridian Books), 1955 (first published 1927).

———, *The Sexual Life of Savages in North-Western Melanesia: An Ethnographic Account of Courtship, Marriage and Family Life Among the Natives of the Trobriand Islands, British New Guinea*. New York: Harcourt, Brace & World, 1929.

———, "Culture," in *Encyclopedia of the Social Sciences*, Vol. IV, 621–646. New York: The Macmillan Company, 1930.

———, *Coral Gardens and Their Magic*. New York: American Book, 1935.

———, *The Dynamics of Culture Change*. New Haven: Yale University Press, 1945.

———, *The Dilemma of Contemporary Linguistics*, in Dell Hymes, ed., *Language in Culture and Society*. New York: Harper & Row, 1964.

Mandelbaum, David, ed., *Collected Writings of Edwin Sapir*. Berkeley: University of California Press, 1949.

Manis, Jerome G., "Agricultural Migration and Population Prediction," *Rural Sociology*, XXIV (1959), 29–34.

——— and Bernard N. Meltzer, eds. *Symbolic Interaction*. Boston: Allyn & Bacon, 1967.

Mann, Floyd C. and L. K. Williams, "Automation in the Office," in Charles R. Walker, ed., *Technology, Industry and Man*. New York: McGraw-Hill, 1968, pp. 147–158.

Mannheim, Karl, *Man and Society in an Age of Reconstruction*, Part I. New York: Harcourt, Brace, 1940.

Manning, Peter K., "Problems in Interpreting Interview Data," *Sociology and Social Research*, LI (1967).

———, *Metaphors as Mirrors*. Unpublished papers, Michigan State University, 1968.

March, James C. and Herbert A. Simon, *Organizations*. New York: Wiley, 1958.

Marcuse, Herbert, *One-Dimensional Man*. Boston: Beacon Press, 1964.

———, "The New Forms of Control," in Jack D. Douglas, ed., *Freedom and Tyranny: Social Problems in a Technological Society*. New York: Knopf, 1970.

Marler, Peter, "Communications in Monkeys and Apes," in Irven DeVore, ed., 1965, pp. 544–584.

Marquis, Stewart, "Co-systems, Societies, and Cities," *American Behavioral Scientist*, XI, No. 6 (July-August 1968), 11–15.

Marsh, Robert, *Comparative Sociology*. New York: Harcourt, Brace & World, 1967.

Marshall, T. H., *Class, Citizenship and Social Development*. New York: Doubleday, 1964.

Martindale, Don, *The Nature and Types of Sociological Theory*. Boston: Houghton Mifflin, 1960.

Maruyana, Magoroh, "The Second Cybernetics: Deviation-Amplifying Mutual Causal Processes," in Walter Buckley, ed., *Modern Systems Research for the Behavioral Scientist*. Chicago: Aldine, 1968.

Marx, Karl, *Capital: A Critique of Political Economy*. Moscow: Foreign Languages Publishing House, 1954.

———, *Economic and Philosophical Manuscripts of 1844*. Moscow: Foreign Languages Publishing House, 1961.

———, *Economics and Political Manuscripts of 1864*. New York: International Publishers, 1964.

——— and Friedrich Engels, *The Communist Manifesto*. Chicago: Regnery, 1954.

Mason, Stephen, *A History of the Sciences*, rev. ed. New York: Collier, 1963.

Massie, Joseph L., "Management Theory," in James G. March, ed., *Handbook of Organizations*. Chicago: Rand McNally, 1965, pp. 387–422.

Matson, Floyd, *The Broken Image*. Garden City: Doubleday Anchor, 1966.

Matza, David, *Becoming Deviant*. Englewood Cliffs, N.J.: Prentice-Hall, 1969.

Mayer, Kurt B. and Walter Buckley, *Class and Society*. New York: Random House, 1970.

Mayhew, Leon, "Ascription in Modern Societies," *Sociological Inquiry*, XXXVIII (Spring 1969), 105–120.

Mayo, Elton and George W. Lombard, *Teamwork and Labor Turnover in the Aircraft Industry of Southern California*. Boston: Graduate School of Business Administration, Harvard University, 1944.

McBride, Glenn, *A General Theory of Social Organization and Behavior*. St. Lucia, Australia: University of Queensland Press, 1964.

McCandless, B., "Childhood Socialization," in D. Goslin, ed., *Handbook of Socialization Theory and Research*. Rand McNally, 1969.

McCartney, James L., "On Being Scientific: Changing Styles of Presentation in Sociological Research," *American Sociologist*, V (1970), 30–35.

McCord, William et al., "Some Effects of Paternal Absence on Male Children," *Journal of Abnormal and Social Psychology*, LXIV (1962), 361–369.

McGill, Thomas E., ed., *Readings in Animal Behavior*. New York: Holt, Rinehart & Winston, 1965.

McHugh, Peter, *Defining the Situation*. Indianapolis: Bobbs-Merrill, 1968.

McLuhan, Marshall, *Understanding Media: The Extensions of Man*. New York: McGraw-Hill, 1964.

———, "Cybernation and Culture," in C. R. Dechert, ed., *The Social Impact of Cybernetics*. New York: Simon & Schuster, 1966, pp. 95–108.

McNeill, David, *The Acquisition of Language*. New York: Harper & Row, 1970, chs. 3, 5.

Mead, George Herbert, "The Social Self," *Journal of Philosophy, Psychology, and Scientific Methods*, X (January-December 1913), 374–380.

———, *Mind, Self and Society*, Charles W. Morris, ed. Chicago: University of Chicago Press, 1934.

———, *George Herbert Mead on Social Psychology: Selected Papers*, Anselm Strauss, ed. Chicago: University of Chicago Press, 1964.

Mead, Margaret, *Sex and Temperament in Three Primitive Societies*. New York: New American Library (Mentor Book), 1950 (first published 1935).

———, *Male and Female: A Study of the Sexes in a Changing World*. New York: New American Library (Mentor Book), 1955.

Meissner, Martin, *Technology and the Worker*. San Francisco: Chandler, 1969.

Merble, Judith A., "The Taylor Strategy: Organizational Innovation and Class Structure," *Berkeley Journal of Sociology*, XIII (1968), 59–81.

Merritt, Richard and Stein Rokkan, eds., *Comparing Nations*. New Haven: Yale University Press, 1966.

Merton, Robert K., *Social Theory and Social Structure*, rev., enlarged ed. New York: The Free Press, 1957.

———, "Sociological Ambivalence," in Edward Tiryakian, ed., *Sociological Theory, Values, and Sociocultural Change*. New York: The Free Press, 1963.

Messinger, Sheldon L., Harold Sampson, and Robert D. Towne, "Life as Theater: Some Notes on the Dramaturgic Approach to Social Reality," *Sociometry*, XXV (1962), 98–110.

Meyer, Marshall W., "Automation and Bureaucratic Structure," *American Journal of Sociology*, LXXIV (November 1968), 256–264.

Meyerson, Martin and Edward C. Banfield, *Politics, Planning and the Public Interest: The Case of Public Housing in Chicago*. New York: The Free Press, 1955.

Michael, Donald N., "Cybernation: The Silent Conquest," in Morris Phillipson, ed., *Automation: Implications for the Future*. New York: Vintage, 1962, pp. 78–128.

Michels, Robert, *Political Parties.* New York: Crowell-Collier, 1962 (originally published 1911).

Mikva, Zorita Wise, "The Neighborhood Improvement Association: A Counterforce to the Expansion of Chicago's Negro Population." Unpublished M.A. dissertation, Department of Sociology, University of Chicago, 1951.

Miliband, Ralph, *The State in Capitalist Society.* New York: Basic Books, 1969.

Mill, John Stuart, *A System of Logic.* London: Longmans, 1843.

Miller, Arthur R., "Personal Privacy in the Computer Age: The Challenge of a New Technology in an Information-Oriented Society," *Michigan Law Review,* LXVII (1969), 1091–1246.

Miller, George A., "Professionals in Bureaucracy: Alienation Among Industrial Scientists and Engineers," *American Sociological Review,* XXXII (October 1967), 755–768.

Miller, Herman P., "Annual and Lifetime Income in Relation to Education: 1939–1959," *American Economic Review,* L (1960), 962–986.

———, *Income Distribution in the United States.* Washington, D.C.: Government Printing Office, 1966.

Miller, Stephen J., "The Social Base of Sales Behavior," *Social Problems,* XII (1964), 15–24.

Miller, Walter, "Lower Class Culture as a Generating Milieu of Gang Delinquency," *Journal of Social Issues,* XIV, No. 3 (1958), 5–19.

Mills, C. Wright, *The Power Elite.* New York: Oxford University Press, 1959a.

———, *The Sociological Imagination.* New York: Oxford University Press, 1959b.

———, *The Marxists.* New York: Dell, 1962.

———, "The Professional Ideology of Social Pathologists," *Power, Politics and People.* New York: Ballantine, 1963.

Mills, Theodore M., "Some Hypotheses on Small Groups from Simmel," in Lewis Coser, ed., *Georg Simmel.* Englewood Cliffs, N.J.: Prentice-Hall, 1965.

Mischel, Theodore, *Cognitive Development and Epistemology.* New York: Academic Press, 1971.

Moeller, Gerald, "Bureaucracy and the Teacher's Sense of Power," *School Review,* LXXII (1964), 137–157.

Moller, Herbert, "Youth as a Force in the Modern World," in *Comparative Studies in Society and History,* 1960.

Molotch, Harvey, "Toward a More Human Human Ecology," *Land Economics,* XLIII, No. 3 (August 1967), 336–341.

———, "Oil in Santa Barbara and Power in America," *Sociological Inquiry*, XL (Winter 1970), 131–144.

Montagu, M. F. Ashley, ed., *Man and Aggression*. New York: Oxford University Press, 1968.

Moore, Barrington, Jr., *Soviet Politics—The Dilemma of Power*. Cambridge: Harvard University Press, 1956.

———, *Social Origins of Dictatorship and Democracy*. Boston: Beacon Press, 1966.

Moreno, J. L., *Who Shall Survive?* (rev. and enlarged ed.). New York: Beacon House, 1953. Originally published in 1934.

Morgan, G., and H. Ricciutti, "Infant Responses to Shapes During the First Year," in B. M. Foss, ed., *Determinants of Infant Behavior*, Vol. IV. London: Methuen, 1968.

Morris, Charles W., *Signs, Language and Behavior*. Englewood Cliffs, N.J.: Prentice-Hall, 1946.

Morris, Desmond, ed., *Primate Ethology*. London: Weidenfeld & Nicolson, 1967.

———, *The Naked Ape*. Toronto: Bantam Books, 1969.

Motz, Annabelle B., "The Family as a Company of Players," *Trans-Action*, II (1965), 27–30.

Mouzelis, Nicos P., *Organization and Bureaucracy: An Analysis of Modern Theories*. Chicago: Aldine, 1967.

Moynihan, Daniel, *Maximum Feasible Misunderstanding*. Glencoe, Ill.: The Free Press, 1969.

Murchison, Carl, *Handbook of Social Psychology*. Worcester, Mass.: Clark University, 1935.

Murdock, George Peter, *Social Structure*. New York: The Macmillan Company, 1949.

Murtagh, John M. and Sara Harris, *Cast the First Stone*. New York: McGraw-Hill, 1957.

Mussen, P., and E. Rutherford, "Parent-Child Relations and Parental Personality in Relation to Young Children's Sex Role Preferences," *Child Development*, XXXIV (1963), 589–607.

Myrdal, Gunnar, *Challenge to Affluence*. New York: Pantheon, 1963.

———, with assistance of Richard Sterner and Arnold Rose, *An American Dilemma: The Negro Problem and Modern Democracy*. New York: Harper & Brothers, 1944.

Nadworny, Milton J., *Scientific Management and the Unions*. Cambridge: Harvard University Press, 1955.

Natanson, Maurice, *Literature, Philosophy and the Social Sciences*. The Hague: Martinus Nijhoff, 1962.

Needham, Rodney, Introduction to E. Durkheim and M. Mauss, *Primitive Classification*. Chicago: University of Chicago Press, 1967.

Nef, John U., *Cultural Foundations of Industrial Civilization*. Cambridge, England: Cambridge University Press, 1958.

Neubauer, Deane, "Some Conditions of Democracy," *American Political Science Review*, LXI (December 1967), 1002–1009.

Nimmo, Dan, *Newsgathering in Washington*. New York: Atherton, 1964.

Nisbet, Robert, *Social Change and History*. New York: Oxford University Press, 1969.

Nissen, H. W. and M. P. Crawford, "A Preliminary Study of Food-Sharing Behavior in Young Chimpanzees," *Journal of Comparative Psychology*, XXII (1936), 383–419 (cited in Michael Argyle, 1969, p. 34).

North, C. C. and Paul K. Hatt, *Job and Occupation: A Popular Evaluation*. Chicago: National Opinion Research Center, University of Chicago, 1947.

Oettinger, Anthony G., *Run, Computer, Run*. Cambridge: Harvard University Press, 1969.

Ogburn, William, *Social Change with Respect to Culture and Original Nature*. New York: Viking Press, 1950 (originally published 1922).

Okazaki, A., *Kekkon to Jinko*. Tokyo: Chikuro Shobo, 1941 (as quoted in Gardner Lindzey, 1967).

Oliver, Bernard J., Jr., *Sexual Deviation in American Society: A Social Psychological Study of Sexual Non-Conformity*. New Haven: College and University Press, 1967.

O'Neill, William L., *Divorce in the Progressive Era*. New Haven: Yale University Press, 1967.

Orans, Martin, "Surplus," *Human Organization*, XXV, No. 1 (Spring 1966), 24–32.

Orne, Martin T., "On the Social Psychology of the Psychological Experiment: With Particular Reference to Demand Characteristics and Their Implications," *American Psychologist*, XVII (November 1962), 776–783.

────── and Frederick Evans, Jr., "Social Control in the Psychological Experiment: Antisocial Behavior and Hypnosis," *Journal of Personality and Social Psychology*, I (March 1965), 189–200.

Orwell, George, *Down and Out in Paris and London*. London: Secker & Warburg, 1951.

Packard, E. P. W., *The Prisoner's Hidden Life*. Chicago: Published by the author, 1868 (as cited in Thomas Szasz, 1970, pp. 14–15).

Park, Robert E., "Human Ecology," *American Journal of Sociology*, XLII (July 1936), 1–15.

———, "The Nature of Race Relations," in Edgar T. Thompson, ed., *Race Relations and the Race Problem: A Symposium on a Growing National and International Problem with Special References to the South*. Durham: Duke University Press, 1939.

———, *On Social Control and Collective Behavior*. Chicago: Phoenix, 1965.

——— and Ernest W. Burgess, *Introduction to the Science of Sociology*. Chicago: University of Chicago Press, 1921.

Parke, Robert, Jr., and Paul C. Glick, "Prospective Changes in Marriage and the Family," *Journal of Marriage and the Family*, XXIX (1967), 249–256.

Parkhill, Douglas F., *The Challenge of the Computer Utility*. Reading, Mass.: Addison-Wesley, 1966.

Parry, Hugh J. and Helen M. Crossley, "Validity of Responses to Survey Questions," *Public Opinion Quarterly*, XIV (Spring 1950), 61–80.

Parsons, Talcott, *The Social System*. New York: The Free Press, 1951.

———, *A Revised Analytical Approach to the Theory of Social Stratification*. Glencoe, Ill.: The Free Press, 1953.

——— and Edward A. Shils, eds., *Toward a General Theory of Social Action*. Cambridge: Harvard University Press, 1954.

———, "Some Considerations on the Theory of Social Change," *Rural Sociology*, XXVI (1961), 219–239.

———, "Certain Primary Sources and Patterns of Aggression in the Social Structure of the Western World," *Essays in Sociological Theory*, rev. ed. New York: The Free Press, 1964.

———, "Full Citizenship for the American Negro," in Talcott Parsons and Kenneth B. Clark, eds., *The Negro American*. Boston: Houghton Mifflin, 1966a.

———, *Societies: Evolutionary and Comparative Perspectives*. Englewood Cliffs, N.J.: Prentice-Hall, 1966b.

———, "On the Concept of Value-Commitments," *Sociological Inquiry*, XXXVIII (Spring 1968), 135–159.

———, "Some Considerations on the Theory of Social Change," *Rural Sociology*, XXVI (1961), 219–239.

———, "The Position of Identity in the General Theory of Action," in Chad Gordon and Kenneth Gergen, eds., *The Self in Social Interaction*, Vol. I, Classic and Contemporary Perspectives. New York: Wiley, 1968.

Pascal, Blaise, *Thoughts*. Garden City, N.Y.: Doubleday, 1961.

Peabody, Robert L. and Francis E. Rourke, "Public Bureaucracies," in James G. March, ed., *Handbook of Organizations*. Chicago: Rand McNally, 1965, pp. 802–837.

Pearson, Harry W., "The Economy Has No Surplus: Critique of a Theory of Development," in C. M. Arensburg and H. W. Pearson, eds., *Trade and Markets in the Early Empires*. New York: The Free Press, 1957, pp. 320–341.

Peck, R. F., and R. Havighurst, *The Psychology of Character Development*. New York: Wiley, 1960.

Piaget, Jean, *The Moral Judgment of the Child*. New York: The Free Press, 1948.

———, *The Child's Conception of the World*. New York: Humanities Press, 1951.

———, *Judgment and Reasoning in the Child*. New York: Humanities Press, 1952.

———, *The Child's Conception of Number*. New York: Humanities Press, 1952.

———, *The Origins of Intelligence in Children*. New York: International University Press, 1952.

———, *The Construction of Reality in the Child*. New York: Basic Books, 1954.

———, *The Language and Thought of the Child*. New York: Humanities Press, 1959.

———, *The Child's Conception of Physical Causality*. Paterson, N.J.: Littlefield, 1960.

———, *Play, Dreams, and Imitation in Childhood*. New York: Norton, 1962.

——— and B. Inhelder, *The Psychology of the Child*. New York: Basic Books, 1969.

Pittinger, Robert E., Charles F. Hochett, and John J. Daneby, *The First Five Minutes: A Sample of Microscopic Interview Analysis*. Ithaca, N.Y.: Martineau, 1960.

Platt, Anthony, *The Child Savers: The Invention of Juvenile Delinquency in the United States*. Chicago: University of Chicago Press, 1970.

Polanyi, Karl, *The Great Transformation*. Boston: Beacon Press, 1945.

Pool, Ithiel de Sola, Robert P. Abelson, and Samuel L. Popkin, *Candidates, Issues, and Strategies*. Cambridge: M.I.T. Press, 1965.

Popper, Karl, *The Open Society and Its Enemies*. New York: Harper & Row, 1962.

Popplestone, John A., "The Horseless Cowboys," *Trans-Action*, May-June 1966, pp. 25–27.

Porter, William, "Journalism," *International Encyclopedia of the Social Sciences,* VIII (1967), 265–276.

Portman, Adolph, *Animals as Social Beings.* New York: Viking Press, 1961.

Psathas, George, "Ethnomethodology and Ethno-Science." Paper presented to ASA, 1967.

—— and James Henslin, "Dispatched Orders and the Cab Driver," *Social Problems,* XIV (1967).

Radcliffe-Browne, A. R., *Structure and Function in Primitive Society.* New York: The Free Press, 1952.

Rainwater, Lee and William Yancey, *The Moynihan Report and the Politics of Controversy.* Cambridge: M.I.T. Press, 1968.

Ramsey, Charles and Robert Smith, "Japanese and American Perceptions of Occupations," *American Journal of Sociology,* LXV (March 1960), 475–482.

Redfield, Robert, *Tepoztlan, A Mexican Village.* Chicago: University of Chicago Press, 1930.

Reynolds, Vernon and Frances, "Chimpanzees in the Budongo Forest," in Irven DeVore, ed., 1965, pp. 368–424.

Rhee, H. A., *Office Automation in Social Perspective.* Oxford: Blackwell, 1968.

Robinson, W. S., "Ecological Correlations and the Behavior of Individuals," *American Sociological Review,* XV (June 1950), 351–357.

Roethlisberger, Fritz J. and William J. Dickson, *Management and the Worker.* Cambridge: Harvard University Press, 1939.

Rogoff, Natalie, *Recent Trends in Occupational Mobility.* Glencoe, Ill.: The Free Press, 1953.

Rokkan, Stein, *Citizens, Elections and Parties.* New York: David McKay, 1970.

Romano, V. O. I., "Donship in a Mexican-American Community in Texas," *American Anthropologist,* LXII (1960), 966–976.

Rorvik, David M., "Cloning: Asexual Human Reproduction?" *Science Digest,* 1969, pp. 6–13.

Rose, Arnold M., ed., *Human Behavior and Social Processes.* Boston: Houghton-Mifflin, 1962.

Rosenberg, Hans, *Bureaucracy, Aristocracy, and Autocracy.* Cambridge: Harvard University Press, 1958.

Rosenberg, Harold and David M. White, *Mass Culture.* New York: The Free Press, 1959.

Rosenthal, Douglas E., "Client Participation in Professional Decisions: The

Lawyer-Client Relationship in Personal Injury Cases." Unpublished doctoral dissertation, Department of Political Science, Yale University, 1970.

Rosenthal, Robert, *Experimenter Effects of Behavioral Research.* New York: Appleton-Century-Crofts, 1966.

——— and Lenore Jacobson, *Pygmalion in the Classroom.* New York: Holt, Rinehart, & Winston, 1968.

Rossi, Peter and Robert Dentler, *The Politics of Urban Renewal: The Chicago Findings.* New York: The Free Press, 1961.

Rosten, Leo, *The Washington Correspondents.* New York: The Macmillan Company, 1937.

Rotenstreich, Nathan, "On the Ecstatic Sources of the Concept of Alienation," *Review of Metaphysics,* XVI (March 1963), 550–555.

Roth, Guenther, "Personal Rulership, Patrimonialism, and Empire Building in the New States," in Reinhard Bendix et al., eds., *State and Society.* Boston: Little, Brown, 1968, pp. 581–591.

Rowell, T. E., "Variability in the Social Organization of Primates," in Desmond Morris, ed., 1967, pp. 219–235.

Rowland, L. W., "Will Hypnotized Persons Try to Harm Themselves or Others?" *Journal of Abnormal and Social Psychology,* XXXIV (January 1939), 114–117.

Ruesch, Hans, *Top of the World.* New York: Permabooks, 1959.

Ruesch, Jurgen and Gregory Bateson, *Communication.* New York: Norton, 1951.

Ruggles, Richard, John de J. Pemberton, Jr., and Arthur R. Miller, "Symposium: Computers, Data Banks, and Individual Privacy," *Minnesota Law Review,* LIII (1968), 211–245.

Russell, Claire and W. M. S. Russell, *Violence, Monkeys and Man.* London: The Macmillan Company, 1968.

Russell Sage Foundation, "Guidelines for the Collection, Maintenance, and Dissemination of Pupil Records." New York, 1970.

Russett, Bruce, *World Handbook of Political and Social Indications.* New Haven: Yale University Press, 1964.

Sahlins, Marshall, "The Origin of Society," *Scientific American Zoo,* September 1960, pp. 2–13 (reprint pagination).

——— and Elman Service, eds., *Evolution and Culture.* Ann Arbor: University of Michigan Press, 1960.

Samuel, A. L., "Some Studies in Machine Learning Using the Game of Checkers," in E. A. Feigenbaum and J. Feldman, eds., *Computers and Thought.* New York: McGraw-Hill, 1963, pp. 71–105.

Sansom, William, *A Contest of Ladies*. London: Hogarth, 1956.

Sapir, Edward, *Language*. New York: Harcourt, Brace, 1921.

Scanzoni, John, "A Re-inquiry into Marital Disorganization," *Journal of Marriage and the Family*, XXVII (1965), 483–491.

Schachter, Stanley, *The Psychology of Affiliation: Experimental Studies in the Sources of Gregariousness*. Stanford: Stanford University Press, 1959.

Schaller, George B., *The Mountain Gorilla: Ecology and Behavior*. Chicago: University of Chicago Press, 1963.

——— and Gordon R. Lowther, "The Relevance of Carnivore Behavior to the Study of Early Hominids," *Southwestern Journal of Anthropology*, XXV (Winter 1969), 307–541.

Schattschneider, E. E., *The Semisovereign People*. New York: Holt, Rinehart, & Winston, 1960.

Scheff, Thomas J., *Being Mentally Ill: A Sociological Theory*. Chicago: Aldine, 1966.

Schegloff, Emanuel, "On Sequencing in Conversation," in H. Garfinkel and H. Sachs, eds., *Contributions in Ethnomethodology*. Bloomington: University of Indiana Press, forthcoming.

Schein, E., I. Schneier, and C. H. Barker, *Coercive Persuasion*. New York: Norton, 1961.

Schelling, Thomas B., *The Strategy of Conflict*. New York: Oxford University Press, 1963, pp. 83–118.

Scheuch, Erwin, "Cross-national Comparisons Using Aggregate Data: Some Substantive and Methodological Problems," in Richard Merritt and Stein Rokkan, eds., *Comparing Nations*. New Haven: Yale University Press, 1966.

Schjelderup-Ebbe, T., "Social Behavior in Birds," in Carl Murchison, 1935, Ch. 20 (cited in Roger Brown, 1965, pp. 16–21).

Schlesinger, Joseph A., "Political Party Organization," in James G. March, ed., *Handbook of Organizations*. Chicago: Rand McNally, 1965, pp. 764–801.

Schneirla, T. C., "Instinct and Aggression," reprinted in Ashley Montagu, 1968, pp. 59–64.

Schramm, Wilbur A., *Mass Communications*. Urbana: University of Illinois Press, 1960.

———, J. Lyle, and E. Parker, *Television in the Lives of Our Children*. Stanford: Stanford University Press, 1961.

Schulze, Robert O., "The Bifurcation of Power in a Satellite City," in Morris Janowitz, ed., *Community Political Systems*. New York: The Free Press, 1961, pp. 19–81.

Schumpeter, Joseph, *Capitalism, Socialism and Democracy*. New York: Harper & Brothers, 1942.

Schurmann, H. Franz, Peter Dale Scott, and Reginald Zelnick, *The Politics of Escalation in Vietnam*. Boston: Beacon Press, 1966.

Schutz, Alfred, *Collected Papers*, Vol. I. The Hague: Martinus Nijhoff, 1962.

———, *Collected Papers*, Vol. II, *Studies in Social Theory*, A. Brodersen, ed. The Hague: Martinus Nijhoff, 1964.

———, *Collected Papers*, Vol. III, *Studies in Phenomenological Philosophy*, I. Schutz, ed. The Hague: Martinus Nijhoff, 1966.

———, *The Phenomenology of the Social World*, trans. G. Walsh, and F. Lehnert. Evanston: Northwestern University Press, 1967.

———, *On Phenomenology and Social Relations*, H. R. Wagner, ed. Chicago: University of Chicago Press, 1970.

Scott, John Paul, *Animal Behavior*. Chicago: University of Chicago Press, 1958.

———, "That Old-Time Aggression, 1967," reprinted in Ashley Montagu, 1968, pp. 51–58.

Scott, John W. and Mohamed El-Assal, "Multiversity, University Size, University Quality, and Student Protest," *American Sociological Review*, XXXIV (October 1969), 702–709.

Scott, Marvin, *The Racing Game*. Chicago: Aldine, 1968.

——— and Stanford Lyman, "Accounts, Deviance, and Social Order," in Jack D. Douglas, ed., *Deviance and Respectability: The Social Construction of Moral Meanings*. New York: Basic Books, 1970.

Scott, Robert, *The Making of Blind Men*. New York: Russell Sage, 1968.

Seale, Patrick and Maureen McConville, *Red Flag/Black Flag*. New York: Putnam, 1968.

Sebeok, Thomas A., ed., *Style in Language*. Cambridge: M.I.T. Press, 1960.

———, "Review of: Communication Among Social Bees; Porpoises and Sonar; Man and Dolphin," *Language*, XXXIX (October-December 1963), 448–466.

Sebold, Hans, ed. *Adolescence: A Sociological Analysis*. New York: Appleton-Century-Crofts, 1968.

Secord, P. and C. Backman, *Social Psychology*. New York: McGraw-Hill, 1964.

Seeley, John, *Crestwood Heights*. Toronto: University of Toronto Press, 1956.

Seeman, Melvin, "On the Meaning of Alienation," *American Sociological Review*, XXIV (December 1959), 783–791.

———, "On the Personal Consequences of Alienation in Work," *American Sociological Review*, XXXII (April 1967), 273–285.

Seligman, Ben B., *Most Notorious Victory: Man in an Age of Automation*. New York: The Free Press, 1966.

Sellin, Thorstein, *Culture Conflict in Crime*. New York: Social Science Research Council, 1938.

Selznick, Phillip, *TVA and the Grass Roots*. Berkeley: University of California Press, 1949.

———, *Leadership in Administration*. Evanston: Row, Peterson, 1957.

Service, Elman R., *Primitive Social Organization: An Evolutionary Perspective*. New York: Random House, 1962.

Sewall, William and Vinal P. Shah, "Socioeconomic Status, Intelligence and the Attainment of High Education," *Sociology of Education*, Winter 1967, pp. 1–23.

Shanas, Ethel, Peter Townsend, Dorothy Wedderturn, Henning Friis, Paul Milhoj, and Jan Stehouwer, *Old People in Three Industrial Societies*. New York: Atherton Press, 1968.

Sherif, Muzafer, "Group Influences upon the Formation of Norms and Attitude," in Theodore M. Newcomb et al., ed., *Readings in Social Psychology*. New York: Henry Holt, 1947.

Sherrill, Robert, *Gothic Politics in the Deep South*. New York: Putnam, 1968.

Shibutani, Tamotsu, *Society and Personality*. Englewood Cliffs, N.J.: Prentice-Hall, 1961.

——— and Kian Moonkwan, *Ethnic Stratification, A Comparative Approach*. New York: The Macmillan Company, 1965.

Shils, Edward, "On the Comparative Study of New States," in Clifford Geertz, ed., *Old Societies and New States*. New York: The Free Press, 1963.

Sibley, Elbridge, *The Education of Sociologists in the United States*. New York: Russell Sage Foundation, 1963.

Silberman, Charles E., *The Myths of Automation*. New York: Harper & Row, 1966.

Silvers, Ronald J., "The Modern Artist's Associability: Constructing a Situated Moral Revolution," in Jack D. Douglas, ed., *Deviance and Respectability*. New York: Basic Books, 1970.

Simmel, Georg, "How Is Society Possible?" *American Journal of Sociology*, XVI (November 1910), 372–391.

———, *The Sociology of George Simmel*, K. Wolff, ed. Glencoe, Ill.: The Free Press, 1962.

Simmons, Jerry L., "Public Stereotypes of Deviants," *Social Problems,* XIII (1965), 223–232.

Simon, Herbert, *Administrative Behavior,* 2nd ed. New York: The Macmillan Company, 1957.

———, *The Shape of Automation.* New York: Harper & Row, 1965.

Simpson, George E. and J. Milton Finger, "The Sociology of Race and Ethnic Relations," in Robert K. Merton, Leonard Broom, and Leonard S. Cottrell, Jr., eds., *Sociology Today: Problems and Perspectives.* New York: Basic Books, 1959.

Sjoberg, Gideon, "The Preindustrial City," *American Journal of Sociology,* LX (March 1955), 438–445.

Skinner, B. F., *Verbal Behavior.* New York: Appleton-Century-Crofts, 1957.

Skolnick, Jerome H., *The Politics of Protest.* New York: Ballantine Books, 1969.

Slater, Philip E., "Role Differentiation in Small Groups," *American Sociological Review,* XX (June 1955), 300–310.

———, "On Social Regression," *American Sociological Review,* XXVIII (June 1963), 339–364.

Slobin, Dan I., "The Acquisition of Russian as a Native Language," in Frank Smith and George Miller, eds., *The Genesis.* Cambridge: M.I.T. Press, 1966, pp. 129–148.

Smelser, Neil, *Social Change in the Industrial Revolution: An Application of Theory to the British Cotton Industry.* Chicago: University of Chicago Press, 1959.

———, "Mechanisms of Change and Adjustment to Change," in Wilbert Moore and Bert Hoselitz, eds., *Industrialization and Society.* New York: UNESCO, 1966.

Smith, Adam, *The Wealth of Nations.* New York: Modern Library, 1937.

Smith, Thomas, "Merit as Ideology in the Okugawa Period," in Ronald Dore, ed., *Aspects of Social Change in Modern Japan.* Princeton: Princeton University Press, 1967.

Soderberg, C. Richard, "The American Engineer," in Kenneth S. Lynn, ed., *The Professions in America.* Boston: Beacon Press, 1967, pp. 203–230.

Sorokin, Pitirim A., *Contemporary Sociological Theories.* New York: Harper & Brothers, 1928.

———, *Fads and Foibles in Modern Sociology.* Chicago: Regnery, 1956.

Southwick, Charles H., ed., *Primate Social Behavior.* Princeton: Van Nostrand, 1963.

Spady, William, "Educational Mobility and Access: Growth and Paradoxes," *American Journal of Sociology*, November 1967, pp. 273–286.

Sparks, John, "Allogrooming in Primates: A Review," in Desmond Morris, ed., 1967, pp. 148–175.

Spectorsky, A. C., *The Exurbanites*. Philadelphia: Lippincott, 1955.

Spencer, Herbert, *Essays Scientific, Political and Speculative*. New York: D. Appleton, 1891.

———, *The Principles of Ethics*. London: Williams & Norgate, 1904.

Spiro, Melford, *Children of the Kibbutz*. New York: Schocken Books, 1965.

Spitz, R. A., "Hospitalism: An Inquiry into the Genesis of Psychiatric Conditions in Early Childhood," *The Psychoanalytic Study of the Child*, I (3rd ed.). New York: International University Press, 1959.

Spock, Benjamin, *Baby and Child Care*. New York: Pocket Books, 1967.

Spottiswoode, R., *A Grammar of the Film*. Berkeley: University of California Press, 1950.

Spykman, Nicholas J., *The Social Theory of Georg Simmel*. New York: Atherton Press, 1966.

Stampp, Kenneth M., *The Pauliss Institution: Slavery in the Ante-Bellum South*. New York: Knopf, 1956.

Stein, Maurice, *The Eclipse of Community*. Princeton: Princeton University Press, 1960.

Stember, Charles H., *Education and Attitude Change*. New York: American Jewish Committee, 1961.

Sternliev, George, *The Tenement Landlord*. New Brunswick: Rutgers State University, 1966.

Stewart, Omer C., "Lorenz/Margolin on the Ute," in Ashley Montagu, ed., 1968, pp. 103–110.

Stinchcombe, Arthur, *Constructing Social Theories*. New York: Harcourt, Brace, & World, 1968.

Stone, Gregory, "Appearance and the Self," in Arnold M. Rose, ed., *Human Behavior and Social Processes: An Interactionist Approach*. New York: Houghton Mifflin, 1962.

——— and Harvey A. Faberman, "On the Edge of Rapprochement: Was Durkheim Moving Toward the Perspective of Symbolic Interactionism?" *Sociological Quarterly*, VIII (Spring 1967), 149–164.

——— and Harvey A. Faberman, eds., *Social Psychology from the Standpoint of Symbolic Interactionism*. Waltham, Mass.: Blaisdell, 1970.

Stone, Philip J., Dexter C. Dunphy, Marshall S. Smith, and Daniel M. Ogilvie, *The General Inquirer: A Computer Approach to Content Analysis*. Cambridge: M.I.T. Press, 1966.

Stouffer, Samuel A., *Communism, Conformity, and Civil Liberties*. New York: Doubleday, 1955.

Strauss, Anselm L., *Mirrors and Masks*. Glencoe, Ill.: The Free Press, 1959a.

———, ed., *The Social Psychology of George Herbert Mead*. Chicago: University of Chicago Press, 1959b.

———, Leonard Schatzman, Rue Bucher, Danute Ehrlich, and Melvin Sabshin, "The Hospital and Negotiated Order," in Eliot Freidson, ed., *The Hospital in Modern Society*. New York: The Free Press, 1963.

———, Leonard Schatzman, Rue Bucher, Danute Ehrlich, and Melvin Sabshin, *Psychiatric Ideologies and Institutions*. New York: The Free Press, 1964.

Strodtbeck, Fred L., "Husband-Wife Interaction Over Revealed Differences," *American Sociological Review*, XVI (August 1951), 468–473.

——— and Richard D. Mann, "Sex Role Differentiation in Jury Deliberations," *Sociometry*, XIX (March 1956), 3–11.

Struik, Dirk J., *Yankee Science in the Making*, rev. ed. New York: Collier, 1962.

Sudnow, D., *Passing On: The Social Organization of Dying*. Englewood Cliffs, N.J.: Prentice-Hall, 1967.

Sumner, William Graham, *Folkways: A Study of the Sociological Importance of Usages, Manners, Customs, Mores, and Morals*. Boston: Ginn, 1940.

Sutherland, E., *The Professional Thief*. Chicago: University of Chicago Press, 1957.

Suttles, Gerald D., *The Social Order of the Slum: Ethnicity and Territory in the Inner City*. Chicago: University of Chicago Press, 1968.

Swanson, Guy E., "Mead and Freud: Their Relevance for Social Psychology," *Sociometry*, XXIV (December 1961), 319–339.

———, J. Coleman, and A. F. C. Wallace, "Symposium," *American Sociological Review* (1968), 13.

Sykes, G., *Society of Captives*. New York: Atheneum, 1965.

Szasz, Thomas S., *The Myth of Mental Illness*. New York: Harper & Row, 1961.

———, *The Manufacture of Madness: A Comparative Study of the Inquisition and the Mental Health Movement*. New York: Harper & Row, 1970.

Tachi, Minorv and Yoichi Okazaki, "Economic Development and Population Growth," *Developing Economics*, III (December 1965), 497–515.

Taeuber, Karl and Alma Taeuber, *Negroes in Cities*. Chicago: Aldine, 1965.

Task Force Report on Organized Crime. Washington, D.C.: Government Printing Office, 1967.

Taylor, Frederick W., *Shop Management.* New York: Harper & Brothers, 1919.

Teggart, Frederick, *The Theory and Processes of History.* Berkeley: University of California Press, 1941.

Terman, Lewis M., *Psychological Factors in Marital Happiness.* New York: McGraw-Hill, 1938.

——— and Miles, *Sex and Personality Studies in Masculinity and Femininity.* New York: McGraw-Hill, 1936.

Theodorson, George A., *Studies in Human Ecology.* New York: Harper & Row, 1961.

Thibaut, John W. and Harold H. Kelley, *The Social Psychology of Groups.* New York: Wiley, 1959.

Thomas, William I., *The Unadjusted Girl.* Boston: Ginn, 1923.

———, *The Child in America.* New York: Knopf, 1928.

——— and Florian Znaniecki, *The Polish Peasant in Europe and America.* New York: Dover Publications, 1958.

Thompson, Edward T., "The Grammar of Society," *Sociology and Social Research,* 1935.

Tiger, Lionel, *Men in Groups.* London: Nelson, 1969.

——— and Robin Fox, "The Zoological Perspective in Social Science," *Man,* I (March 1966), 75–81.

Timasheff, Nicholas, *Sociological Theory: Its Nature and Growth.* New York: Random House, 1961.

Tinbergen, N., *Social Behaviour in Animals.* London: Methuen, 1953.

Tiryakian, Edward A., *Sociologism and Existentialism: Two Perspectives on the Individual and Society.* Englewood Cliffs, N.J.: Prentice-Hall, 1962.

Tocqueville, Alexis de, *Democracy in America.* New York: Vintage, 1954 (originally published 1836).

———, *The Old Regime and the French Revolution.* New York: Doubleday, 1955 (originally published 1856).

Todd, Richard, "You Are an Interfacer of Black Boxes," *Atlantic,* CCXXV (1970), 64–70.

Tönnies, Ferdinand, *Gemeinschaft and Gesellschaft,* trans. and ed. by Charles P. Loomis as *Fundamental Concepts of Sociology.* New York: American Book, 1940 (1st ed. 1887).

Truffaut, F., *Hitchcock.* New York: Simon & Schuster, 1967.

Tumin, Melvin, "Some Social Consequences of Research on Racial Relations," in Jack D. Douglas, ed., *The Impact of Sociology*. New York: Appleton-Century-Crofts, 1970.

Turner, Ralph, "The Theme of Contemporary Social Movements," *British Journal of Sociology*, XX (December 1969), 390–405.

Turner, Roy, "Some Formal Properties of Therapy Talk," in David Sudnow, ed., *Studies in Social Interaction*. New York: The Free Press, 1972.

Tyler, Stephen, ed., *Cognitive Anthropology*. New York: Holt, Rinehart, & Winston, 1970.

Udy, Stanley, Jr., *Organization of Work, A Comparative Analysis of Production Among Nonindustrial Peoples*. New Haven: Human Relations Area File Press, 1959.

Ulam, Adam, *The Unfinished Revolution*. New York: Random House, 1960.

United States Department of Health, Education, and Welfare, *The Story of the White House Conferences on Children and Youth*. Washington, D.C.: Government Printing Office, 1967.

Useem, John, "Notes on the Sociological Study of Language," *Social Science Research Council Items*, XVII, September 1963.

Vahinger, Hans, *The Philosophy of "As If."* New York: Harcourt, Brace, 1927.

Valentine, Charles, *Culture and Poverty*. Chicago: University of Chicago Press, 1968.

Van Dyck, Jules and Mart Van Oers, "Sur quelques dimensions empiriques de l'aliénation," *Sociologie du Travail*, XI (January-March 1969), 44–60.

Vigotsky, L. S., *Thought and Language*. Cambridge: M.I.T. Press, 1962.

Vold, George B., *Theoretical Criminology*. New York: Oxford University Press, 1958.

Vonnegut, Kurt, Jr., *Piano Player*. New York: Holt, Rinehart, & Winston, 1952.

Wade, Richard, *Slavery in the Cities, The South 1820–1860*. New York: Oxford University Press, 1964.

Waitzkin, Howard, "Truth's Search for Power: The Dilemmas of the Social Sciences," *Social Problems*, vol. 15, no. 4, pp. 408–419.

Walker, Charles R., *Toward the Automatic Factory*. New Haven: Yale University Press, 1957.

Wallace, Walter L., ed., *Sociological Theory*. Chicago: Aldine, 1969.

Ward, Lester F., *Applied Sociology: A Treatise on the Conscious Improvement of Society by Society*. Boston: Ginn, 1905.

———, "Dynamic Sociology," in Henry Steele Commager, ed., *Lester Ward and the Welfare State*. Indianapolis: Bobbs-Merrill, 1967.

Ward, Robert and D. A. Rustow, *Political Modernization of Japan and Turkey*. Princeton: Princeton University Press, 1964.

Warner, W. Lloyd, *Yankee City*. New Haven: Yale University Press, 1963.

────── et al., *The Emergent American Society: Large Scale Organization*, Vol I. New Haven: Yale University Press, 1967.

Washburn, S. L., ed., *Social Life of Early Man*. New York: Viking Fund Publications in Anthropology (No. 31), 1961.

────── and Phyllis C. Jay, eds., *Perspective on Human Evolution* (I). New York: Holt, Rinehart & Winston, 1968.

Weber, Max, *From Max Weber: Essays in Sociology*, trans. H. H. Gerth and C. Wright Mills. New York: Oxford University Press, 1946.

──────, *Max Weber, The Theory of Social and Economic Organization*, trans. A. M. Henderson and Talcott Parsons. New York: Oxford University Press, 1947 (originally published 1922).

──────, *From Max Weber*. New York: Oxford University Press, 1958a.

──────, *The Protestant Ethic and the Spirit of Capitalism*. New York: Charles Scribner's Sons, 1958b.

──────, *The Theory of Social and Economic Organization*. New York: The Free Press, 1965.

──────, *Economy and Society*. New York: Bedminster Press, 1968.

──────, "Science as a Vocation," in Jack D. Douglas, ed., *The Relevance of Sociology*. New York: Appleton-Century-Crofts, 1970.

Weick, Karl E., "Systematic Observational Methods," in Gardner Lindzey and Elliot Aronson, eds., *The Handbook of Social Psychology*, Vol. II. Reading, Mass.: Addison-Wesley, 1968.

Weinberg, Ian, "The Problem of the Convergence of Industrial Societies: A Critical Look at the State of a Theory," *Comparative Studies in Society and History*, X (October 1968), 1–15.

Weinberg, Martin S., "The Situated Morality of a Nudist Camp," in Jack D. Douglas, ed., *Deviance and Respectability: The Social Construction of Moral Meanings*. New York: Basic Books, 1970.

Weinberg, S. Kirson, *Incest Behavior*. New York: Citadel Press, 1955.

Weisberger, Bernard, *The American Newspaperman*. Chicago: University of Chicago Press, 1961.

Welter, Rush, *Popular Education and Democratic Thought in America*. New York: Columbia University Press, 1962.

Werner, H., *Comparative Psychology of Mental Development*. Chicago: Fawcett, 1948.

Wertheim, W. F., "Sociological Aspects of Corruption in Southeast Asia," in Reinhard Bendix et al., eds., *State and Society*. Boston: Little, Brown, 1968, pp. 561–580.

Werthmann, Carl and Irving Pilavin, "Gang Members and the Police," in David Bordua, ed., *The Police*. New York: Wiley, 1967.

Westie, Frank R., "Race and Ethnic Relations," in R. E. L. Faris, ed., *Handbook of Sociology*. Chicago: Rand McNally, 1964.

Westin, Allen F., *Privacy and Freedom*. New York: Atheneum, 1967.

White, Morton G., *Foundations of Historical Knowledge*. New York: Harper Torch, 1965.

——— and Lucia White, *The Intellectual Versus the City*. Cambridge: Harvard University Press, 1962.

Whitehill, Arthur, Jr., and Shin'ichi Takezawa, *The Other Worker*. Honolulu: East-West Center Press, 1968.

Whorf, Benjamin, *Language, Thought and Reality*, John B. Carroll, ed. Cambridge: M.I.T. Press, 1956.

Whyte, William Foote, *Street Corner Society*. Chicago: University of Chicago Press, 1943.

———, *Money and Motivation*. New York: Harper & Brothers, 1955.

———, "Elton Mayo," *International Encyclopedia of the Social Sciences*, X (1968), 82–83.

Whyte, William H., Jr., *The Organization Man*. Garden City, N.Y.: Doubleday, 1956.

Wildavsky, Aaron, *The Politics of the Budgetary Process*. Boston: Little, Brown, 1964.

Wilensky, Harold L., "Human Relations in the Workplace: An Appraisal of Some Recent Research," in C. M. Arensberg, ed., *Research in Industrial Human Relations*. New York: Harper & Brothers, 1957, pp. 25–54.

Wiley, Norbert, "America's Unique Class Politics: The Interplay of the Labor, Credit, and Community Markets," *American Sociological Review*, XXXII (August 1967), 529–541.

Williams, Robin, *American Society*. New York: Knopf, 1960.

Winch, Peter, *The Idea of a Social Science*. London: Routledge & Kegan Paul, 1958.

Wirth, Louis, "Social Interaction: The Problem of the Individual and the Group," *American Journal of Sociology*, XLIV (May 1939), 965–979.

———, "The Problem of Minority Groups," in Ralph Linton, ed., *The Science of Man in the World Crisis*. New York: Columbia University Press, 1945.

———, *The Ghetto*. Chicago: University of Chicago Press, 1956.

———, "Urbanism as a Way of Life," in Albert Reiss, Jr., ed., *Louis Wirth on Cities and Social Life*. Chicago: University of Chicago Press, 1964.

Wittgenstein, L., *The Blue and Brown Books*. London: Blackwell, 1958.

———, *Tractatus Logico-Philosophicus*. London: Routledge & Kegan Paul, 1961.

———, *Philosophical Investigations*. New York: The Macmillan Company, 1967.

Wolfe, Eric, *Peasant Wars of the Twentieth Century*. New York: Harper & Row, 1969.

Wolff, Kurt H., ed. and trans., *The Sociology of Georg Simmel*. Glencoe, Ill.: The Free Press, 1950.

———, ed., *Georg Simmel, 1895–1918*. Columbus: Ohio State University Press, 1959.

Wood, Robert C., *1400 Governments: The Political Economy of the New York Metropolitan Region*. Cambridge: Harvard University Press, 1961.

Woodward, Joan, *Industrial Organization: Theory and Practice*. London: Oxford University Press, 1965.

Wrong, Dennis, "The Oversocialized Conception of Man in Modern Sociology," *American Sociological Review*, XXVI (1960), 184–193.

Wynne-Edwards, V. C., *Animal Dispersion in Relation to Social Behaviour*. Edinburgh and London: Oliver & Boyd, 1962.

Young, P. C., "Antisocial Uses of Hypnosis," in L. M. LeCron, ed., *Experimental Hypnosis*. New York: The Macmillan Company, 1952.

Zajone, Robert B., ed., *Animal Social Psychology*. New York: Wiley, 1969.

Zimmer, Heinrich, *Philosophies of India*. New York: Meridian Books, 1956.

Zimmerman, Don H. and Melvin Pullner, "The Everyday World as a Phenomenon," in Jack D. Douglas, ed., *Understanding Everyday Life*. Chicago: Aldine, 1970.

Zimmerman, L. J., *Poor Lands, Rich Lands: The Widening Gap*. New York: Random House, 1965.

Znaniecki, Florian, "Social Groups as Products of Participating Individuals," *American Journal of Sociology*, XLIV (May 1939), 799–811.

Index

Ackoff, Russell L., 434
Action (social), 32–34, 51–56, 67, 79, 82, 84, 97, 100–114, 218–20, 293–94
Adams, Robert, 501
Adorno, T. W., 482–84
Affiliation, 133–36, 213–15, 509, 553
Age-status, 493–96
Aiken, Michael, 429
Albert, Ethel M., 142
Alienation, 402–4, 428–31, 437
Almond, Gabriel, 392
Alsop, Stewart, 321
Animal behavior, 118–38
Anomie, 34–36, 541–45
Anshen, Melvin, 434
Appearance, 232–38, 241–42, 246–48
Ardrey, Robert, 120, 123
Argyle, Michael, 136
Aries, Philippe, 494–95
Aristotle, 27–28
Asch, Solomon, 66–67
Ascription, 170, 367–68, 390–91
Ashworth, A. E., 423
Attitude, 76–79, 89, 91
Audience, 231, 243, 248
Ausubel, D. P., 200
Authority, 53, 75, 213, 333–36, 343–54, 390, 413–17, 424
Authoritarian personality, 482–84
Automation, 425–27, 432–36, 439–69
Axelrod, Morris, 508

Bachrach, Peter, 520, 523
Backman, C., 206

Backstages, 232–34
Bagdikian, Ben H., 324
Baily, L., 199
Bain, Read, 215
Bales, Robert F., 71, 257–59, 292
Ballard, Hoyt B., 372
Bancroft, Frederick, 155
Bandura, Albert, 195, 199
Banfield, Edward C., 323, 331, 518, 519
Baran, 384
Baratz, Morton, 520, 523
Barber, Bernard, 375
Baritz, Loren, 22, 420
Barnard, Chester, 312, 344
Barnett, S. A., 124
Bauer, Raymond A., 313
Beals, Ralph L., 142, 146
Beatty, John, 124
Becker, Howard, 97, 204, 220–21, 243, 476, 549–50
Behaviorism, 63–76, 174–75
Bell, Daniel, 18–19, 347, 379, 529, 563
Bellah, Robert, 394–95
Bendix, Reinhard, 336, 339, 352, 369, 389, 390, 397, 402, 420, 425
Benedict, Ruth, 147–48
Benjamin, Roger, 402–3
Berelson, Bernard, 254–55
Berger, Peter L., 110–11
Bernstein, Basil M., 197
Berry, Brewton, 482
Bias (statistical), 449
Biggs, Mae A., 243–45
Birnbaum, Norman, 49

637

Bittner, Egon, 114
Blau, Peter M., 72, 74, 75, 202, 413, 417, 435
Blauner, Robert, 428–30, 433
Boomfield, L., 174
Blumer, Herbert, 102, 211, 216–17, 400, 437, 487–88
Bolzano, Bernard, 104
Boorstin, Daniel, 61, 521
Bourgeoisie, 48
Breed, Warren, 321
Brentano, Franz, 104
Brickman, William, 457
Bright, James R., 432, 435
Brinton, Crane, 539
Brown, Julia, 393, 447
Brown, Roger, 132, 133, 176, 182, 183, 185, 283, 288–89, 290–91
Bruce, Donald, 292
Bruner, Jerome, 66, 183, 285
Brzezinski, Zbigniew, 397–98
Bucher, Rue, 223
Buck, Roy C., 453
Buckingham, Walter, 456
Bureaucracies, 350–52, 391, 410–38
Burgess, Ernest, 512–14
Burke, Kenneth, 103

Campbell, E. Q., 203, 462
Cantril, Hadley, 67–69
Caplow, Theodore, 414, 514, 526
Caprio, Frank S., 143
Carey, James T., 137
Carroll, John B., 282
Carstens, Arthur, 432
Carter, Loren, 493–94
Cater, Douglass, 319, 320
Cavan, Sherri, 299–300
Census, 264–65
Chambliss, William J., 220
Chapin, F. Stuart, 31–32
Charismatic legitimacy, 53, 334–36, 380
Chicago sociology, 62–64, 87–97, 512, 543–44
Childe, V. Gordon, 501
Chinoy, Ely, 428
Chomsky, Noam, 174–77
Cicourel, Aaron, 179, 197, 205, 297
Clark, Joseph S., 345
Class, 48–49, 196, 357, 362–66, 372–80
Class conflict, 37, 46, 48
Cloning, 162

Coale, Ansley J., 504
Coding, 442–46
Cohen, Albert, 548–49
Cohen, Bernard, 321
Coleman, James S., 200, 203, 344, 347, 462
Collingwood, R. G., 52
Collins, Randall A., 335
Common sense, 3, 6–13, 22–23, 106–9, 557–58
Comparative psychology, 121–22, 387–407
Computers, 432–36, 439–69
Comte, Auguste, 29, 39–42
Conant, James B., 205
Conduct, 110–11, 218
Conflict, 48, 330–32
Conklin, 284
Content analysis, 254–56
Cooley, Charles H., 98–102, 215, 219, 246
Coser, Lewis, 56, 213
Cox, Oliver C., 373
Craftsmanship, 425
Cremin, Lawrence A., 201
Cressey, Donald, 529
Cross-sectional studies, 392–93
Crozier, Michael, 413, 436
Cultural interest groups, 341–42
Cultural relativism, 41
Culture, 126, 128, 295, 513
Cuzzort, R. P., 247
Cybernetics, 454, 455

Dahrendorf, Ralf, 49
Dalton, Melville, 96, 344, 417, 422
Davis, Kingsley, 135, 375–78, 504, 505, 542
De Beauvoir, Simone, 151
De Bell, Garret, 491
Dechert, Charles R., 467
Definition of the situation, 101, 177, 338, 474–97
Denzin, Norman, 99, 215–18
Deutsch, Karl, 310, 342
Deutscher, Irwin, 79, 291
Deutsher, Isaac, 346
Deviance, 81, 111, 476, 537–59
DeVore, Irven, 129, 132
Dexter, Lewis A., 313
Dickson, W. J., 418–19
Display behaviors, 122–23

Dodd, Stuart, 31–32
Domhoff, G. William, 372
Dominance orders, 127, 129, 131–33
Douglas, Jack D., 97, 545, 565
Dramaturgical analysis, 103–4
Dramaturgical discipline, 246
Dramaturgical loyalty, 245–46
Dramaturgical model, 228–48
Durkheim, Emile, 29, 33, 34–36, 38–39, 45, 46, 80, 81, 99, 170, 210–12, 282–83, 507, 541–42
Dysfunction, 81

Ecological theory, 543–48
Economic determinism, 46–48, 376–77
Ego, 106
Egoism, 35, 541
Ehrlich, Danute, 223
Eisenstadt, S. N., 401
Ellis, Robert A., 204
Ellul, Jacques, 436
Encounter, 109, 171, 218–19, 222, 230–31
Equilibrium, 81
Erikson, Kai T., 543, 546–47
Ervin-Tripp, Susan, 182
Et cetera assumption, 180, 187
Ethnocentrism, 480
Ethnography, 141–49
Ethnomethodology, 104–15, 294, 296–301, 487
Ethology, 120–24
Etzioni, Amitai, 429
Eufunction, 81, 542
Evans, Frederick, Jr., 271–74
Everyday life, 6–13, 24, 87–115, 224–49, 278–304, 564–65
Existentialism, 104–15, 170–73, 224–25
Exogamy, 145
Experimentation, 268–74, 292
Expression given, 229–30
Expression given off, 229–30
Expressive aspect of behavior, 246–47

Face-to-face interaction, 109–11, 278–302
Family life, 110, 140–63, 193–98, 212
Family of orientation, 145
Family of procreation, 145
Fanon, Frantz, 400
Farberman, Harvey A., 210
Faunce, William A., 425, 432, 437

Fayol, Henri, 427
Feagin, Joe R., 202
Feldman, Arnold, 397
Field research, 36–38, 63, 87–97, 105, 564
Fink, Donald G., 446, 447
Firey, Walter, 514
Fisher, Lloyd C., 420
Fitzhugh, George, 60
Flavell, J., 179
Folkways, 60–62, 89
Foster, George, 508
Frazier, E. Franklin, 481
Freud, Sigmund, 170
Friedrich, Carl, 388
Friedrichs, Robert W., 10–11
Fromm, Erich, 429
Fronts, 234–39, 241
Frontstage, 231–34
Froomkin, Joseph N., 432
Frumkin, Robert M., 150, 152–55
Fuller, Richard C., 478–79
Functionalism, 210–12, 309–10, 375–78, 541–48

Gans, Herbert J., 11–12, 14, 93–95, 508, 526
Garfinkel, Harold, 108, 113–14, 292, 298–99, 476
Gebhart, Paul, 158
Geertz, Clifford, 342, 394, 508
Gemeinschaft, 68, 70, 507
Generalized other, 101, 111
Gerard, Ralph W., 457, 460, 461
Gerschenkron, Alexander, 394, 399
Gesellschaft, 68, 70, 507
Gilman, Albert, 133
Gilmartin, Brian, 393, 447
Glaser, Barney G., 223, 224
Glazer, Nathan, 511, 528
Glick, Paul C., 162
Glossing, 180, 187
Glueck, Eleanor, 196
Glueck, Seldon, 196
Goffman, Erving, 103, 109, 188, 206, 218, 224, 228–48, 299, 476, 557
Goodall, Jane, 129, 131
Goodenough, Ward, 295
Goodman, Paul, 533–34
Goodman, Percival, 533–34
Gordon, Mitchell, 524
Gorer, Geoffrey, 124

640 Index

Gouldner, Alvin W., 8, 12–13, 94, 421–25, 474–75
Greer, Scott, 517
Gross, Edward, 344
Group marriage, 145–46

Hafez, E. S. E., 136
Hage, Jerald, 429
Hagstrom, Warren O., 424
Hall, K. R. L., 125, 129, 130, 132
Hall, Max W., 316
Hall, Oswald, 523
Hall, Richard, 429, 435
Handlin, Oscar, 425
Hare, A. Paul, 71
Harlow, Harry, 134–35, 194
Harlow, Margaret, 134–35, 194
Harris, Seymour E., 238
Hartshorne, H., 189
Hass, C. Glenn, 201
Hatt, Paul K., 367
Hauser, Philip, 499, 502
Havighurst, A. R., 189, 200
Hawthorne studies, 418–19
Heidegger, Martin, 105
Heilbroner, Robert L., 436
Henslin, James M., 243–45, 292
Hereditarians, 121
Herskovitz, Melville J., 501
Hierarchy, 127, 423, 424
  See also Status
Himmelweit, H. T., 199
Hintze, Otto, 352
Historicism, 30, 50–54, 390
Hodge, Robert, 405
Hoijer, Harry, 142, 146
Holt, John, 204
Homans, George C., 72–74, 419, 450
Homology, 120
Hoos, Ida R., 434
Horowitz, Irving, 504
Hunter, Floyd, 519
Huntington, Samuel P., 352, 397–98
Husserl, Edmund, 104–7, 476
Hymes, Dell, 295
Hypothesis, 251–74

"I," 101, 102
Ichheiser, Gustav, 228
Ideal types, 54, 351–52, 413–14

Identity, 212, 236–39, 293
Identity kits, 238
Impression management, 228–31, 337
Index, 77–78
Indexicality, 180, 184–85, 187
Industrialization, 88–91, 160, 359–62, 390, 391, 396–405, 503–5
Inhelder, B., 179
Inkeles, Alex, 392, 396, 405
Institutionalization, 110–11
Instrument aspect of behavior, 246–47
Interaction process analysis, 71, 257–59, 292
Interest groups, 338–43, 528
Internalization, 111, 170
Interviewing, 257–58, 261, 266–68
Iron law of oligarchy, 343–45

Jacobs, Jane, 94, 524–26
Jacobs, Jerry, 202
Jacobson, Lenore, 203
Jaki, Stanley L., 453
Jensen, Arthur, 197–98
Johnson, John M., 13, 554–55
Jonassen, Christen T., 514
Jouvenal, Bertrand de, 18

Karpman, Benjamin, 141
Katz, Elihu, 309
Kautsky, John, 402–3
Kerr, Clark, 343, 396, 420
Kerr, N., 204
Key, V. O., 348
Keyfitz, Nathan, 502, 503
Kindleberger, C. D., 395
Kinsey, Alfred Charles, 158
Kitsuse, John I., 205
Kjolseth, Rolf, 292
Klapper, Joseph T., 309
Klietsch, Ronald G., 246
Kluckhohn, Clyde, 126
Kohl, Herbert, 203, 204
Kohlberg, L., 188–89
Kolko, Gabriel, 363, 365
Kon, Igor S., 429
Kornhauser, William, 424, 427
Kozol, Jonathan, 203, 204
Kraft, Robert E., 320
Kroeber, A. L., 126
Kuhn, Manford, 214, 215

Kuhn, Thomas, 10, 23
Kuznets, Simon, 360, 393

LaBarre, Weston, 140, 142, 146, 147
Labeling theory, 550–51
Lampe, Keith, 491–92
Lampman, Robert J., 363
Lane, Robert E., 204, 511
Language, 174–75, 182–85, 211, 216, 278–302
Lastrucci, Carlo L., 119
Laswell, Harold, 310
Law, 45, 252, 540–58
Lazarsfeld, Paul, 309
Lea, Henry C., 152
Leach, Edmond R., 124
LeBon, Gustave, 48
Lee, Rose Hum, 481
Legitimacy, 53, 75, 110–11, 213, 333–36, 338, 380, 390, 474
Lehrer, Stanley, 457
Lemert, Edwin, 476, 479, 549
Lenneberg, Eric H., 182
Lenski, Gerhard, 357–62
Le Play, Frederic, 38, 68
Lerner, Daniel, 310
Levinger, George, 160
Levi-Strauss, Claude, 147, 283–85
Levy, Marion, 396
Lewin, Kurt, 160
Lewis, Oscar, 506, 508–9
Liebow, Elliot, 508
Light, Ivan, 457
Lind, A. W., 548
Lindesmith, Alfred, 220–21, 284, 289, 549
Lindzey, Gardner, 141, 143
Linguistics, 174–75, 285–88
Lipset, Seymour M., 332, 339, 341, 344, 347, 369
Litwak, Eugene, 220
Long, Norton, 522–23
Lorenz, Konrad, 120, 121, 123–24
Lowenthal, Leo, 255–56
Lowie, Robert H., 243
Lowther, Gordon R., 129
Luckmann, Thomas, 110–11
Lundberg, Ferdinand, 31–32
Lyle, J., 198
Lyman, Stanford M., 172, 173, 481, 482, 486, 488

Lynd, Helen, 88–90
Lynd, Robert S., 18, 88–91, 373

MacDonald, Dwight, 315
Maccoby, E., 195
Macrae, Norton, 530
Macrosociology, *see* Social structure
Madge, John, 255
Malinowski, Bronislaw, 144, 148–49, 211
Mandelbaum, David, 282
Manis, Jerome G., 205
Mann, Floyd C., 257, 434
Manner, 238–39, 241
Mannheim, Karl, 504
Manning, Peter, 112
Marcuse, Herbert, 49, 429–31
Marquis, Stewart, 532
Marriage, 145–49
Marsh, Robert, 392
Marshall, T. H., 402, 403
Martin, Clyde, 158
Martindale, Don, 211
Marx, Karl, 29, 31, 37, 46–50, 342, 359, 362–63, 429, 475, 476
Marxism, 30, 46–50, 373–75, 399–401, 475
Mass media, 198–200, 303–26, 489–90
Massie, Joseph L., 427
Matza, David, 87, 107, 172, 551–53
May, M., 189
Mayer, Kurt B., 364
Mayo, Elton, 419–21
McCandless, B., 201
McConville, Maureen, 338
McCord, William, 196
McKenzie, R. D., 89
McLuhan, Marshall, 317, 456, 466
McPartland, Thomas S., 214
"Me," 101, 102
Mead, George Herbert, 98, 214–17, 246, 290, 291
Mead, Margaret, 149
Meanings, 32, 45, 51–56, 65, 67, 77, 84–85, 87–97, 100–114, 171–72, 188–90, 212–13, 278–302, 487, 551–57, 564–65, 568
Mechanistic theories, 31
Meissner, Martin, 428, 432, 435
Meritt, Richard, 392
Merkle, Judith A., 418

Merton, Robert K., 67, 80, 81, 83, 211, 436, 542, 544–45
Meyer, Marshall W., 435
Meyerson, Martin, 518
Michael, Donald N., 435
Michels, Robert, 343–45
Mikva, Zorita Wise, 516
Miles, 195
Miliband, Ralph, 372, 373
Mill, John Stuart, 252, 254–55
Miller, Arthur, 462, 464, 466
Miller, George, 427
Miller, Herman, 205, 392
Miller, Walter, 549
Mills, C. Wright, 3, 15, 20, 46, 49, 50–51, 371–73, 521, 566
Mills, Theodore, 214
Mobility, 368–70, 376
Mobilization, 500–503
Moeller, Gerald, 204
Molotch, Harvey, 490, 514, 521
Monogamy, 145–46, 157
Moore, Barrington, Jr., 375, 382, 400
Moore, Wilbert, 397
Moral entrepreneur, 551
Moreno, J. L., 69, 72
Mores, 62, 145, 540–58
Morris, Desmond, 120, 121
Morselli, Henri, 34
Mouzelis, Nicos P., 417
Mowrer, Ernest R., 89
Moynihan, Daniel, 20, 322–23, 511, 528, 529
Murdock, George, 145–47, 155–56
Murtagh, John M., 238
Mussen, P., 195
Myers, Richard R., 478–79
Myrdal, Gunnar, 479, 484–86

Nadworny, Milton J., 418
Natason, Maurice, 280
Natural history, 293–94
Needham, Rodney, 295
Neoimperialism, 375
Neubauer, Deane, 392
News, *see* Mass media
Nisbet, Robert, 401
Norms, 65–66, 71, 90, 170, 215, 293, 474, 548, 556
North, C. C., 367
Nuclear family, 141, 157

Objectivity, 102, 111
Ogburn, William, 31–32
Okazaki, A., 143
Oliver, Bernard J., Jr., 141
O'Neill, William L., 165
Opinion poll, 77
Orans, Martin, 502
Organicism, 30, 42–46, 474–75
Orne, Martin T., 119, 271–74

Packard, E. P. W., 242
Pareto, Vilfredo, 55–56
Park, Robert E., 87, 88, 478, 481, 482
Parke, Robert, Jr., 162
Parker, E., 198
Parkhill, Douglas F., 456
Parsons, Talcott, 12, 81, 170, 211, 212, 217, 375, 390, 401, 482, 485, 486–87, 507, 543
Participant observation, 87–97, 105, 257, 508–10, 539, 547–48, 550–51
Pearson, Harry W., 502
Peck, R. F., 200
Performance, 109, 231, 238–39, 243–48
Performing self, 247
Personal front, 234–39, 242
Personality system, 211–12
Phenomenological sociology, 104–15, 549–53
Phenomenology, 477, 487–88
Piaget, Jean, 176, 178–82, 283, 285, 289
Plato, 42
Pluralism, 371, 519, 523
Polanyi, Karl, 502
Politics, 328–55
Polyandry, 145–47
Polygamy, 145
Polygyny, 145–46
Pomeroy, Wardell, 158
Pool, Ithiel de Sola, 313
Popper, Karl, 23
Popplestone, John A., 235
Porter, William, 320
Positivism, 30, 38–42, 475
Postman, Leo, 66
Power, 75, 357, 370–72, 374
Power elite, 49–51, 371–72, 519–24
Power groups, 55, 79, 340–45
Pressure groups, 477
Primary groups, 68
Primate behavior, 125–30

Program, 442–46, 454, 456, 461
Proletariat, 48, 363
Protologues, 120
Psathas, George, 292

Quantification, 392
Quantitative sociology, 30–36
Questionnaires, 76–79
Quetelet, Adolphe, 33

Rainwater, Lee, 323
Random sampling, 260–261
Rational-legal legitimacy, 53, 334–36
Reciprocal dependence, 145
Reciprocal familiarity, 245
Reciprocity of perspectives, 179–80, 184
Redfield, Robert, 507
Reductionism, 75
Regions, 231–34
Relative deprivation, 359–62
Replications, 97, 264, 271–72
Representative sample, 77, 264
Research, 36–38, 61, 63, 87–97, 105, 250–75, 393–95, 564
Reynolds, Frances, 129
Reynolds, Vernon, 129
Rhee, H. A., 434
Robinson, W. S., 525
Roethlisberger, F. J., 418–19
Rogoff, Natalie, 259
Rokkan, Stein, 388, 390, 392, 398, 404
Role conflict, 83, 145
Role playing, 69–70, 82–83, 103, 247–48
Role sets, 83
Role taking, 100–101
Roles, 69, 71, 82–84, 95, 96, 110, 144, 170, 176, 213, 236, 293, 300, 390–91
Romano, V. O. I., 293–94
Rorvik, David M., 162
Rosenthal, Robert, 203, 266–68, 274
Rossi, Peter, 405
Rotenstreich, Nathan, 429
Roth, Guenther, 351
Rowell, T. E., 129
Rowland, L. W., 271–72
Ruggles, Richard, 464
Rules, 45, 109, 112, 188, 217–18, 221–22, 224, 235–36, 293, 296, 411, 423, 424, 427, 457–58, 538–59
Ruling class, 372
Russell, Claire, 126

Russell, W. M. S., 126
Russett, Bruce, 392
Rutherford, E., 195

Sabshin, Melvin, 223
Saint-Simon, Henri de, 29, 39, 40, 475
Sanctions, 540
Sansom, William, 229
Sapir, Edward, 282, 283
Scanzoni, John, 160
Schacter, Stanley, 133
Schaller, George B., 129, 139
Schattschneider, E. E., 520
Schatzman, Leonard, 223
Schein, E., 207
Schelling, Thomas B., 334
Schjelderup-Ebbe, T., 131
Schlesinger, Joseph A., 345
Schneirla, T. C., 124
Schramm, Wilbur A., 198
Schulze, Robert O., 521
Schumpeter, Joseph, 339
Schutz, Alfred, 104, 106, 476
Scott, John Paul, 124, 132
Scott, Marvin B., 172, 173, 486, 488
Scott, Richard W., 413, 417
Seale, Patrick, 338
Secondary groups, 68
Secord, P., 206
Seeman, Melvin, 429–31
Self, 98–104, 190–92, 209–48, 289–90
Seligman, Ben, 435
Sellin, Thorstein, 548
Selznick, Phillip, 341, 352
Serial monogamy, 157
Sewall, William, 203
Sexual behavior, 139–65
Shah, Vinal P., 203
Shaw, Clifford, 89
Sherif, Muzafer, 65–66
Sherrill, Robert, 348
Shils, Edward, 390
Sibley, Elbridge, 201
Siegal, Abraham, 343
Signs, 280, 289, 298
Sign-vehicles, 228–31
Silberman, Charles E., 436, 457
Simmel, Georg, 56, 210, 213–15, 224
Simon, Herbert, 434, 456, 457
Simulation, 450–51
Situations, 109, 112, 128–30, 168–275

Skinner, B. F., 22, 74, 176
Slater, Philip E., 133
Small, Albion, 62, 64
Smelser, Neil, 401
Social Darwinism, 62, 478, 480–82
Social disorganization, 11–13, 75, 78, 87, 543–48
Social facts, 13–18, 210–11
Social interaction, 63, 71–76, 89, 91–92, 109–11, 133–36, 171–72, 177–82, 212–26, 278–302, 549–53, 557
Social organization, 11–14, 78, 92–94, 130–31, 514–17
Social psychology, 62–71, 76–79, 99, 308–9
Social reality, 36, 217–26, 351–52
Social structure, 15–18, 24, 41, 44–45, 82, 107–8, 216, 293–94
Social system, 41, 129–30, 211–12
Socialization, 48, 81, 111, 168–208, 212, 217, 225–26
Sociology of knowledge, 9, 108, 110
Sociology of sociology, 9–13
Sociometry, 69, 72–73
Soderberg, C. Richard, 452
Sorel, George, 48
Sorokin, Pitirim A., 31
Spady, William, 203
Spencer, Herbert, 29, 42–44, 60, 401, 480
Spitz, R. A., 193–94
Spykman, Nicholas J., 213
Status, 170, 357, 366–68, 373–80
Stein, Maurice, 88
Sternlieb, George, 513
Stewart, Omer C., 124
Stone, Gregory, 210, 223, 236–38, 239
Stratification, 356–86
Strauss, Anselm L., 217, 223, 224, 284, 289
Strodtbeck, Fred L., 257
Structural-functional sociology, 79–85, 210, 474
Struik, Dirk J., 452
Subculture theories, 548–49
Sumner, William Graham, 60–62, 480–81
Surveys, 76–79, 257–65, 449–50
Sutherland, E., 549
Suttles, Gerald D., 12, 16–17, 94, 510–11, 525
Sweezy, 384

Symbolic interactionism, 85, 87, 97–104, 210, 246, 487
Symbols, 99, 100, 127, 246–47, 279–83
Szeleny, Ivan, 220

Taba, H., 189
Tabulation, 261–63
Taylor, Frederick W., 417, 427
Team performances, 243–46
Terman, Lewis M., 161, 195
Thomas, W. I., 77–78, 87, 172, 482
Thrasher, Frederick, 544
Thrasher, M., 89
Tiger, Lionel, 120, 121
Tinbergen, N., 131
Tocqueville, Alexis de, 37–38, 352, 402, 408
Todd, Richard, 454
Tönnies, Ferdinand, 46, 68, 70, 507
Total institutions, 238
Toynbee, Arnold, 37
Traditional legitimacy, 53, 334–36, 380
Transsituation, 9, 10, 171, 186–87, 192, 565
Treiman, Donald, 405
Trow, Martin, 344, 347
Tumin, Melvin, 18
Turing, A. M., 448
Tyler, Stephen, 295–96, 297
Typification, 178, 182–88, 197–98

Ulam, Adam, 400
Urban sociology, 87, 498–536
Useem, John, 293

Vahinger, Hans, 119
Valentine, Charles, 549
Value-free sociology, 7–8
Values, 7–9, 23, 45, 53, 65–66, 77, 78, 81, 84, 90, 391, 376–77, 474
Van Dyck, Jules, 429
Van Oers, Mart, 429
Variables, 292, 391, 507
Vaux, Clotilde de, 41
Verba, Sidney, 392
Verstehen, 54, 106
Vigotsky, L. S., 183, 289
Vincent, George E., 64

Wade, Richard, 528
Walker, Charles R., 428, 433

Walters, Richard H., 195, 199
Ward, Lester F., 62, 63, 473, 480–81
Warner, W. Lloyd, 10, 91
Warren, Carol A. B., 232–33, 240–41
Watson, John B., 64
Weber, Max, 7–8, 29, 37, 46, 50–54, 202, 212–13, 334–36, 349, 351, 352, 378–80, 390, 391, 413–14, 476, 502
Weick, Karl E., 256
Weinberg, Ian, 393, 397
Weinberg, Martin, 556
Weisberger, Bernard, 313
Weiss, 223
Welles, Orson, 67–69
Werner, H., 284
Wertheim, W. F., 351
Westin, Allen F., 462
White, Lucia, 524
White, Morton G., 316, 524
Whorf, Benjamin, 282, 283
Whorfian hypothesis, 447

Whyte, William Foote, 92–93, 419, 508
Wiener, Norbert, 454, 455, 467–68
Wildavsky, Aaron, 352
Wilensky, Harold L., 420
Wiley, Norbert, 340, 379
Williams, Robin, 84, 434
Wirth, W. I., 87, 223, 481, 506–8, 544
Wittgenstein, Ludwig, 187, 286–88, 476
Wolfe, Eric, 400
Wolff, Kurt, 213
Wood, Robert C., 527
Woodward, Joan, 427, 431, 433, 435
Wrong, Dennis, 212
Wynne-Edwards, 123–24, 130

Yancey, William, 323
Young, P. C., 271–72

Zajonc, Robert B., 119, 121, 130
Znaniecki, Florian, 77–78, 223
Zorbaugh, Harvey W., 87, 89